**Communications
in Computer and Information Science** 2136

Series Editors

Gang Li ⓘ, *School of Information Technology, Deakin University, Burwood, VIC,
Australia*
Joaquim Filipe ⓘ, *Polytechnic Institute of Setúbal, Setúbal, Portugal*
Ashish Ghosh ⓘ, *Indian Statistical Institute, Kolkata, West Bengal, India*
Zhiwei Xu, *Chinese Academy of Sciences, Beijing, China*

Rationale

The CCIS series is devoted to the publication of proceedings of computer science conferences. Its aim is to efficiently disseminate original research results in informatics in printed and electronic form. While the focus is on publication of peer-reviewed full papers presenting mature work, inclusion of reviewed short papers reporting on work in progress is welcome, too. Besides globally relevant meetings with internationally representative program committees guaranteeing a strict peer-reviewing and paper selection process, conferences run by societies or of high regional or national relevance are also considered for publication.

Topics

The topical scope of CCIS spans the entire spectrum of informatics ranging from foundational topics in the theory of computing to information and communications science and technology and a broad variety of interdisciplinary application fields.

Information for Volume Editors and Authors

Publication in CCIS is free of charge. No royalties are paid, however, we offer registered conference participants temporary free access to the online version of the conference proceedings on SpringerLink (http://link.springer.com) by means of an http referrer from the conference website and/or a number of complimentary printed copies, as specified in the official acceptance email of the event.

CCIS proceedings can be published in time for distribution at conferences or as post-proceedings, and delivered in the form of printed books and/or electronically as USBs and/or e-content licenses for accessing proceedings at SpringerLink. Furthermore, CCIS proceedings are included in the CCIS electronic book series hosted in the SpringerLink digital library at http://link.springer.com/bookseries/7899. Conferences publishing in CCIS are allowed to use Online Conference Service (OCS) for managing the whole proceedings lifecycle (from submission and reviewing to preparing for publication) free of charge.

Publication process

The language of publication is exclusively English. Authors publishing in CCIS have to sign the Springer CCIS copyright transfer form, however, they are free to use their material published in CCIS for substantially changed, more elaborate subsequent publications elsewhere. For the preparation of the camera-ready papers/files, authors have to strictly adhere to the Springer CCIS Authors' Instructions and are strongly encouraged to use the CCIS LaTeX style files or templates.

Abstracting/Indexing

CCIS is abstracted/indexed in DBLP, Google Scholar, EI-Compendex, Mathematical Reviews, SCImago, Scopus. CCIS volumes are also submitted for the inclusion in ISI Proceedings.

How to start

To start the evaluation of your proposal for inclusion in the CCIS series, please send an e-mail to ccis@springer.com.

Rosa Meo · Fabrizio Silvestri
Editors

Machine Learning and Principles and Practice of Knowledge Discovery in Databases

International Workshops of ECML PKDD 2023
Turin, Italy, September 18–22, 2023
Revised Selected Papers, Part IV

Springer

Editors
Rosa Meo 📖
University of Turin
Turin, Italy

Fabrizio Silvestri 📖
Sapienza University of Rome
Rome, Italy

ISSN 1865-0929   ISSN 1865-0937 (electronic)
Communications in Computer and Information Science
ISBN 978-3-031-74639-0   ISBN 978-3-031-74640-6 (eBook)
https://doi.org/10.1007/978-3-031-74640-6

© The Editor(s) (if applicable) and The Author(s), under exclusive license
to Springer Nature Switzerland AG 2025

This work is subject to copyright. All rights are solely and exclusively licensed by the Publisher, whether the whole or part of the material is concerned, specifically the rights of translation, reprinting, reuse of illustrations, recitation, broadcasting, reproduction on microfilms or in any other physical way, and transmission or information storage and retrieval, electronic adaptation, computer software, or by similar or dissimilar methodology now known or hereafter developed.
The use of general descriptive names, registered names, trademarks, service marks, etc. in this publication does not imply, even in the absence of a specific statement, that such names are exempt from the relevant protective laws and regulations and therefore free for general use.
The publisher, the authors and the editors are safe to assume that the advice and information in this book are believed to be true and accurate at the date of publication. Neither the publisher nor the authors or the editors give a warranty, expressed or implied, with respect to the material contained herein or for any errors or omissions that may have been made. The publisher remains neutral with regard to jurisdictional claims in published maps and institutional affiliations.

This Springer imprint is published by the registered company Springer Nature Switzerland AG
The registered company address is: Gewerbestrasse 11, 6330 Cham, Switzerland

If disposing of this product, please recycle the paper.

Preface

The European Conference on Machine Learning and Principles and Practice of Knowledge Discovery in Databases (ECML PKDD 2023) is the premier European conference on Machine Learning and Data Mining. ECML PKDD took place in Torino, Italy, on September 18–22, 2023.

The program included an exceptionally large number of workshops that spanned many different specialized topics held during the first and last day of the conference. They received 515 submissions sent for review by the reviewers of the program committee. 200 of them were accepted for presentation. Some of them are included in these Post-Workshop proceedings.

The Workshops are organized by topics and are divided into the following five volumes:

1. Volume 1970: Interpretable and Explainable AI: Responsible Models, Bias, Law and Society
2. Volume 1971: Natural Domains and Knowledge Informed Machine LearningEthical AI, Social Good, Multimedia Forensics, Hybrid Learning and Uncertainty
3. Volume 1972: Machine Learning with recent advances and their applicationsAdvancing Explainable and Sustainable AI, Knowledge Discovery and Graph Learning
4. Volume 1973: AI in Applied Sciences: Healthcare, Manufacturing, Causal Modeling, Simplification, Efficiency and Adaptation to Change
5. Volume 1974: Emerging Trends in AI: Large Language Models, Blockchain, Federated learning, Financial, Cybersecurity, Neuromorphic, Edge and Embedded Machine Learning

November 2023

Rosa Meo
Fabrizio Silvestri

Organization

General Chairs

Elena Baralis Politecnico di Torino, Italy
Francesco Bonchi CENTAI, Italy

Steering Committee

Massih-Reza Amini Université Grenoble Alpes, France
Annalisa Appice University of Bari, Italy
Elena Baralis Politecnico di Torino, Italy
Peggy Cellier INSA Rennes, France
Tania Cerquitelli Politecnico di Torino, Italy
Tias Guns KU Leuven, Belgium
Alípio Mário Guedes Jorge University of Porto, Portugal
Fernando Perez-Cruz Technical University of Madrid, Spain
Claudia Plant University of Vienna, Austria
Manuel Gomez Rodriguez Max Planck Institute for Software Systems, Germany
Grigorios Tsoumakas Aristotle University of Thessaloniki, Greece

Program Committee Chairs

Rosa Meo University of Torino, Italy
Fabrizio Silvestri Sapienza University of Rome, Italy

Program Committee for the Volume 1970: Interpretable and Explainable AI: Responsible Models, Bias, Law and Society

- *Advances in Interpretable Machine Learning and Artificial Intelligence – Joint Workshop and Tutorial*

Adrien Bibal	InferLink, USA
Tassadit Bouadi	University of Rennes, France
Jerôme Fink	University of Namur, Belgium
Benoît Frenay	University of Namur, Belgium
Luis Galarraga	IRISA/Inria Rennes, France
Megha Khosla	Delft University of Technology, Netherlands
Jose Oramas	Internet Data Lab, University of Antwerp, Belgium

- *BIAS 2023 - 3rd Workshop on Bias and Fairness in AI*

Toon Calders	University of Antwerp, Belgium
Daphne Lenders	University of Antwerp, Belgium
Eirini Ntoutsi	University of the Bundeswehr Munich, Germany
Akis Papadopoulos	Centre for Research and Technology Hellas, Greece
Mykola Pechenizkiy	Technical University of Eindhoven, Netherlands

- *Biased Data in Conversational Agents*

Francesca Grasso	University of Turin, Italy
Giovanni Siragusa	University of Turin, Italy

- *Explainable Artificial Intelligence: From Static to Dynamic*

Barbara Hammer	Bielefeld University, Germany
Eyke Hüllermeier	LMU Munich, Germany
Fabian Fumagalli	Bielefeld University, Germany
Maximilian Muschalik	LMU Munich, Germany

- *ML, Law and Society*

Mattia Cerrato	Johannes Gutenberg University Mainz, Germany
Marius Köppel	Johannes Gutenberg University Mainz, Germany
Alesia Vallenas Coronel	Johannes Gutenberg University, Germany
Carlo Alberto Barbano	University of Turin, Italy - Télécom Paris, France
Marco Grangetto	University of Turin, Italy

Enzo Tartaglione   Télécom Paris - Institut Polytechnique de Paris, France
Roberto Nai   University of Turin, Italy
Emilio Sulis   University of Turin, Italy
Galileo Sartor   University of Turin, Italy
Francesca Gennari   Scuola Superiore Sant'Anna, Italy

Program Committee for the Volume 1971: Natural Domains and Knowledge Informed Machine LearningEthical AI, Social Good, Multimedia Forensics, Hybrid Learning and Uncertainty

- *RKDE 2023: 1st International Tutorial and Workshop on Responsible Knowledge Discovery in Education*

Daniela Rotelli	University of Pisa, Italy
Mirko Marras	EPFL, Switzerland
Paola Mejia	EPFL, Switzerland
Agathe Merceron	Berlin University of Applied Sciences, Germany
Anna Monreale	University of Pisa, Italy

- *SoGood 2023 – 8th Workshop on Data Science for Social Good*

Irena Koprinska	University of Sydney, Australia
Ricard Gavaldà	Universitat Politècnica de Catalunya, Spain
Joao Gama	INESC TEC - LIAAD, Portugal
Rita P. Ribeiro	INESC TEC, Portugal

- *Towards Hybrid Human-Machine Learning and Decision Making (HLDM)*

Andrea Passerini	University of Trento, Italy
Fabio Casati	Servicenow, Switzerland
Burcu Sayin	University of Trento, Italy
Anna Monreale	University of Pisa, Italy
Roberto Pellungrini	University of Pisa, Italy
Paula Gürtler	Centre for European Policy Studies, Belgium

- *Uncertainty Meets Explainability in Machine Learning*

Vasilis Gkolemis	Athena Research Center, Greece
Christos Diou	Harokopio University of Athens, Greece

- *Workshop: Deep Learning and Multimedia Forensics. Combating Fake Media and Misinformation*

Mauro Barni	University of Siena, Italy
Giovanna Maria Dimitri	University of Siena, Italy
Benedetta Tondi	University of Siena, Italy

Program Committee for the Volume 1972: Machine Learning with Recent Advances and Their Applications Advancing Explainable and Sustainable AI, Knowledge Discovery and Graph Learning

- *XAI-TS: Explainable AI for Time Series: Advances and Applications*

Amal Saadallah	TU Dortmund, Germany
Matthias Jakobs	TU Dortmund, Germany
Emmanuel Müller	TU Dortmund, Germany

- *XKDD 2023: 5th International Workshop on eXplainable Knowledge Discovery in Data Mining*

Przemyslaw Biecek	Warsaw University of Technology, Poland
Riccardo Guidotti	University of Pisa, Italy
Francesca Naretto	Scuola Normale Superiore di Pisa, Italy
Tania Cerquitelli	Politecnico di Torino, Italy
Daniele Regoli	Intesa Sanpaolo, Italy

- *Deep Learning for Sustainable Precision Agriculture*

Marcello Chiaberge	Politecnico di Torino, Italy
Matteo Matteucci	Politecnico di Milano, Italy
Marco Piras	Politecnico di Torino, Italy
Renato Ferrero	Politecnico di Torino, Italy
Karl Mason	University of Galway, Ireland
Abdul Wahid	University of Galway, Ireland
Simone Angarano	Politecnico di Torino, Italy
Mauro Martini	Politecnico di Torino, Italy

- *Knowledge Guided Machine Learning*

Simone Monaco	Politecnico di Torino, Italy
Daniele Apiletti	Politecnico di Torino, Italy
Lia Morra	Politecnico di Torino, Italy

- *MACLEAN: MAChine Learning for EArth ObservatioN*

Dino Ienco	INRAE, Montpellier, France
Thomas Corpetti	CNRS, Rennes, France
Roberto Interdonato	CIRAD - UMR TETIS, Montpellier, France
Minh-Tan Pham	IRISA-UBS, Université Bretagne Sud, IUT de Vannes, France

- *MLG: Mining and Learning with Graphs*

Alice Moallemy-Oureh	University of Kassel, Germany
Maximilian Thiessen	TU Wien, Austria
Pascal Welke	TU Wien, Austria
Thomas Gärtner	TU Wien, Austria

- *Neuro Explicit AI and Expert Informed ML for Engineering and Physical Sciences*

Mitra Baratchi	University of Leiden, Netherlands
Anna Krause	University of Würzburg, Germany
Nikola Simidjievski	University of Cambridge, UK
Philipp Slusallek	German Research Center for Artificial Intelligence (DFKI) & Saarland University, Germany
Ivo Couckuyt	Ghent University, Belgium
Sebastian Rojas Gonzalez	Ghent University, Belgium
Henry B. Moss	Secondmind, UK
Patrick Gallinari	Sorbonne University, Criteo, France
Yuan Yin	Sorbonne University, France

- *New Frontiers in Mining Complex Patterns*

Paolo Mignone	University of Bari Aldo Moro, Italy
Graziella De Martino	University of Bari Aldo Moro, Italy
Elio Masciari	University of Naples, Italy
Ettore Ritacco	ICAR-CNR, Italy

Program Committee for the Volume 1973: AI in Applied Sciences: Healthcare, Manufacturing, Causal Modeling, Simplification, Efficiency and Adaptation to Change

- *PharML, Machine Learning for Pharma and Healthcare Applications Joint with MARBLE Workshop*

Lee Cooper	Northwestern University, USA
Naghmeh Ghazaleh	La Roche Ltd., Switzerland
Jonas Richiardi	Lausanne University Hospital (CHUV), Switzerland
Damian Roqueiro	ETH Zurich, Switzerland
Diego Saldana	Novartis Institutes for BioMedical Research, Switzerland
Konstantinos Sechidis	Novartis Institutes for BioMedical Research, Switzerland

- *Simplification, Compression, Efficiency and Frugality for Artificial Intelligence*

Enzo Tartaglione	Télécom Paris - Institut Polytechnique de Paris, France
Attilio Fiandrotti	Università di Torino, Italy
Giovanna Varni	University of Trento, Italy

- *Workshop on Uplift Modeling and Causal Machine Learning for Operational Decision Making*

Wouter Verbeke	KU Leuven, Belgium
Szymon Jaroszewicz	Institute of Computer Science, Polish Academy of Sciences, Poland
Eustache Diemert	Criteo AI Lab, France

- *6th Workshop on AI in Aging, Rehabilitation and Intelligent Assisted Living (ARIAL)*

Shehroz Khan	University Health Network, Toronto, Canada
Luca Romeo	University of Macerata, Italy
Ali Abedi	University Health Network, Toronto, Canada

- *Adapting to Change: Reliable Multimodal Learning Across Domains*

Raffaello Camoriano	Politecnico di Torino, Italy
Tatiana Tommasi	Politecnico di Torino, Italy
Carlo Masone	Politecnico di Torino, Italy
Giuseppe Averta	Politecnico di Torino, Italy
Francesca Pistilli	Politecnico di Torino, Italy

- *AI4M: AI for Manufacturing*

Jefrey Lijffijt	Ghent University, Belgium
Dimitra Gkorou	ASML, Netherlands
Pieter Van Hertum	ASML, Netherlands
Mykola Pechenizkiy	TU Eindhoven, Netherlands

Program Committee for the Volume 1974: Emerging Trends in AI: Large Language Models, Blockchain, Federated learning, Financial, Cybersecurity, Neuromorphic, Edge and Embedded Machine Learning

- *Challenges and Opportunities of Large Language Models in Real-World Machine Learning Applications*

Enrico Palumbo	Spotify, Italy
Daniele Amberti	Amazon Alexa, Italy
Davide Bernardi	Amazon, Italy

Alessandro Manzotti   Amazon, Italy
Hugues Bouchard   Spotify, USA

- *Deep Learning Meets Neuromorphic Hardware Discovery Challenge*

Andrea Ceni   University of Pisa, Italy
Claudio Gallicchio   University of Pisa, Italy
Gianluca Milano   Istituto Nazionale di Ricerca Metrologica, Italy

Chairs of *Discovery Challenge:*

Danilo Giordano   Politecnico di Torino, Italy
André Panisson   CENTAI, Torino, Italy

- *ITEM: IoT, Edge, and Mobile for Embedded Machine Learning*

Gregor Schiele   University of Duisburg-Essen, Germany
Holger Froening   University of Heidelberg, Germany
Franz Pernkopf   Graz University of Technology, Austria
Michaela Blott   XILINX Research, Ireland
Kazem Shekofteh   Heidelberg University, Germany

- *LIMBO - LearnIng and Mining for BlOckchains*

Sabrina Gaito   Universitá degli Studi di Milano, Italy
Roberto Interdonato   CIRAD, UMR Tetis, France
Andrea Tagarelli   University of Calabria, Italy
Matteo Zignani   Università degli Studi di Milano, Italy

- *Machine Learning for Cybersecurity (MLCS 2023)*

Giuseppina Andresini   University of Bari Aldo Moro, Italy
Annalisa Appice   University of Bari Aldo Moro, Italy
Ibéria Medeiros   Universidade de Lisboa, Portugal
Luca Demetrio   Universitá di Genova, Italy
Pedro M. Ferreira   University of Lisbon, Portugal

- *MIDAS - The 8th Workshop on MIning DAta for Financial ApplicationS*

Ilaria Bordino   UniCredit R&D, Italy
Ivan Luciano Danesi   UniCredit, Italy
Francesco Gullo   University of L'Aquila, Italy
Giovanni Ponti   ENEA, Italy
Lorenzo Severini   UniCredit, Italy

- *Workshop on Advancements in Federated Learning*

Roberto Esposito   Università di Torino, Italy
Fabio Pinelli   IMT Lucca, Italy
Mirko Polato   Università di Torino, Italy
Gabriele Tolomei   Sapienza University of Rome, Italy

We would like to thank all participants, the program committees and reviewers, and the ECML PKDD conference and workshop chairs who contributed to making the workshops a successful event. We are also grateful to Springer for their help in publishing this volume.

April 2024

Rosa Meo and Fabrizio Silvestri
on behalf of the volume editors

Contents – Part IV

PharML, Machine Learning for Pharma and Healthcare Applications

CORKI: A Correlation-Driven Imputation Method for Partial Annotation
Scenarios in Multi-label Clinical Problems 3
   *Ricardo Santos, Bruno Ribeiro, Isabel Curioso, Marília Barandas,
André V. Carreiro, Hugo Gamboa, Pedro Coelho, José Fragata,
and Inês Sousa*

Neuro-symbolic Artificial Intelligence for Patient Monitoring 19
   Ole Fenske, Sebastian Bader, and Thomas Kirste

Direct One-to-All Lead Conversion on 12-Lead Electrocardiogram 26
   *Samir Braga Chaves, José Antônio Fernandes de Macedo,
Régis Pires Magalhães, Lívia Almada Cruz,
and Bruna Raynara Maia Batista*

Unveiling Driver Modules in Lung Cancer: A Clustering-Based
Gene-Gene Interaction Network Analysis 41
   *Golnaz Taheri, Marcell Szalai, Mahnaz Habibi,
and Panagiotis Papapetrou*

Benchmarking Collaborative Learning Methods Cost-Effectiveness
for Prostate Segmentation 59
   *Lucia Innocenti, Michela Antonelli, Francesco Cremonesi,
Kenaan Sarhan, Alejandro Granados, Vicky Goh, Sebastien Ourselin,
and Marco Lorenzi*

Predicting Sepsis Onset with Deep Federated Learning 73
   Lena Mondrejevski, Daniel Azzopardi, and Ioanna Miliou

A Workflow for Creating Multimodal Machine Learning Models
for Metastasis Predictions in Melanoma Patients 87
   *Franco Rugolon, Korbinian Randl, Maria Bampa,
and Panagiotis Papapetrou*

Molecular Fingerprints-Based Machine Learning for Metabolic Profiling 103
   *Christel Sirocchi, Federica Biancucci, Muhammad Suffian,
Riccardo Benedetti, Matteo Donati, Stefano Ferretti,
Alessandro Bogliolo, Mauro Magnani, Michele Menotta,
and Sara Montagna*

Simplification, Compression, Efficiency and Frugality for Artificial Intelligence

Neural Networks Comprising Sequentially Semiseparable Matrices with One Dimensional State Variable are Universal Approximators 115
   Matthias Kissel and Klaus Diepold

TinyMetaFed: Efficient Federated Meta-learning for TinyML 126
   Haoyu Ren, Xue Li, Darko Anicic, and Thomas A. Runkler

On the Potentials of Input Repetition in CNN Networks for Reducing Multiplications 138
   Laura Medina and Jose Flich

The Quest of Finding the Antidote to Sparse Double Descent 153
   Victor Quétu and Marta Milovanović

Unveiling the Potential of Tiny Machine Learning for Enhanced People Counting in UWB Radar Data 168
   Massimo Pavan, Luis González Navarro, Armando Caltabiano, and Manuel Roveri

Towards Comparable Knowledge Distillation in Semantic Image Segmentation 185
   Onno Niemann, Christopher Vox, and Thorben Werner

Combining Primal and Dual Representations in Deep Restricted Kernel Machines Classifiers 201
   Francesco Tonin, Panagiotis Patrinos, and Johan A. K. Suykens

Addressing Limitations of TinyML Approaches for AI-Enabled Ambient Intelligence: Position Paper 217
   Antoine Bonneau, Frédéric Le Mouël, and Fabien Mieyeville

Leveraging Low Rank Filters for Efficient and Knowledge-Preserving Lifelong Learning 226
   Muhammad Tayyab and Abhijit Mahalanobis

Learning When to Observe: A Frugal Reinforcement Learning Framework for a High-Cost World 242
   Colin Bellinger, Isaac Tamblyn, and Mark Crowley

Workshop on Uplift Modeling and Causal Machine Learning for Operational Decision Making

Exploiting Causal Knowledge During CATE Estimation Using Tree Based Metalearners 261
    Roger Pros and Jordi Vitrià

A Parameter-Free Bayesian Framework for Uplift Modeling Application on Telecom Data 277
    Mina Rafla, Nicolas Voisine, and Bruno Crémilleux

A Churn Prediction Dataset from the Telecom Sector: A New Benchmark for Uplift Modeling 292
    Théo Verhelst, Denis Mercier, Jeevan Shestha, and Gianluca Bontempi

6th Workshop on AI in Aging, Rehabilitation and Intelligent Assisted Living (ARIAL)

Semi-supervised Co-teaching for Monitoring Motor States of Parkinson's Disease Patients 303
    Kamer Ali Yuksel, Golara Javadi, and Ahmet Gunduz

Explainable Artificial Intelligence in Medical Diagnostics: Insights into Alzheimer's Disease 312
    Ali Nawaz and Amir Ahmad

Cross-Modal Video to Body-Joints Augmentation for Rehabilitation Exercise Quality Assessment 320
    Ali Abedi, Mobin Malmirian, and Shehroz S. Khan

Multimodal Sensor Fusion for Daily Living Activity Recognition in Active Assisted Living for Older Adults 328
    Kang Wang, Himalaya Sharma, Jasleen Kaur, Shi Cao, and Plinio Morita

Modeling and Detecting Urinary Anomalies in Seniors from Data Obtained by Unintrusive Sensors 336
    Yueyi Ge, Ingrid Zukerman, Mahsa Salehi, and Mor Vered

Assessing Frailty Using Behavioral and Physical Health Data in Everyday Living Settings 345
    Chao Bian, Shehroz S. Khan, and Alex Mihailidis

Synthesizing Diabetic Foot Ulcer Images with Diffusion Model 353
    Reza Basiri, Karim Manji, Harton Francois, Alisha Poonja, Milos R. Popovic, and Shehroz S. Khan

Engaging Older Adults at Meal-Time Through AI-Empowered Socially
Assistive Robots 361
   *Berardina De Carolis, Corrado Loglisci, Nicola Macchiarulo,
and Giuseppe Palestra*

Investigating the Dynamics of Cardio-Metabolic Comorbidities and Their
Interactions in Ageing Adults Through Dynamic Bayesian Networks 369
   *Erica Tavazzi, Chiara Roversi, Martina Vettoretti,
and Barbara Di Camillo*

Adapting to Change: Reliable Multimodal Learning Across Domains

Harnessing Error Patterns to Estimate Out-of-Distribution Performance 381
   Thomas Bonnier and Benjamin Bosch

HAVE-Net: Hallucinated Audio-Visual Embeddings for Few-Shot
Classification with Unimodal Cues 390
   *Ankit Jha, Debabrata Pal, Mainak Singha, Naman Agarwal,
and Biplab Banerjee*

CAD Models to Real-World Images: A Practical Approach to Unsupervised
Domain Adaptation in Industrial Object Classification 399
   *Dennis Ritter, Mike Hemberger, Marc Hönig, Volker Stopp,
Erik Rodner, and Kristian Hildebrand*

EMG Subspace Alignment and Visualization for Cross-Subject Hand
Gesture Classification 416
   *Martin Colot, Cédric Simar, Mathieu Petieau,
Ana Maria Cebolla Alvarez, Guy Cheron, and Gianluca Bontempi*

Adapting Classifiers to Changing Class Priors During Deployment 424
   Natnael Daba, Bruce McIntosh, and Abhijit Mahalanobis

AI4M: AI for Manufacturing

Applying Machine Learning Models on Metrology Data for Predicting
Device Electrical Performance 435
   *Bappaditya Dey, Anh Tuan Ngo, Sara Sacchi, Victor Blanco,
Philippe Leray, and Sandip Halder*

Comparing Deep Reinforcement Learning Algorithms in Two-Echelon
Supply Chains 454
   Francesco Stranieri and Fabio Stella

Reinforcement Learning for Segmented Manufacturing 470
  Nathalie Paul, Alexander Kister, Thorben Schnellhardt,
  Maximilian Fetz, Dirk Hecker, and Tim Wirtz

Automatic Tool Wear Inspection by Cascading Sensor and Image Data 486
  Robbert Verbeke, Lars De Pauw, Fabian Fingerhut, Tom Jacobs,
  Toon Goedemé, and Elena Tsiporkova

Author Index 503

PharML, Machine Learning for Pharma and Healthcare Applications

CORKI: A Correlation-Driven Imputation Method for Partial Annotation Scenarios in Multi-label Clinical Problems

Ricardo Santos[1,2](✉) ⓘ, Bruno Ribeiro[1], Isabel Curioso[1], Marília Barandas[1,2], André V. Carreiro[1], Hugo Gamboa[1,2], Pedro Coelho[3,4], José Fragata[3,4], and Inês Sousa[1]

[1] Associação Fraunhofer Portugal Research, Porto, Portugal
ricardo.santos@fraunhofer.pt
[2] LIBPhys-UNL, NOVA School of Science and Technology, Caparica, Portugal
[3] Comprehensive Health Research Center, NOVA Medical School, Lisboa, Portugal
[4] Hospital de Santa Marta, Centro Hospitalar Universitário Lisboa Central, Lisboa, Portugal

Abstract. Multi-label classification tasks are relevant in healthcare, as data samples are commonly associated with multiple interdependent, non-mutually exclusive outcomes. Incomplete label information often arises due to unrecorded outcomes at planned checkpoints, varying disease testing across patients, collection constraints, or human error. Dropping partially annotated samples can reduce data size, introduce bias, and compromise accuracy. To address these issues, this study introduces CORKI (Correlation-Optimised and Robust K Nearest Neighbours Imputation for Multi-label Classification), a data-centric method for partial annotation imputation in Multi-label data. This method employs proximity measures and an optional weighting term for outcome prevalence to tackle imbalanced labels. Additionally, it leverages different modalities of correlation that consider not only variable values but also missingness patterns. CORKI's performance was compared with a domain-knowledge-based rule system and the standard sample-dropping approach on three public and one private cardiothoracic surgery datasets with diverse missing label rates. CORKI yielded performances comparable to those of the domain-knowledge approach, establishing itself as a reliable method, while being highly generalizable. Moreover, it was able to maintain imputation accuracy in demanding partial annotation scenarios, presenting drops of only 5% for missing rates of 50%.

Keywords: Multi-label Classification · Missing Label Imputation · Correlation · K-Nearest Neighbours

1 Introduction

Multi-label classification (MLC) is useful to address intricate real-world problems, as it allows for the simultaneous association of multiple class labels to individual instances. MLC has been employed in diverse domains, such as biomedical research for protein function prediction [22] or natural language processing for topic classification [7]. Harnessing the potential of a single learning task to address multiple interdependent and non-mutually exclusive targets allows for the modelling of intricate relationships between classes, which is not possible in single-label classification. This is especially relevant in clinical contexts, as distinct physiological manifestations are commonly related, and therefore can benefit from being studied simultaneously.

Nevertheless, some challenges arise in MLC. In large label spaces, the computational costs of more complex models tend to increase [8]. Also, Multi-label datasets often exhibit imbalanced label distributions [24]. Moreover, real-world data collection faces annotation challenges. Obtaining a comprehensive set of labels can be impractical or infeasible, resulting in incomplete or missing annotations. Healthcare environments are particularly susceptible to this problem, especially when predicting multiple health outcomes concurrently or over varying time horizons, as these situations may involve unrecorded outcomes. Decision Support Systems (DSS) must be robust and resilient to this inconsistency.

A standard procedure to address incomplete labels is sample dropping, which reduces the dataset size and may cause data bias. Using domain knowledge allows estimating partial labels with more certainty, but it is not always an option.

This study addresses the need for effective strategies to handle missing labels in MLC from a data-level perspective, applicable to different Machine Learning (ML) algorithms. We present CORKI (Correlation-Optimised and Robust K Nearest Neighbors Imputation for MLC), an innovative label imputation technique that incorporates different types of feature-label correlation into a K Nearest Neighbours (KNN) strategy. CORKI strives towards the development of resilient clinical DSS that provide reliable insights and promote personalized healthcare practices. Despite being applicable to other domains, CORKI was carefully designed to account for the specifications of medical contexts, regarding both incomplete records and severely imbalanced data distributions.

To evaluate the proposed method, three public databases on electrocardiography (ECG) Multi-label disease diagnosis and a cardiothoracic surgery dataset for long-term risk prediction were studied. Imputation accuracy and performance impact on MLC tasks were assessed, as CORKI was compared to a conventional sample-dropping approach and a domain-knowledge imputation scheme.

2 Related Work

The problem of Multi-label Learning with Missing Labels (MLML) [27] has been studied in the literature, through data and model-based approaches.

At the model level, Jain et al. [14] presented a generative framework for MLC which computes the likelihood of a negative value corresponding to a missing label. Ben-Baruch et al. [3] proposed an asymmetric loss that weights imputed labels, initially performed by balancing their probability in an instance and among the data. Ibrahim et al. [13] tested a similar strategy that weights loss according to confidence measures. Durand et al. [6] exploited label proportion to adapt the loss function and a curriculum learning strategy to predict missing labels.

From a data-level perspective, a common approach is to study inter-label relations to infer missing labels. Huang et al. [11] used pairwise label correlation to fill in missing labels, while Cheng and Zeng [4] used both positive and negative label correlations. Recent work showed that considering information from the feature matrix is beneficial. Rastogi and Mortaza [19] proposed a method that leverages both the correlation between labels and the structural proximity of samples in the feature matrix, achieving state-of-the-art results. Zhang et al. [29] used both feature and label embeddings to achieve an enriched version of the labels, without missing values. Tan et al. [23] partitioned data samples into several small groups by leveraging granular computing principles and used that information to achieve better missing-label value estimations.

Although successful in different learning tasks, these methods present limited applicability. Firstly, many techniques were designed considering image or text data problems, and while most of them are theoretically compatible with other modalities such as tabular data or time series, validation tests rarely consider those [1,12,14,27,28]. Secondly, methods that focus on model adaptations are typically associated with complex architectures, which might be problematic in terms of scalability and explainability [3,6,13,14]. Lastly, regarding healthcare scenarios, which are the focus of this work, the few studies that considered use cases from this domain resorted exclusively to clinical text datasets [11,12,29]. Moreover, they used these data for evaluation purposes only and did not consider distinctive attributes of healthcare data such as severe label imbalance.

This work addresses literature gaps by proposing a novel data-centric method that considers imbalanced clinical use cases and uses a new type of correlation to achieve accurate label imputations in the context of MLML, while also including a dimensionality reduction process that improves scalability. CORKI is grounded on the recent work of Curioso et al. [5], who studied the impact of using correlation measurements between data missingness patterns and known values for missing feature imputation.

3 CORKI: Correlation-Optimized and Robust KNN Imputation for Multi-label Classification

In MLC, the learning problem is associated with multiple interdependent and non-mutually exclusive labels. Real-world MLC scenarios may involve partial annotations or missing labels, which traditional algorithms do not consider.

In this scope, we propose CORKI, a label imputation method for MLC. This method is built upon a KNN imputation strategy, typically used to replace missing values in the features matrix, based on proximity measures such as the Euclidean distance [25]. CORKI first performs a correlation-based dimensionality reduction, to exclusively capture information from features that are most correlated with the label being imputed. Rather than just resorting to the traditional correlation between variable values, CORKI also explores the potential of incorporating the correlation between values and the missingness pattern of each label, i.e. the configuration of observed and missing elements. As missing labels can be due to similar motives, their missingness patterns may provide insights into the imputation process. Additionally, CORKI addresses imbalanced settings by integrating an optional weighting term that considers class prevalence.

3.1 Correlation

Pearson's correlation, one of the most used measurements in medical research, assesses the strength of a linear relationship between two numeric, random variables [18]. This work resorts to two coefficients based on Pearson's correlation.

The Phi coefficient, ϕ, measures the linear correlation between two binary variables:

$$\phi = \sqrt{\frac{\chi^2}{N}} \tag{1}$$

where χ^2 is the chi-square statistic for the 2×2 contingency table of the two variables and N is the number of observations.

The point biserial correlation coefficient, r_{pbi}, measures the strength of association between a numeric variable X and a binary nominal variable Y:

$$r_{\text{pbi}} = \frac{\bar{X}_1 - \bar{X}_0}{\sigma_X} \sqrt{p_1 p_0} \tag{2}$$

where p_1 and $p_0 = 1 - p_1$ denote the proportion of samples with $Y = 1$ and $Y = 0$, respectively. $\bar{X}_1$ and $\bar{X}_0$ are respectively the means of X given $Y = 1$ and $Y = 0$, and σ_X is the standard deviation of X.

3.2 Notation

Let us consider a Multi-label tabular dataset with G features, L labels and N samples. g_i represents the values of the ith feature, where $i \in \{1, 2, ..., G\}$, and l_j the values of the jth label, where $j \in \{1, 2, ..., L\}$. $l_{\text{miss},j}$ denotes the missingness pattern of the jth label, a binary array indicating for each data sample, whether the label was annotated or not, assuming values of 0 or 1, respectively.

C_{vv} is a $(G \times L)$ matrix, which contains the correlation coefficient between every feature, g_i, and label, l_j. Considering that each label l_j may have a variable number of missing annotations, C_{vv} is computed through pairwise deletion, where the correlation between the values of each feature and the available values within each label is obtained iteratively. This procedure removes any dependency on a complete data subset during training, both in terms of features and labels.

Analogous to C_{vv} in structure, we define C_{vm}, which contains the correlation between each feature g_i and the missingness pattern of the jth label, $l_{\text{miss},j}$.

3.3 Methodology

The CORKI method employs correlation measurements between feature values and both label values and missingness patterns. This information is used to improve a KNN-based approach for selecting proximal samples for label estimation. Instead of computing the distance between all features, CORKI performs a preliminary feature selection based on correlation, which reduces data dimensionality and enhances the method's scalability for large datasets.

CORKI is also robust to label imbalance by incorporating a weighting term to reflect the prevalence of positives when defining each neighbour's contribution. The following step-by-step outlines the implementation of CORKI's method:

1. Consider a dataset X, with G features and N instances, which relates to Multi-label outcomes Y, with L labels with partial annotations.
2. Compute C_{vv}, with the correlations between feature and label values, and C_{vm}, with the correlations between feature values and label missingness patterns. Figure 1 offers a graphical illustration of these two types of correlation. CORKI takes into account the absolute value of the correlations, thereby considering the strength of the association, rather than its direction.
3. For each label l_j, select from X the subset X_{miss_j}, which includes all samples where l_j is missing, i.e., where the missingness pattern, $l_{\text{miss},j}$, assumes the value 1. Additionally, create the subset X_{obs_j}, with samples where l_j is observed, i.e., when $l_{\text{miss},j}$ is equal to 0. If X_{miss_j} is empty, skip to the next label.
4. Compute the coefficient $r_{Cj,i}$ between label l_j and the ith attribute of X using the correlation matrices. This coefficient is identical for all samples within the subset X_{miss_j} and is calculated as follows:

$$r_{Cj,i} = \frac{1}{2} \times (C_{vv}[i,j] + C_{vm}[i,j]), \quad 0 \leq r_{Cj,i} \leq 1 \qquad (3)$$

5. Remove from X_{miss_j} and X_{obs_j} all features with $r_{Cj,i} < 0.7$. This value was defined as a threshold for high correlation, based on Schober et al. [21]. If all features are removed then this method cannot be applied, but in any case it would not be worth using a correlation-based method on a set of variables without significant correlations.
6. For each sample, find the K nearest neighbours of each sample in X_{miss_j}, within the updated subset X_{obs_j}, using the Euclidean distance.
7. For each instance of X_{miss_j}, replace the missing label l_j by a weighted mode between the K nearest neighbours' labels. The weight of the kth neighbour, $w_{j,k}$, is given by the inverse of the Euclidean distance, $d_{j,k}$, and the prevalence of its class, p_k, defined by:

$$w_{j,k} = \frac{1}{d_{j,k} \times p_k}, \qquad (4)$$

For each label l_j, the prevalence p_k is a ratio between the number of instances from class k and the total number of instances. The distance $d_{j,k}$ was previously scaled into a range from 0 to 1, where 1 corresponds to the distance of the farthest neighbour among K. While the prevalence of each neighbour's class addresses dataset imbalance, it can be ignored if considered irrelevant. Then, the weight of the kth neighbour, $w_{j,k}$, only depends on the normalized Euclidean distance:

$$w_{j,k} = \frac{1}{d_{j,k}}, \tag{5}$$

In both cases the weights are normalized, i.e. sum up to 1.

8. Repeat Steps 4–8 until all missing values from all labels have been imputed.

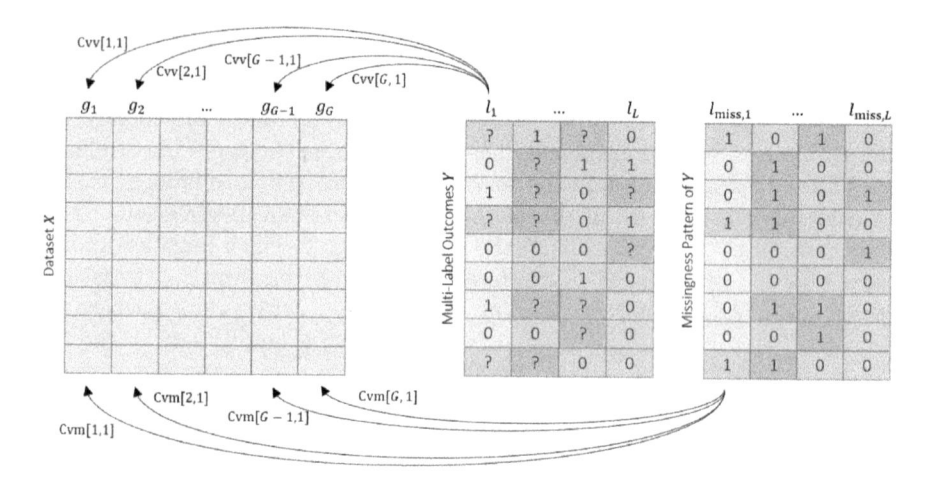

Fig. 1. Graphical depiction of the two types of correlation computed in CORKI. This example only looks at the correlation values for the first label, i.e. $j = 1$.

4 Datasets

Two healthcare use cases evaluated CORKI as an imputation method for partial annotations: the ECG-based MLC of cardiovascular diseases (CVD) and the longitudinal prediction of post-surgery risk of complications.

4.1 ECG Multi-label Classification

The ECG is a non-invasive test to record the heart's electrical activity, used to diagnose CVD commonly through ML-based MLC techniques [20].

The PhysioNet/Computing in Cardiology (CinC) Challenge 2020 provided numerous datasets for the evaluation of automated ECG classification pipelines [2]. This open-source database was used as the baseline tool to evaluate CORKI, from which three standardised datasets were leveraged: the China Physiological Signal Challenge 2018 (CPSC) [16], followed by the Physikalisch Technische Bundesanstalt XL (PTB-XL) [26], and the Georgia 12-lead ECG Challenge (G12EC) [9] Database. All three datasets encompass data from 12-lead ECG signals, demographic information (age and sex), and Multi-label annotations.

Nine common labels were selected and a similar preprocessing framework was applied to all datasets. The signals were resampled to 250 Hz and a 10-second window was retrieved from the centre of each ECG, as extremities typically contain lower-quality signals. Then, the ECG signals underwent a 2nd order bandpass Butterworth filter with a range of 1 to 40 Hz, followed by a z-normalisation.

Morphological features, wavelet descriptors and time intervals were computed based on R peak detection, resulting in a total of 80 features [17]. Also, age and sex were used as demographic data. A 5-fold split was performed on each dataset using either the provided folds (when available) or a random stratification approach, which balanced labels concerning the positive class, age and sex. The last fold was used as a test set, while the remaining were employed during cross-validation. Table 1 describes the target CVDs and the available sample count.

Table 1. Records and label distribution in the CPSC, PTB-XL and G12EC datasets.

Disease	Acronym	CPSC	PTB-XL	G12EC	Total
Normal ECG	NORM	918	9 514	1 735	12 167
Atrial fibrillation	AF	1 220	1 514	568	3 302
First-degree atrioventricular block	I-AVB	722	795	766	2 283
Left bundle branch block	LBBB	235	536	231	1 002
Premature atrial contraction	PAC	614	398	636	1 648
Premature ventricular contraction	PVC	699	1 153	41	1 893
Right bundle branch block	RBBB	1 857	542	554	2 953
ST-segment depression	STD	868	1 009	38	1 915
ST-segment elevated	STE	220	28	134	382
No. Recordings (Total)		6 871	13 932	4 301	25 104
No. Positive Labels (Total)		7 353	15 489	4 703	27 544
No. Positive Labels (Average)		817	1 721	522.4	3 060.4
Positive Class Prevalence (Average)		11.9%	12.4%	12.1%	12.2%

Since these datasets have complete annotations for all diseases, artificial missing labels were injected. To evaluate the effectiveness of CORKI across different rates of partial annotations, 3%, 5%, 10%, 25% and 50% of the labels were randomly removed. This strategy creates a pattern typical of a Missing Completely at Random (MCAR) mechanism, where the missingness origin is not related to the data values, either missing or observed [15].

4.2 Cardiothoracic Surgery Long-Term Risk Prediction

A second scenario was included, following a cardiothoracic surgery department use case, where clinicians from a Portuguese hospital collected a retrospective anonymised dataset for long-term risk prediction of post-surgery complications.

The dataset adheres to the European Association for Cardio-Thoracic Surgery (EACTS) Adult Cardiac Database fields, a European standard for cardiac surgery data collection [10]. The Cardiothoracic Surgery (CTS) dataset comprises a cohort of adult patients who underwent open-heart surgery between 2008 and 2019, excluding those who died in-hospital or did not respond to phone calls. It encompasses 105 variables, including patient demographics, pre-surgery conditions, procedure details, hospital stay duration, and in-hospital post-surgery complications. The clinicians also documented major events through phone calls at 30, 90, 180, and 365 days post-discharge, noting complications from mild to severe. These serve as Multi-label objectives, focusing on the identification of patients at a high risk of developing severe complications between contact points.

Incomplete labels arose from missed calls or post-mortem intervals. Table 2 presents the main statistics of the dataset, disclosing the extremely imbalanced prevalence of complications (average 2.8%). Also, the number of missing samples surpasses the number of positive samples. Although the origin of these partial annotations cannot be determined, they are likely to follow either a Missing at Random (MAR) mechanism, in which the missingness is associated with the observed data values, or a Missing Not at Random (MNAR) mechanism, where the unobserved values themselves lead to the missingness [15].

Table 2. Records, label and missing values distribution in the CTS dataset.

Interval	CTS
$[0, 30]$ days	196
$]30, 90]$ days	184
$]90, 180]$ days	141
$]180, 365]$ days	146
No. Recordings (Total)	5 890
No. Missing Labels (Total)	735
No. Missing Labels (Average)	183.8
Missing Rate (Average)	3.1%
No. Positive Labels (Total)	667
No. Positive Labels (Average)	166.8
Positive Class Prevalence (Average)	2.8%

The CTS dataset has a different validation approach. Given the extensive collection period, which may have seen changes in medical procedures, an external test set was created, including all surgeries performed in the last year, 2019.

Additionally, a standard test set was obtained by randomly selecting a patient-stratified group comprising 30% of the data from 2008 to 2018. The remaining training set was divided into five folds using the same strategy.

5 Experiments

The performance and robustness of CORKI were evaluated in the previous use cases, against the sample-dropping approach. The first experiment assessed the accuracy of imputations by comparing the imputation values delivered by CORKI with the ground truth ones. Then, in order to evaluate the impact of imputation on MLC, datasets processed with CORKI and the sample-dropping approach, as well as the original dataset when available, were used to train classifiers and their performance was compared.

CORKI was tested considering different parameter configurations. Regarding K, the number of neighbour samples to consider during imputation, the values of 5, 20, and 50 were used. To assess the impact of considering the positive class prevalence, CORKI was applied both adopting and disregarding the weighting term, as detailed in Sect. 3.3.

In the CTS dataset, a domain-knowledge imputation rule was also tested: (i) missing labels of post-mortem periods were replaced with 1, and (ii) the remaining with 0. This assumes similarities between deceased patients and those with complications, while unconfirmed deaths are considered low-risk periods.

5.1 Imputation Accuracy

The fully annotated datasets (CPSC2018, PTB-XL and G12EC) were subject to artificial missing label injection, to assess the quality of the generated imputations. These were compared to the ground truth values, and their accuracy was computed given the binary nature of label classes. This procedure was repeated for five rates of artificially generated missing annotations (3%, 5%, 10%, 25% and 50%). This evaluation was conducted in the test sets only, as feature-label correlations had been computed from the training sets. The CTS dataset was not included in this particular experiment, as it contains naturally missing annotations with no ground truth available.

5.2 Classification Performance Impact

A second experiment assessed the impact of CORKI on MLC model performance in both use cases of Sect. 4. Four Multi-label-compatible ML classifiers were used: Decision Tree (DT), Random Forest (RF), Multi-Layer Perceptron (MLP), and KNN. To minimise the influence of external factors on label imputation, an optimisation pipeline performed hyperparameter tuning through grid search, forward sequential feature selection, and decision threshold optimisation.

The best hyperparameters and features were selected according to the macro average of the area under the Receiver Operating Characteristic curve (AUROC).

For the public datasets, these were optimised on the complete versions of the data and applied to every experiment, due to computational constraints. Nevertheless, this option faithfully captures the original conditions of the problem. For the CTS dataset, the optimisation pipeline was implemented for each experiment, as no complete dataset reference is available. Threshold optimization was performed for every label in all use cases, by selecting the one that maximized the sum between specificity and sensitivity. The optimization was conducted through a k-fold grouped stratified cross-validation strategy.

MLC performance metrics were obtained from test sets where no label imputation took part. Since the CTS dataset has originally missing labels, these were dropped for metrics computation. Results were evaluated in terms of AUROC, sensitivity, specificity and F1-score.

6 Results

6.1 Imputation Accuracy

The efficacy of label imputation was assessed by the accuracy of imputations in the test set. Since the labels of the ECG MLC use case are binary, this measure consists of an average of the hit-or-miss imputation accuracy across all labels, weighted according to each label's prevalence. As described in Sect. 3.3, two versions of CORKI were tested: a standard one based solely on distance, and a second one weighted by prevalence. Table 3 presents the obtained results for various MR and datasets, reported by the mean and standard deviation for all labels, i.e., diseases, and tested K number of neighbours used by CORKI.

Table 3. ECG imputation results from CORKI for the test set in the G12EC, CPSC2019 and PTB-XL datasets. The Total column presents the average and pooled standard deviation across all datasets. Results are presented as a percentage (%) in terms of balanced accuracy. CORKI P. refers to the disease prevalence weighting.

MR	Strategy	G12EC	CPSC2018	PTB-XL	Total
3	CORKI	62.8 ± 17.9	67.8 ± 20.6	63.7 ± 17.3	64.9 ± 18.6
	CORKI P.	68.8 ± 24.0	71.7 ± 11.6	**78.9 ± 13.4**	73.1 ± 17.2
5	CORKI	60.6 ± 13.3	61.5 ± 15.6	64.6 ± 17.5	62.2 ± 15.6
	CORKI P.	**70.4 ± 20.4**	**73.3 ± 10.3**	78.1 ± 12.6	**73.9 ± 15.1**
10	CORKI	59.4 ± 12.9	58.1 ± 9.2	64.3 ± 17.1	60.6 ± 13.5
	CORKI P.	67.2 ± 16.4	70.6 ± 12.3	78.6 ± 12.6	72.1 ± 13.9
25	CORKI	58.8 ± 12.0	60.3 ± 9.1	57.9 ± 11.2	59.0 ± 10.8
	CORKI P.	67.2 ± 11.0	72.6 ± 8.8	70.9 ± 14.4	70.2 ± 11.6
50	CORKI	58.8 ± 10.8	58.5 ± 8.8	57.2 ± 10.7	58.2 ± 10.1
	CORKI P.	68.4 ± 9.74	68.9 ± 9.1	69.3 ± 13.3	68.9 ± 10.9

The highest average imputation accuracy recorded against all data, (73.9 ± 15.1)%, was achieved by the prevalence-weighted CORKI for an artificial MR of 5%. On the other hand, the lowest average accuracy, (58.2 ± 10.1)%, was obtained for an MR of 50% using the non-weighted CORKI version. These MR were selected to capture a wide range of potential missing label scenarios.

The PTB-XL dataset exhibited the best imputations across various MR among all datasets, with the overall maximum accuracy of (78.9 ± 13.4)% being achieved at an MR of 3%. This tendency was particularly evident for the prevalence-weighted CORKI and might be a result of the superior size of this dataset when compared to the remaining (see Table 1). With more data samples, correlation and proximity measures tend to get more realistic, which positively impacts the accuracy of imputation values computed through CORKI.

The tested datasets are imbalanced, with an average positive class prevalence of 12.2%. As so, the higher balanced accuracies achieved by the weighted versions suggest that CORKI is more robust to data imbalance. However, standard deviations have a similar magnitude, indicating great variability between labels.

As expected, imputation accuracy decreases with higher MR, as less information is available to retrieve meaningful correlations. Curiously, standard deviations tend to decrease with increasing MR. Nevertheless, the drop in performance with prevalence weighting only reaches 5.0% between 3% and 50% of MR.

6.2 Classification Performance Impact

Table 4 draws the results from the ECG classification use case against different MR. For each combination, the results refer to the pipeline with the highest cross-validation AUROC and the best number of neighbours K. For each dataset, CORKI prevalence-weighted and unweighted versions were compared to the original data and to sample dropping. The AUROC, sensitivity, specificity and F1-score are shown, obtained following threshold optimization.

The complete dataset generally achieves the highest classification performance, only surpassed by a maximum of 0.1% in terms of AUROC. Sometimes, imputation strategies can prompt higher performances than those attained with original samples, as the artificial values are more likely to follow expected data distributions [5]. Nevertheless, strategies can be compared to this baseline performance. From the tested classifiers (DT, RF, MLP and KNN), the MLP exhibited superior performance in all scenarios except two. The optimal K does not show a consistent trend, although 5 neighbours were the most common.

CORKI achieved performances comparable to the complete dataset in most cases up to 25% MR, while sample dropping maintained such values only up to 10% MR. As instances with missing labels are removed, the data distribution changes with the loss of information, leading to biased learning. This phenomenon is emphasized at higher missing rates, which explains the worse performances through dropping in those conditions. With a 50% MR, this strategy removed all samples from the train set in several cases, preventing any models from training, and making CORKI the only viable option in such a scenario.

Table 4. ECG classification results for the test set in the G12EC, CPSC2019 and PTB-XL datasets. Results are presented as percentage (%) in terms of AUROC, sensitivity, specificity and F1-score, as the mean and standard deviation of all labels. CORKI P. refers to the disease prevalence weighting. MLP was generally selected as the best model, except in cases marked with *, where KNN was selected.

	MR	Strategy	K	AUROC	Sensitivity	Specificity	F1-Score
G12EC		Original	-	86.5 ± 13.4	73.6 ± 20.7	85.7 ± 6.2	44.8 ± 30.5
	3	Drop	-	85.7 ± 12.1	70.6 ± 23.7	82.8 ± 13.4	44.6 ± 32.1
		CORKI	20	86.2 ± 13.9	71.2 ± 20.2	83.1 ± 11.7	45.1 ± 31.8
		CORKI P.	5	85.4 ± 14.8	70.1 ± 21.6	84.4 ± 9.6	44.5 ± 30.6
	5	Drop	-	85.1 ± 13.8	69.5 ± 23.5	81.7 ± 16.8	44.9 ± 31.7
		CORKI	5	85.9 ± 14.6	72.8 ± 19.4	85.4 ± 7.0	45.4 ± 30.9
		CORKI P.	5	84.8 ± 15.9	70.7 ± 24.1	83.5 ± 8.8	44.1 ± 31.4
	10	Drop	-	82.4 ± 16.1	70.2 ± 22.8	82.1 ± 7.8	42.1 ± 30.1
		CORKI	50	86.2 ± 13.7	74.6 ± 22.4	84.5 ± 8.3	**45.6 ± 32.0**
		CORKI P.	5	84.4 ± 15.0	72.4 ± 20.0	82.1 ± 9.6	43.1 ± 31.1
	25	Drop	-	65.7 ± 22.9	31.4 ± 25.2	**92.1 ± 7.8**	30.1 ± 24.8
		CORKI	20	84.8 ± 16.5	67.4 ± 26.5	86.9 ± 6.4	45.3 ± 29.8
		CORKI P.	50	82.7 ± 13.2	**78.5 ± 18.1**	73.5 ± 11.1	37.0 ± 28.1
	50	Drop	-	-	-	-	-
		CORKI	20	83.7 ± 15.9	71.1 ± 23.1	84.4 ± 4.9	43.8 ± 29.6
		CORKI P.	5	81.4 ± 14.0	76.2 ± 17.9	71.0 ± 11.6	35.2 ± 27.5
CPSC2018		Original	-	92.9 ± 3.9	83.6 ± 8.5	88.3 ± 6.7	61.2 ± 16.7
	3	Drop	-	92.9 ± 3.9	83.0 ± 7.6	89.4 ± 4.6	61.2 ± 16.4
		CORKI	50	**93.0 ± 3.9**	85.3 ± 6.3	87.0 ± 8.9	59.1 ± 21.1
		CORKI P.	5	92.5 ± 4.0	85.3 ± 6.9	85.9 ± 10.0	57.8 ± 22.7
	5	Drop	-	92.6 ± 4.1	82.6 ± 10.4	**90.0 ± 5.5**	60.6 ± 21.7
		CORKI	50	**93.0 ± 3.8**	85.3 ± 4.8	87.7 ± 7.8	59.5 ± 20.4
		CORKI P.	5	92.4 ± 4.0	84.5 ± 6.4	87.1 ± 6.9	57.9 ± 22.0
	10	Drop	-	92.0 ± 4.0	81.9 ± 9.1	89.3 ± 4.2	59.3 ± 15.6
		CORKI	20	92.7 ± 3.9	83.1 ± 8.1	89.1 ± 6.8	**62.0 ± 15.7**
		CORKI P.	5	92.3 ± 3.8	86.0 ± 7.0	85.8 ± 8.3	57.4 ± 18.9
	25	Drop*	-	81.0 ± 9.2	57.4 ± 30.9	79.1 ± 21.0	38.5 ± 23.6
		CORKI	50	92.1 ± 4.4	81.6 ± 10.2	89.2 ± 4.6	59.6 ± 15.9
		CORKI P.	50	89.4 ± 5.2	**87.4 ± 7.5**	70.6 ± 6.9	40.4 ± 18.8
	50	Drop	-	-	-	-	-
		CORKI*	50	87.4 ± 6.6	73.8 ± 13.3	89.3 ± 4.3	55.7 ± 16.2
		CORKI P.	5	87.4 ± 5.9	84.0 ± 11.5	71.7 ± 11.1	40.4 ± 18.2
PTB-XL		Original	-	91.6 ± 8.6	86.2 ± 5.9	82.5 ± 16.5	45.1 ± 28.9
	3	Drop	-	90.6 ± 11.1	79.4 ± 13.7	86.8 ± 9.3	**46.1 ± 28.9**
		CORKI	50	90.3 ± 12.4	80.8 ± 13.1	83.0 ± 16.8	45.6 ± 28.9
		CORKI P.	5	90.3 ± 11.5	84.3 ± 8.6	80.5 ± 20.3	44.1 ± 28.9
	5	Drop	-	90.7 ± 10.1	81.5 ± 13.0	85.5 ± 8.2	44.0 ± 29.3
		CORKI	5	90.5 ± 12.2	84.0 ± 8.4	83.0 ± 16.2	45.8 ± 28.9
		CORKI P.	5	90.3 ± 12.1	85.3 ± 9.0	81.7 ± 15.3	44.2 ± 28.4
	10	Drop	-	85.8 ± 16.2	72.2 ± 28.6	**87.8 ± 8.7**	43.8 ± 29.4
		CORKI	5	**90.8 ± 10.8**	84.2 ± 8.4	83.6 ± 13.4	44.6 ± 28.2
		CORKI P.	5	90.3 ± 11.2	87.2 ± 8.5	80.0 ± 15.9	42.4 ± 28.8
	25	Drop	-	-	-	-	-
		CORKI	5	90.2 ± 11.9	84.3 ± 9.1	81.7 ± 16.4	43.9 ± 27.4
		CORKI P.	5	89.8 ± 10.2	89.4 ± 10.6	75.5 ± 14.2	37.6 ± 27.7
	50	Drop	-	-	-	-	-
		CORKI	50	90.0 ± 10.1	87.5 ± 8.5	78.9 ± 20.8	43.1 ± 29.1
		CORKI P.	5	87.7 ± 10.9	**90.0 ± 9.6**	72.1 ± 12.0	33.6 ± 28.7

Contrary to what was observed in the first experiment, the results for prevalence weighting in CORKI were overall inferior when compared to the standard version. Still, sensitivity tends to increase at the cost of specificity, particularly in the CPSC2018 and PTB-XL datasets. This may be associated with a higher number of positive labels imputed, positively affecting true positives and negatively impacting false positives, resulting in a decrease in the F1-score.

Longitudinal risk prediction performance using the CTS dataset is summarized in Table 5. Two test sets were evaluated: one randomly split (Test) and another with all surgeries from the last year available (Test 2019). This dataset is severely imbalanced and has a natural MR of 3.1%. MLP and K set to 50 consistently achieved the best AUROC. Due to severe imbalance, the F1-scores are low, as models favour the positive class, leading to many false positives.

In addition to sample dropping, domain knowledge imputation was tested. While the former led to the worst results in terms of the AUROC, the latter produced the highest. In the first set, the prevalence-weighted version of CORKI can match the domain knowledge performance, with higher sensitivity. CORKI imputation always surpasses the sample-dropping strategy, especially in the first test set. This tendency was unclear in the results gathered for the public datasets, for the similar MR of 3%. This might come as a consequence of the extremely low representation of positive samples in the CTS dataset (2.8%), which makes the loss of positive samples through dropping much more impactful.

All methods presented considerably worse performance when tested against the Test 2019 of the CTS dataset, which suggests the presence of temporal drift at feature or label levels. The fact that the weighted version of CORKI produced worse results when compared to the standard version increases this suspicion. In a scenario where class distributions change over time, the benefits of applying this technique are lost, and the quality of imputations is likely to be affected.

Table 5. Longitudinal risks estimation in cardiothoracic surgery classification results for the CTS test sets. Results are presented as percentage (%) in terms of AUROC, sensitivity, specificity and F1-score, as the mean and standard deviation of all labels. CORKI P. refers to the disease prevalence weighting. MLP was always selected as the best model. * corresponds to the same outcome in all three tested K.

		Strategy	K	AUROC	Sensitivity	Specificity	F1-Score
CTS	Test	Drop	-	57.3 ± 2.6	43.4 ± 20.8	64.2 ± 10.1	5.9 ± 1.3
		Domain	-	**67.9 ± 4.7**	53.4 ± 7.6	**70.1 ± 2.2**	**9.0 ± 2.8**
		CORKI	*	66.3 ± 4.1	51.7 ± 5.9	68.4 ± 1.8	8.3 ± 2.6
		CORKI P.	50	**67.9 ± 5.9**	**57.1 ± 14.0**	66.3 ± 5.0	8.6 ± 2.9
	Test 2019	Drop	-	55.6 ± 3.5	40.5 ± 13.2	64.8 ± 13.4	6.5 ± 0.7
		Domain	-	**60.5 ± 3.2**	44.6 ± 3.5	66.8 ± 3.4	7.5 ± 1.2
		CORKI	*	58.6 ± 1.6	**47.3 ± 4.7**	**69.4 ± 2.0**	**8.5 ± 1.2**
		CORKI P.	50	57.0 ± 3.7	37.9 ± 9.3	67.4 ± 6.4	6.5 ± 1.3

7 Discussion

Partial annotations in MLC can arise from decisions and errors made by humans or machines, or simply due to the characteristics of real-world data subject to crowdsourcing annotations. The method proposed in this work, CORKI, aims to provide a general solution for MLC pipelines by leveraging correlation measures in the feature-label level, distance estimations and class prevalence.

Our evaluation shows that CORKI performs well in terms of imputation accuracy, despite the high class imbalance of the ECG classification use case. However, the evaluation was limited to three datasets with similar characteristics, so tests should be further extended. Additionally, the weighted version of CORKI produces more accurate imputations at all MR, which reflects the importance of considering class prevalence in label imputation.

In terms of classification performance, CORKI generated similar results to those achieved with the original versions of the data, despite the loss of information. Compared to a standard sample dropping, CORKI becomes more relevant with higher MR. Also, the prevalence-weighted version produces contradictory results between tests and different K neighbours that emerged from the optimal combinations, which suggests that prevalence weighting and K should be optimized for each specific context. Future work might focus on studying the behaviour of the method as this parameters change. Moreover, upcoming research should address the lack of comparison with more complex baselines beyond the naive dropping of samples, which constitutes a limitation of this work.

Especially in healthcare, it is common for the collection of data to be intermittent, following specific clinical events or monitoring needs. By leveraging not only relationships between variables but also missingness patterns, CORKI accounts for the underlying context of data collection, aiming at more accurate estimations. On another note, the results attained by the prevalence-weighted version of CORKI reflect a tendency to benefit sensitivity over specificity, especially at higher missing rates, which is desirable in many healthcare use cases, as the cost of false negatives is usually much higher than that of the false positives. Nevertheless, the trustworthiness of such estimations should be accounted for in future work by resorting to methods such as uncertainty estimations.

As a final note, CORKI constitutes a promising label imputation method to address partial annotations in MLC with promising results. This method tackles certain gaps in the literature by (i) accounting for scalability, since it consists of a data-centric approach involving a dimensionality reduction step, (ii) addressing the applicability of MLML to the clinical domain, by accounting for specific characteristics of health data such as severe class imbalance, and (iii) introducing a new type of feature-label correlation for missing label estimation, involving the patterns of missingness in the label matrix. CORKI can potentially have a positive impact in healthcare contexts, where missing labels and imbalanced distributions are common and accurate imputation methods are essential for developing reliable clinical DSS.

8 Conclusion

This work addressed the challenges of Multi-label learning with partial annotations in healthcare contexts, focusing on the data level to make traditional Multi-label ML pipelines viable. CORKI is proposed, a label imputation method that leverages feature-label correlations, proximity measures, and positive class prevalence to produce accurate estimations. CORKI was evaluated through ECG classification and longitudinal post-surgery risk prediction use cases, demonstrating its effectiveness in imbalanced clinical scenarios in terms of imputation accuracy and classification performance.

Results indicate that CORKI outperforms sample-dropping strategies, enhancing learning performance in low- to high-missing label settings. These findings establish CORKI as a promising method to deal with partial annotations in clinical contexts, as it consists of a resource-effective alternative when domain expertise is scarce or impractical. Nevertheless, additional tests are recommended to validate CORKI's generalization using benchmark datasets, as well as comparisons with alternative methods from the literature.

Acknowledgements. This work was supported by European funds through Plano de Recuperação e Resiliência, project "Center for Responsible AI" with project number 62_C645008882-00000055.

References

1. Akbarnejad, A., Baghshah, M.S.: An efficient semi-supervised multi-label classifier capable of handling missing labels. IEEE Trans. Knowl. Data Eng. **31**, 229–242 (2019)
2. Alday, E.A.P., et al.: Classification of 12-lead ECGs: the physionet/computing in cardiology challenge 2020. Physiol. Meas. **41**(12), 124003 (2020)
3. Ben-Baruch, E., et al.: Multi-label classification with partial annotations using class-aware selective loss. In: Proceedings of the IEEE/CVF Conference on Computer Vision and Pattern Recognition, pp. 4764–4772 (2022)
4. Cheng, Z., Zeng, Z.: Joint label-specific features and label correlation for multi-label learning with missing label. Appl. Intell. **50**(11), 4029–4049 (2020). https://doi.org/10.1007/s10489-020-01715-2
5. Curioso, I., et al.: Addressing the curse of missing data in clinical contexts: A novel approach to correlation-based imputation. J. King Saud Univ. Comput. Inf. Sci. **35**(6), 101562 (2023)
6. Durand, T., Mehrasa, N., Mori, G.: Learning a deep convnet for multi-label classification with partial labels. In: Proceedings of the IEEE/CVF Conference on Computer Vision and Pattern Recognition, pp. 647–657 (2019)
7. Fei, H., et al.: Topic-enhanced capsule network for multi-label emotion classification. IEEE/ACM Trans. Audio Speech Lang. Process. **28**, 1839–1848 (2020)
8. Gibaja, E., Ventura, S.: Multi-label learning: a review of the state of the art and ongoing research. Wiley Interdiscip. Rev. Data Min. Knowl. Discov. **4**(6), 411–444 (2014)

9. Goldberger, A.L., et al.: PhysioBank, PhysioToolKit, and PhysioNet: components of a new research resource for complex physiologic signals. Circulation **101**(23), e215–e220 (2000)
10. Head, S.J., et al.: The European association for cardio-thoracic surgery (EACTS) Database: an introduction. Euro. J. Cardiothorac. Surg. **44**(3), e175–e180 (2013)
11. Huang, J., et al.: Improving multi-label classification with missing labels by learning label-specific features. Inf. Sci. **492**, 124–146 (2019)
12. Huang, J., et al.: Multi-label learning with missing and completely unobserved labels. Data Min. Knowl. Disc. **35**(3), 1061–1086 (2021). https://doi.org/10.1007/s10618-021-00743-x
13. Ibrahim, K.M., et al.: Confidence-based weighted loss for multi-label classification with missing labels. In: Proceedings of the 2020 International Conference on Multimedia Retrieval (2020)
14. Jain, V., Modhe, N., Rai, P.: Scalable generative models for multi-label learning with missing labels. In: International Conference on Machine Learning (2017)
15. Little, R.J., Rubin, D.B.: Statistical Analysis with Missing Data, vol. 793. Wiley (2019)
16. Liu, F., et al.: An open access database for evaluating the algorithms of electrocardiogram rhythm and morphology abnormality detection. J. Med. Imag. Health Inf. **8**(7), 1368–1373 (2018)
17. Mondéjar-Guerra, V., et al.: Heartbeat classification fusing temporal and morphological information of ECGs via ensemble of classifiers. Biomed. Signal Process. Control **47**, 41–48 (2019)
18. Mukaka, M.M.: A guide to appropriate use of correlation coefficient in medical research. Malawi Med. J. **24**(3), 69–71 (2012)
19. Rastogi, R., Mortaza, S.: Multi-label classification with missing labels using label correlation and robust structural learning. Knowl. Based Syst. **229**, 107336 (2021)
20. Sai, Y.P., et al.: A review on arrhythmia classification using ECG signals. In: 2020 IEEE International Students' Conference on Electrical, Electronics and Computer Science (SCEECS), pp. 1–6. IEEE (2020)
21. Schober, P., Boer, C., Schwarte, L.A.: Correlation coefficients: appropriate use and interpretation. Anesth. Analg. **126**(5), 1763–1768 (2018)
22. Tahzeeb, S., Hasan, S.: A neural network-based multi-label classifier for protein function prediction. Eng. Technol. Appl. Sci. Res. **12**(1), 7974–7981 (2022)
23. Tan, A., et al.: Weak multi-label learning with missing labels via instance granular discrimination. Inf. Sci. **594**, 200–216 (2022)
24. Tarekegn, A.N., Giacobini, M., Michalak, K.: A review of methods for imbalanced multi-label classification. Pattern Recogn. **118**, 107965 (2021)
25. Troyanskaya, O., et al.: Missing value estimation methods for DNA microarrays. Bioinformatics **17**(6), 520–525 (2001)
26. Wagner, P., et al.: PTB-XL, a large publicly available electrocardiography dataset. Sci. data **7**(1), 154 (2020)
27. Wu, B., et al.: Multi-label learning with missing labels. In: 2014 22nd International Conference on Pattern Recognition, pp. 1964–1968 (2014)
28. Xu, L., et al.: Learning low-rank label correlations for multi-label classification with missing labels. In: 2014 IEEE International Conference on Data Mining, pp. 1067–1072 (2014)
29. Zhang, C., et al.: Hybrid noise-oriented multilabel learning. IEEE Trans. Cybern. **50**, 2837–2850 (2020)

Neuro-symbolic Artificial Intelligence for Patient Monitoring

Ole Fenske[✉][iD], Sebastian Bader[iD], and Thomas Kirste[iD]

Rostock University, Albert-Einstein-Str. 22, 18059 Rostock, Germany
{ole.fenske,sebastian.bader,thomas.kirste}@uni-rostock.de
https://www.mmis.informatik.uni-rostock.de/en/

Abstract. In this paper we argue that Neuro-Symbolic AI (NeSy-AI) should be applied for patient monitoring. In this context, we introduce patient monitoring as a special case of Human Activity Recognition and derive concrete requirements for this application area. We then present a process architecture and discuss why NeSy-AI should be applied for patient monitoring. To further support our argumentation, we show how NeSy-AI can help to overcome certain technical challenges that arise from this application area.

Keywords: neuro-symbolic · symbolic-subsymbolic · neural-symbolic · patient monitoring · human activity recognition

1 Introduction

The intuition behind Neuro-Symbolic AI (NeSy-AI) is to integrate low-level perception with high-level reasoning by utilising (deep) neural networks (NNs) and symbolic systems respectively [11,13]. Here, the symbolic systems refer to explicit knowledge representation (e.g., graphs, ontologies, formal logic) and symbol manipulation algorithms. There are three existing approaches to realize NeSy-AI:

- **Extraction**: Learn from raw data with a neural network and extract the learned information to model it as symbolic knowledge.
- **Embedding**: Embed symbolic knowledge right into the neural network.
- **Hybrid**: Combine both methods (neural and symbolic) such that they exist as co-routines next to each other.

The intuition behind such an integration is to complement both methods in their advantages and shortcomings. For instance, neural networks, on one hand, are proven to learn from raw data and are able to tackle noise and inconsistencies. Thus, applications requiring raw data analysis and information extraction can benefit from neural networks. However, the blackbox nature, i.e., inability to interpret the decision making process and learned knowledge, of such networks can be problematic in many applications such as healthcare.

On the other hand, symbolic AI is interpretable by design where the decision process is transparent and accessible for humans. The transparent nature of symbolic AI can therefore be useful in complementing the mentioned blackbox nature of neural networks. Nevertheless, symbolic AI also suffers from certain drawbacks. For instance, processing raw data is problematic as such methods are prone to observation errors, inconsistencies and data outliers. Moreover, training symbolic AI systems, as we do with neural networks, is much harder.

The contributions of this paper are: In Sect. 2 we introduce patient monitoring as an important use case within Human Activity Recognition and several requirements are provided. In Sect. 3 we derive a process architecture for patient monitoring and justify our intuition behind applying Nesy-AI. Furthermore, we outline the concrete challenges to be expected and strategies to tackle these challenges through Nesy-AI on an abstract and theoretical level. Finally, in the last section, we conclude our work by summarizing the core insights of this paper and giving a short outlook.

2 Patient Monitoring as a Special Case of Human Activity Recognition

Human Activity Recognition (HAR) aims at recognizing activities of interest based on sensor information [16]. Depending upon the type of sensor used, HAR can be classified into vision and sensor based [12]. Vision based approaches rely on cameras whereas sensor based methods can be further divided into wearable sensors and environmental sensors. Wearable sensors are often attached to humans or objects that are part of the activity i.e. cooking utensils, whereas environmental sensor are placed in the surroundings.

In this context, patient monitoring can be seen as a special case of HAR, because we want to monitor the current state at a patients bedside (e.g. nurse and patient next to bed) as well as specific high-level activities (e.g. changing bedsheets) in hospitals. Therefore, we deploy non-invasive sensors (e.g. thermal, time-of-flight) within the environment of a hospital, to span a so called (virtual) *patient zone* around the patients bed. These sensors have a low resolution, because this makes them a) cheap and thus more affordable for the hospitals and b) more energy-efficient and easy deployable, because they need no extra energy-supply.

Of course, this specific setup comes at a cost. Because of the low resolution, the recognition task itself becomes more challenging due to low-quality data. Also the spatial environment might vary for different locations. A patient room can be arranged in various ways, so that sensor data for the same scene can look differently. Therefore, one-fits-all solution for a recognition system is infeasible and a rather generalised approach is required to accommodate multiple environmental settings. Also the fact that we are in a clinical environment plays a crucial role, when it comes to recording training data for the system. In such an environment we cannot expect to have much training data, what makes the recognition task even harder.

Besides the information extracted from the sensor data, domain knowledge is also available. This can be provided by experts in terms of best practises for states or by semi-formal specifications for high-level activities. The challenging aspect here is, that the best practices for states differ between hospitals due to specific setups, personnel situation, etc., whereas the semi-formal specifications of activities stay the same, as they are specific in laws and global rules. Also the domain knowledge is not readily available as well-structured and annotated data, rather, such information is often possessed by respective people. Therefore, a formalised version of such knowledge is required to be operable by computers.

Another aspect is, that the overall system must be easily usable and intelligible for users with no technical background such as hospital staff. Moreover, the before mentioned heterogeneity needs to be addressed as well. For example, the hospital staff must be enabled to customise the system by redefining processes or incorporating additional architectural information of the hospital, such that the system is easily modified to fit the local requirements.

To summarise, our goal is to provide a low-training system, which a) is able to make use of different sensor modalities with low resolution, b) can make use of additional domain knowledge, and c) is easily accessible and customizable for non-technical users, This system can then serve as a baseline for further clinical use cases, such as, the entry and exit of persons into the patient zone (a virtual monitoring zone), fall detection, bed preparation, pressure sore risks or hands-disinfection recognition for hygiene management.

3 Patient Monitoring as a Use Case for NeSy-AI

As explained in Sect. 2, we want to integrate domain background knowledge with sensor data to infer corresponding states and activities.

To account for the different types of domain knowledge (as outlined in Sect. 2) we divide the overall monitoring process into multiple levels, as shown in the Fig. 1.

In the first level, we extract abstract information from the observations available through the sensor data. Here, an observation corresponds to the information that can be drawn directly from the respective sensor data, for instance, "There are two persons and an occupied bed".

At the second level, we infer semantic states derived from the observations. They correspond to fine-grained semantic states, which can be inferred from observations by utilising the additional domain knowledge, specifying the concrete setup within the hospital. Referring back to example observation "There are two persons and an occupied bed", we can derive the state as "Nurse + Patient" using the (domain) knowledge of being in a hospital environment.

In the third level, high-level activities are detected, which are defined as a sequence of states. Again, background knowledge is used at this level to infer activities. Lets continue our example and have a look at the next state in Fig. 1. From the given state sequence we can conclude the activity "nurse aids patient" and that the next activity could be "bed preparation". Here, domain knowledge from nursing science is utilised to map sequential states into more complex high-level activities and to predict future activities as well.

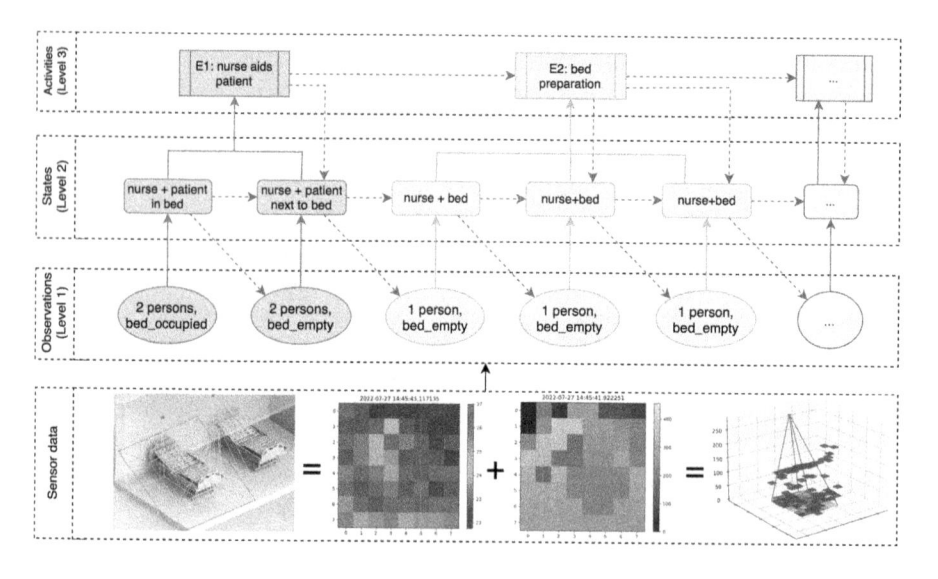

Fig. 1. The different levels of the patient monitoring process.

As the domain knowledge is either informal or semi-formal, a knowledge model is required to formalise it such that it can be used in AI methods. As described in Sect. 1, symbolic AI is the appropriate methodology for knowledge-modelling in an interpretable and formalized manner. Moreover, as mentioned already, to analyse sensor data, we will use neural networks as they are proven to be robust against noise and inconsistencies in raw data.

As this is in line with the overall goal of NeSy-AI, we argue that it should be applied to patient monitoring. To further underpin our argumentation, we describe some specific challenges which arise from the requirements we identified in Sect. 2 and we will also explain how NeSy-AI can be used to address them.

Sample Efficiency: As outlined before, neural networks are well established for low-level perception. However, they rely on high quantity of underlying training data. Therefore, in order for such networks to be applicable, samples for each possible activity with its corresponding states and observations need to be recorded as well. This conflicts our pivotal low-training requirement (Sect. 2). Since additional background knowledge is available, we should utilise it to address the problem. In this regard, several NeSy-AI approaches are available: Logic Tensor Networks (LTNs) [8] for example, integrate neural networks with first-order fuzzy logic to learn efficiently while requiring fewer data samples. In our context, we could potentially use fuzzy logic to model domain knowledge to achieve similar results. Similarly DeepProbLog [15] take one step further. Preliminary experiments[1] have shown that DeepProbLog can even be used to reduce the complexity of the learning task itself, and thus the amount of training data required. Here, the domain knowledge can be used to model interdependence among observations (e.g., number of persons or bed), states (e.g., nurse + bed or nurse + bed + patient) and the activities (e.g., changing bed sheets or patient being asleep) associated. Therefore, by logically modelling the domain knowledge and integrating it with the neural networks, we can restrict the learning task to observations only. Thus, the respective states and activities could be inferred from the logical model while learning the low-level observations from the raw sensor data by neural networks.

Uncertainty: One of the most prominent frameworks for high-level reasoning is logic, however, it is restricted by crisp (e.g. Boolean) decisions. This becomes problematic in the presence of uncertainty as in noisy sensor data and, therefore, needs to be accounted for in the overall monitoring process. The corresponding research in the NeSy-AI field [2,7,15] argue in favour of integrating probability as its third component. With ProbLog [6,10] for example, a dedicated language was designed to assign Prolog clauses with their probability of being true. In similar context, Computational State Space Models (CSSMs) use probabilistic filters for doing the inference and reasoning, and they are proven to handle problems with big state spaces well [14]. The main problem with both approaches is, that they don't integrate with neural networks to generate observations. To address this, DeepProbLog [15] uses so-called neural predicates to model the probability of a clause being true or taking a particular value by a neural network (with a Softmax output layer). Thus, we are able to account for uncertainty resulting from the sensor data in the further monitoring process. Also the system is end-to-end full differentiable, hence, the overall system can be trained on annotated data to learn the probabilities of the respective (neural and probabilistic) clauses.

Explainability: Resulting from the previously outlined requirements, i.e., enabling the non-technical users for the proposed system, explainability becomes pivotal. As described before, neural networks' decision making framework acts as a blackbox and, therefore, can not be explained. Hence, we require a symbolic part of the system. Several NeSy approaches (e.g., [1,3–5,9]) use ontologies or knowledge graphs as their symbolic component to support the intelligibility of such systems. One approach [5] for example, generates the knowledge graph from labeled training samples and use it in combination with WordNet to (a) enrich the labels of the (training) dataset itself and (b) refine the predictions of the neural component, such that the knowledge graph constraints are adhered. The *X-NeSyL* [9] approach aims to increase the overall system performance, in addition to its explainability. It uses a knowledge graph (which reflects expert information and serves as a gold standard) where individual nodes are associated with a neural network to guide its learning process in such a way that the expert

---

[1] https://github.com/vac-mmis/Neuro-SymbolicArtificialIntelligenceforPatientMonitoring.

knowledge is not violated. In other words, the knowledge graph serves as a so-called feature attribution graph and reflects the information if a certain neural network feature contributes negatively or positively towards a prediction during training and reasoning. Another related work which can be stated here is again DeepProbLog [15]. By using a logic program to model the domain knowledge, the knowledge base as well as the inference process are interpretable by design.

4 Conclusion

With this paper, we aim at initiating further research and development in patient monitoring using NeSy-AI. For this, we first provided a general introduction to NeSy-AI and then introduced a process architecture for patient monitoring to account for the different levels of domain knowledge used. Additionally, a number of important requirements for patient monitoring were presented and based on those requirements, we outlined the potential challenges and their possible solution with NeSy-AI for patient monitoring. The presented work, therefore, should enable NeSy techniques to be applicable in the patient monitoring domain. We believe that our work will not only benefit the application domain, but also the research within the NeSy community as well. Moreover, the presented techniques were mostly applied to toy-examples, hence, an application to real-world problems still remains an open question in the NeSy community and thus might reveal new interesting insights in further developments. Moreover, the presented work could be used for other assistance scenarios such as elderly care or for patients with mobility issues.

Acknowledgement. We want to thank GWA Hygiene for providing us with the sensors as well as the additional infrastructure which is necessary for a project like this.

References

1. Bennetot, A., Laurent, J.L., Chatila, R., Díaz-Rodríguez, N.: Towards explainable neural-symbolic visual reasoning.(2019). In: IJCAI19 Neural-Symbolic Learning and Reasoning Workshop (2019). https://sites.google.com/view/nesy2019/home
2. Besold, T.R., et al.: Neural-symbolic learning and reasoning: a survey and interpretation. In: Neuro-Symbolic Artificial Intelligence: The State of the Art, pp. 1–51. IOS Press (2021)
3. Bollacker, K., Díaz-Rodríguez, N., Li, X.: Extending knowledge graphs with subjective influence networks for personalized fashion. In: Portmann, E., Tabacchi, M.E., Seising, R., Habenstein, A. (eds.) Designing Cognitive Cities, pp. 203–233. Studies in Systems, Decision and Control, Springer International Publishing, Cham (2019). https://doi.org/10.1007/978-3-030-00317-3_9
4. Confalonieri, R., Weyde, T., Besold, T.R., Moscoso del Prado Martín, F.: Using ontologies to enhance human understandability of global post-hoc explanations of black-box models. Artif. Intell. **296**, 103471 (2021).https://doi.org/10.1016/j.artint.2021.103471. https://www.sciencedirect.com/science/article/pii/S0004370221000229

5. Daniels, Z.A., Frank, L.D., Menart, C., Raymer, M., Hitzler, P.: A framework for explainable deep neural models using external knowledge graphs. In: Pham, T., Solomon, L., Rainey, K. (eds.) Artificial Intelligence and Machine Learning for Multi-Domain Operations Applications II, pp. 73. SPIE, Online Only, United States, April 2020. https://doi.org/10.1117/12.2558083
6. De Raedt, L., Kimmig, A., Toivonen, H.: Problog: a probabilistic prolog and its application in link discovery. In: IJCAI 2007, Proceedings of the 20th International Joint Conference on Artificial Intelligence, pp. 2462–2467. IJCAI-INT JOINT CONF ARTIF INTELL (2007)
7. De Raedt, L., Manhaeve, R., Dumancic, S., Demeester, T., Kimmig, A.: Neurosymbolic= neural+ logical+ probabilistic. In: NeSy'19@ IJCAI, the 14th International Workshop on Neural-Symbolic Learning and Reasoning (2019)
8. Donadello, I., Serafini, L., d'Avila Garcez, A.: Logic tensor networks for semantic image interpretation. In: Proceedings of the Twenty-Sixth International Joint Conference on Artificial Intelligence, pp. 1596–1602. International Joint Conferences on Artificial Intelligence Organization, Melbourne, Australia, August 2017. https://doi.org/10.24963/ijcai.2017/221
9. Díaz-Rodríguez, N., Lamas, A., Sanchez, J., Franchi, G., Donadello, I., Tabik, S., Filliat, D., Cruz, P., Montes, R., Herrera, F.: EXplainable Neural-Symbolic Learning (X-NeSyL) methodology to fuse deep learning representations with expert knowledge graphs: The MonuMAI cultural heritage use case. Information Fusion **79**, 58–83 (Mar 2022) https://doi.org/10.1016/j.inffus.2021.09.022, https://linkinghub.elsevier.com/retrieve/pii/S1566253521001986
10. Fierens, D., Broeck, G.V.d., Renkens, J., Shterionov, D., Gutmann, B., Thon, I., Janssens, G., De Raedt, L.: Inference and learning in probabilistic logic programs using weighted Boolean formulas. Theory and Practice of Logic Programming **15**(3), 358–401 (2015). https://doi.org/10.1017/S1471068414000076, http://arxiv.org/abs/1304.6810, arXiv:1304.6810 [cs]
11. Hitzler, P., Eberhart, A., Ebrahimi, M., Sarker, M.K., Zhou, L.: Neuro-symbolic approaches in artificial intelligence. National Sci. Rev. **9**(6), nwac035 (2022). https://doi.org/10.1093/nsr/nwac035
12. Hussain, Z., Sheng, M., Zhang, W.E.: Different approaches for human activity recognition: a survey. J. Network Comput. Appl. **167**, 102738 (2020). https://doi.org/10.1016/j.jnca.2020.102738. http://arxiv.org/abs/1906.05074, arXiv:1906.05074 [cs]
13. Kamruzzaman Sarker, M., Zhou, L., Eberhart, A., Hitzler, P.: Neuro-symbolic artificial intelligence: Current trends. arXiv e-prints pp. arXiv–2105 (2021)
14. Krüger, F., Nyolt, M., Yordanova, K., Hein, A., Kirste, T.: Computational State Space Models for Activity and Intention Recognition. A Feasibility Study. PLOS ONE **9**(11), e109381 (2014). https://doi.org/10.1371/journal.pone.0109381
15. Manhaeve, R., Dumančič, S., Kimmig, A., Demeester, T., De Raedt, L.: DeepProbLog: Neural Probabilistic Logic Programming. In: Advances in Neural Information Processing Systems. vol. 31. Curran Associates, Inc. (2018). https://papers.nips.cc/paper/2018/hash/dc5d637ed5e62c36ecb73b654b05ba2a-Abstract.html
16. Yang, J., Lee, J., Choi, J.: Activity recognition based on rfid object usage for smart mobile devices. J. Comput. Sci. Technol. **26**(2), 239–246 (2011)

Direct One-to-All Lead Conversion on 12-Lead Electrocardiogram

Samir Braga Chaves[✉], José Antônio Fernandes de Macedo, Régis Pires Magalhães, Lívia Almada Cruz, and Bruna Raynara Maia Batista

Federal University of Ceará, Fortaleza, Brazil
samirchaves@insightlab.ufc.br

Abstract. The Electrocardiogram (ECG) test is instrumental in daily clinical practice. It comprises the signal from different leads jointly analyzed by the cardiologist to conclude the diagnosis. However, the complete set of ECG signals needs to be collected in a clinical environment with the help of professionals and appropriate equipment. With the emergence of smartwatches, users can perform the ECG test more comfortably and easily. Although collecting one lead at a time is possible, more is needed for a complete clinical analysis. Some works sought to facilitate obtaining the ECG test by reconstructing a set of leads from a smaller set. Most works start from more than one lead, and others have also carried out this reconstruction from a single lead, but with restrictions like considering aligned segments of a single beat or segments of fixed length. The present work achieved the best results in the literature for reconstructing several of the 11 leads from lead I, considering segments without fixed size. These results were possible through a neural network architecture for the direct conversion (point-by-point) of ECG leads, with the following advantages over other alternatives: the possibility of being trained with signal segments of different sampling frequencies and durations without changing the architecture, complexity adjustment to avoid overfitting on small datasets and ability to deal with raw data. Our architecture achieved the average value of Pearson correlation of 0.75 on a cross-database evaluation against the current value of 0.39.

Keywords: Conversion · Deep learning · Recurrent Layers · Electrocardiogram (ECG) · Leads

1 Introduction

The Electrocardiogram (ECG) test, despite having more than 100 years [19], is instrumental in daily clinical practice for diagnosing different types of diseases and supporting decision-making in other contexts [4]. As seen in the following sections, the test comprises the signal from different leads, and the cardiologist performs a joint analysis of these leads to conclude the diagnosis. Despite being relatively accessible, ECG signals still need to be collected in a clinical environment with the help of professionals and appropriate equipment, resulting in significant time consumption and high costs.

With the emergence of wearable devices capable of performing the ECG test, such as smartwatches, users can perform this procedure in an entirely more comfortable and easy way and already receive feedbacks on possible health problems [1]. When the smartwatch is worn in its natural placement, it captures the electrical potential difference between the two arms, generating the lead I signal. However, this setup limits the collection to only one lead at a time. Although it is already valuable for identifying some arrhythmias, more is needed for a complete clinical analysis [12].

Some works aim to obtain the ECG test by reconstructing a set of leads from a smaller set. Most works start from a number of leads greater than one [7,16]. However, other authors have also carried out this reconstruction from a single lead, but with some restrictions like considering aligned segments of just a single beat [10] or segments of fixed length [2].

The objective of the current study is to reconstruct the entire set of 12 leads from a single lead, considering segments of variable length and sampling frequency. For that task, we achieved the best results in the existing literature for reconstructing multiple out of the remaining 11 leads solely based on lead I, utilizing arbitrary segments.

Our primary contribution is the proposal of a neural network architecture specifically designed for the direct conversion of ECG leads from a single lead, offering several advantages over existing alternatives in the literature:

- Flexibility to be trained with signal segments of varying frequencies and durations without requiring modifications to the architecture.
- Adaptability to prevent overfitting when dealing with small datasets.
- Capability to handle raw data without the need for applying noise filters.

We also bring geometric and probabilistic modeling of the problem to support the architecture choices for a point-by-point conversion, which can help future research.

2 ECG Background

The electrocardiogram (ECG) is a diagnostic test that captures the heart's electrical activity. Electrodes are placed on the skin to detect and record these signals. The resulting electrocardiogram provides valuable information about heart rate, rhythm, and can aid in the diagnosis of heart conditions. ECG is a non-invasive procedure widely employed for diagnosing and monitoring heart diseases. In the following section, we will discuss the collection of ECG signals and the configuration of the lead system used in the process.

2.1 Signal Collection

The collection of the ECG signal occurs through electrodes strategically placed on the patient's body. Each pair of electrodes measures, over time, the electrical potential difference (voltage) between the regions where they are placed. This pair of electrodes is called a lead, and given a set of electrodes, different leads arise from the combination of different pairs. The signals from the different leads together make up an ECG test.

How many electrodes will be used, where will they be positioned, and the leads formed from them form a Lead System. Some Lead Systems have been proposed and used over the years; however, the most applied currently is the 12-Lead System [20], presented below.

2.2 12-Lead System

As the name suggests, this system comprises signals from 12 leads from nine electrodes. Three electrodes are placed on the patient's limbs, generating the six limb leads, and the other six electrodes are on his chest, each generating a single lead called chest leads or precordial leads. The first set, referring to the members, is formatted by leads LI, LII, LIII, aVl, aVr, and aVf, while the second set contains leads V1, V2, ..., and V6.

Figure 1 illustrates the arrangement of leads on two planes. The leads of this system lie on two perpendicular planes: frontal and horizontal. The limb leads are on the frontal plane, while the precordial leads are on the horizontal. The position of the limb leads obeys an expected angulation and needs to be correct due to its use in diagnosis medical evaluation [17]. The determination of angles is not considered for precordial leads since the placement of their respective electrodes is greatly influenced by the anatomy of the patient's body [8].

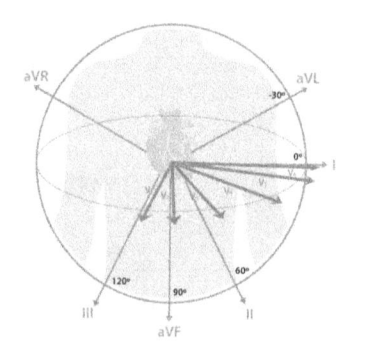

(a) Leads placement relative to the human body.

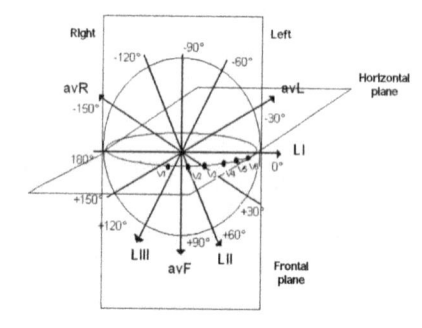

Source: https://www.cablesandsensors.com

(b) Planes in 12-Lead System

Source: https://cardiopapers.com.br

Fig. 1. Illustration of the 12-Lead system and its planes

3 Mathematical Analysis of the Problem

3.1 Algebraic Interpretation of the ECG

As the frontal plane leads are arranged on expected angles, it is possible to perform a deterministic conversion between them [6,21], disregarding noise from the signal collection or poor positioning of the electrodes. In the generic interpretation made here, it is necessary to have at least two leads and perform algebraic calculations to recover the remaining four from them. Since limb leads come from three electrodes, it is possible to assume that they are on the same plane, which does not occur with precordial leads where the horizontal plane is only theoretical in this context.

Consider the representation illustrated in Fig. 2. Each lead L represents the sequence of voltages measured in millivolts over time. At any instant t, the voltage value in t to L is l. Consider that the frontal plane represents a two-dimensional vector space V; its origin also represents the point where the voltage value equals 0 in all its leads. Also consider a system of polar coordinates P with a coincident pole to the origin of V. Thus, being Θ_L the angle of the lead L, there is a point in P of polar coordinates (l, Θ_L) which, when converted to cartesian coordinates, corresponds to a vector $\vec{v}$ in V, where $|\vec{v}| = l$.

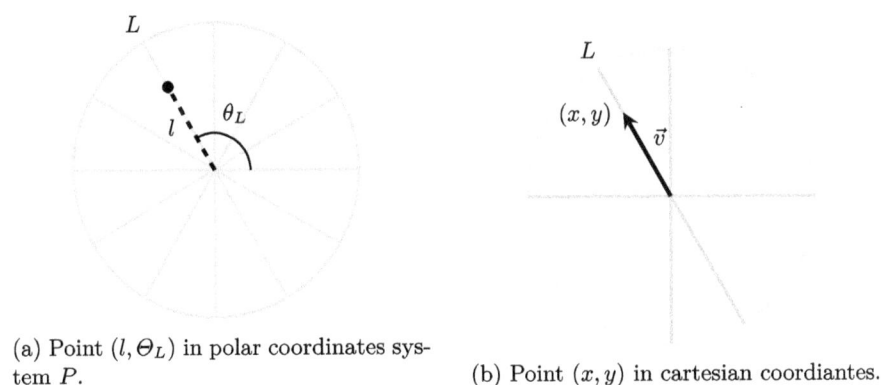

(a) Point (l, Θ_L) in polar coordinates system P.

(b) Point (x, y) in cartesian coordiantes.

Fig. 2. Algebraic representation of the voltage value at instant t in lead L

Therefore, it is possible to determine the vector in V that characterizes the voltage at instant t for any lead L on the frontal plane once its angle is known.

The many leads show different perspectives of the same event: the heart's electrical activity over time [11]. This activity can be recorded as a three-dimensional trajectory (for example, through a vectocardiogram [20]). However, it is possible to project each point belonging to it in the frontal plane, thus generating a 2D trajectory. The vector associated with each new point can be projected again onto the line passing through the origin with an angle equal to the angle of the lead L. By converting this last projected vector to the polar coordinate system P, we have a point whose radius of its coordinate exactly corresponds to the L voltage of at instant t. In other words, with the theoretical position of the electrical pulse projected in the frontal plane, it is possible to obtain the voltage value of all six limb leads.

Despite not having the information on this trajectory initially, retrieving it from any two leads is possible. Consider two leads $L1$ and $L2$, with respective angles θ_{L1} and θ_{L2}. At instant t, their voltage are l_1 and l_2, respectively. As shown earlier, it is possible to interpret this information as points in the polar coordinate system P and convert them to the vectors $\vec{v_1}$ and $\vec{v_2}$ in the vector space V.

$$\vec{v_1} = (x_1, y_1) = (l_1 \cos(\theta_{L1}), l_1 \sin(\theta_{L1}))$$
$$\vec{v_2} = (x_2, y_2) = (l_2 \cos(\theta_{L2}), l_2 \sin(\theta_{L2}))$$

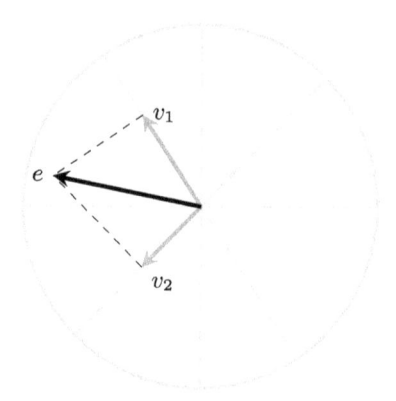

Fig. 3. Visual representation of the relationship between the vectors $\vec{v_1}$, $\vec{v_2}$ and $\vec{e}$. The vector $\vec{e}$ is at the intersection of the lines perpendicular to the vectors $\vec{v_1}$ and $\vec{v_2}$.

As illustrated in Fig. 3, having these two vectors is enough to find the single vector $\vec{e} = (e_x, e_y)$ which, when projected on the lines that pass by the origin with angles θ_{L1} and θ_{L2}, results in the vectors $\vec{v_1}$ and $\vec{v_2}$. We can find it by solving the linear system below:

$$\begin{pmatrix} x_1 & y_1 \\ x_2 & y_2 \end{pmatrix} \begin{pmatrix} e_x \\ e_y \end{pmatrix} = \begin{pmatrix} x_1^2 + y_1^2 \\ x_2^2 + y_2^2 \end{pmatrix}$$

3.2 Uncertainty on Conversion of Leads

As seen previously, we can interpret the nature of the leads as one-dimensional perspectives, aligned in time, of three-dimensional information. Therefore, as the problem treated here is converting a single lead into others, the information provided is insufficient for an exact solution. For example, consider a circular trajectory in two-dimensional space projected onto one of the space axes, as in Fig. 4. The projected trajectory is one-dimensional, and using it to recover the original trajectory is only possible when the mathematical function that originates it is known. Otherwise, recovering the 2D point from the 1D point will have an uncertainty factor related to the lost dimension in the projection.

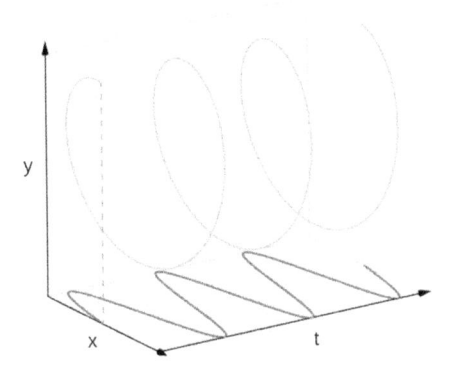

Fig. 4. Example of a 2D circular trajectory over time (t axis) and its projection on the x axis.

The uncertainty about this point at instant t may decrease once we consider the historical information of the path before and after t. Observing the example of Fig. 4, it is possible to notice that the uncertainty can be further reduced in cyclical trajectories, given the proximity of the trajectory points between the cycles, for example, in a supervised learning task. The trajectory captured on ECG leads is also cyclical, and we can apply the same intuition.

Illustrating the problem as projecting a trajectory is essential only to understand the uncertainty present in the task of lead conversion. However, the solution proposed here does not have the reconstruction of any trajectory as an intermediate step. The strategy is to leave the mapping between the leads and the quantification of this uncertainty to the model.

To do so, consider the set $\mathcal{L}$ below of missing leads that are targets of the conversion:

$$\mathcal{L} = \{\text{LII}, \text{LIII}, \text{aVl}, \text{aVr}, \text{aVf}, \text{V1}, \text{V2}, \text{V3}, \text{V4}, \text{V5}, \text{V6}\}$$

And that each lead $L \in \mathcal{L}$ is another set $\{l_1, ..., l_T\}$ where $|L| = T$.

Assume the notation $L(t) = l_t$ for the voltage of the lead L at time t. It is possible to model the quoted uncertainty as probability distributions. It follows that the joint probability of the ECG signal for lead L, given the sign of lead I, can be obtained from the product of conditional probabilities:

$$p(L \mid \mathrm{LI}) = \prod_{t=1}^{T} p(L(t) \mid \mathrm{LI}(1), ..., \mathrm{LI}(T)); \ \forall L \in \mathcal{L} \qquad (1)$$

And that the joint probability of $\mathcal{L}$ is the product of the probabilities of each missing lead:

$$p(\mathcal{L} \mid \mathrm{LI}) = \prod_{L \in \mathcal{L}} p(L \mid \mathrm{LI}) = \prod_{L \in \mathcal{L}} \prod_{t=1}^{T} p(L(t) \mid \mathrm{LI}(1), ..., \mathrm{LI}(T)) \qquad (2)$$

4 Related Works

The main related work is the paper by Beco et al. [2], which proposes a strategy based on the U-Net model [15] for converting ECG signal segments with fixed length. This conversion also focuses on the 12-Lead System and assumes only a single lead as input and the remaining 11 as output. As the U-Net architecture is based on encoding-decoding, the work presents two variations for the evaluated model: the first uses a shared encoder for all leads, and the second uses an encoder for each lead. They made the evaluations using the same three datasets presented in Sect. 6.2.

As far as the authors of the present work know, Beco et al. [2] present the best results in the literature for converting the LI lead into the remaining 11 leads from arbitrary segments; therefore, we use it to compare results. There are other related works, such as those cited by [2] and presented below.

The work by Grande-Fidalgo et al. [7] used linear regression and dense neural networks to reconstruct the standard 12-lead set from a subset of three input leads. Sohn et al. [16] used LSTMs to perform 12-lead reconstruction from a three-lead patch-type device. Both of these works use more than a single lead as input to their models, so their results cannot be directly compared to solutions using a single lead.

The work by Lee et al. [10] was one of the few that used only a single lead as input. For this, they used a Generative Adversary Network (GAN). However, the input segments had to be single heartbeats and must be aligned in time, which required a preprocessing of the signal.

5 Proposed Solution

As seen in Sect. 3.2, the lead conversion problem requires consideration of historical information from the ECG signal. Therefore, the proposed solution models the distribution presented in Eq. 2 using recurrent neural network layers, as shown below.

5.1 The Proposed Architecture

The GRU (Gated Recurrent Unit) architecture, which excels in capturing long-term dependencies and temporal patterns, was found to yield the best results in empirical tests. Therefore, in this study, we employ the GRU as the recurrent layer for our model. The input to the model is the ECG signal specifically related to lead I. As illustrated in Fig. 5, this signal is passed parallel to the two bidirectional GRUs: Bi-GRU$_1$ receives a signal of dimension 1 and generates another signal of dimension λ_1 as output, whereas Bi-GRU$_2$ receives this same signal and returns another one of dimension $\lambda_1 \times \lambda_2$. The variables λ_1 and λ_2 are hyperparameters that control the complexity of the model. Later sections show their different values and where they have been applied. The output tensors of each Bi-GRU are scaled to four dimensions: the first two dimensions are equivalent, respectively, to the size of the minibatch (**b**) and the length of the sequence (**s**), and the last two represent the dimensions of an array. A multiplication of these matrices is performed, and the tensor resulting from this operation is brought back to three dimensions.

The matrix multiplication operation represents a linear transformation $f(x) = xW$ at each of the points of the output time series of the GRUs, where x is generated by Bi-GRU$_1$ and W is generated by Bi-GRU$_2$. Therefore, at the instant t, we have that $f_t(x_t) = x_t W_t$. As bidirectional GRUs, x_t and W_t have accumulated information referring to points before and after t. Thus, the new point generated by f_t is indirectly influenced by all other points in the LI signal.

Finally, the tensor resulting from the matrix multiplication operation mentioned above is passed through another GRU, this time unidirectional. The role of the last GRU is to map the intermediate dimension set by the hyperparameter λ_2 to 11, the number of leads remaining. This mapping relates the latent space resulting from the previously mentioned linear transformations with the space of the 11 output signals of the conversion, where this relation considers the temporality of the points thanks to the GRU recurrence operation.

The main idea behind the whole flow is to expand the dimensionality of internal tensors from the single feature input signal. We can see the Bi-GRU$_1$ and Bi-GRU$_2$ as two heads thinking independently and extracting two sets of features. The Bi-GRU$_1$ is responsible for pondering the features extracted by the Bi-GRU$_2$ when combining those two feature sets in a single one using the matrix multiplication operation. Therefore, the last GRU establishes a relationship from those latent features to the output space of 11 leads.

In addition to λ_1 and λ_2, there are other hyperparameters present in the model that also impact its complexity:

- **number of GRU layers**: Each GRU used is multilayer, and the amount of stacked internal layers can be chosen independently.
- **dropout**: Each multilayer GRU allows adding a dropout layer to the outputs of each internal layer, except for the last one. This parameter defines the dropout probability of these intermediate layers and can be used as a regularization parameter. This setting is only present in GRUs if there is more than one stacked layer.

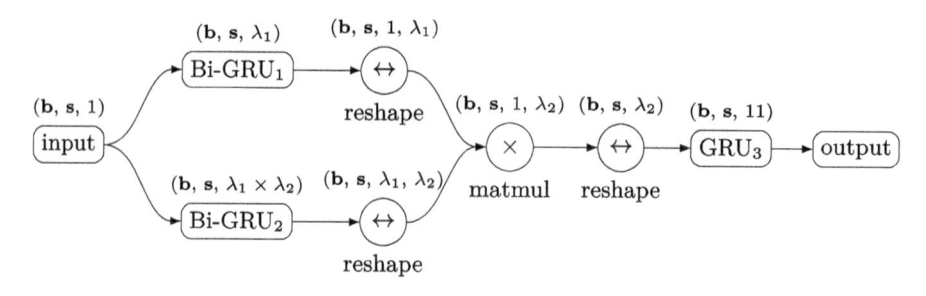

Fig. 5. Proposed architecture. Each dimension in parentheses represents the output dimension of the respective node. Let **b** be the size of the minibatch and **s** the length of the signal sequence.

We decided to create this new architecture instead of other approaches, like pre-trained models, due to a focus on the lightness and straightness of the solution. Some existing architectures for signal problems, like Transformers [9] and GAN [5], often require heavy data preprocessing or huge models, which can make the solution much more complex and slow. Our model is based purely on recurrent layers, and the only necessary data treatment it needs is normalization.

6 Experiments and Results

The first part of the experiments aims to compare the techniques applied in the present work and those applied in the work of Beco et al. [2], as well as its results. The second part explores the solution's flexibility in different scenarios. We use the following metrics for evaluation: Pearson's correlation coefficient (r), the root mean square error (RMSE), and the Structural Similarity Index Measure (SSIM). Finally, the third part compares the diagnosis using reconstructed signals.

6.1 Experiment Environment

All experiments were carried out in the Google Colab environment, which has 12.7 GB of system RAM and 15 GB of GPU RAM. The GPU version used was the Nvidia Tesla T4.

6.2 Data Sources

We used three sets of ECG data, which contain, among other information, the 12 leads explained in Sect. 2.2.

The PTB database [3] contains 549 records from 290 subjects, with ages ranging from 17 to 87. Each record consists of 15 signals: the 12 conventional leads and the 3 Frank lead ECGs (vx, vy, vz). The signals are digitized at 1000 samples per second, with 16-bit resolution ranging from ± 16.384 mV. Most ECG records have a detailed clinical summary in the header file, including age, gender, diagnosis, and information on medical history, medication, interventions, coronary artery pathology, ventriculography, echocardiography, and hemodynamics.

The PTB-XL ECG dataset [18] consists of 21,799 12-leas ECG records of 10 s from 18,869 patients. The dataset was annotated by up to two cardiologists, covering 71 different ECG statements. All the annotation statements have been grouped into five superclasses: NORM (normal ECG), MI (myocardial infarction), STTC (ST/T change), CD (conduction disturbance), and HYP (hypertrophy). Moreover, the dataset includes extensive metadata on demographics, infarction characteristics, likelihoods for diagnostic ECG statements, and annotated signal properties.

The INCART database consists of 75 annotated recordings captured using a Holter. Each record has a duration of 30 min and contains 12 standard leads with a sampling frequency of 257 Hz. The included records in the database were, preferably, from subjects with consistent ECGs and diagnoses such as ischemia, coronary artery disease, conduction abnormalities, and arrhythmias.

6.3 Result Comparison

Beco et al. [2] bring the results of their model applied to PTB-XL and INCART datasets after being trained on the PTB dataset. We use in this work the same preprocessing on all the involved datasets: division into 5-second segments, application of the second-order Butterworth filter with cutoff frequency $f_c = [1, 40]\ Hz$, and all left at the same frequency. In this case, the sampling frequency used here is 500 Hz instead of the 1 kHz used by Beco et al. [2]. However, we calculate all metrics with an amplified version of 1 kHz for a fair comparison.

For the PTB-XL dataset, we chose only the 16.272 ECGs that do not have conflicting superclass annotations. Finally, all signals had their magnitudes normalized in the interval $[-1, 1]$, using MinMax scaling. The maximum and minimum amplitude values were always extracted from the training sets and then used in the test sets for normalization. The model was trained with values of $\lambda_1 = 4$, $\lambda_2 = 8$ and $dropout = 0.3$ in Bi-GRU$_2$ and in Bi-GRU$_2$, which had 2 layers each. GRU$_3$ had only one layer. This hyperparameter configuration was the best among the empirically evaluated variations.

Table 1 shows the result comparison in the three metrics used when evaluating the model with the PTB-XL dataset. The present work produces a better result in all leads for the r and RMSE metrics, and for the SSIM metric, the average of the values of the leads still presents a better result.

The results were slightly different when performing the same evaluation with the INCART dataset, as seen in Table 2. The average of the r (avg.) and RMSE metric values are even higher in this work. However, for the SSIM metric, the work by Beco et al. [2] is higher by 0.01.

Figure 6 shows the visual comparison between the original and the reconstructed signals of an example record from the test set of the PTB-XL dataset. The segment has 5 s of duration.

Table 1. A comparison between the results of the study conducted by Beco et al. [2] and the current work is depicted for evaluating different datasets. The training was conducted using the PTB dataset, while the evaluation was performed using the PTB-XL dataset.

Lead	r (avg.)		SSIM		RMSE	
	Beco et al.	This work	Beco et al.	This work	Beco et al.	This work
II	0.60	**0.76**	0.23	**0.59**	0.33	**0.08**
III	0.31	**0.44**	**0.43**	0.30	0.38	**0.08**
aVR	−0.61	**0.93**	0.09	**0.78**	0.74	**0.05**
aVL	−0.63	**0.81**	0.11	**0.62**	0.75	**0.04**
aVF	0.29	**0.47**	0.23	**0.36**	0.41	**0.08**
V1	0.79	**0.84**	**0.91**	0.47	0.16	**0.09**
V2	0.71	**0.77**	**0.84**	0.50	0.22	**0.17**
V3	0.65	**0.72**	**0.64**	0.54	0.29	**0.17**
V4	0.62	**0.76**	0.30	**0.61**	0.32	**0.15**
V5	0.76	**0.85**	0.35	**0.69**	0.24	**0.11**
V6	0.80	**0.89**	0.53	**0.71**	0.20	**0.08**
Average	0.39	**0.75**	0.42	**0.56**	0.37	**0.10**

Table 2. Comparison between the results of the work by Beco et al. [2] and the present work for an evaluation between different datasets (training performed with PTB and evaluation performed with INCART).

Lead	r (avg.)		SSIM		RMSE	
	Beco et al.	This work	Beco et al.	This work	Beco et al.	This work
II	0.36	**0.53**	0.19	**0.45**	0.37	**0.27**
III	0.17	**0.19**	**0.28**	0.27	0.43	**0.28**
aVR	0.67	**0.71**	**0.83**	0.58	0.22	**0.14**
aVL	**0.36**	0.33	**0.47**	0.31	0.35	**0.14**
aVF	0.17	**0.36**	0.22	**0.34**	0.41	**0.28**
V1	0.57	**0.68**	**0.79**	0.44	0.24	**0.16**
V2	0.50	**0.56**	**0.73**	0.32	0.28	**0.26**
V3	0.36	**0.51**	**0.44**	0.33	0.37	**0.26**
V4	0.34	**0.42**	0.19	**0.38**	0.41	**0.23**
V5	0.45	**0.61**	0.11	**0.49**	0.35	**0.23**
V6	0.45	**0.64**	0.21	**0.49**	0.34	**0.24**
Average	0.40	**0.50**	**0.41**	0.40	0.34	**0.22**

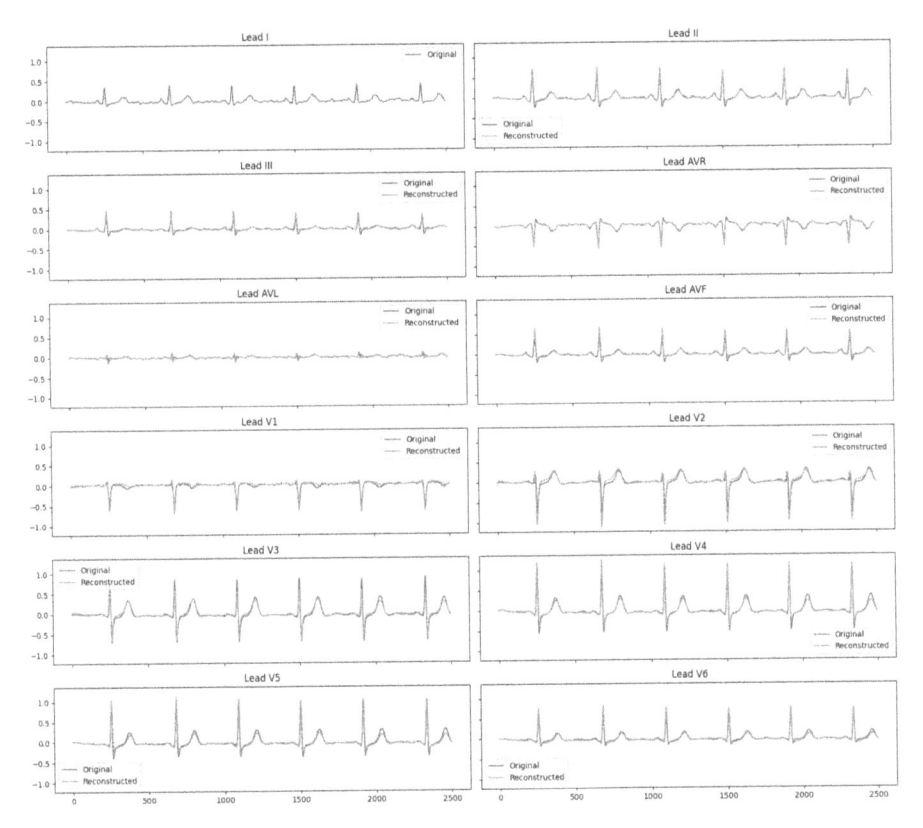

Fig. 6. Example of one-to-all lead reconstruction. The orange signals are the reconstruction, while the blue ones are the original. The horizontal axis corresponds to time in milliseconds, and the vertical axis indicates the original signal amplitude in millivolts. (Color figure online)

6.4 Flexibility Evaluation

As a direct conversion is made between the points of the lead signals, the same architecture can be applied to sequences of longer lengths. To evaluate this flexibility, we chose the PTB-XL dataset, whose segments are initially 10 s long and have a sampling frequency of 500 Hz. We used the same selection of ECGs without superclass annotation conflict and divided the selected ECGs into training (80%) and test (20%) sets. Table 3 shows the results for training the model with values of $\lambda_1 = 12$, $\lambda_2 = 11$, $dropout = 0.25$ in all GRUs, which had two stacked layers each. Again, this hyperparameter configuration was the best in the empirical tests performed.

We evaluated with the original signal, without applying the previously mentioned second-order Butterworth filter, and with the filtered version. The model performs better in all metrics for all leads when applying the filter, but it still achieves a close result even without its application.

Table 3. Results for the proposed architecture trained and evaluated on the PTB-XL dataset.

Lead	r (avg.)		SSIM		RMSE	
	No filter	With filter	No filter	With filter	No filter	With filter
II	0.73	**0.77**	0.50	**0.60**	0.09	**0.08**
III	0.44	**0.48**	0.25	**0.34**	0.10	**0.08**
aVR	0.90	**0.93**	0.67	**0.77**	0.05	**0.04**
aVL	0.81	**0.82**	0.51	**0.58**	0.05	**0.04**
aVF	0.46	**0.51**	0.32	**0.40**	0.09	**0.07**
V1	0.80	**0.83**	0.46	**0.48**	0.10	**0.09**
V2	0.77	**0.77**	0.49	**0.53**	0.18	**0.16**
V3	0.74	**0.76**	0.54	**0.56**	0.18	**0.16**
V4	0.77	**0.81**	0.56	**0.63**	0.16	**0.13**
V5	0.83	**0.86**	0.60	**0.64**	0.12	**0.10**
V6	0.74	**0.90**	0.58	**0.70**	0.13	**0.07**
Average	0.73	**0.77**	0.50	**0.57**	0.11	**0.09**

6.5 Diagnosis Using a Reconstructed Signal

Beco et al. [2] used an adapted version of the model proposed by Nguyen et al. [13] to perform a classification task of disease diagnosis on ECG signal. For that, they trained the classification model on eighty percent of the PTB-XL using the original signal of the lead I. Then they used the remaining twenty percent for evaluation. The classification targets are the five superclasses from PTB-XL dataset. They also evaluated the model trained on the original signals with the reconstructed signal of lead I (obtained using the lead conversion U-Net model using lead II as input).

They achieved an accuracy of 54.13% when using original signals and 45.71% when using reconstructed signals. For the balanced accuracy, the results were 46.58% and 37.56%, respectively.

We repeated the same procedure and used the same model described above, but we used the lead aVr for diagnosis since lead I is used by us as input. We achieved an accuracy of 55.26% when using original signals and 55.21% for reconstructed signals. For the balanced accuracy, our results were 54.12% and 45.61%, respectively. This behavior denotes the same bias towards the NORM class pointed out by Beco et al. [2], even though it is smaller than the one noticed by them.

7 Conclusion and Future Work

In this paper, we propose a deep learning architecture to perform a direct one-to-all conversion on leads of the ECG 12-lead system. By employing this architecture, we can achieve the most favorable outcomes reported in the existing literature for the reconstruction of multiple leads out of the remaining 11, solely based on lead I, utilizing arbitrary segments. Our experiments demonstrate that we achieved relevant improvements when compared to the most related work [2] in cross-database evaluation.

Moreover, the proposed architecture demonstrates the flexibility to be trained with signal segments of two different durations without requiring modifications to the architecture. We could also see that the model is able to prevent overfitting when dealing with small datasets due to the tuning of the λ_1 and λ_2 hyperparameters. Finally, the model was capable of handling raw data without the need for applying noise filters, with close result values when comparing both cases.

It is still necessary to investigate the sensibility of the model to signals of many different segment lengths and sampling frequencies. Related to diagnosis using the reconstructed signals, the results still need to be improved, given the bias towards a "normal" state. Other deep learning models must be investigated to perform this diagnosis, since even the original signal's accuracy was low to be applied in a real-world scenario.

Regarding future research opportunities for the direct conversion of ECG signals, we believe that the distribution $P(L(t) \mid LI)$ for some lead $L \in \mathcal{L}$ can be modeled with other non-recurrent neural network architectures, such as the Causal Convolutional Networks used in the WaveNet model [14]. Even though it is generally applied to predict data from the same space used as input (such as generating new audio snippets), one can use these layers to model the correlation between the spaces of the different leads, given the temporal dynamics of the input signal data.

Acknowledgements. Part of the results presented in this article were carried out within the scope of the project "CENTRO DE EXCELENCIA EM INTELIGENCIA ARTIFICIAL - AI4WELLNESS" which is funded by Samsung Eletronica da Amazonia Ltda, under terms of Brazilian Federal Law No. 8,248/1991. The authors thank the contribution of the research team who provided feedback on this study and supported this work.

References

1. Abdou, A., Krishnan, S.: Horizons in single-lead ECG analysis from devices to data. Front. Sig. Process. **2** (2022). https://doi.org/10.3389/frsip.2022.866047
2. Beco, S.C., Pinto, J.R., Cardoso, J.S.: Electrocardiogram lead conversion from single-lead blindly-segmented signals. BMC Med. Inf. Decis. Mak. **22**(1) (2022). https://doi.org/10.1186/s12911-022-02063-6
3. Bousseljot, R., Kreiseler, D., Schnabel, A.: Nutzung der ekg-signaldatenbank cardiodat der ptb über das internet. Biomed. Eng. **40**(s1), 317–318 (1995). https://doi.org/10.1515/bmte.1995.40.s1.317
4. Drew, B.J., et al.: Prevention of torsade de pointes in hospital settings. Circulation **121**(8), 1047–1060 (2010). https://doi.org/10.1161/CIRCULATIONAHA.109.192704

5. Golany, T., Radinsky, K.: PGANs: personalized generative adversarial networks for ECG synthesis to improve patient-specific deep ECG classification. In: Proceedings of the AAAI Conference on Artificial Intelligence, vol. 33, no. 1, pp. 557–564 (2019)
6. Goldberger, E.: The aVl, aVr, and aVf leads: a simplification of standard lead electrocardiography. Am. Heart J. **24**(3), 378–396 (1942). https://doi.org/10.1016/S0002-8703(42)90821-4
7. Grande-Fidalgo, A., Calpe, J., Redón, M., Millán-Navarro, C., Soria-Olivas, E.: Lead reconstruction using artificial neural networks for ambulatory ECG acquisition. Sensors **21**(16), 5542 (2021). https://doi.org/10.3390/s21165542
8. Ilg, K.J., Lehmann, M.H.: Importance of recognizing pseudo-septal infarction due to electrocardiographic lead misplacement. Am. J. Med. **125**(1), 23–27 (2011)
9. Lan, E.: Performer: a novel PPG-to-ECG reconstruction transformer for a digital biomarker of cardiovascular disease detection. In: 2023 IEEE/CVF Winter Conference on Applications of Computer Vision (WACV), pp. 1990–1998. IEEE Computer Society, Los Alamitos, CA, USA (2023). https://doi.org/10.1109/WACV56688.2023.00203
10. Lee, J., Oh, K., Kim, B., Yoo, S.K.: Synthesis of electrocardiogram V-lead signals from limb-lead measurement using R-peak aligned generative adversarial network. IEEE J. Biomed. Health Inform. **24**(5), 1265–1275 (2020). https://doi.org/10.1109/JBHI.2019.2936583
11. Malmivuo, J., Plonsey, R.: Bioelectromagnetism. 16. Vectorcardiographic Lead Systems, pp. 290–306 (1995)
12. Mohammed, W.R., Hussein, A.F.: The optimization of ECG-leads based cardiovascular abnormal detection scheme. In: 2022 2nd International Conference on Computing and Machine Intelligence (ICMI), pp. 1–5 (2022). https://doi.org/10.1109/ICMI55296.2022.9873695
13. Nguyen, Q.H., Nguyen, B.P., Nguyen, T.B., Do, T.T., Mbinta, J.F., Simpson, C.R.: Stacking segment-based CNN with SVM for recognition of atrial fibrillation from single-lead ECG recordings. Biomed. Sig. Process. Control **68**, 102672 (2021). https://doi.org/10.1016/j.bspc.2021.102672
14. van den Oord, A., et al.: WaveNet: a generative model for raw audio. arXiv preprint arXiv:1609.03499 (2016)
15. Ronneberger, O., Fischer, P., Brox, T.: U-Net: convolutional networks for biomedical image segmentation. In: Navab, N., Hornegger, J., Wells, W.M., Frangi, A.F. (eds.) MICCAI 2015. LNCS, vol. 9351, pp. 234–241. Springer, Cham (2015). https://doi.org/10.1007/978-3-319-24574-4_28
16. Sohn, J., Yang, S., Lee, J., Ku, Y., Kim, H.C.: Reconstruction of 12-lead electrocardiogram from a three-lead patch-type device using a LSTM network. Sensors **20**(11), 3278 (2020). https://doi.org/10.3390/s20113278
17. Tung, R.T.: Electrocardiographic limb leads placement and its clinical implication. Kansas J. Med. **14**(3), 229–230 (2021). https://doi.org/10.17161/kjm.vol14.15259
18. Wagner, P., et al.: PTB-XL, a large publicly available electrocardiography dataset. Sci. Data **7**(1), 154 (2020). https://doi.org/10.1038/s41597-020-0495-6
19. Waller, A.D.: A demonstration on man of electromotive changes accompanying the heart's beat. J. Physiol. **8**(5), 229–234 (1887)
20. Yang, H., Bukkapatnam, S.T., Komanduri, R.: Spatiotemporal representation of cardiac vectorcardiogram (VCG) signals. Biomed. Eng. Online **11**, 1–15 (2012). https://doi.org/10.1186/1475-925X-11-16
21. Zeisler, E.B.: A critique of Einthoven's law in electrocardiography. Proc. Soc. Exp. Biol. Med. **28**, 12–15 (1930)

Unveiling Driver Modules in Lung Cancer: A Clustering-Based Gene-Gene Interaction Network Analysis

Golnaz Taheri[1(✉)], Marcell Szalai[1], Mahnaz Habibi[2], and Panagiotis Papapetrou[1]

[1] Department of Computer and Systems Sciences, Stockholm University, Stockholm, Sweden
{golnaz.taheri,panagiotis}@dsv.su.se
[2] Department of Mathematics, Qazvin Branch, Islamic Azad University, Qazvin, Iran

Abstract. Lung cancer, which is the leading cause of cancer-related death worldwide and is characterized by genetic changes and heterogeneity, presents a significant treatment challenge. Existing approaches utilizing Machine Learning (ML) techniques for identifying driver modules lack specificity, particularly for lung cancer. This study addresses this limitation by proposing a novel method that combines gene-gene interaction network construction with ML-based clustering to identify lung cancer-specific driver modules. The methodology involves mapping biological processes to genes and constructing a weighted gene-gene interaction network to identify correlations within gene clusters. A clustering algorithm is then applied to identify potential cancer-driver modules, focusing on biologically relevant modules that contribute to lung cancer development. The results highlight the effectiveness and robustness of the clustering approach, identifying 110 unique clusters ranging in size from 4 to 10. These clusters surpass evaluation requirements and demonstrate significant relevance to critical cancer-related pathways. The identified driver modules hold promise for influencing future approaches to lung cancer diagnosis, prognosis, and treatment. This research expands our understanding of lung cancer and sets the stage for further investigations and potential clinical advancements.

Keywords: Lung Cancer · Driver Modules · Machine Learning · Gene-Gene Interaction Network

1 Introduction

Lung cancer stands as the foremost contributor to cancer-related mortality globally, accounting for an estimated 1.8 million deaths in 2020, which represents almost 18.4% of all cancer deaths [1]. Unfortunately, the prognosis for lung cancer remains unfavorable, with only 18.6% of patients surviving beyond five years [2]. Smoking is responsible for the majority of cases, while a notable percentage occurs in non-smokers [3,4]. Environmental factors like asbestos, radon gas, and pollution also contribute to lung cancer [5]. There are two main types: small cell lung cancer (SCLC) and non-small cell lung cancer (NSCLC), with NSCLC being the most common and having high incidence and mortality rates [6]. In 2020 an estimate of 2,206,771 new cases of NSCLC was reported, while the mortality rate for this cancer in the same year reached 1,796,144 individuals. NSCLC is further categorized into adenocarcinoma, squamous cell carcinoma, and large cell carcinoma [7]. Genomic studies have revealed the complex molecular landscape associated with lung tumors influenced by factors, such as smoking and environmental exposures [7]. Advancements in deep sequencing technologies, exemplified by projects like The Cancer Genome Atlas (TCGA) [9], have generated extensive cancer genomics data. This wealth of information presents unprecedented opportunities to comprehend the mechanisms of carcinogenesis. Identifying cancer-related somatic mutations, driver modules, and functionally interconnected gene alterations is crucial for understanding cancer initiation, progression, and development. Driver modules actively contribute to cancer's hallmark characteristics and uncovering them enhances our understanding of cancer and aids in designing effective treatment strategies [10].

Various computational approaches have emerged to prioritize genes independently and identify candidate driver genes, which are genes causally linked to different diseases and oncogenesis [11–14]. These methods combine somatic mutation data with additional information, such as interaction networks or gene expression data, to generate gene rankings. While these rankings offer valuable insights into potential genes of interest, it is important to note that mutations at different genomic loci can contribute to the same disease [15]. This genetic variation might point to an underlying biological process in which genes linked to cancer could operate as possible driver modules and functional pathways. For the purpose of finding such candidate modules, several computational techniques have been developed. [16,17].

Related Work. Mutual exclusivity refers to the non-random occurrence of genomic alterations without co-occurrence. MEMo is a computational method introduced by Ciriello et al. [18] to identify mutually exclusive alteration sets. MEMo compares observed co-occurrence frequencies with a null model, considering alteration frequencies and sample cohort size. It successfully highlights mutually exclusive modules and identifies promising genes selectively altered in tumors. However, MEMo relies on existing biological knowledge and stringent filters, limiting its ability to discover associations between less-studied genes. While useful for evaluating mutation combinations, mutual exclusivity has limitations. It does not encompass all possibilities, as concurrent driver mutations can occur and the pattern applies only within the same pathway, not across different pathways. Therefore, mutual exclusivity alone is inadequate for characterizing all functional mutation combinations. Detecting cancer-driving mutations among infrequently mutated genes is challenging. Cho et al. [19] introduced MUFFINN, a pathway-focused technique that considers mutations in both individual genes and their functional network neighbors. MUFFINN demonstrates increased sensitivity compared to gene-focused analyses, making it valuable for prioritizing cancer genes. Importantly, it remains effective even with smaller patient populations, enhancing cancer genome projects. Advanced computational techniques utilize biological pathways and networks to identify cancer driver mutations and pathways. De novo methods analyze somatic mutation patterns across tumors to infer cancer-related genes and pathways. Dimitrakopoulos et al. [20] discuss recent advancements, limitations, and future challenges in detecting cancer genes and pathways, emphasizing the need for de novo approaches to overcome biases in prior knowledge-based methods. Pathway-based methods rely on reference databases, while network-based methods favor well-studied genes. In contrast, techniques identifying combinatorial mutation patterns learn pathways from scratch, enhancing sensitivity by managing noise and evaluating statistical uncertainties. Zhang et al. [21] developed an integrated approach that combines mutual exclusivity, coverage, and protein-protein interaction data to construct an edge-weighted network. It outperformed other methods in identifying known cancer driver modules and demonstrated high precision in distinguishing normal and tumor samples using pan-cancer data.

These studies have a limitation in their broad-spectrum approach to cancer, which lacks specificity for particular types of cancer like lung cancer. While the findings are generally promising, their applicability to specific cancers, including lung cancer, remains untested and uncertain. The success observed in these studies may not necessarily translate to equally successful outcomes when applied to lung cancer or other specific types of cancer. This limitation highlights the importance of further research that focuses on individual cancer types to gain a more nuanced understanding of the disease.

Contributions. This research introduces a novel approach for identifying statistically significant gene clusters using a graph-based representation of gene interactions. It addresses limitations in current broad-spectrum cancer studies and focuses specifically on lung cancer. By utilizing clustering techniques, this study aims to identify unique driver modules specific to lung cancer, providing valuable insights at the molecular level. This targeted method enhances personalized treatment strategies and bridges the gap between general and specific cancer research, improving the precision and relevance of findings for lung cancer patients. The main contributions of this work are summarized as follows:

- **Novelty.** This study introduces a novel approach to overcome limitations in current broad-spectrum cancer studies. Existing research lacks specificity, making it uncertain for specific cancer types like lung cancer. This study focuses on identifying unique driver modules in lung cancer using clustering, providing a more targeted understanding at the molecular level and may lead to more reliable insights and personalized treatment strategies.
- **Significance.** The identification of statistically significant gene clusters provides a fresh perspective on gene-based indicators of cancer, indicating that modules of various sizes can contribute to lung cancer development. Additionally, identifying commonly occurring genes across multiple clusters helps identify significant contributors to lung cancer.

– **Clinical Investigation.** The study's findings have practical implications for understanding the genetic landscape of lung cancer. This knowledge can impact diagnostics, prognosis, and the development of targeted therapies, enhancing our understanding of the role of genes and modules in lung cancer and their implications for therapeutic interventions.

2 A Workflow for Clustering-Based Gene-Gene Interaction Network Analysis

In this section, we introduce a workflow for identifying driver modules in lung cancer, which involves two key steps. Firstly, a set of mutated genes specific to lung cancer is selected, and a gene-gene interaction weighted network is constructed using relevant Gene Ontology (GO terms or biological processes). Secondly, a clustering algorithm is applied to detect dense clusters with high weights, resulting in the identification of significant modules associated with lung cancer with high P-values based on cancer-related pathways.

2.1 Step I: Gene Selection and Gene-Gene Interaction Network Construction

We construct a lung cancer network with a set of genes with high-frequency mutations associated with lung cancer, with g_i denoting the ith gene. We extend this set of genes with respect to the biological processes in which each gene g_i participates. Specifically, genes g_i and g_j were connected in the lung cancer network, if and only if, there exists at least one GO term in which both genes participate at the same time. This process leads to the creation of an extended graph of n nodes (corresponding to the total number of genes) and m edges.

More formally, let $V = \{g_1, ..., g_n\}$ represent the set of lung cancer network genes. For each gene g_i, we define $\mathcal{GO}(g_i)$ as the set of GO terms related to the biological processes in which gene g_i participates. Based on the presence of genes in the GO terms, we define a weighted mutated network $G = <V, E, \omega>$. The weight of the edge between two connected genes g_i and g_j, denoted as $\omega(g_i g_j)$, is determined as follows:

$$\omega(g_i g_j) = |\mathcal{GO}(g_i) \cap \mathcal{GO}(g_j))|, \text{ for all } g_i, g_j \in V,$$

with $|X|$ denoting the cardinality or the number of elements in the set X. The algorithm to construct the graph for each mutated cancer gene is described in Algorithm 1. In Fig. 1, a section of the original graph we obtained in our experimental evaluation is illustrated, specifically showcasing the initial 100 genes along with their corresponding edges.

2.2 Step II: Community Detection in the Gene-Gene Interaction Graph

The second step of our workflow involves the identification of clusters in the gene-gene interaction graph. Without loss of generality, any community detection algorithm can be employed. In this paper, we chose the Leiden algorithm, as

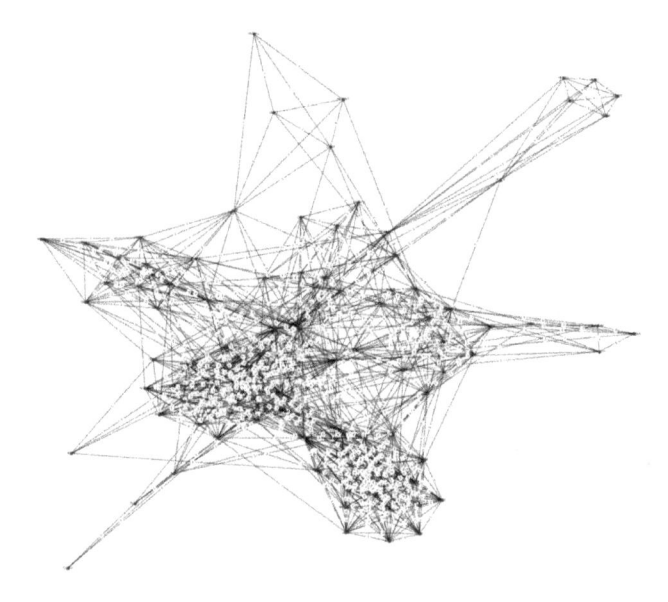

Fig. 1. Subgraph of the original gene-gene interaction graph used in our experimental evaluation. In this subgraph we showcase the graph for the first 100 genes.

it is widely recognized for its effectiveness in community detection. The algorithm optimizes a quality function to identify densely connected groups of nodes [24], and comprises three main phases: (1) local node movement, (2) partition refinement, and (3) network aggregation based on the refined partition. The algorithm initially performs local node movements, followed by refinement of the partition. Finally, the non-refined partition is used to create an initial partition for the aggregate network during the aggregation phase.

Let $\mathcal{G} = (\mathcal{V}, \mathcal{E})$ be a graph with $n = |\mathcal{V}|$ nodes and $m = |\mathcal{E}|$ edges. Graphs are assumed to be undirected. For simplicity, our mathematical notation assumes graphs to be unweighted but all the mathematical parts are valid for weighted graphs like our constructed graph in the previous section. A partition $\mathcal{P} = \{C_1, ..., C_r\}$ consists of $r = |\mathcal{P}|$ communities, where each community $C_i \subseteq \mathcal{V}$ consists of a set of nodes such that $\mathcal{V} = \bigcup_i C_i$ and for all $i \neq j$, $C_i \cap C_j \neq \emptyset$.

The Leiden algorithm incorporates a refinement phase to obtain a partition $\mathcal{P}_{refined}$, which is a more detailed version of the initial partition $\mathcal{P}$ resulting from the local moving phase. The Leiden algorithm creates an aggregate network based on $\mathcal{P}_{refined}$ instead of $\mathcal{P}$, allowing for the identification of higher-quality partitions. The refinement phase involves merging nodes within communities of $\mathcal{P}_{refined}$ while ensuring sufficient connectivity to their communities in $\mathcal{P}$. This process may split communities in $\mathcal{P}$ into multiple communities in $\mathcal{P}_{refined}$. During the refinement phase, node mergers are not solely based on maximizing the increase in the quality function. Instead, a node can be merged with any community, which leads to an increase in the quality function, with the selection of the community being randomized. The likelihood of selecting a community is

Algorithm 1. Step I: Constructing the gene-gene interaction graph
---
Require: Dataframe $\mathcal{D}$: which contains the information about genes and their corresponding GO terms
Ensure: Graph $\mathcal{G}\{V, E\}$
1: **procedure** CONSTRUCT_GRAPH($\mathcal{D}$)
2:    $\mathcal{G} \leftarrow$ create an empty graph
3:    **for** $\forall$ row r in $\mathcal{D}$ **do**
4:       $\mathcal{N} \leftarrow$ all elements in r except 'nan'
5:       **for** $\forall$ node n_1 in $\mathcal{N}$ **do**
6:          **for** $\forall$ node n_2 in $\mathcal{N}$ **do**
7:             **if** $n_1 \neq n_2$ **then**
8:                **if** $(n_1, n_2) \notin \mathcal{G}$ **then**
9:                   add edge (n_1, n_2) to $\mathcal{G}$ with weight $w_{n_1, n_2} = 1$
10:                **else**
11:                   $w_{n_1, n_2} = w_{n_1, n_2} + 1$
12:                **end if**
13:             **end if**
14:          **end for**
15:       **end for**
16:    **end for**
17:    convert $\mathcal{G}$ to iGraph graph
18:    **return** $\mathcal{G}$
19: **end procedure**

influenced by the magnitude of the increase in the quality function. The level of randomness in community selection is controlled by a parameter $\theta > 0$, enabling the exploration of a broader partition space. This algorithm (Algorithm 2) offers scalability, enabling the analysis of large graphs that may be computationally demanding for alternative methods. Moreover, the algorithm demonstrates stability by minimizing randomness, ensuring consistent outcomes when applied to the same graph.

3 Experimental Results

3.1 Datasets

Two different datasets were utilized in this study. The first dataset was used to extract the mutation network, while the second dataset provided the relevant biological process annotations specifically related to lung cancer. All the Materials and implementations are available at our GitHub repository [8].

Mutated Genes: The extraction of significantly mutated genes is a crucial step in identifying driver genes and modules associated with lung cancer. To achieve this, researchers have accessed various datasets containing genetic alterations in patients with bronchus and lung cancer. Among these datasets, the TCGA dataset is particularly reliable [9]. We also obtained a dataset comprising

Algorithm 2. Step II: Finding communities in the graph

Require: Graph $\mathcal{G}\{V, E\}$, Integer maximum_cluster_size: limit cluster hierarchy by setting maximum cluster size
Ensure: List $\mathcal{R}$: resulting clusters
1: **procedure** PERFORM_CLUSTERING($\mathcal{G}$, maximum_cluster_size)
2:     $\mathcal{R} \leftarrow$ empty list
3:     **for** $i =$ maximum_cluster_size to 4, decrement by 1 **do**
4:         $\mathcal{P} \leftarrow$ LEIDEN_CLUSTERING($\mathcal{G}$, i)
5:         **for** $\forall$ cluster $\in \mathcal{P}$ **do**
6:             sort elements in the cluster
7:             **if** $\neg$IS_SUBSET(cluster, $\mathcal{R}$) **then**
8:                 $\mathcal{R} \leftarrow \mathcal{R} \cup$ cluster
9:             **end if**
10:         **end for**
11:     **end for**
12:     **return** $\mathcal{R}$
13: **end procedure**

mutated genes in lung cancer patients, along with pertinent biological information. From this dataset, we focused on the top 100 genes exhibiting the highest mutation frequency, considering genetic modifications present in multiple cases.

Gene Ontology: To identify driver genes and modules in lung cancer, we utilized GO terms from the UniProt database [22]. This extensively curated human-centric database comprises 20,422 entries, providing valuable insights into biological processes and associated proteins. Leveraging the resources within the UniProt database, we conducted a thorough analysis of human proteins, exploring their roles and interactions. We used general GO terms without any filtering, and then we expanded the pool of 100 highly mutated genes for lung cancer with the help of these GO terms. The extended set of genes consists of genes that are functionally related to the mutated lung cancer genes. This approach allowed us to comprehensively explore genes that may not possess genetic alterations but could still contribute to lung cancer.

3.2 Setup

The primary objective of this study is to identify modules specifically associated with lung cancer. To achieve this goal, we introduced dense clusters with high weights as potential candidate driver modules related to lung cancer. Our approach involved considering genes within 61 cancer-related biological processes defined by GO terms, resulting in a set of 100 genes with high mutation frequency from TCGA [9]. To identify the candidate set of driver modules related to lung cancer, we applied community detection (using the Leiden algorithm) and subsequently filtered the clusters based on their weights. We generated unique dense clusters of sizes 4, 5, 6, 7, 8, 9, and 10, resulting in a total of 4,694 dense clusters. This specific range is chosen based on the understanding that biological modules typically consist of at least 4 genes, as smaller groupings may lack the necessary complexity and functionality associated with modular systems in biology [23,25,26]. Conversely, clusters with more than 10 genes are considered excessively broad and tend to provide less informative insights. Their larger size compromises their specificity, making it challenging to discern the distinct functional roles of individual genes within the broader biological context [25]. Thus, by focusing on clusters within the 4–10 member range, we aim to strike a balance between complexity and specificity, facilitating a more nuanced understanding of gene interactions and their functional significance. Furthermore, our approach focuses on the identification of clusters that are not part of any other cluster. The objective is to uncover distinct and exclusive groups of genes that exhibit unique characteristics or functionalities. By doing so, we aim to identify exceptional clusters that possess specific properties or perform specialized functions, separate from the influence of larger clusters. This approach allows us to uncover novel insights into the intricate dynamics of the genetic network by uncovering hidden patterns and novel insights into the underlying biology of lung cancer modules. Next, from the obtained dense clusters, we selected the top 5% of clusters with the highest average weight, which are considered as the candidate driver module set. The candidate driver modules are dense clusters and good clusters in the sense of clustering quality. We showed them in 7 tables as supplementary materials in our GitHub repository [8]. In this study, we are looking for biologically meaningful modules related to lung cancer; therefore, we defined the P-value score to measure the association of these modules with cancer-related pathways, and then we selected 110 modules from this candidate set based on the P-value of the cancer-related pathways associated with each module. These modules represent subsets of genes that demonstrate significant involvement in cancer pathways and we presented these filtered modules in Tables 1, 2, 3, 4, respectively.

3.3 Evaluation of Modules Related to Lung Cancer

Extensive research has unraveled the intricate signaling pathways involved in cancer development. Disruption of these pathways is critical to driving cancer progression. Building upon Ahmad et al. [27], we have compiled a comprehensive list of cancer-related signaling pathways, which provides valuable insights into the molecular mechanisms underlying cancer progression. These pathways govern crucial cellular responses like survival, proliferation, migration, differentiation, and apoptosis, forming the foundation of our investigation into lung cancer-specific modules.

ERBB Signaling Pathway: The ERBB family plays a crucial role in cancer-related signaling pathways, including proliferation, survival, angiogenesis, and metastasis. These receptors are frequently amplified, mutated, or overexpressed in cancer cases, making them attractive targets for cancer treatment. Dysregulation and mutations within the ERBB family have been found to play a significant role in evading anti-tumor immune responses, further emphasizing their importance in cancer progression [27].

Estrogen Receptor Signaling Pathway: Estrogen's involvement in lung cancer has been studied [29]. Recent research has explored its impact on lung cancer development, signaling pathways, and the connection between estrogen receptor (ER) and epidermal growth factor receptor (EGFR). Clinical trials combining ER and EGFR antagonists have been discussed. The detrimental effects of tobacco smoking on estrogen and the role of environmental endocrine-disrupting chemicals targeting ER in lung carcinogenesis are also significant considerations.

FOXO Signaling Pathway: FOXOs are crucial players in cell fate decisions and tumor suppression across various cancer types. The PI3K/AKT pathway is a key player in the interaction with FOXOs and is implicated in several types of cancer. Additionally, other pathways such as Ras-MEK-ERK, IKK are associated with FOXOs in tumorigenesis.

MAPK Signaling Pathway: The MAPK pathway is a tightly controlled part that plays a vital role in diverse cellular processes, including migration, cell proliferation, differentiation, and survival [30]. Dysregulation of this pathway has been implicated in various types of cancer. Additionally, parallel or redundant pathways, such as the PI3K/Akt pathway, are frequently disrupted in cancer.

mTOR Signaling Pathway: The mTOR pathway regulates crucial cellular processes like cell survival, metabolism, growth, and protein synthesis. Dysregulation of mTOR signaling frequently occurs in various malignancies, including lung cancer [31]. Hyperactivation of the mTOR pathway promotes cell proliferation and metabolism, contributing to tumor initiation and progression. Furthermore, mTOR signaling negatively regulates autophagy through multiple mechanisms.

P53 Signaling Pathway: p53 gene mutations are commonly found in human neoplasms, including lung cancer, and are linked to aggressive tumor characteristics and lower overall survival rates. Acting as a tumor suppressor, p53 plays a vital role in maintaining cancer control and inhibiting abnormal cell growth [32]. Post-translational modifications, like ubiquitination, are key in regulating the activity and stability of wild-type p53.

PI3K/Akt Signaling Pathway: The EGFR-mediated signaling pathway includes the PI3K/AKT pathway, which is frequently dysregulated in various human malignancies [28]. Extensive research has shown that PI3Ks are crucial in regulating essential cellular processes involved in cancer development, including metabolism, cell survival, proliferation, differentiation, and motility [28]. The PI3K/AKT pathway is governed by multiple oncogenes and growth factor receptors, such as KIT, MET, EGFR, and ERBB, playing a significant role in intracellular physiological processes [27].

Ras/Raf Signaling Pathway: Targeting the Ras/Raf signaling pathway and its upstream activators has gained attention in cancer research. Abnormal activation of this pathway, particularly through EGFR activation, is highly prevalent

[27]. Ras proteins, central to this pathway, are frequently implicated in oncogenesis, with their mutations associated with cancer development [28].

VEGF Signaling Pathway: VEGF signaling in lung cancer extends beyond angiogenesis, impacting various aspects of tumor progression. This pathway enables carcinoma cells to evade apoptosis and advance toward invasive and metastatic states [33]. Cells with active VEGF signaling gain a survival advantage and promote lung cancer dissemination. These findings emphasize the potential of targeting VEGF and its receptors to directly address tumor cells.

Wnt Signaling Pathway: The Wnt signaling pathway holds a crucial role in the regulation of embryonic organ development and cancer progression. Emerging studies have shown its importance in various aspects, including therapeutic resistance, maintenance of stemness, regulation of the immune microenvironment, and shaping of the cancer phenotype [34].

For evaluation, we used the Gene Set Enrichment Analysis (GSEA) formula to calculate the P-value of candidate modules with respect to the mentioned cancer-related pathways. Suppose that $P = \{p_1, ..., p_M\}$ is a collection of the above-mentioned pathways related to cancer and H is a candidate module (cluster) for lung cancer. The GSEA equation is employed to determine the P-value of cluster H in relation to pathway P_i, described as follows:

$$P - value = \frac{\binom{k}{h_0}\binom{m-k}{a-h_0}}{\binom{m}{a}}$$

In this formula, m represents the total genes present in the lung cancer network and a is the number of genes in the cluster. Furthermore, k shows the number of genes in pathway p_i, and h_0 indicates the number of genes in the cluster found within the assumed pathway. A cluster was identified as a lung cancer driver module if it exhibited a significant P-value, high density, and an elevated average score. A threshold of 0.05 was set for the P-value, and a module was identified as a cancer driver if it had a P-value below this threshold for at least three distinct cancer-related pathways.

Table 1. Statistically significant lung cancer driver modules of size 4.

Genes within the module				P-values corresponding to the signaling pathways implicated in cancer development									# of P-values below
				ERBb	Estrogen	FoxO	MAPK	mTOR	p53	PI3K	Ras	VEGF	Wnt	the 0.05 threshold
CDKN2A	CDKN2B	CDKN1A	HRAS	0.000	0.034	0.000	0.074	0.041	0.000	0.003	0.058	0.015	0.956	7
EGFR	ID1	EGF	ERBB2	0.000	0.034	0.000	0.000	0.959	0.981	0.000	0.001	0.984	0.956	6
GSK3B	GSK3A	CSNK1A1	CSNK2A3	0.022	0.965	0.965	0.923	0.041	0.981	0.086	0.941	0.984	0.000	3
FGFR2	WNT2	FGF9	TMIE	0.977	0.965	0.965	0.002	0.041	0.981	0.003	0.001	0.984	0.044	5
NODAL	SP3	CITED2	JUN	0.022	0.034	0.965	0.074	0.959	0.981	0.911	0.941	0.984	0.044	3
FST	FGF10	FGF7	NKX2-1	0.977	0.965	0.965	0.002	0.959	0.981	0.003	0.001	0.984	0.956	3
SMPD3	PDGFB	PDGFA	NR4A3	0.977	0.965	0.965	0.002	0.959	0.981	0.003	0.001	0.984	0.956	3
CSF1R	CSF1	IL34	DOK7	0.977	0.965	0.965	0.002	0.959	0.981	0.003	0.001	0.984	0.956	3
TP53	TIGAR	MDM2	RPL26	0.977	0.965	0.034	0.074	0.959	0.000	0.003	0.941	0.984	0.044	4
MAPK14	MAP3K20	MAPK11	DYM	0.977	0.965	0.000	0.000	0.959	0.981	0.003	0.941	0.000	0.956	3
BCL2	IL7	IL9	RAG2	0.977	0.034	0.034	0.923	0.959	0.019	0.003	0.941	0.984	0.956	4
PIK3CG	GPR183	PIK3CD	TREM1	0.022	0.034	0.034	0.923	0.041	0.981	0.003	0.058	0.015	0.956	6

Table 2. Statistically significant lung cancer driver modules of size 5.

Genes within the module					P-values corresponding to the signaling pathways implicated in cancer development									# of P-values below the 0.05 threshold
					ERBb	Estrogen	FoxO	MAPK	mTOR	p53	PI3K	Ras	VEGF	Wnt	
SRC	PDGFB	PTK2	FGR	FGF7	0.000	0.043	0.957	0.004	0.949	0.976	0.000	0.002	0.000	0.945	6
MAPK3	HOXA3	MAPK1	PRKCQ	HESX1	0.000	0.001	0.001	0.004	0.001	0.976	0.005	0.002	0.000	0.945	8
AKT1	STK11	AKT2	PIK3CA	IRS2	0.000	0.000	0.000	0.004	0.000	0.976	0.000	0.000	0.000	0.945	8
VEGFA	EFNB2	KDR	FLT4	EPAS1	0.972	0.956	0.957	0.000	0.949	0.976	0.000	0.000	0.000	0.945	4
TP53	CHEK2	FOXO3	CDKN1A	BRCA2	0.028	0.956	0.001	0.091	0.949	0.000	0.000	0.927	0.981	0.054	4
AIFM1	BCL2	BCL2L1	MCL1	MUC17	0.972	0.043	0.957	0.905	0.949	0.000	0.000	0.071	0.981	0.945	3
MAP6	MAP2K2	MAP2K1	BRAF	DIXDC1	0.000	0.001	0.000	0.000	0.000	0.976	0.005	0.002	0.000	0.945	8
VEGFC	FBXW7-AS1	NUS1	VEGFD	VEGFB	0.972	0.956	0.957	0.000	0.949	0.976	0.000	0.000	0.000	0.981	3
KRAS	NF1	ALS2	PLK2	SYNGAP1	0.028	0.043	0.001	0.004	0.050	0.976	0.105	0.000	0.019	0.945	6
NFKBIA	RELA	IKBKB	TMSB4X	NFKB1	0.972	0.956	0.042	0.000	0.050	0.976	0.000	0.000	0.000	0.981	0.945	4
CSF1R	CSF1	CEBPE	IL31RA	IL34	0.972	0.956	0.957	0.004	0.949	0.976	0.005	0.002	0.981	0.945	3
INSR	INS	PPIA	IL1A	EDN3	0.972	0.956	0.001	0.000	0.001	0.976	0.005	0.002	0.981	0.945	5
MAPK14	PENK	ATF2	MAPK11	CALR	0.972	0.043	0.001	0.000	0.949	0.976	0.105	0.927	0.000	0.945	4
PRKCG	GRIN2A	GRIN2C	OBP2B	GPRASP3	0.028	0.956	0.957	0.091	0.050	0.976	0.890	0.002	0.019	0.054	3
FGFR4	TAB1	FGF18	FGFR1	FLT1	0.972	0.956	0.957	0.000	0.949	0.976	0.000	0.000	0.981	0.945	3
RPS6KB1	CFLAR	ERRFI1	EPRS1	EIF4E	0.028	0.956	0.957	0.905	0.001	0.976	0.005	0.927	0.981	0.945	3
AREG	IQGAP1	EREG	BTC	PIGR	0.000	0.956	0.957	0.004	0.949	0.976	0.005	0.927	0.981	0.945	3
PIK3CB	PIK3CG	TYRO3	CSRP1	MYL12A	0.028	0.043	0.042	0.905	0.050	0.976	0.005	0.071	0.019	0.945	5
IGF1R	PDGFD	PDGFC	CBL	CSPP1	0.028	0.956	0.042	0.000	0.050	0.976	0.000	0.000	0.981	0.945	5

3.4 Results

The results are presented in this subsection in 7 tables according to the size of the modules and their corresponding P-value in each of the cancer-related signaling pathways. In all tables, the first column indicates the list of gene names, columns 2–11 display the corresponding P-values for each selected signaling pathway and

Table 3. Statistically significant lung cancer driver modules of size 6.

Genes within the module			P-values corresponding to the signaling pathways implicated in cancer development										# of P-values below the 0.05 threshold
			ERBb	Estrogen	FoxO	MAPK	mTOR	p53	PI3K	Ras	VEGF	Wnt	
SRC PDGFRB	ENPP2 THBS1	PDGFB TXNIP	0.033	0.051	0.948	0.005	0.939	0.028	0.000	0.003	0.023	0.934	6
MTOR RRAGD	CLEC16A LARS1	RPTOR H3-5	0.033	0.948	0.948	0.887	0.000	0.972	0.007	0.913	0.977	0.934	3
PTH INS	OSBPL8 IGF1	INSR CLTCL1	0.966	0.948	0.000	0.000	0.000	0.028	0.000	0.000	0.977	0.934	6
TP53 MUC1	PML PPP2R5C	CDKN1A GML	0.033	0.948	0.050	0.107	0.939	0.000	0.000	0.913	0.977	0.064	3
COL1A1 PDGFA	MMP14 MMP2	PDGFRA ANKRD11	0.966	0.051	0.948	0.005	0.939	0.972	0.000	0.003	0.977	0.934	3
CSF1R FLT3	KIT AHSP	ERBB4 ZNF160	0.033	0.948	0.948	0.000	0.939	0.972	0.000	0.000	0.977	0.934	4
FGF2 FGF9	WNT4 AKT3	APLN FRS2	0.033	0.051	0.050	0.000	0.002	0.972	0.000	0.000	0.023	0.064	6
AREG HBEGF	EREG KIF16B	BTC GAB1	0.000	0.051	0.948	0.005	0.939	0.972	0.007	0.084	0.977	0.934	3
PTPN2 NFAM1	PIK3R1 RHOQ	PIK3R2 DCAF1	0.000	0.001	0.001	0.887	0.002	0.972	0.007	0.003	0.000	0.934	7
PTK2B LAMA3	PTK2 CYTIP	ABL2 LMO7	0.000	0.948	0.948	0.887	0.939	0.972	0.007	0.084	0.023	0.934	3
CASP8 TNFRSF10A	BAD HABP4	NFKB1 TMEM150C	0.033	0.948	0.948	0.107	0.939	0.000	0.007	0.003	0.023	0.934	5
EPM2AIP1 PIK3CA	AKT1 PPP1R3G	ADTRP PGM2L1	0.000	0.001	0.001	0.107	0.002	0.972	0.007	0.003	0.000	0.934	7
IGF1R HRAS	PDGFD HCST	PDGFC MACC1	0.033	0.051	0.001	0.000	0.002	0.972	0.000	0.000	0.023	0.934	7

Table 4. Statistically significant lung cancer driver modules of size 7.

Genes within the module				P-values corresponding to the signaling pathways implicated in cancer development										# of P-values below the 0.05 threshold
				ERBb	Estrogen	FoxO	MAPK	mTOR	p53	PI3K	Ras	VEGF	Wnt	
HSPA5 PRKAA2	XBP1 ERN1	PRKAA1 KCNB1	MLXIPL	0.961	0.940	0.002	0.870	0.002	0.967	0.010	0.899	0.973	0.924	3
ITGB3 PDGFC	PDGFB HDGF	PDGFA ELK3	PDGFD	0.961	0.940	0.940	0.000	0.929	0.967	0.000	0.000	0.973	0.924	3
PTK2B BCAR1	SRC FES	HGF AATK	PTK2	0.001	0.059	0.940	0.123	0.929	0.967	0.010	0.097	0.000	0.924	3
INSR PRKCZ	INS CFLAR	IGF1 MYDGF	IGF1R	0.961	0.940	0.000	0.000	0.000	0.033	0.000	0.000	0.973	0.924	6
NQO1 AREG	CASP8 ANXA1	GJB2 CASP3	CASP9	0.039	0.940	0.940	0.007	0.929	0.000	0.010	0.899	0.027	0.924	5
MTOR MAPK8	TARDBP MAPK9	MAPK10 KDM5B	SRRD	0.000	0.940	0.000	0.000	0.069	0.967	0.140	0.000	0.973	0.000	5
KIT FLT1	PDGFRB TOPAZ1	PDGFRA DCBLD2	CSRNP1	0.961	0.940	0.940	0.000	0.929	0.967	0.000	0.000	0.973	0.924	3
TP53 CDKN1A	KRAS GTSE1	NF1 NES	KIFAP3	0.001	0.059	0.002	0.000	0.069	0.000	0.000	0.004	0.027	0.074	7
ERBB4 NTN5	ERBB3 TGFA	NRG1 EPGN	ERBB2	0.000	0.059	0.940	0.000	0.929	0.967	0.000	0.097	0.973	0.924	3
FGF2 FGFR1	SETX FLRT3	FGF18 SHCBP1	FGFR3	0.961	0.940	0.940	0.000	0.929	0.967	0.000	0.000	0.973	0.924	3
PIK3CB PIK3CA	KBTBD2 PEAR1	AKT1 ZNF568	IGF2	0.000	0.000	0.000	0.007	0.000	0.967	0.000	0.000	0.000	0.924	8
CSNK2A2 PRKCA	TAF1 CSNK2B	HIPK2 DYRK2	HIPK1	0.039	0.940	0.940	0.123	0.069	0.967	0.140	0.097	0.027	0.000	3
KDR FLT4	CLEC14A TEK	CD34 MCAM	STK40	0.961	0.940	0.940	0.000	0.929	0.967	0.000	0.000	0.027	0.924	4
FGF4 HMX2	FGF6 RNF43	SHOX2 FGF3	FGF9	0.961	0.940	0.940	0.000	0.929	0.967	0.000	0.000	0.973	0.074	3
THBS1 ANGPT2	RPS6KB1 GPI	PKLR RPS6KB2	FOXP1	0.001	0.940	0.940	0.123	0.002	0.033	0.000	0.097	0.973	0.924	4
SEC13 AKT3	WDR59 BMT2	WDR24 SIK3	MIOS	0.039	0.059	0.058	0.123	0.000	0.967	0.140	0.097	0.027	0.924	3
GRB2 PTPRA	SOS1 ZNF106	HRAS TNFSF8	SOS2	0.000	0.000	0.000	0.000	0.000	0.967	0.000	0.000	0.027	0.924	8

the last column indicates the number of signaling pathways in which the module's P-value falls below the 0.05 threshold.

Table 1 shows the significant modules with 4 genes and emphasizes the significance of proposed clusters in terms of their biological relevance. The presence of multiple modules showing statistical significance concerning the predefined pathways supports this observation. We successfully identified 12 distinct clusters, each consisting of 4 genes, and a considerable proportion of these clusters exhibited statistical significance across three or more pathways, as indicated in the last column. Similarly, Table 2 presents the statistically significant modules consisting of 5 genes. Unlike Table 1, Table 2 exhibits a distinct characteristic, as it contains several modules that show statistical significance for eight different pathways. This represents the highest number of pathways identified for any cluster size, although this feature is not exclusive to Table 2. Table 3 provides an overview of modules comprising 6 genes that demonstrate statistical significance. This table contains several modules that show statistical significance for seven different pathways. Table 4 shows lung cancer driver modules consisting of 7 genes. This table contains several modules that show statistical significance for more than five different pathways. Table 5 displays the modules

Table 5. Statistically significant lung cancer driver modules of size 8.

Genes within the module				P-values corresponding to the signaling pathways implicated in cancer development									# of P-values below
				ERBb	Estrogen	FoxO	MAPK	mTOR	p53	PI3K	Ras	VEGF	Wnt	the 0.05 threshold
PRKCG	CLN3	GRIN2A	GRIN2C	0.044	0.931	0.932	0.138	0.078	0.962	0.830	0.000	0.030	0.083	3
GRIN1	GRIN2B	TSHZ3	MPP2											
ABL1	VEGFA	ITGB1BP1	PTPRJ	0.044	0.931	0.932	0.010	0.919	0.962	0.013	0.006	0.030	0.913	5
NRP1	NRP2	NR4A1	SCG2											
PTH	EPM2AIP1	AKT1	ADTRP	0.001	0.002	0.000	0.000	0.000	0.962	0.001	0.000	0.000	0.913	8
INS	AKT2	IRS2	SORBS1											
MAPK3	MYC	SRF	MAPK1	0.000	0.002	0.000	0.000	0.000	0.962	0.001	0.006	0.000	0.083	8
BRAF	GRHL2	HMBOX1	ZNF512B											
IL5	ERBB4	PDGFB	FG2	0.044	0.067	0.932	0.000	0.919	0.962	0.000	0.000	0.969	0.913	4
PDGFRB	ESR1	LRRK1	ARPC1B											
RCAN1	PPP3CB	PPP3CC	PPP3CA	0.955	0.931	0.932	0.000	0.919	0.962	0.830	0.885	0.000	0.000	3
PPP3R2	NFAT5	ADGRB2	NFATC3											
MYCN	FGF4	NGFR	FGF10	0.955	0.931	0.932	0.000	0.919	0.962	0.000	0.000	0.969	0.913	3
FGF7	TP63	FGF18	ZNF219											
PRKAA1	CDK1	PRKAA2	MAPK8	0.044	0.931	0.000	0.138	0.003	0.037	0.013	0.109	0.969	0.083	5
NFE2L2	ACACA	DIP2B	HTD2											
MAPK14	MAP3K20	MAP3K5	MAPK11	0.044	0.931	0.000	0.000	0.919	0.001	0.157	0.885	0.000	0.913	5
PBK	CHEK2	CDKN1A	MAP3K13											
FGFR2	PDGFA	PDGFD	PDGFC	0.955	0.931	0.932	0.000	0.919	0.962	0.000	0.000	0.969	0.913	3
PIK3R5	PIK3R6	AKAP13	NEK10											
WNT3A	GSK3B	AXIN1	FOXO1	0.044	0.931	0.066	0.852	0.003	0.962	0.157	0.885	0.969	0.000	3
GSK3A	RNF180	RNF19A	ZNF106											
PTPN2	PIK3R1	PIK3R2	SOGA1	0.000	0.000	0.000	0.852	0.000	0.962	0.001	0.000	0.000	0.913	7
BCAR3	PIK3R3	RHOQ	IRS4											
SPINK1	NTRK3	IL1A	ERBB2	0.000	0.067	0.932	0.000	0.919	0.962	0.000	0.006	0.969	0.913	4
EREG	TGFA	FGF1	EPGN											
KDR	STK40	FLT1	FLT4	0.955	0.931	0.932	0.000	0.919	0.962	0.000	0.000	0.030	0.913	4
PGF	CCBE1	PIFO	EPHA6											
PAK3	NPFFR2	PAK1	EPHA4	0.000	0.931	0.932	0.010	0.919	0.962	0.830	0.000	0.969	0.913	3
CHN1	SIPA1L1	BRSK2	PAK2											
MAP2K6	ATF2	MAP2K4	MAP3K7	0.000	0.002	0.066	0.000	0.078	0.962	0.001	0.006	0.030	0.083	6
MAP2K7	NFKB1	FGF14	HRAS											
SMPD3	LOX	IGF1	RPS6KB1	0.001	0.931	0.066	0.010	0.000	0.037	0.000	0.006	0.969	0.913	6
IGF2	PEAR1	PHIP	RPS6KB2											
PDCD10	CAMK1	RAF1	MAP2K2	0.000	0.000	0.000	0.000	0.000	0.962	0.000	0.000	0.000	0.913	8
MAP2K1	MMRN2	MTCP1	TCL1A											
CDKN1B	CDC34	CCNE2	CCNE1	0.044	0.931	0.066	0.852	0.919	0.001	0.001	0.885	0.969	0.913	3
MNAT1	CDKN3	CDC6	ZNF827											
FOS	FOSL1	JUND	LRP11	0.044	0.002	0.932	0.000	0.919	0.962	0.830	0.885	0.969	0.003	4
TXNIP	CAPN2	JUN	CSN1S1											
ERBB3	INSR	IGF1R	PRR5	0.044	0.931	0.002	0.000	0.000	0.962	0.001	0.006	0.969	0.083	6
PRR5L	UNC5B	ROR1	UNC5A											
PTK2B	TNXB	PTK2	ABL2	0.001	0.931	0.932	0.852	0.919	0.962	0.001	0.109	0.030	0.913	3
SPINK5	LAMA4	LMO7	TNXA											

of size 8. Notably, the gene PDGFB appears most frequently, appearing in a total of 7 clusters. It is followed by CDKN1A, INS, INSR, IGF1R, and AKT1, which each appear in 6 clusters. Among the various cluster sizes explored, as evident in Table 5, which contains the highest number of modules (a total of 22). Table 5 contains several modules that show statistical significance for eight different pathways. Table 6 presents the lung cancer driver modules, consisting of 9 genes. This table contains several modules that show statistical significance for seven different pathways. Table 7 illustrates the largest modules, consisting of 10 genes. This table contains several modules that show statistical significance for more than five different pathways. These modules provide a foundation for further investigations, such as exploring potential combinations between modules and examining the implications of their statistical assessment.

Table 6. Statistically significant cancer driver modules of size 9.

Genes within the module					P-values corresponding to the signaling pathways implicated in cancer development									# of P-values below the 0.05 threshold
					ERBb	Estrogen	FoxO	MAPK	mTOR	p53	PI3K	Ras	VEGF	Wnt	
TP53 USP47	BCL2 BID	CASP9 BEX3	BAX CASP8AP2	BAK1	0.950	0.074	0.924	0.152	0.909	0.000	0.001	0.872	0.034	0.093	3
PDGFB PDGFD	PDGFRB DDR2	EGFR HRAS	PDGFA S100A11	ESR1	0.001	0.000	0.003	0.000	0.087	0.958	0.000	0.000	0.034	0.903	7
MAPK3 MAPKAPK5	MAPK1 NAF1	PRKCQ PKIB	NEK2 SPATA4	NEK7	0.001	0.003	0.003	0.001	0.004	0.958	0.016	0.007	0.001	0.903	8
PPP3CB AKAP5	PPP3CC DRD4	PPP3R1 STIMATE	PPP3CA CBARP	PPP3R2	0.950	0.923	0.924	0.000	0.909	0.958	0.811	0.872	0.000	0.000	3
IL5 CD4	ERBB4 FLT1	PDGFRA TEK	ERBB2 EPHB6	FGFR3	0.001	0.923	0.924	0.000	0.909	0.958	0.000	0.000	0.965	0.903	4
FGFR2 ZFPM2	SHOX2 EVC	FGF9 HMX2	PRRX1 TEDC1	FOXF1	0.950	0.923	0.924	0.012	0.909	0.958	0.016	0.007	0.965	0.903	3
MAPK14 MAPKAPK2	MAP3K20 MAPK11	MAP2K3 PBK	MAP2K6 PRELP	MAP3K5	0.950	0.923	0.003	0.000	0.909	0.958	0.811	0.872	0.000	0.903	3
INS GCK	AKT2 PRKCI	PRKCZ SORBS1	IRS2 ITLN1	PGP	0.049	0.074	0.000	0.012	0.004	0.958	0.016	0.007	0.034	0.903	7
AKT1 IGF1R	ADTRP PIK3C2B	INSR IFIT2	PDPK1 NPY5R	IGF2	0.049	0.074	0.000	0.000	0.000	0.958	0.000	0.000	0.034	0.903	7
IRS1 PREX2	IGF1 SERPINA12	PIK3R1 PIK3R5	PIK3R2 RTN1	PRR5L	0.001	0.003	0.000	0.152	0.000	0.042	0.000	0.000	0.001	0.903	8
RGCC MNAT1	CCND1 CCNG1	CCND2 SPDYE17	CCND3 CDK3	CCNH	0.950	0.923	0.003	0.835	0.909	0.000	0.001	0.872	0.965	0.000	4
OSM HAX1	ANGPT1 EVI2B	HCLS1 CSF3	ANGPT4 UNC5A	UNC5B	0.950	0.923	0.924	0.012	0.909	0.958	0.000	0.007	0.965	0.903	3
CDKN2B CNPPD1	CDKN1B MEN1	CDKN1A TP53I13	CDKN2C S100G	CDK7	0.001	0.923	0.000	0.835	0.909	0.042	0.016	0.872	0.965	0.903	4
MTOR CD68	MEAK7 KLHL22	RPTOR ZNF143	PRR5 PEAK3	RICTOR	0.049	0.923	0.924	0.835	0.000	0.958	0.016	0.872	0.965	0.903	3

In total, this work identified 110 cancer-driver modules that are both statistically and biologically significant. Among these, 46 modules are associated with 3 different pathways, 18 modules with 4 pathways, 11 modules with 5

Table 7. Statistically significant cancer driver modules of size 10.

Genes within the module					P-values corresponding to the signaling pathways implicated in cancer development									# of P-values below the 0.05 threshold
					ERBb	Estrogen	FoxO	MAPK	mTOR	p53	PI3K	Ras	VEGF	Wnt	
MAPK3 HESX1	MAPK1 DENND10	RAF1 TBC1D10C	MAP2K2 ATP6AP1L	MAP2K1 C3orf33	0.000	0.000	0.000	0.000	0.000	0.953	0.000	0.000	0.000	0.893	8
KIT IGF1R	PDGFB KITLG	PDGFRB PIK3AP1	INSR MYDGF	IGF1 TOPAZ1	0.944	0.915	0.000	0.000	0.000	0.046	0.000	0.000	0.962	0.893	6
PRKD2 FLT4	SMOC2 TEK	PRKD1 VASH2	PRKCA AAMP	KDR RIN2	0.054	0.915	0.916	0.000	0.096	0.953	0.000	0.000	0.001	0.102	4
FGF4 FGF8	FGF2 PHF14	FGFR2 FRS2	FGF10 GREB1L	GATA2 TMEM59L	0.944	0.915	0.916	0.000	0.900	0.953	0.000	0.000	0.962	0.893	3
ACVRL1 GCNT2	SMAD4 GLIPR2	RGCC AMHR2	TGFBR2 ANGPT2	TGFBR1 PXN	0.944	0.915	0.000	0.001	0.900	0.953	0.187	0.132	0.038	0.102	3
RELA CHUK	IKBKB ZNF675	MAP3K7 TRAF2	TRAF6 NLRP2	MALT1 COMMD7	0.944	0.915	0.003	0.000	0.005	0.953	0.001	0.000	0.962	0.102	5
PIK3CB PIK3CG	PIRT CA8	PIK3C2A PI4KA	PIK3CD GAB2	PIK3C2B PI4KAP1	0.001	0.003	0.003	0.819	0.005	0.953	0.020	0.000	0.001	0.893	7
SMPD3 PIK3CA	AKT1 IRS2	ADTRP C1QTNF12	INS SLC39A14	RPS6KB1 ZNF236	0.000	0.003	0.000	0.015	0.000	0.953	0.000	0.000	0.001	0.893	8
CDC42 RHOBTB3	RAC2 RND2	RHOG PARVG	RHOH FSCN2	RHOQ PEAK3	0.944	0.915	0.916	0.015	0.900	0.953	0.792	0.009	0.001	0.102	3
SUV39H1 PRKAG1	PRKAA1 PRKAG3	PRKAA2 ACSM1	ACACA SIK1B	PRKAB2 ACSM5	0.944	0.915	0.000	0.819	0.005	0.953	0.020	0.859	0.962	0.893	3
VEGFC FBXW7-AS1	IL1A VEGFD	NKX3-1 VEGFB	HDGF GKN1	PGF PROK1	0.944	0.915	0.916	0.000	0.900	0.953	0.000	0.000	0.962	0.893	3
MAPK14 MNT	MAP3K5 MAPK10	MAP2K4 MAPK9	MAPK11 KAT6A	PRMT5 PRELP	0.000	0.915	0.000	0.000	0.900	0.953	0.792	0.009	0.001	0.005	6
ABI2 WASF2	AKIRIN1 BRK1	CYFIP1 DBNL	RAC1 RHOU	RAC3 NISCH	0.944	0.915	0.916	0.015	0.900	0.953	0.187	0.009	0.001	0.005	4

pathways, 13 modules with 6 pathways, 10 modules with 7 pathways, and 12 modules with 8 pathways. These findings highlight the diversity and complexity of the molecular mechanisms involved in cancer development and progression. It is worth noting that out of the 10 pathways analyzed, the PI3K pathway demonstrated the highest statistical significance with P-values below the 0.05 threshold for a total of 89 or 80.9% of all modules. On the other hand, the Wnt pathway showed the least statistical significance, appearing in only 13 modules, which corresponds to 11.8% of all modules generated by this clustering method. Figure 2 provides a comprehensive visualization, presenting the P-values associated with each module within various pathways. The heatmap offers valuable insights into the statistical significance and relative strengths of these modules.

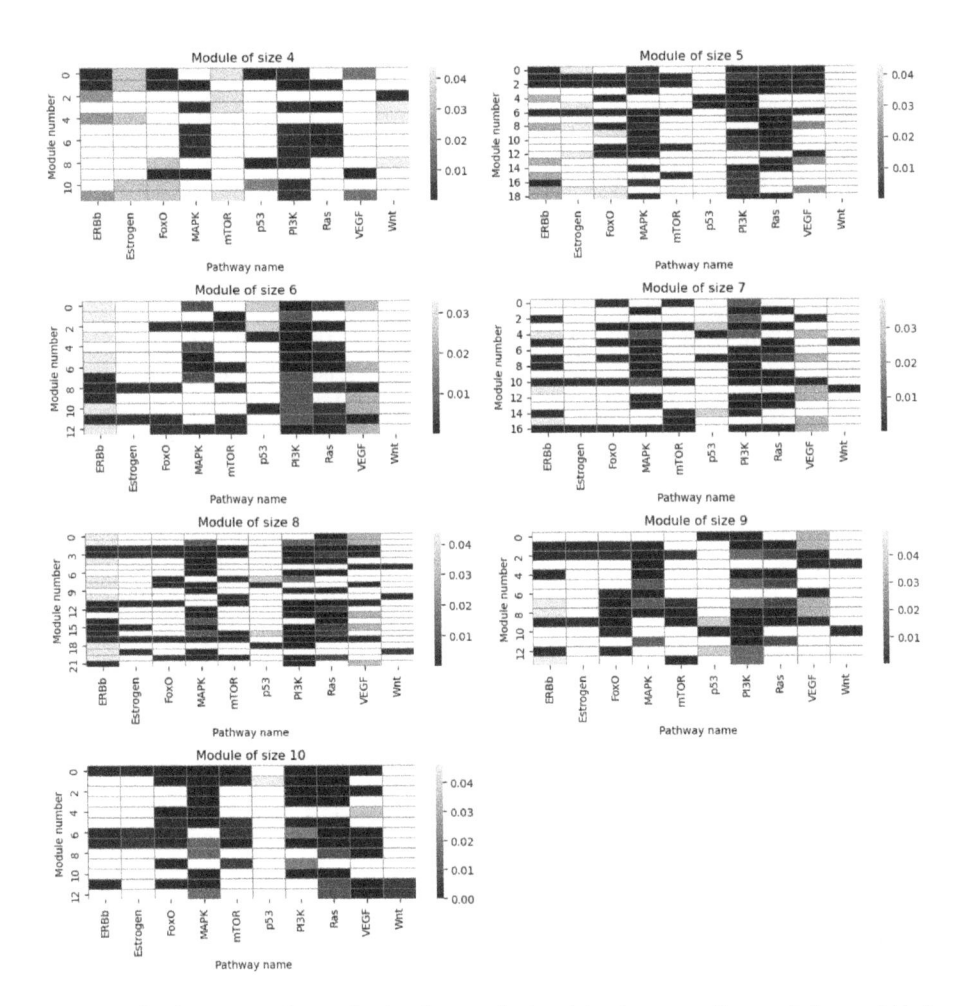

Fig. 2. The heatmap, shows the intricate relationships between the modules and their corresponding pathway P-values

In summary, the analysis of the 110 distinct modules identified has revealed their statistical significance across a minimum of three selected signaling pathways. Remarkably, a majority of these modules surpass this minimum requirement, demonstrating statistical relevance in up to eight pathways. The interconnected nature of each module suggests their involvement in multiple biological processes, with no module being a subset of another. These findings are highly satisfactory, providing substantial insights into the field of lung cancer research and highlighting the significance of these modules in understanding the disease.

4 Conclusions

Lung cancer, a leading cause of cancer-related mortality globally, poses a significant challenge in terms of treatment due to its genetic alterations and heterogeneity. In this study, our focus was on identifying driver modules associated with lung cancer. By utilizing a collection of mutated genes found in lung cancer patients, we identified the key genes responsible for driving lung cancer. To construct a biological network that represents the mutated gene set, we assigned network nodes to the mutated genes, and the network edge between the two genes shows the number of GO terms that both genes participated in at the same time. Next, we introduced a clustering method as a machine-learning approach. This algorithm facilitated the identification of high-density sub-networks with significant weight within the lung cancer network. We discovered the top 5% of clusters with the highest average weight and calculated the P-value for each of these obtained modules based on well-established cancer pathways. Consequently, we presented 110 significant modules in Tables 1, 2, 3, 4, 5, 6, 7 showcasing their extensive coverage within cancer pathways. The identification of driver genes and modules in lung cancer offers a comprehensive understanding of the causes and progression of this disease.

References

1. Hanahan, D., Weinberg, R.A.: Hallmarks of cancer: the next generation. Cell **144**(5), 646–674 (2011)
2. Noone, A.M., Cronin, K.A., Altekruse, S.F., Howlader, N., et al.: Cancer incidence and survival trends by subtype using data from the surveillance epidemiology and end results program, 1992–2013. Cancer Epidemiol. Biomark. Prev. **26**(4), 632–41 (2017)
3. Ridge, C.A., McErlean, A.M., Ginsberg, M.S.: Seminars in Interventional Radiology, pp. 093–098. Thieme Medical Publishers (2013)
4. Thun, M.J., Hannan, L.M., Adams-Campbell, L.L., Boffetta, P., et al.: Lung cancer occurrence in never-smokers: an analysis of 13 cohorts and 22 cancer registry studies. PLoS Med. **5**(9), e185 (2008)
5. Cruz, C.S., Tanoue, L.T., Matthay, R.A.: Lung cancer: epidemiology, etiology, and prevention. Clin. Chest Med. **32**(4), 605–44 (2011)
6. Pikor, L.A., Ramnarine, V.R., Lam, S., Lam, W.L.: Genetic alterations defining NSCLC subtypes and their therapeutic implications. Lung Cancer **82**(2), 179–89 (2013)

7. Chen, Z., Fillmore, C.M., Hammerman, P.S., Kim, C.F., Wong, K.K.: Non-small-cell lung cancers: a heterogeneous set of diseases. Nat. Rev. Cancer **14**(8), 535–46 (2014)
8. Lung Cancer Modules Repository. https://github.com/Golnazthr/LungCancer Modules
9. Cancer Genome Atlas (TCGA) Research Network: Comprehensive genomic characterization defines human glioblastoma genes and core pathways. Nature **455**(7216), 1061 (2008)
10. Vogelstein, B., Papadopoulos, N., Velculescu, V.E., Zhou, S., Diaz, L.A., Jr., Kinzler, K.W.: Cancer genome landscapes. Science **339**(6127), 1546–1558 (2013)
11. Taheri, G., Habibi, M.: Using unsupervised learning algorithms to identify essential genes associated with SARS-CoV-2 as potential therapeutic targets for COVID-19. bioRxiv **5**(1) (2022)
12. Taheri, G., Habibi, M.: Identification of essential genes associated with SARS-CoV-2 infection as potential drug target candidates with machine learning algorithms. Sci. Rep. **13**(1), 15141 (2023)
13. Dopazo, J., Erten, C.: Graph-theoretical comparison of normal and tumor networks in identifying BRCA genes. BMC Syst. Biol. **1**(11), 1–7 (2017)
14. Yang, H., Wei, Q., Zhong, X., Yang, H., Li, B.: Cancer driver gene discovery through an integrative genomics approach in a non-parametric Bayesian framework. Bioinformatics **33**(4), 483–90 (2017)
15. Vanunu, O., Magger, O., Ruppin, E., Shlomi, T., Sharan, R.: Associating genes and protein complexes with disease via network propagation. PLoS Comput. Biol. **6**(1), e1000641 (2010)
16. Deng, Y., Luo, S., Deng, C., Luo, T., Yin, W., Zhang, H., et al.: Identifying mutual exclusivity across cancer genomes: computational approaches to discover genetic interaction and reveal tumor vulnerability. Brief. Bioinform. **20**(1), 254–266 (2019)
17. Zhang, J., Zhang, S.: The discovery of mutated driver pathways in cancer: models and algorithms. IEEE/ACM Trans. Comput. Biol. Bioinf. **15**(3), 988–998 (2018)
18. Ciriello, G., Cerami, E., Sander, C., Schultz, N.: Mutual exclusivity analysis identifies oncogenic network modules. Genome Res. **22**(2), 398–406 (2012)
19. Cho, A., Shim, J.E., Kim, E., Supek, F., Lehner, B., Lee, I.: MUFFINN: cancer gene discovery via network analysis of somatic mutation data. Genome Biol. **17**(1), 1–6 (2016)
20. Dimitrakopoulos, C.M., Beerenwinkel, N.: MUFFINN: computational approaches for the identification of cancer genes and pathways. Syst. Biol. Med. **9**(1), e1364 (2017)
21. Zhang, W., Wang, S.L., Liu, Y.: Identification of cancer driver modules based on graph clustering from multiomics data. J. Comput. Biol. **28**(10), 1007–1020 (2021)
22. Habibi, M., Taheri, G.: Topological network based drug repurposing for Coronavirus 2019. PLoS ONE **16**(7), e0255270 (2021)
23. Habibi, M., Taheri, G.: A new machine learning method for cancer mutation analysis. PLoS Comput. Biol. **18**(10), e1010332 (2022)
24. Traag, V.A., Waltman, L., Van Eck, N.J.: From Louvain to Leiden: guaranteeing well-connected communities. Sci. Rep. **9**(1), 5233 (2019)
25. Spirin, V., Mirny, L.A.: Protein complexes and functional modules in molecular networks. In: Proceedings of the National Academy of Sciences, pp. 12123–12128 (2010)
26. Taheri, G., Habibi, M., Wong, L., Eslahchi, C.: Disruption of protein complexes. J. Bioinform. Comput. Biol. **11**(03), 1341008 (2013)

27. Ahmad, A.: Breast Cancer Metastasis and Drug Resistance: Challenges and Progress. Springer (2019)
28. Taheri, G., Habibi, M.: A novel machine learning method for mutational analysis to identifying driver genes in breast cancer. bioRxiv **11**(01), 1341008 (2022)
29. Stabile, L.P., Siegfried, J.M.: Estrogen receptor pathways in lung cancer. Curr. Oncol. Rep. **6**(01), 259–267 (2004)
30. Taheri, G., Habibi, M.: Comprehensive analysis of pathways in Coronavirus 2019 (COVID-19) using an unsupervised machine learning method. Appl. Soft Comput. **128**, 109510 (2022)
31. Ekman, S., Wynes, M.W., Hirsch, F.R.: The mTOR pathway in lung cancer and implications for therapy and biomarker analysis. J. Thorac. Oncol. **7**(06), 947–953 (2012)
32. Hao, X.L., Han, F., Zhang, N., Chen, H.Q., et al.: TC2N, a novel oncogene, accelerates tumor progression by suppressing p53 signaling pathway in lung cancer. Cell Death Differ. **26**(7), 1235–1250 (2019)
33. Frezzetti, D., Gallo, M., Maiello, M.R., D'Alessio, A., Esposito, C., et al.: EGF as a potential target in lung cancer. Expert Opin. Ther. Targets **21**(10), 959–66 (2017)
34. Stewart, D.J.: Wnt signaling pathway in non-small cell lung cancer. J. Natl. Cancer Inst. **106**(1), 1–11 (2014)

Benchmarking Collaborative Learning Methods Cost-Effectiveness for Prostate Segmentation

Lucia Innocenti[1,2](✉), Michela Antonelli[2], Francesco Cremonesi[1], Kenaan Sarhan[2], Alejandro Granados[2], Vicky Goh[2], Sebastien Ourselin[2], and Marco Lorenzi[1]

[1] Epione Research Group, Inria, Sophia Antipolis, France
[2] King's College London, London, UK
lucia.innocenti@inria.fr

Abstract. Healthcare data is often split into medium/small-sized collections across multiple hospitals and access to it is encumbered by privacy regulations. This brings difficulties to use them for the development of machine learning and deep learning models, which are known to be data-hungry. One way to overcome this limitation is to use collaborative learning (CL) methods, which allow hospitals to work collaboratively to solve a task, without the need to explicitly share local data.

In this paper, we address a prostate segmentation problem from MRI in a collaborative scenario by comparing two different approaches: federated learning (FL) and consensus-based methods (CBM).

To the best of our knowledge, this is the first work in which CBM, such as label fusion techniques, are used to solve a problem of collaborative learning. In this setting, CBM combine predictions from locally trained models to obtain a federated strong learner with ideally improved robustness and predictive variance properties.

Our experiments show that, in the considered practical scenario, CBMs provide equal or better results than FL, while being highly cost-effective. Our results demonstrate that the consensus paradigm may represent a valid alternative to FL for typical training tasks in medical imaging.

Keywords: Collaborative Learning · Cost-Effectiveness · Prostate Segmentation

1 Introduction

Prostate cancer is the most frequently diagnosed cancer in men in more than half of the countries worldwide [1]. While accurate prostate segmentation is crucial for effective radiotherapy planning [2], traditional manual segmentation is

---

Supplementary Information The online version contains supplementary material available at https://doi.org/10.1007/978-3-031-74640-6_5.

expensive, time-consuming, and dependent on the observer [3]. Automated or semi-automated methods are needed for efficient and reliable prostate segmentation [4], and deep learning is nowadays the main tool for solving the segmentation task [5]. Hospital data are highly sensitive and are difficult to collect in data silos for centralized training. This makes their use in notoriously data-hungry deep learning systems problematic. For this reason, collaborative learning (CL) is emerging as a powerful approach: it allows different decentralized entities to collaborate in solving a task, and researchers are exploring ways to do this by keeping the local data private [6].

Federated learning (FL) [7] has gained great attention since the first apparition. FL solves a collaborative training problem in which a model is collectively optimized by different clients, each of them owning a local private dataset [8]. Through different training rounds, a server orchestrates local optimization and aggregation of trained parameters across clients. Since training data is kept on the client's side, FL addresses the problems of data privacy and governance. Nevertheless, FL still poses several challenges in real-world applications [9,10], consisting of 1) the sensitivity of the optimization result to the heterogeneity of system and data distribution across clients, and 2) the need for a large number of communication rounds, making communication cost a critical aspect. Moreover, from a practical perspective, FL systems are costly, since they are based on the setup and maintenance of complex computational infrastructures in hospitals, and thus require the availability of local resources and personnel [11–13].

Consensus-based methods (CBM) are a class of algorithms widely explored in machine learning, where the outputs from an ensemble of weak-predictors are aggregated to define a strong-predictor, outperforming the weak experts in terms of predictive robustness [14]. In medical imaging, CBM are often at the core of state-of-the-art approaches for image segmentation tasks [15,16].

In this paper, we propose a comparison of these two different collaborative methods. Our specific focus is on collaborative prostate segmentation applied to magnetic resonance images (MRI). Differently from FL, in CBM independent models are locally trained by each client only once and, at testing time, a strong predictor is obtained by aggregating the output of the local models. Contrarily to FL, the setup of a CBM system in a hospital is straightforward, since no coordination in training is needed. Moreover, CBM provides data privacy and governance guarantees akin to FL, because no private information is shared during training, and model parameters are shared only once after training. Note that CBM has been coupled to FL training in previous works [17–19,19–22]. Nevertheless, most of these approaches are still based on distributed optimization, and thus they require setting up the whole FL infrastructure in hospitals, while the CBM we are analyzing here overtaken this limitation.

We present in this work a thorough benchmark of these models based on a cross-silo collaborative prostate segmentation task. The contributions of this paper are the following:

- We generate a distributed scenario based on natural data splits from a large collection of prostate MRI datasets currently available to the community, thus defining a realistic federated simulation.
 - We define novel metrics to compare FL and CBM in terms of accuracy, robustness, cost-effectiveness, and utility.
 - We apply the two CL approaches to this federated scenario and evaluate them in terms of accuracy and new-proposed metrics.

The paper is structured as follows. In Sect. 2 we present the data and the learning models used for the benchmark, i.e. federated learning and consensus-based methods, and present the experiments and evaluation methods adopted in this work. Section 3 presents the experiment setting and results. Finally, Sect. 4 discusses our findings and future perspectives.

2 Benchmark Definition

Starting from a large publicly available collection of data for prostate segmentation, we first define the federated setting by partitioning the data based on image acquisition characteristics and protocols. This allows us to obtain splits with controlled inter-center heterogeneity, thus simulating a realistic collaborative training scenario. We further define experiments to evaluate segmentation accuracy, cost-effectiveness, robustness to data heterogeneity, and utility for clients. Finally, we apply the differential privacy (DP) paradigm to different methods and we analyze how they respond to it.

2.1 Distributed Scenario

We gathered data provided by 3 major publicly available datasets on prostate cancer imaging analysis, and by 1 private dataset:

 - **Medical Segmentation Decathlon - Prostate** [23] provides 32 prostate MRIs for training.
 - **Promise12** [24] consists of 50 training cases obtained with different scanners. Of those, 27 cases were acquired by using an endorectal coil.
 - **ProstateX** [25] contains prostate MRIs acquired by using two different scanners (Skyra and Triotim, both from Siemens). Segmentations of 194 cases are available [26].
 - **Private Hospital Dataset** (PrivateDS) is composed of 36 MRIs collected by using a Siemens Aera scanner during a project on active surveillance for prostate cancer detection. An expert radiologist produced prostate masks. This dataset is used as an independent test set.

Datasets were split as in Table 1, to define centers characterized by specific image acquisition properties, thus allowing to obtain heterogeneous image distributions among centers. The common preprocessing pipeline applied to all the data comprised of flipping, cropping/padding to the same dimension, and intensity normalization. N4-bias-correction has also been applied to the data from Promise12 in N03 in order to compensate for the intensity artifacts introduced by the endorectal coil.

Table 1. Description of the different centers here considered for the distributed learning scenario, derived by partitioning the four dataset Decathlon, ProstateX, Promise12, and PrivateDS.

ID	#Samples	Dataset	Subset Selection	Training	Test
N01	32	Decathlon	Full Dataset	Y	Y
N02	23	Promise12	No Endorectal Coil	Y	Y
N03	27	Promise12	Only Endorectal Coil	Y	Y
N04	184	ProstateX	Only Scanner Skyra	Y	Y
N05	5	ProstateX	Only Scanner Triotim	N	Y
N06	36	PrivateDS	Full Dataset	N	Y

2.2 Collaborative Learning Frameworks

In our scenario we consider M hospitals, each having a local dataset $\mathcal{D}_i = \{z_{k,i}\}_{k=1}^{N_i}$. Given z, a volumetric MRI, and a vector of parameters θ, we define a segmentation problem in which a model g produces binary masks $h_z = g(z, \theta)$. Each hospital is a client indexed by $i \in [0, M]$, and the local training consists in solving the loss minimization problem, considering a loss function $f(\cdot)$.

Federated Learning. FL is a collaborative optimization problem defined by:

$$\theta_g = \arg\min_{\theta}(\mathcal{L}(\theta)) \text{ s.t. } \mathcal{L}(\theta) := \sum_{i=1}^{n} p_i \mathcal{L}_i(\theta_i). \qquad (1)$$

In FL, local losses are weighted by p_i, such that $\sum_{i=1}^{n} p_i = 1$, where the weights p_i are arbitrarily set, for example, based on the local dataset size. Different strategies on how to optimize the weights have been proposed in the literature, with the aim of mitigating the impact of data heterogeneity or client drift. In this paper, we consider the following FL strategies from the state-of-the-art:

- **FedAvg** [27] is the backbone of FL optimization where, at round r, each client locally executes a number of stochastic gradient descent steps, and sends the partially optimized model θ_i^r to the server. The received models are weighted and averaged by the server into a global one, θ_g^{r+1}, which is then sent back to the clients to initialize the next optimization round. This process is repeated for R rounds until convergence.
- **FedProx** [28] tackles the problem of federated optimization with data heterogeneity across clients. This approach extends FEDAVG by introducing a proximal term to the local objective function to penalize model drift from the global optimization during local training. The proximal term is controlled by a trade-off hyperparameter, μ, through the following optimization problem:

$$\mathcal{L}_i(\theta)^r := \frac{1}{N_i} \sum_{k=1}^{N_i} \mathcal{L}(z_{k,i}, \theta_i^r) + \frac{\mu}{2} ||\theta_i^r - \theta_g^r||^2. \qquad (2)$$

Consensus-Based Methods. With CBM, a global federated ensemble of weak predictors is composed by aggregating the outputs from the different local models. During *training*, each client fully optimizes the segmentation model $g(z, \theta_i)$ on its local dataset D_i, by independently minimizing the local objective function $\mathcal{L}_i$. Trained local models are subsequently centralized and, for a given test image z' at *inference* time, the segmentation masks from all the local models are computed and aggregated by applying an ensembling strategy:

$$h_{z'} = \texttt{ensembling}(\{h_i(z')\}|_{i=1}^{M}) \text{ s.t. } h_i(z') = g(z', \theta_i). \qquad (3)$$

Among the different approaches to ensembling proposed in the literature [29], in this work we consider:

- **Majority Voting** [30] (MV) is a simple merging method that assigns to each voxel the label predicted by the majority of the local models.
- **Staple** [31] optimizes a consensus based on Expectation-Maximization (E-M) defined by the following iterative process:
    - the E-step computes a probabilistic estimate of the true segmentation, that is a weighted average of each local prediction;
    - the M-step assigns a performance level to each individual segmentation, which will be used as weights for the next E-step.
- **Uncertainty-Based Ensembling** (UBE) is based on weighted averaging of local decisions, in which the weights represent the uncertainty of each local model on the prediction task. As uncertainty can be quantified in different ways, in this work we adopt dropout [32] to compute a measure of the global uncertainty of each local model for the segmentation of a testing image z. In particular, here the uncertainty is computed as the total voxel-wise variance at inference time, defined as: $p_i = \sum_{x \in \Omega} \text{Var}\left(g(z, \theta_i)\right)[x]$, where Ω is the set of voxels in z, $\text{Var}(\cdot)[x]$ is the sampling variance estimated from S stochastic forward passes of the model, computed at voxel x.

2.3 Experiments Details

The benchmark is based on four experiments, quantifying a different aspect for comparison between different strategies. The experiments are characterized by the same baseline model used for segmentation, which is presented below.

Segmentation Accuracy was quantified through 5-fold cross-validation across all nodes, by testing all training strategies for each unique combination of training/testing split. The final result was obtained by averaging across all splits.

Additionally, N05 and N06 from Table 1 were not used for training, and exclusively reserved for use as independent test set. The performance of the trained model was evaluated using the Dice Score (DSC) and a Normalised Surface Distance (NSD), following the guidelines from the Decathlon Segmentation Challenge [33].

We benchmarked the following strategies. *Local*: model trained only on the data from a single node, without aggregation; *Centralized*: model trained on the aggregated data from all the centers; *Federated*: federated training using both FEDAVG and FEDPROX as FL strategies; *Consensus*: ensembling of prediction using the CBMs strategies presented above.

Cost-Effectiveness was investigated in terms of training and inference time and communication bandwidth [34–36]. For estimating the bandwidth we consider the amount of data exchanged through the network during the training phase; this value depends on the model size, that in our setting is constant among all the experiments, and the number of exchanges, which is strategy-dependent.

Model Robustness was assessed to compare FL and CBM with respect to varying data heterogeneity across clients. To this end, we evaluated the change in performance of the methods when removing N03 from the experiment. We expect a large variation in performance depending on the presence of N03, being this client the only one with images acquired with an endorectal coil, thus introducing large heterogeneity in the collaborative segmentation task.

Clients Utility refers to the evaluation of how beneficial it is for an individual client to participate in a collaborative method, and which specific method would bring the most value to that client. To determine this, we consider the accuracy of different models on various test sets.

Let's consider a client labeled as l. We have two models: a local model denoted as $\mathcal{M}_l$, and a collaborative model denoted as $\mathcal{M}_c$. We evaluate the performance of these models on two different test sets: $\mathcal{T}_l$, which is the local test set specific to client l, and $\mathcal{T}_e$, which is the union of all test sets excluding $\mathcal{T}_l$.

To compare the utility of the two models, we examine two metrics:

- variation in accuracy on the local test set: This is computed as the difference between the accuracy of the collaborative model on the local test set ($\text{DSC}_{\mathcal{M}_c, \mathcal{T}_l}$) and the accuracy of the local model on the same test set ($\text{DSC}_{\mathcal{M}_l, \mathcal{T}_l}$).
- variation in accuracy on the external test sets: This is calculated as the difference between the accuracy of the collaborative model on the combined external test sets ($\text{DSC}_{\mathcal{M}_c, \mathcal{T}_e}$) and the accuracy of the local model on the same combined external test sets ($\text{DSC}_{\mathcal{M}_l, \mathcal{T}_e}$).

By analyzing these two metrics, we can quantify the impact of using either the local or collaborative methods on both internal and external datasets. Ideally, a positive value for both metrics indicates that collaboration is beneficial for the client in all scenarios. However, it is more common to observe that collaboration improves model generalization but may affect local performance. Therefore, striking a balance between these two values is crucial.

In summary, the client's utility aims to determine the most advantageous approach for a client by comparing the accuracy variations of local and collaborative models on local and external test sets, respectively.

Privacy Mechanisms such as differential privacy (DP) [37] have been proposed in the literature to quantify the privacy that a protocol provides and to train a model in a privacy-preserving manner. In the context of DP, the term "budget" refers to the amount of privacy protection available for the entire federated learning process, and represents the cumulative privacy loss allowed during

| FedAVG | UBE | MAV | Centralized |

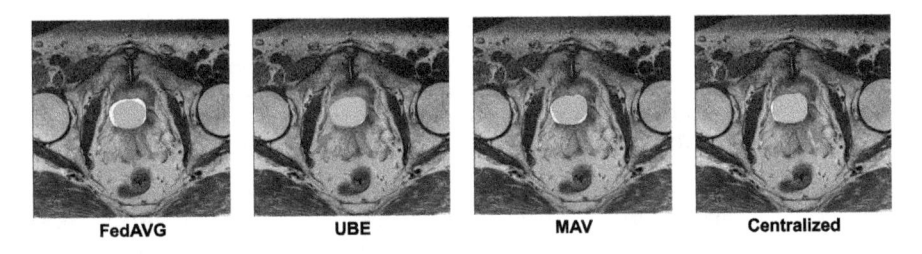

Fig. 1. A representation of the segmentation task on a sample image using different strategies. In white, the ground truth; in red, the segmentation provided by each training approach. (Color figure online)

the training phase. This budget is typically defined as a function of ϵ, where ϵ is used to control the strength of privacy guarantees for each round of federated learning updates. Here we compared the accuracy we can obtain by spending a fixed privacy budget ϵ while protecting different collaborative methods.

A common **baseline model** was defined to obtain comparable results across strategies. We employed a 3D UNet architecture with residual connections [5]. The training was based on the optimization of the DICE Loss, by using the ADAMW optimizer for all experiments [38]. The UNet implementation is available in the MONAI library[1]. We fixed model hyper-parameters and maintained consistency in the amount of training, loss type, and optimizer used across all configurations. Hyperparameter search was performed by varying training parameters for all experiments (see Appendix Table 5) and selecting those performing averagely better on the local models, obtaining a learning rate of 0.001, a batch size of $B = 8$, and a dropout value of 0.3. All the experiments were executed using Fed-BioMed [39], an open-source platform that simulates the FL infrastructure. The code for running the experiments is available on the GitHub page of the author.

The number of epochs and rounds were defined using a standard strategy [40], which ensured comparable numbers of training steps among local and federated training for each node. Specifically, the number of rounds R for FL methods was defined as follows: $R = E \cdot N_T/M/B/s$, where E is the number of epochs required to train the model locally, $s = 20$ is the fixed number of local SGD steps, and N_T is the total number of samples in the training set.

3 Results

Segmentation Accuracy. Table 2 presents the average DSC among the 5-Fold evaluations obtained with the different collaborative learning strategies, while an illustrative example of the results on a sample image is available in Fig. 1. The best results are indicated in **bold**. Similar results are obtained with the

---

[1] https://monai.io/index.html.

Table 2. Comparison of the 5-fold DSC obtained in the segmentation task by different training strategies.

	Local N01 N02 N03 N04	Centralized	Federated FEDAVG FEDPROX	Consensus UBE STAPLE MV
N01-test	0.86 0.64 0.49 0.44	0.92	0.85 0.70	**0.89** 0.83 0.84
N02-test	0.80 0.69 0.66 0.73	0.90	0.82 0.75	0.85 **0.87** **0.87**
N03-test	0.64 0.72 0.75 0.44	0.83	0.70 0.75	0.73 0.75 **0.76**
N04-test	0.79 0.66 0.62 0.88	0.91	**0.88** 0.84	0.87 0.86 0.86
N05	0.57 0.68 0.71 0.73	0.77	0.71 0.67	**0.72** 0.68 0.68
N06	0.75 0.63 0.61 0.75	0.83	**0.82** 0.80	0.80 **0.82** **0.82**
Average	0.73 0.67 0.64 0.66	0.86	0.80 0.75	**0.81** 0.80 0.80

Table 3. Comparison of costs of different training strategies in terms of training and inference time and training bandwidth.

	Local N01 N02 N03 N04	Centralized	Federated FEDAVG FEDPROX	Consensus UBE STAPLE MV
Train. time (min)	22 35 38 36	421	116 116	**38** **38** **38**
Inf. time (sec)	0.4 0.4 0.4 0.4	0.4	**0.3** **0.3**	16.3 3.7 **0.9**
Train. Bandwidth (MB)	30 30 30 30	0	9600 9600	**120** **120** **120**

NSD metric and can be found in Appendix Table 1 and Table 2. Details about standard deviation among the K runs can be found in Appendix Table 3.

Overall, CBM obtain better or at least comparable results than FL: the last row in Table 2 shows that UBE is on average the best-performing method, but all the CBM provide very similar results. In general, distributed methods highly outperform local methods, which fail to generalize.

Cost-Effectiveness. We consider the total training time for FL and the longest time for local training across clients for CBM. Federated training is roughly three times longer than CBM training ($\sim$ 2 hours vs $\sim$ 30 minutes). Among the CBM methods, UME is associated with the largest testing time, having to perform many inferences to estimate the uncertainty map. MAV is the most efficient and takes two times longer than the average FL (though still in the order of seconds). However, we note that testing time is a magnitude lower than training time, making its impact irrelevant in a real case application. The amount of exchanged data for FL is equal to $2 \cdot M \cdot m_s \cdot R$, where R is the number of rounds and m_s is the model size. For CBM, is only $M \cdot m_s$, resulting in a difference of $C \cdot m_s \cdot (2 \cdot R - 1)$. Considering the UNet used in the experiment, $m_s = 30MB$, the difference between FL and CBM is roughly of 9.25 GBytes.

Model Robustness. The performance of local models reported in Table 2 (panel "Local") allows to appreciate the heterogeneity across clients. As expected, N03 emerges as the client with the highest heterogeneity from this

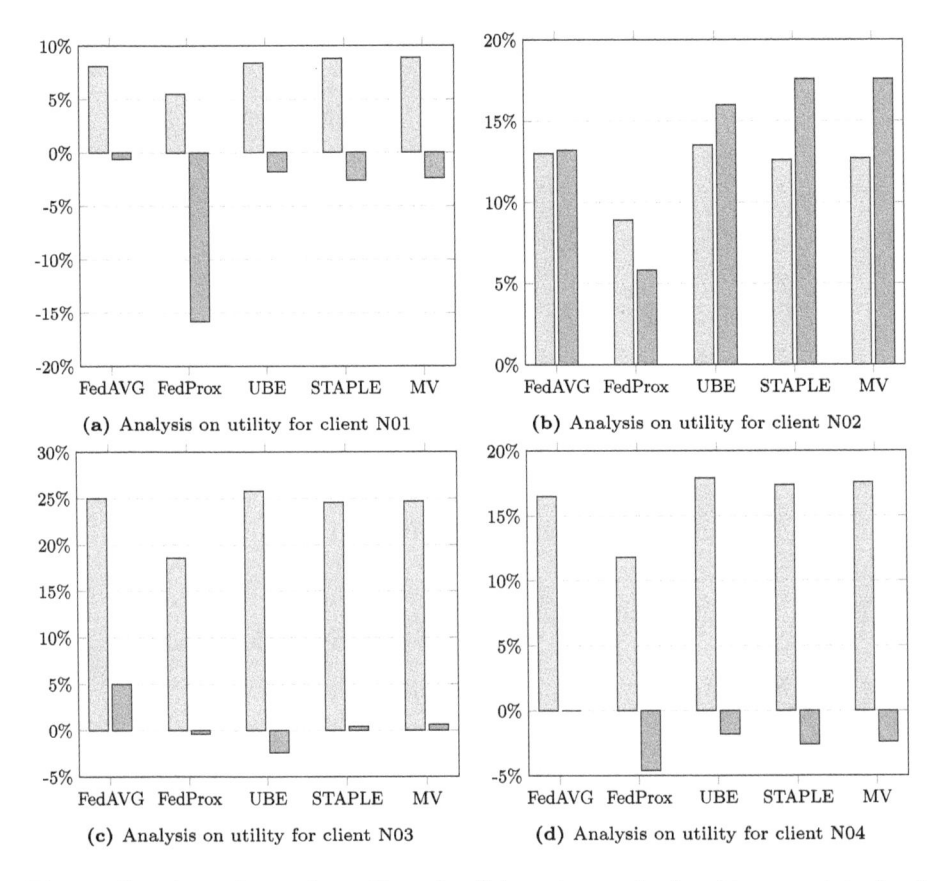

Fig. 2. The chart shows the utility of collaborative methods with respect to local models when used on the local test sets (red bar) or external test sets (blue bar) for each client indicated in the sub-captions. Each histogram corresponds to a different client. For all clients, collaborative methods improved generalization by a difference of up to 25%, while decreasing local performance by at most 15% and in some cases even improving it. A significant degree of heterogeneity can be observed in the impact on generalization and local performance among different test sets as well as different methods. (Color figure online)

analysis, given the drop in testing performance of the models locally trained on the other clients. As shown in Appendix Table 4, CBM leads to an average absolute DSC variation of 1.7%, 2.4%, and 2.7%, for respectively UBE, MV, and Staple, as compared to the 3.1% and 5.7% DSC change respectively associated with FEDAVG and FEDPROX. A graphical representation of this property is available in Appendix Figure 1. This result denotes the improved robustness of CBM to clients' heterogeneity. The overall results obtained after removing N03 are compatible with those shown in Table 2, and confirm the positive performances of CBM as compared to FL.

Clients Utility. Fig. 2 presents a comparison of the utility of different collaborative methods for the four clients in the experiment.

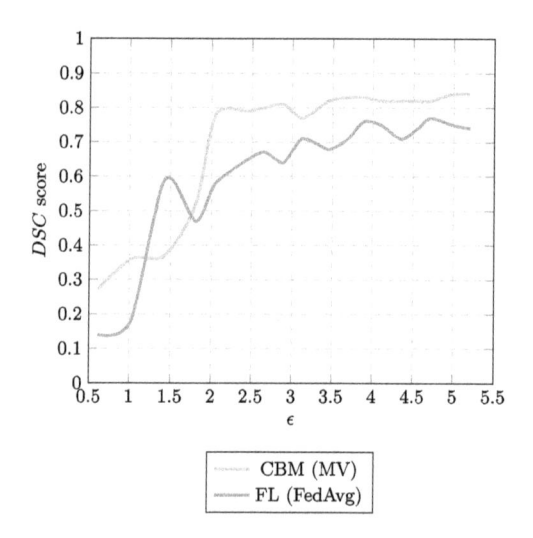

Fig. 3. The chart compares the accuracy reached by different methods when spending a privacy budget ϵ for differential privacy. The two compared methods are majority voting (MV) for CBM and federated averaging (FedAvg) for FL. CBM obtain on average better performances when ϵ is fixed, and it already reaches the plateau with $\epsilon \approx 3$.

For all clients and all methods, collaborative methods lead to improvements in model generalization when evaluated on external test sets. This implies that collaborating with other clients helps to enhance the overall performance of the models on unseen data. Additionally, it is worth noting that even for small clients like N02, collaborative methods also result in improved local performance. This suggests that even clients with limited local data can benefit from participating in the collaboration. Surprisingly, even the largest client, N04, still experiences advantages by joining the collaboration. This indicates that size alone does not diminish the benefits of collaborative methods and that even clients with substantial local datasets can gain value from collaboration. Overall, in this particular experiment, the performance of CBM is comparable to that of FL. However, UBE method consistently demonstrates the most substantial improvements across various metrics, making it the preferred choice among the collaborative methods evaluated.

Privacy Mechanisms. The privacy analysis is performed in the framework of Rényi Differential Privacy (RDP) [41], a relaxation of the classical definition [42] allowing a convenient way to keep track of the cumulative privacy loss. This allows us to quantify the privacy budget ϵ corresponding to SGD optimization with parameters defined as for the baseline model of Sect. 2.3.

Following [43], the DP Gaussian mechanism was defined with noise $\sigma = 4$. One can show that the privacy budget for obtaining the results presented in Table 2 is $\epsilon_{CBM} = 5.2$ in the CBM scenario, and $\epsilon_{FL} = 7.9$ in the federated one, denoting the lower privacy cost of CBM. CBM is also characterized by a lower privacy cost in relation to our chosen performance metric: DSC. We compared how DSC on unseen data evolved for the ensembling method MV and the FedAVG aggregation strategy when the privacy budget ϵ varied between 0.5 and 5.5. Figure 3 shows that the CMB method achieved a higher DSC than FL with a lower privacy budget: CBM reached a plateau at roughly $\epsilon = 3$ while FL reached a plateau only after $\epsilon > 4$, and at a lower DSC value.

4 Conclusions

In this paper, we proposed a realistic benchmark for collaborative learning methods for prostate segmentation. To this end, we used a collection of large public and private prostate MRI datasets to simulate a realistic distributed scenario across hospitals and we defined experiments and metrics to compare local training with different collaborative learning methods, namely FL and CBM, in terms of performances, cost-effectiveness, robustness and privacy of the models. For the considered scenario of cross-silo federated prostate segmentation, our results show that CBM represent a reliable alternative to FL in terms of performances, while being highly competitive in terms of robustness, and superior in cost-effectiveness when considering the practical implementation and required resources. Indeed, CBM avoid synchronization of training across hospitals, while the setup of an FL infrastructure is costly and time-consuming, and often prohibitive for typical hospital applications.

By simply sharing locally trained models and applying CBM to local predictions, we can rely on established theory from the state-of-the-art of multi-atlas segmentation to obtain competitive results at much less cost, as CBM avoid synchronization of training across hospitals.

Our preliminary results on privacy-preserving methods based on differential privacy show that CBM can guarantee a stronger level of privacy protection.

Moreover, secure aggregation techniques could be used at inference time for CBM in order to avoid sharing the whole model, adding another privacy layer to the framework. Other FL schemes could be included in our benchmark, such as SCAFFOLD [44] or FedOpt [45], to better account for heterogeneity. Nevertheless, given previous benchmark results on similar medical imaging tasks [40], we do not expect a substantial change in the overall message of this study, especially concerning the comparison of cost-effectiveness between FL and CBM paradigms. Different consensus strategies could be implemented in the future, for example, to account for voxel-wise uncertainty across local models. The benchmark here proposed focuses on a cross-silo setup, typical of FL applications in hospitals proposed so far. Future investigations could extend our study to include a larger number of clients, thus allowing to better exploit the robustness guarantees associated with consensus strategies.

References

1. Sung, W.W.Y., et al.: A cost-effectiveness analysis of systemic therapy for metastatic hormone-sensitive prostate cancer. Front. Oncol. **11**, 627083 (2021)
2. Khan, Z., et al.: Recent automatic segmentation algorithms of MRI prostate regions: a review. IEEE Access **9**, 97878–97905 (2021)
3. Korsager, A.S., et al.: The use of atlas registration and graph cuts for prostate segmentation in magnetic resonance images. Med. Phys. **42**(4), 1614–1624 (2015)
4. Castellino, R.A.: Computer aided detection (CAD): an overview. Cancer Imag. **5**(1), 17 (2005)
5. Ronneberger, O., Fischer, P., Brox, T.: U-Net: convolutional networks for biomedical image segmentation. In: Medical Image Computing and Computer-Assisted Intervention–MICCAI (2015)
6. McMahan, B., et al.: Communication-efficient learning of deep networks from decentralized data. In: Artificial Intelligence and Statistics (2017)
7. Rieke, N., et al.: The future of digital health with federated learning. NPJ Digital Med. **3**(1), 1–7 (2020)
8. Zhang, C., et al.: A survey on federated learning. Knowl. Based Syst. **216**, 106775 (2021)
9. Li, T., et al.: Federated learning: challenges, methods, and future directions. IEEE Sig. Process. Mag. **37**(3), 50–60 (2020)
10. Kairouz, P., et al.: Advances and open problems in federated learning. Found. Trends Mach. Learn. **14**(1–2), 1–210 (2021)
11. Li, W., et al.: Privacy-preserving federated brain tumour segmentation. In: Machine Learning in Medical Imaging: 10th International Workshop, MLMI 2019, Held in Conjunction with MICCAI 2019, Shenzhen, China, October 13, 2019 (2019)
12. Chhikara, P., et al.: Federated learning meets human emotions: a decentralized framework for human-computer interaction for IoT applications. IEEE Internet Things J. **8**(8), 6949–6962 (2020)
13. Huang, L., et al.: Patient clustering improves efficiency of federated machine learning to predict mortality and hospital stay time using distributed electronic medical records. J. Biomed. Inform. **99**, 103291 (2019)
14. Lars Kai Hansen and Peter Salamon: Neural network ensembles. IEEE Trans. Pattern Anal. Mach. Intell. **12**(10), 993–1001 (1990)
15. Dang, T., et al.: Weighted ensemble of deep learning models based on comprehensive learning particle swarm optimization for medical image segmentation. In: 2021 IEEE Congress on Evolutionary Computation (CEC) (2021)
16. Dang, T., et al.: Ensemble of deep learning models with surrogate-based optimization for medical image segmentation. In: 2022 IEEE Congress on Evolutionary Computation (CEC) (2022)
17. Xu, A., et al.: Closing the generalization gap of cross-silo federated medical image segmentation. In: Proceedings of the IEEE/CVF Conference on Computer Vision and Pattern Recognition (2022)
18. Shi, N., et al.: Fed-ensemble: improving generalization through model ensembling in federated learning. arXiv preprint arXiv:2107.10663 (2021)
19. Hamer, J., Mohri, M., Suresh, A.T.: Fedboost: a communication-efficient algorithm for federated learning. In: International Conference on Machine Learning (2020)
20. Guha, N., Talwalkar, A., Smith, V.: One-shot federated learning. In: Workshop on Machine Learning on the Phone and other Consumer Devices (NeurIPs) (2018)

21. Lin, T., et al.: Ensemble distillation for robust model fusion in federated learning. Adv. Neural. Inf. Process. Syst. **33**, 2351–2363 (2020)
22. Casado, F.E., et al.: Ensemble and continual federated learning for classification tasks. Mach. Learn. **112**(9), 1–41 (2023)
23. Antonelli, M., et al.: The medical segmentation decathlon. Nat. Commun. **13**(1), 4128 (2022). http://medicaldecathlon.com/
24. Litjens, G., et al.: Evaluation of prostate segmentation algorithms for MRI: the promise12 challenge. Med. Image Anal. **18**(2) (2014). https://promise12.grand-challenge.org/
25. Armato III, S.G., et al.: Prostatex challenges for computerized classification of prostate lesions from multiparametric magnetic resonance images. J. Med. Imag. **5**(4), 044501 (2018). https://prostatex.grand-challenge.org/
26. Cuocolo, R., et al.: Quality control and whole-gland, zonal and lesion annotations for the prostatex challenge public dataset. Eur. J. Radiol. **138**, 109647 (2021)
27. Warfield, S.K., Zou, K.H., Wells, W.M.: Simultaneous truth and performance level estimation (STAPLE): an algorithm for the validation of image segmentation. IEEE Trans. Med. Imag. **23**(7) (2004)
28. Li, T., et al.: Federated optimization in heterogeneous networks. Proc. Mach. Learn. Syst. **2**, 429–450 (2020)
29. Dong, X., et al.: A survey on ensemble learning. Front. Comp. Sci. **14**, 241–258 (2020)
30. Kittler, J., et al.: On combining classifiers. IEEE Trans. Pattern Anal. Mach. Intell. **20**(3), 226–239 (1998)
31. Warfield, S.K., Zou, K.H., Wells, W.M.: Simultaneous truth and performance level estimation (STAPLE): an algorithm for the validation of image segmentation. IEEE Trans. Med. Imag. **23**(7), 903–921 (2004)
32. Gal, Y., Ghahramani, Z.: Dropout as a Bayesian approximation: Representing model uncertainty in deep learning. In: International Conference on Machine Learning, pp. 1050–1059 (2016)
33. Antonelli, M., et al.: The medical segmentation decathlon. Nat. Commun. **13**(1), 4128 (2022)
34. Luo, B., et al.: Cost-effective federated learning design. In: IEEE INFOCOM 2021-IEEE Conference on Computer Communications (2021)
35. Nguyen, H.T., et al.: Fast-convergent federated learning. IEEE J. Sel. Areas Commun. **39**(1), 201–218 (2020)
36. Chen, M., et al.: Convergence time optimization for federated learning over wireless networks. IEEE Trans. Wireless Commun. **20**(4), 2457–2471 (2020)
37. Ziller, A., et al.: Medical imaging deep learning with differential privacy. Sci. Rep. **11**(1), 1–8 (2021)
38. Loshchilov, I., Hutter, F.: Decoupled weight decay regularization. In: arXiv preprint arXiv:1711.05101 (2017)
39. Silva, S., et al.: Fed-BioMed: a general open-source frontend framework for federated learning in healthcare. In: Domain Adaptation and Representation Transfer, and Distributed and Collaborative Learning: Second MICCAI Workshop, DART 2020, and First MICCAI Workshop, DCL 2020, Held in Conjunction with MICCAI 2020, Lima, Peru, October 4–8, 2020, Proceedings 2 (2020)
40. Ogier du Terrail, J., et al.: Flamby: datasets and benchmarks for cross-silo federated learning in realistic healthcare settings. arXiv preprint arXiv:2210.04620 (2022)
41. Mironov, I.: Rényi differential privacy. In: 2017 IEEE 30th Computer Security Foundations Symposium (CSF) (2017)

42. Dwork, C., et al.: Calibrating noise to sensitivity in private data analysis. In: Third Theory of Cryptography Conference (2006)
43. Abadi, M., et al.: Deep learning with differential privacy. In: Proceedings of the 2016 ACM SIGSAC Conference on Computer and Communications Security, pp. 308–318 (2016)
44. Karimireddy, S.P., et al.: Scaffold: stochastic controlled averaging for federated learning. In: International Conference on Machine Learning (2020)
45. Asad, M., Moustafa, A., Ito, T.: Fedopt: towards communication efficiency and privacy preservation in federated learning. Appl. Sci. **10**(8), 2864 (2020)

Predicting Sepsis Onset with Deep Federated Learning

Lena Mondrejevski, Daniel Azzopardi, and Ioanna Miliou(✉)

Department of Computer and Systems Sciences, Stockholm University, Stockholm, Sweden
{lena.mondrejevski,daaz9860,ioanna.miliou}@dsv.su.se

Abstract. Life-threatening conditions like sepsis are a leading cause of hospital mortality. The early identification of sepsis onset allows for timely intervention aiming to save patient lives. Although showing great promise for early sepsis onset prediction, Centralized Machine Learning applications are hindered by privacy concerns. Federated Learning has the potential to counteract the mentioned limitation as it trains a global model utilizing distributed data across several hospitals without sharing the data. This research explores the potential of Federated Learning to provide a more privacy-preserving and generalizable solution for predicting sepsis onset using a Deep Federated Learning setup. Patients from the MIMIC-III dataset are classified as either septic or non-septic using relevant patient features, and sepsis onset is identified at the first hour of a detected 5-hour SIRS interval for patients diagnosed with sepsis. We compare the predictive performance of different combinations of classifiers (LSTM and GRU), *patient history window* lengths, *prediction window* lengths, and Federated Learning clients, using the metrics AUROC, AUPRC, and F1-Score. Our results show that the Centralized Machine Learning and Federated Learning setups are on par in terms of predictive performance. In addition, on average, the best-performing Federated Learning model is GRU, with a five-hour *patient history window* and a three-hour *prediction window*. Overall, the study demonstrates that the proposed Federated Learning setup can predict sepsis onset comparably to state-of-the-art centralized deep learning algorithms for varying numbers of clients, enabling healthcare institutions to collaborate on mutually beneficial tasks without sharing isolated sensitive patient information.

Keywords: Sepsis Onset Prediction · Federated Learning · Recurrent Neural Network · Classification · Supervised Learning · MIMIC-III

1 Introduction

Despite the vast availability of technology at our disposal, severe life-threatening conditions like sepsis are still among the leading causes of patient mortality in hospitals worldwide, with 30 million people contracting sepsis every year [5,21].

As an autoimmune disease, sepsis arises "when the body's response to an infection damages its own tissues"[1], causing abnormal organ function. Early sepsis onset prediction, where sepsis onset is defined as the beginning of the patient's sepsis episode, gives physicians a crucial head start to plan and preemptively administer the necessary treatment. However, the complex nature of this disease makes it hard for physicians to identify sepsis onset timely.

Current literature has proposed various approaches for predicting sepsis onset with a traditional Machine Learning (ML) approach [2,18], where a central model is built in a centralized environment using joined data. However, most ML applications for healthcare are still hindered by privacy concerns in those Centralized Machine Learning (CML) approaches as it requires the aggregation of several datasets. Alternatively, ML models can be trained solely based on smaller local datasets. Apart from the possible accuracy and generalizability limitations of ML models trained on those smaller demographic-specific datasets, these approaches also result in limited implementations of industry-applied solutions [16].

Federated Learning (FL) [9] has become increasingly popular in healthcare applications [10,22] for its ability to train a global model from data distributed across several clients without sharing the data, thus counteracting the mentioned limitations of training models locally or in a centralized environment. This enables data-siloed healthcare institutions to collaborate and utilize all available data while maintaining patient anonymity and complying with data protection regulations, with the added benefit of seamless integration into existing healthcare infrastructure [13,22].

Related Work. The approach to classify in-hospital sepsis proposed by Calvert et al. [2] is still regarded as a gold standard by several researchers [17,19,24], although outdated. It uses nine patient parameters from the MIMIC-II dataset [18], together with traditional ML techniques, for predicting sepsis. Meanwhile, several state-of-the-art approaches for predicting sepsis onset using Deep Learning (DL) techniques have emerged in the past few years. DL is a branch of ML consisting of multi-layer neural networks eliminating some of the data pre-processing and feature extraction typically associated with traditional ML approaches by attempting to simulate human behavior, making the process faster and less complex. A class of DL neural networks called Recurrent Neural Networks (RNNs) can be used to recognize patterns and predict possible future scenarios from sequential data. Several approaches involve implementations of RNNs, such as Long Short-Term Memory (LSTM) [4,20,24] and Gated Recurrent Unit (GRU) [19] in a CML setup for sepsis onset prediction. Overall, a review by [6] identified that neural networks outperformed ensembles and decision trees across 130 traditional ML models for sepsis onset prediction. Similar to the approach used by Calvert et al. [2], the RNN-based model proposed by Scherpf et al. [19] determines sepsis onset using respective International

---

[1] https://www.mayoclinic.org/diseases-conditions/sepsis/symptoms-causes/syc-20351214.

Classification of Diseases 9 (ICD-9)[2] codes and a five-hour Systemic Inflammatory Response Syndrome (SIRS) interval.

A review by Xu et al. [22] showed an increasing number of FL approaches for healthcare applications that have been published in recent years. Despite the limited availability of sizeable datasets for FL implementations, applications vary from phenotyping and brain imaging data analysis to arrhythmia detection and mortality prediction [12,14,15]. For example, the research by Mondrejevski et al. [12] proposed an FL setup for Intensive Care Unit (ICU) mortality prediction using the MIMIC-III dataset. They showed that as the number of clients increased (resulting in fewer data available for each client), performance was comparable to CML, while it decreased for the local models that were based on each client's individual data.

To the best of our knowledge, there are currently no implementations describing the prediction of sepsis onset using Deep Federated Learning. The closest application to an FL application employed on sepsis data was proposed by Xue et al. [23]. However, it is important to note that the federated clinical decision system proposed by the authors employed a reinforcement learning approach, which is not the focus of this study.

Contributions. This research expands upon existing research to provide a Deep FL solution to sepsis onset prediction and serve as a benchmark for future studies. The primary contributions of this study are:

(i) A Deep Federated Learning solution for the prediction of sepsis onset;
(ii) The comparison of different temporal DL model architectures (GRU and LSTM) in terms of predictive performance;
(iii) An evaluation of varying *patient history windows* (5h, 10h, and 24h), *prediction windows* (3h, 6h, and 12h), and participating FL clients (2, 4, and 8) based on the predictive performance.

2 Problem Formulation

This paper formulates sepsis onset prediction as a binary classification problem, where the system assigns a *sepsis* label for patients that will become septic in h hours, or a *non-sepsis* label if the patient is not going to become septic in h hours. We denote with p the number of ICU patients and M the collection of multivariate time series, such that $|M| = p$. For each ith ICU patient in M, where $M_i \in M$, M_i describes a set of patient vital signs and lab tests in the form of time series. The length of the jth time series M_{ij} varies depending on the sampling rate used to collect each patient parameter.

For CML, a function $f_{CML}(\cdot)$ is learned using M, such that given one ICU patient, the system predicts whether sepsis onset will occur in h hours. The FL function $f_{FL}(\cdot)$ is built using local models $f_{FL}^c(\cdot)$, where c is a client in the FL system, with $c \in \{1, 2, \cdots, C\}$, and C is the number of clients. Here,

---
[2] https://www.cdc.gov/nchs/icd/icd9.htm.

each client c trains a set of weights w^c using local data $\mathcal{M}^c \in \mathcal{M}$, such that $\mathcal{M}^a \cap \mathcal{M}^b = \emptyset, \forall (a,b) \in [1,C] \times [1,C]$. The global classifier is then built as a function of the local weights: $f_{FL}(w^1, \cdots, w^C)$.

3 Methods

A Deep Federated Learning approach for predicting sepsis onset is proposed, with the goal of identifying, in a distributed setup, whether patients will develop sepsis during their ICU stay or not.

3.1 Definition of Sepsis Onset

In this study, we focus on the prediction of sepsis onset during patients' stay in the ICU. As the sepsis diagnosis does not suffice to determine this point in time, we need to define the time of the onset itself. We regard the gold standard proposed by Calvert et al. [2] for defining the sepsis onset as the beginning of the patient's first 5-hour SIRS interval, which is the "zero-hour" of the patient's sepsis episode, thus indicating the *sepsis onset*. The 5-hour SIRS interval is defined as a range in the temporal data where at least two of the criteria described below are present for at least 5 consecutive hours in a patient's hospital stay. The following SIRS criteria and corresponding thresholds are used:

- **Body Temperature** *(under 36°C or over 38°C)*
- **Heart Rate** *(more than 90 beats per minute)*
- **Respiratory Rate** *(greater than 20 breaths per minute)* or **Partial Pressure of** CO_2 *(less than 32 mmHg)*
- **Leukocyte (White Blood Cell) count** *(less than 4000/μL or more than 12,000/μL)*

3.2 Definition of Patient History Window and Prediction Window

We define two windows that complement the prediction setup (see Fig. 1):

- The *patient history window* W represents the timespan between the first and last data points of the multivariate time series used for predicting sepsis onset. According to the *patient history window* W, we extract the patient data $\mathcal{M}$ (see Sect. 2). $\mathcal{M}$ is used to predict whether a sepsis onset will occur.
- The *prediction window* H represents the timespan between the latest value in the *patient history window* and the sepsis onset itself, with length of h hours (see Sect. 2).

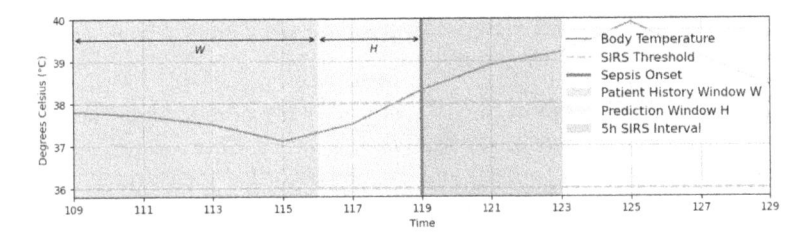

Fig. 1. Sample SIRS feature describing the relationship between the *patient history window* W (annotated with blue color), the *prediction window* H (annotated with yellow color), the 5-hour SIRS Interval (annotated with red color), and the time of sepsis onset (annotated with a red vertical line) (adapted from [19]). (Color figure online)

3.3 FL Modelling

We implement two different Recurrent Neural Network architectures, namely LSTM and GRU, for predicting sepsis onset. These specific architectures allow for better exploitation of the temporal patterns hidden in the patient data.

For each classifier, the input layer is followed by two hidden layers, each with 40 neurons and a recurrent dropout of 0.2, and finally, a dense, sigmoid-activated output layer (based on Scherpf et al. [19]). Adam is used as an optimization algorithm, as it can handle sparse gradients on noisy data [8]. Furthermore, since the prediction of sepsis onset is treated as a binary classification problem, binary cross-entropy is used as the loss function to optimize the RNNs.

Our FL model training is based on the Federated Averaging (FedAvg) algorithm [11], which was shown to be a robust FL algorithm for healthcare implementations, demonstrating reasonable performance, and is commonly employed in setups handling deep neural network architectures and non-IID (Independent and Identically Distributed) data [3].

In our FL approach, we initialize the global model with w_0 and communicate it to the clients, followed by a number of FL rounds. In each FL round, each of the C clients trains their local model $f_{FL}^c(\cdot)$ using their individual patient dataset M^c and the received global model weights. The model parameters of the locally trained models are then sent back to the global server, where the received weights are averaged, building the updated global model. Finally, the global server shares the global model with the federated clients again, thus starting a new FL round. This process is repeated until convergence, using loss as the convergence criteria.

4 Empirical Evaluation

4.1 Data Description

In this study, we use the MIMIC-III dataset (v1.4) [7], which contains anonymized data of patients admitted to the Beth Israel Deaconess Medical Center in Boston, Massachusetts, within the period 2001 to 2012. The database consists of diverse data points of 46520 ICU patients across 58976 admissions.

Patient Selection. Several criteria are used to determine which patients and admissions are suitable for the study:

1. Firstly, similar to Scherpf et al. [19], only patients admitted to the ICU aged 18 and older are included in the study.
2. Secondly, patients need to have at least one recorded measurement available for *admission age, systolic blood pressure, diastolic blood pressure, heart rate, body temperature, respiratory rate, partial pressure of* CO_2, *blood oxygen saturation, white blood cell count* and *blood pH*, which are necessary for the SIRS criteria as well as for the classifier (see Table 1).
3. Thirdly, we exclude admissions with a positive sepsis diagnosis but with an undetected beginning of sepsis. The criteria necessary to satisfy the presence of varying grades of septic infection are defined as a diagnosis of sepsis, severe sepsis, or septic shock having the ICD-9 codes 995.91, 995.92, and 785.52, respectively, during a patient's ICU stay. In addition, the SIRS criteria are necessary to define sepsis onset (see Sect. 3.1).
4. Finally, admissions with a positive sepsis diagnosis must have the necessary length to fit the *patient history window*, the *prediction window*, and the 5-hour SIRS interval, at the least.

Table 1. Patient features used for predicting sepsis onset.

Type	Patient Features
Demographic information	Admission Age *(years)*
Vital signs	Systolic Blood Pressure *(mmHg)*, Diastolic Blood Pressure *(mmHg)*, Heart Rate *(beats per minute)*, Body Temperature (°C), Respiratory Rate *(breaths per minute)*, Blood Oxygen Saturation *(%)*
Laboratory test results	White Blood Cell count *(cells per µL)*, Blood Potential Hydrogen *(pH)*

Feature Extraction and Preprocessing. We first extract in total 9 patient features, based on Calvert et al. [2] and the SIRS parameters (see Table 1). Following, the features are re-sampled in 1h time intervals with mean as aggregation function to obtain a single value per 1h. Subsequently, we populate missing values in the temporal data of a patient's registered ICU stay using forward and then backward imputation, starting from the beginning of the ICU stay. As a result of the Patient Selection process, there are no patients with empty features.

Labeling. The patient selection process results in a set of adult patients that were admitted to the ICU and either diagnosed with sepsis as well as having a prevalent sepsis onset, or not diagnosed with sepsis (see Table 2). The latter is assigned to the *non-sepsis* class, while the former belong to the *sepsis* class.

Window Extraction. For each selected patient in the cohort, we extract M_i based on the length of the *patient history window* W. For the sepsis class, we first identify the point of interest, sepsis onset. In accordance with the time of sepsis onset, we specify different *prediction windows* H (with lengths 3h, 6h, and 12h) and we extract M for different *patient history windows* W (with lengths 5h, 10h, and 24h) for experimentation.

Patient history windows W for the *non-sepsis* class are picked randomly from the whole ICU admission, once per admission, having the same length as W of the *sepsis* class.

The window extraction process results in an imbalanced class distribution between *sepsis* and *non-sepsis* classes for all combinations of *patient history window* and *prediction window*, as seen in Table 2.

Table 2. Patient distribution from inclusion criteria for varying *patient history window* and *prediction window* lengths for the non-sepsis class (*0*) and for the sepsis class (*1*).

Prediction	Data					
	5h		10h		24h	
	0	1	0	1	0	1
3h	28764	4043	28841	3966	29075	3732
6h	28813	3994	28894	3913	29123	3684
12h	28907	3990	28995	3812	29240	3567

4.2 Evaluation Strategy

Similar to the approach proposed by Scherpf et al. [19], the model instances are evaluated using 4-fold stratified cross-validation, where the resulting average is reported. Each fold consists of 25% of the dataset, where in each of the four cross-validation rounds, one of the folds serves as the test dataset, and the remaining three folds are used for training and validation. In CML, the three folds are then split into 75% training and 25% validation dataset, whereas in FL, the three folds are first split equally depending on the number of FL clients to simulate an FL environment, and then each clients data is again split into 75% training and 25% validation dataset. Subsequently, data for the CML and FL approach are standardized using the mean and standard deviation of either the CML's training data or each client's training data. It is important to note that since the amount of data available is limited, all the simulated clients (healthcare institutions) are used to train the FL model. Finally, to adhere to the approach by Scherpf et al. [19], due to a more significant number of samples in the *non-sepsis class* (see Table 2), sepsis cases are oversampled to balance the training data. A fixed random seed ensures that the distributions across clients are replicated throughout the evaluation process.

The predictive performance of both LSTM and GRU architectures is evaluated using varying *patient history window* lengths (5h, 10h, 24h) and *prediction window* lengths (3h, 6h, 12h). Furthermore, several numbers of FL clients are used for evaluation (2, 4, and 8), similar to what was done by Mondrejevski et al. [12]. It is important to note that both the CML and FL model combinations are evaluated on the same data (cross-validation splits) for the varying parameters to ensure a fair comparison. Additionally, we set the mini-batch size to 256 and the learning rate to 0.01 with a maximum of 50 FL rounds, where each client's local model is trained for three epochs. The models of both CML and FL were monitored for early stopping on the validation loss with a patience value of 20.

Finally, we use multiple metrics to measure the predictive performance: AUPRC, F1-Score, and AUROC. The most commonly used metric for evaluating models predicting sepsis onset is AUROC. However, AUPRC and F1-Score are common alternatives and better suited for highly imbalanced data. The AUROC metric measures the probability of a random positive sample having a higher probability of being predicted as positive compared to a random negative sample by calculating the area under the curve, measuring the false positive against the true positive rates at different thresholds. In contrast, the AUPRC metric measures how well a model can identify true positives with minimal false positives by calculating the area under the curve, measuring precision against recall at different thresholds. Furthermore, the F1-Score is measuring the harmonic mean of precision and recall.

4.3 Setup

For the proposed analysis, the MIMIC-III was set up and queried from a local PostgreSQL database server. TensorFlow is the primary library used for building the models and the FL environment. Furthermore, Python 3.9 was used and ran on a local machine with the following specifications: Intel Core i3-5005U CPU at 2GHz with 8 GB RAM.

4.4 Results and Discussion

To tackle the task of predicting sepsis onset using a Deep FL solution, the FL setup was evaluated on 54 different combinations of *patient history window* lengths (5h, 10h, and 24h), *prediction window* lengths (3h, 6h, and 12h), numbers of federated clients (2, 4, and 8), and RNN architectures, namely LSTM and GRU. Furthermore, the performance of the FL setup was evaluated against the CML implementation proposed by Scherpf et al. [19]. The performance of each model, for the described combinations and training parameters, in terms of the AUROC, AUPRC, and F1-Score metrics can be found in Table 3.

Table 3. AUROC, AUPRC, and F1-Score for the CML model and the evaluated FL model combinations for 2, 4 and 8 clients.

AUROC

Patient History (hours)	Prediction (hours)	CML		2FL		4FL		8FL	
		GRU	LSTM	GRU	LSTM	GRU	LSTM	GRU	LSTM
5	3	0.84	0.84	0.83	0.79	0.79	0.78	0.79	0.77
	6	0.82	0.82	0.78	0.78	0.78	0.77	0.78	0.76
	12	0.80	0.80	0.77	0.76	0.77	0.72	0.75	0.72
10	3	0.84	0.83	0.79	0.77	0.78	0.77	0.76	0.75
	6	0.81	0.82	0.77	0.78	0.77	0.77	0.76	0.75
	12	0.79	0.80	0.81	0.80	0.78	0.77	0.77	0.76
24	3	0.81	0.82	0.85	0.82	0.78	0.78	0.77	0.77
	6	0.77	0.81	0.83	0.82	0.77	0.79	0.77	0.77
	12	0.77	0.81	0.76	0.78	0.76	0.75	0.76	0.74

AUPRC

Patient History (hours)	Prediction (hours)	CML		2FL		4FL		8FL	
		GRU	LSTM	GRU	LSTM	GRU	LSTM	GRU	LSTM
5	3	0.47	0.47	0.47	0.39	0.38	0.36	0.37	0.37
	6	0.44	0.45	0.37	0.36	0.36	0.35	0.37	0.32
	12	0.39	0.42	0.35	0.34	0.35	0.26	0.33	0.27
10	3	0.46	0.47	0.37	0.35	0.36	0.35	0.31	0.30
	6	0.41	0.42	0.33	0.35	0.34	0.34	0.32	0.30
	12	0.35	0.39	0.42	0.41	0.36	0.33	0.34	0.34
24	3	0.38	0.45	0.46	0.45	0.35	0.35	0.33	0.33
	6	0.33	0.41	0.45	0.44	0.33	0.37	0.32	0.35
	12	0.33	0.40	0.32	0.35	0.31	0.30	0.31	0.31

F1 Score

Patient History (hours)	Prediction (hours)	CML		2FL		4FL		8FL	
		GRU	LSTM	GRU	LSTM	GRU	LSTM	GRU	LSTM
5	3	0.43	0.46	0.44	0.40	0.38	0.36	0.38	0.35
	6	0.42	0.44	0.38	0.38	0.37	0.36	0.36	0.32
	12	0.38	0.40	0.36	0.35	0.35	0.30	0.34	0.27
10	3	0.43	0.45	0.38	0.37	0.37	0.36	0.35	0.33
	6	0.39	0.42	0.35	0.36	0.35	0.33	0.33	0.30
	12	0.37	0.39	0.42	0.38	0.35	0.35	0.34	0.32
24	3	0.37	0.41	0.46	0.42	0.35	0.35	0.35	0.35
	6	0.34	0.40	0.41	0.40	0.35	0.37	0.34	0.35
	12	0.32	0.38	0.32	0.35	0.32	0.32	0.32	0.30

GRU vs LSTM. Comparing the results of the models based on the two classifier architectures in the FL setup showed that GRU overall performed only marginally better than LSTM for the same number of FL clients. This is apparent from the AUROC, AUPRC, and F1-Score metrics presented in Table 3. Conversely, for the CML approach, LSTM outperformed GRU on average. It is also interesting to note that LSTM in CML and FL with two clients showed a slower performance degradation (when that occurred) with an increased *prediction window* length than the GRU alternative. However, this did not apply to the FL models with a higher number of clients.

Patient History Windows and Prediction Windows. To capture a more holistic view of the FL and CML models' performance, varying *patient history window* lengths and *prediction window* lengths were evaluated against each other. Although it would be expected to see that as the *patient history window* length decreases, the performance would also decrease, the results observed in Table 3 showed that for FL, there was no performance degradation when considering the overall reported AUROC, AUPRC, and F1-Score metrics. Surprisingly, even with a five-hour *patient history window*, the models show a good predictive performance indicating that five hours of data suffice to predict sepsis onset for varying *prediction windows*.

Furthermore, as expected, we observe a performance decrease for increasing *prediction window* lengths. Despite a prevalent decrease, the extent of it is minimal. Across the evaluated FL clients, on average, the best combination of *patient history window* and *prediction window* for the proposed setup are a five-hour *patient history window* and a three-hour *prediction window* (see Fig. 2). Similarly, for CML, on average, the model with the shorter five-hour *patient history window* and the three-hour *prediction window* achieved the best performance.

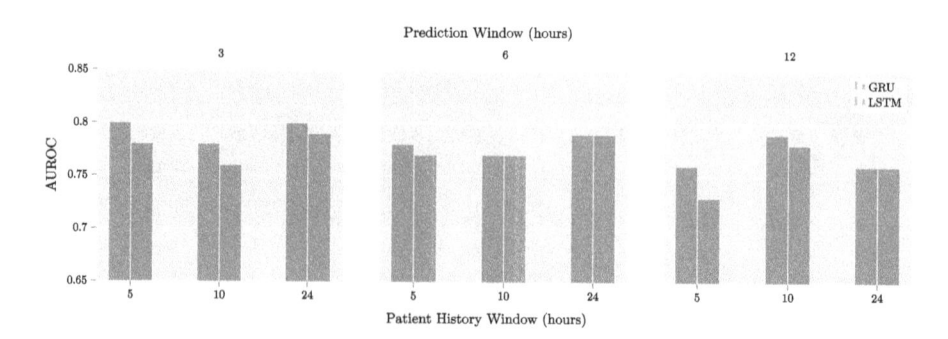

Fig. 2. AUROC performance of FL GRU and LSTM models, averaged across FL clients for varying *patient history windows* and *prediction windows* (AUPRC and F1-Score metrics followed a similar trend).

Federated Learning Clients. For the FL approach, the evaluation was performed with 2, 4, and 8 FL clients, each representing a healthcare institution where relevant data would be held locally or on private, secure servers. As demonstrated in Table 3, although AUROC, AUPRC, and F1-Score metrics did not vary significantly across the different numbers of clients for the same *patient history window* and *prediction window*, an overall decrease in performance can be observed as the number of clients increases, for both GRU and LSTM (see also Fig. 3). We observe that the best-performing FL model was for two clients and used a GRU architecture with a *patient history window* of 24 h and a three-hour *prediction window*.

From Fig. 3, it is interesting to note that the metrics AUPRC and F1-Score showed a more significant drop in the average performance for an increasing number of FL clients compared to AUROC. The overall performance decrease for an increasing amount of clients could be due to an insufficient amount of data, as Budrionis et al. [1] show that when sufficient amounts of data are available, the performance of CML and FL implementations should not be affected, irrespectively of the number of clients. Although the system would benefit from further improvements to reduce the rate of performance degradation when the dataset is possibly not big enough, the more stable AUROC rate is advantageous for implementations in a healthcare environment as lower probabilities of false negatives mean that although the model might not be highly accurate, the chances of positive sepsis cases being missed are lower, enabling physicians to carry out the necessary checks pre-emptively before the patient is in a critical state.

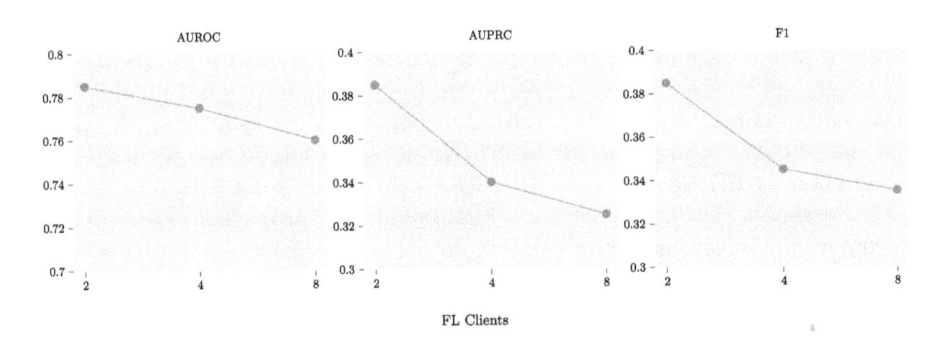

Fig. 3. Average performance (GRU and LSTM performance for the different windows) for increasing FL clients.

Centralized Learning and Federated Learning. The federated sepsis onset prediction solution proposed in this study is evaluated against the centralized approach proposed by [19]. Based on the results presented in Table 3, both the CML and FL models perform well despite a significant imbalance between the *sepsis* and *non-sepsis* classes. In addition, the CML and FL setups show to be on par in terms of predictive performance. As mentioned previously, the best-performing FL model was for two FL clients and used a GRU architecture with a *patient history window* of 24 h, and a three-hour *prediction window*, resulting in an AUROC of 0.85, an AUPRC of 0.46, and an F1-Score of 0.46. Comparatively, the best-performing CML model is based on GRU and used a five-hour *patient history window* and a three-hour *prediction window*, achieving an AUROC of 0.84, an AUPRC of 0.47, and an F1-Score of 0.43.

Although the best-performing models for both the CML and FL approaches are on par, the CML approach showed, on average, a better performance than the FL approach with an increased number of clients.

Model Computation. The FL models took around 1.5 to 2.5 h each to train, while the CML models took an average of 30 min each. In the meanwhile, while the training time varied slightly between LSTM and GRU, the strongest training time indicators were *patient history window* length and the number of FL clients. This increase in time was caused by the fact that the FL setup was simulated on a single machine, and the local models of each client were trained sequentially. Although real-world FL setups would incur additional training time due to weights being transferred between the clients and the global server, the overall time could decrease significantly if the clients train the models in parallel.

5 Conclusions

This research expands upon existing studies by exploring a Deep Federated Learning solution for sepsis onset prediction, based on the MIMIC-III dataset. We provided a comparison of temporal DL model architectures (GRU and LSTM) and an evaluation on varying *patient history windows* (5h, 10h, and 24h), *prediction windows* (3h, 6h, and 12h), and number of participating FL clients (2, 4, and 8). We found that the best-performing model, on average for different numbers of FL clients, was GRU, with a five-hour *patient history window* and a three-hour *prediction window*, thus providing a promising and replicable benchmark for sepsis onset prediction in an FL environment. Finally, this study demonstrated that a Deep FL setup is capable of predicting sepsis onset comparably to state-of-the-art CML algorithms without sharing isolated patient data, enabling healthcare institutions to collaborate on mutually beneficial tasks.

There are several possibilities for future extensions, such as enhancing the study by optimizing the FL setup via, for example, exploring alternative hyperparameters or FL algorithms. In addition, we could improve our study by using more data representing other regions and patient demographics or personalizing the model for each client to reflect local patient demographics better. Finally, we could consider more realistic patient distributions (in terms of class or diagnosis distribution), as it is quite unlike in a real-world scenario that the patient data are homogeneously distributed across clients. Finally, using explainability techniques, a more transparent decision support tool could be built, potentially increasing the acceptance rate amongst clinicians.

Although certain improvements are yet to be made in this area before a Federated Learning setup can be used for developing ML models to predict sepsis onset in a real-world healthcare environment, the research has shown promising results, thus enabling physicians to identify sepsis onset timely and improve patient outcomes. In addition, the Federated Learning setup would enable healthcare institutions to collaborate on mutually beneficial tasks without sharing isolated sensitive patient information.

References

1. Budrionis, A., Miara, M., Miara, P., Wilk, S., Bellika, J.G.: Benchmarking PySyft federated learning framework on MIMIC-III dataset. IEEE Access **9**, 116869–116878 (2021)
2. Calvert, J.S., et al.: A computational approach to early sepsis detection. Comput. Biol. Med. **74**, 69–73 (2016)
3. Chen, Y., Lu, W., Wang, J., Qin, X., Qin, T.: Federated learning with adaptive batchnorm for personalized healthcare (2021)
4. Fagerström, J., Bång, M., Wilhelms, D., Chew, M.S.: LiSep LSTM: a machine learning algorithm for early detection of septic shock. Sci. Rep. **9**(1) (2019)
5. Fleischmann, C., et al.: Assessment of global incidence and mortality of hospital-treated sepsis current estimates and limitations. Am. J. Respir. Crit. Care Med. **193**(3), 259–272 (2016)
6. Fleuren, L.M., et al.: Machine learning for the prediction of sepsis: a systematic review and meta-analysis of diagnostic test accuracy. Intensive Care Med. **46**(3), 383–400 (2020). https://doi.org/10.1007/s00134-019-05872-y
7. Johnson, A.E., et al.: MIMIC-III, a freely accessible critical care database. Sci. Data **3**(1), 1–9 (2016)
8. Kingma, D.P., Ba, J.: Adam: a method for stochastic optimization. arXiv preprint arXiv:1412.6980 (2014)
9. Konečný, J., McMahan, H.B., Yu, F.X., Richtárik, P., Suresh, A.T., Bacon, D.: Federated learning: strategies for improving communication efficiency (2016)
10. Lee, G.H., Shin, S.Y.: Federated learning on clinical benchmark data: performance assessment. J. Med. Internet Res. **22**(10), e20891 (2020)
11. McMahan, B., Moore, E., Ramage, D., Hampson, S., y Arcas, B.A.: Communication-efficient learning of deep networks from decentralized data. In: Artificial Intelligence and Statistics, pp. 1273–1282. PMLR (2017)
12. Mondrejevski, L., Miliou, I., Montanino, A., Pitts, D., Hollmén, J., Papapetrou, P.: FLICU: a federated learning workflow for intensive care unit mortality prediction. In: 2022 IEEE 35th International Symposium on Computer-Based Medical Systems (CBMS), pp. 32–37. IEEE (2022)
13. Pfitzner, B., Steckhan, N., Arnrich, B.: Federated learning in a medical context: a systematic literature review. ACM Trans. Internet Technol. **21**(2), 1–31 (2021)
14. Prayitno, et al.: A systematic review of federated learning in the healthcare area: from the perspective of data properties and applications. Appl. Sci. **11**(23), 11191 (2021)
15. Rand, K., Armengol, N.L., Mondrejevski, L., Miliou, I.: Early prediction of the risk of ICU mortality with deep federated learning. In: 2023 IEEE 36th International Symposium on Computer-Based Medical Systems (CBMS). IEEE (2023)

16. Rieke, N., et al.: The future of digital health with federated learning. NPJ Digital Med. **3**(1) (2020)
17. Rosnati, M., Fortuin, V.: MGP-AttTCN: an interpretable machine learning model for the prediction of sepsis. PLoS ONE **16**(5), e0251248 (2021)
18. Saeed, M., Lieu, C., Raber, G., Mark, R.: MIMIC II: a massive temporal ICU patient database to support research in intelligent patient monitoring. In: Computers in Cardiology, pp. 641–644 (2002)
19. Scherpf, M., Gräßer, F., Malberg, H., Zaunseder, S.: Predicting sepsis with a recurrent neural network using the MIMIC III database. Comput. Biol. Med. **113**, 103395 (2019)
20. Svenson, P., Haralabopoulos, G., Torres, M.T.: Sepsis deterioration prediction using channelled long short-term memory networks. In: Artificial Intelligence in Medicine, pp. 359–370. Springer (2020)
21. Vincent, J.L., et al.: Assessment of the worldwide burden of critical illness: the intensive care over nations (ICON) audit. Lancet Respir. Med. **2**(5), 380–386 (2014)
22. Xu, J., Glicksberg, B.S., Su, C., Walker, P., Bian, J., Wang, F.: Federated learning for healthcare informatics. J. Healthc. Inf. Res. **5**(1), 1–19 (2020)
23. Xue, Z., et al.: A resource-constrained and privacy-preserving edge-computing-enabled clinical decision system: a federated reinforcement learning approach. IEEE Internet Things J. **8**(11), 9122–9138 (2021)
24. Zhang, D., Yin, C., Hunold, K.M., Jiang, X., Caterino, J.M., Zhang, P.: An interpretable deep-learning model for early prediction of sepsis in the emergency department. Patterns **2**(2), 100196 (2021)

A Workflow for Creating Multimodal Machine Learning Models for Metastasis Predictions in Melanoma Patients

Franco Rugolon(✉)[ID], Korbinian Randl[ID], Maria Bampa[ID], and Panagiotis Papapetrou[ID]

Department of Computer and Systems Sciences, Stockholm University, Stockholm, Sweden
franco.rugolon@dsv.su.se

Abstract. Melanoma is the most common form of skin cancer, responsible for thousands of deaths annually. Novel therapies have been developed, but metastases are still a common problem, increasing the mortality rate and decreasing the quality of life of those who experience them. As traditional machine learning models for metastasis prediction have been limited to the use of a single modality, in this study we aim to explore and compare different unimodal and multimodal machine learning models to predict the onset of metastasis in melanoma patients to help clinicians focus their attention on patients at a higher risk of developing metastasis, increasing the likelihood of an earlier diagnosis. We use a patient cohort derived from an Electronic Health Record, and we consider various modalities of data, including static, time series, and clinical text. We formulate the problem and propose a multimodal ML workflow for predicting the onset of metastasis in melanoma patients. We evaluate the performance of the workflow based on various classification metrics and statistical significance. The experimental findings suggest that multimodal models outperform the unimodal ones, demonstrating the potential of multimodal ML to predict the onset of metastasis.

Keywords: Multimodal predictions · Machine learning · Melanoma · Metastasis · EHR

1 Introduction

Melanoma is the most common form of skin cancer and can be caused by a combination of factors, including increased sun exposure, exposure to ultraviolet light, genetic disposition, and immune suppression [17,32]. Despite newly available forms of treatments that managed to decrease the mortality rate, melanoma remains the fifth most common form of cancer and has been responsible for over 7600 deaths in the United States in 2022 [28]. With the development of novel treatments, patient survival has significantly improved; however, patients in advanced stages often experience recurrences after treatment [21]. For example, malignant melanoma can metastasize to multiple sites, including the lung, liver, brain, bone, and lymph nodes [3].

While a few established risk factors exist, modern and systematic patient data collections and repositories, such as Electronic Health Records (EHRs), could enable us to uncover previously unknown risk factors, or predict the risk of a patient developing metastasis [10]. An EHR includes the key administrative and clinical data related to patient care over time, including demographics, progress notes, medications, vital signs, past medical history, and laboratory data. Given the increased availability of EHRs, Machine Learning (ML) can be leveraged to predict the insurgence of metastasis in melanoma patients by exploiting the patient's clinical history [19]. In that way, an improved diagnostic process for melanoma patients can lead to earlier, more timely care and potentially to higher survival rates and better quality of life for the patients [15].

Traditionally, ML methods and models have been limited to using data of single types and forms [38], which can differ according to the underlying data generation process, called modality [36]. However, EHRs contain, by nature, heterogeneous and multimodal data, reflecting the complexity of real-world medical and clinical information [36]. The modalities that exist in EHRs can, for example, be structured (e.g., medications and diagnostic codes over a time period, demographics, and other static patient information), time series (e.g., lab measurements and interventions over time), or unstructured (e.g., free text written by healthcare professionals). Clinicians usually interpret EHRs by integrating and synthesizing data from all these modalities concurrently to reach their decisions [38]. Nonetheless, these modalities could have complex interactions; for instance, a patient's family history should be considered when establishing the risk for a patient to develop conditions that show hereditary patterns. Taking into consideration patient information and modeling the various modalities jointly, could be beneficial for an ML model. To the best of our knowledge, there is still a scarcity of studies applying multimodal ML methods that can exploit the inherent complexity of EHR data and investigate critical conditions, such as the onset of metastasis in melanoma patients.

Contributions In this paper, we propose a workflow for multimodal learning from EHRs, making the source code available on GitHub[1]. We further demonstrate the feasibility and efficacy of the proposed workflow on the EHRs of patients with melanoma to predict the onset of metastasis in these patients. Moreover, we compare our approach with alternative solutions that employ subsets of one or more data modalities. Our main goal is to highlight patients with a higher risk of developing metastasis so that clinicians can increase the surveillance of these patients and potentially reach an earlier diagnosis.

---

[1] https://github.com/FoxtrotRomeo/melanoma_metastasis

2 Background

2.1 Problem Formulation

Consider a set of I patients, and let $\mathcal{H} = \{\mathcal{E}_1, \ldots, \mathcal{E}_I\}$ denote the set of their corresponding EHRs, with $\mathcal{E}_i$ being the EHR of patient i. Moreover, each EHR comprises four components, i.e., $\mathcal{E}_i = \{\mathcal{D}_i, \mathcal{M}_i, \mathcal{L}_i, \mathcal{T}_i\}$. These components are either static, i.e., they remain constant over time, or sequential, i.e., they evolve over time. The static components in our study include:

- $\mathcal{D}_i$: the set of diagnoses for patient i, such that $\mathcal{D}_i \in \mathcal{D}$, with $\mathcal{D}$ being the set of all diagnoses in the dataset, in the form of International Classification of Diseases, 10th Revision (ICD10 codes); and
- $\mathcal{M}_i$: the set of medications for patient i, such that $\mathcal{M}_i \in \mathcal{M}$, with $\mathcal{M}$ being the set of all medications in the dataset, in the form of Anatomical Therapeutic Chemical (ATC) codes of medications prescribed to the patient.

Moreover, the sequential components in our study include:

- $\mathcal{L}_i$: the sequence of Nomenclature for Properties and Units (NPU) lab codes with their corresponding values over time, for patient i, denoted as $\{\mathcal{L}_{i1}, \mathcal{L}_{i2}, \ldots, \mathcal{L}_{iJ(i)}\}$. Each $\mathcal{L}_{ij}$ is the set of lab codes and lab values registered at time point j, while the total number of laboratory exam code instances for patient i is denoted as $J(i)$.
- $\mathcal{T}_i$: the sequence of clinical notes over time for patient i, denoted as $\mathcal{T}_i = \{\mathcal{T}_{i1}, \mathcal{T}_{i2}, \ldots, \mathcal{T}_{iK(i)}\}$. Each $\mathcal{T}_{ik}$ is a clinical note written by a healthcare professional at time point k, with $K(i)$ denoting the total number of notes in the sequence.

Finally, for each patient i, we denote the day of metastasis diagnosis or the patient's last visit (if the patient never developed metastasis) as t_{0i}.

Multimodal Learning for Melanoma Metastasis Prediction. Given a training set of EHRs of I patients $\mathcal{H}_{train} = \{\mathcal{E}_1, \ldots, \mathcal{E}_I\}$ comprising static and sequential components, a critical time point of interest t_{0i} for each patient i, and a time constraint t_{min}, we want to train a multimodal binary classifier $f(\cdot)$, such that

$$f(\mathcal{H}_{train}, t_{0i}, t_{min}, i) \rightarrow \begin{cases} 1, & \text{metastasis at time point } t_{0i} \text{ for patient } i \\ 0, & \text{otherwise} \end{cases}$$

by taking into consideration all data modalities in the training set.

Next, we present the related work in the area of multimodal learning with a focus on EHR data and melanoma prediction.

2.2 Related Work

The use of ML for melanoma prediction has been studied in the literature using either genomic and photographic data [13,18] or EHR data [13,19,29,30].

Genomic data has been utilized to identify the genes most commonly correlated with melanoma development and to differentiate between different subclasses of melanoma. Conversely, other works utilize clinical photographs and photographic data as input to the ML algorithms to predict melanoma; although informative for melanoma predictions, such models often encounter problems in performing predictions on patients with darker skin tones or in photographs with non-optimal lighting conditions [13, 18]. While these methods have achieved some success, according to the review by Ma et al., the majority of them report their results using metrics such as accuracy [18]; however, accuracy would be an inappropriate metric to report, given that the problem of predicting the onset of metastasis is imbalanced. Additionally, these methods rely on expensive analysis conducted by specialized personnel, which might cause a delay in the performing of the tests, an increased expense for the sanitary system, and the need for the patient to travel to specialized centers in case the exams cannot be performed at the facilities in their proximity.

Various studies have used EHR data to improve the diagnosis and treatment of melanoma patients. Some of these studies used Natural Language Processing [19] and other techniques to extract information from EHRs, and highlighted how the performance of the algorithms decreased with increased linguistic variability of the clinical reports [29], confirming the difficulty of dealing with unstructured information. Other papers focused on the use of EHRs to conduct retrospective studies, trying to identify associations between different risk factors and incidence of melanoma [25], survival in melanoma patients [30], or to categorize and stratify the patients according to the characteristics of the melanoma [12]. These studies used EHRs as a source of patient information; however, they often considered only one modality or source of data in the EHR [19, 29], or they reduced the complexity of the task aggregating continuous variables [12]. While this approach might be necessary when traditional statistical methods are involved, ML allows us to incorporate in the learning model data with different modalities and sources, enabling a complete representation of the patients and, potentially, better results in terms of prediction strength [38].

A few studies have applied multimodal ML methods to EHRs [26, 27, 33, 37], with a focus on different tasks: predicting mortality and length of stay [26], the procedures that will be performed on the patients [33], the diagnosis that a patient will present on the next visit [27], or identifying sub-types of a particular disease which can lead to specific treatments. Some papers only integrate clinical codes and clinical text [27], while some others integrate static data (e.g. demographics), with time series data (e.g. vital signs and laboratory exam results) [26, 37], and some others integrate time series data with clinical text [33]. The previously mentioned studies highlight the potential given by multimodal ML to achieve results that are comparable to or better than other approaches [26, 33] but also underline the challenges related to working with sparse, irregular data with missing values [26, 27, 37].

3 MultiModal Learning from EHRs Using Stacked Classifiers

We propose a multimodal learning workflow for predicting the onset of metastasis in melanoma patients. The workflow comprises two steps: (1) patient representation and (2) multimodal learning using stacking. Next, we describe each step in detail.

3.1 Patient Representation

The first step of our workflow focuses on creating different representations for each of the four considered data types, i.e., diagnoses, medications, labs, and clinical text.

Diagnoses. For each distinct medical event in $\mathcal{E}_i$ that corresponds to the set of diagnoses $\mathcal{D}_i$, we apply a one-hot-encoding transformation that maps $\mathcal{D}$ to a binary matrix B, with $B_{ij} = 1$, if $\mathcal{E}_i$ contains at least one occurrence of the medical event on the jth day and 0 otherwise. Since the clinical records recorded all the inpatient and outpatient visits for all patients in the dataset, including visits completely unrelated to melanoma, the diagnoses for which the codes did not start with C43 (i.e., the code corresponding to "Malignant melanoma of skin" [35]) were included only if at least ten patients presented that specific diagnostic code, in an effort to filter out outliers.

Medications. For each medical event in $\mathcal{E}_i$ that corresponds to the set of medications in $\mathcal{M}_i$, we count the number of occurrences and assign these values as the features for this modality. Additionally, we aggregate the medications belonging to the same pharmacological subgroup, exploiting the hierarchical structure of the ATC codes to reduce the number of features, while maintaining a similar mechanism of action for each group of medications. Consecutively, we apply normalization, using Robust Scaler, which removes the median and scales the data according to the quantile range [24], but without losing generality, any normalization technique can be used here.

Labs. In our workflow, the medical events comprising $\mathcal{L}_i$ are represented as a time series, as the temporal nature of this data is deemed to be a potential indicator of the progression of the illness. Given that the patients are not, in general, in an ICU setting with frequent and repeated measurements, the time series are represented with different granularities: we aggregate values daily, weekly, or every two, three, or four weeks, in order to study which representation is more appropriate in this particular setting. More concretely, if the time series has a weekly granularity, we take the weekly average value of each event in $\mathcal{L}_i$ during the considered 90 days. Finally, we normalize the data, again using a Robust Scaler.

Clinical Text. As clinical texts tend to describe a patient's status at a specific time rather than correspond to a timespan, resampling and imputing this modality might distort the encoded information. Therefore, we sort each medical event in the set of clinical texts in $\mathcal{T}_i$ in chronological order (newest first) and treat them as a natural series of events disregarding the time gaps in between. Each text in the resulting sequence is then tokenized using a WordPiece tokenizer built on a special vocabulary for SweDeClin-BERT [34].

3.2 Classification Process

In order to combine the aforementioned different modalities, we propose a two-stage stacked classifier: on the first stage of this model, we extract a probabilistic prediction for each of the modalities presented in the sets of ICD10 codes $\mathcal{D}_i$, ATC codes $\mathcal{M}_i$, NPU codes $\mathcal{L}_i$, and clinical texts $\mathcal{T}_i$. The second stage consists of a logistic regression classifier trained on the outputs of the best models individuated during stage one, producing a single binary label.

For classifying the inputs $\mathcal{D}_i$ and $\mathcal{M}_i$, we compare a Support Vector Machine (SVM) [23], a Decision Tree (DT) [5], a Random Forest (RF) [4], a Gradient Boosting Classifier (GBC) [11], and Logistic Regression (LR). In addition, we also employ a fully connected Neural Network (NN). The networks are built with an input layer, followed by one to three blocks formed by a dense layer and a dropout layer, followed by a layer for batch normalization and a single perceptron, using the *sigmoid* activation function. The optimal number of blocks and the optimal activation function of the hidden layers is determined during hyperparameter optimization on the validation data. Furthermore, we optimize the dropout ratio, the values for l1 and l2 regularization, and the learning rate based on the validation scores.

For classifying the inputs $\mathcal{L}_i$, in the form of Time Series, we compared a K-Nearest Neighbors (KNN), a Catch22 classifier [2], MUSE [31], a Shapelet Transform classifier [2], a Canonical Interval Forest [20], and Rocket [9]. Additionally, we try a Long Short-Term Memory (LSTM) [14], and a bidirectional LSTM (BiLSTM), both built using Tensorflow [1]. For LSTM and BiLSTM we use the same structure and hyperparameter optimization strategy as for the NN. The only difference is in the type of layer and in the activation function for the hidden layers: we change the type of layer from Dense to LSTM or to Bidirectional LSTM, and we only initialize the activation function as *tangens hyperbolicus*, to allow for the use of graphical acceleration during the training process.

For the clinical notes $\mathcal{T}_i$, we use SweDeClin-BERT [34], a BERT model pre-trained for Swedish clinical texts. The pooled output of this transformer is fed into a single RNN layer with *tangens hyperbolicus* as the activation function, followed by a dropout layer (dropout rate = 0.2) to avoid over-fitting, and finally a single perceptron with a sigmoid activation function. For the RNN we use a size of 768 units, which is the size of SweDeClin-BERT's output. Furthermore, we evaluate the model with LSTM, GRU [7], and BiLSTM as the type of the RNN layer.

4 Empirical Evaluation

4.1 Dataset

For this study, we use data from the research infrastructure the Health Bank - the Swedish Health Records Research Bank [8]. The data is called Stockholm EPR Structured and Unstructured ADE corpus (SU-ADE Corpus)[2], and are patient records based on the TakeCare EPR records, containing data on more than two million patients treated at Karolinska Hospital in Stockholm, Sweden, between 2006 and 2014. The dataset includes ICD10 codes for diagnoses, ATC codes for the drugs administered to each patient, laboratory exams and values, and unstructured information, like clinical text written in daily and discharge notes. The dataset does not include explicit demographic data. Therefore we could not provide a patient overview here.

This work focuses on studying whether a melanoma patient will have an onset of metastasis. From the set of patients' EHRs $\{\mathcal{E}_1, \ldots, \mathcal{E}_I\}$ in the Health Bank, we include in the patient cohort only patients that have been diagnosed with melanoma; that is, for a record $\mathcal{E}_i$ if the set $\mathcal{D}_i$ includes an ICD10 starting with "C43" (i.e., the code corresponding to "Malignant melanoma of skin" [35]) then $\mathcal{E}_i$ is included in the melanoma cohort. The resulting cohort is labeled based on whether a patient has metastasis: if the term "metastas" is present in the clinical notes of $\mathcal{E}_i$, we label patient i with a positive class. Otherwise, we assign the negative class. This process was necessary given the lack of an ICD10 code indicating the presence or absence of metastasis. For patients in the positive class, we only consider the 90 days before the first appearance of "metastas" (excluding the day of the first appearance). For the patients who do not have this term in their clinical notes, the day of the last recorded event in their clinical history is taken as a termination day, and the 90 days before this event are included in the data.

4.2 Set Up

We create a stratified split made of a train set, a test set for the unimodal models, and a test set for the multimodal models from the filtered data. The two test sets are completely disjunct: since the individual models are trained on the train set, and the best model is selected based on its performance on the unimodal test set, using the same test set for the multimodal model could lead to overfitting. Our strategy is aimed at minimizing this risk. The train set and the test sets include data from the same patients across all modalities. All included patients have data in all modalities, so the stacked classifier can later combine the output of the unimodal models. The numbers and proportions of positive and negative patients in the three sets are shown in Table 1.

---

[2] This research has been approved by the Regional Ethical Review Board in Stockholm under permission no. 2014/1882-31/5.

Table 1. Class distribution of the filtered data.

	Negative	Positive	Total	Percentage
Train	52	159	211	69.9%
Test_unimodal	11	34	45	14.9%
Test_multimodal	12	34	46	15.2%
Total	75	227	302	
Percentage	24.8%	75.2%		100.0%

(i) In the first step we train the unimodal classifiers on the training data available for each modality. This step involves extensive hyperparameter optimization, and we select the best model for each data source based on their performance on the test set for the unimodal classifiers. A representation of this process can be seen in Fig. 1; **(ii)** As a second step, we train the stacked linear-regression classifier on the unimodal classifiers' predictions for the merged train and test set for the unimodal classifiers, and we test it on the test set for the multimodal classifiers. The final model is shown in Fig. 2.

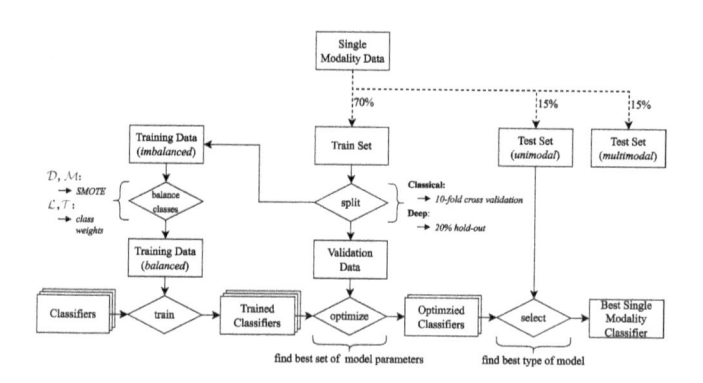

Fig. 1. Training process of the unimodal classifiers.

To speed up the optimization process, we use a Bayesian search strategy on the train set, and we test the performance of each classifier on the unimodal classifier test set. The training process for static data on the traditional classifiers is performed using 10-fold cross-validation and using a Synthetic Minority Oversampling Technique (SMOTE) [6] on the train set to eliminate the problem of data imbalance. To avoid data leakage during the cross-validation process, the SMOTE augmentation is applied to each fold of the cross-validation individually. For time series classifiers, we employ 10-fold cross-validation without SMOTE, training the classifiers directly on the imbalanced data.

Dense NNs, LSTMs and Bidirectional LSTMs are trained using 20% of the data as a validation split, but given the long time needed to train the neural

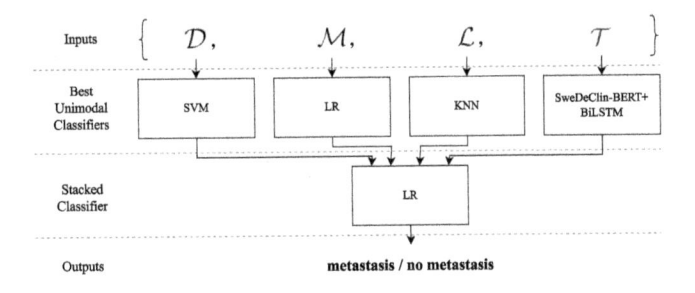

Fig. 2. Structure of the stacked classifier.

networks, we do not apply cross-validation for these classifiers. Instead of performing data augmentation, we use a bias b, calculated as shown in Eq. 1 derived from the proportions of patients belonging to the positive and negative classes while training these models:

$$b = \ln \frac{I_{pos}}{I_{neg}} \qquad (1)$$

Here I_{pos} is the number of patients with metastasis and I_{neg} is the number of patients without metastasis. This bias is used as one of the parameters for the output layer of the NN, LSTM and BiLSTM-based networks, reducing the impact of the class imbalance in the data. For text-based classifiers, the Transformer, LSTMs, BiLSTMs, and GRUs are trained in a similar way as NNs, using class weights w_{pos} and w_{neg}, for the positive and negative classes, respectively, calculated as shown in Eq. 2:

$$\begin{bmatrix} w_{pos} \\ w_{neg} \end{bmatrix} = 0.5 \begin{bmatrix} \frac{I_{pos}+I_{neg}}{I_{pos}} \\ \frac{I_{pos}+I_{neg}}{I_{neg}} \end{bmatrix} \qquad (2)$$

To optimize the model's hyperparameters, we use either cross-validation or a hold-out set: for the classifiers from the scikit-learn and the scikit-time suites, optimization is performed on different hyperparameters, depending on each individual model (see Sect. 3.2).

For the deep models trained on the static and time series data, we use ADAptive Moment Optimization (ADAM) [16], and early stopping on the validation loss with a patience of 10 for the models trained on static and time series data and with a patience of 2 for the models trained on the clinical text, in order to optimize the number of training epochs and avoid overfitting. We repeat this analysis with the same hyperparameter optimization procedure for the data with daily, weekly, biweekly, triweekly, and tetraweekly granularity.

For training the transformer model, we also use the ADAM optimizer, with a learning rate that stays at $2 \cdot 10^{-5}$ for the first two epochs and decreases by a factor of 0.1 after each consecutive epoch.

After training and optimization, the best unimodal classifiers are:

- **On $\mathcal{D}$ data:** SVM with a polynomial kernel, regularization parameter C set to 1, and the kernel coefficient for the polynomial kernel set to 0.1.

- **On $\mathcal{M}$ data:** LR, with the regularization parameter C set to 12, primal formulation, intercept added to the decision function, the maximum number of iterations set to 1000, without the use of l1 or l2 penalty, and using sag as a solver.
- **On $\mathcal{L}$ data:** KNN, trained on data with a triweekly granularity, with the distance parameter set to 'squared', the weights for the neighbors set to constant, and considering 10 neighbors when assigning the output class.
- **On $\mathcal{T}$ data:** the model created combining **SweDeClin-BERT and BiLSTM** to classify the outputs. This model used the pre-trained SweDeClin-BERT model and then passed its outputs to a bidirectional LSTM layer made of 768 units using *tangens hyperbolicus* as activation function, followed by a dropout layer with the dropout value set to 0.2, and a single perceptron using the sigmoid activation function.

4.3 Evaluation Metrics

Given the imbalanced nature of our dataset, the F1 score is used to assess the performance of the classifiers and choose the best-performing classifier for each modality. We also provide precision and recall for the positive class (the patients diagnosed with metastasis) and accuracy. Regarding the F1 score, we also provide the 95% confidence intervals obtained with a random sampling with replacement (bootstrapping), repeated 1000 times.

In addition, we present the results of the Friedman test and of the Nemeny test [22] to establish if there is a significant difference in the performance of the classifiers within each modality, and between the best-performing classifier for each single modality and the multimodal classifier trained on all the modalities.

4.4 Unimodal Classifiers

The results obtained by the three best unimodal classifiers for each modality are presented in Table 2. We observe that SVM with medications $\mathcal{M}$ as input performs significantly better than the other modalities with regards to F1-score, and the best unimodal models with text $\mathcal{T}$ as input achieve an equally high score of 0.88%; the diagnoses $\mathcal{D}$ and lab results $\mathcal{L}$ obtain the lowest results within our classifiers, but still a considerably high F1-score. Additionally, we include the 95% confidence intervals to ensure that the performance obtained by the classifiers is not due to the particular test set we use. We then perform the Friedman test with a 0.05 threshold for statistical significance. The statistic of the Friedman test and the relative p-values on the different modalities can be seen in Table 3. The results indicate statistically significant differences in all the modalities except for the classifiers trained on clinical text. We interpret this as a result of the transfer learning performed on SweDeClin-BERT: the fine-tuning performed by us is only adapting the classifier to our data, but not inherently changing the function of the model. It can be seen that the results of the unimodal classifiers with regard to the p-values are several orders of magnitude lower

Table 2. The precision, recall, accuracy, and F1 score of the different unimodal classifiers on the test set, with 95% confidence intervals reported on F1 score (Lower, Median, and Upper).

Modality	Data source	Model	F1 score Lower	F1 score Median	F1 score Upper	Precision	Recall	Accuracy
Static data	$\mathcal{D}$	SVM	0.8052	**0.8354**	0.8500	0.7556	1.0000	0.7556
		RF	0.7273	0.8235	0.9014	0.8421	0.9412	0.8222
		DT	0.7143	0.7838	0.8462	0.8049	0.9706	0.8000
	$\mathcal{M}$	LR	0.8286	**0.9014**	0.9565	0.8857	0.9118	0.8478
		DT	0.8060	0.8649	0.9167	0.8000	0.9412	0.7826
		Dense NN 2layers	0.8158	0.8571	0.8947	0.7727	1.0000	0.7778
Time series	$\mathcal{L}$	KNN triweekly data	0.8500	**0.8500**	0.8500	0.8095	1.0000	0.8222
		Catch22 tetraweekly data	0.8052	0.8462	0.8831	0.8049	0.9706	0.8000
		BiLSTM, 1 layer weekly data	0.7733	0.8205	0.8500	0.8831	0.7907	0.8000
Text data	$\mathcal{T}$	SweDeClin-BERT+BiLSTM	0.8060	**0.8824**	0.9429	0.8824	0.8824	0.8261
		SweDeClin-BERT+LSTM	0.8000	0.8824	0.9552	0.8824	0.8824	0.8261
		SweDeClin-BERT+GRU	0.7998	0.8788	0.9538	0.9062	0.8529	0.8261

Table 3. The Friedman test's statistic and p-value for tests conducted on the classifiers trained on the single modalities.

Modality	Friedman test Statistic	Friedman test p-value
$\mathcal{D}$	32.9130	7.1289e-08
$\mathcal{M}$	27.6957	9.6820e-07
$\mathcal{L}$	35.6087	1.8521e-08
$\mathcal{T}$	3.1739	0.2046

than the threshold for statistical significance, except for the classifiers trained on clinical text, which produced a p-value above 0.05.

Following that, we conduct the post hoc Nemeny test, which highlights the pairs of classifiers which produce significantly different results. The results of the Nemeny test for the classification results of the unimodal classifiers trained on $\mathcal{D}$ can be seen in Table 6(a), for the classifiers trained on $\mathcal{M}$ in Table 6(b), for the classifiers trained on $\mathcal{L}$ in Table 6(c), and, even if no statistically relevant differences were found, for the classifiers trained on $\mathcal{T}$ the results of the Nemeny test can be found in Table 6(d). In the previously mentioned tables, we highlight the p-values lower than 0.05, which show a statistically significant difference between the results of couples of classifiers. These results show that, apart from the classifiers trained on clinical text, the best-performing classifiers for each modality have statistically significant differences in performance when compared with the other classifiers for the same modality. Nevertheless, an interesting finding is that the LR and DT classifiers trained on the ATC medication codes produce very similar predictions. Finally, we choose the best-performing unimodal classifiers as the components of the multimodal classifiers, as illustrated in Fig. 2.

4.5 Multimodal Classifiers

The results obtained by the multimodal classifiers can be seen in Table 4, in which the results of the classifiers for each combination of two modalities and the results of the classifier trained on all three modalities are presented. This table shows that the stacked classifier trained on all modalities performs considerably better than the combination of static data and time series modalities or the combination of time series and clinical text on all metrics. However, the performance of all modalities performs equally well if we consider the combination of static data and clinical text modalities as input. Following that, we performed the Friedman test on the classification results of the multimodal classifiers trained on all the combinations of two modalities and the classification results of the classifier trained on all three modalities, with an $h0$ similar to the one for the test performed on the unimodal classifiers. The results of this test can be seen in Table 5, and they show how $h0$ can be rejected for both the multimodal classifiers and the comparison between the best unimodal classifier for each modality and the best multimodal classifier.

Following the results of the Friedman test, we perform a Nemeny post hoc test to compare the classification results of all the couples of multimodal classifiers and of the best unimodal classifiers for each modality with those of the best multimodal classifier. The results of these tests can be seen, respectively, in Table 7(a) and in Table 7(b). These results show how there is a statistically significant difference in the performance of the classifiers that include and those that do not include static data (which is composed of data from both $\mathcal{D}$ and $\mathcal{M}$). In particular, comparing this information with the results shown in Table 4, we can see that not including static data in the training data for the multimodal classifiers leads to significantly worse performance for the classifiers. Table 7(b),

Table 4. The precision, recall, accuracy, and F1 score with 95% confidence intervals reported on F1 score (Lower, Median, and Upper) of the stacked classifiers on the different combinations of modalities.

Modality	Data source	Model	F1 score			Precision	Recall	Accuracy
			Lower	Median	Upper			
All modalities	$(\mathcal{D}, \mathcal{M})+\mathcal{L}+\mathcal{T}$	Stacked classifier	0.8831	**0.9189**	0.9577	0.8500	1.0000	0.8696
Static data+Clinical text	$(\mathcal{D}, \mathcal{M})+\mathcal{T}$	Stacked classifier	0.8831	0.9189	0.9577	0.8500	1.0000	0.8696
Static data+Time series	$(\mathcal{D}, \mathcal{M})+\mathcal{L}$	Stacked classifier	0.8493	0.9041	0.9577	0.8462	0.9706	0.8478
Time series+Clinical text	$\mathcal{L}+\mathcal{T}$	Stacked classifier	0.8500	0.8500	0.8500	0.7391	1.0000	0.7391

Table 5. The Friedman test's statistic and p-value for tests conducted on the multimodal classifiers.

Modality	Friedman test	
	Statistic	p-value
Multimodal	25.2261	1.3848e-05
Unimodal and multimodal	48.8522	6.2685e-10

Table 6. The p-values resulting from the Nemeny test performed on the classification results of the best-performing models for the unimodal classifiers trained on (a) $\mathcal{D}$, (b) $\mathcal{M}$, (c) $\mathcal{L}$, and (d) $\mathcal{T}$. Greyed values denote significant difference at $p \leq 0.05$.

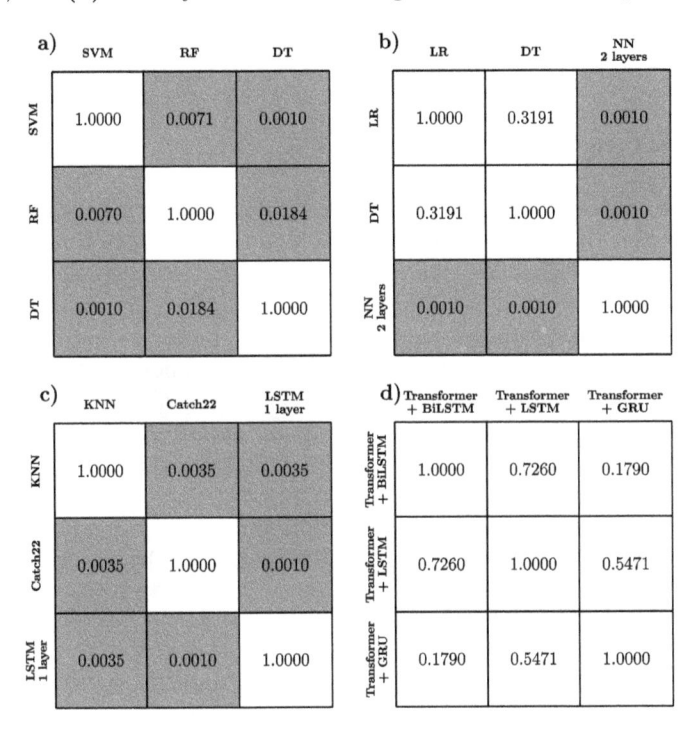

a)

	SVM	RF	DT
SVM	1.0000	0.0071	0.0010
RF	0.0070	1.0000	0.0184
DT	0.0010	0.0184	1.0000

b)

	LR	DT	NN 2 layers
LR	1.0000	0.3191	0.0010
DT	0.3191	1.0000	0.0010
NN 2 layers	0.0010	0.0010	1.0000

c)

	KNN	Catch22	LSTM 1 layer
KNN	1.0000	0.0035	0.0035
Catch22	0.0035	1.0000	0.0010
LSTM 1 layer	0.0035	0.0010	1.0000

d)

	Transformer + BiLSTM	Transformer + LSTM	Transformer + GRU
Transformer + BiLSTM	1.0000	0.7260	0.1790
Transformer + LSTM	0.7260	1.0000	0.5471
Transformer + GRU	0.1790	0.5471	1.0000

Table 7. The p-values resulting from the Nemeny test performed on the classification results of the multimodal classifiers (a) and of the best-performing unimodal classifiers together with the multimodal classifier trained on all the data modalities (b). Greyed values denote significant difference at $p \leq 0.05$.

a)

	Time Series	Static Data Text	Static Data Time Series	All
Time Series Text	1.0000	0.0243	0.0010	0.0594
Static Data Text	0.0243	1.0000	0.1285	0.9000
Static Data Time Series	0.0010	0.1285	1.0000	0.0594
All	0.0594	0.9000	0.0594	1.0000

b)

	$\mathcal{D}$	$\mathcal{M}$	$\mathcal{L}$	$\mathcal{T}$	All
$\mathcal{D}$	1.0000	0.0010	0.0010	0.0010	0.0010
$\mathcal{M}$	0.0010	1.0000	0.8440	0.9000	0.8440
$\mathcal{L}$	0.0010	0.8440	1.0000	0.5447	0.2767
$\mathcal{T}$	0.0010	0.9000	0.5447	1.0000	0.9000
All	0.0010	0.8440	0.2767	0.9000	1.0000

instead, shows that the only significant difference between the performance of the unimodal classifiers and of the multimodal classifier trained on all modalities is between the performance of the classifier trained only on the diagnosis data and the multimodal one. Comparing this result with the performances reported in Tables 2 and 4, we see that the classifiers trained only on diagnoses $\mathcal{D}$ obtain significantly worse results than the one trained on all the modalities.

5 Conclusion

In this paper, we propose a workflow for employing multimodal ML models to predict the onset of metastasis in melanoma patients, possibly improving the chances for these patients to get an earlier diagnosis. We show that employing multiple modalities to train an ML model can positively influence the prediction strength, as the proposed multimodal model performs better than some unimodal ones. Future work could experiment with different methods to fuse the various modalities and potentially work on adding an explainable layer or an uncertainty quantification to the multimodal model. Additionally, it would be beneficial to work closely with clinicians to ensure that the results of the ML models are based on sound medical knowledge, increasing the chances of adoption of these models in the clinical workflow. Lastly, conducting further benchmarks can help to investigate the transferability of this workflow to different kinds of cancer and different clinical settings.

Acknowledgements. This work was supported in part by the Digital Futures EXTREMUM project on "Explainable and Ethical Machine Learning for Knowledge Discovery from Medical Data Sources".

This work has received funding from the Horizon Europe Research and Innovation programme under Grant Agreements No 875351 and 101093026.

References

1. Abadi, M., et al.: TensorFlow: large-scale machine learning on heterogeneous systems, software available from tensorflow.org (2015). https://www.tensorflow.org/
2. Bostrom, A., Bagnall, A.: Binary shapelet transform for multiclass time series classification. Transactions on Large-Scale Data-and Knowledge-Centered Systems XXXII: Special Issue on Big Data Analytics and Knowledge Discovery, pp. 24–46 (2017)
3. Braeuer, R.R., et al.: Why is melanoma so metastatic? Pigm. Cell Melanoma Res. **27**(1), 19–36 (2014)
4. Breiman, L.: Random forests. Mach. Learn. **45**, 5–32 (2001)
5. Breiman, L.: Classification and Regression Trees. Routledge (2017)
6. Chawla, N.V., Bowyer, K.W., Hall, L.O., Kegelmeyer, W.P.: Smote: synthetic minority over-sampling technique. J. Artif. Intell. Res. **16**, 321–357 (2002)
7. Cho, K., van Merrienboer, B., Bahdanau, D., Bengio, Y.: On the properties of neural machine translation: encoder-decoder approaches (2014)

8. Dalianis, H., Henriksson, A., Kvist, M., Velupillai, S., Weegar, R.: Health bank-a workbench for data science applications in healthcare. CAiSE Ind. Track **1381**, 1–18 (2015)
9. Dempster, A., Petitjean, F., Webb, G.I.: Rocket: exceptionally fast and accurate time series classification using random convolutional kernels. Data Min. Knowl. Disc. **34**(5), 1454–1495 (2020)
10. Erdei, E., Torres, S.M.: A new understanding in the epidemiology of melanoma. Expert Rev. Anticancer Ther. **10**(11), 1811–1823 (2010)
11. Friedman, J.H.: Greedy function approximation: a gradient boosting machine. Ann. Stat., 1189–1232 (2001)
12. Green, A.C., Pandeya, N., Morton, S., Simonidis, J., Whiteman, D.C.: Early detection of melanoma in specialised primary care practice in Australia. Cancer Epidemiol. **70**, 101872 (2021)
13. Grossarth, S., et al.: Recent advances in melanoma diagnosis and prognosis using machine learning methods. Curr. Oncol. Rep., 1–11 (2023)
14. Hochreiter, S., Schmidhuber, J.: Long short-term memory. Neural Comput. **9**(8), 1735 (1997)
15. Karimkhani, C., et al.: The global burden of melanoma: results from the global burden of disease study 2015. Br. J. Dermatol. **177**(1), 134–140 (2017)
16. Kingma, D.P., Ba, J.: Adam: a method for stochastic optimization. arXiv preprint arXiv:1412.6980 (2014)
17. Leiter, U., Garbe, C.: Epidemiology of melanoma and nonmelanoma skin cancer—the role of sunlight. In: Sunlight, Vitamin D and Skin Cancer, pp. 89–103 (2008)
18. Ma, E.Z., Hoegler, K.M., Zhou, A.E.: Bioinformatic and machine learning applications in melanoma risk assessment and prognosis: a literature review. Genes **12**(11), 1751 (2021)
19. Malke, J.C., et al.: Enhancing case capture, quality, and completeness of primary melanoma pathology records via natural language processing. JCO Clin. Cancer Inf. **3**, 1–11 (2019)
20. Middlehurst, M., Large, J., Bagnall, A.: The canonical interval forest (CIF) classifier for time series classification. In: 2020 IEEE International Conference on Big Data (Big Data), pp. 188–195. IEEE (2020)
21. Nascentes Melo, L.M., et al.: Advancements in melanoma cancer metastasis models. Pigm. Cell Melanoma Res. **36**(2), 206–223 (2023)
22. Nemenyi, P.B.: Distribution-free Multiple Comparisons. Princeton University (1963)
23. Noble, W.S.: What is a support vector machine? Nat. Biotechnol. **24**(12), 1565–1567 (2006)
24. Pedregosa, F., et al.: Scikit-learn: machine learning in Python. J. Mach. Learn. Res. **12**, 2825–2830 (2011)
25. Pottegård, A., et al.: Use of sildenafil or other phosphodiesterase inhibitors and risk of melanoma. Br. J. Cancer **115**(7), 895–900 (2016)
26. Purushotham, S., Meng, C., Che, Z., Liu, Y.: Benchmarking deep learning models on large healthcare datasets. J. Biomed. Inform. **83**, 112–134 (2018)
27. Qiao, Z., Wu, X., Ge, S., Fan, W.: MNN: multimodal attentional neural networks for diagnosis prediction. Extraction **1**, A1 (2019)
28. Robert, C., et al.: Improved overall survival in melanoma with combined dabrafenib and trametinib. N. Engl. J. Med. **372**(1), 30–39 (2015)
29. Rossi, K.R., Echeverria, D., Carroll, A., Luse, T., Rennix, C.: Development and evaluation of Perl-based algorithms to classify neoplasms from pathology records in synoptic report format. JCO Clin. Cancer Inf. **5**, 295–303 (2021)

30. Sadetsky, N., Chuo, C.Y., Davidoff, A.J.: Development and evaluation of a proxy for baseline ECOG PS in advanced non-small cell lung cancer, bladder cancer, and melanoma: an electronic health record study. Pharmacoepidemiol. Drug Saf. **30**(9), 1233–1241 (2021)
31. Schäfer, P., Leser, U.: Multivariate time series classification with weasel muse. arXiv preprint arXiv:1711.11343 (2017)
32. Siegel, R.L., Miller, K.D., Fuchs, H.E., Jemal, A.: Cancer statistics, 2022. CA Cancer J. Clin. **72**(1), 7–33 (2022)
33. Suresh, H., Hunt, N., Johnson, A., Celi, L.A., Szolovits, P., Ghassemi, M.: Clinical intervention prediction and understanding with deep neural networks. In: Machine Learning for Healthcare Conference, pp. 322–337. PMLR (2017)
34. Vakili, T., Lamproudis, A., Henriksson, A., Dalianis, H.: Downstream task performance of bert models pre-trained using automatically de-identified clinical data. In: Proceedings of the 13th Conference on Language Resources and Evaluation (LREC 2022), pp. 4245 – 4252 (2022)
35. WHO: ICD-10 Version:2016 — icd.who.int (2023). https://icd.who.int/browse10/2016/en#/C43
36. Xu, Z., So, D.R., Dai, A.M.: Mufasa: multimodal fusion architecture search for electronic health records. In: Proceedings of the AAAI Conference on Artificial Intelligence, vol. 35, pp. 10532–10540 (2021)
37. Yin, C., Liu, R., Zhang, D., Zhang, P.: Identifying sepsis subphenotypes via time-aware multi-modal auto-encoder. In: Proceedings of the 26th ACM SIGKDD International Conference on Knowledge Discovery and Data Mining, pp. 862–872 (2020)
38. Zhang, X., et al.: Learning robust patient representations from multi-modal electronic health records: a supervised deep learning approach. In: Proceedings of the 2021 SIAM International Conference on Data Mining (SDM), pp. 585–593. SIAM (2021)

Molecular Fingerprints-Based Machine Learning for Metabolic Profiling

Christel Sirocchi[1](✉), Federica Biancucci[2], Muhammad Suffian[1], Riccardo Benedetti[2], Matteo Donati[1], Stefano Ferretti[1], Alessandro Bogliolo[1], Mauro Magnani[2], Michele Menotta[2], and Sara Montagna[1]

[1] Department of Pure and Applied Sciences, University of Urbino, Piazza della Repubblica 13, 61029 Urbino, Italy
c.sirocchi2@campus.uniurb.it
[2] Department of Biomolecular Sciences, University of Urbino, Via Saffi 2, 61029 Urbino, Italy

Abstract. Metabolomics has emerged as a promising field in pharmaceuticals and preventive healthcare, offering practical applications in disease detection and drug testing. However, the analysis and interpretation of complex metabolic datasets remain challenging, with current methods relying heavily on limited and incompletely annotated biological pathways. To overcome these limitations, we propose a novel approach that involves training machine learning classifiers on fingerprint-based encodings of metabolites to predict their response under specific experimental conditions. In this study, we evaluate our approach using a cellular model for the genetic disease Ataxia Telangiectasia (AT). Remarkably, some of our trained models predict affected metabolites with good performance, providing compelling evidence that the structural properties of metabolites hold predictive power over their response to specific conditions. Additionally, we suggest that evaluating the feature importance of the model can greatly assist researchers in identifying clusters of significant molecules and formulating hypotheses about affected pathways. Notably, our analysis of the AT cellular model identifies distinct groups of metabolites, some of which were already known to participate in the affected pathways, thereby validating existing knowledge. Moreover, we discovered metabolites not previously associated with AT, opening up novel opportunities for further exploration.

Keywords: Ataxia telangiectasia · mass spectrometry · metabolic pathways · untargeted metabolomics · machine learning

1 Introduction

Metabolomics is the quantitative study of small molecule substrates and products of cellular metabolism and provides valuable insights into the state of an organism under specific conditions [10]. Metabolomic profiling of diseased and healthy tissues can help uncover the disease mechanisms of action and identify unique metabolic signatures, aiding in identifying potential drug targets [9]. Therefore, metabolomics serves as an indispensable tool in preventive healthcare as well as pharmaceutical research and development, with the potential to enable timely disease detection and facilitation of drug testing [22].

Leading the progress in metabolomics are the remarkable advancements in liquid chromatography and mass spectrometry [4]. These technologies enable the detection of a vast amount of metabolites simultaneously, thereby facilitating the identification of metabolic changes and the characterisation of novel metabolites. However, the analysis and biological interpretation of the generated large volumes of complex data poses several challenges: the vast majority of metabolites remain unidentified and available data analysis methods primarily focus on changes in individual metabolites or rely on the existing knowledge of biological pathways, which is not comprehensive or fully annotated. To unlock the full potential of metabolomics and achieve a thorough comprehension of cellular metabolism, there is a pressing need for novel approaches that extend beyond known pathways and effectively consider all detected metabolites.

Considering that chemically similar compounds are generally found in metabolic proximity, chemical structures can be analysed to identify enriched structural features within a specific experimental condition [1], thereby providing insights into the affected pathways. Chemical structures can be represented using fingerprints, i.e. vectors that capture the presence or absence of structural properties [8], and Machine Learning (ML) methods can then be used to learn metabolic profiling, i.e. determine if a metabolite is affected in a given experimental condition, based on structural features. Relationships between chemical structures and their metabolic response can then be explored in a data-driven manner, opening new avenues for understanding metabolic processes and identifying biomarkers. Moreover, such ML classifiers also offer a tool to predict the level of metabolites of interest that may have been missed in a given mass spectrometry experiment, thus reducing the need for repeating costly experiments.

This study aims to evaluate the relationship between chemical structure and metabolic response by training ML classifiers on metabolomic data. We specifically focus on Ataxia Telangiectasia, a rare neurodegenerative disorder caused by mutations in the Ataxia Telangiectasia Mutated (ATM) gene and known to disrupt multiple metabolic pathways [19]. Within this context, the study builds upon previous preliminary work encoding metabolites with Morgan fingerprints to explore a wider range of structural encodings [25]. The study shows that classifiers trained on molecular fingerprints can predict with good accuracy whether a given metabolite is significantly suppressed in a diseased sample. This finding confirms that the structural properties of metabolites are predictive of their response to a particular condition. Additionally, we propose to compute feature importance to identify the specific chemical groups that contribute to the classification process, shedding light on the biological pathways affected by the disease. Remarkably, feature importance calculated for one of our best-performing model identified metabolites known to participate in affected pathways, thereby validating existing knowledge, as well as groups of metabolites not previously associated with AT, opening up novel opportunities for further investigation.

2 Background and Related Work

A standard metabolomic approach involves comparing samples obtained from a normal state with samples from a perturbed state, which can result from treatment administration or genetic knockout [4]. The most adopted statistical method to perform such comparison is pathway enrichment analysis, which identifies pathways that exhibit a higher degree of overlap with a set of significantly under or over-expressed metabolites than would be expected by chance, thereby aiding in the identification of affected pathways [12]. Nonetheless, employing this approach presents several challenges. It heavily depends on existing knowledge of biological pathways, which is often incomplete and not fully annotated. Furthermore, its application to metabolomic data should be approached with caution, as the method was primarily developed for transcriptomic data and may necessitate further adaptations [27]. Lastly, it is noteworthy that enrichment results can be sensitive to the pathway definitions used by various metabolomic databases [12].

The complex nature of metabolome data, characterised by nonlinear interactions among numerous metabolites, has driven researchers to increasingly harness the power of ML, although its application in metabolomics is in its early stages [7]. ML is employed in identifying specific metabolites associated with diseases or other conditions, streamlining the biomarker discovery process and contributing to disease diagnosis, the classification of diverse metabolic states, and the automatic discovery of latent patterns [18]. The use of ML is well-established in data preprocessing, a critical step for accurate metabolite annotation and quantification that includes baseline correction, noise filtering, peak detection and alignment, data normalisation and scaling, retention time prediction, and handling of missing data [15]. ML also stands at the forefront of multi-omics integration, as it is capable of harmonising data from various sources, including metabolite concentrations, gene expression profiles, and protein-protein interactions [21]. In elucidating active pathways, enrichment analysis remains a standard practice in metabolic pathway exploration, although ML has been used to augment this approach. Overall, while ML is well-suited for analysing metabolomics data and has demonstrated satisfactory predictive capabilities, it is important to acknowledge that the biological knowledge and interpretation gained from these methods are still limited [15].

ML has instead achieved maturity in the field of drug discovery, with refined and optimised ML pipelines specifically tailored to predict functional properties based on the structural characteristics for extensive and diverse biochemical libraries [14]. In this context, ML has not only demonstrated impressive predictive capabilities but has also contributed to a deeper understanding of the mechanisms of target interaction and valuable drug properties [3]. In conjunction with molecular fingerprinting, which provides a concise representation of chemical structures, ML has revolutionised drug discovery and design by enabling the prediction of drug activity and crucial drug properties such as bioavailability, solubility, and toxicity, suggesting whether a molecule warrants consideration as a potential drug [16]. Additionally, the precise prediction of interactions between drugs and their designated targets aids in elucidating a drug's mechanism of action, providing valuable insights into the disease's underlying pathology [26].

Recognising the urgent need for data analysis methods in metabolomics that can comprehensively analyse all accessible data and provide deeper insights into underlying biological mechanisms, this study harnesses the extensive experience of the drug discovery field in ML, as both drug discovery and metabolomics share a common objective and face similar challenges in studying a diverse array of small biological compounds.

3 Data and Methods

The study used fibroblasts WT AG09429 and AT GM00648 as cellular models for the disease and the control, respectively. Metabolite analysis was conducted in triplicate using the UHPLC Vanquish system with an Accucore 150 amide HILIC column. LC was coupled to an Orbitrap Exploris 240 mass spectrometer equipped with an H-ESI source, operating in positive and negative modes and scanning the 80–800 m/z range. Metabolite identification and quantitation were carried out using Compound Discoverer 3.2 (Thermo Fisher Scientific).

Data processing resulted in the detection and identification of 4643 chemical structures. Duplicate molecules were filtered, retaining only the one with the highest peaks and yielding a set of 2821 distinct metabolites with known structures. Among these metabolites, only 184 were successfully assigned a KEGG ID that would allow for enrichment analysis. The ratios between the measured quantities in the diseased and healthy conditions, along with the corresponding adjusted p-values, were calculated for each metabolite.

For ML classification, the chemical structures were encoded using five fingerprinting techniques. MACCS fingerprint encodes the presence of 166 predefined chemical substructures within molecules and is often adopted for pattern recognition and substructure-based similarity assessments [5]. Morgan fingerprint encodes molecular structure based on substructures within a defined radius around each atom and is suitable for both local and global structural feature extraction [24]. Topological torsion fingerprint quantifies topological torsion angles between pairs of atoms and is better apt at revealing subtle structural nuances affecting molecular properties [20]. Atom pair fingerprint quantifies the occurrences of atoms within a molecule and is often used in similarity searching and virtual screening [2]. Daylight fingerprints represent specific fragments present in a molecule and also find widespread use in virtual screening [11]. All fingerprints were generated using the RDKit library [13]. Fingerprints with variable lengths (all except MACCS) were encoded into 1024 bits, accounting for chirality when applicable. Morgan fingerprints were generated with both radius 2 and 3.

The target class is binary and states whether the metabolite is significantly down-regulated, i.e. its adjusted p-value is below 0.05 and the ratio of diseased to healthy is less than 1. The focus on down-regulation stems from the disease's established tendency to inhibit cellular activities, so it is of interest to explore suppressed pathways. The data exhibits class imbalance, with the positive class accounting for only 17% of the data. The metrics to evaluate the models include Accuracy (A), F1-score $(F1)$, Recall for class 1 (R_1), Matthew's Correlation Coefficient (MCC), and Balanced Accuracy (BA). MCC serves as a more informative statistical measure for unbalanced datasets, while $F1$ and R_1 place emphasis on the models' ability to correctly classify instances of class 1. Six ML algorithms, namely Decision Tree (DT), Random Forest (RF), Support Vector Machine (SVM), Logistic Regression (LR), gaussian Naive Bayes (NB), and XGBoost (XGB), were trained on data by applying 5-fold cross-validation with grid search for parameter optimisation.

4 Results and Discussion

The results of the ML models trained on the six different structural encodings are summarised in Table 1. None of the models exhibited exceptional performance, primarily due to the inherent challenges posed by the dataset: (a) the class imbalance, with only 17% of the samples belonging to class 1, (b) the binary nature of all features, which also hindered the application of standard data augmentation techniques such as SMOTE for unbalanced datasets [6], (c) and the relatively large number of features (1024) compared to the sample size (2821), which could not be addressed with data dimensionality reduction techniques such as PCA as we aimed to preserve the original features for interpretability.

The NB, LR, and SVM models exhibit relatively better overall performance when compared to tree-based algorithms. The latter are characterised by comparable accuracy but lower recall, which can be attributed to the binary nature of the fingerprint data. Morgan fingerprint with radius 3 does not exceed that with radius 2 in terms of overall performance, suggesting that substructures up to a diameter of 4 adequately capture key structural features for predicting metabolic responses. The NB model trained on the topological torsion fingerprint achieved an impressive recall score of 0.76, surpassing all other recall metrics across all models and fingerprints by more than 10%. This notable performance could potentially be attributed to the fact that a large number of metabolites are isomers, which topological torsion can resolve more effectively than conventional fingerprints. However, further investigation is required to elucidate this result. With this exception, different fingerprints exhibit similar performances overall. MACCS fingerprint records higher recall on average, potentially attributed to its lower number of features. Overall, the trained models demonstrate satisfactory performance, providing evidence that the structural properties of metabolites hold predictive power over their response to particular conditions.

To gain insights into the chemical substructures contributing to the classification, we computed feature importance for the NB model trained on the Morgan fingerprint of radius 2 using permutation importance. Figure 1 presents the most important features alongside their corresponding chemical structures. Notably, the influential bits represent chemical configurations contained in nucleic bases (bits 836 and 71), phosphate groups (bits 363 and 795), and amino acids (bits 86, 600, and 750). Upon closer examination of the metabolites in the dataset where these features are present, we observed the presence of various nucleotide-based molecules having the role of coenzymes and signalling molecules, including Acetyl-CoA, Coenzyme A, NAD+, FAD, AMP, and GMP. Notably, NAD+ has been previously associated with the disease as a result of mitochondria dysfunctions, and its identification supports existing knowledge [23]. Interestingly, we also identified a second group of molecules corresponding to dipeptides and other derivatives of protein degradation that have not been previously linked to the disease, emerging as a potential focal point for further investigation.

The proposed approach offers various opportunities for improving model performance. Expanding the metabolic dataset by integrating measurements from different chromatographic columns, such as HILIC and C18, would effectively double the dataset size and enhance its diversity. The features can be reduced by calculating their correlation with the label vector and removing coefficients below a certain threshold. Alternatively, more compact molecular fingerprints could be explored. In addition, unbalanced data can be mitigated by using a less stringent p-value threshold to determine if a metabolite is significantly down-regulated. Lastly, it is important to consider that classification tasks are intrinsically more challenging for complex conditions with multiple affected pathways and a diverse range of affected metabolites like in AT.

Table 1. Performance metrics computed for six ML classifiers trained on 6 fingerprint encodings of metabolomic data

model	Morgan radius 2					Morgan radius 3					DayLight				
	A	F1	R_1	MCC	BA	A	F1	R_1	MCC	BA	A	F1	R_1	MCC	BA
DT	0.77	0.60	0.34	0.20	0.60	0.75	0.59	0.34	0.17	0.59	0.66	0.57	0.57	0.19	0.62
NB	0.68	0.59	0.56	0.22	0.63	0.69	0.59	0.58	0.24	0.65	0.68	0.55	0.39	0.12	0.57
SVM	0.75	0.63	0.51	0.27	0.66	0.77	0.64	0.49	0.29	0.66	0.69	0.59	0.53	0.21	0.63
LR	0.70	0.60	0.57	0.24	0.65	0.72	0.61	0.53	0.24	0.64	0.67	0.57	0.55	0.19	0.62
RF	0.77	0.63	0.42	0.25	0.63	0.79	0.62	0.36	0.24	0.62	0.79	0.64	0.42	0.29	0.65
XGB	0.77	0.62	0.41	0.25	0.63	0.77	0.63	0.42	0.26	0.63	0.78	0.62	0.39	0.24	0.62
model	Atom Pair					Topological Torsion					MACCS				
	A	F1	R_1	MCC	BA	A	F1	R_1	MCC	BA	A	F1	R_1	MCC	BA
DT	0.70	0.57	0.41	0.15	0.59	0.51	0.46	0.55	0.04	0.53	0.60	0.53	0.61	0.16	0.60
NB	0.67	0.58	0.59	0.22	0.64	0.56	0.52	0.76	0.21	0.64	0.63	0.54	0.52	0.14	0.59
SVM	0.69	0.60	0.60	0.25	0.66	0.65	0.56	0.56	0.18	0.62	0.67	0.59	0.65	0.25	0.66
LR	0.70	0.60	0.57	0.25	0.65	0.65	0.57	0.57	0.19	0.62	0.67	0.59	0.63	0.24	0.65
RF	0.70	0.59	0.54	0.22	0.64	0.72	0.58	0.41	0.18	0.60	0.68	0.58	0.57	0.22	0.64
XGB	0.80	0.65	0.42	0.30	0.65	0.70	0.56	0.39	0.13	0.58	0.76	0.64	0.48	0.28	0.65

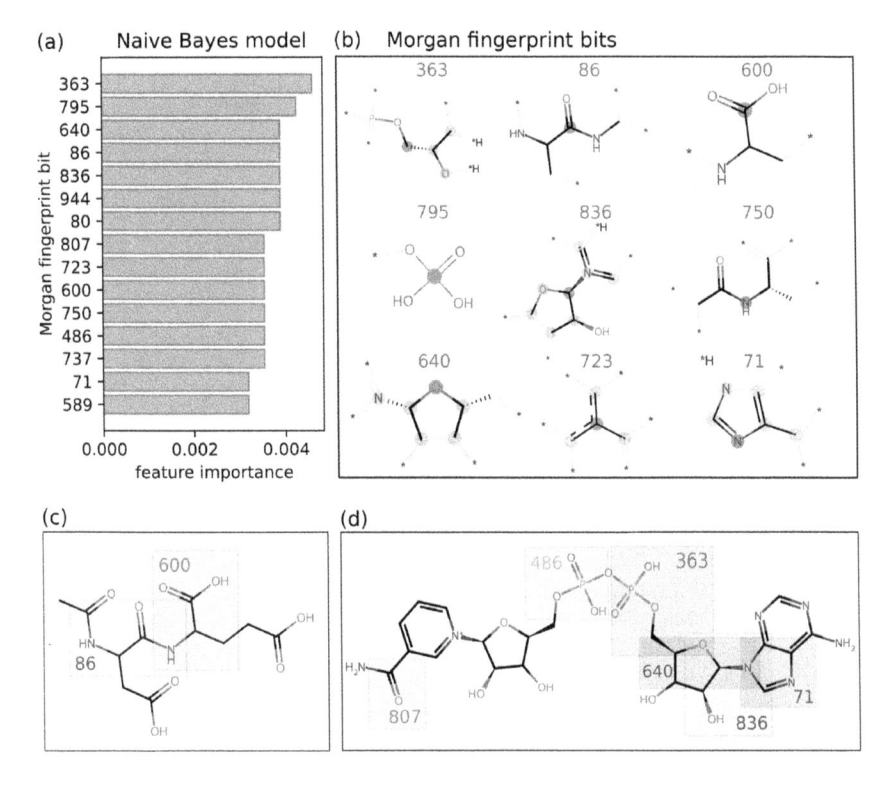

Fig. 1. (a) The 15 fingerprint bits with the highest feature importance for the NB model trained on Morgan fingerprint of radius 2 and (b) the corresponding substructures mapped (c) on a dipeptide and (d) on the coenzyme NAD+.

5 Conclusions and Future Work

This study uses ML trained on a fingerprint-based encoding of metabolites to identify chemical configurations associated with a disease, providing valuable insights into affected pathways. The main advantage of this approach is that it considers all detected metabolites and does not rely on extensive knowledge of metabolic pathways, which is particularly scarce for certain species. Feature importance was used to identify such structures, although more sophisticated eXplainable Artificial Intelligence (XAI) strategies [17] can be deployed for model interpretation to provide deeper insights. The proposed approach can also be applied to uncover the mechanisms of action of novel treatments. For instance, in the case of Ataxia Telangiectasia, the administration of medexamethasone was found to alleviate symptoms, but its action remains unclear. Future work will focus on training classifiers on metabolic data from treatment samples and employing XAI techniques to identify relevant chemical configurations that can shed light on the pathways restored by the treatment administration [23]

Acknowledgements. This work has been funded by the European Union - NextGenerationEU under the Italian Ministry of University and Research (MUR) National Innovation Ecosystem grant ECS00000041 - VITALITY - CUP H33C22000430006.

References

1. Barupal, D.K., Haldiya, P.K., Wohlgemuth, G., Kind, T., Kothari, S.L., Pinkerton, K.E., Fiehn, O.: Metamapp: mapping and visualizing metabolomic data by integrating information from biochemical pathways and chemical and mass spectral similarity. BMC Bioinform. **13**(1), 1–15 (2012)
2. Carhart, R.E., Smith, D.H., Venkataraghavan, R.: Atom pairs as molecular features in structure-activity studies: definition and applications. J. Chem. Inf. Comput. Sci. **25**(2), 64–73 (1985)
3. Carracedo-Reboredo, P., Liñares-Blanco, J., Rodríguez-Fernández, N., Cedrón, F., Novoa, F.J., Carballal, A., Maojo, V., Pazos, A., Fernandez-Lozano, C.: A review on machine learning approaches and trends in drug discovery. Comput. Struct. Biotechnol. J. **19**, 4538–4558 (2021)
4. Drexler, D.M., Reily, M.D., Shipkova, P.A.: Advances in mass spectrometry applied to pharmaceutical metabolomics. Anal. Bioanal. Chem. **399**, 2645–2653 (2011)
5. Durant, J.L., Leland, B.A., Henry, D.R., Nourse, J.G.: Reoptimization of mdl keys for use in drug discovery. J. Chem. Inf. Comput. Sci. **42**(6), 1273–1280 (2002)
6. Fernández, A., Garcia, S., Herrera, F., Chawla, N.V.: Smote for learning from imbalanced data: progress and challenges, marking the 15-year anniversary. J. Artif. Intell. Res. **61**, 863–905 (2018)
7. Galal, A., Talal, M., Moustafa, A.: Applications of machine learning in metabolomics: disease modeling and classification. Front. Genet. **13**, 1017340 (2022)
8. Glen, R.C., Bender, A., Arnby, C.H., Carlsson, L., Boyer, S., Smith, J.: Circular fingerprints: flexible molecular descriptors with applications from physical chemistry to adme. IDrugs **9**(3), 199 (2006)
9. Harrigan, G.G., Goodacre, R.: Metabolic profiling: its role in biomarker discovery and gene function analysis: its role in biomarker discovery and gene function analysis. Springer Science & Business Media (2003)
10. Holmes, E., Wilson, I.D., Nicholson, J.K.: Metabolic phenotyping in health and disease. Cell **134**(5), 714–717 (2008)
11. James, C.A.: Daylight theory manual (2004). http://www.daylight.com/dayhtml/doc/theory/theory.toc.html
12. Karp, P.D., Midford, P.E., Caspi, R., Khodursky, A.: Pathway size matters: the influence of pathway granularity on over-representation (enrichment analysis) statistics. BMC Genomics **22**, 1–11 (2021)
13. Landrum, G.: Rdkit documentation. Release **1**(1–79), 4 (2013)
14. Lavecchia, A.: Machine-learning approaches in drug discovery: methods and applications. Drug Discovery Today **20**(3), 318–331 (2015)
15. Liebal, U.W., Phan, A.N., Sudhakar, M., Raman, K., Blank, L.M.: Machine learning applications for mass spectrometry-based metabolomics. Metabolites **10**(6), 243 (2020)
16. Lo, Y.C., Rensi, S.E., Torng, W., Altman, R.B.: Machine learning in chemoinformatics and drug discovery. Drug Discovery Today **23**(8), 1538–1546 (2018)
17. Lundberg, S.M., Lee, S.I.: A unified approach to interpreting model predictions. Advances in neural information processing systems **30** (2017)

18. Mendez, K.M., Reinke, S.N., Broadhurst, D.I.: A comparative evaluation of the generalised predictive ability of eight machine learning algorithms across ten clinical metabolomics data sets for binary classification. Metabolomics **15**, 1–15 (2019)
19. Menotta, M., Biagiotti, S., Spapperi, C., Orazi, S., Rossi, L., Chessa, L., Leuzzi, V., D'Agnano, D., Soresina, A., Micheli, R., et al.: Atm splicing variants as biomarkers for low dose dexamethasone treatment of at. Orphanet J. Rare Dis. **12**(1), 1–7 (2017)
20. Nilakantan, R., Bauman, N., Dixon, J.S., Venkataraghavan, R.: Topological torsion: a new molecular descriptor for sar applications. comparison with other descriptors. J. Chem. Inf. Comput. Sci. **27**(2), 82–85 (1987)
21. Noor, E., Cherkaoui, S., Sauer, U.: Biological insights through omics data integration. Current Opinion Syst. Biology **15**, 39–47 (2019)
22. Puchades-Carrasco, L., Pineda-Lucena, A.: Metabolomics in pharmaceutical research and development. Curr. Opin. Biotechnol. **35**, 73–77 (2015)
23. Ricci, A., Biancucci, F., Morganti, G., Magnani, M., Menotta, M.: New human atm variants are able to regain atm functions in ataxia telangiectasia disease. Cell. Mol. Life Sci. **79**(12), 601 (2022)
24. Rogers, D., Hahn, M.: Extended-connectivity fingerprints. J. Chem. Inf. Model. **50**(5), 742–754 (2010)
25. Sirocchi, C., et al.: Machine learning-enabled prediction of metabolite response in genetic disorders. In: CEUR Workshop Proceedings, vol. 3578, pp. 1–9 (2023)
26. Staszak, M., Staszak, K., Wieszczycka, K., Bajek, A., Roszkowski, K., Tylkowski, B.: Machine learning in drug design: Use of artificial intelligence to explore the chemical structure-biological activity relationship. Wiley Interdisciplinary Reviews: Computational Molecular Science **12**(2), e1568 (2022)
27. Wieder, C., Frainay, C., Poupin, N., Rodríguez-Mier, P., Vinson, F., Cooke, J., Lai, R.P., Bundy, J.G., Jourdan, F., Ebbels, T.: Pathway analysis in metabolomics: recommendations for the use of over-representation analysis. PLoS Comput. Biol. **17**(9), e1009105 (2021)

Simplification, Compression, Efficiency and Frugality for Artificial Intelligence

Neural Networks Comprising Sequentially Semiseparable Matrices with One Dimensional State Variable are Universal Approximators

Matthias Kissel[✉] and Klaus Diepold

Technical University of Munich, Arcisstr. 21, 80333 Munich, Germany
matthias.kissel@tum.de

Abstract. One approach towards handling the large resource requirements of modern neural networks is to use structured weight matrices. In this paper, we analyze the approximation capabilities of such neural networks. In particular, we investigate sequentially semiseparable (SSS) matrices with one dimensional state variable. This class of matrices is quite limited in their expressiveness, but it facilitates an efficient matrix-vector multiplication algorithm. Our contribution is to prove that neural networks comprising SSS matrices with one dimensional state variable are universal approximators. With our proof, we show that the same approximation capabilities which have been shown for weight matrices of low displacement rank also apply for SSS weight matrices.

Keywords: Matrix Structures · Efficient Inference · Sequentially Semiseparable Matrices

1 Motivation

Modern neural networks achieve remarkable results in several domains. This is based, among other things, on the fact that networks are becoming ever larger and deeper. State-of-the-art networks often comprise millions of parameters [15, 26], requiring large computational resources for training and inference. Some applications even require specialized hardware for using these networks [22].

One approach to deal with this increasing resource consumption is to use structured weight matrices.

Definition 1. *A matrix $A \in \mathbb{R}^{m \times n}$ is called structured, if it is defined by less than $\mathcal{O}(mn)$ parameters.*

In contrast to sparse matrices, structured matrices don't need to contain zeros. Instead, a structured matrix can be dense and is defined by the relationship of few parameters. Besides the apparent memory savings, there are efficient algorithms for some classes of structured matrices that can save computational resources for performing various linear algebra operations.

There are many types of structured matrices. Two prominent examples are hierarchical matrices [2] and matrices of low displacement rank [20]. In this paper, we focus on another structure class that occurs when describing time-varying systems using state-space methods [9]: SSS matrices. The number of parameters defining an SSS matrix is inter alia determined by the dimension of the state variable of the described system. Every matrix can be represented as SSS matrix if the state dimension is large enough. However, matrices defined with low dimensional state variable are of particular interest. For these matrices, there exist an efficient matrix-vector multiplication algorithm [3,13]. This means that memory as well as computational resources can be saved when the matrix is represented as SSS matrix. Matrix-vector multiplications play a major role for the computational cost required for inference with neural networks [19,28]. Therefore, using SSS matrices in neural networks can significantly reduce the computational demands of neural networks.

Typically, it is not evident which matrix structure type is best suited for a given problem. This is, because there is not one single structure which outperforms all others when being used in neural networks. Moreover, there is a trade-off between reduction in parameters, inference time, and prediction accuracy of the resulting model. Therefore, it is important to have a repertoire of possible matrix structures, which can be used in neural networks. By that, different structure types can be tested for the problem at hand. By focusing on SSS matrices in this paper, we give the theoretical foundation needed to add them to the repertoire of matrix structures, which can be used in neural networks.

Many theoretical insights in the field of neural networks build on the universal approximation theorem, proven by Cybenko in [5]. His theorem states that neural networks with sigmoidal activation function can be used to approximate any function to a desired accuracy. In [29], Zhao et al. show that this theorem also holds for neural networks comprising weight matrices of low displacement rank. Based on these results, our main contribution is to prove that Cybenko's [5] universal approximation theorem also holds for neural networks comprising SSS matrices with one dimensional state variable. By that, we show that the same approximation capabilities, which have been shown for neural networks comprising matrices of low displacement rank, also hold for neural networks comprising SSS matrices.

The rest of this paper is organized as follows. We first give an overview over previous work using structured matrices in neural networks. Subsequently, we define sequentially semiseparable matrices and explain how they can be used in neural networks. Our main contribution is given in Sect. 4, in which we show that the universal approximation holds for neural networks comprising sequentially semiseparable matrices with one dimensional state variable. Finally, we summarize our findings and draw a conclusion.

2 Literature Review

The research about semiseparable matrices dates back until 1937 [12,25]. This class of matrices has some interesting properties, and there exist efficient algorithms for several applications. For example, the inverse of a generator representable plus diagonal semiseparable matrix can be computed in an efficient way. Vandebril et al. [25] give a comprehensive overview over the results achieved with semiseparable matrices.

A special member of the class of semiseparable matrices are SSS matrices [9], which occur when describing time-varying systems using a state-space representation. We define SSS matrices formally in Sect. 3. Depending on the properties of the SSS matrix (which refers foremost to the dimension of the state variable), SSS matrices can be efficiently multiplied with vectors. This makes them particularly interesting for use in neural networks, since a large part of the computational costs for the use of neural networks is spent on matrix-vector multiplications. This is why SSS matrices have been used for example in the domain of neural drone control [18], or for approximating large matrices arising in deep convolutional networks [16]. Moreover, Kissel et al. [17] proposed the *backpropagation through states* algorithm, which can be used for training neural networks with SSS weight matrices.

Besides SSS matrices, there are many other types of structured matrices. Some of them have been used in neural networks. For example, Fan et al. [10,11] used hierarchical weight matrices in neural networks, resulting in a multiscale structure. Especially for products of sparse matrices, there have been promising results recently. A product of sparse matrices is in general not sparse. It has been shown that many dense matrices can be well approximated with products of sparse matrices [6–8], showing promising results when applied to neural networks [1,7,27].

The most popular structure class used in neural networks are matrices of low displacement rank. This class includes well known matrix types like Toeplitz, Hankel, Vandermonde, and Cauchy matrices. Even convolutional neural networks can be described as standard neural network with weight matrices of low displacement rank (using sparse Toeplitz matrices). Sindhwani et al. [23] proposed to use Toeplitz-like matrices, which can be trained end-to-end with the rest of the network. Moreover, Thomas et al. [24] trained displacements as well as operator matrices end-to-end as part of the neural network training procedure. Zhao et al. [29] contributed theoretical results regarding neural networks with weight matrices of low displacement rank. They showed that these networks are universal approximators.

The topics of this paper also touch the concepts of structured sparsity learning [14,21]. However, we do not focus on sparse matrices. The structured matrices we consider are usually dense and thus do not contain zeros. This distinguishes our approach from structured sparsity learning, which aims to identify zero entries in a matrix that have some structural relationship to each other. However, it is possible that the concepts used to describe the structure in both approaches do overlap with each other.

3 Sequentially Semiseparable Matrices

In the following, we define SSS matrices based on the matrix-vector product $y = Tu$, where $y \in \mathbb{R}^m$ is the resulting vector, $T \in \mathbb{R}^{m \times n}$ is the SSS matrix, and $u \in \mathbb{R}^n$ is the input vector. Analogous to the results from Zhao et al. [29], we consider square matrices in this paper (i.e. $m = n$). This is, however, not a general limitation for SSS matrices, since they are defined for arbitrary matrix shapes.

SSS matrices occur when describing time-varying systems using a state-space representation. In time-varying system theory, T is called the Toeplitz operator, u are the system inputs, and y are the system outputs. The Toeplitz operator describes the time-varying input-output behavior of the system. That is, for each timestep $k = 1, \ldots, p$, the outputs of this timestep y_k for a causal system are computed based on the inputs u_k and the state of the system at this timestep x_k:

$$y_k = C_k x_k + D_k u_k \tag{1}$$

with

$$x_{k+1} = A_k x_k + B_k u_k. \tag{2}$$

A_k, B_k, C_k and D_k for $k = 1, \ldots, p$ are matrices describing the system behavior. The Toeplitz operator corresponding to the system has a particular structure

$$T = \begin{bmatrix} D_1 & 0 & 0 & 0 \\ C_2 B_1 & D_2 & 0 & 0 \\ C_3 A_2 B_1 & C_3 B_2 & D_3 & 0 \\ C_4 A_3 A_2 B_1 & C_4 A_3 B_2 & C_4 B_3 & D_4 \end{bmatrix}. \tag{3}$$

Since we do not investigate physical systems, we call the number of timesteps p computation stages throughout the paper.

In the following, we restrict the dimensions of inputs, outputs and the state variable to one at each computation stage. This limits the expressiveness of the class considerably. As mentioned before, SSS matrices with arbitrary state variable dimension can represent any matrix. With the limitation to one dimensional input, output, and state variable, this expressiveness is lost, and some matrices can no longer be represented. Moreover, we restrict the SSS matrix to be a lower diagonal matrix (which corresponds to a causal Toeplitz operator). This further restricts the expressiveness of the structure class. However, since the class of lower diagonal SSS matrices is contained in the general class of SSS matrices, a proof for lower diagonal SSS matrices directly also applies to general SSS matrices.

With the aforementioned limitations, we can define SSS matrices.

Definition 2. *A lower triangular SSS matrix $T \in \mathbb{R}^{n \times n}$ with one dimensional input, output and state variable at each computation stage, is defined as*

$$T = D + C(I - ZA)^{-1} ZB, \tag{4}$$

where D, C, A, and B are diagonal matrices

$$A = \begin{pmatrix} a_1 & & & 0 \\ & a_2 & & \\ & & \ddots & \\ 0 & & & a_p \end{pmatrix} \quad (5)$$

(other matrices respectively), and Z is a down-shift matrix defined as

$$Z = \begin{pmatrix} 0 & & & 0 \\ 1 & \ddots & & \\ & \ddots & \ddots & 0 \\ 0 & & 1 & 0 \end{pmatrix}. \quad (6)$$

Note that in the general case, the A, B, C and D matrices are block diagonal matrices. However, since we consider the case that the inputs, outputs and states are one dimensional, the entries on the diagonals of the A, B, C and D matrices result as scalars.

Matrices of the form given in Definition 2 can efficiently be multiplied with a vector using the representation given in Eq. 1 and 2. Here, the index k on matrices refers to the kth entry on the diagonal of the matrix. It can be seen that in our case with one dimensional state variable, the matrix-vector multiplication can be computed with $\mathcal{O}(n)$ operations, compared to $\mathcal{O}(n^2)$ operations required by the standard algorithm [3,13].

We are interested in using matrices as defined in Definition 2 in neural networks. For that, analogously to the approach from Zhao et al. [29], we stack r SSS matrices, and use the resulting matrix as weight matrix in a single layer feed-forward neural network with sigmoidal activation function. The resulting network function is given by

$$N(u) = \sum_{j=1}^{rn} \alpha_j \sigma(w_j^T u + \theta_j). \quad (7)$$

Here, α_j are weighing factors for the outputs at each neuron j and θ_j is the bias of the neuron. The overall weight matrix is defined as

$$W = \begin{bmatrix} T_1 \ldots T_r \end{bmatrix}, \quad (8)$$

where $T_1, \ldots T_r$ are SSS matrices as defined in Definition 2 and w_j denotes the jth column of W.

4 Universal Approximation Theorem

Cybenko [5] proved that single hidden layered neural networks with sigmoidal activation functions are universal approximators. In his proof, he showed that assuming that the set of functions S represented by a neural network is not dense in the space of continuous functions $C(I_n)$ on the n-dimensional unit cube I_n ($[0,1]^n$) results in a contradiction. For that, he used the Hahn-Banach theorem to show that following his assumption that S is not dense in $C(I_n)$, there must be a linear functional L on $C(I_n)$ with the property that $L \neq 0$, but $L(R) = L(S) = 0$ (with R being the closure of S). This then leads to the contradiction, since the discriminatory function $\sigma(y^T x + \theta)$ is in R for all y and θ. Therefore, the subspace S must be dense in $C(I_n)$.

In the following, we show that the universal approximation theorem formulated by Cybenko also applies to networks comprising SSS matrices with one dimensional state variable, as defined in Eq. 7. For that, we show that the two requirements on which the universal approximation theorem for standard feedforward neural networks is based, do also apply for our networks: First, we show that the set of functions of the form $N(u)$ defined in Eq. 7 (P in the following) is a linear subspace of $C(I_n)$. Second, we show that all functions of the form $\sigma(y^T x + \theta)$ are contained in P. Our approach is based on Cybenko's work, and also follows the approach from Zhao et al. [29], who showed that neural networks with weight matrices of low displacement rank are universal approximators.

Lemma 1. *The set of functions P of the form $N(u)$ as defined in Eq. 7 is a linear subspace of $C(I_n)$.*

Proof. We look at the function $N(u)$ defined in Eq. 7. By setting

$$\tilde{\alpha}_j = \beta \alpha_j \quad \forall j, \tag{9}$$

we have

$$\forall \beta \in \mathbb{R} : \forall N(u) \in P : \exists \tilde{N}(u) \in P : \\ \tilde{N}(u) = \beta N(u). \tag{10}$$

With

$$\alpha^{(V)} = \begin{bmatrix} \alpha^{(H)} & \alpha^{(G)} \end{bmatrix} \tag{11}$$

(where $\alpha^{(V)}$ denotes the weighing factors of $V(u)$, other variables respectively),

$$W^{(V)} = \begin{bmatrix} W^{(H)} & W^{(G)} \end{bmatrix}, \tag{12}$$

and

$$\theta^{(V)} = \begin{bmatrix} \theta^{(H)} & \theta^{(G)} \end{bmatrix}, \tag{13}$$

we have

$$\forall H(u), G(u) \in P : \\ V(u) = H(u) + G(u) \in P. \tag{14}$$

Combining the results in Eq. 10 and Eq. 14, it directly follows that

$$\forall H(u), G(u) \in P, \kappa, \gamma \in \mathbb{R} : \\ \kappa H(u) + \gamma G(u) \in P. \tag{15}$$

We now show that the *representation property* [29] is fulfilled by structured matrices as defined in Definition 2. The representation property is fulfilled, if for any vector $v \in \mathbb{R}^n$, there exist a matrix T such that $v \in \mathbb{R}^n$ is a column of T.

Lemma 2. (Representation Property of SSS matrices with one dimensional state variable).

$$\forall y \in \mathbb{R}^n : \exists T = \begin{bmatrix} t_1 \ldots t_n \end{bmatrix} \tag{16}$$

with T of the form as defined in Definition 2 and $t_1 = y$.

Proof. We need to show that it is always possible to have

$$T = D + C(I - ZA)^{-1}ZB = \begin{bmatrix} y * \ldots * \end{bmatrix} \tag{17}$$

Since the state variable is one dimensional, A, B, C and D are diagonal matrices. In the following, we refer to the ith column of a matrix A by $A^{(i)}$. ZB is a diagonal matrix shifted down by one entry, in particular

$$ZB^{(1)} = \begin{bmatrix} 0 & b_1 & 0 & \ldots & 0 \end{bmatrix}^T. \tag{18}$$

Therefore we have

$$C(I - ZA)^{-1}ZB^{(1)} = b_1(C(I - ZA)^{-1})^{(2)}. \tag{19}$$

This can be seen by looking at the product $G(ZB^{(1)})$ with $G = C(I - ZA)^{-1}$

$$\begin{pmatrix} G_{1,1} & G_{1,2} & \ldots & G_{1,n} \\ G_{2,1} & G_{2,2} & \ldots & G_{2,n} \\ \vdots & \vdots & \vdots & \vdots \\ G_{n,1} & G_{n,2} & \ldots & G_{n,n} \end{pmatrix} \begin{pmatrix} 0 \\ b_1 \\ 0 \\ \vdots \\ 0 \end{pmatrix}. \tag{20}$$

As $(I - ZA)$ is a bidiagonal matrix, the entries of $(I - ZA)^{-1}$ can be computed using the Neumann expansion [9], and are given by [4]

$$((I - ZA)^{-1})_{i,j} = \begin{cases} 0 & \text{for } i < j \\ 1 & \text{for } i = j, \\ \prod_{f=j}^{i-1} a_f & \text{for } i > j \end{cases} \tag{21}$$

where a_f denotes the fth element on the diagonal of A. Note that we switched the indices in the original formula from Chatterjee as we are considering a *lower-triangular* bidiagonal matrix - using the fact that

$$(I - ZA)^{-1} = (((I - ZA)^T)^{-1})^T. \tag{22}$$

Now it can be seen that

$$D^{(1)} + b_1(C(I-ZA)^{-1})^{(2)} = \begin{pmatrix} d_1 \\ b_1 c_2 \\ b_1 c_3 \prod_{f=2}^{2} a_f \\ \vdots \\ b_1 c_n \prod_{f=2}^{n-1} a_f \end{pmatrix} \quad (23)$$

Therefore, if we set $a_k = b_k = 1$ for all k, $d_1 = y_1$, $d_k = 0$ for all $k > 1$ and $c_k = y_k$ for all k we have $t_1 = y$.

Based on Lemma 2, we can now show that any function of the form

$$f(x) = \sigma(y^T x + \theta) \quad (24)$$

can be represented with a neural network as defined in Eq. 7, where the number of SSS matrices in the network is limited to one (i.e. $r = 1$).

Corollary 1.
$$\forall y, \theta : \exists T, \tilde{\theta}, \alpha :$$
$$\sum_{j=1}^{n} \alpha_j \sigma(t_j^T x + \tilde{\theta}_j) = \sigma(y^T x + \theta), \quad (25)$$

with $T = \begin{bmatrix} t_1 \ldots t_n \end{bmatrix}$ and T is of the form defined in Definition 2.

Proof. According to Lemma 2, we can chose T such that $t_1 = y$. Moreover, we set $\alpha_1 = 1$ and $\alpha_j = 0$ for all $j \neq 1$ as well as $\tilde{\theta}_j = \theta$ for all j. This results in

$$\sum_{j=1}^{n} \alpha_j \sigma(t_j^T x + \tilde{\theta}_j) = \sigma(t_1^T x + \theta) \quad (26)$$
$$= \sigma(y^T x + \theta).$$

Using Lemma 1 and Corollary 1, it directly follows that Cybenko's theorem [5] also applies for neural networks as defined in Eq. 7.

Theorem 1. (Universal Approximation Theorem for Neural Networks comprising SSS matrices with one dimensional state variable). *Let σ be any continuous discriminatory function. Then functions of the form given in Eq. 7 are dense in $C(I_n)$. In other words, given any $f \in C(I_n)$ and $\epsilon > 0$, there is a function $N(u) \in P$ for which*

$$|N(u) - f(u)| < \epsilon \quad \forall u \in I_n. \quad (27)$$

Proof. Based on Cybenko's universal approximation theorem, this follows directly from Lemma 1 and corollary 1.

5 Discussion

It is evident that neural networks with *arbitrary* SSS weight matrices are universal approximators. This is, because all matrices can be represented exactly as SSS matrices, if the state dimension is large enough. In contrast, it is not straightforward that neural networks comprising SSS matrices with one dimensional state variable are universal approximators. Our results show that neural networks with SSS weight matrices have the same approximation capabilities as neural networks with weight matrices of low displacement rank [29].

However, these results do not directly lead to neural networks with fewer parameters in practice. This is due to two reasons. First, the proof is based on the fact, that there can be multiple SSS matrices in the neural network. This is in line with previous results for matrices of low displacement rank and the standard universal approximation theorem. For practical applications, however, we are more interested in finding structured weight matrices, which perform *sufficiently well* (in contrast to perfectly represent a desired mapping). There is a trade-off between matrices that solve the problem more accurately and matrices for which there are more efficient algorithms for computing the matrix-vector product.

The second reason is that although we proved that neural networks comprising SSS matrices with one dimensional state variable are universal approximators, we did not present an algorithm to find such networks. The recently introduced *backpropagation through states* algorithm [17] can be used to train neural networks with SSS weight matrices. However, it does not provide any guarantees regarding the approximation error. Thus, an algorithm that finds the best structured neural network with guarantees is still lacking.

Nevertheless, it is an important result that neural networks with one dimensional state variable are universal approximators. This provides a framework for finding practically applicable algorithms and structures that will lead to more efficient neural networks. Finding these algorithms is still an ongoing research topic.

6 Conclusion

We showed that the universal approximation theorem holds for neural networks comprising SSS weight matrices with one dimensional state variable. Thus, we have shown that SSS matrices in neural networks have the same approximation capabilities as matrices of low displacement rank. Our results prove that any function can be learned by a neural network with SSS matrices. However, our result does not include an upper bound on the number of parameters needed in practice to accurately approximate a function to a desired degree.

References

1. Ailon, N., Leibovitch, O., Nair, V.: Sparse linear networks with a fixed butterfly structure: theory and practice. In: Proceedings of the Thirty-Seventh Conference on Uncertainty in Artificial Intelligence, vol. 161, pp. 1174–1184. PMLR (2021)
2. Börm, S., Grasedyck, L., Hackbusch, W.: Hierarchical matrices. Lecture Notes **21**, 2003 (2003)
3. Chandrasekaran, S., et al.: Some fast algorithms for sequentially semiseparable representations. SIAM J. Matrix Anal. Appl. **27**(2), 341–364 (2005)
4. Chatterjee, G.: Negative integral powers of a bidiagonal matrix. Math. Comput. **28**(127), 713–714 (1974)
5. Cybenko, G.: Approximation by superpositions of a sigmoidal function. Math. Control Sig. Syst. **2**(4), 303–314 (1989)
6. Dao, T., Gu, A., Eichhorn, M., Rudra, A., Ré, C.: Learning fast algorithms for linear transforms using butterfly factorizations. In: International Conference on Machine Learning, pp. 1517–1527. PMLR (2019)
7. Dao, T., et al.: Kaleidoscope: an efficient, learnable representation for all structured linear maps. In: International Conference on Learning Representations (2020)
8. De Sa, C., Cu, A., Puttagunta, R., Ré, C., Rudra, A.: A two-pronged progress in structured dense matrix vector multiplication. In: Proceedings of the Twenty-Ninth Annual ACM-SIAM Symposium on Discrete Algorithms, pp. 1060–1079. SIAM (2018)
9. Dewilde, P., Van der Veen, A.J.: Time-varying systems and computations. Springer Science & Business Media (1998)
10. Fan, Y., Feliu-Faba, J., Lin, L., Ying, L., Zepeda-Núnez, L.: A multiscale neural network based on hierarchical nested bases. Res. Math. Sci. **6**(2), 1–28 (2019)
11. Fan, Y., Lin, L., Ying, L., Zepeda-Núnez, L.: A multiscale neural network based on hierarchical matrices. Multiscale Modeling Simul. **17**(4), 1189–1213 (2019)
12. Gantmakher, F., Krein, M.: Sur les matrices completement non négatives et oscillatoires. Compos. Math. **4**, 445–476 (1937)
13. Golub, G.H., Van Loan, C.F.: Matrix computations. JHU press (2013)
14. Gui, J., Sun, Z., Ji, S., Tao, D., Tan, T.: Feature selection based on structured sparsity: a comprehensive study. IEEE Trans. Neural Networks Learn. Syst. **28**(7), 1490–1507 (2016)
15. He, K., Zhang, X., Ren, S., Sun, J.: Deep residual learning for image recognition. In: Proceedings of the IEEE Conference on Computer Vision and Pattern Recognition, pp. 770–778 (2016)
16. Kissel, M., Diepold, K.: Deep convolutional neural networks with sequentially semiseparable weight matrices. In: ESANN 2022 Proceedings (2022)
17. Kissel, M., Gottwald, M., Gjeroska, B., Paukner, P., Diepold, K.: Backpropagation through states: training neural networks with sequentially semiseparable weight matrices. In: Proceedings of the 21st EPIA Conference on Artificial Intelligence (2022)
18. Kissel, M., Gronauer, S., Korte, M., Sacchetto, L., Diepold, K.: Exploiting structures in weight matrices for efficient real-time drone control with neural networks. In: Proceedings of the 21st EPIA Conference on Artificial Intelligence (2022)
19. Moczulski, M., Denil, M., Appleyard, J., de Freitas, N.: Acdc: a structured efficient linear layer. arXiv preprint arXiv:1511.05946 (2015)
20. Pan, V.: Structured matrices and polynomials: unified superfast algorithms. Springer Science & Business Media (2001)

21. Qiao, L.B., Zhang, B.F., Su, J.S., Lu, X.C.: A systematic review of structured sparse learning. Front. Inf. Technol. Electron. Eng. **18**, 445–463 (2017)
22. Silver, D., et al.: Mastering the game of go without human knowledge. Nature **550**(7676), 354–359 (2017)
23. Sindhwani, V., Sainath, T.N., Kumar, S.: Structured transforms for small-footprint deep learning. In: Proceedings of the 28th International Conference on Neural Information Processing Systems, vol. 2, pp. 3088–3096 (2015)
24. Thomas, A.T., Gu, A., Dao, T., Rudra, A., Ré, C.: Learning compressed transforms with low displacement rank. Adv. Neural. Inf. Process. Syst. **2018**, 9052 (2018)
25. Vandebril, R., Van Barel, M., Golub, G., Mastronardi, N.: A bibliography on semiseparable matrices. Calcolo **42**(3), 249–270 (2005)
26. Xie, D., Xiong, J., Pu, S.: All you need is beyond a good init: exploring better solution for training extremely deep convolutional neural networks with orthonormality and modulation. In: Proceedings of the IEEE Conference on Computer Vision and Pattern Recognition, pp. 6176–6185 (2017)
27. Xu, Z., Li, Y., Cheng, X.: Butterfly-net2: simplified butterfly-net and fourier transform initialization. In: Mathematical and Scientific Machine Learning, pp. 431–450. PMLR (2020)
28. Yang, Z., Moczulski, M., Denil, M., De Freitas, N., Smola, A., Song, L., Wang, Z.: Deep fried convnets. In: Proceedings of the IEEE international conference on computer vision. pp. 1476–1483 (2015)
29. Zhao, L., Liao, S., Wang, Y., Li, Z., Tang, J., Yuan, B.: Theoretical properties for neural networks with weight matrices of low displacement rank. In: International Conference on Machine Learning, pp. 4082–4090. PMLR (2017)

TinyMetaFed: Efficient Federated Meta-learning for TinyML

Haoyu Ren[1,3](✉), Xue Li[2], Darko Anicic[1], and Thomas A. Runkler[1,3]

[1] Siemens AG, Otto-Hahn-Ring 6, 81739 Munich, Germany
{haoyu.ren,darko.anicic,thomas.runkler}@siemens.com
[2] The University of Queensland, Brisbane, QLD 4072, Australia
xueli@itee.uq.edu.au
[3] Technical University of Munich, Arcisstr. 21, 80333 Munich, Germany

Abstract. The field of Tiny Machine Learning (TinyML) has made substantial advancements in democratizing machine learning on low-footprint devices, such as microcontrollers. The prevalence of these miniature devices raises the question of whether aggregating their knowledge can benefit TinyML applications. Federated meta-learning is a promising answer to this question, as it addresses the scarcity of labeled data and heterogeneous data distribution across devices in the real world. However, deploying TinyML hardware faces unique resource constraints, making existing methods impractical due to energy, privacy, and communication limitations. We introduce TinyMetaFed, a model-agnostic meta-learning framework suitable for TinyML. TinyMetaFed facilitates collaborative training of a neural network initialization that can be quickly fine-tuned on new devices. It offers communication savings and privacy protection through partial local reconstruction and Top-P% selective communication, computational efficiency via online learning, and robustness to client heterogeneity through few-shot learning. The evaluations on three TinyML use cases demonstrate that TinyMetaFed can significantly reduce energy consumption and communication overhead, accelerate convergence, and stabilize the training process.

Keywords: Tiny Machine Learning · Federated Meta-Learning · Edge Computing · Online Learning · Neural Networks · Internet of Things

1 Introduction

Over the past decade, the advancement of ML applications has been propelled by the emergence of big data and enhanced computational capabilities. This has led to a surge in large-scale AI models, such as "ChatGPT," which demands extensive resources and significant power consumption. The growing awareness in the ML community emphasizes the escalating resource requirement and environmental unsustainability associated with big AI models.

Tiny Machine Learning (TinyML) has emerged as a powerful paradigm that bridges the gap between ML and embedded systems. It brings real-time AI capabilities closer to the edge, shifting data processing from data centers to Internet of Things (IoT) devices. TinyML offers sustainability, data privacy, and efficiency advantages by minimizing the need for cloud data transmission. The current estimate suggests that over 250 billion IoT devices are in active use today, with continual rising demand, particularly in the industrial sector[1]. Considering the vast deployment of embedded devices, the question arises: can TinyML applications benefit from sharing and integrating insights gained from these devices?

Federated Learning (FL) offers a distributed ML schema where clients collaborate to train a global model by merging their local updates on a central server without sensitive data leaving devices. However, studies have shown that training a common global model is not always optimal due to non-Independent and Identically Distributed data among devices [23]. The complex and ever-changing deployment environment of TinyML, coupled with the distributed nature of IoT devices, leads to heterogeneous data distribution. A global model trained by FL may exhibit arbitrary performance degradation when applied to a new device. Additionally, each device may have different objectives for its ML task, such as different output classes of interest. The resource constraints and limited availability of labeled data on tiny devices further exacerbate the challenges.

To address these challenges, we present TinyMetaFed in this work, depicted in Fig. 1. We consider a group of devices, each assigned an individual ML task from a distribution of tasks, e.g., one device classifies "dog vs. cat" while another classifies "apple vs. pear." TinyMetaFed learns a Neural Network (NN) model initialization that can be quickly fine-tuned on a new device for its unseen task drawn from the same distribution, e.g., to classify "car vs. airplane." The framework works by iteratively sampling a device, training on its specific task, and moving the initialization toward the trained model on that device. We explore partial local reconstruction to enhance communication efficiency and client privacy where a model is partitioned into global and local parameters. During each round, only the global parameters are communicated between a device and the server, ensuring that local parameters never leave the client. We further reduce communication costs by introducing Top-P% selective communication, where only the P% global parameters with the biggest changes are transmitted to the server. To address resource constraints, we propose online learning in TinyMetaFed, enabling on-device data processing in a streaming fashion. Online learning allows local models to process incoming data as it arrives without storing historical data, aligning with real-world production scenarios. Additionally, we improve model generalization performance by applying learning rate scheduling with cosine annealing.

We evaluate TinyMetaFed on three meta-learning datasets: "Sine-wave example" for regression problem, "Omniglot" for image classification, and "Keywords Spotting" for audio classification. Our results demonstrate the superior convergence speed, computational and communication efficiency, and robustness of TinyMetaFed compared to the state-of-the-art methods while revealing the lim-

---
[1] https://venturebeat.com/ai/why-tinyml-is-a-giant-opportunity/.

Fig. 1. Illustration of the TinyMetaFed workflow. Model weights are divided into global weights g and local weights l. In each round t, a device i use the received global weights $g^{(t)}$ to reconstruct its local weights $l_i^{(t)}$ and updates the global weights subsequently. In this work, a few gradient descent steps perform local weights reconstruction and global weights update. Then, the P% updated global weights $g_i^{(t)}$ with biggest absolute changes $|g_i^{(t)} - g^{(t)}|$ are sent back to the server. Finally, the server aggregates the Top-P% updates to the central global weights using learning rate schedule with cosine annealing.

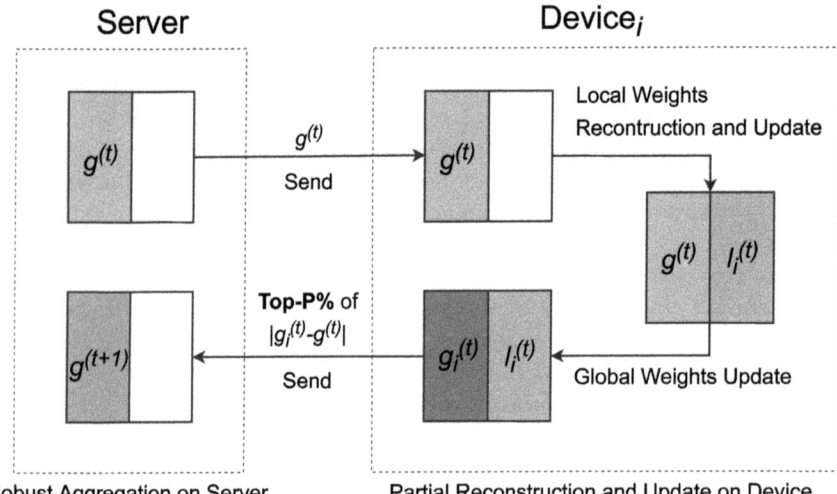

itations of traditional FL architectures when dealing with heterogeneous local data, as shown in Fig. 2.

The rest of the paper is structured as follows: Sect. 2 covers related work on FL, meta-learning, and online learning. Section 3 presents the methodology of TinyMetaFed. Section 4 introduces the benchmarking datasets, describes the experimental settings, and analyzes the results. Finally, Sect. 5 concludes the paper and explores future research directions.

2 Related Work

Federated Learning. FL focuses on training a NN model collaboratively across distributed clients whilst preserving local data privacy. Initial research on FL emerged in 2016, introducing baseline algorithms such as "FedSGD [15]." Since then, numerous advancements have been made, including differential privacy [10], robustness [2], optimization algorithms [22], and communication efficiency [9]. Although some studies have explored FL on edge devices like Raspberry Pi [7], limited attention has been given to applying FL to the TinyML domain. State-of-the-art is limited to a few works [11,13], which have conducted experiments in simulation or controlled environments on a small scale, failing to address real-world challenges in TinyML [8], such as client heterogeneity.

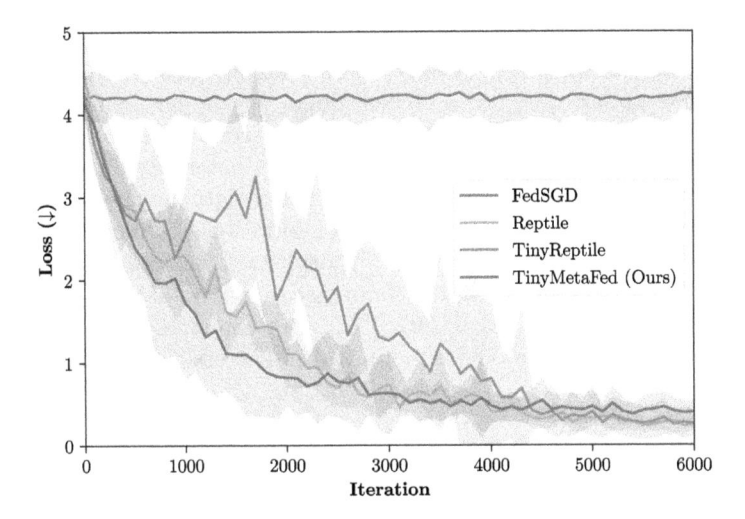

Fig. 2. Demonstration of FedSGD, Reptile, TinyReptile, and TinyMetaFed on the Sine-wave regression example. The model consists of five fully connected layers: 1 → 16 → 16 → 16 → 1. TinyMetaFed attains similar convergence performance as Reptile. However, TinyMetaFed requires significantly lower communication and computational costs per iteration than all other methods, as explained in Sect. 4. While TinyReptile occasionally becomes unstable, TinyMetaFed consistently achieves faster convergence with comparable performance. Besides, traditional FL algorithms like FedSGD struggle with meta-learning settings.

Meta-learning. Meta-learning is an appealing approach for rapid adaptation with minimal data. Unlike transfer learning, which pre-trains a global model and fine-tunes it on small datasets without guaranteed generalization [18], meta-learning aims to train a common model explicitly for easy fine-tuning. The initial advancement in meta-learning, known as "model-agnostic meta-learning" (MAML) [6], introduced gradient-based optimization. However, MAML's requirement for higher-order derivatives makes it computationally intensive. Subsequent research focused on improving performance, such as MAML++ [1], and reducing the computational costs [17]. Relevant work is emerging in the TinyML domain as well [20]. Nevertheless, most approaches require specific setups applicable only to certain models [24] or remain computationally intensive [21], making them unsuitable for tiny devices with severe resource constraints.

On-device Learning. Most ultra-low-power TinyML models have traditionally been trained offline, while edge devices solely perform inference. Although this fashion has demonstrated success across the research community [5] and industry [16], it is increasingly aware that offline-trained models may not be effective in real-world scenarios if data distributions evolve [3]. We believe that on-device learning is crucial for TinyML applications, allowing algorithms to adapt to heterogeneous deployment environments. Some research efforts have been dedicated to this field. For example, J. Lin et al. [12] have applied quantization-aware scaling and sparse update to train a convolutional NN under 256KB of memory. Compared to batch training, online learning has received less attention due to the assumption that data are always available as a batch. By integrating online learning into existing algorithms, we process sensor data one by one and update the model in a streaming fashion, saving computational resources and accelerating the training process. TinyOL [19] incorporates online learning to update the last few layers of a NN against incoming sensor data, keeping the model up to date without saving historical data. Our work combines meta-learning with online learning to enable on-device meta-learning across tiny federated devices.

3 Method

3.1 Federated Meta-learning

In this study, we focus on federated meta-learning. Given limited training data, meta-learning enables a NN to adapt to new tasks or environments quickly. Federated learning employs distributed clients to collectively train a NN by communicating with a central server. Our approach combines meta-learning and federated learning to achieve meta-learning in a federated setting, leveraging resource constrained IoT devices.

Our setup consists of a server and a set of devices. Each device is assigned an ML task t drawn from a distribution of tasks T. While all the tasks share a common pattern with the same number of output classes, such as two-classes image classification, their classification objectives differ. For instance, one task is to classify "dog vs. cat," while another is to classify "apple vs. banana." All devices are deployed with a NN of the same structure for their tasks. For evaluation, we divide these tasks into training tasks $T_{training}$ and testing tasks $T_{testing}$. Our algorithm utilizes $T_{training}$ to find an optimal model initialization ϕ that yields good generalization performance on $T_{testing}$, which have not been encountered during training.

3.2 TinyMetaFed

This section presents TinyMetaFed, a framework that enables federated meta-learning in TinyML. We also discuss several techniques implemented within TinyMetaFed. Figure 1 provides an overview of TinyMetaFed.

Partial Local Reconstruction. In federated learning, transmitting all model weights between devices and a central server can be communication intensive. We propose partial local reconstruction to address the challenge, where models are partitioned into local and global weights. The partition between local and global parameters depends on the use case requirements, privacy needs, and communication limitations. Clients only communicate their global weights with the server while preserving the local weights across iterations by recovering them whenever needed. In each round, a client receives global weights from the server and recovers its local weights through a few gradient decent steps. At the end of a round, the global weights are sent back to the server for aggregation, while local weights can be discarded or retained for local inference.

Top-P% Selective Communication. Instead of sending all the global weights from clients to the server or randomly selecting some of them for transmission, we propose Top-P% selective communication. Here, we assess the importance of each model weight. The approach selects the P% global weights with the largest absolute changes and their indices for transmission in each round.

Online Learning. TinyMetaFed incorporates online learning in local weights reconstruction and global weights update, sequentially processing incoming data, such as sensor data, without storing them. This technique helps to minimize memory usage and keep the models up to date, which differs from traditional batch learning, where models are trained on entire stored datasets in batches.

Learning Rate Scheduling with Cosine Annealing. Traditionally, a fixed learning rate is applied for training optimizers. Annealing the learning rate has proved crucial for achieving state-of-the-art results [14]. Thus, we employ learning rate scheduling with cosine annealing to enhance generalization performance without extensive hyperparameter tuning.

TinyMetaFed, depicted in Algorithm 1, is inspired by the well-known meta-learning algorithm Reptile [17]. The training process in TinyMetaFed operates as follows: in each round t, the server sends the current global weights $g^{(t)}$ to a client i. The client possesses a local dataset D, such as sensor data, specifically for its ML task. The dataset is split into two parts: a support set S and a query set Q, where $D = \langle S, Q \rangle$. The client uses $g^{(t)}$ along with S to reconstruct the local weights $l_i^{(t)}$. Afterward, the client freezes $l_i^{(t)}$ and produces updated global weights $g_i^{(t)}$ using $g^{(t)}$, $l_i^{(t)}$ and Q. The server then receives the Top-P% updated global weights with the largest absolute changes $|g_i^{(t)} - g^{(t)}|$ from the client. Finally, the server applies the learning rate scheduling strategy to aggregate these updates into the global weights $g^{(t+1)}$.

In this framework, local weights reconstruction and global weights update are achieved through k local gradient descent steps in an online learning manner. The training processes are independent of the federated process, enabling clients to reconstruct weights once, store them for inference, and optionally refresh them with new local data. Our framework allows devices to communicate sequentially with the central server without relying on consistent and concurrent connections. Meta-learning strives to find a fast learner, so local datasets $D = \langle S, Q \rangle$ typically contain a limited number of samples, and the training step k is generally defined to a small value. Intuitively, TinyMetaFed aims to bring a model

Algorithm 1. TinyMetaFed

Input: set of clients with tasks drawn from T, set of tasks T with streaming data $D = \langle S, Q \rangle$, server learning rate scheduling function f.
Output: global weights initialization g

1: **ServerUpdate:**
2:   Randomly initialize global weights g
3:   **for** each round t **do**
4:     Sample one available client i with $D_i = \langle S_i, Q_i \rangle$
5:     $g_i^{(t)} \leftarrow$ **ClientUpdate**$(i, g^{(t)})$
6:     $g^{(t+1)} \leftarrow g^{(t)} + f(t)(g_i^{(t)} - g^{(t)})$
7:   **end for**
8:   Return g
9: **ClientUpdate:**
10: $D_i = \langle S_i, Q_i \rangle, g^{(i)}$
11: Freeze $g^{(i)}$
12: $l_i^{(t)} \leftarrow$ **LocalWeightsReconstruction**$(S_i, g^{(t)})$
13: Unfreeze $g^{(i)}$ and freeze $l_t^{(i)}$
14: $g_i^{(t)} \leftarrow$ **GlobalWeightsUpdate**$(Q_i, l_i^{(t)}, g^{(t)})$
15: Send **Top-P%** of $g_i^{(t)}$ with the largest changes $|g_i^{(t)} - g^{(t)}|$ back to the server
16: **LocalWeightsReconstruction/GlobalWeightsUpdate:**
17: Perform k steps of SGD on the streaming data in an online learning way

initialization closer to an optimal point nearest to all tasks/devices, facilitating rapid fine-tuning in new environments. Essentially, TinyMetaFed optimizes for generalization.

4 Experiments and Evaluation

In this section, we assess the performance of TinyMetaFed on regression, image classification, and audio classification tasks. We analyze various performance metrics, such as energy consumption, communication costs, and memory requirement. The NNs from the MLPerf Tiny benchmark [4] are used to ensure consistent comparisons. Table 1 provides an overview of the models for the three tasks. Each experiment is repeated many times, and the results are presented as the mean value with the standard deviation.

Table 1. Overview of the models.

	Task	Model Type	Size	Parameters
Sine-wave Example	Regression	Fully Connected	4.1 KB	593
Omniglot 5-classes	Image Classification	Convolutional	313 KB	80389
Keywords Spotting 3-classes	Audio Classification	Convolutional	71 KB	17251

4.1 Datasets

Sine-Wave. The Sine-wave regression task fits a randomly parameterized sine function $f(x) = a\sin(b\,x + c)$ on each device. The objective is to collectively learn a NN initialization that can be rapidly adapted to new sine functions using a handful of sampled pairs (x, y).

Omniglot. The Omniglot image dataset consists of $C = 1623$ characters from 50 alphabets, with 20 samples per character. In the meta-learning setting, each device is assigned a classification task of M randomly selected characters from C. The goal is to learn good initial weights that can be quickly generalized to new devices with unseen classification tasks based on limited data examples.

Keywords Spotting. The Keywords Spotting dataset contains $C = 35$ distinct keywords, such as "up" and "down," with over 1,000 audio samples per word. Each device is assigned a classification task involving M randomly chosen keywords. The goal is similar to Omniglot, aiming to collaboratively learn a NN initialization that can be fast adapted to a new device with a different keywords classification task of M classes given limited data.

4.2 Baselines and Setup

We compare TinyMetaFed with two state-of-the-art methods, Reptile [17] (serial) and TinyReptile [20]. Reptile, MAML [6], and MAML++ [1] are widely recognized as leading approaches in meta-learning. Compared to MAML and MAML++, Reptile stands out for its simplicity and efficiency. It achieves the goal by repeatedly optimizing the model initialization for different tasks and gradually updating the parameters toward the weights learned for new tasks. Our previous work, TinyReptile, applies the online learning concept to Reptile. This allows TinyReptile to process local data in a streaming fashion without the need to store past data, which saves a significant amount of resources and enables meta-learning on constrained devices. TinyMetaFed builds upon TinyReptile with various improvement strategies introduced in Sect. 3. We exclude other FL and meta-learning algorithms in the experiments since most of them are ineffective or unsuitable in the context of TinyML. We experiment with different hyperparameters that perform well for the given datasets: the Top-P percentage (10%–80%), SGD learning rate β (0.001–0.02), support set size S (1–16), query set size S (1–16), and partitioning of global and local weights. Although, we do not fine-tune them for optimal results. The evaluation is conducted on Arduino Nano BLE 33 microcontroller (MCU)[2] and Raspberry Pi 4 Model B[3].

---

[2] https://docs.arduino.cc/hardware/nano-33-ble-sense.
[3] https://www.raspberrypi.com/products/raspberry-pi-4-model-b/.

4.3 Results

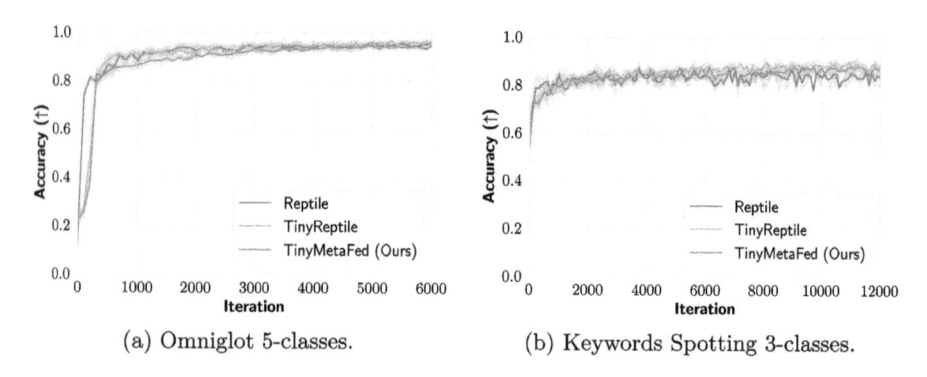

Fig. 3. Training convergence of Reptile, TinyReptile, and TinyMetaFed on the Omniglot and Keywords Spotting datasets. Together with the results from the Sinewave example shown in Fig. 2, we demonstrate that TinyMetaFed can achieve similar convergence performance while significantly reducing energy consumption and communication costs.

We first show the convergence behaviors of the three approaches on the Sinewave, Omniglot image classification, and Keywords Spotting audio classification datasets, as depicted in Figs. 2, 3a, and 3b, respectively. Each experiment is repeated multiple times, and the results are presented as the mean value with the standard deviation. Depending on the datasets, TinyMetaFed demonstrates similar or even better performance than the baselines. For instance, TinyMetaFed exhibits comparable final performance in the Omniglot and Keywords Spotting tasks and demonstrates faster and more stable training progress in the Sine-wave example.

Next, we present the hardware benchmark results for the three tasks, as shown in Tables 2, 3, and 4, respectively. We conduct the experiments on the Sine-wave example using the Arduino MCU and on the Omniglot and Keywords Spotting tasks using the Raspberry Pi. Communication costs are calculated relative to TinyReptile, which serves as the baseline with a value of one, where the entire model is transmitted to the server in each round. Since Reptile employs a batched communication schema, it can require communication with N devices during each iteration. We measure energy consumption by subtracting idle energy consumption from the total energy consumed during algorithm execution using a USB multimeter. The results are measured on one device for one iteration. Our TinyMetaFed empirically improves upon the baseline algorithms in all metrics. For example, it achieves 65% and 59% communication cost savings compared to TinyReptile on the Omniglot and Keywords Spotting datasets and approximately 50% energy saving on both datasets. In Fig. 4, we compare the training progress of these approaches based on the total number of parameters communicated. We observe a clear advantage of TinyMetaFed regarding communication cost saving.

Finally, TinyMetaFed provides a level of protection against privacy attacks. Many attack methods from previous work may not be effective for TinyMetaFed since only the global parameters of the model are communicated to the server, and these updates are directly calculated using a portion of the local support set. TinyMetaFed can be further enhanced in the most privacy-sensitive applications with secure aggregation or differential privacy to provide provable privacy guarantees.

Table 2. Sine-wave: benchmark of one iteration on a Arduino Nano BLE 33.

	Sending	Local Training	Receiving	Total	Communication Cost	Energy Consumption	Memory Requirement
Reptile	0.81 s	6.45 s	0.61 s	7.87 s	1 * N	2.1 J	8.6 KB
TinyReptile	0.81 s	0.32 s	0.61 s	1.74 s	1	0.48 J	2.5 KB
TinyMetaFed (Ours)	**0.76 s**	**0.24 s**	**0.39 s**	**1.39 s**	**0.72**	**0.36 J**	**2.5 KB**

Table 3. Omniglot: benchmark of one iteration on a Raspberry Pi 4.

	Sending	Local Training	Receiving	Total	Communication Cost	Energy Consumption	Memory Requirement
Reptile	4.2 s	9.1 s	2.0 s	15.3 s	1*N	35 J	6517 KB
TinyReptile	4.2 s	5.5 s	2.0 s	11.7 s	1	23 J	79 KB
TinyMetaFed (Ours)	**1.0 s**	**5.2 s**	**0.9 s**	**7.1 s**	**0.35**	**11 J**	**79 KB**

Table 4. Keywords Spotting: benchmark of one iteration on a Raspberry Pi 4.

	Sending	Local Training	Receiving	Total	Communication Cost	Energy Consumption	Memory Requirement
Reptile	2.7 s	9.6 s	1.5 s	13.8 s	1 * N	36 J	11462 KB
TinyReptile	2.7 s	2.7 s	1.5 s	6.9 s	1	15 J	346 KB
TinyMetaFed (Ours)	**0.7 s**	**2.6 s**	**0.8 s**	**4.1 s**	**0.41**	**8 J**	**346 KB**

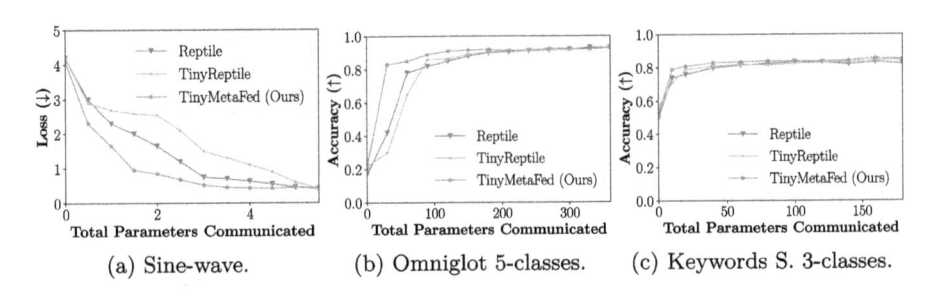

(a) Sine-wave. (b) Omniglot 5-classes. (c) Keywords S. 3-classes.

Fig. 4. Loss or accuracy as a function of total parameters communicated (in millions) between the server and one client across the datasets.

5 Conclusion

Environmental Impact. AI has the potential to benefit society in many ways. However, the rapid development of advanced ML models in recent years has raised concerns about their sustainability and environmental impact. Efforts are underway to improve power consumption and decrease CO_2 emissions in ML operations. TinyML presents opportunities to enable efficient ML applications and address environmental challenges via sustainable computing practices. We believe that the future of ML is bright and tiny[4].

This study proposes TinyMetaFed to facilitate model-agnostic meta-learning on resource-constrained tiny devices in TinyML at scale. We conduct experiments on Arduino MCU and Raspberry Pi, covering three tasks: regression, image and audio classification. Our empirical results show that TinyMetaFed can achieve significant reductions in training time (up to 60%), communication costs (up to 70%), and energy consumption (up to 50%) compared to the baselines. Future work includes enhancing robustness and privacy guarantee, exploring hyperparameters, and deploying in industrial use cases.

Acknowledgment. This work is partially supported by the NEPHELE project (ID: 101070487) that has received funding from the Horizon Europe programme under the topic "Future European Platforms for the Edge: Meta Operating Systems".

References

1. Antoniou, A., Edwards, H., Storkey, A.: How to train your maml (2019)
2. Aramoon, O., Chen, P.Y., Qu, G., Tian, Y.: Meta federated learning (2021)
3. Avi, A., Albanese, A., Brunelli, D.: Incremental online learning algorithms comparison for gesture and visual smart sensors (2022)
4. Banbury, C., et al.: Mlperf tiny benchmark (2021)
5. Dhar, S., Guo, J., Liu, J., Tripathi, S., Kurup, U., Shah, M.: A survey of on-device machine learning: an algorithms and learning theory perspective. ACM Trans. Internet Things **2**(3), 1–49 (2021)
6. Finn, C., Abbeel, P., Levine, S.: Model-agnostic meta-learning for fast adaptation of deep networks. In: Proceedings of the 34th International Conference on Machine Learning, ICML 2017, pp. 1126–1135. JMLR.org, Sydney, NSW, Australia (2017)
7. Gao, Y., et al.: End-to-end evaluation of federated learning and split learning for internet of things. arXiv preprint arXiv:2003.13376 (2020)
8. Imteaj, A., Thakker, U., Wang, S., Li, J., Amini, M.H.: A survey on federated learning for resource-constrained iot devices. IEEE Internet Things J. **9**(1), 1–24 (2022)
9. Ji, S., Jiang, W., Walid, A., Li, X.: Dynamic sampling and selective masking for communication-efficient federated learning. IEEE Intell. Syst. **37**(2), 27–34 (2021)
10. Jiang, B., Li, J., Wang, H., Song, H.: Privacy-preserving federated learning for industrial edge computing via hybrid differential privacy and adaptive compression. IEEE Trans. Industr. Inf. **19**(2), 1136–1144 (2023)

---

[4] https://pll.harvard.edu/course/future-ml-tiny-and-bright.

11. Kopparapu, K., Lin, E., Breslin, J.G., Sudharsan, B.: Tinyfedtl: federated transfer learning on ubiquitous tiny iot devices. In: 2022 IEEE International Conference on Pervasive Computing and Communications Workshops and other Affiliated Events (PerCom Workshops), pp. 79–81 (2022)
12. Lin, J., Chen, W.M., Cai, H., Gan, C., Han, S.: Mcunetv2: memory-efficient patch-based inference for tiny deep learning. arXiv preprint arXiv:2110.15352 (2021)
13. Llisterri Giménez, N., Monfort Grau, M., Pueyo Centelles, R., Freitag, F.: On-device training of machine learning models on microcontrollers with federated learning. Electronics **11**(4) (2022)
14. Loshchilov, I., Hutter, F.: Sgdr: stochastic gradient descent with warm restarts (2017)
15. McMahan, H.B., Moore, E., Ramage, D., Hampson, S., Arcas, B.A.y.: Communication-efficient learning of deep networks from decentralized data. arXiv preprint arXiv:1602.05629 (2016)
16. Montiel, J., et al.: River: machine learning for streaming data in python (2020)
17. Nichol, A., Achiam, J., Schulman, J.: On first-order meta-learning algorithms (2018)
18. Parnami, A., Lee, M.: Learning from few examples: a summary of approaches to few-shot learning (2022)
19. Ren, H., Anicic, D., Runkler, T.A.: Tinyol: Tinyml with online-learning on microcontrollers. In: 2021 International Joint Conference on Neural Networks (IJCNN), pp. 1–8. IEEE (2021)
20. Ren, H., Anicic, D., Runkler, T.A.: Tinyreptile: Tinyml with federated meta-learning. arXiv preprint arXiv:2304.05201 (2023)
21. Rusu, A.A., et al.: Meta-learning with latent embedding optimization. arXiv preprint arXiv:1807.05960 (2018)
22. Singhal, K., Sidahmed, H., Garrett, Z., Wu, S., Rush, J., Prakash, S.: Federated reconstruction: partially local federated learning. Adv. Neural. Inf. Process. Syst. **34**, 11220–11232 (2021)
23. Zhao, Y., Li, M., Lai, L., Suda, N., Civin, D., Chandra, V.: Federated learning with non-iid data. arXiv preprint arXiv:1806.00582 (2018)
24. Zhou, P., Yuan, X., Xu, H., Yan, S., Feng, J.: Efficient meta learning via minibatch proximal update. Advances in Neural Information Processing Systems **32** (2019)

On the Potentials of Input Repetition in CNN Networks for Reducing Multiplications

Laura Medina[✉] and Jose Flich

Universitat Politècnica de València, Valencia, Spain
{laumecha,jflich}@upv.es

Abstract. Convolutional Neural Networks (CNN) are composed of hundreds of millions of dot operations, leading to the emergence of new algorithms to reduce the high computational complexity. This paper introduces input repetition: a new solution to reduce the number of operations of previous quantized CNN models without degrading the accuracy. The input repetition occurs when several identical elements are found in a group of input activations, allowing the reduction of the number of multipliers required to perform the dot operation needed in the convolutional layers. This paper analyzes several strategies to find repetition in the convolution input using quantized state-of-the-art CNN: YoloV3, MobileNET and ResNet50. Results show that input repetition can reduce multiplications by a factor of 2.4x without any performance impact.

1 Introduction

Convolutional Neural Networks (CNNs) are becoming essential in many real-world applications. More precisely, CNNs are vital in the field of object detection [19], image segmentation [14], and facial recognition [13]. Nevertheless, applications must face their computational complexity to achieve the remarkable performance of CNN as they are computationally expensive due to the large number of parameters they contain and the sizes of images they process. Moreover, CNN models comprise convolution operations where small filters are applied over the entire input image. This critical component of CNN requires a large number of multiplications and additions.

In order to reduce the computational complexity of CNN models, several techniques are applied to reduce the size of the CNN models and, for instance, the computations needed to perform the operations. Quantization can be applied to reduce the number of bits of the parameters of the neural network (NN), significantly reducing the model's size and leading to faster inference times and lower power consumption [8]. Another approach commonly used to reduce the size of NN models is pruning. Pruning is a technique that removes unimportant neurons, connections, or filters to reduce the number of parameters in a network, which can lead to a faster and more efficient inference [7]. Although pruning and quantization techniques reduce the models' size and computing requirements, those models are still too large for specific scenarios. In embedded systems with real-time constraints, it is of outmost importance to reduce the computing requirements of such models and to bind the inference time to a determined threshold.

Computational requirements of quantized CNN models make FPGA (Field-Programmable Gate Arrays) devices a good fit for these applications as they provide low power consumption, efficiency and flexibility. FPGAs can also offer low latency and high throughput, critical for real-time applications requiring quick and accurate predictions or applications that set energy efficiency as their primary design goal. However, these devices have limited resources. As the convolutional operations and NN algorithms comprise millions of multiplications and additions, more resources are needed as more parallelism is desired.

In this paper, we propose addressing an alternative redundancy source: exploiting the input redundancy of the models at inference time. We target to reduce the number of multiplications required to perform the convolution operation by identifying the repetition between input activations of convolutions and then performing only the multiplications of the different values. By reducing the multiplications, we aim to reduce the resources needed or maintain the resources but accelerate the process.

Moreover, compression image techniques can be used in NN to reduce the image and, consequently, the number of repeated input pixels to process. Initially, one would think that this technique can worsen the input redundancy. However, for the results of this paper, we identify the input of each convolutional layer, meaning that any previous compression technique that might have been used in the input image is taken into account and will be depicted in the results.

We present an analysis that measures these values' repetition using 8-bit integer (INT8) models. For this study, we analyze different pixels' reorganization using the state-of-the-art quantized models from ONNX Model Zoo [1]. We use Yolo-V3 [15], ResNet-50 [5] and MobileNet [17] models. We demonstrate a significant repetition between the inputs of the convolutional layers, which allows us to reduce 58.3% of the multiplications. This paper demonstrates that it is possible to develop specific accelerators that exploit this repetition, identifying the inputs with the same value and reducing the number of multiplications and, as a result, the number of required resources in FPGAs and speeding up the inference process of NN models. To sum up, this paper makes the following contributions:

1. We analyze the repetition of the values of the inputs of the convolution layers on several state-of-the-art NN INT8 quantized models. For this study, we use different grouping strategies to see how this affects repetition.
2. We design some possible accelerator modules that can be developed to benefit from this repetition, reusing computations from identical inputs.
3. We demonstrate that by reusing input redundancy, we can improve the performance of an inference process by factors up to 2.4 on the target models.

The rest of the paper is organized as follows. Section 2 describes the bibliography related to our topic. Section 3 introduces the concept of repetition at the input and describes the different grouping strategies. Then, Sect. 4 shows the results obtained. Finally, Sect. 5 shows the paper's conclusions.

2 Related Work

Sparsity. Sparsity [10] is applied to NN to reduce the number of operations performed by removing or avoiding the computations of weights or activations set to zero, usually on hiper-parametrized models. However, this approach is not beneficial for quantized models as the values are scaled to fit into a range of values, and the appearances of zero are usually non-exploitable.

Repetition for Pruning. Repetition can also be exploited for another purpose than the one presented in this paper. Previous studies have proposed techniques to reduce the number of computations performed. A pruning method that eliminates convolutional filters by taking the repetition between filters is presented in [3], allowing to reduce the number of computations of the NN.

Repetition for Frame Processing. Other previous studies propose techniques to exploit the repetition of multiple images to reduce the computational requirements of DNNs. In [4,16], propose that if multiple images have identical activations in some parts of the network, it is possible to reuse the intermediate results of these activations rather than recomputing them for each image.

Frequently Input Pattern Computation Reuse. In [9,12], a methodology to reuse frequently input patterns is proposed. The frequent computations patterns are analysed to calculate and save the results to avoid the recomputation of redundant executions. An approximate pattern matching is also presented, where the saved calculations return an inaccurate result rather than the exact computation result.

Weight Computation Reuse. A previous studies [6,18] proposes accelerators that exploits **weight** repetition. In [6], a reduction of 33% in multipliers and memory read is achieved at the cost of storage overhead for the input and weight indirection tables and in [18], a saving of 26% is presented. This proposal is similar to the work presented, as it reduces the number of multiplication by identifying the repeated weights. However, in our study, we exploit the input repetition of convolutions instead of weight repetition without degrading the accuracy.

In this paper, we focus on **input** repetition patterns at convolution layers, which, as far as we know, are not covered by any previous work. Our work is complementary to all the previous works as well.

3 Repetition

The convolution operation consists of multiplying each value of the matrix of input activations (formed by $CI \times H \times W$ elements) by filters (formed by $CO \times$

$KH \times KW$ weights). The convolutional operation (without bias term) is given by:

$$O[c_o, h, w] = \sum_{c_i=0}^{CI-1} \sum_{k_h=0}^{KH-1} \sum_{k_w=0}^{KW-1} I[c_i, h+k_h, w+k_w] \times W[c_o, c_i, k_h, k_w] \quad (1)$$

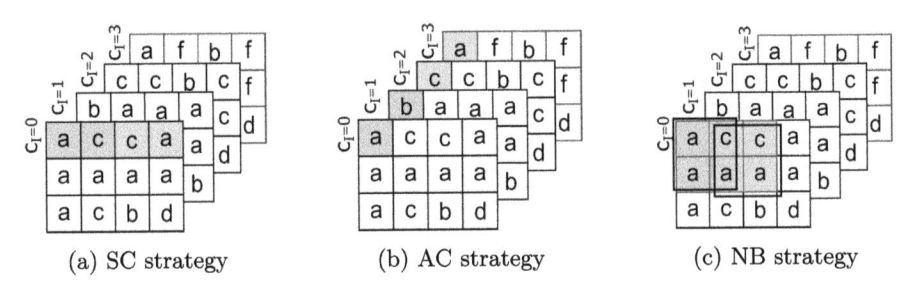

Fig. 1. Examples of grouping strategies of input activations assuming group size $G = 2$. In green, we can see the first group, whereas in blue, we see the next group. A $4 \times 4 \times 3$ input activation tensor is used. (Color figure online)

where O, I and W are outputs, inputs and filters, respectively. Many state-of-the-art NN models quantize these two matrices to INT8 form. Hence, the input and the filter values can only adopt $2^8 = 256$ possible values. Since $CI \times H \times W > 256$, value repetition will be presented in both matrices, necessarily.

Our initial hypothesis is that there is a more significant repetition factor inside the input matrix than in the filter matrix. Indeed, the filters are trained and must be specialized to detect specific image features. Thus, they tend to have different values among them. Also, near pixels of an image have a big probability of having the same or similar values if they represent the same object or pattern, such as a blue sky. Moreover, the input vector of a convolution represents features detected by the previous convolution. Therefore, consecutive or nearby input activations may have the same or similar values. Also, activations at the same location in different input channels may have the same value since they derive from the same activations from the original image. Our hypothesis will be confirmed in the evaluation section, where the results will show that input repetition is much more frequent than weight repetition.

We define the repetition factor (RF) of a group as the number of repetitions within the group. For instance, in a 4-element group with values $\{a, b, b, d\}$ the repetition factor will be set to 1 and for a group with the values $\{a, a, a, a\}$ the repetition factor will be set to 3. Notice that RF will range from 0 to $G - 1$, where G is the group size.

We introduce three approaches for input repetition analysis and optimization on INT8 quantized models. All these approaches will group sets of input activations following a different grouping strategy. Figure 1 shows the three approaches for input repetition: Same-Channel (SC) group (1a), Across-Channels (AC) group (1b) and Nearby (NB) group (1c). Different group sizes will be analyzed. Notice that there is no overlapping of groups in SC and AC strategies. However, in NB, strategy groups overlap.

3.1 Same-Channel Repetition

In Same-Channel (SC) repetition, all the activations for each input channel are read sequentially in groups. The input activations read from an input channel must be multiplied by all the weights of the filters associated with the input channel. As an example, for a $1 \times H \times W$ input (one channel of size $H \times W$), O output channels, and 3×3 filters, an input activation p_x will be multiplied by all the weights of all the filters (assuming typical padding). However, none of those multiplications will be added among them since each multiplication contributes to different output activations and output channels. However, if we identify activations (p_x and p_y) within the same group with the same value ($p_x == p_y$), the multiplication of p_x by w_a can be reused for p_y by w_a.

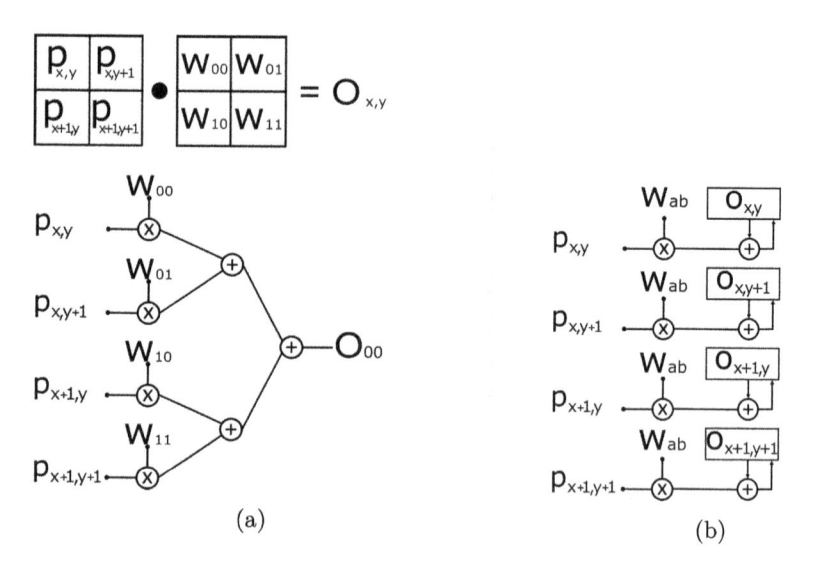

Fig. 2. Standard dot-product operation (a) and distributed dot-product operation (b) in a convolution operation for a 2×2 input frame and a 2×2 filter.

Notice that the additions performed in the dot product operation can be distributed over time while multiplications of other activations are performed. Indeed, multiple dot-product operations can be refactored, and the multiplication and addition phases can be separated. Indeed, assuming an input activation $p_{x,y}$ with coordinates x and y, when multiplied by a weight $w_{a,b}$ of a filter, the output the activation contributes to is $O_{x-a,y-b}$ (assuming stride set to one and not considering padding). Thus, the dot-product operation can be refactored to:

$$O[c_o, x-a, y-b] += I[c_i, x, y] \times W[c_o, c_i, a, b] \qquad (2)$$

Figure 2a shows the standard approach to implement a dot-product operation for a 2×2 input frame and a 2×2 convolution filter. Four products are performed in parallel using the four input activations and the four weights, and a reduction operation is performed using three adders. Notice that, in principle, we can not directly exploit repetition opportunities at the input since all four input activations are multiplied by different weights.

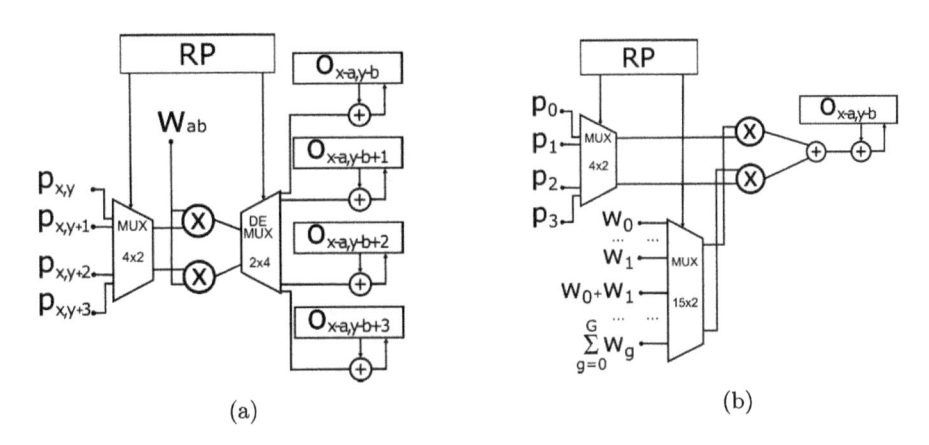

Fig. 3. Dot product implementations using two multipliers with $G=4$ in SC (b) and AC and NB (b).

Instead, In Fig. 2b, we can see how a distributed approach can be used. Now, we multiply four input activations by the same weight. Four multipliers and four adders (one added to the previous case) are used. Notice that we are producing four output activations since none of the multiplications contributes to the same output activation. Thus, four registers are needed to accumulate the outputs of the products. Indeed, the convolution operation can be decomposed into two separate terms: the multiplication phase and the reduction phase.

$$P[c_o, c_i, h, w, k_h, k_w] = I[c_i, h+k_h, w+k_w] \times W[c_o, c_i, k_h, k_w] \qquad (3)$$

$$O[c_o, h, w] = \sum_{c_i=0}^{CI-1} \sum_{k_h=0}^{KH-1} \sum_{k_w=0}^{HW-1} P[c_o, c_i, h, w, kh, kw] \qquad (4)$$

Figure 3a shows the case where we exploit SC repetition. In this case, we still read four consecutive activations from the input and multiply them by the same weight, using four adders to accumulate the outputs. However, now we use a reduced number of multipliers, two. Therefore, we may need two cycles to compute the four multiplications and addition. However, now, we detect the repetition pattern of the four input activations. We can use one cycle to perform the four multiplications and additions if they have the same value ($RF = 3$) or even if they have two differing values ($RF = 2$). Thus, we potentially gain two cycles when reducing the number of multipliers. Notice that either we can reduce the number of multipliers while keeping the performance (inference time), or we can keep the number of multipliers and then improve the performance (reduce the inference time).

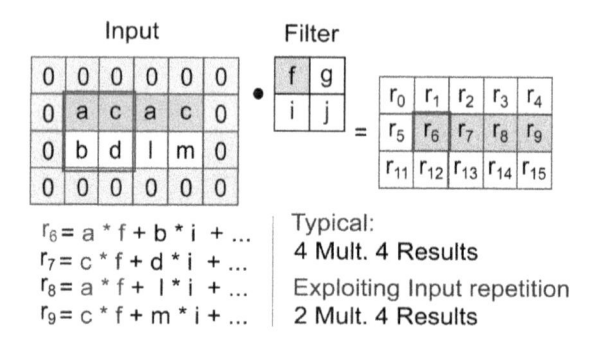

$r_6 = a * f + b * i + ...$
$r_7 = c * f + d * i + ...$
$r_8 = a * f + l * i + ...$
$r_9 = c * f + m * i + ...$

Typical:
4 Mult. 4 Results

Exploiting Input repetition
2 Mult. 4 Results

Fig. 4. SC example. $G = 4$. The green colour represents padding. The red box represents the frame input activations required to obtain the results of the r6 output activation. (Color figure online)

The repeat pattern (RP) module in the SC strategy can be implemented differently. One first approach is to use bitwise comparators in order to assess whether input activations have the same value. As this may affect performance, a better approach is to use those comparators at the output of the convolution layer. Indeed, the output of a convolution layer is used as the input for the following convolution layer in most CNNs.

Figure 4 represents a simplified example for SC on a convolution operation on a $1 \times 2 \times 4$ input with 1×1 padding and 2×2 filters. In this example, each non-padding activation will be multiplied by each filter weight. As we can see, we exploit input repetition by grouping the first four elements as the $a \times f$ and the $c \times f$ multiplications can be reused, needing two multiplications instead of four.

3.2 Across-Channels Repetition

In Across-channels (AC) repetition, the elements are grouped by the same H and W index from different consecutive channels. In this case, the group size corresponds to the number of channels grouped. In AC each input activation must be multiplied by a different weight. This means that, in contrast to the SC strategy, the multiplications must be added among them. So, in order to exploit

AC repetition, we can use the distributive property:

$$p_{h,w}^{i_0} \times w_{a,b}^{i_0} + p_{h,w}^{i_1} \times w_{a,b}^{i_1} = p_{h,w}^{i_0} \times (w_{a,b}^{i_0} + w_{a,b}^{i_1}) \qquad (p_{h,w}^{i_0} == p_{h,w}^{i_1}) \qquad (5)$$

In this case, if we find repetition across channels, we can distribute the operation to reduce the number of multiplications.

Figure 3b shows a possible implementation of the AC strategy. Notice that two differences exist compared to SC. First, the weights also need to be selected. Those weights are precomputed at model load time. Second, the outputs of the two multipliers are added since the four input activations contribute to the same output activation.

Figure 5 shows an example of AC repetition of a convolution operation for a $2 \times 2 \times 2$ input and one output channel, thus we have two filters (one for each input channel). In this case, the intermediate results (represented as $M_{x,y}$) will be added among them, giving as a result, O_a. As the figure describes, we can save one multiplication by exploiting AC repetition to compute O_0.

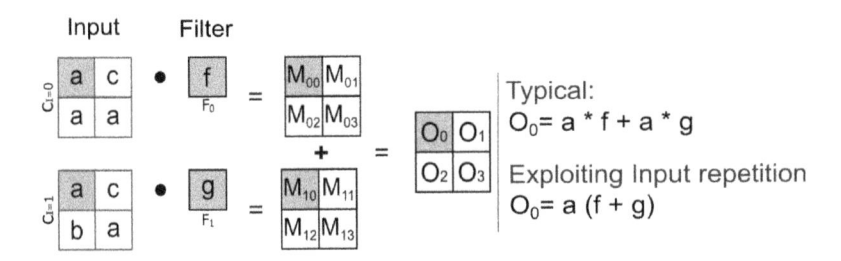

Fig. 5. AC example with a $G = 2$.

3.3 Nearby Repetition

The Nearby (NB) repetition aims to exploit the repetition of nearby activations of the same channel. In this case, nine activations are selected, forming a 3×3 frame. Notice that this frame size is aligned with typical filter sizes (3×3) used in convolution layers. After performing the convolution of the frame with the corresponding filter, a new frame is selected, shifting the frame one column to the left or one row down. The frame is convolved with the filter as in the standard dot-product operation. However, in this case, with NB, the repetition pattern is identified and fewer multiplications are used. In order to exploit NB repetition, weights need to be pre-added. Figure 3b describes the possible implementation of the strategy, which is identical to the AC strategy.

Figure 6 shows an example of NB repetition in place for a $1 \times 3 \times 3$ input and 2×2 filter. Two multiplications are performed instead of four.

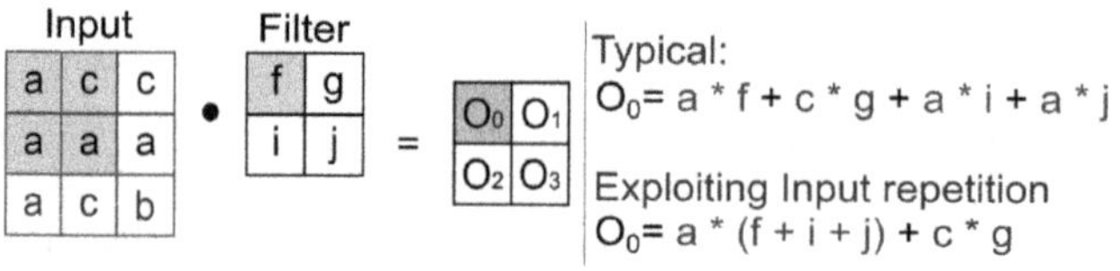

Fig. 6. NB example with $G = 2$.

3.4 SC, AC, and NB Savings and Cost

In a convolution operation (see Eq. 3), one multiplication is performed for every combination of the input channel (CI), output channel (CO), input activation (H and W), and filter weight (KH and KW), where the total number of multiplications is given by:

$$Muls = CI \times CO \times H \times W \times KH \times KW \qquad (6)$$

When exploiting input repetition, the number of multiplications performed is reduced. We define the Speedup factor (S) within a group of size G and a given value of RF as:

$$S = \frac{G}{G - RF} \qquad (7)$$

As a result, in input repetition exploitation, the number of multiplications to perform is:

$$Muls = \frac{CI \times CO \times H \times W \times KH \times KW}{S_{avg}} \qquad (8)$$

where S_{avg} is the average speedup achieved for all the input activation groups. Notice that the different strategies may achieve different performances as they will find a different RF. Also, the group size will determine the performance.

AC repetition may have inherited costs based on the order in which multiplications are performed. However, this depends on how the accelerator or algorithm for convolution operations may be designed, basically determining the order multiplications are scheduled on an engine (either on an FPGA, GPU or even an ASIC). The three grouping strategies can be selected based on the target approach. For instance, if the parallelism is exploited at the input channel level (multiple channels read in parallel), then the AC strategy can be used. On the contrary, if parallelism is exploited at input activation levels (multiple inputs from the same channel are read in parallel), then the SC strategy can be used. Finally, if the dot-product operation is performed, then NB can be used.

Nonetheless, the AC strategy does not perform multiple reads of the input activations, thus not facing extra energy costs for memory reads. The clear overhead is at the operation's output, where multiple output activations may be computed simultaneously. This necessitates extra registers to accumulate the results. However, the number of registers depends exclusively on the group size

(G). The cost of the multiplexer, demultiplexer and RP module also depends on the group size. Small group sizes of 4 or 8 do not significantly increase area and cost. As we will see, small group sizes will have good performance.

On the other hand, in AC and NB strategies, the RP module performs the same comparison of input activations as performed in the SC strategy. Now, the overhead may be incurred in the precomputation of weight sums. However, notice that these sums can be performed offline at load time. As occurs in SC, AC and NB strategy costs are directly related to the group size (G).

4 Evaluation

We have chosen state-of-the-art CNN models used in real-world applications: ResNet-50 and MobileNet-V2, both oriented to perform image classification and Yolo-V3 for real-time object detection segmentation. We use the INT8 quantised version of these models available in the ONNX Model Zoo, which adds an acceptable error compared to floating point versions. For the datasets, we use Imagenet [2] for the ResNet-50 and MobileNet-V2 inference and COCO [11] for Yolo-V3 inference.

4.1 Input Repetition Analysis

Firstly, we analyse the RF of the targeted models using the studies described in the previous section. For the following results, we use the targeted models by extracting the input tensors of each convolution. Then, we perform the study with 50 different images and extract the average of each RF for each layer.

Figure 7 shows the analysis of the three models with the SC strategy with a group size equal to 4 ($G = 4$), representing with colours the percentage of RF calculated to process the input convolution of each layer in the model. The same set of input images has been used for ResNet-50 and MobileNet. In blue, we show the percentage of groups with RF set to three, which means the percentage of times that all four elements within the group present the same value. In yellow, we show the percentage of groups with RF set to 2. Similarly, green and red colours show the percentages for RF set to one and zero, respectively. With RF set to zero, all the group elements differ in value.

The first thing to note is that the RF distribution is not constant across layers and models. The repetition between the input activations of convolution layers is more influenced by the topology of the network than the image itself, as Fig. 7 and Fig. 7b represents the inference of the same images of the dataset but using two different topologies. ResNet-50 model presents a significantly bigger percentage of repetition. The first layer in ResNet-50 and MobileNet models shows a low percentage of repetition. The repetition pattern gets more frequent in successive layers in those models, although more noticeable in the ResNet-50 model. Contrary to this, in Yolo-V3, the repetition pattern is more frequent at the first layers of the model. Nonetheless, the percentage of RF set to three and two is more than 50% in ResNet-50 and Yolo-V3, slightly lower in MobileNet.

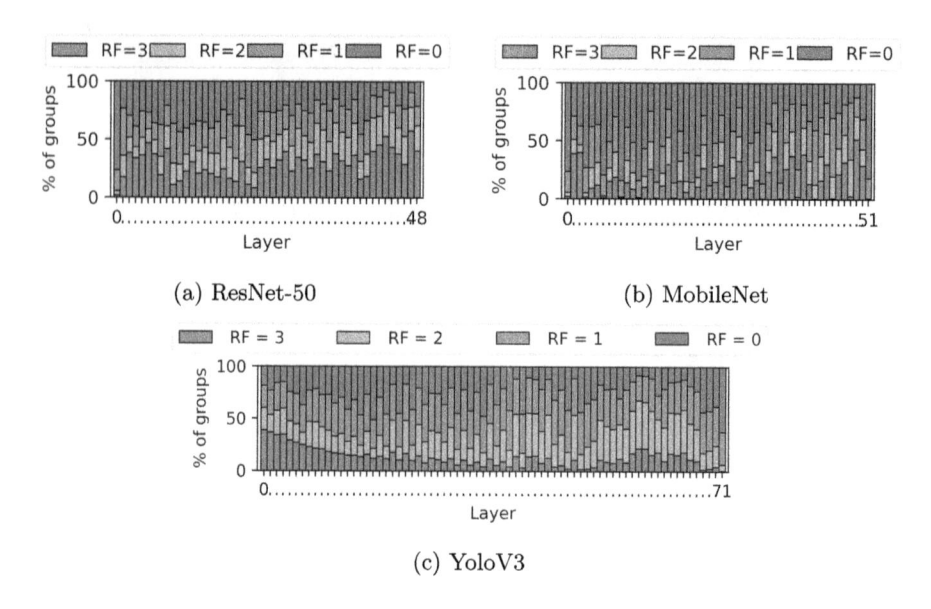

Fig. 7. Repetition factor in SC in different CNN models. $G = 4$.

Table 1 extends the analysis to different group sizes and grouping strategies. This table shows the average RF of each model for each grouping strategy and group size. These results show a considerable activation repetition that can be exploited. The table shows that the repetition factor is improved with a bigger group size. However, incrementing the group size means incrementing the complexity of the possible accelerator.

Table 1. Average RF for each model and grouping strategy

Group size	SC					AC					NB
	4	8	16	32	64	4	8	16	32	64	9
ResNet-50	1.40	3.48	8.41	19.50	44.72	1.10	3.00	7.49	17.71	41.39	4.29
Yolo-V3	1.40	3.48	12.42	22.39	50.89	1.21	2.29	6.80	18.50	45.82	4.69
MobileNet	1.18	3.09	9.39	18.32	43.08	0.69	2.41	6.36	16.31	41,46	4.69

4.2 Average Speedup

In input repetition, the maximum theoretical reduction that can be accomplished is equal to the group size. The RF results shown before confirming a significant input repetition opportunity in all the models studied, which means we could benefit from this by implementing a specialised accelerator or algorithm. In

(a) ResNet-50

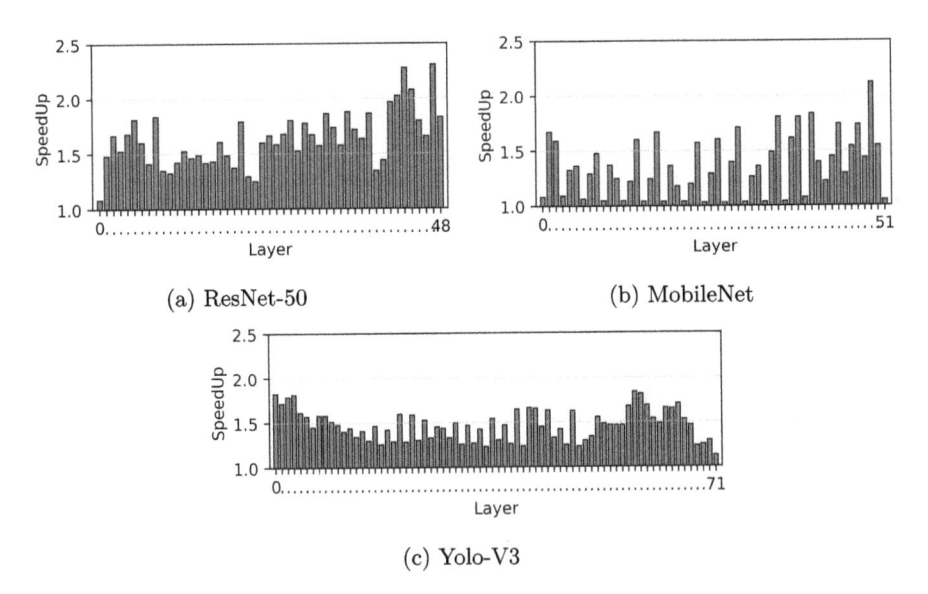

(b) MobileNet

(c) Yolo-V3

Fig. 8. Speedup for SC on each model layer. $G = 4$. Different models.

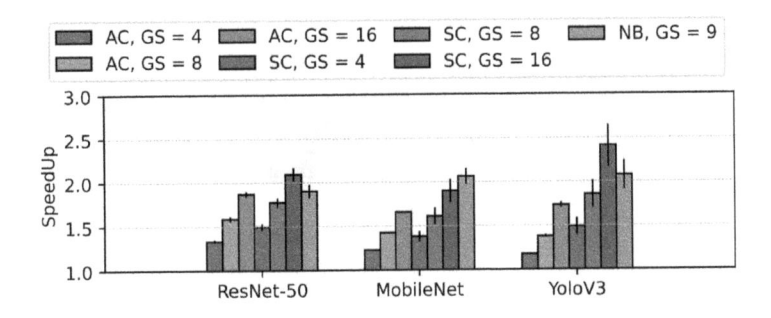

Fig. 9. SpeedUp for each maping strategy. Different models and group sizes.

Fig. 8, we can see each layer's multiplication speedup resulting by exploiting the SC repetition of a group size of 4 in each model.

As we can observe, in all the layers for all models, we obtain speedup results higher than one. Notice the more benefits obtained in both ResNet-50 and Yolo-V3. Also, remarkable is the effect in the MobileNet with layers with almost no benefit ($S = 1$) mixed with layers with good speedup ($S = 1.5$). Notice that each layer has a different number of input activations and filters. Therefore, these results do not directly translate to the final speedup of the whole model inference time.

Figure 9 shows each mapping strategy speedup where the layer's size has been considered for the computation. This figure also shows the error bar representing the standard deviation of the input repetition between images. We can see that the AC strategy better exploits input repeatability. With the smallest group size

($G = 4$), we have an overall speedup of 1.5, 1.4 and 1.5 on each model, respectively. Alternatively, we can save the number of resources for multiplications by 33.3%, 28.6% and 33.3% for each model, respectively. With the largest group size ($G = 16$), we observe with SC an overall speedup of 2.1, 1.9 and 2.4 for each model, which means 52%, 47,4% and 58.3% of multiplications saving while preserving the model accuracy. The error bars represented in this figure show that the repetition is also influenced by the image studied. For instance, the NB strategy is the one with the highest variation by input image, followed by the SC strategy.

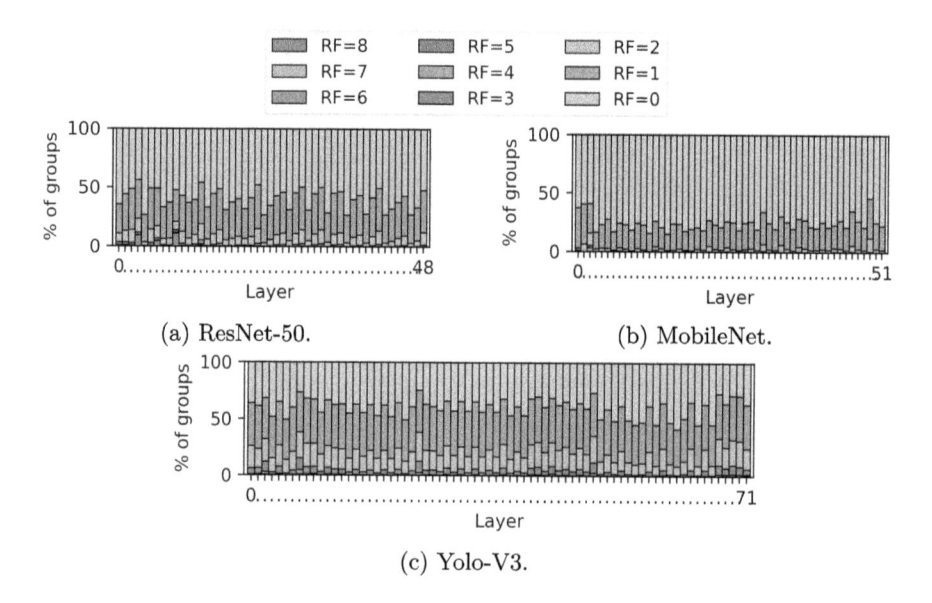

Fig. 10. Weights repetition with $G = 9$.

4.3 Weight Repetition

In this final analysis, we compare the repetition factor found in the model filters, known as weight repetition (as exploited in [6]). Figure 10 shows the weight repetition of the three models. As we can observe, the RF set to zero and one prevails in weight repetition, representing approximately 90% in ResNet-50, 97% in MobileNet and 75% in Yolo-V3. These results show that, by exploiting input repetition, the number of multiplications saved is considerably larger. For example, if we compare the NB results with the weight repetition result, the average RF in NB with $G = 9$ is equal to 4.29, 4.69 and 4.69 in the three respective models. In contrast, in weight repetition, the average RF are equal to 0.5, 0.4, and 0.9 for Resnet, Mobilenet and Yolo-V3, respectively.

5 Conclusions

In this paper, we have presented a repetition data analysis of the input of convolutional layers of 8-bit quantised CNN models. We have used Yolo-V3, ResNet-50 and MobileNet-v1 models, which are state-of-the-art CNNs. This study shows that it is feasible to create a future hardware accelerator that reduces the number of multiplication operators by exploiting the input repetition and, as a result, reducing the resources needed while maintaining execution time and accuracy. We demonstrate that there is an exploitable redundancy at the input, and we calculate the theoretical reduction factor by analysing three different grouping strategies. Results show that it is possible to reduce 52%, 47.4% and 58.3% of multiplications for ResNet-50, MobileNet-v1 and Yolo-V3, respectively, while preserving their complete accuracy.

Acknowledgements. This work has received funding from the Valencian government project "Ifac: Implementing Fault-Tolerant Autonomous Computers (CISEJI/2022/30)".

References

1. ONNX model zoo. https://github.com/onnx/models. Accessed 27 Feb 2023
2. Deng, J., et al.: ImageNet: a large-scale hierarchical image database. In: 2009 IEEE Conference on Computer Vision and Pattern Recognition, pp. 248–255. IEEE (2009)
3. Geng, L., Niu, B.: Pruning convolutional neural networks via filter similarity analysis. Mach. Learn. **111**(9), 3161–3180 (2022)
4. Gonçalves, L.R., Draghetti, L.K., Rech, P., Carro, L.: Using frame similarity for low energy software-only IoT video recognition. In: Pnevmatikatos, D.N., Pelcat, M., Jung, M. (eds.) SAMOS 2019. LNCS, vol. 11733, pp. 157–168. Springer, Cham (2019). https://doi.org/10.1007/978-3-030-27562-4_11
5. He, K., et al.: Deep residual learning for image recognition. In: Proceedings of the IEEE Conference on Computer Vision and Pattern Recognition, pp. 770–778 (2016)
6. Hegde, K., et al.: UCNN: exploiting computational reuse in deep neural networks via weight repetition. In: 2018 ACM/IEEE 45th Annual International Symposium on Computer Architecture (ISCA), pp. 674–687. IEEE (2018)
7. Hoefler, T., et al.: Sparsity in deep learning: pruning and growth for efficient inference and training in neural networks. J. Mach. Learn. Res. **22**(1), 10882–11005 (2021)
8. Hubara, I., et al.: Quantized neural networks: training neural networks with low precision weights and activations. J. Mach. Learn. Res. **18**(1), 6869–6898 (2017)
9. Jiao, X., et al.: Energy-efficient neural networks using approximate computation reuse. In: 2018 Design, Automation and Test in Europe Conference and Exhibition (DATE), pp. 1223–1228 (2018)
10. Kang, S., et al.: An overview of sparsity exploitation in CNNs for on-device intelligence with software-hardware cross-layer optimizations. IEEE J. Emerg. Sel. Top. Circuits Syst. **11**(4), 634–648 (2021)

11. Lin, T.-Y., et al.: Microsoft COCO: common objects in context. In: Fleet, D., Pajdla, T., Schiele, B., Tuytelaars, T. (eds.) ECCV 2014, Part V. LNCS, vol. 8693, pp. 740–755. Springer, Cham (2014). https://doi.org/10.1007/978-3-319-10602-1_48
12. Ma, D., et al.: AXR-NN: approximate computation reuse for energy-efficient convolutional neural networks, pp. 363–368 (2020)
13. Meng, Z., et al.: Identity-aware convolutional neural network for facial expression recognition. In: 2017 12th IEEE International Conference on Automatic Face & Gesture Recognition (FG 2017), pp. 558–565. IEEE (2017)
14. Minaee, S., et al.: Image segmentation using deep learning: a survey. IEEE Trans. Pattern Anal. Mach. Intell. **44**(7), 3523–3542 (2021)
15. Redmon, J., Farhadi, A.: Yolov3: An incremental improvement. arXiv preprint arXiv:1804.02767 (2018)
16. Riera, M., et al.: Computation reuse in DNNs by exploiting input similarity. In: 2018 ACM/IEEE 45th Annual International Symposium on Computer Architecture (ISCA), pp. 57–68 (2018)
17. Sandler, M., et al.: MobileNetV2: inverted residuals and linear bottlenecks. In: Proceedings of the IEEE Conference on Computer Vision and Pattern Recognition, pp. 4510–4520 (2018)
18. Yasoubi, A., et al.: Power-efficient accelerator design for neural networks using computation reuse. IEEE Comput. Archit. Lett. **16**(1), 72–75 (2016)
19. Zhiqiang, W., Jun, L.: A review of object detection based on convolutional neural network. In: 2017 36th Chinese Control Conference (CCC), pp. 11104–11109. IEEE (2017)

The Quest of Finding the Antidote to Sparse Double Descent

Victor Quétu(✉) and Marta Milovanović

LTCI, Télécom Paris, Institut Polytechnique de Paris, Palaiseau, France
{victor.quetu,marta.milovanovic}@telecom-paris.fr

Abstract. In energy-efficient schemes, finding the optimal size of deep learning models is very important and has a broad impact. Meanwhile, recent studies have reported an unexpected phenomenon, the sparse double descent: as the model's sparsity increases, the performance first worsens, then improves, and finally deteriorates. Such a non-monotonic behavior raises serious questions about the optimal model's size to maintain high performance: the model needs to be sufficiently over-parametrized, but having too many parameters wastes training resources.

In this paper, we aim to find the best trade-off efficiently. More precisely, we tackle the occurrence of the sparse double descent and present some solutions to avoid it. Firstly, we show that a simple ℓ_2 regularization method can help to mitigate this phenomenon but sacrifices the performance/sparsity compromise. To overcome this problem, we then introduce a learning scheme in which distilling knowledge regularizes the student model. Supported by experimental results achieved using typical image classification setups, we show that this approach leads to the avoidance of such a phenomenon.

Keywords: Sparse double descent · pruning · regularization · knowledge distillation · deep learning

1 Introduction

The field of computer vision has undergone a remarkable transformation with the advent of deep neural networks (DNNs). These models possess the ability to learn high-level representations of features from raw input data [13]. Compared to conventional machine learning algorithms, DNNs have demonstrated superior performance across various visual recognition tasks. Notably, they have achieved state-of-the-art results in challenging areas such as segmentation [9]. Moreover, DNNs have excelled in image classification [4], as well as in object detection [28]. DNNs have the capacity to process large amounts of data, enabling them to capture intricate patterns and details. By training on extensive datasets, DNNs can generalize their learned knowledge to effectively recognize and interpret novel, previously unseen examples. This ability to generalize contributes to their robustness and adaptability in real-world scenarios.

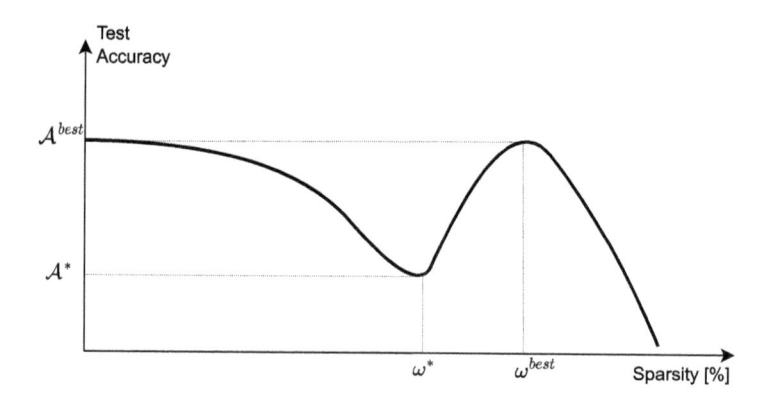

Fig. 1. The Sparse Double Descent phenomenon: as the model's sparsity increases, the performance first worsens, then improves, and finally deteriorates.

However, a significant disadvantage of DNNs is that they are prone to overfitting; as a result, learning procedures need to be created to counteract it. The most direct solution would be to increase the dataset size, as deep learning techniques are well-known for their data hunger. Since they usually optimize some objective function through gradient descent, having a larger training set helps the optimization process to find the most appropriate set of features, resulting in high performance on unseen data. But, such an approach presents two shortcomings: it requires enormous computational power for training and large annotated datasets. While addressing the first drawback remains an actual research topic [7,15], the second is broadly explored with approaches like transfer learning [26] or self-supervised learning [38].

In reality, large datasets are typically unavailable: in the context of *frugal AI*, techniques requiring a small amount of data need to be used, arising research questions on the enlargement of available datasets or the transfer of knowledge from similar tasks. However, it brings also into question the optimal dimension of the deep learning model to be trained. As opposed to what the bias-variance trade-off suggests, the *double descent* (DD) phenomenon can be observed in a very over-parameterized network [5]: given some set of parameters w for the model with accuracy value $\mathcal{A}$, adding parameters will first improve the performance until a local maximum $\mathcal{A}^{best}$ beyond which, adding even more parameters, will worsen the performance until a local minimum $\mathcal{A}^*$, before going back increasing. Regularly reported in the literature [17,42], this phenomenon raises the challenge of finding the best set of parameters, avoiding entering an over-parametrized or under-parameterized regime. Similar to this, a *sparse double descent* (SDD) phenomenon is exhibited when the model shifts via parameter pruning from an over-parametrized towards a sparser regime [20], displayed in Fig. 1. Finding w^{best} is a problem requiring a lot of computation, or extremely over-sizing the model, which are the two possible solutions to address this challenge. Since neither of these two approaches are suitable for a frugal setup, we are investigating if a solution to address this problem can be found.

Our work is structured as follows. First, we highlight the occurrence of the sparse double descent phenomenon in traditional image classification setups (Sect. 3). Then, we show that a standard regularization method like ℓ_2 regularization can help to eschew sparse double descent and we underline its limits (Sect. 4). Moreover, to overcome these limits, we introduce a learning scheme in which a student model is regularized by distilling knowledge from a sparse teacher in its best validation accuracy region (or even with a dense teacher) observing that the student is shunning such a phenomenon (Sect. 5). Finally, we discuss the environmental impact and the potential future directions of our work (Sect. 6).

2 Related Works

Noisy Data in the Real World. In the real world, the acquisition of data or the labeling process can typically lead to a noisy data collection [18]. Numerous works have addressed the issue of annotation noise and suggested ways to avoid learning the incorrect feature sets. For instance, [25] proposes a unified distillation framework that uses the knowledge gained from a small, clean dataset and a semantic knowledge graph to correct noisy labels. The advantages of noise on the neurological system are used as inspiration in other works to discover solutions: in [3], it has been demonstrated how adding constructive noise to the collaborative learning framework at various levels makes it possible to train the model effectively and extract desirable traits from the student model. As a single image might be classified under multiple categories, distinct samples might have label noise of varied intensities. The normalized knowledge distillation feature, which introduces the sample-specific correction factor to replace the temperature, was proposed by [44]. By using a teacher-student strategy, [22] was able to estimate the noise in the training data using Otsu's technique and determine the border between overfitting and good generalization. Other studies concentrate more on the accuracy of the label's prediction. For example, [40] presented a straightforward technique that, by introducing noise and perturbing the teacher's logit outputs, improves student learning and yields results that are more similar to the teacher network. Because it is present in the loss layer in this configuration, the noise replicates a multi-teacher environment and has the effect of a regularizer. A common method is to manually introduce noise into some well-annotated, well-known datasets, such as MNIST and CIFAR-10/100, in order to simulate noise in the labels [20,32]. A similar approach is used in AI security studies, where noise is parametrically inserted to assess the model's resilience to attacks. This approach is known as "adversarial learning" [30] because these attacks offer adversarial interpretations of the data and evaluate the performance of the model.

From Double Descent to Sparse Double Descent in Classification Tasks. Given the existence of labeling noise, the threat posed by DD is real. Multiple machine learning models, including decision trees, random features [29], linear regression [31], and deep neural networks [45], have already reported the existence of the DD phenomenon. For classification tasks, standard deep neural networks, such as the ResNet architecture, trained on image classification datasets consistently follow a double descent curve both when label noise is injected (CIFAR-10), and in some cases, even without any label noise injection (CIFAR-100) [45]. The study [32] demonstrates that double descent happens as a function of both the number of training epochs and as the model size when the model width is increased. Indeed, the double descent phenomenon has been thoroughly investigated within the context of over-parametrization [8,32]. As opposed to the DD phenomenon, the SDD phenomenon occurs when a dense model is unstructurely pruned, in the transition from the complex model to the sparse, pruned model (as illustrated in Fig. 1) [20]. Given that SDD renders many criteria, such as when to stop the pruning, uncertain, it has consequences for model selection, regularization methods, and understanding the behavior of complicated models in high-dimensional contexts.

Frugal AI and Sparse Double Descent. Frugality involves working with limited resources and it manifests in different ways [14]. One may consider input frugality, which focuses on the costs associated with data and it may involve a reduced amount of training data or fewer features than in the non-frugal scenario. Another type is learning process frugality, which emphasizes the costs associated with the learning process itself, including computational and memory resources. Finally, model frugality focuses on the costs associated with storing or using machine learning models (e.g. classifiers or regression models), driven by resource constraints like low memory or processing power. Frugal models for supervised learning may need less memory and generate predictions with less computing power than what is necessary for optimal prediction quality.

To reduce the computational footprint of models at training and inference, the training of sparse neural networks has been studied for resource-constrained settings [41]. Indeed, sparse double descent is closely linked to frugality. Such a phenomenon typically occurs while training sparse models and it raises the challenge of finding the best set of parameters during model pruning.

In the next section, we will present and show the occurrence of the SDD phenomenon.

3 Occurrence of Sparse Double Descent

Exposing Sparse Double Descent. We present an algorithm to expose the sparse double descent phenomenon in Algorithm 1. First, the dense model, represented by its parameters w, is trained on the learning task Ξ, eventually with a ℓ_2 regularization weighted by λ (line 2). Then, the model is pruned (line 4), using an unstructured pruning method called magnitude-based pruning popularized by [19] in which a given amount of weights ζ^{iter}, below some specific threshold, are pruned. At each pruning iteration, a fixed ζ^{iter} amount of weights from the model is removed. Magnitude-based pruning is used because of its competitiveness in terms of both effectiveness and computational simplicity [16]

Algorithm 1. Iterative magnitude pruning algorithm to expose SDD: **P**rune, **T**rain, **R**epeat.

1: **procedure PTR** (w^{init}, Ξ, λ, ζ^{iter}, ζ^{end})
2:     $w \leftarrow$ Train(w^{init}, Ξ, λ)
3:     **while** Sparsity(w, w^{init}) $< \zeta^{end}$ **do**
4:         $w \leftarrow$ Prune(w, ζ^{iter})
5:         $w \leftarrow$ Train(w,Ξ, λ)
6:     **end while**
7: **end procedure**

despite the existence of more complex pruning methods. Since after pruning the performance of the model is affected, the model is retrained using the same original policy (line 5). Recent works have shown that this approach leads to the best performance at the highest sparsities [36]. Once the sparsity's model reaches ζ^{end}, the pruning process ends.

Setup. The same approach as He et al. [20] is followed for the experimental setup. The first model we train is ResNet-18, trained on CIFAR-10 & CIFAR-100, for 160 epochs, optimized with SGD, having momentum 0.9, a learning rate of 0.1 decayed by a factor 0.1 at milestones 80 and 120, batch size 128 and λ equal to 1e−4. The second model is ViT, with 4 patches, 8 heads, and 512 embedding dimensions, trained on CIFAR-10 and CIFAR-100 for 200 epochs, optimized with SGD, having a learning rate of 1e−4 with a cosine annealing schedule and λ equal to 0.03. For each dataset, a percentage ε of symmetric, noisy labels is introduced: the labels of a given proportion of training samples are flipped to one of the other class labels, selected with equal probability [27]. In our experiments, we set $\varepsilon \in \{10\%, 20\%, 50\%\}$. Moreover, we also conduct experiments without adding synthetic noise, as it has clean structures which greatly enable statistical analyses but often fail to model real-world noise patterns. Towards this end, we carry out experiments also on CIFAR-100N, a dataset presented by [43], which is formed by the CIFAR-100 training dataset equipped with human-annotated real-world noisy labels collected from Amazon Mechanical Turk. Thus, we use the same architectures and learning policies presented above. In all experiments, we use ζ^{iter} to 20% and $\zeta^{end} > 99.8\%$.

Occurrence of Sparse Double Descent. Figure 2 displays the results of ResNet-18 and ViT, on CIFAR-10 and CIFAR-100. As in He et al. [20] work, the double descent consists of 4 phases. First, at low sparsities, the network is overparameterized, thus pruned network can still reach similar accuracy to the dense model. The second phase is a phase near the "interpolation threshold", where training accuracy is going to drop, and test accuracy is about to first decrease and then increase as sparsity grows. The third phase is located at high sparsities, where test accuracy is rising. The final phase happens when both training and test accuracy drop significantly. For all the investigated noise rates ε, whether on CIFAR-10 or CIFAR-100, the sparse double descent phenomenon occurs both

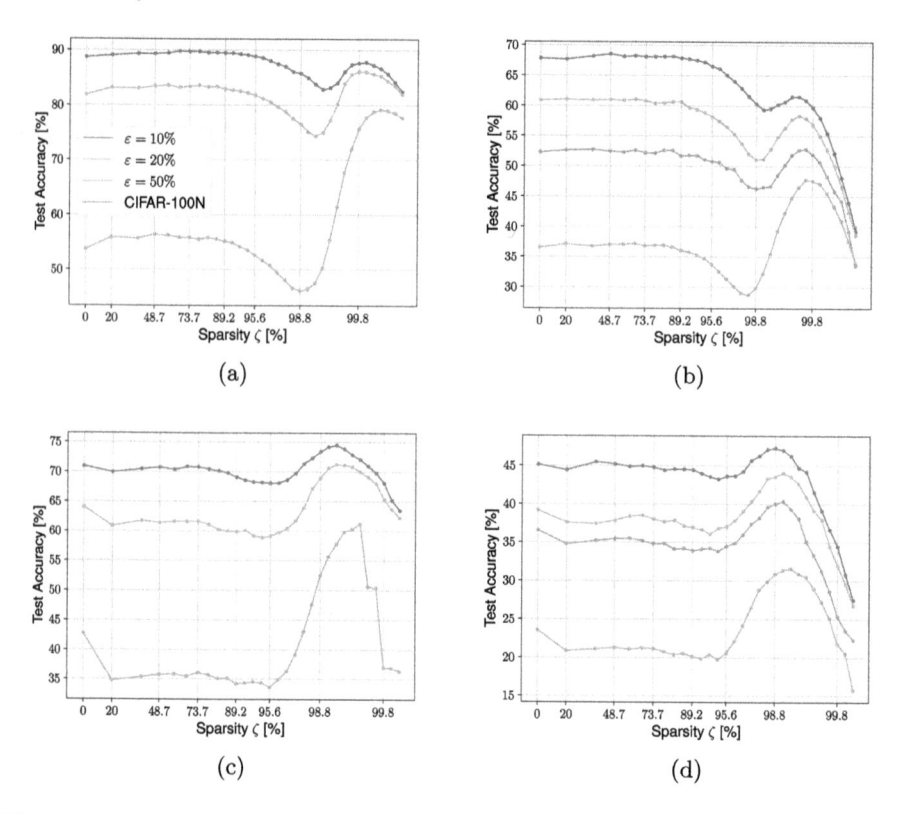

Fig. 2. Test accuracy of ResNet-18 on CIFAR-10 (a) and CIFAR-100 (b) ($\lambda = 1 \times 10^{-4}$), and on ViT on CIFAR-10 (c) and CIFAR-100 (d) ($\lambda = 0.03$).

for ResNet and ViT. We observe a similar phenomenon in the simulated ε of the human-annotated CIFAR-100N.

Looking at the curves in Fig. 2, it is clear that it is difficult to define the traditional early stopping criteria. Indeed, they may make the mistake of stopping the algorithm when the model reaches a minimum performance in the second phase, whereas it increases again during the next phases. Avoiding the sparse double descent phenomenon would allow us to use the traditional stopping criteria. Indeed, if the performance becomes monotonic, we can stop the algorithm when the performance starts deteriorating, knowing that it will never improve again after that point, enabling us to save computational training costs and find easily the best performance/sparsity trade-off.

Toward this end, we present in the next section an approach using ℓ_2 regularization to avoid SDD.

4 ℓ_2 Regularization Helps to Lessen the Sparse Double Descent

The Positive Contribution of ℓ_2 Regularization. Recently, it has been shown that, for certain linear regression models with isotropic data distribution, optimally-tuned ℓ_2 regularization can achieve monotonic test performance as either the sample size or the model size is grown. Nakkiran et al. [33] demonstrated it analytically and established that optimally-tuned ℓ_2 regularization can mitigate double descent for general models, including neural networks like Convolutional Neural Networks. However, for classification tasks, this problem is not easily alleviated. In our study [37], it has been shown that the more challenging the dataset and classification task, the harder it is to avoid DD. In fact, we show that, for simple setups like a LeNet-300-100 trained on MNIST dataset, the sparse double descent is disappearing when the ℓ_2 regularization is used. However, for more complex tasks, like ResNet-18 on CIFAR datasets, whether the regularization is employed or not, the sparse double descent occurs and is present in both cases. Indeed, an ablation study over λ confirms that even for high values of λ, the phenomenon is not dodged: the overall performance of the model drops because the imposed regularization becomes too strong to allow the model to learn the training set entirely. However, our recent work [35] shows that an optimally-tuned ℓ_2 regularization relieves sparse double descent in vision transformers (ViT). Carrying out an ablation study over λ, we demonstrate that incrementing λ smoothens the bump of the test loss, and at some point, i.e. for λ_{opt}, the test loss becomes flat and behaves monotonically: the phenomenon is dodged. Note that for $\lambda > \lambda_{opt}$, sparse double descent is also avoided but the performance worsens as the regularization is stronger.

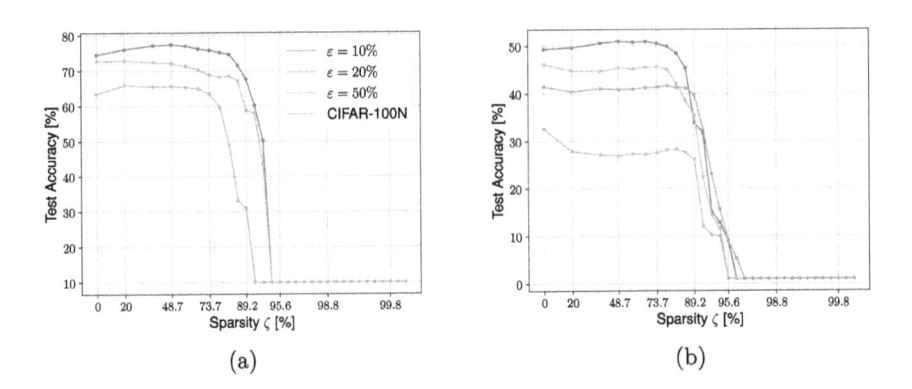

Fig. 3. Test accuracy of ViT with different amount of noise ε on CIFAR-10 (a) and CIFAR-100 (b) with $\lambda = 1$ ($\varepsilon \in \{10\%, 20\}$), $\lambda = 3$ ($\varepsilon = 50\%$).

Dodging the Sparse Double Descent. To illustrate these facts, the results of ViT on CIFAR-10/CIFAR-100 with $\varepsilon \in \{10\%, 20\%, 50\%\}$ with λ_{opt} are portrayed in Fig. 3. With $\lambda = 1$, for small noise rates, i.e. $\varepsilon \leq 20\%$, the phenomenon vanishes and performance is enhanced. However, for higher noise rates, like $\varepsilon = 50\%$, the sparse double descent is mitigated, but still present. Even if it already helps, the strength of the regularization is not high enough to completely avoid the phenomenon but with a higher value of λ, i.e., equal to 3, the performance becomes monotonic.

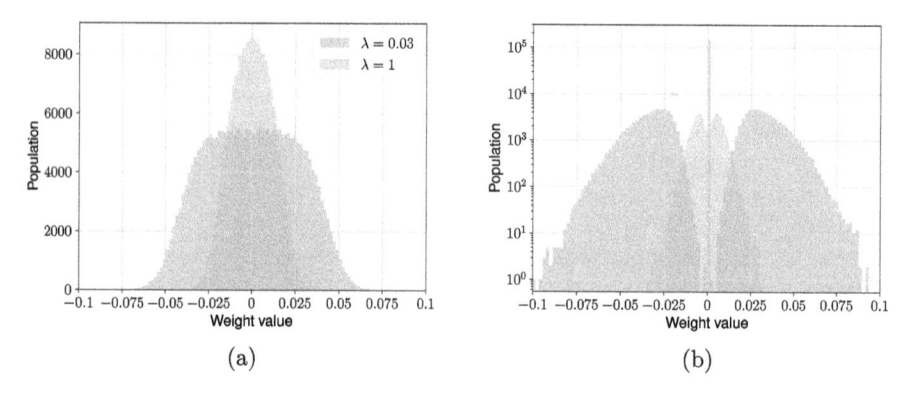

Fig. 4. Histogram of the weights of ViT for $\varepsilon = 10\%$ on CIFAR-10, with $\zeta = 0\%$ (a) and $\zeta = 48.8\%$ (b).

Performance/Sparsity Trade-Off. We show in Table 1 a comparison between the use of an optimal ℓ_2 regularization and regular techniques on CIFAR-10 with $\varepsilon = 10\%$ regarding performance, sparsity and computational cost. Vanilla training joined with traditional early stopping criteria, costing more than 289 PFLOPs (second line), leads to a model with harmed performance and lower sparsity in comparison with the entire pruning process, requiring 443 PFLOPs (first line). On the other hand, the use of the optimal ℓ_2 regularization enabling the model to dodge sparse double descent results in a model with the lowest sparsity and worse performance than the full pruning process, but needs fewer FLOPs than the other approaches. Indeed, as visible in Fig. 3, at high sparsity i.e., $> 90\%$, the performance is very deteriorated and even reaches random guess when λ_{opt} is used: when we avoid SDD, the capacity of the model to be compressed suffers at high regularization regimes. This behavior is a result of the strong prior we impose on the distribution of the parameters of the model. The greater this prior, the fewer degrees of freedom we are able to eliminate from our system. The distribution of the parameters for one of the possible training setups, for $\lambda = 0.03$ and $\lambda = 1$, without pruning and after two pruning stages is shown in Fig. 4 as a visual example to illustrate this behavior. With stronger regularization, the parameters have less variance despite being removed in the same amount, which has the dual effect of making them more robust to injected noise (due to the strong regularization), but also making this distribution more sensitive to compression by pruning. Thus, we draw the conclusion that, if we aim for a robust and well-generalizing model, we should avoid SDD and use strong ℓ_2 regularization. On the other hand, if we aim for compressibility, we should prefer SDD because the better generalizing region is pushed to the highly compressed regions.

Table 1. Performance and training computational cost between the different approaches for ViT on CIFAR-10 with $\varepsilon = 10\%$.

Early stop	λ_{opt}	Training cost [PFLOPs] (↓)	CO_2 emissions [g] (↓)	Test accuracy [%] (↑)	Sparsity [%] (↑)
		443.68	563.5	74.47 ± 0.01	99.26
✓		289.33	367.5	68.07 ± 0.02	95.60
✓	✓	192.89	245.0	71.48 ± 0.06	86.58

Although a standard regularization approach like ℓ_2, is already positively contributing to dodging the sparse double descent, it also presents some flaws. In some setups, like ResNet-18 on CIFAR datasets, the sparse double descent is still noticeable even if ℓ_2 regularization is used [37]. Moreover, this regularization has the big drawback of sacrificing the performance/sparsity trade-off. Thus, the need to design a custom regularization towards avoidance of sparse double descent is becoming apparent. In the next section, we present a learning scheme in which a student model is regularized by distilling knowledge from a sparse teacher in its best validation accuracy region (or even with a dense teacher), observing that the student is dodging SDD.

5 Distilling Knowledge Shuns Sparse Double Descent

Combining Knowledge Distillation and Network Pruning. The combination of knowledge distillation (KD) and pruning has already been examined in various studies. The study [46] proposes a "progressive feature distribution distillation" to improve generalization when working with a smaller training set. This method entails obtaining a student network by pruning a trained network, followed by distilling the feature distribution into the student network. The size reduction of the final model is a primary goal of studies combining the two approaches. For instance, [12] use structured pruning and dense knowledge distillation approaches to drastically compress an initial large language model into a compressed shallow (but still deep) network. The study [24] revealed that standard KD applied to word-level prediction can be useful for Neural Machine Translation. Therein, on top of KD, weight pruning was used to reduce the number of parameters. Studies [10] and [1] are examples of efforts in the area of image processing that are more practical and aimed at improving performance on a sparsified model. Moreover, the study [34] provides a number of examples where the "prune, then distill" approach is highly effective, drawing on the advantageous, well-generalizing qualities of both pruning and KD.

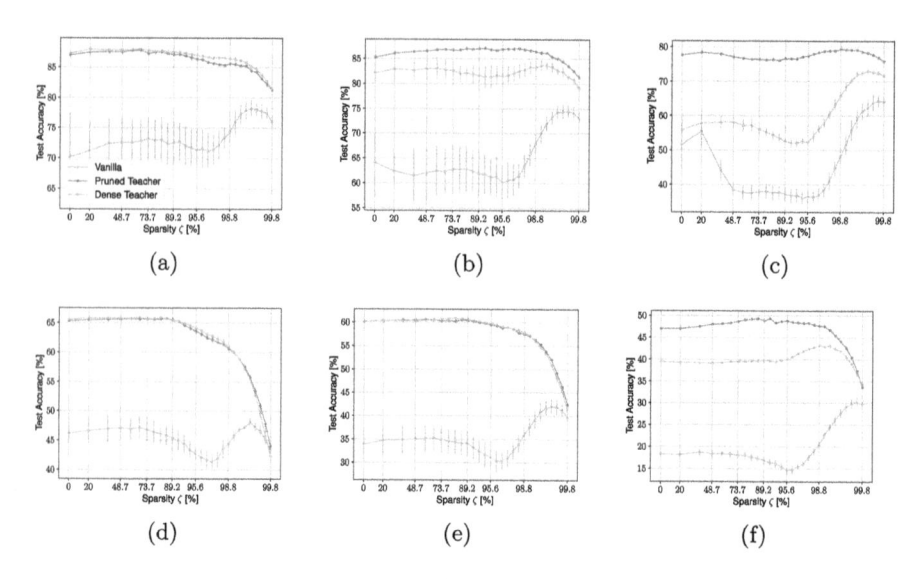

Fig. 5. Performance of the VGG-like model on CIFAR-10 (a, b, c) and CIFAR-100 (d, e, f) for different label noises. **Left.** $\varepsilon = 10\%$ **Middle.** $\varepsilon = 20\%$ **Right.** $\varepsilon = 50\%$

Working on a related research subject, the authors of [8] explored whether it could be more practical to train a small model directly or rather first train a larger one and then prune it, highlighting the significance of additional research on the SDD. The authors of this work offer persuasive proof that the latter tactic is successful in improving model performance in sparsified regimes. The DD phenomenon in a self-supervised setting was used to give pseudo-labels to a large held-out dataset [11]. Whilst this approach attempted to exploit DD, our aim, in contrast to this work, is to avoid the sparse double descent in order to improve performance on the final student model on the same task and dataset as the teacher. Motivated by [39] and building on top of [34] (although in a very different context), we present in the next paragraph our approach that will drive our quest towards the dodging of SDD.

Approach. In an image classification setup, inside a KD framework, the typical objective function minimized to train a tinier student network is a linear combination of the standard cross-entropy loss $\mathcal{L}_{CE}$, using "hard" ground truth labels, and the Kullback-Leibler divergence loss $\mathcal{L}_{KL}$, calculated between the teacher's predictions $\boldsymbol{y}^t$ and the student's ones $\boldsymbol{y}^s$, scaled by a temperature τ:

$$\mathcal{L} = (1-\alpha)\mathcal{L}_{CE}(\boldsymbol{y}^s, \hat{\boldsymbol{y}}) + \alpha\mathcal{L}_{KL}(\boldsymbol{y}^s, \boldsymbol{y}^t, \tau) \quad (1)$$

where $\hat{\boldsymbol{y}}$ stands for the ground truth target, and α is the distillation hyperparameter weighting the average between the two losses. Our KD scheme employs the same formulation loss as in [21,23].

To train and sparsify the student model, the same procedure- but changing the objective function to (1)- as in Algorithm 1 is employed. The teacher used to distill its knowledge can be either a pruned model in its best-fit regime (*i.e.*, with the best validation accuracy) or its dense (*i.e.*, unpruned) version.

Results. To conduct the following experiments, a "VGG-like" model is defined characterized by its depth δ (the larger, the deeper the model) and the number of convolutional filters per layer 2^γ (the larger, the wider the model) following [36]. The results on CIFAR-10 and CIFAR-100 with $\varepsilon \in \{10\%, 20\%, 50\%\}$ are portrayed in Fig. 5. A ResNet-18 teacher, whose performance can be found in Fig. 2, is used to distill the knowledge in a VGG-like student model with $\gamma = 32$ and $\delta = 5$. For every value of ε, the sparse double descent phenomenon is always revealed by the student model trained with a vanilla-training setup. Nonetheless, the same student model trained within our KD scheme is consistently eschewing this phenomenon, whether the knowledge is distilled from the pruned or the dense teacher.

Table 2. Performance and training computational cost between traditional approaches and our scheme for a VGG-like model on CIFAR-10 with $\varepsilon = 20\%$.

Early stop	Distillation	Distillation from pruned teacher	Training FLOPs [PFLOPs] (↓)	CO_2 emissions [g] (↓)	Test accuracy [%] (↑)	Sparsity [%] (↑)
			48.84	510	74.52 ± 1.20	99.62
✓			4.88	51	60.23 ± 3.37	36.00
✓	✓		35.82	374	81.52 ± 1.85	99.26
✓	✓	✓	35.82	374	86.89 ± 0.16	99.26

Computation/Performance Trade-Off. The comparison between our approach and traditional techniques on CIFAR-10 with $\varepsilon = 20\%$ regarding performance achieved and computational cost at training time is presented in Table 2. Vanilla training joined with traditional early stopping criteria, (second line) leads to a model with low sparsity and poor performance. To reach decent performance, the whole pruning process has to be entirely completed until all of its parameters are completely removed, which costs more than 48 PFLOPs (first line). On the other hand, our method produces a model with high sparsity achieving more than 10% improvement in performance with approximately 25% less computation. We believe this to be a core practical contribution in real-world scenarios, particularly when working with limited and noisy annotated datasets, where SDD can easily occur.

6 Environmental Impact

Carbon Emissions at Training Time. Besides comparing the training cost, in terms of FLOPs required to achieve the models with the different mentioned approaches above, we also present the estimation of emitted CO_2 at training time using [2] in Tables 1 and 2.

Despite leading to a model with a worse performance/sparsity trade-off, the use of an optimal ℓ_2 regularization is the greener approach, as it can be observed in Table 1, saving at least 30% of carbon emissions compared to the two other methods. Indeed, the vanilla approach without early stopping criteria, is offering the best performance/sparsity compromise but is the biggest emitter of CO_2 with more than 550g of carbon emissions.

Concerning our KD scheme, vanilla training joined with traditional early stopping criteria is the greener approach, emitting 51g of CO_2, but has the big drawback to lead to a model with low sparsity and poor performance, as given in Table 2. Since the whole pruning process has to be entirely completed until all of its parameters are completely removed to achieve better performance, the vanilla approach is the biggest polluter with more than 500g of carbon emissions. On the other hand, our method, producing a model with high sparsity and achieving more than 10% improvement in performance, saves more than 25% of CO_2 emissions.

CO_2 at Inference Time. Our presented approaches already enable us to reduce the carbon footprint at training time. However, since a neural network is going to be used multiple times for inference, it is also important to lessen the CO_2 emissions related to this use. Indeed, the chosen unstructured pruning technique is only limited to the identification of the portion of the parameters that can be set to zero. Therefore, it offers very few, if any, practical benefits when it comes to the deployment of the model in a resource-constrained system. To make the most of it in real-life scenarios and address this problem, a study to optimally deploy our models onto an edge device should be carried on, and the use of specifically designed libraries like [6] can be of great help to meet this type of need. We leave this aspect for future work.

7 Conclusion

In this paper, we have proposed two approaches to shun the sparse double descent phenomenon: a simple ℓ_2 regularization and a learning scheme involving knowledge distillation. While standard regularization methods like ℓ_2 are positively contributing to lessening such a phenomenon, they are revealing some limits, which can be resolved by leveraging a knowledge distillation scheme. Thanks to that scheme, the good generalization properties of the teacher are transmitted to the student model, which is no longer suffering from sparse double descent.

Sparse double descent is impacting the determination of the optimal model size required to maintain the performance of over-parametrized models. With this study, we hope to inform the community about this risk that various deep neural networks might face in compression schemes.

References

1. Aghli, N., Ribeiro, E.: Combining weight pruning and knowledge distillation for CNN compression. In: Proceedings of the IEEE/CVF Conference on Computer Vision and Pattern Recognition, pp. 3191–3198 (2021)

2. Anthony, L.F.W., Kanding, B., Selvan, R.: Carbontracker: tracking and predicting the carbon footprint of training deep learning models. In: ICML Workshop on Challenges in Deploying and monitoring Machine Learning Systems, July 2020. arXiv:2007.03051
3. Arani, E., Sarfraz, F., Zonooz, B.: Noise as a resource for learning in knowledge distillation. In: Proceedings of the IEEE/CVF Winter Conference on Applications of Computer Vision, pp. 3129–3138 (2021)
4. Barbano, C.A., Tartaglione, E., Berzovini, C., Calandri, M., Grangetto, M.: A two-step radiologist-like approach for Covid-19 computer-aided diagnosis from chest X-ray images. In: Sclaroff, S., Distante, C., Leo, M., Farinella, G.M., Tombari, F. (eds.) ICIAP 2022, Part I. LNCS, vol. 13231, pp. 173–184. Springer, Cham (2022). https://doi.org/10.1007/978-3-031-06427-2_15
5. Belkin, M., Hsu, D., Ma, S., Mandal, S.: Reconciling modern machine-learning practice and the classical bias-variance trade-off. Proc. Natl. Acad. Sci. **116**(32), 15849–15854 (2019)
6. Bragagnolo, A., Barbano, C.A.: Simplify: a python library for optimizing pruned neural networks. SoftwareX **17**, 100907 (2022). https://doi.org/10.1016/j.softx.2021.100907. https://www.sciencedirect.com/science/article/pii/S2352711021001576
7. Bragagnolo, A., Tartaglione, E., Grangetto, M.: To update or not to update? Neurons at equilibrium in deep models. In: Advances in Neural Information Processing Systems (2022)
8. Chang, X., Li, Y., Oymak, S., Thrampoulidis, C.: Provable benefits of overparameterization in model compression: from double descent to pruning neural networks. In: Proceedings of the AAAI Conference on Artificial Intelligence, vol. 35, pp. 6974–6983 (2021)
9. Chaudhry, H.A.H., et al.: Lung nodules segmentation with deephealth toolkit. In: Mazzeo, P.L., Frontoni, E., Sclaroff, S., Distante, C. (eds.) ICIAP 2022, Part I. LNCS, vol. 13373, pp. 487–497. Springer, Cham (2022). https://doi.org/10.1007/978-3-031-13321-3_43
10. Chen, L., Chen, Y., Xi, J., Le, X.: Knowledge from the original network: restore a better pruned network with knowledge distillation. Complex Intell. Syst. **8**(2), 709–718 (2022)
11. Cotter, A., Menon, A.K., Narasimhan, H., Rawat, A.S., Reddi, S.J., Zhou, Y.: Distilling double descent. arXiv preprint arXiv:2102.06849 (2021)
12. Cui, B., Li, Y., Zhang, Z.: Joint structured pruning and dense knowledge distillation for efficient transformer model compression. Neurocomputing **458**, 56–69 (2021)
13. Dosovitskiy, A., et al.: An image is worth 16x16 words: transformers for image recognition at scale. In: International Conference on Learning Representations (2021)
14. Evchenko, M., Vanschoren, J., Hoos, H.H., Schoenauer, M., Sebag, M.: Frugal machine learning. arXiv preprint arXiv:2111.03731 (2021)
15. Frankle, J., Carbin, M.: The lottery ticket hypothesis: finding sparse, trainable neural networks. In: International Conference on Learning Representations (2019). https://openreview.net/forum?id=rJl-b3RcF7
16. Gale, T., Elsen, E., Hooker, S.: The state of sparsity in deep neural networks. arXiv preprint arXiv:1902.09574 (2019)
17. Geiger, M., et al.: Jamming transition as a paradigm to understand the loss landscape of deep neural networks. Phys. Rev. E **100**(1), 012115 (2019)
18. Gupta, S., Gupta, A.: Dealing with noise problem in machine learning data-sets: a systematic review. Procedia Comput. Sci. **161**, 466–474 (2019)

19. Han, S., Pool, J., Tran, J., Dally, W.: Learning both weights and connections for efficient neural network. Adv. Neural Inf. Process. Syst. **28** (2015)
20. He, Z., Xie, Z., Zhu, Q., Qin, Z.: Sparse double descent: where network pruning aggravates overfitting. In: International Conference on Machine Learning, pp. 8635–8659. PMLR (2022)
21. Hinton, G., Vinyals, O., Dean, J., et al.: Distilling the knowledge in a neural network. arXiv preprint arXiv:1503.02531 **2**(7) (2015)
22. Kaiser, T., Ehmann, L., Reinders, C., Rosenhahn, B.: Blind knowledge distillation for robust image classification. arXiv preprint arXiv:2211.11355 (2022)
23. Kim, T., Oh, J., Kim, N., Cho, S., Yun, S.Y.: Comparing Kullback-Leibler divergence and mean squared error loss in knowledge distillation. arXiv preprint arXiv:2105.08919 (2021)
24. Kim, Y., Rush, A.M.: Sequence-level knowledge distillation. arXiv preprint arXiv:1606.07947 (2016)
25. Li, Y., Yang, J., Song, Y., Cao, L., Luo, J., Li, L.J.: Learning from noisy labels with distillation. In: Proceedings of the IEEE International Conference on Computer Vision, pp. 1910–1918 (2017)
26. Liu, T., Xie, S., Yu, J., Niu, L., Sun, W.: Classification of thyroid nodules in ultrasound images using deep model based transfer learning and hybrid features. In: 2017 IEEE International Conference on Acoustics, Speech and Signal Processing (ICASSP), pp. 919–923. IEEE (2017)
27. Ma, X., et al.: Dimensionality-driven learning with noisy labels. In: International Conference on Machine Learning, pp. 3355–3364. PMLR (2018)
28. Mazzeo, P.L., Frontoni, E., Sclaroff, S., Distante, C.: Image Analysis and Processing. ICIAP 2022 Workshops: ICIAP International Workshops, Lecce, Italy, May 23–27, 2022, Revised Selected Papers, Part I, vol. 13373. Springer, Cham (2022). https://doi.org/10.1007/978-3-031-13321-3
29. Meng, X., Yao, J., Cao, Y.: Multiple descent in the multiple random feature model. arXiv preprint arXiv:2208.09897 (2022)
30. Miller, D.J., Xiang, Z., Kesidis, G.: Adversarial learning targeting deep neural network classification: a comprehensive review of defenses against attacks. Proc. IEEE **108**(3), 402–433 (2020). https://doi.org/10.1109/JPROC.2020.2970615
31. Muthukumar, V., Vodrahalli, K., Subramanian, V., Sahai, A.: Harmless interpolation of noisy data in regression. IEEE J. Sel. Areas Inf. Theory **1**(1), 67–83 (2020)
32. Nakkiran, P., Kaplun, G., Bansal, Y., Yang, T., Barak, B., Sutskever, I.: Deep double descent: where bigger models and more data hurt. In: International Conference on Learning Representations (2020). https://openreview.net/forum?id=B1g5sA4twr
33. Nakkiran, P., Venkat, P., Kakade, S.M., Ma, T.: Optimal regularization can mitigate double descent. In: International Conference on Learning Representations (2021)
34. Park, J., No, A.: Prune your model before distill it. In: Avidan, S., Brostow, G., Cissé, M., Farinella, G.M., Hassner, T. (eds.) ECCV 2022. LNCS, vol. 13671, pp. 120–136. Springer, Cham (2022). https://doi.org/10.1007/978-3-031-20083-0_8
35. Quétu, V., Milovanović, M., Tartaglione, E.: Sparse double descent in vision transformers: real or phantom threat? In: Foresti, G.L., Fusiello, A., Hancock, E. (eds.) ICIAP 2023. LNCS, vol. 14234, pp. 490–502. Springer, Cham (2023). https://doi.org/10.1007/978-3-031-43153-1_41
36. Quétu, V., Tartaglione, E.: Dodging the sparse double descent. arXiv preprint arXiv:2303.01213 (2023)

37. Quétu, V., Tartaglione, E.: Can we avoid double descent in deep neural networks? arXiv preprint arXiv:2302.13259 (2023)
38. Ravanelli, M., et al.: Multi-task self-supervised learning for robust speech recognition. In: ICASSP 2020-2020 IEEE International Conference on Acoustics, Speech and Signal Processing (ICASSP), pp. 6989–6993. IEEE (2020)
39. Saglietti, L., Zdeborová, L.: Solvable model for inheriting the regularization through knowledge distillation. In: Mathematical and Scientific Machine Learning, pp. 809–846. PMLR (2022)
40. Sau, B.B., Balasubramanian, V.N.: Deep model compression: distilling knowledge from noisy teachers. arXiv preprint arXiv:1610.09650 (2016)
41. Schwarz, J., Jayakumar, S., Pascanu, R., Latham, P.E., Teh, Y.: Powerpropagation: a sparsity inducing weight reparameterisation. Adv. Neural. Inf. Process. Syst. **34**, 28889–28903 (2021)
42. Spigler, S., Geiger, M., d'Ascoli, S., Sagun, L., Biroli, G., Wyart, M.: A jamming transition from under-to over-parametrization affects generalization in deep learning. J. Phys. A: Math. Theor. **52**(47), 474001 (2019)
43. Wei, J., Zhu, Z., Cheng, H., Liu, T., Niu, G., Liu, Y.: Learning with noisy labels revisited: a study using real-world human annotations. In: International Conference on Learning Representations (2022)
44. Xu, K., Rui, L., Li, Y., Gu, L.: Feature normalized knowledge distillation for image classification. In: Vedaldi, A., Bischof, H., Brox, T., Frahm, J.-M. (eds.) ECCV 2020. LNCS, vol. 12370, pp. 664–680. Springer, Cham (2020). https://doi.org/10.1007/978-3-030-58595-2_40
45. Yilmaz, F.F., Heckel, R.: Regularization-wise double descent: why it occurs and how to eliminate it. In: 2022 IEEE International Symposium on Information Theory (ISIT), pp. 426–431. IEEE (2022)
46. Zhou, Z., Zhou, Y., Jiang, Z., Men, A., Wang, H.: An efficient method for model pruning using knowledge distillation with few samples. In: ICASSP 2022-2022 IEEE International Conference on Acoustics, Speech and Signal Processing (ICASSP), pp. 2515–2519. IEEE (2022)

Unveiling the Potential of Tiny Machine Learning for Enhanced People Counting in UWB Radar Data

Massimo Pavan[1]([✉]), Luis González Navarro[3], Armando Caltabiano[2], and Manuel Roveri[1]

[1] Politecnico di Milano, Milan, Italy
{massimo.pavan,manuel.roveri}@polimi.it
[2] Truesense s.r.l., Milan, Italy
armando.caltabiano@truesense.it
[3] Universidad Politécnica de Madrid, Madrid, Spain
luis.gnavarro@alumnos.upm.es

Abstract. Tiny Machine Learning (TinyML) allows to move the intelligence processing as close as possible to where data are generated, hence reducing the latency with which a decision is made and being able to process data even when remote connection is scarce or absent. In this technological scenario, Ultra-Wideband (UWB) radar data represent a new and challenging source of data providing relevant information, while guaranteeing the privacy of users. This paper introduces a novel TinyML solution able to count the number of people in a given area by processing UWB radar data. This novel solution was carefully designed to guarantee a high counting accuracy, while reducing the memory and computational demand so as to be executed on tiny devices. Experimental results on a real-world UWB radar dataset show the effectiveness of the proposed solution.

Keywords: Tiny Machine Learning · Ultra-Wideband (UWB) radar · People Counting

1 Introduction

In the most recent technological landscape, tiny devices are becoming one of the main areas of technological breakthrough. As Internet-of-Things (IoT) units, embedded systems, and edge devices become more present in the technological environment, the scientific trend reflects the displacement of data processing closer to where the data are generated. This aims to increase the autonomy of tiny devices since decisions can be taken locally, while reducing the energy consumption (since transmitting is far more energy-demanding than processing the data), the required bandwidth, and the latency of decision-making. Designing Machine Learning (ML) models meant to operate on tiny devices requires to completely redesign the traditional ML models and algorithms due to the severe technological constraints on memory, computation and energy consumption [4, 5, 27].

This is exactly where Tiny Machine Learning (TinyML) comes into play by introducing tiny models and algorithms as well as approximate computing mechanisms (e.g., quantization and pruning) to design ML solutions able to satisfy the aforementioned technological constraints of tiny devices [2, 23].

One of the most promising applications for TinyML is *presence detection*, aiming at identifying the presence of one or more persons in a given environment. However, current solutions rely on the processing of images taken from video cameras or microphones [7, 26], hence potentially impacting on the privacy of users.

In order to deal with and address this privacy issue in detecting and counting people, we introduce the use of Ultra-Wideband (UWB) radar, which shows to be a promising radar technology for human activity recognition [10, 15]. From the technological point-of-view, UWB radar devices are characterized by precise recordings (in the order of the mm), low energy consumption (generally below 0.1 W) and fast acquisition of data (in fractions of seconds), making them valuable solutions even for tiny devices. In this perspective, TinyML solutions for UWB-radar will pave the way for a large number of interesting applications based on tiny devices and will guarantee the privacy of users. Very few examples of TinyML solutions operating on UWB radar data are available in the literature [19, 20] and currently none of these solutions addresses the problem of people counting.

The aim of this paper is to introduce a novel TinyML solution for people counting in UWB radar data. The core of the proposed solution, which is inspired by the solutions described in [19, 20], comprises a suitably-defined preprocessing phase to extract relevant information from radar data and a novel family of Convolutional Neural Networks (CNNs) characterized by a custom design of tiny dilated convolutional blocks and the use of quantization mechanisms to reduce the computational and memory demands. The people counting problem has been reformulated, for the first time in the literature, as a regression problem to estimate the number of people present in the radar data and the considered application scenario referred to person counting inside a car. The UWB radar signals, in the form of range-Doppler maps, have been collected in real-world conditions with a microcontroller unit that includes a UWB radar module. These signals have been acquired inside a car, so as to count the number of passengers present in the backseat.

The presented solution targets tiny devices with extremely limited amounts of memory, computational power, and power consumption budgets. This characteristic makes the solution interesting for application scenarios in which:

- a continuous source of energy is not available, e.g., inside of a car;
- the cost of the device is relevant, e.g., when a lot of devices need to be deployed inside of an entire building to control smart lighting and air conditioning systems;

– other types of sensors do not work, e.g., cameras don't work well in the dark, while microphones don't work in space.

The effectiveness of the proposed solution has been experimentally evaluated on the acquired UWB radar dataset for people counting and the memory and computational demand of the proposed solution revealed to be compatible with the technological constraints of the considered microcontroller unit.

The paper is organized as follows. Section 2 introduces the related literature, Sect. 3 describes the proposed solution and Sect. 4 details the experimental results. Conclusions and future works are finally draws in Sect. 5.

2 Related Literature

This section includes a thorough analysis of the current state of the art on the field of UWB and UWB-radar data processing in deep learning and TinyML.

2.1 People Counting with Radar Data

The usage of radar data for various human-monitoring tasks has recently become central in the scientific community. Notable examples of tasks addressed with this technology include presence detection [10,12,15] and human activity recognition (HAR) [13,14,18,25].

Nevertheless, the literature shows a large variety in terms of the technical solutions for the radar (e.g., UWB-radar, MFCC frequency modulated radar), the number of radar devices used, the number of antennas embedded in each device, and the family of the proposed algorithmic solution - e.g., Digital Signal Processing (DSP), Machine Learning (ML), Deep Learning (DL).

The same variety is present also for the task of people counting using radar data. For example, in [28] multiple MFCC radar were deployed in a room to perform people counting by using a DSP algorithm.

Various works that use UWB-radar data are also present in the literature. [6,15] proposed to use a ML algorithm based on clustering techniques to perform people counting for single antennas radar and Multiple-Input-Multiple-Output (MIMO) radar, respectively. Other works explored the usage of DL algorithms, and in particular CNN, used in conjunction with the spectrograms of the signal [21,29]. These works modeled the problem of people counting as a classification task.

Despite the interesting approaches proposed by the literature, none of the works for people counting with UWB-radar data is tailored for the porting to a real-world embedded device.

2.2 Tiny Machine Learning

TinyML is a field of study that combines Embedded Systems and Machine Learning. It explores ML models and architectures to be executed on small and low-power devices. In order to design these kinds of solutions, strong constraints in terms of memory, computation and power have to be taken into account [27]. The literature in this field focuses on the design of *approximated deep learning solutions* [8,24]. Techniques such as weight quantization [11], pruning [16] and Gate-Classification CNNs [9] have been developed in order to make the porting of such algorithms possible [23]. For example [3] combines both pruning and precision scaling were combined to make large CNNs able to be executed in IoT units.

Some notable applications of TinyML that have received a lot of attention in recent years include the analysis of audio [26] and visual data [7] to perform tasks that aim at detecting the presence of people in an environment. These solutions are usually limited to perform detection, which is a binary task to only distinguish between the presence or absence of the target. Recent solutions [17] expanded the field by introducing the task of object detection in the TinyML context, aiming to detect the presence and position of multiple targets in pictures.

2.3 UWB-Radar Usage in TinyML

In the context of TinyML, UWB-radar data were recently exploited to perform tasks of presence detection and subject recognition [19,20]. These works introduced a family of Convolutional Neural Networks, called *TyCNN*, specifically designed for the analysis of UWB-radar data on tiny devices. Despite not being designed for people counting, these solutions will be considered in the design of the proposed solution, as described in the next section.

3 People Counting in UWB Radar: The Proposed Solution

The proposed solution for people counting in UWB radar relies on a convolutional neural network for regression, called *TyCNN-R* that has been suitably designed to deal with UWB radar data. One of the distinguishing features of *TyCNN-R* is that the final layer is a single-neuron final dense layer, which is meant to provide an estimate of the amount of people present in a UWB recording. We emphasize that *TyCNN-R* extends TyCNNs, which is the family of the state-of-the-art CNNs for presence detection [20] and subject recognition [19] on UWB-radar data for tiny devices.

The rest of the section is organized as follows. The problem formulation and the technological setting are introduced in Sect. 3.1. Section 3.2 describes the preprocessing of UWB radar data, while the architecture of the proposed *TyCNN-R* is detailed in Sect. 3.3. The computational and memory demand of *TyCNN-R* are provided in Sect. 3.4.

3.1 Problem Formulation and Technological Setting

The problem of people counting has been formalized as a regression task with discrete dependent variables associated to the people count. In particular, the task consist in associating to an input UWB record I a label $y_I \in \mathbb{N}$:

y_I : the number of people are present in the record I.

In our specific case, due to the limited size of the considered space (i.e., the backseat of a car), y_I can assume only values in $\{0, 1, 2, 3\}$.

Since the maximum amount of people present in the record is fixed, such a formalization could share some similarities with a classification task, but we opted for a "discrete" regression task, since the "distance" among the classes is meaningful.

Data have been acquired in an in-car setting by an ESP32 microcontroller unit with a UWB radar module, equipped with a couple of TX and RX antennas. From the technological point of view, the considered radar module is capable of performing a scan of the environment and returning a 65-values-long vector of imaginary values representing energy intensities, where the values at position 1 and 65 represent the closest and the furthest spatial bin, respectively. The radar can detect subjects in a 60° cone and its working range of distance is set to 0–3 m. During the acquisition phase, a 20-s radar scan at 10 Hz is considered, resulting on a range-time map of 65 × 200 for each dataset sample. A description of the dataset and further technological details about UWB radar can be found in [20].

A sample of the dataset in which one person is present in the seat closer to the radar is shown in Fig. 1. We emphasize that, as detailed above, the sample is organized into a 65 × 200 matrix and that the figure shows the absolute value of the complex values.

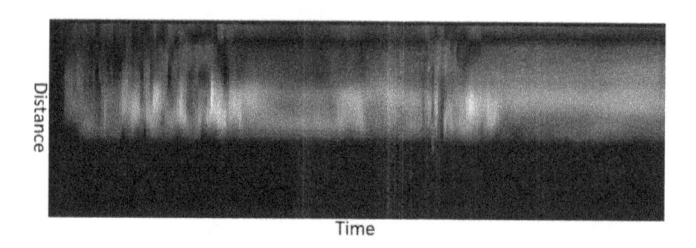

Fig. 1. A sample of the dataset. The sample is organized into a 65 × 200 matrix and represented values refers to the absolute value of the complex values. In this specific case the person captured is represented by a higher signal intensity in the top part of the image, being closer to the sensor

3.2 UWB Radar Data Preprocessing

The UWB radar data preprocessing, which is detailed in what follows, comprises four main steps: Fast Fourier Transform, scaling, bin selection, and frequency selection. All the preprocessing steps considered for the acquired UWB radar data rely on the research carried out in [19, 20]:

1. The Fast Fourier Transform (FFT) algorithm is applied to the raw data acquired by UWB radar. The result is a 65 × 256 range-Doppler map, where the y-axis represents frequency instead of time. The change in size, i.e., from 200 to 256 width, refers to the limitations of the on-device FFT processing, where data used as input to the FFT needs to be arranged in a power-of-two shape. In order to address the requirement the input data of the range-time maps are zero-padded and a Hann window is used to smooth the transition between zeros and actual data.
2. The outcomes of the FFT are then scaled logarithmically and the norm of the imaginary values is computed. This results in the transformation of the FFT data into real values.
3. The first 12 horizontal bins are removed due to the high presence of noise in the bins closer to the device. The outcome of this step is a 53 × 256 range-Doppler map.
4. Finally a frequency selection step is carried out. This step consists in removing the frequencies above 1.66 Hz, hence keeping only the frequencies between 0 Hz and 1.66 Hz since this frequency range typically covers human-related activities. This allows to remove two thirds of the data in the range-Doppler maps, hence reducing the size of the input of *TyCNN-R* and, consequently, the memory demand on the device. The outcome of this step is a 53 × 86 matrix. Figure 2 shows an example of the outcome of this step.

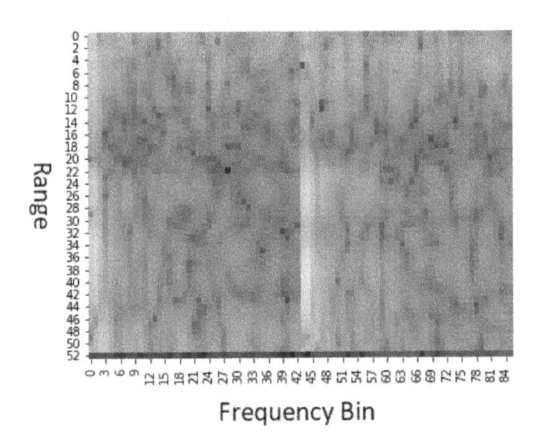

Fig. 2. 53 × 86 range-Doppler map after preprocessing step 4

We emphasize that finally a Z-score normalization is performed before providing the data to the network [30].

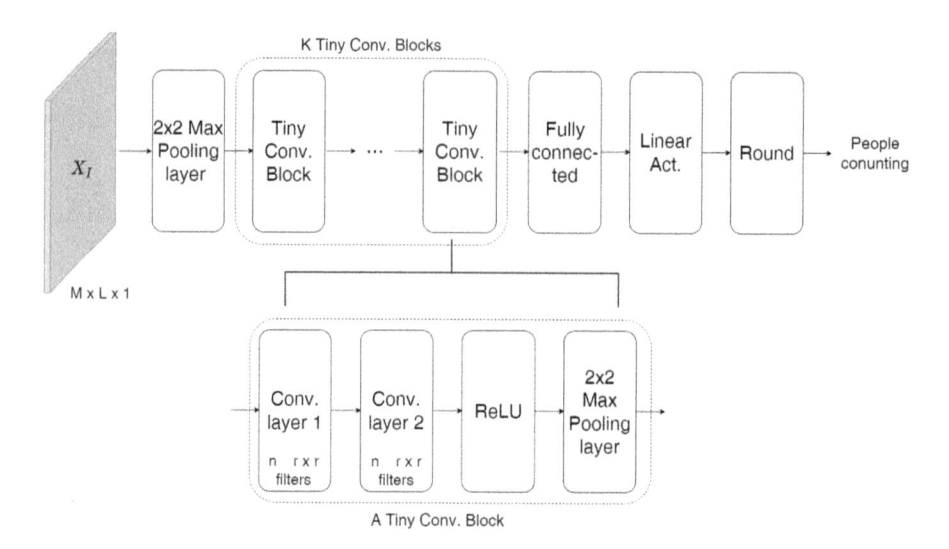

Fig. 3. An overview of the proposed *TyCNN-R* for people counting in UWB radar.

3.3 TyCNN-R: The Proposed CNN for People Counting in UWB Radar

An overview of the proposed *TyCNN-R* is given in Fig. 3. More specifically, *TyCNN-R* receives in input a $M \times L \times 1$ image X_I, being $M = 53$ and $L = 86$ as detailed in Sect. 3.2, and produces in output $y_I \in \mathbb{N}$ representing the people counting in X_I.

In more detail, the proposed *TyCNN-R* for people counting in UWB radar comprises three main phases:

- the initial phase comprises a 2×2 Max Pooling layer aiming at reducing the input activation size and, consequently, reducing the number of weights and the computational demand of the remaining two phases of *TyCNN-R*;
- the convolutional phase comprises a sequence of K Tiny Convolutional Blocks (TCBs). Each TCB is organized into two consecutive convolutional layers (characterized by a number n of $r \times r$ square filters, possibly dilated with a dilation factor d) to extract the main features of the image, a ReLU activation function, and a Max Pooling layer, used to reduce the dimension of the activation map;
- the final regression phase comprises a flattening layer, a dropout layer (with dropout rate $= 0.3$) and a regression dense layer with linear activation. The dense layer computes a single floating point value, which is consequently rounded to assign the number of people present.

Summarizing, the main architectural parameters of *TyCNN-R* are the following:

- **the number of TCBs K**: it reports the number of TCBs present in the network;

- **the convolutional kernel size** r: it represents both height and width of the 2D convolution filters. The model uses square convolution filters of odd dimensions. The value of r is fixed for all the convolutional layers in the network;
- **the number of filters** n: it accounts for the number of filters for each convolutional layer. The value of n is the same for all the convolutional layers;
- **the dilation rate** d: an integer specifying the dilation rate of the convolutional layers.

3.4 Computational Load and Memory Footprint Evaluation

In this section, we evaluate the computational and memory demands of the proposed *TyCNN-R* network. To address this goal, we followed the definition for the memory footprint m and computational load c introduced in [20], which is defined as follows:

$$c = n_{ops}$$

$$m = (\hat{m_w} + \hat{m_a}) \cdot m_p$$

being n_{ops} the number of multiplications required to compute the inference, $\hat{m_w}$ the number of the parameters of *TyCNN-R*, $\hat{m_a}$ the number of values of the activations and m_p the memory (in Bytes) required to store a parameter or an activation value. In our case, since both the weights of the network and the input data are quantized, m_p is equal to 1 Byte. Furthermore, since we are only performing the inference of *TyCNN-R*, $\hat{m_a}$ can be optimized by reusing the same memory space for all the activations. By using this optimization, $\hat{m_a}$ can be reduced up to the maximum sum of the activations of two consecutive layers.

In order to obtain the values of memory footprint and number of operations for each layer of the network, a specific analytic analysis has been conducted. The detailed calculation for each type of layer can be found in [20], while a detailed breakdown with the number of operations and memory footprint of *TyCNN-R* layer by layer can be found in Table 1, where the notation introduced in Sect. 3.3 is used.

The volumes of each intermediate activation are also visualized in Fig. 4.

4 Experimental Results

The experiments and analyses carried out to prove the effectiveness of *TyCNN-R* are described in this section. The technological requirements imposed by the target device for this application are introduced in Sect. 4.1. Section 4.2 describes the training and evaluation of the proposed *TyCNN-R*, while a description of the comparison used to evaluate the performance of the model is provided in Sect. 4.3. Finally, we provide and comment the results of the experiments in Sect. 4.4.

Table 1. Memory footprint and computational demand of the proposed *TyCNN-R* architecture

	Memory footprint (Bytes)	Number of operations
Input	$M \cdot L \cdot 1$	–
Pool0 (Weights)	–	–
Input-Pool0 (Activations)	$\frac{M}{2} \cdot \frac{L}{2} \cdot 1$	$2 \cdot 2 \cdot M \cdot L$
Conv1_00 (Weights)	$r^2 \cdot n + n$	–
Conv1_00 (Activations)	$\frac{M}{2} \cdot \frac{L}{2} \cdot n$	$r^2 \cdot n \cdot \frac{M}{2} \cdot \frac{L}{2}$
Conv1_01 (Weights)	$r^2 \cdot n^2 + n$	–
Conv1_01 (Activations)	$\frac{M}{2} \cdot \frac{L}{2} \cdot n$	$r^2 \cdot n^2 \cdot \frac{M}{2} \cdot \frac{L}{2}$
Pool1 (Weights)	–	–
Pool1 (Activations)	$\frac{M}{4} \cdot \frac{L}{4} \cdot n$	$2 \cdot 2 \cdot \frac{M}{2} \cdot \frac{L}{2}$
ConvK_00 (Weights)	$r^2 \cdot n^2 + n$	–
ConvK_00 (Activations)	$\frac{M}{2^K} \cdot \frac{L}{2^K} \cdot n$	$r^2 \cdot n^2 \cdot \frac{M}{2^K} \cdot \frac{L}{2^K}$
ConvK_01 (Weights)	$r^2 \cdot n^2 + n$	–
ConvK_01 (Activations)	$\frac{M}{2^K} \cdot \frac{L}{2^K} \cdot n$	$r^2 \cdot n^2 \cdot \frac{M}{2^K} \cdot \frac{L}{2^K}$
PoolK (Weights)	–	–
PoolK (Activations)	$\frac{M}{2^{K+1}} \cdot \frac{L}{2^{K+1}} \cdot n$	$2 \cdot 2 \cdot \frac{M}{2^K} \cdot \frac{L}{2^K}$
FC Classifier (Weights)	$\frac{M}{2^{K+1}} \cdot \frac{L}{2^{K+1}} \cdot n \cdot 1 + 1$	–
FC Classifier (Activations)	1	$\frac{M}{2^{K+1}} \cdot \frac{L}{2^{K+1}} \cdot n \cdot 1$

4.1 Technological Requirements

The designed people-counting application is expected to run on the same board used to collect the dataset. This device is equipped with an ESP32 Microcontroller, a Flash memory of size 4 MB, two RAM memories, sized 520 KB SRAM and 16 KB SRAM respectively (in RTC), and a 1800 mAh battery.

However, not all the resources on the device can be dedicated to the inference of *TyCNN-R*, since the memory space and the computational power required by the firmware and the rest of the application must be taken into account as well. The actual requirements that *TyCNN-R* needs to meet to be ported on the target device are summarized in Table 2.

Table 2. Maximum available memory dedicated to the neural network in the microcontroller

Resource	Requirement
Flash Memory	<3 MB
RAM	<150 KB
Execution time	<2 s

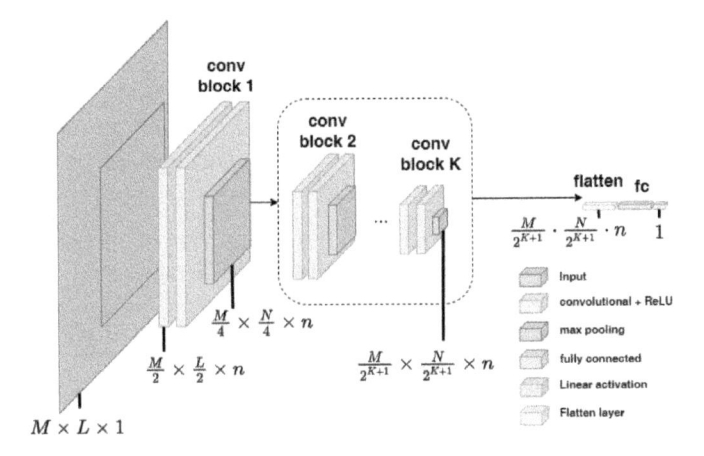

Fig. 4. The volumes of each intermediate activation of the proposed *TyCNN-R* architecture.

These requirements were used as targets for the proposed algorithms. From the memory point of view, the RAM memory requirements have proven to be the bottleneck, and, for this reason, we provide for the proposed algorithm and the comparison the memory footprint m, a reliable estimation of the peak RAM memory usage.

From the computational point of view, we provide as a proxy of the actual execution time the total amount of operations c. Indeed, these two parameters are related, and in former experiments the board has proven to be able to execute roughly $12 \cdot 10^6$ Op/s during neural network inference [20].

4.2 Training and Evaluating TyCNN-R for People Counting

In order to provide unbiased results, the dataset is split into a training set (85% of the available data) and a test set (15%).

The training set is initially used to select the best parameter configuration for *TyCNN-R*, by performing a grid search over the parameters described in Sect. 3.3 and detailed in Table 3. A 10-fold cross-validation approach was used to evaluate each parameter configuration and the one providing the largest accuracy was selected.

Table 3. Grid search parameter range

Parameter	tested values
K	{2, 3, 4}
r	{5, 7}
n	{12, 14, 16, 18, 20, 22}
d	{1, 2}

We emphasize that all the values in the range selected for the grid search guarantee to meet the computational and memory limitations of the target device and the available training time and resources. Indeed, the increase of convolutional block K number and dimension of the filter r induce an increase of both the training time and the amount of on-device memory needed to run inference.

Table 4. Memory footprint and computational demand of the proposed *TyCNN-R* network (an asterisk marks the activations re-using such arrays)

	Memory footprint (Bytes)	Number of operations
Input	$*53 \cdot 86 \cdot 1 = 4558$	–
Pool0 (Weights)	–	–
Input-Pool0 (Activations)	$*26 \cdot 43 \cdot 1 = 1118$	$2 \cdot 2 \cdot 53 \cdot 86 = 18232$
Conv1_00 (Weights)	$49 \cdot 12 + 12 = 600$	–
Conv1_00 (Activations)	$26 \cdot 43 \cdot 12 = 13416$	$49 \cdot 12 \cdot 26 \cdot 43 = 657384$
Conv1_01 (Weights)	$49 \cdot 144 + 12 = 7086$	–
Conv1_01 (Activations)	$26 \cdot 43 \cdot 12 = 13416$	$49 \cdot 144 \cdot 26 \cdot 43 = 7888608$
Pool1 (Weights)	–	–
Pool1 (Activations)	$*13 \cdot 21 \cdot 12 = 3276$	$2 \cdot 2 \cdot 26 \cdot 43 = 9116$
Conv2_00 (Weights)	$49 \cdot 144 + 12 = 7086$	–
Conv2_00 (Activations)	$*13 \cdot 21 \cdot 12 = 3276$	$49 \cdot 144 \cdot 13 \cdot 21 = 1926288$
Conv2_01 (Weights)	$49 \cdot 144 + 12 = 7086$	–
Conv2_01 (Activations)	$*13 \cdot 21 \cdot 12 = 3276$	$49 \cdot 144 \cdot 13 \cdot 21 = 1926288$
Pool2 (Weights)	–	–
Pool2 (Activations)	$*6 \cdot 10 \cdot 12 = 720$	$2 \cdot 2 \cdot 13 \cdot 21 = 1092$
Conv3_00 (Weights)	$49 \cdot 144 + 12 = 7086$	–
Conv3_00 (Activations)	$*6 \cdot 10 \cdot 12 = 720$	$49 \cdot 144 \cdot 6 \cdot 10 = 423360$
Conv3_01 (Weights)	$49 \cdot 144 + 12 = 7086$	–
Conv3_01 (Activations)	$*6 \cdot 10 \cdot 12 = 720$	$49 \cdot 144 \cdot 6 \cdot 10 = 423360$
Pool3 (Weights)	–	–
Pool3 (Activations)	$*3 \cdot 5 \cdot 12 = 180$	$2 \cdot 2 \cdot 6 \cdot 10 = 240$
FC Classifier (Weights)	$3 \cdot 5 \cdot 12 \cdot 1 + 1 = 181$	–
FC Classifier (Activations)	$*1$	$3 \cdot 5 \cdot 12 \cdot 1 = 180$
Total	55957	13274688

The best parameter configuration obtained by the grid search is $K = 3$, $r = 7$, $n = 12$ and $d = 1$.

Then, the entire training set was used to train a *TyCNN-R* with the selected parameter configuration, and its accuracy was evaluated on the test set. The experiment is repeated 10 times with different initializations of the weights of

TyCNN-R and shuffling of the training data. The results are detailed in Table 6, reporting the average accuracy results along with the 95% confidence interval.

For the training we considered the MSE as loss function, while Adam was used as optimizer. The learning rate was set to 0.3e−4, and *TyCNN-R* was trained for 400 epochs. After the training, the full-integer post-training weight quantization algorithm was considered [11]. The quantization algorithm has been applied both to inputs and activations to minimize the memory footprint m of the network. The memory footprint m and the computational demand c of the *TyCNN-R* used for the experiments are reported in Table 4.

4.3 The Proposed Comparisons

In this section, as a comparison, we introduce a naive baseline and the *TyCNN-C* architecture proposed in [19], suitably adapted to the problem of people counting. We highlight the fact that *TyCNN-C* was originally proposed for a different task, but being the only architecture working on radar data that matches the constraints of tiny devices, it was adapted in this work to tackle the problem of people counting and used as a comparison. In more detail, in our experimental setting, we compared our solution with:

Table 5. Memory footprint and computational demand of the *TyCNN-C* classification network (an asterisk marks the activations re-using such arrays)

	Memory footprint (Bytes)	Number of operations
Input	$*53 \cdot 86 \cdot 1 = 4558$	–
Pool0 (Weights)	–	–
Input-Pool0 (Activations)	$*26 \cdot 43 \cdot 1 = 1118$	$2 \cdot 2 \cdot 53 \cdot 86 = 18232$
Conv1_00 (Weights)	$49 \cdot 22 + 22 = 1100$	–
Conv1_00 (Activations)	$26 \cdot 43 \cdot 22 = 24596$	$49 \cdot 22 \cdot 26 \cdot 43 = 1205204$
Conv1_01 (Weights)	$49 \cdot 484 + 22 = 23738$	–
Conv1_01 (Activations)	$26 \cdot 43 \cdot 22 = 24596$	$49 \cdot 484 \cdot 26 \cdot 43 = 26514488$
Pool1 (Weights)	–	–
Pool1 (Activations)	$*13 \cdot 21 \cdot 22 = 6138$	$2 \cdot 2 \cdot 26 \cdot 43 = 4472$
Conv2_00 (Weights)	$49 \cdot 484 + 22 = 23738$	–
Conv2_00 (Activations)	$*13 \cdot 21 \cdot 22 = 6006$	$49 \cdot 484 \cdot 13 \cdot 21 = 6474468$
Conv2_01 (Weights)	$49 \cdot 484 + 22 = 23738$	–
Conv2_01 (Activations)	$*13 \cdot 21 \cdot 22 = 6006$	$49 \cdot 484 \cdot 13 \cdot 21 = 6474468$
Pool2 (Weights)	–	–
Pool2 (Activations)	$*6 \cdot 10 \cdot 22 = 1386$	$2 \cdot 2 \cdot 13 \cdot 21 = 1092$
FC Classifier (Weights)	$6 \cdot 10 \cdot 22 \cdot 4 + 4 = 5284$	–
FC Classifier (Activations)	$*4$	$6 \cdot 10 \cdot 22 \cdot 4 = 5280$
Total	126791	40697704

- **naive baseline:** We considered a simple algorithm that assigns the most represented class in the training set to every datum in the test set;
- **TyCNN-C for people counting:** the *TyCNN-C* solution encompasses an architecture similar to the one of the *TyCNN-R*, with the notable exception of using a different classification head that manages the problem as a classification task. The classification task consists in associating to the input I to a categorical class $y_I \in \{0, 1, 2, 3\}$ where:

$$\begin{cases} 0: & \text{No person present in the record} \\ 1: & \text{One person is present in the record} \\ 2: & \text{Two people are present in the record} \\ 3: & \text{Three people are present in the record} \end{cases} \quad (1)$$

In order to make a fair comparison, a grid search over the parameter described in Sect. 3.3 has been carried out on *TyCNN-C* as well, so as to select the parameter configuration providing the largest accuracy. The outcome of the grid search is the parameter configuration $K = 2$, $r = 7$, $n = 22$ and $d = 1$. The *TyCNN-C* was trained using categorical cross-entropy as loss function, Adam as optimizer, learning rate equal to 0.3e-4, and 400 learning epochs. As for *TyCNN-R*, it was quantized after the training. The memory and computational load of this model are detailed in Table 5. These values are computed following the instruction provided in the paper proposing the network architecture [19].

4.4 Experimental Results

Table 6 compares the accuracies of the Naive Baseline, of the *TyCNN-C* model and the proposed *TyCNN-R* model, along with a comparison of the total memory usage and amount of operations and estimates of the time and energy required by a single inference with each model. The experiments have been repeated 10 times with different initializations of the weights and order of the training data, and the provided intervals are computed as 95% confidence intervals. Furthermore, the confusion matrices of the proposed *TyCNN-R* and the comparison *TyCNN-C* are reported in Fig. 5 and Fig. 6, respectively.

Table 6. Experimental results comparison for UWB radar people counting

Architecture	Accuracy (%)	Memory (kB)	Ops. (10^6)	time (s)	Energy (J)
Naive Baseline	0.406	–	–	–	–
TyCNN-C (adapted)	0.680 ± 0.038	123.8	40.70	3.39	1.70
TyCNN-R (proposed solution)	0.714 ± 0.025	54.65	13.27	1.11	0.56

The results clearly show that the *TyCNN-R* model outperformed *TyCNN-C* by more than 3%, and it is far beyond the Naive Baseline. Moreover, *TyCNN-R* is also characterized by smaller memory and computational demand. The experimental results highlight that modeling the task of people counting as a regression task, compared to modeling it as a classification task, shows promising results when using constrained devices. The regression approach was in fact capable of achieving the highest accuracy with less parameters on this dataset.

Fig. 5. The confusion matrix for the *TyCNN-R* architecture.

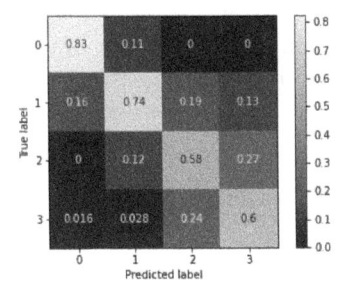

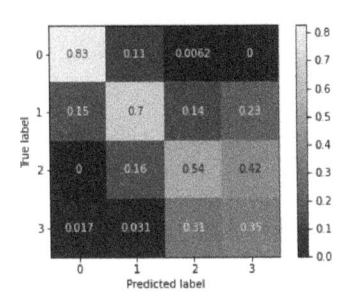

Fig. 6. The confusion matrix for the *TyCNN-C* architecture.

Finally, from the confusion matrix of *TyCNN-R*, it is possible to notice that the errors committed by the model tend to concentrate on "close" classes. This property is enforced by the regression approach, since the distance among the classes is considered during the learning phase. The confusion matrices highlight also that the proposed *TyCNN-R* performs better in situations where there are multiple targets present in the record.

5 Conclusion

The aim of this paper was to introduce, for the first time in the literature, a TinyML solution for people counting based on UWB-radar. To achieve this goal we proposed *TyCNN-R*, a new evolution of the TyCNN network design previously used for presence detection and subject recognition. The effectiveness and efficiency of the proposed solution have been successfully evaluated on a real-world scenario for in-car people counting.

Future works will encompass the analysis of multi-antenna radar data, the exploration of alternative methods for performing people counting, incremental learning mechanisms to support the on-device learning, and the extension of the use of UWB-radar to anomaly detection scenarios.

Environmental Impact

5.1 Execution

Considering a battery of 1800 mAh dedicated just to the execution of the algorithm, with the tension of execution of the device set to 5 V, the inference with the proposed solution could be executed roughly 58000 times before needing to be recharged. Considering executing inference 2 times per minute, an estimated life of such a device would be 29000 min or approximately 20 days. These estimates do not include the collection of the data through the sensor nor consumption while the device is in sleep mode, so it needs to be taken as an upper bound of the expected life of a real-world device.

Given some of the possible applications of our solution (e.g., smart buildings) highlighted in Sect. 1, we do believe that the adoption of tinyml-based solutions like ours can have an overall positive environmental impact, as previously highlighted by [22].

5.2 Training

The training and evaluation of the proposed solution *TyCNN-R* was performed on a cloud server encompassing an Intel(R) Xeon(R) Gold 5318S CPU @ 2.10 GHz, an NVIDIA A40 GPU and a ram total size of 378 GB. Various metrics concerning the environmental impact of this machine were tracked during the training with the use of codecarbon.io [1]. The server is a shared machine that is used by multiple researchers at the same time, so the following measures should be considered an upper bound. The metrics measured during the training and testing of a single parameter configuration are reported in Table 7.

Table 7. Environmental impact metrics for the training of a single parameter configuration.

Metric	value
duration	802.033193 s
emissions	0.009262 kg CO_2eq
emissions rate	0.000012 kg/s
energy consumed	0.040946 kW

Having tried a total of 60 parameter configurations, a rough estimate of the total amount of emissions and energy consumed is reported in Table 8.

Table 8. Environmental impact metrics the training of all the parameter configurations.

Metric	value
emissions	0.55572 kg CO_2eq
energy consumed	2.45676 kW

Acknowledgments. The authors would like to thank Gabriele Viscardi, Pierpaolo Lento and Alessandro Basso for the valuable support in the development of this work. This paper is supported by PNRR-PE-AI FAIR project funded by the NextGeneration EU program.

References

1. Codecarbon. https://codecarbon.io/. Accessed 30 Sept 2010
2. Alippi, C., Disabato, S., Roveri, M.: Moving convolutional neural networks to embedded systems: the AlexNet and VGG-16 case. In: 2018 17th ACM/IEEE International Conference on Information Processing in Sensor Networks (IPSN), pp. 212–223 (2018). https://doi.org/10.1109/IPSN.2018.00049
3. Alippi, C., Disabato, S., Roveri, M.: Moving convolutional neural networks to embedded systems: the AlexNet and VGG-16 case. In: 2018 17th ACM/IEEE International Conference on Information Processing in Sensor Networks (IPSN), pp. 212–223. IEEE (2018)
4. Alippi, C., Fantacci, R., Marabissi, D., Roveri, M.: A cloud to the ground: the new frontier of intelligent and autonomous networks of things. IEEE Commun. Mag. **54**(12), 14–20 (2016). https://doi.org/10.1109/MCOM.2016.1600541CM
5. Alippi, C., Roveri, M.: The (not) far-away path to smart cyber-physical systems: an information-centric framework. Computer **50**(4), 38–47 (2017). https://doi.org/10.1109/MC.2017.111
6. Choi, J.W., Yim, D.H., Cho, S.H.: People counting based on an IR-UWB radar sensor. IEEE Sens. J. **17**(17), 5717–5727 (2017). https://doi.org/10.1109/JSEN.2017.2723766
7. Chowdhery, A., Warden, P., Shlens, J., Howard, A., Rhodes, R.: Visual Wake Words Dataset. arXiv:1906.05721 [cs, eess] (2019). http://arxiv.org/abs/1906.05721, arXiv: 1906.05721
8. David, R., Duke, J., et al.: TensorFlow lite micro: embedded machine learning for TinyML systems. Proc. Mach. Learn. Syst. **3**, 800–811 (2021)
9. Disabato, S., Roveri, M.: Reducing the computation load of convolutional neural networks through gate classification. In: 2018 International Joint Conference on Neural Networks (IJCNN), pp. 1–8. IEEE (2018)
10. Ha, T., Kim, J.: Detection and localization of multiple human targets based on respiration measured by IR-UWB radars. In: 2019 IEEE SENSORS, pp. 1–4 (2019). https://doi.org/10.1109/SENSORS43011.2019.8956687. ISSN 2168-9229
11. Jacob, B., Kligys, S., et al.: Quantization and training of neural networks for efficient integer-arithmetic-only inference. In: Proceedings of the IEEE Conference on Computer Vision and Pattern Recognition, pp. 2704–2713 (2018)
12. Kim, Y., Moon, T.: Human detection and activity classification based on micro-doppler signatures using deep convolutional neural networks. IEEE Geosci. Remote Sens. Lett. **13**(1), 8–12 (2016). https://doi.org/10.1109/LGRS.2015.2491329
13. Koks, D.: How to create and manipulate radar range–doppler plots, p. 95 (2014)
14. Lang, Y., Hou, C., Yang, Y., Huang, D., He, Y.: Convolutional neural network for human micro-doppler classification. In: European Microwave Conference (2017)
15. Liang, F., et al.: Detection of multiple stationary humans using UWB MIMO radar. Sensors **16**, 1922 (2016). https://doi.org/10.3390/s16111922
16. Liu, J., Tripathi, S., Kurup, U., Shah, M.: Pruning algorithms to accelerate convolutional neural networks for edge applications: a survey. arXiv preprint arXiv:2005.04275 (2020)

17. Louis Moreau, M.K.: Announcing FOMO (faster objects, more objects) (2022). https://www.edgeimpulse.com/blog/announcing-fomo-faster-objects-more-objects
18. Park, J., Javier, R.J., Moon, T., Kim, Y.: Micro-doppler based classification of human aquatic activities via transfer learning of convolutional neural networks. Sensors **16**(12), 1990 (2016). https://doi.org/10.3390/s16121990. https://www.mdpi.com/1424-8220/16/12/1990
19. Pavan, M., Caltabiano, A., Roveri, M.: On-device subject recognition in UWB-radar data with tiny machine learning. In: CEUR Workshop Proceedings (2022)
20. Pavan, M., Clatabiano, A., Roveri, M.: TinyML for UWB-radar based presence detection. In: Proceedings of WCCI 2022, p. 5. IEEE, July 2022
21. Pham, C.T., Luong, V.S., Nguyen, D.K., Vu, H.H.T., Le, M.: Convolutional neural network for people counting using UWB impulse radar. J. Instrum. **16**(08), P08031 (2021). https://doi.org/10.1088/1748-0221/16/08/P08031. https://dx.doi.org/10.1088/1748-0221/16/08/P08031
22. Prakash, S., et al.: Is TinyML sustainable? Assessing the environmental impacts of machine learning on microcontrollers (2023)
23. Ray, P.P.: A review on TinyML: state-of-the-art and prospects **34**(4), 1595–1623 (2022). https://doi.org/10.1016/j.jksuci.2021.11.019. https://www.sciencedirect.com/science/article/pii/S1319157821003335
24. Sanchez-Iborra, R., Skarmeta, A.F.: TinyML-enabled frugal smart objects: challenges and opportunities. IEEE Circuits Syst. Mag. **20**(3), 4–18 (2020)
25. Shao, Y., Guo, S., Sun, L., Chen, W.: Human motion classification based on range information with deep convolutional neural network. In: 2017 4th International Conference on Information Science and Control Engineering (ICISCE), pp. 1519–1523 (2017). https://doi.org/10.1109/ICISCE.2017.317
26. Warden, P.: Speech commands: a dataset for limited-vocabulary speech recognition. arXiv:1804.03209 [cs] (2018). http://arxiv.org/abs/1804.03209, arXiv: 1804.03209
27. Warden, P., Situnayake, D.: TinyML: Machine Learning with TensorFlow Lite on Arduino and Ultra-Low-power Microcontrollers. O'Reilly (2020). Google-Books-ID: sB3mxQEACAAJ
28. Weiß, J., Pérez, R., Biebl, E.: Improved people counting algorithm for indoor environments using 60 GHz FMCW radar. In: 2020 IEEE Radar Conference (RadarConf 2020), pp. 1–6 (2020). https://doi.org/10.1109/RadarConf2043947.2020.9266607. ISSN 2375-5318
29. Yang, X., Yin, W., Zhang, L.: People counting based on CNN using IR-UWB radar. In: 2017 IEEE/CIC International Conference on Communications in China (ICCC), pp. 1–5 (2017). https://doi.org/10.1109/ICCChina.2017.8330453
30. Zach: Z-score normalization: definition & examples (2021). https://www.statology.org/z-score-normalization/

Towards Comparable Knowledge Distillation in Semantic Image Segmentation

Onno Niemann[1(✉)], Christopher Vox[2], and Thorben Werner[1]

[1] University of Hildesheim, 31141 Hildesheim, Germany
onno.niemann@posteo.de
[2] Volkswagen AG, Berliner Ring 2, 38440 Wolfsburg, Germany

Abstract. Knowledge Distillation (KD) is one proposed solution to large model sizes and slow inference speed in semantic segmentation. In our research we identify 25 proposed distillation loss terms from 14 publications in the last 4 years. Unfortunately, a comparison of terms based on published results is often impossible, because of differences in training configurations. A good illustration of this problem is the comparison of two publications from 2022. Using the same models and dataset, Structural and Statistical Texture Distillation (SSTKD) reports an increase of student mIoU of 4.54 and a final performance of 29.19, while Adaptive Perspective Distillation (APD) only improves student performance by 2.06% points, but achieves a final performance of 39.25. The reason for such extreme differences is often a suboptimal choice of hyperparameters and a resulting underperformance of the student model used as reference point. In our work, we reveal problems of insufficient hyperparameter tuning by showing that distillation improvements of two widely accepted frameworks, Structured Knowledge Distillation (SKD) and Intra-class Feature Variation Distillation (IFVD), vanish when hyperparameters are optimized sufficiently. To improve comparability of future research in the field, we establish a solid baseline for three datasets and two student models and provide extensive information on hyperparameter tuning. We find that only two out of seven techniques can compete with our simple baseline on the ADE20K dataset.

Keywords: Knowledge Distillation · Efficient Semantic Segmentation · Model Compression

1 Introduction

Advances in Deep Learning techniques for Semantic Image Segmentation brought major performance improvements to fields such as autonomous driving, medical image analysis, robotic perception and video surveillance. As these performance gains often came at the price of increased model complexity and required computational power, efficient deep learning techniques have become increasingly relevant [18].

Two techniques, which start with a large model and make it more efficient are model Pruning and Quantization. Pruning shrinks a model by dropping less important nodes and Quantization reduces the numerical precision of weights. Knowledge Distillation takes a different approach and does not change model efficiency during training. Instead it starts with a small model (student) and improves its performance by leveraging guidance from a more complex model (teacher). Teacher model weights are frozen and knowledge is distilled into the student by making an addition to the student loss, which penalizes differences in student and teacher output. Incentivizing the student to mimic the more complex behaviour of the teacher can significantly lift its performance.

KD was introduced in the image classification domain and originally the distillation loss was applied to student and teacher only at output-level. The extension of teacher guidance to intermediate layers and the transfer to semantic segmentation have been studied in various publications. Re-using the most basic, output-level distillation loss in a segmentation context is straightforward, as it can be applied on pixel instead of image-level in the student and teacher output. However, several papers criticize that this naive approach treats pixels in isolation and introduce more complex techniques. Most of them build upon the naive pixel-wise distillation by adding loss terms to it. A problem with these published methods is that a significant share focuses solely on performance improvement in their own training framework and fails to provide a good baseline for comparison against other literature.

The dimension of this comparability problem is illustrated by the overview over important publications in Table 1. The comparison clearly shows that the baseline performance of the student model varies strongly between publications, making it hard to compare the quality of the proposed techniques based on the lift they provide. To address this problem of comparability, we perform an extensive hyperparameter optimization of the most fundamental of KD frameworks for semantic segmentation and provide detailed information on optimal hyperparameters for training of two student models on three datasets. As a byproduct of this optimization, we find that the temperature parameter used to "soften" student and teacher output in image classification can improve distillation in segmentation, although many publications in the field ignore it.

In summary, we point out challenges in comparing different methods and present a training procedure, which sets the ground for a fair comparison of KD techniques. We further put the performance of three commonly used loss terms into perspective by comparing them to our achieved results.

2 Related Work

Semantic Segmentation. Most earlier image segmentation techniques were based on Partial Differential Equations or Random Forest methods [10], before the advent of deep learning sparked a series of publications leveraging the powers of Convolutional Neural Networks (CNNs). The majority of this early CNN-based segmentation research focuses on improving model performance, which is achieved by adding skip connections [17] and decoder networks [2,19,24], or concatenating convolutions at different scales in the pyramid pooling module of Pyramid Science Parsing Networks (PSPNets) [44]. More recent publications investigate the application of transformer based models [28,33,45].

Another branch of segmentation research focuses on model efficiency. Real-time semantic segmentation aims for fast inference speed while maintaining performance [15,21,37,43]. There is always a trade-off between performance and efficiency.

Knowledge Distillation in Classification. KD aims to increase the performance of a compact student model by leveraging guidance from a large teacher model during training. It is one of the most widely used model compression techniques due to its broad applicability [31]. KD imposes no requirements on teacher or student model architectures [3] and allows leveraging unlabelled data by training the student on soft labels generated by the teacher [31].

Generally, the teacher model weights are frozen during student training and the student is encouraged to mimic the teacher's output logits by training on a weighted combination of standard cross entropy and KD loss [4,13] (Eq. 1). The cross entropy term (Eq. 2) ensures performance on the labeled training data while the distillation term (Eq. 3) penalizes deviations from the teacher output. The weight of the distillation loss, λ, is a hyperparameter of student training. Scaling output logits of both models by $\tau > 1$ is crucial for a successful distillation of knowledge in image classification [13] and extending the level of student teacher matching to intermediate feature layers can give a further boost [23,40].

$$L_S = L_{CE} + \lambda * L_{KD} \qquad (1)$$

$$L_{CE}(z_s, y) = -\sum_{c=1}^{C} y_c \log \sigma_c(z_s) \qquad (2)$$

$$L_{KD}(z_s, z_t) = -\tau^2 \sum_{c=1}^{C} \sigma_c(\frac{z_t}{\tau}) \log \sigma_c(\frac{z_s}{\tau}) \qquad (3)$$

Despite the simplicity of the classical KD framework, the underlying mechanisms are still not well-understood. Commonly, the success of KD is associated with the information contained in teacher predictions for wrong classes, referred to as "dark knowledge" [39]. However, phenomena such as students outperforming teachers when trained solely on teacher output and high disagreement between student and teacher predictions suggest there might be other reasons for the success of KD [27]. Two alternative explanations are that teacher guidance has a regularizing effect similar to label smoothing [39] and that teacher output provides a sample-wise importance weighting, making the student focus on samples of low teacher confidence [8].

KD in Image Segmentation. Applying the classical KD framework to semantic image segmentation problems is straight-forward. The distillation loss in Eq. 3

is usually applied on image-level, summing over all classes, but since image segmentation is essentially pixel-wise classification, it can be applied to each pixel in the image instead. This most basic distillation loss is referred to as pixel-wise distillation (L_{PI}) and is a useful baseline for more complex distillation schemes. Since pixel-wise distillation treats each pixel in isolation and ignores the fact that segmentation depends strongly on contextual information, various alternative distillation techniques exist, many of which use pixel-wise distillation as one part of their framework.

The earliest proposed technique investigates a "consistency" loss comparing regional differences in student and teacher output [34] aiming for a more contextual distillation of knowledge by matching the distance of the center pixel and an 8-neighborhood. Instead of a direct matching of student and teacher output, in Knowledge Adaptation (KA) [12] teacher output is compressed to a more dense latent space by an autoencoder before being compared to student logits. Additionally, an affinity loss term is introduced to better capture long-range dependencies.

Structured Knowledge Distillation (SKD) [16] is the most cited publication in the field and uses a combination of three loss terms, one of them the basic pixel-wise loss. Again the other two loss terms are supposed to focus more on contextual information in both intermediate and output layers. The pair-wise loss (L_{PA}) is based on a pair-wise Markov random field framework and encourages students to mimic the teacher at intermediate layers. The holistic loss (L_{HO}) requires an additional discriminator model with the task to differentiate student and teacher output. Student and discriminator compete with each other following a similar training protocol as used to train Generative Adversarial Networks [9], ultimately leading to the student output being as similar as possible to the teacher output [16].

Building upon SKD, Intra-Class Feature Variation Distillation (IFVD) [32] also uses the pixel-wise and holistic loss terms, but replaces the pair-wise loss with the new IFV loss, L_{IFV}. Per-class prototypes are calculated and the distance of intermediate features to the respective prototype is aligned between student and teacher. Another suggested approach, CSCACE [20], introduces a Channel and Spatial Correlation (CSC) and an Adaptive Cross Entropy (ACE) term. CSC calculates correlation matrices between intermediate features and can be understood as an extension of the pair-wise loss of SKD. ACE combines the classic pixel-wise KD loss with the ground truth label by only using the teacher output when the teacher prediction is correct.

As one of the few approaches that modify the pixel-wise distillation loss, Channel-Wise Distillation (CWD) [26] proposes a channel/class-wise normalization of student and teacher outputs before calculating the pixel-wise distillation loss. This idea is assumed by several later methods. Double Similarity Distillation (DSD) [7] introduces a pixel-wise similarity loss, which matches intermediate student and teacher features by utilizing self-attention maps across multiple layers. A category-wise similarity distillation loss makes the student mimic the teacher at output level by minimizing the L2 distance between correlation matrices of student and teacher output. Masked Generative Distillation (MGD) [36] is a more general technique, which can also be used for knowledge distillation in image classification or object detection. The proposed method masks some parts of the input while still requiring the student to mimic the full teacher output.

Inter-Class Distance Distillation (IDD) [41] and Feature-Augmented Knowledge Distillation (FAKD) [38] use the pixel-wise-distillation loss with channel-wise normalization as suggested in CWD [26]. IDD additionally includes all terms introduced by SKD and an inter-class feature distance loss following a similar reasoning as IFVD. FAKD does not introduce additional loss terms but proposes the perturbation of intermediate student features in multiple ways and training the student to mimic the teacher despite the applied perturbations.

Structural and Statistical Texture Knowledge Distillation (SSTKD) [14] and Adaptive Perspective Distillation (APD) [30] use the pixel-wise distillation loss. SSTKD additionally includes the holistic loss of SKD and two novel loss terms, which encourage the student to mimic low-level texture information of the teacher [14]. The authors of APD argue that segmentation networks learn to generalize and thus acquire a universal perception. Their introduced adaptive perspective includes calculating class-wise average features of individual images. According to the authors, this process distills contextual information more explicitly. APD is the only reviewed technique that updates part of the teacher model during student training.

Self-attention and Self-distillation [1] introduces a self-attention loss term to make the student learn contextual information from the teacher and a layer-wise context distillation loss. The second term is different from other discussed techniques, as it is applied across student layers to ensure a consistent representation of contextual information in shallow layers. Cross-Image Relational Knowledge Distillation (CIRKD) [35] again uses the pixel-wise distillation loss and uses three more loss terms. Unique about this method is the introduction of a pixel queue to make student models mimic the teachers distance to output for pixels of the same class from previous images.

3 Related Work Comparison

A comparison of the discussed knowledge distillation frameworks is rarely straightforward. A very common problem is differences in student and teacher architectures. Especially earlier methods use a variety of models and results cannot be compared to recent literature. Table 1 presents the results of distillation frameworks that report performance on the most common choice of student and teacher model, PSPNets with ResNet101 and ResNet18 backbone, respectively. This choice of models has been the standard in the field since the publication of SKD [16], but Consistency [34], CSCACE [20], KA [12] and SALC [1] use other architectures and are not included in the comparison.

Even though the techniques in Table 1 use the same model architectures we can observe significant performance differences for both the student-only training ("S only") and the full KD framework ("+T"). While the differences in "+T" are

Table 1. Comparison of reported student Mean Intersection over Union (mIoU) of various techniques following the most common architectural setup. The "Ls" column refers to the number of loss terms in addition to the CE loss. "S only" shows the performance of the student model trained without teacher. "+T" contains the best performance reported in the publication applying all proposed loss terms. Methods followed by * use the L_{PI}, the ones followed by † additionally do channel-wise normalization, as introduced in CWD [26].

	Ls	ADE20K		Cityscapes	
		S only	+ T	S only	+ T
SKD [16]*	3	33.82	36.55	69.10	72.67
IFVD [32]*	3	–	–	69.10	74.54
CWD [26]†	1	24.65	26.80	70.09	75.90
DSD [7]	2	33.80	38.00	69.42	73.20
MGD [36]	1	–	–	69.85	74.10
IDD [41]†	6	24.65	27.69	70.09	77.59
FAKD [38]†	1	29.42	35.30	68.99	74.75
SSTKD [14]*	4	24.65	29.19	69.10	75.15
APD [30]*	3	37.19	39.25	74.15	75.68
CIRKD [35]	4	–	–	72.55	74.73

to be expected for different KD algorithms, the inconsistent baseline performance of the student model makes it very hard to compare methods.

Additionally, the listed techniques often propose a number of loss terms ("Ls"), but do not provide comprehensive ablation studies that isolate the effect of individual terms across datasets. Finally, many results in recent literature are reported without standard deviations, SKD being the only exemption in Table 1. This introduces another complicating factor when comparing results of KD algorithms.

For a specific example we look at APD vs. DSD: Judging only by the final performance of 39.25, APD outperforms all other techniques on ADE20K. Considering its starting point of 37.19, however, student performance is only lifted by 2.06. As DSD achieves a lift of 4.20 using one loss term less, but only achieves a final performance of 38.00, it is unclear, which of the two techniques is superior.

4 Methodology

In this work, we present a series of experiments highlighting the importance of individual hyperparameter tuning for every combination of datasets and models. We grid search initial learning rate $\mu(0)$ and weight decay γ for student with and without teacher model separately to ensure the best performance possible in both settings. In this way we guarantee a fair performance comparison when measuring the lift from KD. In a second step, we optimize the temperature parameter τ of the combined student and teacher training.

We also fine-tune the weight of the pixel-wise distillation loss, λ_{PI}, and find an optimal performance for $\lambda_{PI} = 1e-1$ for all experiments. Finally, we test different proposed loss terms in isolation to measure their effect on student performance by optimizing their respective loss weights.

5 Experiments

5.1 Datasets and Evaluation Metric

We evaluate our approach on three public semantic segmentation benchmark datasets, PascalVOC [6], Cityscapes [5], and ADE20K [46]. All datasets have pixel-wise annotations.

Cityscapes is an urban street scene understanding dataset showing street scenes recorded in 50 cities. It contains 5,000 images with labels from 19 classes. All images have dimension 2048 × 1024 and train, validation and test set contain 2,975, 500 and 1,525 images, respectively.

ADE20K is a complex scene understanding dataset containing images of objects, parts of objects and stuff from varying contexts. Pixels are assigned one of 150 object and stuff class labels. The 25,000 images are of varying sizes and train, validation and test set contain 20,000, 2,000 and 3,000 images, respectively.

PascalVOC contains 1,464 images for training, 1,449 images for validation and a private test set. It has 20 different object classes and images are of varying size.

Mean Intersection over Union is the metric used in all our experiments.

5.2 Implementation Details

As most other relevant methods, we follow the architectural setup and training procedure of SKD [16]. For the choice of student and teacher models, this means using PSPNets [44] with different backbones. The teacher backbone is a ResNet101 [11] and for the student backbone we test a ResNet18 [11] and an EfficientNet-B0 [29]. For simplicity we will refer to the two student models as ResNet and EffNet students. As in SKD, we use an SGD optimizer with decaying learning rate $\mu(i)$ over training steps according to Eq. 4.

$$\mu(i) = \mu(0) * (1 - \frac{i}{\eta})^{0.9}; \qquad i := [1 \ldots \eta] \qquad (4)$$

η is the total number of training batches and i is the current batch. Unless otherwise stated the ResNet and EffNet student backbones are initialized with weights pre-trained on ImageNet. The pre-trained student weights were obtained from the torchvision package (v0.12) of the PyTorch library [22] for both backbones and the teacher weights were taken from [16] for Cityscapes and from [42] for the other datasets.

All experiments are conducted with a batch size of 8 and students are trained with crops of size 512 × 512 on Cityscapes and 473 × 473 on ADE20K and PascalVOC.

All experimental results are calculated on the validation datasets of Cityscapes, PascalVOC and ADE20K.

5.3 The Impact of Temperature

The authors of the original KD framework [13] strongly emphasize the importance of logit scaling by a temperature parameter $\tau > 1$ in image classification, the main reason for its success being the "softening" of teacher output class distributions [13]. To show that teacher output distributions are "hard" also in image segmentation we analyze the effect of different values of τ on the Shannon Entropy [25] of teacher output. When all probability mass is assigned to one class the Shannon Entropy is zero and when the probability mass is distributed evenly over all classes Shannon Entropy is maximal.

We generate teacher output for 800 randomly selected images from the Cityscapes dataset, resulting in probability distributions over the 19 classes for 209,715,200 pixels. These distributions are scaled with different temperature values according to Eq. 3. The shares of Shannon Entropies over all pixels for different temperatures are shown in Fig. 1. Temperatures of 1, 2, 4, 8, and 16 were chosen as [13] report successful distillation for values up to 20. An important observation is that when the teacher output is not scaled ($\tau = 1$), the entropy strongly spikes at 0. More than 60% of pixels are classified with a confidence close to 1, suggesting that teacher output might be too "hard" for efficient distillation of knowledge and higher temperatures might help. On the other hand, for a value of $\tau = 16$ almost 100% of distributions have an entropy of approximately 2.9, indicating an almost even distribution of probability mass over all classes.

5.4 Hyperparameter Optimization

We optimize hyperparameters separately for student only and the combined student and teacher training. The results of the grid search for initial learning rate $\mu(0)$ and weight decay γ for both students on Cityscapes are presented in Table 2a. Right of it in Table 2b are the optimal hyperparameters for all datasets.

We use the same grid for the student and teacher training and set the temperature parameter to $\tau = 1$. The results are shown in Tables 3 where again the left shows the detailed grid for Cityscapes and the right the optimal hyperparameters for all students and datasets.

In a second stage of hyperparameter optimization, we tune the temperature parameter τ. The tested values and their responses for all models and datasets can be found in Table 4. A choice of $\tau = 1$ appears to work well on PascalVOC and ADE20K, but greater values yield performance gains on Cityscapes.

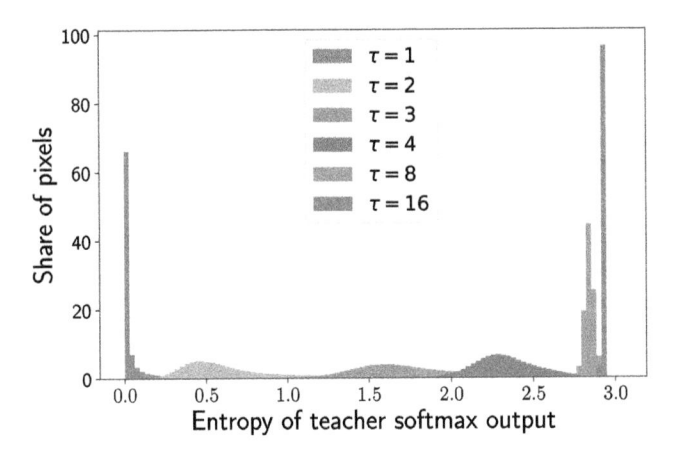

Fig. 1. Effect of logit scaling on Shannon Entropy of teacher output probability distributions over classes. The histograms are based on class probability distributions of randomly selected pixels from Cityscapes. Without scaling ($\tau = 1$) over 60% of pixels are assigned one class with a probability close to 1.

Table 2. Grid search results for student-only training. a) shows the whole grid for Cityscapes, b) the best hyperparameters for all datasets. The best performance in a) is highlighted in bold.

(a) Cityscapes Grid Search								(b) All Datasets				
	\multicolumn{7}{c}{$\mu(0)$}			EffNet		ResNet	
	EffNet				ResNet				$\mu(0)$	γ	$\mu(0)$	γ
γ	1e−1	5e−2	1e−2	5e−3	5e−2	1e−2	5e−3	PascalVOC	1e−2	5e−4	5e−3	5e−4
5e−4	35.0	43.9	59.8	60.1	68.89	**70.55**	67.95	Cityscapes	1e−1	5e−6	1e−2	5e−4
5e−5	62.2	63.6	61.1	60.1	69.74	69.48	67.98	ADE20K	5e−3	5e−5	1e−2	5e−5
5e−6	**64.6**	63.6	61.1	59.4	**70.55**	67.65	67.09					

Table 3. Grid search results for student and teacher training. a) shows the whole grid for Cityscapes, b) the best hyperparameters for all datasets. The best performance in a) is highlighted in bold.

(a) Cityscapes Grid Search								(a) All Datasets				
	\multicolumn{7}{c}{$\mu(0)$}			EffNet		ResNet	
	EffNet				ResNet				$\mu(0)$	γ	$\mu(0)$	γ
γ	1e−1	5e−2	1e−2	5e−3	5e−2	1e−2	5e−3	PascalVOC	1e−2	5e−6	5e−3	5e−5
5e−4	40.4	46.9	62.8	61.1	66.44	**71.64**	70.54	Cityscapes	5e−2	5e−6	1e−2	5e−4
5e−5	62.1	65.6	63.2	62.0	67.19	70.82	68.42	ADE20K	1e−2	5e−5	1e−2	5e−5
5e−6	65.0	**66.1**	63.1	61.6	70.02	69.72	68.64					

Table 4. Impact of the temperature parameter τ on segmentation performance. The best performances are highlighted in bold. Results within one standard deviation of the best result are underlined. Experiments on ADE20K were run only once.

τ	PascalVOC		Cityscapes		ADE20K	
	EffNet	ResNet	EffNet	ResNet	EffNet	ResNet
1	**66.24 ± 0.46**	**65.22 ± 0.44**	65.26 ± 0.59	71.33 ± 0.85	**36.32**	**37.74**
2	<u>66.08 ± 0.16</u>	64.37 ± 0.08	64.62 ± 0.77	72.15 ± 0.10	35.51	36.85
3	65.91 ± 0.26	63.30 ± 0.44	65.08 ± 0.63	**72.75 ± 0.29**	34.87	36.04
4	65.02 ± 0.82	63.42 ± 0.54	65.26 ± 0.43	<u>72.44 ± 0.31</u>	35.02	36.34
6	<u>66.11 ± 0.67</u>	63.65 ± 0.51	64.52 ± 0.45	<u>72.49 ± 0.43</u>	35.23	36.49
8	<u>66.11 ± 0.13</u>	64.18 ± 0.36	**65.58 ± 0.03**	72.09 ± 0.50	34.91	36.51

5.5 Additional Losses

The Losses L_{PA} [16], L_{HO} [16], and L_{IFV} [32] are part of many KD algorithms, but their individual contribution to the student's learning behavior when hyperparameters are optimal is unclear in literature. We use the optimal hyperparameters of the combined training in Table 3b and optimize the weight of each individual loss term. The results for the Cityscapes dataset are presented in Table 5.

Table 5. Impact of individual loss terms on segmentation performance on Cityscapes. The results for three loss terms, L_{PA}, L_{HO} and L_{IFV} are presented in tables a), b) and c), respectively. The best mIoU is highlighted in bold for each student model.

(a) L_{PA}

λ_{PA}	EffNet	ResNet
1e−3	65.08	70.51
1e−2	**65.17**	70.28
1e−1	63.09	**72.98**
1e+0	13.49	71.88
1e+1	3.211	69.34

(b) L_{HO}

λ_{HO}	EffNet	ResNet
1e−4	**65.84**	70.35
1e−3	65.48	70.81
1e−2	64.70	**72.50**
1e−1	41.53	28.20

(c) L_{IFV}

λ_{IFV}	EffNet	ResNet
1e−4	65.78	70.25
1e−3	**66.01**	71.70
1e−2	65.80	**71.75**
1e−1	64.31	71.48
1e+0	65.03	**71.75**
1e+1	65.52	70.60
5e+1	64.76	71.21
1e+2	62.70	70.20

5.6 Final Performance Comparison

Table 6 shows the results of the additional loss experiments in comparison to student-only or simple pixel-wise distillation training. It is clear that adding the teacher model and the pixel-wise distillation loss, L_{PI}, improves student performance, while none of the three tested additional loss terms provides a further lift. An exception is the PascalVOC dataset, where the conclusion is less clear.

Table 6. Evaluation of L_{PA}, L_{HO}, and L_{IFV} when added to $L_{CE} + L_{PI}$ with optimal hyperparameters. Best results are highlighted in bold; results within one standard deviation of the best result are underlined.

L_{PI}	L_{PA}	L_{HO}	L_{IFV}	Pascal Voc EffNet	Pascal Voc ResNet	Cityscapes EffNet	Cityscapes ResNet	ADE20K EffNet	ADE20K ResNet
				65.43 ± 0.38	64.50 ± 0.34	64.42 ± 0.46	70.45 ± 0.10	34.10	35.23
x				66.24 ± 0.46	65.22 ± 0.44	**65.58 ± 0.03**	**72.75 ± 0.29**	**36.32**	**37.74**
x	x			66.40 ± 0.35	**65.84 ± 0.35**	64.94 ± 0.28	71.77 ± 1.05	34.98	36.57
x		x		**66.72 ± 0.21**	65.21 ± 0.28	65.00 ± 0.73	71.87 ± 1.14	35.22	36.50
x			x	66.38 ± 0.23	<u>65.83 ± 0.39</u>	65.24 ± 0.70	70.96 ± 1.03	35.41	37.09

Comparing our results to the related work in Table 1 shows that our student model with a performance of 37.74 clearly outperforms five out of seven methods on ADE20K, even though it was trained using only the most basic distillation loss. As the ADE20K dataset is the most complex dataset with 150 classes, this observation is surprising.

6 Ablation Study

Another hyperparameter of KD is the initialization of student weights. The effect of pre-training student backbone models on the ImageNet dataset compared to random weight initialization has been studied with varying conclusions. The authors of SKD find KD to be more efficient when the student is initialized randomly [16]. CWD [26] contradicts this by stating that the pre-trained weights help distillation, but calls the lift in student performance less significant compared to the randomly initialized case. The provided reason for this statement is that the relative improvement of the student is smaller since the model was better when trained without a teacher. CIRKD [35] and FAKD [38] also report a higher absolute improvement for random initialization. APD [30] is very unclear on the subject of weight initialization, stating in a sketch of their algorithm that student weights are initialized randomly, while the performance of student models trained without a teacher suggests an initialization with pre-trained weights.

Our investigation of student weight initialization suggests that distillation of teacher knowledge by the simple pixel-wise distillation loss does not improve the performance of a randomly initialized student, while it does improve the pretrained one. Table 7 compares our findings to the results of SKD and CWD. Our experiments find the validation mIoU of the student trained without a teacher to be 63.68, averaged over four runs. This result is in line with CWD, but 6.18% points higher than what is reported by SKD. Also similar to CWD, we find no improvement in performance due to KD when student weights are initialized randomly.

Table 7. mIoU of randomly initialized ResNet student trained on Cityscapes compared to literature. The best mIoU is highlighted in bold.

Method	SKD	CWD	Ours
Teacher	78.56	78.5	78.24
L_{CE}	57.50	63.63	**63.68**
$L_{CE} + L_{PI}$	58.63	–	63.34
$L_{CE} + L_{PI} + L_{PA} + L_{HO}$	63.24	63.20	–

7 Environmental Impact

KD is an effective technique to reduce energy consumption at inference time, as the student model requires less energy than the larger teacher. On the other hand, energy consumption during student training is increased compared to training the student without teacher. These two phenomena result in two trade-offs: the first is performance loss compared to teacher vs. reduced energy consumption during inference and the second is increased performance compared to student-only vs. increased energy consumption during training. The decision about when to use KD always depends on the exact use case. If a model is expected to be deployed on a large number of devices, which all process images at a high rate, energy use during training might be negligible compared to inference and thus KD might be extremely beneficial.

The CO_2 emissions of training and inference of our experiments with the ResNet student on Cityscapes are shown in Table 8. The codecarbon.io tool was used for calculations.

Training the student on its own takes 0.841kWh, which with the German electricity conditions means 298g of emitted CO_2. As expected, the addition of the teacher in KD leaves energy consumption during inference unchanged, but increases energy consumption and emissions during training to almost the threefold. Comparing student and teacher reveals that the ResNet student emits only 57g of CO_2 per 10,000 images at inference compared to 146g for the teacher model. This means, if we accept the decrease in performance we could save over 60% of CO_2 emission during inference time.

Table 8. CO_2 emissions of different model combinations at training and inference on Cityscapes. S and T are the ResNet student and the teacher trained in isolation; S+T refers to pixel-wise knowledge distillation. Numbers for inference correspond to inference on 10,000 images.

Model	mIoU	training		inference	
		energy (kWh)	CO_2 (kg)	energy (kWh)	CO_2 (kg)
S	70.45	0.841	0.298	0.161	0.057
S+T	72.75	2.52	0.891	0.161	0.057
T	78.24	3.01	1.06	0.413	0.146

8 Conclusion

In this work, we point out a significant comparability problem in the field of KD for semantic segmentation, which will grow in relevance as more techniques are published. We argue that comparibility can be improved by thoroughly optimizing training hyperparameters and show that doing so eliminates the gains from two accepted techniques, SKD and IFVD, on the two more complex of the three investigated datasets. To facilitate an easier comparison in the future we provide a detailed training protocol including optimal hyperparameters for two student models and three datasets. As part of the hyperparameter tuning we investigate the temperature parameter τ, which most publications in the field ignore and set to 1. We investigate the entropy of class probability distributions of teacher output to visualize the softening effect of $\tau > 1$ and show that the temperature parameter can be beneficial to the distillation of teacher knowledge in semantic segmentation.

Following up on this work and using the presented training with optimized hyperparameters, it would be useful to provide a fair comparison of the other loss terms in Table 1. Additionally, the understanding of KD in segmentation could be deepened by an analysis of factors that decide when logit scaling is helpful and why it improves distillation on Cityscapes and not on the other datasets.

Disclaimer. The results, opinions and conclusions expressed in this publication are not necessarily those of Volkswagen Aktiengesellschaft.

Funded by the Lower Saxony Ministry of Science and Culture under grant number ZN3492 within the Lower Saxony "Vorab" of the Volkswagen Foundation and supported by the Center for Digital Innovations (ZDIN).

References

1. An, S., Liao, Q., Lu, Z., Xue, J.H.: Efficient semantic segmentation via self-attention and self-distillation. IEEE Trans. Intell. Transp. Syst. **23**(9), 15256–15266 (2022)
2. Badrinarayanan, V., Kendall, A., Cipolla, R.: SegNet: a deep convolutional encoder-decoder architecture for image segmentation. CoRR **abs/1511.00561** (2015)
3. Beyer, L., Zhai, X., Royer, A., Markeeva, L., Anil, R., Kolesnikov, A.: Knowledge distillation: a good teacher is patient and consistent. In: Proceedings of the IEEE/CVF Conference on Computer Vision and Pattern Recognition (CVPR), pp. 10925–10934 (2022)
4. Bucila, C., Caruana, R., Niculescu-Mizil, A.: Model compression. In: Proceedings of the 12th ACM SIGKDD International Conference on Knowledge Discovery and Data Mining, KDD 2006, pp. 535–541. Association for Computing Machinery, New York (2006)
5. Cordts, M., et al.: The cityscapes dataset for semantic urban scene understanding. In: Proceedings of the IEEE Conference on Computer Vision and Pattern Recognition (CVPR) (2016)
6. Everingham, M., Gool, L.V., Williams, C.K.I., Winn, J.M., Zisserman, A.: The pascal visual object classes (VOC) challenge. Int. J. Comput. Vis. **88**(2), 303–338 (2010)
7. Feng, Y., Sun, X., Diao, W., Li, J., Gao, X.: Double similarity distillation for semantic image segmentation. IEEE Trans. Image Process. **30**, 5363–5376 (2021)
8. Furlanello, T., Lipton, Z.C., Tschannen, M., Itti, L., Anandkumar, A.: Born again neural networks (2018)
9. Goodfellow, I.J., et al.: Generative adversarial networks (2014)
10. Hao, S., Zhou, Y., Guo, Y.: A brief survey on semantic segmentation with deep learning. Neurocomputing **406**, 302–321 (2020)
11. He, K., Zhang, X., Ren, S., Sun, J.: Deep residual learning for image recognition. In: Proceedings of the IEEE Conference on Computer Vision and Pattern Recognition, pp. 770–778 (2016)
12. He, T., Shen, C., Tian, Z., Gong, D., Sun, C., Yan, Y.: Knowledge adaptation for efficient semantic segmentation (2019)
13. Hinton, G., Vinyals, O., Dean, J.: Distilling the knowledge in a neural network (2015)
14. Ji, D., Wang, H., Tao, M., Huang, J., Hua, X., Lu, H.: Structural and statistical texture knowledge distillation for semantic segmentation. In: 2022 IEEE/CVF Conference on Computer Vision and Pattern Recognition (CVPR), pp. 16855–16864 (2022)
15. Li, H., Xiong, P., Fan, H., Sun, J.: DFANet: deep feature aggregation for real-time semantic segmentation. In: Proceedings of the IEEE/CVF Conference on Computer Vision and Pattern Recognition (CVPR) (2019)
16. Liu, Y., Chen, K., Liu, C., Qin, Z., Luo, Z., Wang, J.: Structured knowledge distillation for semantic segmentation. In: 2019 IEEE/CVF Conference on Computer Vision and Pattern Recognition (CVPR), pp. 2599–2608 (2019)
17. Long, J., Shelhamer, E., Darrell, T.: Fully convolutional networks for semantic segmentation. CoRR **abs/1411.4038** (2014). http://arxiv.org/abs/1411.4038
18. Menghani, G.: Efficient deep learning: a survey on making deep learning models smaller, faster, and better. CoRR **abs/2106.08962** (2021). arXiv:2106.08962

19. Noh, H., Hong, S., Han, B.: Learning deconvolution network for semantic segmentation (2015). arXiv:1505.04366
20. Park, S., Heo, Y.S.: Knowledge distillation for semantic segmentation using channel and spatial correlations and adaptive cross entropy. Sensors **20**(16) (2020). https://www.mdpi.com/1424-8220/20/16/4616
21. Paszke, A., Chaurasia, A., Kim, S., Culurciello, E.: ENet: a deep neural network architecture for real-time semantic segmentation. arXiv preprint arXiv:1606.02147 (2016)
22. Paszke, A., et al.: PyTorch: an imperative style, high-performance deep learning library. In: Advances in Neural Information Processing Systems, vol. 32, pp. 8024–8035. Curran Associates, Inc. (2019). http://papers.neurips.cc/paper/9015-pytorch-an-imperative-style-high-performance-deep-learning-library.pdf
23. Romero, A., Ballas, N., Kahou, S.E., Chassang, A., Gatta, C., Bengio, Y.: FitNets: hints for thin deep nets (2015)
24. Ronneberger, O., Fischer, P., Brox, T.: U-Net: convolutional networks for biomedical image segmentation. CoRR **abs/1505.04597** (2015). http://arxiv.org/abs/1505.04597
25. Shannon, C.E.: A mathematical theory of communication. Bell Syst. Tech. J. **27**(3), 379–423 (1948). https://doi.org/10.1002/j.1538-7305.1948.tb01338.x
26. Shu, C., Liu, Y., Gao, J., Yan, Z., Shen, C.: Channel-wise knowledge distillation for dense prediction (2020). arXiv:2011.13256
27. Stanton, S., Izmailov, P., Kirichenko, P., Alemi, A.A., Wilson, A.G.: Does knowledge distillation really work? (2021). arXiv:2106.05945
28. Strudel, R., Garcia, R., Laptev, I., Schmid, C.: Segmenter: transformer for semantic segmentation (2021). arXiv:2105.05633
29. Tan, M., Le, Q.: EfficientNet: rethinking model scaling for convolutional neural networks. In: International Conference on Machine Learning, pp. 6105–6114. PMLR (2019)
30. Tian, Z., et al.: Adaptive perspective distillation for semantic segmentation. IEEE Trans. Pattern Anal. Mach. Intell. **45**(2), 1372–1387 (2023). https://doi.org/10.1109/TPAMI.2022.3159581
31. Turc, I., Chang, M., Lee, K., Toutanova, K.: Well-read students learn better: the impact of student initialization on knowledge distillation. CoRR **abs/1908.08962** (2019). arXiv:1908.08962
32. Wang, Y., Zhou, W., Jiang, T., Bai, X., Xu, Y.: Intra-class Feature Variation Distillation for Semantic Segmentation, pp. 346–362 (2020). https://doi.org/10.1007/978-3-030-58571-6_21
33. Xie, E., Wang, W., Yu, Z., Anandkumar, A., Alvarez, J.M., Luo, P.: Segformer: simple and efficient design for semantic segmentation with transformers (2021). arXiv:2105.15203
34. Xie, J., Shuai, B., Hu, J.F., Lin, J., Zheng, W.S.: Improving fast segmentation with teacher-student learning (2018). arXiv:1810.08476
35. Yang, C., Zhou, H., An, Z., Jiang, X., Xu, Y., Zhang, Q.: Cross-image relational knowledge distillation for semantic segmentation (2022). arXiv:2204.06986
36. Yang, Z., Li, Z., Shao, M., Shi, D., Yuan, Z., Yuan, C.: Masked generative distillation (2022). arXiv:2205.01529
37. Yu, C., Wang, J., Peng, C., Gao, C., Yu, G., Sang, N.: BiSeNet: bilateral segmentation network for real-time semantic segmentation. In: Ferrari, V., Hebert, M., Sminchisescu, C., Weiss, Y. (eds.) ECCV 2018. LNCS, vol. 11217, pp. 334–349. Springer, Cham (2018). https://doi.org/10.1007/978-3-030-01261-8_20

38. Yuan, J., Qi, Q., Du, F., Intra, Z., Wang, F., Liu, Y.: FAKD: feature augmented knowledge distillation for semantic segmentation (2022). arXiv:2208.14143
39. Yuan, L., Tay, F.E.H., Li, G., Wang, T., Feng, J.: Revisit knowledge distillation: a teacher-free framework. CoRR **abs/1909.11723** (2019). arXiv:1909.11723
40. Zagoruyko, S., Komodakis, N.: Paying more attention to attention: improving the performance of convolutional neural networks via attention transfer (2017)
41. Zhang, Z., Zhou, C., Tu, Z.: Distilling inter-class distance for semantic segmentation (2022). arXiv:2205.03650
42. Zhao, H.: semseg (2019). https://github.com/hszhao/semseg
43. Zhao, H., Qi, X., Shen, X., Shi, J., Jia, J.: ICNet for real-time semantic segmentation on high-resolution images. In: Ferrari, V., Hebert, M., Sminchisescu, C., Weiss, Y. (eds.) ECCV 2018. LNCS, vol. 11207, pp. 418–434. Springer, Cham (2018). https://doi.org/10.1007/978-3-030-01219-9_25
44. Zhao, H., Shi, J., Qi, X., Wang, X., Jia, J.: Pyramid scene parsing network. In: Proceedings of the IEEE Conference on Computer Vision and Pattern Recognition, pp. 2881–2890 (2017)
45. Zheng, S., et al.: Rethinking semantic segmentation from a sequence-to-sequence perspective with transformers (2020). arXiv:2012.15840
46. Zhou, B., Zhao, H., Puig, X., Fidler, S., Barriuso, A., Torralba, A.: Scene parsing through ADE20K dataset. In: 2017 IEEE Conference on Computer Vision and Pattern Recognition (CVPR), pp. 5122–5130 (2017). https://doi.org/10.1109/CVPR.2017.544

Combining Primal and Dual Representations in Deep Restricted Kernel Machines Classifiers

Francesco Tonin[✉], Panagiotis Patrinos, and Johan A. K. Suykens

ESAT-STADIUS, KU Leuven, 3001 Heverlee, Belgium
{francesco.tonin,panos.patrinos,johan.suykens}@esat.kuleuven.be

Abstract. In the context of deep learning with kernel machines, the deep Restricted Kernel Machine (DRKM) framework allows multiple levels of kernel PCA (KPCA) and Least-Squares Support Vector Machines (LSSVM) to be combined into a deep architecture using visible and hidden units. We propose a new method for DRKM classification coupling the objectives of KPCA and classification levels, with the hidden feature matrix lying on the Stiefel manifold. The classification level can be formulated as an LSSVM or as an MLP feature map, combining depth in terms of levels and layers. The classification level is expressed in its primal formulation, as the deep KPCA levels, in their dual formulation, can embed the most informative components of the data in a much lower dimensional space. The dual setting is independent of the dimension of the inputs and the primal setting is parametric, which makes the proposed method computationally efficient for both high-dimensional inputs and large datasets. In the experiments, we show that our developed algorithm can effectively learn from small datasets, while using less memory than the convolutional neural network (CNN) with high-dimensional data and that models with multiple KPCA levels can outperform models with a single level. On the tested larger-scale datasets, DRKM is more energy efficient than CNN while maintaining comparable performance.

Keywords: Kernel methods · Manifold learning · Primal-Dual Representations

1 Introduction

The deep Restricted Kernel Machine (DRKM) was introduced in [18] to find synergies between kernel methods and deep learning. While recent research has focused on leveraging RKM in generative models [16,17] and unsupervised learning [20–22], there has been little investigation into the use of DRKM for classification problems. The *single*-level RKM classification framework was used in [10] to propose a multi-modal classification method based on tensor learning using a single model weight tensor with all the modes sharing a common latent space. The *semi*-supervised RKM was used in conjunction with message-passing kernel

PCA (KPCA) levels in [1] for semi-supervised node classification in graphs using *only* the dual representation. In [18], deep reduced set kernel-based models were applied to classification datasets, and an unconstrained DRKM with a primal-estimation scheme using a Least-Squares Support Vector Machines (LSSVM) classifier was evaluated on two UCI datasets. However, its unconstrained formulation introduces additional stabilization terms in the objective and does not combine primal and dual in the same model. A DRKM for multi-level kernel PCA (DKPCA) was introduced in [22] as a method for unsupervised representation learning employing multiple levels of kernel PCA with orthogonality constraints. However, this method does not consider a classification objective and only employs the dual representation. Overall, effective classification algorithms for deep (i.e., with multiple levels) RKMs are still an open problem and previous studies have only considered either primal or dual models.

In this paper, we propose a new DRKM classifier employing multiple levels of KPCA and an LSSVM or MLP classification level. We combine the dual representation of the KPCA with the primal representation of the LSSVM/MLP: the dual representation is better suited for the kernel trick and feature extraction, while the primal representation is more computationally efficient for larger datasets and can directly take advantage of the nonlinear embedding from the multiple KPCA levels. Given that the size of the kernel matrix is independent of the dimension of the inputs, the dual problem is typically suited for handling problems with high-dimensional input data, while solving the primal is often suitable for large numbers of data. Combining the parametric primal representation and the kernel-based dual in the DRKM provides a powerful framework for efficient algorithms for both high-dimensional inputs and larger-scale datasets. Therefore, the model is well-suited for Frugal AI, where the non-parametric levels can handle high-dimensional data with computational resources that are independent of the number of inputs, possibly reducing the dimensionality of the input space, such that the parametric classification level can be efficiently trained in a much lower dimensional space. Note that we employ the dual framework for the unsupervised KPCA levels and the primal framework for the supervised classification level. Employing unsupervised levels is advantageous when training with limited labelled data, as the model is built on unsupervised core models that can effectively induce patterns and representations from the unlabelled data. Our main contributions are as follows.

- We propose a new method for DRKM classification that couples the objectives of KPCA and LSSVM/MLP classification levels to create a deep architecture. Our method integrates the kernel-based dual representation in the unsupervised part and the parametric primal representation in the supervised part. In this way, the final model is applicable to general data in the sense that the DRKM can be applied to limited and larger amounts of data in either low or high dimensional inputs spaces.
- We define a constrained optimization problem with orthogonality constraints on the hidden features of the unsupervised levels and illustrate a training algorithm based on Projected Gradient Descent. In particular, we investigate how

end-to-end training compares with unsupervised initialization of the KPCA levels followed by fine-tuning.
- We empirically evaluate our method on benchmark datasets comparing with the LSSVM/MLP classifiers alone, showing that increased depth can benefit performance in kernel methods when limited training data is available. Our approach is frugal in that it can effectively learn from limited training data thanks to its unsupervised KPCA core, and it can also efficiently deal with larger datasets thanks to the primal classification level. We additionally empirically show lower environmental impact than the CNN on a number of UCI datasets with thousands of dimensions, thanks to the employed non-parametric dual representation, with similar classification performance.

2 Background

Consider the training data $\{(x_i, y_i)\}_{i=1}^N$, where $x_i \in \mathbb{R}^d$ and $y_i \in \{-1, 1\}$. The objective of RKM binary classification [18] is:

$$J_0 = \sum_{i=1}^N \left(1 - y_i \left(\varphi(x_i)^T w + b\right)\right) h_i - \frac{\lambda}{2} h_i^2 + \frac{\eta}{2} w^T w, \qquad (1)$$

where $\varphi(x) \in \mathbb{R}^l$ is the feature map, $w \in \mathbb{R}^l$ is the weight vector, $h_i \in \mathbb{R}$ are the hidden features, and $\lambda, \eta > 0$ are regularization constants. It can be shown that (1) is a lower bound to the LSSVM classification objective [18,19]. In the shallow case where there is no other level, the solution of (1) in the conjugated features h_i is given by a linear system obtained from the stationarity of J_0 [18].

Regarding the KPCA level, let s be the number of selected principal components. In the LS-SVM setting, the KPCA problem can be written as minimizing a regularization term and finding directions of maximum variance [19]:

$$\underset{W, e_i}{\text{minimize}} \quad \tilde{J}_{\text{KPCA}} = \frac{\eta}{2} \text{Tr}\left(W^\top W\right) - \frac{1}{2} \sum_{i=1}^N e_i^\top \Lambda^{-1} e_i$$

$$\text{subject to} \quad e_i = W^\top \varphi(x_i), \quad i = 1, \dots, N,$$

where $W \in \mathbb{R}^{l \times s}$ is the interconnection matrix, $e_i \in \mathbb{R}^s$ are the score variables along the selected s projection directions, and $\Lambda = \text{diag}\{\lambda_1, \dots, \lambda_s\} \succ 0, \eta > 0$ are regularization hyperparameters. The RKM formulation of KPCA [18] is given by an upper bound of $\tilde{J}_{\text{KPCA}}$ obtained component-wise with the Fenchel-Young inequality $\frac{1}{2\lambda}e^2 + \frac{\lambda}{2}h^2 \geq eh$, $\forall e, h \in \mathbb{R}$ which introduces the hidden features h and leads to the following objective with *conjugate feature duality*:

$$J_{\text{KPCA}} = -\sum_{i=1}^N \varphi(x_i)^\top W h_i + \frac{1}{2}\sum_{i=1}^N h_i^\top \Lambda \, h_i + \frac{\eta}{2} \text{Tr}\left(W^\top W\right), \qquad (2)$$

where $h_i \in \mathbb{R}^s$ are the conjugated hidden features corresponding to each training sample x_i; in representation learning, h_i is also known as the latent representation of x_i consisting of s latent variables or of s hidden features. By characterizing the stationary points of J_{KPCA} in (2), the following eigenvalue problem is obtained

$$\frac{1}{\eta} KH = H\Lambda,$$

where $K \in \mathbb{R}^{N \times N}$ denotes the kernel matrix induced by the positive-definite kernel function $k : \mathbb{R}^d \times \mathbb{R}^d \mapsto \mathbb{R}$ with $k(x_i, x_j) = \varphi(x_i)^\top \varphi(x_j)$ and the matrix $H = [h_1, \ldots, h_N]^\top$ incorporates the conjugate hidden features for all N data points. Since the primal form in (2) is not directly suitable for minimization because it is unbounded below, [21] derived a rewriting of (2) in the dual by introducing orthogonality constraints on the hidden features and eliminating the interconnection matrix. Using the stationarity of J_{KPCA} and the kernel trick, the first term of (2) can be rewritten as $-\frac{1}{\eta}\text{Tr}\left(H^T K H\right)$, and the third term can be rewritten as $\frac{1}{2\eta}\text{Tr}\left(H^T K H\right)$. Derivation details are given in [21]. A deep KPCA (DKPCA) framework combining multiple KPCA levels in a single objective was proposed in [22]. In that work, the principal components of multiple KPCA levels are coupled in their hidden units creating both forward and backward dependency across levels, showing greater representation efficiency for unsupervised learning. In this work, we propose a new method for classification based on a DKPCA architecture coupled with a classification level with end-to-end training combining dual and primal representations.

2.1 Related Work

Deep kernel learning tackles multiple latent spaces for greater flexibility, more informative hierarchical investigation of the data, and kernel-based interpretations. [14] considers the representation learned by successive network layers. In particular, they consider a deep neural network (DNN) of L layers $f(x) = f_L \circ \cdots \circ f_1(x)$ and analyze the induced kernels $k_0 = k_{\text{RBF}}(x, x')$, $k_1 = k_{\text{RBF}}(f_1(x), f_1(x'))$, ..., $k_L = k_{\text{RBF}}(f_L \circ \cdots \circ f_1(x), f_L \circ \cdots \circ f_1(x'))$, with k_{RBF} indicating the Gaussian kernel. In other words, each layer of the DNN is associated with a kernel defined on the output of that layer. Conversely, in this paper we consider several feature maps over multiple levels. In other words, following the terminology used in [18], in [14] deep learning is only performed over *layers*, while in our approach depth is given by multiple *levels*, each associated with a different feature map possibly consisting of multiple layers. For instance, a DRKM can consist of multiple DNNs, each associated with the feature map φ_j of level j. Therefore, in the framework of DRKM, [14] performs shallow learning, as it works with a single DNN. Additionally, in the DRKM the levels are coupled in terms of their hidden features, while in [14] the considered architecture is a composition of the outputs of each layer. A concatenation of operator-valued kernel layers was considered for data autoencoding in [12], but no extension to supervised learning was considered. In [6], shallow PCA is conducted to extract principal components, which are then applied to another KPCA, where each KPCA independently and sequentially optimizes its variance maximization. PCA is firstly performed to extract principal components of the data and then further dimensionality reduction is sequentially applied to the extracted features from the previous (K)PCA layer. This serial approach makes each layer straightforwardly maximize its variance objective, which is independent of other layers.

3 Proposed Method

In this section, we describe the proposed combination of KPCA levels in the dual and a classification level in the primal. The former part extracts multiple levels of the most informative components of the given data through multiple feature maps. After such transformations, the classification level can effectively learn a decision boundary in a much lower dimensional subspace, motivating its representation in the primal. We start by describing the model formulation where the primal classifier is an LSSVM classifier following one ore more KPCA levels. Next, we derive the model for the MLP classifier. Finally, we discuss the optimization algorithm and multiple initialization procedures.

3.1 Shallow RKM Primal LSSVM Classifier

We start by defining a DRKM classifier with a single KPCA level, i.e., the shallow RKM. Its architecture is the following.

- Level 1 consists of KPCA using as input the sample x_i. The features extracted by this level are characterized by its hidden features $h_i^{(1)}$.
- Level 2 consists of LSSVM classification using as input the hidden features $h_i^{(1)}$ from the previous level and with output data y_i. This level is characterized by its weights w.

The training objective of the above architecture is obtained from the representation learning optimization problem of RKM with one KPCA level and an LSSVM classifier written in its RKM formulation. The solution in terms of the h_i of the latter is given by a linear system in the shallow case; however, in the case of multiple levels, end-to-end learning cannot be performed by solving the linear system. We propose an alternative training strategy for the deep case. First of all, we eliminate h_i in (1): from the stationarity of J_0 it follows that

$$h_i = \frac{1}{\lambda}\left(1 - y_i\left(w^T \varphi(x_i) + b\right)\right). \tag{3}$$

Replacing (3) in (1),

$$J_0 = \sum_{i=1}^{N} \frac{1}{2\lambda}\left(1 - y_i\left(w^T \varphi(x_i) + b\right)\right)^2 + \frac{\eta}{2} w^T w.$$

We propose to combine one level of KPCA in the RKM formulation with the objective of an LSSVM classifier in the following optimization problem:

$$\min_{h_i^{(1)}, w, b} J_1 = -\frac{1}{2\eta_1} \text{Tr}\left(H^{(1)^T} K^{(0)} H^{(1)}\right) + \frac{\eta}{2} w^T w$$

$$+ \frac{1}{2\lambda} \sum_{i=1}^{N} \left(1 - y_i(w^T \varphi(h_i^{(1)}) + b)\right)^2 \quad (4)$$

$$\text{s.t.} \quad H^{(1)^T} H^{(1)} = I.$$

The objective of (4) consists of a KPCA term written in the dual formulation and a classification term in the primal. The former problem is independent of the input dimensionality due to the dual formulation; we use the primal formulation for the latter term because $h_i^{(1)}$ is usually low-dimensional, as the number of principal components s_1 is generally small. The classifier is expressed in the primal as $\hat{y} = \text{sign}\left(w^T \varphi(h^{(1)}) + b\right)$, where $\hat{y}$ is the estimated label of an input sample x and h_i is computed following (3) with input $h^{(1)}$, which is the latent representation of x. Regarding the choice of φ, one can employ a linear mapping as often done in the last layer of deep neural network classifiers; the full model is still non-linear due to the first KPCA level. Moreover, the formulation in (4) is intended for binary classification problems; multiclass problems with p classes can be solved with a one-vs-all approach by training p binary classifiers.

Remark 1 (Orthogonality constraints). Contrary to the classifier proposed in [18], we use orthogonality constraints on the hidden features of the kernel PCA level. In the field of neural networks, it was shown that orthogonality constraints can lead to better performance [2] and better regularization [4,5]. For example, [4] shows that, if the weights of the neural network are points of the Grassmann manifold $\mathcal{G}(1, n)$, minimizing the soft orthogonality constraint $L(\alpha, W) = \frac{\alpha}{2} ||W^T W - I||_F^2$, where $W \in \mathbb{R}^{n \times p}$ is the weight matrix of the neural network, also minimizes a model complexity loss, introduced in [7], based on the KL divergence $D_{\text{KL}}(Q(w|\beta) || P(w|\alpha))$ between the posterior $Q(w|\beta)$ and the prior $P(w|\alpha)$ distribution of the neural network weights. In contrast to [4], our method is based on kernel methods.

3.2 Deep RKM Primal LSSVM Classifier

We now define the DRKM classifier with n_{levels} KPCA levels: increased classifier depth may lead to a more compact representation of the target function and thus to better performance for complex classification problems. The architecture, illustrated in Fig. 1, is as follows.

- Level 1 consists of KPCA using as input the sample x_i. The features extracted by this level are characterized by its hidden features $h_i^{(1)}$.
- Level j, $2 \leq j \leq n_{\text{levels}}$ consists of KPCA using as input the hidden features $h_i^{(j-1)}$ from the previous level. The features extracted by this level are characterized by its hidden features $h_i^{(j)}$.

```
┌─────────┐      ┌──────────────┐   Level n_L    ┌──────────┐ Classification Level
│ Level 1 │ H^(1)│              │ H^(n_L-1)      │          │ H^(n_L)
│         │ ───► │  H^(n_L-1)   │ ─────────────► │          │ ─────►  w^T φ(h^(n_L)) + b
│ K^(0)(X)│      │              │                │K^(n_L-1) │
│         │      │              │                │(H^(n_L-1)│
└─────────┘      └──────────────┘                └──────────┘
                                                                       ▲
                                                                       │ y
```

Fig. 1. Diagram of the proposed DRKM of (5) with n_L KPCA levels in dual and one final LSSVM classification level in primal. Each green arrow goes from the level that is characterized by the corresponding hidden features to the level where it is used as input. $K^{(0)}(X)$ indicates the kernel matrix of the input data.

- Level $n_{\text{levels}} + 1$ consists of LSSVM classification using as input the hidden features $h_i^{(n_{\text{levels}})}$ from the previous level and with output data y_i. This level is characterized by its weights w.

The proposed objective to be minimized for $n_{\text{levels}} \geq 2$ of KPCA levels is:

$$J_{n_{\text{levels}}}(h_i^{(1)}, \ldots, h_i^{(n_{\text{levels}})}, w, b) = -\frac{1}{2\eta_1} \text{Tr}\left(H^{(1)T} K^{(0)} H^{(1)}\right) \quad (5)$$

$$-\sum_{j=2}^{n_{\text{levels}}} \frac{1}{2\eta_j} \text{Tr}\left(H^{(j)T} K^{(j-1)}(H^{(j-1)}) H^{(j)}\right)$$

$$+\frac{1}{2\lambda} \sum_{i=1}^{N} \left(1 - y_i(w^T \varphi(h_i^{(n_{\text{levels}})}) + b)\right)^2 + \frac{\eta}{2} w^T w,$$

where $H^{(j)} = [h_1^{(j)}, \ldots, h_N^{(j)}]^T \in \mathbb{R}^{N \times s_j}$ incorporates the hidden features conjugated along s_j projection directions for all N data points, where s_j is the number of selected principal components by the j-th level. The kernel matrices are obtained as follows: $K^{(0)} \in \mathbb{R}^{N \times N}$ is attained as $(K^{(0)})_{ik} = k^{(0)}(x_i, x_k)$ and $K^{(j-1)} \in \mathbb{R}^{N \times N}$ as $(K^{(j-1)})_{ik} = k^{(j-1)}(h_i^{(j-1)}, h_k^{(j-1)})$, where $k^{(0)} : \mathbb{R}^d \times \mathbb{R}^d \mapsto \mathbb{R}$ is the kernel function of the first level and $k^{(j-1)} : \mathbb{R}^{s_{j-1}} \times \mathbb{R}^{s_{j-1}} \mapsto \mathbb{R}$ is the kernel function of level $j = 2, \ldots, n_{\text{levels}}$. The projection directions of shallow KPCA are uncorrelated due to the orthogonality of different principal components; similarly, we impose $H^{(j)T} H^{(j)} = I$ in (5). Following [21], orthogonality between the hidden features of two different levels can be imposed to encourage the levels to learn new features of the data instead of repeating the same features in every level. The number of levels is an hyperparameter to be tuned in addition to the kernel hyperparameters and the number of components in each level. One can tune these hyperparameters using standard techniques such as defining a separate validation set or employing cross-validation. In general, the minimum number of levels required for good performance on a given set of observations depends on the complexity of the training dataset. For an out-of-sample x^*, multiple strategies to compute its latent representation have been proposed in the context of RKMs [15,18,21,22]. Based on [17], we propose to apply a kernel smoother approach [9] $h^{(n_{\text{levels}})\star} = \frac{\sum_{i=1}^{N} \tilde{k}(x_i, x^\star) h_i^{(n_{\text{levels}})}}{\sum_{i=1}^{N} \tilde{k}(x_i, x^\star)}$, where $\tilde{k}$ is a localized kernel such as the Gaussian kernel with design parameter $\tilde{\sigma}$, representing the width of the considered local neighborhood. A larger $\tilde{\sigma}$ gives lower variance, as more observed points are considered, but also higher bias. With smaller bandwidth, the similarity measure expressed by $\tilde{k}$ is more local, so $h^{(n_{\text{levels}})\star}$ is closer to the latent representation of training points that are similar to $x^\star$. Using this approach, the predicted class of $x^\star$ expressed in the primal model representation is:

$$\hat{y}^\star = \text{sign}\left[w^T \varphi\left(\frac{\sum_{i=1}^{N} \tilde{k}(x_i, x^\star) h_i^{(n_{\text{levels}})}}{\sum_{i=1}^{N} \tilde{k}(x_i, x^\star)}\right) + b\right]. \tag{6}$$

Note that $h_i^{(n_{\text{levels}})}$ depends on the hidden features of the previous levels $h_i^{(n_{\text{levels}}-1)}, \ldots, h_i^{(1)}$ as they are jointly optimized in (5). The final architecture of the proposed DRKM is therefore a combination of non-parametric modeling through the hidden features of the last KPCA level computed through (6) and the parametric classifier with parameters w, b.

3.3 Deep RKM Primal MLP Classifier

The classification DRKM can also be constructed with multiple KPCA levels in the RKM formulation and a final MLP classification level, instead of the LSSVM classifier described in the previous subsection. The MLP classifier is a single level that consists of a multi-layer feature map. Note here the difference between depth given by multiple KPCA levels and depth in the MLP: in the latter case deep learning is only performed over layers, while in the former case depth is given by multiple levels, each associated with a different feature map possibly consisting of multiple layers.

The training objective of the DRKM with a final MLP $f_\theta(h_i^{(n_{\text{levels}})}) : \mathbb{R}^{s_{n_{\text{levels}}}} \to \mathbb{R}^p$ parametrized by W, b as classification level with p classes is:

$$J(h_i^{(1)}, \ldots, h_i^{(n_{\text{levels}})}, W, b, \theta) = -\frac{1}{2\eta_1} \text{Tr}\left(H^{(1)T} K^{(0)} H^{(1)}\right) \tag{7}$$

$$- \sum_{j=2}^{n_{\text{levels}}} \frac{1}{2\eta_j} \text{Tr}\left(H^{(j)T} K^{(j-1)}(H^{(j-1)}) H^{(j)}\right)$$

$$+ \frac{1}{2\lambda N} \sum_{i=1}^{N} \mathcal{L}(f_\theta(h_i^{(n_{\text{levels}})}), y_i) + \frac{\eta}{2} \text{Tr}\, W^T W,$$

where $\mathcal{L}(\hat{y}_i, y_i) = -\sum_{k=1}^{p} y_{i,k} \log \frac{\exp \hat{y}_{i,k}}{\sum_{j=1}^{p} \exp \hat{y}_{i,j}}$ is the cross entropy loss with $\hat{y}_i = f_\theta(h_i^{(n_{\text{levels}})})$ and $y_{i,k}$ a binary indicator of input x_i belonging to class k.

The logits predicting the class of an out-of-sample point $x^\star$ are given by $f_\theta(h^{(n_{\text{levels}})})$, where $h^{(n_{\text{levels}})}$ is obtained through the kernel smoother approach.

One motivation to employ the MLP classification level is that the MLP approach also naturally handles the multi-class case, resulting in multiple logits, one for each class. The next subsection describes the optimization algorithm for the DRKM classifier consisting of multiple KPCA levels and a final LSSVM or MLP classification level.

3.4 Optimization

The nonlinear optimization problem with objective (5) or (7) has at least one global minimum due to the Weierstrass theorem, as the objective function is continuous and the feasible set is compact, and it may have multiple local minima since it is a non-convex problem. The constraint set is a Stiefel manifold $\text{St}(s, N)$, so one of the algorithms that have been proposed for optimization on the Stiefel manifold could be employed. For instance, one could exploit the Cayley transform to determine the search curve, such as in the algorithms proposed in [23,24]. However, as explained in [21], these methods could be numerically problematic because determining the search curve requires a matrix inversion at each iteration. Therefore, we propose to employ the Projected Gradient Descent (PGD) algorithm, which specifies an iterative algorithm projecting H onto the Stiefel manifold at each iteration k. The iterates for minimizing (5) are specified by

$$H^{k+1} = \Pi_{\text{St}(s,N)}(H^k - \alpha_k \nabla J_2(H^k, w^k, b^k)),$$
$$w^{k+1} = w^k - \alpha_k \nabla J_{n_{\text{levels}}}(H^k, w^k, b^k),$$
$$b^{k+1} = b^k - \alpha_k \nabla J_{n_{\text{levels}}}(H^k, w^k, b^k),$$

where $\Pi_{\text{St}(s,N)}$ is the Euclidean projection onto the Stiefel manifold and α_k is the stepsize selected via backtracking. This projection is computed using the compact SVD of H^k, while the weights w and bias b of the LSSVM classifier level are not projected onto the Stiefel manifold. The objective (7) with MLP classifier is also optimized with PGD, where the weights of the MLP are not projected on the Stiefel manifold but are trained using Adam [11].

The variables can be initialized randomly from the standard normal distribution and *end-to-end* training or with unsupervised initialization with *fine-tuning*. In the unsupervised initialization scheme, the KPCA levels are first trained in the DKPCA unsupervised setting [22] by considering only the unsupervised terms of the objective (5); after convergence, the full model is fine-tuned using labels.

4 Experimental Evaluation

In this section, we conduct numerical experiments on standard benchmark datasets to evaluate the DRKM classifier and explore its properties. Specifically, we focus on efficient learning for small and large datasets in low- and high-dimensions.

4.1 Experimental Setup

We compare our method with a standard LSSVM classifier with RBF kernel, and a multilayer perceptron (MLP), and a Convolutional Neural Network (CNN). We test on MNIST [13], two UCI datasets, ARCENE [8] and Sonar, on the bioinformatics dataset Protein, on the RCV1 dataset [3], and on the IMDB Drama dataset.

Table 1. Tested datasets.

Dataset	N	N_{test}	d	p
MNIST	4000	10000	28 × 28	10
ARCENE	112	60	10000	2
Sonar	166	42	60	2
Protein	1489	13406	357	3
RCV1	16193	4049	47236	2
IMDB	96735	24184	1002	2

To assess that the proposed DRKM can effectively learn from small amount of training data, we chose a train/test split with few training samples; details are given in Table 1, where N and N_{test} are the number of used training and test instances, respectively, d the input dimension, and p the number of classes. We train all models for a maximum of 100 iterations. In the DRKM objective, we fix $\eta = \eta_j = 1$, $j = 1, ..., n_{\text{levels}}$ and $\lambda = 0.5$. The MLP has one hidden layer with 10 neurons and ReLU activation. For the CNN, we employ 2D convolution for 2-dimensional datasets and 1D convolution for 1D datasets.

4.2 Experimental Results

Do Deeper Models Perform Better? The classification accuracy on the test set of MNIST attained by a DRKM classifier with one, two, and three KPCA levels and one linear LSSVM classification level for multiple N (number of training points) is shown in Table 2. All models use the same overall number of components: $s_1 = 6$ for 1-level, $s_1 = 3$ and $s_2 = 3$ for 2-level, $s_1 = s_2 = s_3 = 2$ for 3-level. The variance is due to random initialization and different selection of the subset of training points. The mean accuracy of the two-level

Table 2. Mean classification accuracy (%) on the test set of MNIST according to the number of KPCA levels. Each column corresponds to a training set size.

Method	$N = 50$	$N = 100$	$N = 250$	$N = 500$	$N = 750$	$N = 1000$
1-level	57.27 (5.75)	59.76 (4.51)	71.24 (5.74)	75.15 (7.47)	79.68 (7.01)	80.59 (7.64)
2-level	**61.05** (1.24)	**65.97** (1.03)	**75.74** (0.50)	81.11 (1.22)	83.89 (0.23)	**85.29** (0.45)
3-level	61.02 (1.23)	65.64 (1.70)	75.69 (0.49)	**81.35** (0.43)	**83.90** (0.20)	**85.29** (0.69)

Table 3. Classification accuracy (%) in the small-data regime.

Method	MNIST	ARCENE	Sonar	Protein
MLP	87.33	74.67	77.85	57.29
CNN	**95.80**	80.33	85.71	59.87
LSSVM	91.75	79.67	88.09	57.30
DRKM (DKPCA initialization, no fine-tuning)	92.72	79.67	81.95	60.13
DRKM (DKPCA initialization, with fine-tuning)	92.73	82.00	84.71	61.24
DRKM (end-to-end training, random initialization)	92.78	**82.33**	**90.27**	**61.48**

model is higher than that for the one-level model across all N, suggesting that the increased depth led to better generalization. For instance, for $N = 500$ the mean performance of the one-level model is 75.15%, while for the two-level model it is 81.11%. The three-level model performs similarly to the two-level model. The three-level model keeps only two principal components per level, which may not be enough to get improved results. Furthermore, a deeper architecture may be useful on datasets more difficult than MNIST with, for instance, multiple more realistic objects and a complex background, where greater model complexity could boost classification accuracy. In general, the variance of the model with one level is significantly larger than that of the models with two and three levels, which means that different initializations have a greater influence on the model with the lowest depth. In conclusion, classification performance can benefit from architectures with multiple levels (Fig. 2).

Method	Protein (full)	RCV1	IMDB
MLP	63.01	93.38	97.88
CNN	67.33	**94.83**	**98.88**
LSSVM	58.33	94.27	97.78
DRKM	**67.61**	**94.83**	**98.88**

Fig. 2. Classification accuracy (%) for larger-scale data.

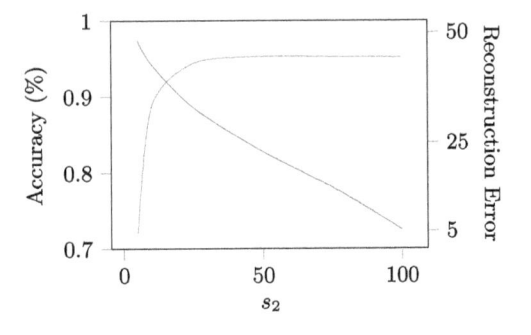

Fig. 3. Test classification accuracy (%) and training reconstruction error of DRKM on MNIST with varying s_2.

How Does the Proposed Method Perform Compared to Related Techniques? Table 3 compares the classification accuracy (%) of a two-level DRKM with $s_1 = s_2 = 10$ with MLP classification level against an MLP classifier, a

CNN, and a standard nonlinear LSSVM classifier. Results are averaged over five runs. The two-level DRKM outperforms the LSSVM classifier on all datasets, showing that increased depth and end-to-end training can result in better performance. In general, the experiments suggest that the proposed model is well suited for both low-dimensional datasets such as Sonar, as the KPCA levels can derive a higher number of features than the dimension of the input dataset, and high-dimensional datasets such as ARCENE, because the formulations in (5) and (7) do not depend on the dimension d of the input space thanks to the combination of the dual and primal representations. This is not the case for the CNN, which achieves significantly better performance only with spatial data such as the MNIST 2D images. Table 2 evaluates DRKM with end-to-end training on larger datasets, where *Protein (full)* indicates the Protein dataset with $N = 11916$ training points. The results show that the proposed method can be applied effectively to both small-scale datasets and larger datasets, for both lower-dimensional data (Protein) and higher-dimensional data (RCV1, IMDB). To further evaluate the performance on high-dimensional data, we train DRKM on MNIST for varying number of components s_2 keeping fixed $s_1 = 100$ with cosine kernel. The test classification performance and the training reconstruction error (MSE) are shown in Fig. 3. It can be seen that an initial sharp increase in accuracy corresponds to a distinctive drop in reconstruction error; further increasing s_2 leads to a decrease in training reconstruction error but small improvement in test accuracy, showing that small values of s_2 are enough to achieve good performance on MNIST.

What is the Effect of Fine-Tuning? We compare end-to-end training to fine-tuning after DKPCA unsupervised initialization in Table 3. In addition, we consider a linear classifier trained on the deep features extracted by DKPCA [22], i.e., a DRKM with DKPCA initialization but no fine-tuning and a linear classification level. On Sonar and ARCENE, fine-tuning the hidden units initialized using unsupervised DKPCA initialization results in significantly higher performance compared to simply training a linear classifier on the feature extracted by DKPCA. Note that while random initialization give unfeasible initial points, the unsupervised initialization gives a feasible point. On the other hand, on the more complex MNIST dataset, DKPCA initialization already performs quite well compared to the other initialization schemes. While on MNIST the proposed optimization algorithm converges to a similar minimum when the initial $h_i^{(1)}, h_i^{(2)}$ are found by DKPCA, on ARCENE end-to-end training with random initialization considerably outperforms the other initialization schemes, showing that the effect of the initialization schemes is dependent on the dataset at hand.

What is the Environmental Impact? The experiments above show that the combination of unsupervised KPCA in dual and supervised level in primal is effective when training with limited data. In efficient AI, it is also important to consider computational efficiency and the corresponding environmental impact of Machine Learning algorithms. In Table 4, we report the energy consumption in the small-data regime in Wh tracked using CodeCarbon.io[1]. Overall, DRKM

---

[1] https://codecarbon.io/.

Table 4. Energy consumption in Wh when training with limited data.

Method	MNIST	ARCENE	Sonar	Protein
MLP	0.0075	0.0007	0.001	0.000002
CNN	0.1540	0.3746	0.036	0.00016
LSSVM	0.1304	0.0002	0.00001	0.000008
DRKM (DKPCA initialization, no fine-tuning)	0.0610	0.0006	0.0009	0.000007
DRKM (DKPCA initialization, with fine-tuning)	1.177	0.0044	0.021	0.0012
DRKM (end-to-end training, random initialization)	0.316	0.0051	0.016	0.00026

Table 5. Efficiency comparisons on running time and memory consumption on the limited data benchmarks where training time (s) and peak training memory usage (MB) are given.

Method	Time (s)				Memory (MB)			
	MNIST	ARCENE	Sonar	Protein	MNIST	ARCENE	Sonar	Protein
MLP	1.57	0.22	0.03	0.53	12.29	22.07	2.88	8.38
CNN	4.55	11.36	0.33	2.88	74.46	5127.45	86.27	289.12
LSSVM	0.91	0.07	0.002	0.05	50.41	22.08	0.59	0.60
DRKM	0.98	0.15	0.07	0.42	67.89	43.52	5.24	40.53

Table 6. Efficiency comparisons on running time and memory consumption on the larger-scale benchmarks.

Method	Time (s)			Memory (MB)		
	Protein (full)	RCV1	IMDB	Protein (full)	RCV1	IMDB
MLP	5.26	5.92	23.80	10.32	5.18	32.44
CNN	25.79	99.18	372.64	326.43	720.43	700.12
LSSVM	0.95	1.42	8.26	10.88	16.68	19.26
DRKM	16.46	33.72	365.17	139.20	148.78	1343.54

has comparable or lower energy consumption than CNN while showing higher performance on the 1D datasets. The evaluations on the larger-scale data are presented in Table 7, where DRKM shows lower energy consumption than CNN while maintaining competitive performance.

We evaluate the efficiency of DRKM by comparing in terms of running time and memory consumption with three commonly used methods: MLP, CNN, and LSSVM. The results are presented in Tables 5 and 6. Table 5 shows the efficiency comparisons when

Table 7. Energy consumption (Wh) for larger-scale data.

Method	Protein (full)	RCV1	IMDB
MLP	0.020	0.029	0.076
CNN	0.115	0.44	2.96
LSSVM	0.0023	0.003	0.017
DRKM	0.052	0.092	1.87

limited data is available, where we measured the training time (in seconds) and peak training memory usage (in megabytes). We can observe that the combination of non-parametric and parametric levels makes it possible for the DRKM to achieve competitive results, with significantly lower memory consumption compared to CNN. For instance, in the high-dimensional ARCENE datasets, the DRKM uses 43.52 MB compared to 5127.45 MB used by CNN. The significant advantage in memory usage is due to the dual KPCA levels, whose dimension is independent of the input dimensions. The KPCA levels can perform dimensionality reduction such that the parametric classification level in the DRKM operates from an input space of much lower dimension. This indicates that our DRKM method strikes a balance between computational efficiency and memory utilization, making it a favorable choice compared to the CNN for applications where data has thousands of dimensions but memory resources are limited. Table 6 presents the efficiency comparisons on larger-scale benchmarks. The results demonstrate that DRKM exhibits favorable efficiency characteristics, with lower training times compared to CNN. Moreover, despite the larger dataset sizes, DRKM maintains a reasonable memory consumption, outperforming CNN in this regard in all tested datasets except the largest one. Overall, the experimental results demonstrate that the DRKM approach shows competitive efficiency in terms of both energy consumption, running time and memory usage when compared to established methods, suggesting its potential as an effective and resource-efficient solution in Frugal AI applications.

5 Conclusion

We propose a DRKM classifier based on the DKPCA representation learning method in its dual representation combined with a primal classification level expressed as LSSVM or as MLP. Our proposed DRKM classifier exhibits several advantageous characteristics that make it well-suited for Frugal AI. Firstly, the integration of unsupervised KPCA levels in our model enables superior performance compared to both LSSVM and MLP/CNN when dealing with tabular classification datasets with limited training points. This indicates the ability of our model to extract meaningful features from scarce data, making it particularly useful in resource-constrained scenarios. Moreover, our study demonstrates that employing multiple KPCA levels in the DRKM classifier surpasses the performance of using a single KPCA level. This finding highlights the significance of incorporating multiple perspectives in representation learning, leading to enhanced classification accuracy. Finally, our method showcases versatility in handling datasets of varying input dimensions and number of samples. We show that DRKM has lower energy consumption than the CNN on a number of higher-dimensional UCI datasets thanks to the employed dual representation, whose dimension is independent of the number of inputs. The combination of dual and primal components of the DRKM allows for efficient learning across different data settings, as the kernel-based levels are better suited for high-dimensional data and the parametric classification level is suitable for larger number of data.

Overall, the above findings demonstrate the suitability of the DRKM classifier for Frugal AI applications, where limited resources and diverse data dimensions are common challenges. By leveraging its dual and primal components, our model demonstrates promising capabilities in achieving good performance and efficient training in Frugal AI scenarios. Future work can investigate the performance of the DRKM classifier with fixed-size methods [19] to further improve its scalability on very large-scale datasets with millions of samples, such as ImageNet. For computer vision tasks, it would also be interesting to explore the application of specific kernels to enhance its performance on image data.

Acknowledgements. This work is jointly supported by ERC Advanced Grant E-DUALITY (787960), iBOF project Tensor Tools for Taming the Curse (3E221427), Research Council KU Leuven: Optimization framework for deep kernel machines C14/18/068, KU Leuven Grant CoE PFV/10/002, and Grant FWO G0A4917N, EU H2020 ICT-48 Network TAILOR (Foundations of Trustworthy AI - Integrating Reasoning, Learning and Optimization), and the Flemish Government (AI Research Program), and Leuven.AI Institute. This work was also supported by the Research Foundation Flanders (FWO) research projects G086518N, G086318N, and G0A0920N; Fonds de la Recherche Scientifique – FNRS and the Fonds Wetenschappelijk Onderzoek – Vlaanderen under EOS Project No. 30468160 (SeLMA).

References

1. Achten, S., Tonin, F., Patrinos, P., Suykens, J.A.K.: Semi-supervised classification with graph convolutional kernel machines. arXiv (2023)
2. Bansal, N., Chen, X., Wang, Z.: Can we gain more from orthogonality regularizations in training deep CNNs? In: NeurIPS (2018)
3. Chang, C.C., Lin, C.J.: LIBSVM: a library for support vector machines. ACM Trans. Intell. Syst. Technol. (TIST) **2**(3), 1–27 (2011)
4. Cho, M., Lee, J.: Riemannian approach to batch normalization. In: NeurIPS (2017)
5. Cogswell, M., Ahmed, F., Girshick, R., Zitnick, L., Batra, D.: Reducing overfitting in deep networks by decorrelating representations. In: ICLR (2016)
6. Deng, X., Tian, X., Chen, S., Harris, C.J.: Deep principal component analysis based on layerwise feature extraction and its application to nonlinear process monitoring. IEEE Trans. Control Syst. Technol. **27**(6), 2526–2540 (2019). https://doi.org/10.1109/TCST.2018.2865413
7. Graves, A.: Practical variational inference for neural networks. In: NeurIPS (2011)
8. Guyon, I., Gunn, S.R., Ben-Hur, A., Dror, G.: Result analysis of the NIPS 2003 feature selection challenge. In: NeurIPS (2004)
9. Hastie, T., Tibshirani, R., Friedman, J.: The Elements of Statistical Learning: Data Mining, Inference, and Prediction. Springer, New York (2009). https://doi.org/10.1007/978-0-387-84858-7
10. Houthuys, L., Suykens, J.A.: Tensor-based restricted kernel machines for multi-view classification. Inf. Fusion **68**, 54–66 (2021)
11. Kingma, D.P., Ba, J.L.: Adam: a method for stochastic optimization. In: ICLR (2015)
12. Laforgue, P., Clémençon, S., d'Alché-Buc, F.: Autoencoding any data through kernel autoencoders. In: International Conference on Artificial Intelligence and Statistics. PMLR (2019)

13. LeCun, Y., Cortes, C., Burges, C.: MNIST handwritten digit database (2010). http://yann.lecun.com/exdb/mnist
14. Montavon, G., Braun, M.L., Müller, K.R.: Kernel analysis of deep networks. J. Mach. Learn. Res. **12**(9), 2563–2581 (2011)
15. Pandey, A., Schreurs, J., Suykens, J.A.K.: Robust generative restricted kernel machines using weighted conjugate feature duality. In: LOD (2020)
16. Pandey, A., Schreurs, J., Suykens, J.A.K.: Generative Restricted Kernel Machines: a framework for multi-view generation and disentangled feature learning. Neural Netw. **135**, 177–191 (2021)
17. Schreurs, J., Suykens, J.: Generative kernel PCA. In: ESANN, pp. 129–134 (2018)
18. Suykens, J.A.K.: Deep restricted kernel machines using conjugate feature duality. Neural Comput. **29**(8), 2123–2163 (2017)
19. Suykens, J.A.K., Van Gestel, T., De Brabanter, J., De Moor, B., Vandewalle, J.: Least Squares Support Vector Machines. World Scientific (2002)
20. Tonin, F., Pandey, A., Patrinos, P., Suykens, J.A.K.: Unsupervised energy-based out-of-distribution detection using Stiefel-restricted kernel machine. In: IJCNN (2021)
21. Tonin, F., Patrinos, P., Suykens, J.A.K.: Unsupervised learning of disentangled representations in deep restricted kernel machines with orthogonality constraints. Neural Netw. **142**, 661–679 (2021)
22. Tonin, F., Tao, Q., Patrinos, P., Suykens, J.A.K.: Deep kernel principal component analysis for multi-level feature learning. arXiv (2023)
23. Wen, Z., Yin, W.: A feasible method for optimization with orthogonality constraints. Math. Program. **142**(1), 397–434 (2013)
24. Zhu, X.: A Riemannian conjugate gradient method for optimization on the Stiefel manifold. Comput. Optim. Appl. **67**(1), 73–110 (2017)

Addressing Limitations of TinyML Approaches for AI-Enabled Ambient Intelligence
Position Paper

Antoine Bonneau[1,2](✉)[iD], Frédéric Le Mouël[1][iD], and Fabien Mieyeville[2][iD]

[1] Univ Lyon, INSA Lyon, Inria, CITI, EA3720, 69621 Villeurbanne, France
{antoine.bonneau,frederic.le-mouel}@insa-lyon.fr
[2] Univ Lyon, Université Claude Bernard Lyon 1, INSA Lyon, Ecole Centrale de Lyon, CNRS, Ampére, UMR5005, 69622 Villeurbanne, France
fabien.mieyeville@univ-lyon1.fr

Abstract. The integration of Artificial Intelligence (AI) and Ambient Intelligence (AmI) has emerged as a promising approach to creating responsive and contextually aware environments. AmI creates contextually aware environments by seamlessly integrating intelligent technologies, while AI develops algorithms for autonomous learning and decision-making. However, embedding AI within AmI environments faces challenges due to limited resources and energy constraints. While recent research on embedded AI has primarily focused on specific tasks of AmI, our goal is to develop a comprehensive framework encompassing all the necessary components for practical use cases. Through this endeavor, we aim to explore power-aware designs and distributed learning as fundamental approaches to address limited computational resources, energy constraints, and dynamic context variations challenges.

Keywords: On-Device Learning · Intermittent Learning · Federated Learning · TinyML · Power Consumption

1 Introduction

In the past decade, the fields of Artificial Intelligence (AI) and Ambient Intelligence (AmI) have experienced rapid advancements as two complementary domains. AmI [10] is a paradigm that enables responsive and contextually aware environments by seamlessly integrating intelligent technologies into everyday surroundings. It involves the creation of intuitive systems capable of perceiving, reasoning, and adapting to human presence, needs, and preferences, thereby enhancing user experiences and simplifying interactions with the digital world. AmI has found a natural ally in AI, the domain of computer science concerned with developing intelligent systems capable of performing tasks that typically require human intelligence. It encompasses the development of algorithms and models that enable machines to learn, reason, and make decisions autonomously, mimicking cognitive processes. The intertwining of AI and AmI has been a natural progression [7], as their combined potential holds the promise of unlocking new frontiers in intelligent systems.

How can AmI and AI combination be beneficial? Local data processing and analysis at the deep edge with AI reduces reliance on continuous connectivity and centralized infrastructure, enhancing resilience against network disruptions and limiting personal data exposure. Deploying ML on resource-constrained sensor bring intelligence into AmI hardware. Even though entirely autonomous systems are still out of reach, working on infrastructural bricks is essential in developing AmI's ubiquitous network and can benefit Wireless Sensors Networks Monitoring (WSN) applications. Installing sensors within agricultural fields [18] can facilitate optimized irrigation, fertilization, and pest control. Similarly, in marine ecosystems [35], WSN could help monitor water quality or detect harmful algal blooms [15]. Critical civilian infrastructure elements are prone to damage resulting from environmental factors and operational conditions. The domain of Structural Health Monitoring (SHM) [12] could improve the detection of anomalies or strains by enabling WSN to locally analyze this data, promptly identifying potential issues, and triggering timely maintenance or repairs. In pursuing knowledge and exploring remote and extreme environments like deep space [29], humanity requires safe camps; hence, these isolated habitats can yield substantial benefits to AmI to monitor environmental conditions and resource usage and ensure the safety of explorers.

The integration of AI and AmI presents several challenges. AmI, being inherently integrated into the environment, necessitates miniaturized hardware, thereby imposing constraints on computational resources and autonomy because of the reduced possible size of the battery. Embedded devices, including microcontroller units (MCUs) and sensors, have limited processing power and memory. In the meantime, AI algorithms, particularly Machine Learning (ML) ones, tend to be computationally demanding. Energy consumption is critical for energy-harvesting (EH) and battery-powered devices. The typical efficiencies of energy harvesting techniques suitable for AmI devices range from 10^{-5} to 10^{-2} W [34], while the power consumption of these devices during operational tasks necessary for performing computations, is on the order of 10^{-1} W. Nevertheless, the nodes can operate despite an unfavorable ratio, as they spend a significant portion of their lifespan in standby mode. Few studies look at power consumption, and even fewer take physical measurements, preferring estimates based on datasheets [31], and the few that do only measure microcontroller [23] power consumption neglecting the rest of the hardware. ML models, especially Deep Learning (DL) models, can be large and complex, requiring significant memory and storage resources severely limited in embedded devices. AmI environments are dynamic and subject to context variations. Thus, AI models deployed on embedded devices should be adaptable to such variations and robust enough to handle uncertainties and noisy sensor data.

To address resource limitations in embedding AI within AmI environments, we propose combining Federated Learning and Intermittent Learning with

TinyML. Federated Learning enables collaborative model training and resource sharing across multiple devices. Discontinuously powered devices require Intermittent Learning to be usable. When integrated with TinyML, these approaches enable lightweight and efficient deployment of machine learning models on embedded devices, ensuring privacy and adaptability in AmI settings.

2 Background and Motivations

2.1 Current Implementation of Ambient Intelligence

The integration of sensors and AI has transformed computing. Initially, sensors relied on rule-based frameworks but have now advanced to ML-based approaches. They have transitioned from plugged-into power sources to mobile with energy harvesting or charging stations. For instance, researchers develop wearable health monitoring devices powered through energy harvesting for continuous operation, while autonomous vacuum cleaners recharge at dedicated stations.

Semantic AI is a branch of AI that focuses on understanding and interpreting the meaning of data and information. It involves using rules and algorithms to process and analyze data to make intelligent decisions and take appropriate actions. AmI implementations traditionally leveraged this AI to emulate contextual intelligence [22]. For instance, intelligent agents equipped with semantic knowledge can autonomously control home appliances. In healthcare, Semantic AI is being utilized to assist individuals in their daily activities, such as reminding them to take medication.

ML-based AI [10] has improved the performance and complexity of tasks previously performed with semantic AI and introduced new possibilities such as language, gesture, emotion, and human activity recognition. Current models are mostly trained using supervised or reinforcement techniques. Nevertheless, rule-based systems or supervised learning lack the necessary robustness to effectively adapt to a continuously evolving real-world environment that deviates from its initial design and deployment conditions.

2.2 Energy Consumption Concerns in TinyML

The essence of intelligent sensors lies in their ability to learn, which is now facilitated by TinyML techniques [11,25]. On-device learning empowers the local processing of information, primarily focusing on inference tasks, following the refinement of a pre-trained model [37]. On the other hand, autonomous systems and EH technologies enable self-powered AmI applications but imply a tight energy budget and have to cope with inevitable power shortages. The energy storage supporting EH [27] is a challenge in itself: batteries have higher energy density and provide constant (but relatively high) voltage, while supercapacitors have low energy density and provide unstable (but relatively low) voltage. On the other hand, supercapacitors are exposed to significant depletion, while batteries have only a few charge/discharge cycles. Due to the compact size of the sensors, the batteries employed must be small, typically ranging from 600 to 700 mAh [4]. Consequently, these batteries can only sustain an always-on device's requirements on a daily timescale or monthly, considering periods of sleep.

Previous works have shown that it is possible to use advanced AI solutions despite the memory constraints of low-end devices [20,25]. Lin et al. [17] has successfully fine-tuned a human recognition model on an STM32F746, a 32 bits microcontroller typical of low-end devices using less than 256 KB of RAM and 1 MB of Flash. Sudharsan et al. [31,32] employed smaller models and trained them from scratch using a reformable offline approach [24] on low-end MCUs. However, their approach solely relied on the datasheet information to estimate the computational requirements for training and inference processes. Profentzas et al. [23] optimized a pre-trained activity-recognition neural network on an nRF-52840 SoC featuring: a 32-bit ARM Cortex-M4 with FPU at 64 MHz, 256 KB of RAM and 1 MB of Flash physically measuring energy consumption. However, they limited their instrumentation to the MCU and did not reflect the actual energy-guzzling components consumption of a board such as the voltage regulator.

3 Concrete Use Cases

When establishing a cloud link for WSN proves to be arduous, cloud processing of ML models may be impossible. In certain circumstances, monitoring applications assume criticality while simultaneously encountering challenges in terms of connectivity. The accessibility of these environments to human presence may present challenges or render them permanently inaccessible once the devices are activated.

Environmental Monitoring. Utilizing ML on sensors within agricultural fields [18] can facilitate optimized irrigation, fertilization, and pest control. Similarly, in marine ecosystems [35], ambient intelligence implemented in a WSN would help monitor water quality, tidal behavior changes, detect harmful algal blooms, and contribute to conservation efforts. Civil Engineering critical infrastructure elements such as bridges and dams are prone to potential damage from various environmental factors, operational conditions, and daily interactions with multiple agents. This is the domain of Structural Health Monitoring (SHM) [12].

Habitats Optimized for Missions of Exploration. In the pursuit of knowledge and exploration of remote and extreme environments like deep space [29], or ocean depths, humanity requires safe camp infrastructure to accomplish missions. By deploying sensor networks, these habitats can be monitored for environmental conditions, resource usage, and the safety of explorers. Embedded intelligence enables local analysis on the sensor nodes, facilitating anomaly identification and timely alerts. This proactive approach ensures the success of exploration missions and the well-being of personnel in challenging environments.

4 Challenges and Elements of a Conceptual Framework

In the realm of embedded systems, limited memory and power outages pose significant challenges. We want to develop a cross-platform framework departing from a lightweight RTOS addressing presented issues. We want to compare low-level programming ease, relevant frameworks [14,21], and microcontroller operating systems [1] to analyze associated overhead. To facilitate comprehensive evaluations, we propose assessing energy consumption in MCU boards within the context of AmI by focusing on individual tasks that can be examined independently. We will evaluate data acquisition and cleaning processes (Sect. 4.1), analyze trade-offs of ML models for classification and regression in a power-aware context (Sect. 4.2), and assess the energy consumption of various communication protocols and distributed learning (Sect. 4.3).

4.1 Minimizing Hardware Requirements Through Data Reduction

Employing data reduction techniques can decrease the volume of manipulated data by selectively extracting helpful information from input signals, thereby mitigating memory constraints. A consequential advantage of data reduction is the reduction in processing time needed for analysis or computation.

Adaptive Sampling [28,33] entails the dynamic selection of representative data points from large datasets, which efficiently utilizes computational resources. The computational burden is significantly reduced by intelligently sampling only the most informative data instances. Moreover, adaptive sampling reduces the overall time required for model training and inference, enabling time-sensitive applications to operate effectively within the limitations of embedded systems.

TimeSeries Segmentation. [6,13,19] involves partitioning time-varying data into smaller, more manageable segments based on characteristic patterns and behaviors. This technique enables the selective analysis of specific segments rather than processing the entire time series data. The segmentation or *change point detection* methods are similar to feature extraction and would help focus on relevant portions without requiring a demanding Convolutional Neural Network (CNN).

4.2 Meeting Short and Long-Term Time Constraints

One significant resulting challenge of EH systems is the occurrence of power shortages that may hinder continuous operation. By carefully considering power availability and adapting system behavior accordingly, embedded computing can effectively operate within energy-limited environments. Limited device accessibility and updates make it imperative to imbue devices with self-assessment capabilities during the design stage. This challenge entails enabling devices to evaluate and analyze their understanding of the environment. By incorporating self-assessment and adaptation mechanisms, devices can autonomously maintain and update their understanding of the environment, ensuring effective operation even in dynamic or disrupting circumstances.

Intermittent Learning. refers to a learning paradigm that manages irregular or sporadic availability of training data or computational resources. Lee et al. [16] introduced Intermittent Learning as a way for EH computing platforms to perform machine learning tasks effectively and efficiently. Among the frameworks for intermittent learning that later emerged, [2] developed *REHASH*, a tool helping design adaptive IoT workflow heuristics. They evaluated their work by running activity recognition and greenhouse monitoring applications using an MSP430FR5994 Launchpad.

Incremental/Continual Learning refers to a machine learning paradigm that focuses on the ability of a model to learn from new data incrementally over time without requiring retraining from scratch [30]. Ren et al. [26] have tested their incremental online learning algorithm TinyOL on an Arduino 33 BLE board in a default detection application for USB fan vibrations data. Continual learning involves updating and expanding the model's knowledge while preserving previously learned information, enabling adaptation to new tasks or concepts without significant performance degradation. Until recent advances, retraining a model that has experienced concept drift in its evaluated data entails transmitting the data through the internet to a server responsible for generating a new model [24] subsequently redistributed to the hardware executing inferences.

4.3 Enabling Devices Collaboration Using Federated Learning

Federated Learning (FL) addresses the challenge of distributed data storage by allowing entities to collaboratively train models without sharing their data. FL is classified into two categories: Centralized Federated Learning (CFL) and Decentralized/Distributed/Serverless Federated Learning (DFL) [3,36]. CFL uses a central server, while DFL enables decentralized aggregation of model parameters. DFL finds significant utility in overcoming AmI device constraints disconnected from the internet and centralized servers. In such scenarios, DFL serves as a means to overcome these individual deficiencies by leveraging the collective power of the network. DFL allows for collaboratively training models and achieving higher intelligence without relying on solid individual capabilities. This collective approach could virtually circumvent computational weaknesses and memory constraints, providing a robust solution for AmI systems if in-situ and collaborative processing are balanced enough to justify communication overhead.

Some works have already started addressing the constraints imposed on intelligent sensors and the distribution of AI calculations in embedded systems. Dai et al. [9], with *DispFL*, have proposed to act on communication costs using personalized FL and decentralized learning. Costa et al. [8] designed a framework to enable the deployment of decentralized learning in resource-constrained devices.

They evaluated their contribution on a STM32L4R5ZIT6 MCU over some Artificial Neural Network models.

In the context of AmI, the implementation of FL necessitates addressing the inherent challenges posed by the fluctuating size of the learning network and the varying availability of energy resources among participants. Learning occurs exclusively among active nodes, which may vary across iterations. Hence, adopting specific strategies to ensure the FL process's reliability and expeditious convergence is imperative.

5 Conclusion and Future Work

We claim that the challenges linked to incorporating AI into Ambient Intelligence (AmI) settings can be successfully resolved by integrating Federated Learning, Intermittent Learning, and TinyML [5]. Combining those approaches and data reduction techniques enables collaborative model training and resource sharing across devices while addressing the sporadic availability of training data and computational power. Overall, this approach holds great potential to enhance the performance and resilience of embedded systems in resource-constrained environments, enabling the advancement of intelligent systems in AmI and unlocking new possibilities. We will evaluate solutions on a testbed composed of piezoelectric patches on an aluminum plate. TinyML sensors must collect and analyze data to identify vibration sources and distance and evaluate default type and severity. We then want to focus on distributed learning strategies for SHM tasks with separate processing nodes for piezoelectric signals.

References

1. Baccelli, E., et al.: RIOT: an open source operating system for low-end embedded devices in the IoT. IEEE Internet of Things J. **5** (2018). https://doi.org/10.1109/JIOT.2018.2815038
2. Bakar, A., Ross, A.G., Yildirim, K.S., Hester, J.: REHASH: a flexible, developer focused, heuristic adaptation platform for intermittently powered computing. ACM Interactive, Mobile, Wearable Ubiq. Tech. (2021). https://doi.org/10.1145/3478077
3. Beltrán, E.T.M., et al.: Decentralized Federated Learning: Fundamentals, State-of-the-art, Frameworks, Trends, and Challenges (Nov 2022). https://doi.org/10.48550/arXiv.2211.08413
4. Blaauw, D., et al.: IoT design space challenges: Circuits and systems. In: Symposium on VLSI Technology: Digest of Technical Papers (Jun 2014). https://doi.org/10.1109/VLSIT.2014.6894411
5. Bonneau, A., Le Mouël, F., Mieyeville, F.: Energy-efficient in-situ monitoring using on-device and distributed learning. In: Green Days, Lyon, France (Mar 2023)
6. Chiappa, S.: A bayesian approach to switching linear gaussian state-space models for unsupervised time-series segmentation. In: 7th ICML. IEEE (2008). https://doi.org/10.1109/ICMLA.2008.109
7. Chin, J., Callaghan, V., Allouch, S.B.: The Internet-of-Things: reflections on the past, present and future from a user-centered and smart environment perspective. J. Ambient Intell. Smart Environ. **11** (2019). https://doi.org/10.3233/AIS-180506

8. Costa, D., Costa, M., Pinto, S.: Train me if you can: decentralized learning on the deep edge. Applied Sciences **12**(9) (2022). https://doi.org/10.3390/app12094653
9. Dai, R., Shen, L., He, F., Tian, X., Tao, D.: DisPFL: Towards Communication-Efficient Personalized Federated Learning via Decentralized Sparse Training (May 2022). https://doi.org/10.48550/arXiv.2206.00187
10. Dunne, R., Morris, T., Harper, S.: A survey of ambient intelligence. ACM Comput. Surv. **54** (2022). https://doi.org/10.1145/3447242
11. Dutta, D.L., Bharali, S.: TinyML meets IoT: a comprehensive survey. Internet of Things **16** (2021). https://doi.org/10.1016/j.iot.2021.100461
12. Flah, M., Nunez, I., Ben Chaabene, W., Nehdi, M.L.: Machine learning algorithms in civil structural health monitoring: a systematic review. Arch. Comput. Methods Eng. **28** (2021). https://doi.org/10.1007/s11831-020-09471-9
13. Gąsior, K., Urbańska, H., Grzesiek, A., Zimroz, R., Wyłomańska, A.: Identification, decomposition and segmentation of impulsive vibration signals with deterministic components : a sieving screen case study. Sensors **20** (2020). https://doi.org/10.3390/s20195648
14. Han, H., Siebert, J.: TinyML: a systematic review and synthesis of existing research. In: ICAIIC (Feb 2022). https://doi.org/10.1109/ICAIIC54071.2022.9722636
15. Khan, R.M., Salehi, B., Mahdianpari, M., Mohammadimanesh, F., Mountrakis, G., Quackenbush, L.J.: A meta-analysis on harmful algal bloom detection and monitoring: a remote sensing perspective. Remote Sensing **13** (2021). https://doi.org/10.3390/rs13214347
16. Lee, S., Islam, B., Luo, Y., Nirjon, S.: Intermittent learning: on-device machine learning on intermittently powered system. ACM Interactive, Mobile, Wearable and Ubiq. Tech. (2019). https://doi.org/10.1145/3369837
17. Lin, J., Zhu, L., Chen, W.M., Wang, W.C., Gan, C., Han, S.: On-device training under 256 KB memory. In: ANIPS, vol. 35 (Jul 2022). https://doi.org/10.48550/arXiv.2206.15472
18. Mohinur Rahaman, M., Azharuddin, M.: Wireless sensor networks in agriculture through machine learning: a survey. Comput. Electr. Agricul. **197** (2022). https://doi.org/10.1016/j.compag.2022.106928
19. Monte, G., Huang, V., Liscovsky, P., Marasco, D., Agnello, A.: Standard of things, first step: understanding and normalizing sensor signals. In: IECON (Nov 2013). https://doi.org/10.1109/IECON.2013.6699121
20. Ojo, M.O., Giordano, S., Procissi, G., Seitanidis, I.N.: A review of low-end, middle-end, and high-end iot devices. IEEE Access **6** (2018). https://doi.org/10.1109/ACCESS.2018.2879615
21. Osman, A., Abid, U., Gemma, L., Perotto, M., Brunelli, D.: TinyML platforms benchmarking (Nov 2021). https://doi.org/10.48550/arXiv.2112.01319
22. Perera, C., Zaslavsky, A., Christen, P., Georgakopoulos, D.: Context aware computing for the internet of things: a survey. IEEE Commun. Surv. Tutorials **16** (2014). https://doi.org/10.1109/SURV.2013.042313.00197
23. Profentzas, C., Almgren, M., Landsiedel, O.: MiniLearn: On-device learning for low-power IoT devices. In: EWSN (2022). https://doi.org/10.5555/3578948.3578949
24. Rajapakse, V., Karunanayake, I., Ahmed, N.: Intelligence at the extreme edge: a survey on reformable TinyML. ACM Comput. Surv. (2023). https://doi.org/10.1145/3583683

25. Ray, P.P.: A review on TinyML: State-of-the-art and prospects. J. King Saud Univer. - Comput. Inform. Sci. **34** (2022). https://doi.org/10.1016/j.jksuci.2021.11.019
26. Ren, H., Anicic, D., Runkler, T.A.: TinyOL: TinyML with online-learning on microcontrollers. In: IJCNN (Jul 2021). https://doi.org/10.1109/IJCNN52387.2021.9533927
27. Riaz, A., Sarker, M.R., Saad, M.H.M., Mohamed, R.: Review on comparison of different energy storage technologies used in micro-energy harvesting, WSNs, low-cost microelectronic devices: Challenges and recommendations. Sensors **21** (2021). https://doi.org/10.3390/s21155041
28. Rodriguez-Pabon, C., Riva, G., Zerbini, C., Ruiz-Rosero, J., Ramirez-Gonzalez, G., Corrales, J.C.: An adaptive sampling period approach for management of IoT energy consumption: case study approach. Sensors **22** (2022). https://doi.org/10.3390/s22041472
29. Rollock, A.E., Klaus, D.M.: Defining and characterizing self-awareness and self-sufficiency for deep space habitats. Acta Astronautica **198** (2022). https://doi.org/10.1016/j.actaastro.2022.06.002
30. Shaheen, K., Hanif, M.A., Hasan, O., Shafique, M.: Continual learning for real-world autonomous systems: algorithms, challenges and frameworks (May 2021). https://doi.org/10.48550/arXiv.2105.12374
31. Sudharsan, B., Breslin, J.G., Ali, M.I.: Edge2Train: a framework to train machine learning models (SVMs) on resource-constrained IoT edge devices. In: 10th Intl. Conference on the Internet of Things (Oct 2020). https://doi.org/10.1145/3410992.3411014
32. Sudharsan, B., et al.: TinyML benchmark: executing fully connected neural networks on commodity microcontrollers. In: IEEE 7th World Forum on Internet of Things (WF-IoT) (Jun 2021). https://doi.org/10.1109/WF-IoT51360.2021.9595024
33. Trihinas, D., Pallis, G., Dikaiakos, M.D.: AdaM: an adaptive monitoring framework for sampling and filtering on IoT devices. In: 2015 IEEE International Conference on Big Data (Oct 2015). https://doi.org/10.1109/BigData.2015.7363816
34. Williams, A.J., et al.: Survey of energy harvesting technologies for wireless sensor networks. IEEE Access (2021). https://doi.org/10.1109/ACCESS.2021.3083697
35. Xu, G., Shen, W., Wang, X.: Applications of wireless sensor networks in marine environment monitoring: a survey. Sensors **14** (2014). https://doi.org/10.3390/s140916932
36. Yuan, L., Sun, L., Yu, P.S., Wang, Z.: Decentralized federated learning: a survey and perspective (Jun 2023). https://doi.org/10.48550/arXiv.2306.01603
37. Zhu, S., Voigt, T., Ko, J., Rahimian, F.: On-device Training: a first overview on existing systems (Dec 2022). https://doi.org/10.48550/arXiv.2212.00824

Leveraging Low Rank Filters for Efficient and Knowledge-Preserving Lifelong Learning

Muhammad Tayyab[1](✉) and Abhijit Mahalanobis[2]

[1] University of Central Florida, Orlando, FL 32816, USA
muhammad.tayyab@ucf.edu
[2] Department of ECE, University of Arizona, Tucson, AZ, USA

Abstract. We propose a low rank filter approximation based continual learning approach which decomposes convolution filters into compact basis filters and remixing coefficients. For lifelong learning, we keep the same basis filters to allow knowledge sharing, but add separate coefficients for each new task. Task specific feature maps are computed by a sequence of convolutions, first with shared basis filters and followed by the task specific coefficients. This method enables the model to preserve the previously learned knowledge, thus avoiding the problem of catastrophic forgetting. Additionally, choosing compact basis lets us get away with using a small number of basis filters which enables reduction in FLOPs and number of parameters in the model. To demonstrate efficiency of the proposed approach, we evaluate our model on a variety of datasets and network architectures. With Resnet18 based architecture, we report performance improvement on CIFAR100 with significantly low FLOPs and parameters as compared to other methods. For ImageNet our method achieves comparable performance to other recent methods with reduced FLOPs.

Keywords: Neural network compression · Continual Learning · Convolutional neural networks · Image classification

1 Introduction

Recent progress in machine learning research has led to impressive advances and has enabled many practical applications of the deep learning models [1,2]. These conventional methods however assume that all training data is available at once which is hardly the case in real world applications. For instance, imagine a warehouse robot tasked with visually scanning items. If traditional training pipeline is used, every time a set of new items classes are added to the inventory the model will need to be trained again from scratch, with all previous and newly available data. This process is not only time consuming but also needlessly computationally expensive. Additionally, previous training data may not be available now. Naively training the model on new dataset alone makes the

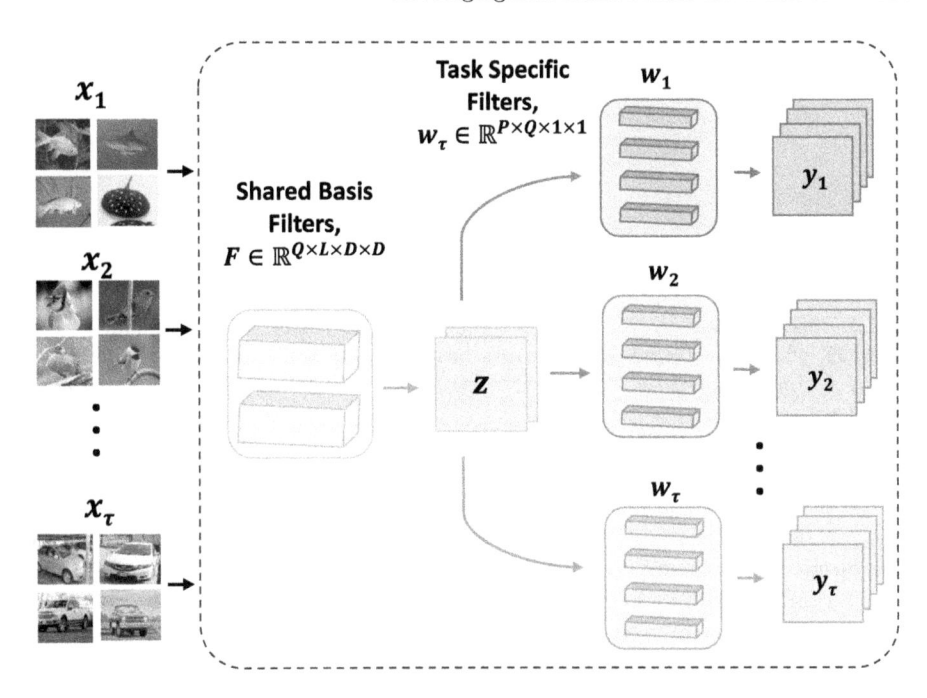

Fig. 1. Our Efficient Lifelong Learning (ELL) method. We substitute the original filters **H** with shared basis filters **F** and a set of task specific coefficients $\mathbf{w_t}$. Combination of these two lets us compute task specific features throughout the network.

model encounter *catastrophic forgetting*, where the model forgets the previously learned representations while adapting to new data only. This limitation is one of the major barriers hindering the widespread adoption of deep learning methods.

This problem (referred to as continual learning or lifelong learning in the literature) is an active area of research. Lifelong learning aims to train a model incrementally, as new data becomes available while also preserving the previously learned representations. To solve this problem several methods have been introduced among them, network expansion based methods work have shown potential. These methods add dedicated parameters to the model for each new task which can be used to calculate the task specific feature maps, thus avoiding forgetting. For example Rusu et al. [3], Yoon et al. [4] and Jerfel et al., 2019 [5] proposed incrementally adding parameters to the model for each new task. Vinay et al. [6] suggested adding several task specific feature map transformation layers to the model which add a small number of additional parameters. Similarly, Miao et al. [7] proposed a low rank sub-space based approach which decompose original filters into a set of task specific atoms and shared coefficients. Task specific filters are obtained at inference time by multiplying the shared coefficients with corresponding filter atoms.

To address the problem of Life Long Learning, we propose a filter decomposition based approach. Our method enables knowledge sharing between tasks using

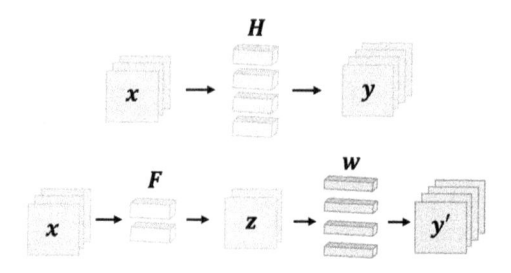

Fig. 2. Illustration of low rank filter decomposition. On top is the 2D convolution with filters **H**, which can be decomposed into basis filters **F** and coefficients **w** as shown below. A convolution with **F** followed by **w** yields **y'** that approximates the original output **y**.

shared basis filters while task specific coefficients enable the model to compute task specific feature maps. We leverage the low rank approximation of convolution filters **H** to decompose them into compact basis filters **F** and coefficients **w**. We share the filters **F** among all tasks while new coefficients (**w**) are added to the model for each additional task. In contrast to Miao et al. [7], task specific feature maps are computed by a sequence of convolutions with **F** followed by $\mathbf{w_t}$, as depicted in Fig. 1. Finally choosing compact basis to represent **H** lets us get away with using a small number of basis filters. This enables significant reduction in FLOPs and number of parameters in the model.

To demonstrate efficiency of the proposed approach, we evaluate our model on a variety of datasets and network architectures. With Resnet18 [1] based architecture, we report performance improvement on CIFAR100 [8] with significantly low FLOPs and parameters as compared to other methods. While for ImageNet [9] our method achieves comparable performance to the recent methods.

2 Related Work

2.1 Lifelong Learning

A lot of research has been done on lifelong learning in recent years. We have followed Delange et al. [10] to divide these methods into following groups based on the way they tackle forgetting of the previously learned knowledge.

Network Expansion methods are most relevant to our proposed approach. These methods prevent catastrophic forgetting by adding dedicated parameters for each new task to calculate the task specific feature maps. However unconstrained parameter growth can very quickly overwhelm the memory resources, so the rate of parameter growth is a matter of concern here.

Rusu et al. [3], Yoon et al. [4] and Jerfel et al., 2019 [5] proposed incrementally adding parameters to the model. While Mallaya et al. [11] prunes the previous tasks parameters before introducing new task. Similarly, Wortsman et al., 2020 [12] presented a masking mechanism to train separate subnetwork for each task.

Algorithm 1. Training procedure of the proposed method

TRAIN($\mathbf{H}$, k, $\mathcal{D}_1$ ... $\mathcal{D}_T$)
    Train model using $\mathcal{D}_1$, acc. to Eq. 3
    Decompose $\mathbf{H}$ in each Conv2D layer into $\mathbf{F}$ and $\mathbf{w}$
    Truncate k% filters in $\mathbf{F}$ and update $\mathbf{w}$ accordingly
    for (task: $t = 1$ to T) **do**
        if ($t == 1$)
            $\mathbf{w}_1 \leftarrow \mathbf{w}$
            Finetune $\mathbf{F}$ and $\mathbf{w}_1$ using $\mathcal{D}_1$, acc. to Eq. 4
        else
            $\mathbf{w}_t \leftarrow \mathbf{w}_1$
            Train $\mathbf{w}_t$ using $\mathcal{D}_t$, acc. to Eq. 5
        end if
    end for
    return ($\mathbf{F}$, $\mathbf{w}_1$ .. $\mathbf{w}_T$)

Recently, Vinay et al. [6] suggested adding several task specific feature map transformation layers to the model which add a small number of additional parameters. Miao et al. [7] proposed a low rank sub-space based approach which decompose original filters into a set of task specific atoms and shared coefficients. Task specific filters are obtained at inference time by multiplying the shared coefficients with corresponding filter atoms.

Replay Methods assign a small memory to store a subset of previous task samples or train a generator model to synthesise pseudo-samples. These samples are then used to train the model along with new task data to make sure that previously learned knowledge is retained. Storing samples from previous tasks however raises privacy concerns which is a drawback of these methods.

Shin et al. [13] proposed training a generative model to produce samples for previous tasks. Rebuffi et al. [14] stores a subset of exemplars per class, selected to best approximate class means in the learned feature space. Rolnick et al. [15] suggest a sampling strategy to limit size of the memory buffer. Yan et al. [16] proposed combining the network expansion with a memory buffer to store previous task samples.

Regularization-based methods avoid storing any samples and instead add a regularization term to the loss function meant to prevent the drift in previous task's loss landscape. These methods need to carefully balance the plasticity vs stability of the model to make sure the new information is ingested properly while also preventing catastrophic forgetting.

Li et al. [17] propose a knowledge distillation based technique, where previous task outputs as the soft labels to mitigate forgetting and transfer knowledge. Kirkpatrick et al. EWC [18] estimate the Fisher information matrix which is used to identify the important parameters for previous tasks. Training algorithm then selectively penalizes changes to these parameters. Similarly, Aljundi et al. MAS [19] suggest unsupervised importance estimation using gradient magnitude.

Finally, Titsias et al. [20] introduced Bayesian functional approach which avoids forgetting by constructing an approximate posterior belief of previous tasks.

2.2 Low Rank Approximation

Our work takes inspiration from class of techniques that rely on low-rank approximations to represent the convolution filters. Jaderberg et al. [21] replace the pretrained 4D filter tensor by a set of separable rank-1 filters and proposed to approximate the response of the original filters by minimizing a L2 norm. In Denton et al. [22], the authors form clusters in the higher filter layers, and then approximate the clusters using a sum of the outer-products of separable 1D filters. Zhang et al. [23] have employed a similar linear combination architecture to ours, but they approximate the response of the filters at each layer. Finally Qiu et al. [24] also proposes an convolutional filter decomposition as a truncated expansion with prefixed basis filters.

3 Method

Our lifelong learning method has been inspired from low rank filter decomposition-based methods [21,22]. We show that this formulation can not only be used to compress the pretrained convolution layer but also naturally extends to adapt the model for lifelong learning problem setting. It has been observed by [22] that task parameters lie in low dimensional sub space of the convolutional filters. We have exploited this fact for CNN compression by substituting the trained convolutional filters, of the first task, with compact filter basis $\mathbf{F}$ and coefficients $\mathbf{w}$, as shown in Fig. 2. For lifelong learning problem setting the basis filters are shared (and are kept fixed) while separate coefficients are added and trained for each new task. The combination of shared basis filters and task specific coefficients enables the model to preserve previously learned knowledge and avoid forgetting altogether.

3.1 Low Rank Approximations of Filters

To find these compact basis filters and coefficients, consider the fundamental 2D convolution operation in a CNN. Assume that an input tensor x is convolved with a set of filters $\mathbf{H} \in \mathbb{R}^{P \times L \times D \times D}$, where P is the number of filters in H and with each filter of size $L \times D \times D$. The output y, of this convolution operation is expressed as

$$y = x * \mathbf{H} \qquad (1)$$

We know that eigen decomposition results in a compact basis that minimizes the reconstruction error achieved by a linear combination of basis functions. We therefore choose $\mathbf{F}$ as the eigen filters that represent the sub-space in which the original filters $\mathbf{H}$ lie. The method for obtaining these is also well-known and straightforward. To approximate the compact sub-space these filters are flattened

(a) 20-split CIFAR100

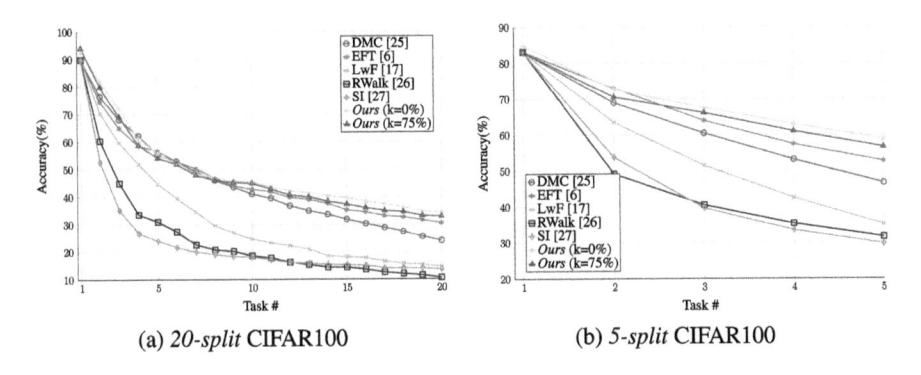

(b) 5-split CIFAR100

Fig. 3. Comparison of CIL accuracy with Resnet18 architecture on CIFAR100 dataset.

Table 1. Comparison of CIL accuracy with Resnet18 architecture on *10-split* CIFAR100 dataset.

Method/Task ID	t1	t2	t3	t4	t5	t6	t7	t8	t9	t10	Avg.
LwF [17]	88.5	70.1	54.8	45.7	39.4	36.3	31.4	28.9	25.5	23.9	44.5
EWC [18]	88.5	52.4	48.6	38.4	31.1	26.4	21.6	19.9	18.8	16.4	36.2
SDC [28]	88.5	78.8	75.8	73.1	71.5	60.7	53.9	43.5	29.5	19.3	59.5
SI [27]	88.5	52.9	40.7	33.6	31.8	29.4	27.5	25.6	24.7	23.3	37.8
MAS [19]	88.5	42.1	36.4	35.1	32.5	25.7	21.0	19.2	17.7	15.4	33.4
RWalk [26]	88.5	55.1	40.7	32.1	29.2	25.8	23.0	20.7	19.5	17.9	35.3
DMC [25]	88.5	76.3	67.5	62.4	57.3	52.7	48.7	43.9	40.1	36.2	57.4
EFT [6]	90.2	76.2	70.1	63.1	57.9	53.6	52.1	49.6	47.6	45.5	60.6
Ours (k = 0%)	92.4	76.3	67.1	63.6	62.0	58.6	56.4	54.3	52.1	49.8	**63.3**
Ours (k = 75%)	89.1	74.7	65.1	61.6	59.8	55.6	53.7	51.4	49.4	47.3	60.8

and arranged as columns of the matrix $\tilde{\mathbf{H}} \in \mathbb{R}^{P \times A}$, where $A = LD^2$. We then compute its singular value decomposition as $\tilde{\mathbf{H}} = \mathbf{U}\mathbf{S}\mathbf{V}^T$ and initialize $\tilde{\mathbf{F}}$ with the columns of $\mathbf{V}^T$ corresponding to non zero eigen values. This leads to $\tilde{\mathbf{w}} = \tilde{\mathbf{F}}^T \tilde{\mathbf{H}}$ and finally appropriate reshaping of $\tilde{\mathbf{F}}$ and $\tilde{\mathbf{w}}$ lets us rewrite the convolution operation defined in Eq. 1 as a sequence of two successive convolutions:

$$y' = (x * \mathbf{F}) * \mathbf{w} \qquad (2)$$

where $\mathbf{F} \in \mathbb{R}^{P \times L \times D \times D}$ and $\mathbf{w} \in \mathbb{R}^{P \times P \times 1 \times 1}$. We refer to the construct introduced in Eq. 2 as *decomposed convolution*. This representation is typically used to compress the model in terms of FLOPs and number of parameters however in its current form it actually increases FLOPs and parameters. To compress the model we discard $k\%$ the basis filters in $\mathbf{F}$ corresponding to the smallest eigen values. This results in $\mathbf{F} \in \mathbb{R}^{Q \times L \times D \times D}$ and correspondingly $\mathbf{w} \in \mathbb{R}^{P \times Q \times 1 \times 1}$, where $Q = \lceil P - kP/100 \rceil$. Analysis of FLOPs and parameters required for implementing Eq. 2 is presented in Sect. 3.3.

3.2 Efficient Lifelong Learning

The objective of lifelong learning algorithm is to incrementally train the model on a set of disjoint classes with some data availability constraints. Formally, the model observes data $(\mathcal{X}_t, \mathcal{Y}_t)$ randomly drawn from distribution $\mathcal{D}_t$, corresponding to task t. Where $\mathcal{X}_t$ and $\mathcal{Y}_t$ represents the input images and corresponding ground truth labels respectively. The goal of a continual learning algorithm is to train model on $\mathcal{D}_t$ while also preserving the previously learned knowledge. However, this data availability constraint introduces the problem of catastrophic forgetting [17,18] where model *forgets* the previous knowledge and ends up performing poorly on previous tasks.

We seek to solve this catastrophic forgetting problem by using the *decomposed convolution* structure. We initially train first task on a vanilla neural network with convolution filters **H**, given the data samples $(\mathcal{X}_1, \mathcal{Y}_1)$.

Table 2. Comparison of TIL accuracy with AlexNet architecture on *10-split* ImageNet.

Method/Task ID	t1	t2	t3	t4	t5	t6	t7	t8	t9	t10	Avg.
LwF [17]	27.6	37.2	42.0	44.4	50.5	56.6	57.9	61.2	62.0	62.7	50.2
IMM [29]	68.5	53.6	52.1	51.7	52.5	55.5	54.7	53.5	54.2	51.8	54.8
EWC [18]	21.8	26.5	29.5	32.9	35.6	40.4	40.0	44.7	47.8	61.1	38.0
PackNet [11]	67.5	65.8	62.2	58.4	58.6	58.7	56.0	56.5	54.1	53.6	59.1
EFT [6]	69.0	63.2	60.1	62.5	53.6	57.2	55.1	52.8	55.7	62.5	59.4
Ours (k = 0%)	65.6	63.3	60.7	63.9	56.5	57.4	55.0	52.8	55.7	64.1	59.5
Ours (k = 25%)	65.0	63.0	59.7	62.8	55.5	56.3	54.5	52.4	55.0	63.5	58.8

Table 3. Comparison of TIL accuracy with VGG16 architecture on *10-split* TinyImageNet.

Method/Task ID	t1	t2	t3	t4	t5	t6	t7	t8	t9	t10	Avg.
LfL [30]	32.4	35.4	43.4	44.1	45.0	55.9	49.4	51.1	58.6	61.4	47.7
LwF [17]	45.1	45.5	53.5	57.6	56.2	65.7	63.5	58.4	59.6	58.5	56.4
IMM [29]	50.6	38.5	44.7	49.2	47.5	51.9	53.7	47.7	50.0	48.7	48.3
EWC [18]	33.9	35.4	43.6	46.7	49.5	52.5	47.8	50.2	56.6	61.4	47.8
HAT [31]	46.8	49.1	55.8	58.0	53.7	61.0	58.7	54.0	54.6	50.3	54.2
PackNet [11]	52.5	49.7	56.5	59.8	55.0	64.7	61.7	55.9	55.2	52.5	56.4
TFM [32]	48.2	47.7	56.7	58.2	54.8	62.2	61.5	57.3	58.5	54.8	56.0
EFT [6]	67.2	62.5	69.4	62.6	68.3	69.6	59.0	67.8	71.5	70.1	66.8
Ours (k=0%)	64.3	64.6	70.8	65.9	68.0	70.6	60.2	69.4	71.2	69.0	67.4
Ours (k=50%)	64.2	64.6	69.1	64.0	68.4	68.7	60.4	67.5	72.1	69.7	66.9

Table 4. Average CIL with Resnet32 architecture on non uniform *6-split* and *11-split* CIFAR100. Dataset is divided into tasks such that first task contains 50 classes and remaining are equally divided into 5 or 10 sets.

Method	6-split	11-split
LwF [17]	57.03	56.82
EWC [18]	56.28	55.41
iCaRL [14]	57.17	52.57
SDC [28]	57.10	56.80
BiC [33]	59.36	54.20
Rebalancing [34]	63.12	60.14
FAS-a [7]	60.23	55.54
FAS-b [7]	65.44	62.48
Ours (k = 0%)	66.65	62.54
Ours (k = 25%)	62.73	59.23

Table 5. Average TIL accuracy and task prediction accuracy for Resnet32, trained on non-uniform split CIFAR100.

Method	6-split	11-split
TIL (K = 0%)	88.6	93.4
TIL (K = 25%)	87.5	93.0
Task Prediction (K = 0%)	79.1	74.5
Task Prediction (K = 25%)	76.7	73.2

$$\underset{\mathbf{H}}{\operatorname{argmin}} \sum_{\mathcal{D}_1} \ell(f(\mathcal{X}_1; \mathbf{H}), \mathcal{Y}_1) \tag{3}$$

where $f(:)$ represents model function and l is the loss function. Once the model is trained we decompose and compress the trained filters as described in Sect. 3.1. Compact nature of basis filters allows us to discard up to 25% of the total filters corresponding to the smallest eigen values, without an adverse affect on model's performance. However with even higher levels of compression model encounters performance degradation. To counter that we fine tune $\mathbf{F}$ and $\mathbf{w_1}$ to minimize the same loss as before.

$$\underset{\mathbf{F}, \mathbf{w_1}}{\operatorname{argmin}} \sum_{\mathcal{D}_1} \ell(f(\mathcal{X}_1; \mathbf{F}, \mathbf{w_1}), \mathcal{Y}_1) \tag{4}$$

It is important to note that initial training and fine tuning is done using $\mathcal{D}_1$ only. For each new task $t > 1$, we add additional task specific coefficients $\mathbf{w_t}$ and initialize them with $\mathbf{w_1}$. This is followed by training the model using $\mathcal{D}_t$ as follows.

$$\underset{w_t}{\operatorname{argmin}} \sum_{\mathcal{D}_t} \ell(f(\mathcal{X}_t; w_t), \mathcal{Y}_t) \tag{5}$$

To compute the task specific feature maps, we first convolve the input tensor with the shared basis filters followed by a convolution with corresponding task specific coefficients, as depicted in Fig. 1. Since shared basis filters are only trained once, this formulation allows us to preserve the learned task specific representations perfectly through out the model and thus avoids the catastrophic forgetting problem entirely.

3.3 Flops and Parameter Growth

In this section we present a theoretical analysis of the impact of our method on FLOPs and parameter growth in the model. Depending on the values of P and Q, the proposed compression scheme lead to substantial reduction in the number of multiplication operations. If the size of the filters is $D \times D \times L$, and the size of the input data is $M \times N \times L$, It is easy to show that $O = LD^2(M-D+1)(N-D+1)$. Therefore, multiplications required in Eq. (1) is

$$A = PO = PLD^2(M - D + 1)(N - D + 1) \tag{6}$$

while multiplications required to obtain output of Eq. (2) is

$$\begin{aligned} B &= QLD^2(M - D + 1)(N - D + 1) + \\ & \quad PQ(M - D + 1)(N - D + 1) \\ &= Q[L^2 + P](M - D + 1)(N - D + 1) \end{aligned} \tag{7}$$

We see that the ratio of the two is

$$\begin{aligned} \frac{A}{B} &= \frac{PLD^2(M - D + 1)(N - D + 1)}{Q[LD^2 + P](M - D + 1)(N - D + 1)} \\ &= \frac{PLD^2}{Q[LD^2 + P]} \end{aligned} \tag{8}$$

Thus, as long as $LD^2 >> P$, the number of multiplications will be reduced by a factor close to P/Q (i.e. the ratio of the original number of filters and the number of basis filters used).

New recall that number of parameters in the original filters is LD^2. Since there are P such filters, the total number of original parameters is PLD^2. However, the total number of parameters for *decomposed convolution* is (QLD^2+QP) (depicted in Fig. 1 as a Q basis filters with LD^2 parameters and P one-dimensional filters of length Q). Therefore, the reduction in the number of parameters is $PLD^2/Q(LD^2 + P)$. If $LD^2 >> P$, the number of parameters is also reduced by a factor of P/Q. Finally since each new task adds additional coefficients $\mathbf{w_t}$, so parameters growth is proportional to PQ.

4 Experiments

We evaluated our method on two lifelong learning scenarios; Task Incremental Learning (TIL) and Class Incremental Learning (CIL). These two scenarios differ in the manner in with new task is treated at inference time. In TIL it is assumed that the task ID is known at inference time which can be used to select the corresponding $\mathbf{w_t}$ to calculate task specific representations. In CIL task ID is not provided and has be to predicted at inference time. We adopted a simple entropy based strategy to predict the task ID, where task ID of an unknown sample is chosen to be the ID of classification head with least entropy.

We also evaluated our method for compression (in Sect. 3.3) by calculating the FLOPs and parameters required for a given model. We opted FLOPs over wall clock time as a measure of model's efficiency, since FLOPs are machine and implementation independent and can be easily estimated in Pytorch.

To train the models, we used SGD optimizer with momentum 0.9, weight decay of 5E-4 and starting learning rate of 0.1. We divided the learning rate by 10 at 100, 150 and 200 epoch mark and train the model for 250 epochs with a batch size of 64.

4.1 Class Incremental Learning (CIL)

Resnet18: To evaluate our method on CIL we first adopted Resnet18 network architecture and train it on three uniform splits of CIFAR100. Specifically we divide the 100 classes into 5, 10 and 20 sets of tasks and refer to them as *5-split*, *10-split* and *20-split respectively*. These splits cover a wide range of problem difficulty as *20-split* CIFAR100 tests models ability to adapt to large number of new tasks while 5-split setting tests model's ability to train on a larger number of classes per task. For each one of these splits we trained Resenet18 at two compression levels with value of k set to 0% and 75% (k is the percentage of basis filters discarded). Results of these experiments are summarised in Table 1 and Fig. 3. We notice that our method outperform others even with very high levels of compression. When compared with EFT [6] our Resnet18 with $k = 75\%$ performs slightly better with 60.8% average CIL accuracy as compared to EFT's 60.6%. Additionally truncation of large number of basis filters significantly reduces the FLOPs and number of parameters in the model (detailed comparison in Sect. 4.5).

Table 6. Comparison of average test accuracy and forgetting for *20-split* CIFAR100 and *20-split* miniImageNet datasets using ResNet18 architecture.

Method	20-split CIFAR100		20-split miniImageNet	
	Accuracy	Forgetting	Accuracy	Forgetting
EWC [18]	43.2	26	34.8	24
ICARL [14]	46.4	16	44.2	24.7
AGEM [35]	60.3	11.0	42.3	17.0
ER-Ring [36]	59.6	0.1	49.8	12.0
Ortho sub [37]	63.4	8.4	51.4	10.0
Adam-NSCL [38]	74.3	9.5	57.9	13.4
IBP-WF [39]	68.3	0	55.8	0
ITLIR [40]	68.5	0	59.3	0
Ours (k = 0%)	**91.3**	0	**85.4**	0
Ours (k = 95%)	87.4	0	79.8	0
Parallel full-rank	92.7	0	94.5	0

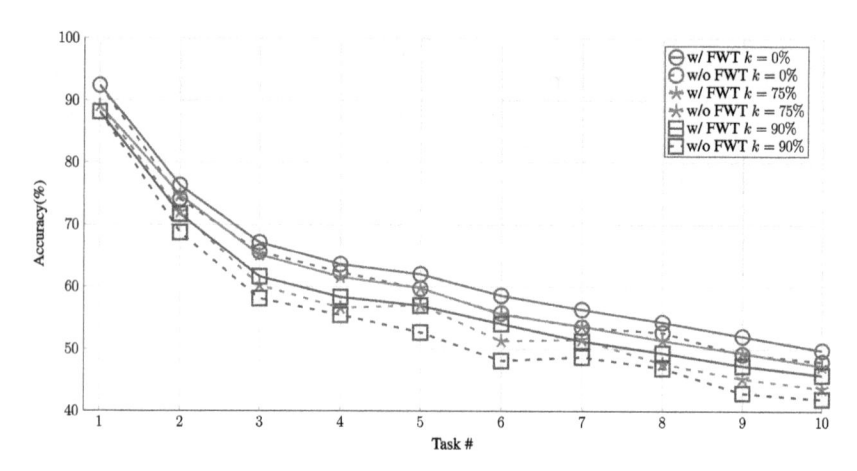

Fig. 4. Evaluation of Forward Knowledge Transfer (FWT). We conducted two experiments for three values of k (0%, 75% and 90%). In one set of experiments we initialize task specific coefficients w_i randomly (w/o FWT) while for the other one we initialized it with w_{i-1} (w/ FWT). As we can see, models using w_{i-1} initialization perform better then the ones using random initialization

Resnet32: For evaluating Resnet32 on CIFAR100 where followed the FAS's [7] non uniform split. This split is different form the previous ones because here the first tasks always contains 50 classes while the remaining 50 are divided into sets of 5 or 10. This experiment evaluates a significantly different and harder problem as now we have very uneven number of classes per task. As we can see in Table 4 our method with $k = 0$ out performs other methods. However due to non-uniformity of the splits our method does not perform equally well with high compression. This performance degradation mainly comes from the failure of task prediction mechanism as shown in Table 5.

4.2 Task Incremental Learning (TIL)

We tested our method on TIL with AlexNet and VGG16 architectures. We trained these models on uniform *10-split* ImageNet [9] and TinyImageNet datasets respectively. ImageNet is a classification dataset containing 1000 classes, while TinyImageNet is a smaller subset of ImageNet dataset containing 200 classes, downsampled to 64 × 64 spatial resolution. The results of these experiments are shown in the Tab. 2 and Tab. 3. We can see that, for both ImageNet and TinyImageNet our uncompressed models ($k = 0\%$) achieves better average accuracy compared to the other methods. While the compressed variants attain results comparable to the previous SOTA.

For TIL we also evaluated our method on Resnet18 architecture with *20-split* CIFAR100 and miniImageNet datasets. For this set of experiments, along with the average accuracy we also report the model's *forgetting*. Forgetting is defined in literature [37] as follows. Let $a_{t,j}$ be the test accuracy of task

Table 7. Ablation on k for CIL with Resnet18 architecture on *10-split* CIFAR100

k/Task ID	t1	t2	t3	t4	t5	t6	t7	t8	t9	t10	Avg.
0%	92.4	76.3	67.1	63.6	62.0	58.6	56.4	54.3	52.1	49.8	63.3
25%	90.4	76.3	65.7	61.75	61.0	58.2	55.9	53.3	50.9	48.9	62.2
75%	89.1	74.7	65.1	61.6	59.8	55.6	53.7	51.4	49.4	47.3	60.8
90%	88.1	71.6	61.6	58.3	56.9	54.0	51.2	49.3	47.3	45.8	58.4

$j < t$ after the model has finished learning task $t \in \{1, ..., T\}$ in a incremental manner. Forgetting F_t is the decrease in the accuracy of a task after its training, and after one or several tasks are learned incrementally and is defined as $F_t = \frac{1}{t-1} \sum_{j=1}^{t-1}(a_{j,j} - a_{t,j})$. Table 6 summarizes the results of these experiments. Our method demonstrates a substantial improvement in comparison to compared approaches. Of particular interest is [40], which employs a filter decomposition structure similar to ours. However, our method diverges by compressing the model subsequent to training on the first task, rather than truncating randomly initialized filters. As a result, our shared basis filters learn more meaningful representations for continual learning, thereby improving the overall model's accuracy.

4.3 Forward Transfer (FWT)

Forward transfer (FWT) is an important metric of the quality of representations learned by a lifelong learning system. It measures the ability of the model to positively influence a future task's performance based on the existing representations. FWT is formally defined in Eq. 4 by Lopez-Paz et al. [41]. However we followed the experimental setup proposed in EFT [6] to informally present this metric. We argue that our model enables FWT by two mechanisms, first by sharing basis filters among all tasks and second, by initializing w_i with previously trained w_{i-1}. To empirically show this, we conducted two experiments for three values of k (0%, 75% and 90%). In one set of experiments we initialize task specific coefficients w_i randomly (w/o FWT) while for the other one we initialized it with w_{i-1} (w/ FWT). As we can see in the Fig. 4, models using w_{i-1} initialization perform better then the ones using random initialization. Secondly the gap between these curves increase for larger values of k. Form these experiments we deduce that our model should get better at FWT with increasing compression.

4.4 Selection of k

Value of k impact the number of parameters in the model which consequently impacts the model's accuracy. For all experiments we have reported results for an uncompressed model (with $k = 0\%$) and we empirically select another value of k which is competitive with other methods in terms of accuracy. Table 7 presents additional results with Resnet18 for different values of k.

4.5 Analysis of Flops and Parameters

In this section we have compared the FLOPs and parameters of various network architectures used in our experiments. For our method, number of total tasks does not impact the FLOPs of a single input image. As can be deduced from Eq. 2, output at each layer is obtained by convolving the input tensor with the shared basis filters followed by the convolution with a single task specific $\mathbf{w_t}$. However as more tasks are added to the model, additional coefficients and classification heads increase the number of parameters in the model drastically. For our comparisons we picked the Resnet18, VGG16 and ALexNet to contain 10 task specific $\mathbf{w_t}$'s in each layer. Table 8 show the FLOPs and parameters for 4 levels of compression.

We can see that our Resnet18 trained for CIL, with $k = 75\%$ needs 0.32 Billion FLOPs and 7.24 Million parameters. In comparison EFT [6] performs equally well but needs 1.21 Billion FLOPs and 11.60 Million parameters. Similarly our Resnet32 with $k = 0\%$ outperforms FAS-b [7] on non-uniform split CIFAR100 and needs only 0.15 Billion FLOPs as compared to 0.28 Billion required by FAS-b [7].

Table 8. Comparison of FLOPs and parameters for various models used in our experiments.

k	FLOPs (Billions)				Params (Millions)			
	Resnet18	Resnet32	VGG16	AlexNet	Resnet18	Resnet32	VGG16	AlexNet*
Baseline	1.11	0.14	2.50	1.74	11.16	0.46	14.76	2.88
0%	1.25	0.15	2.84	2.00	26.84	0.80	33.24	9.77
25%	0.95	0.12	2.10	1.50	20.61	0.60	25.05	8.36
50%	0.64	0.08	1.43	1.00	14.38	0.41	16.86	6.94
75%	0.32	0.04	0.72	0.48	7.24	0.21	8.66	5.52

5 Conclusion

We propose a method for continual learning which leverages ideas from neural network compression and applies them to incrementally learn new tasks. Our method takes inspiration from filter decomposition-based methods and we show that this formulation naturally extends to the continual learning domain. It is well known that task parameters lie in low dimensional sub space of the convolutional filters, this fact can be exploited to represent the convolutional filters in a compact form by using the basis filters and remixing coefficients. For continual learning problem setting the basis filters are shared while separate coefficients are added for each new task. This enables the model to perfectly preserve the previously learned knowledge, thus avoiding the catastrophic forgetting entirely.

We applied this method to several image classification based continual learning problems and show that our method obtains performance gains with uncompressed model while achieving competitive results when a large number of basis filters are discarded.

References

1. He, K., Zhang, X., Ren, S., Sun, J.: Deep residual learning for image recognition. In: Proceedings of the IEEE Computer Society Conference on Computer Vision and Pattern Recognition. IEEE Computer Society (2016)
2. Redmon, J., Farhadi, A.: Yolov3: An incremental improvement (2018). https://arxiv.org/abs/1804.02767
3. Rusu, A.A., et al.: Progressive neural networks, arXiv preprint arXiv:1606.04671 (2016)
4. Yoon, J., Yang, E., Lee, J., Hwang, S.-J.:Lifelong learning with dynamically expandable networks. In: International Conference on Learning Representations (2018)
5. Jerfel, G., Grant, E., Griffiths, T., Heller, K.A.: Reconciling meta-learning and continual learning with online mixtures of tasks. Adv. Neural Inform. Process. Syst. **32** (2019)
6. Verma, V.K., Liang, K.J., Mehta, N., Rai, P., Carin, L.: Efficient feature transformations for discriminative and generative continual learning. In: Proceedings of the IEEE Computer Society Conference on Computer Vision and Pattern Recognition, pp. 13860–13870 (2021)
7. Miao, Z., Wang, Z., Chen, W., Qiu, Q.: Continual learning with filter atom swapping. In: International Conference on Learning Representations (2022)
8. Krizhevsky, A., Hinton, G.: Learning multiple layers of features from tiny images, Tech. Rep. (2009)
9. Deng, J., Dong, W., Socher, R., Li, L.-J., Li, K., Fei-Fei, L.: Imagenet: a large-scale hierarchical image database. In: Proceedings of the IEEE Computer Society Conference on Computer Vision and Pattern Recognition (2009)
10. Delange, M., et al.: A continual learning survey: Defying forgetting in classification tasks IEEE Trans. Pattern Analy. Mach. Intell. (2021)
11. Mallya, A., Lazebnik, S.: Packnet: adding multiple tasks to a single network by iterative pruning. In: 2018 IEEE/CVF Conference on Computer Vision and Pattern Recognition, pp. 7765–7773 (2018)
12. Wortsman, M., et al.: Supermasks in superposition. Adv. Neural. Inf. Process. Syst. **33**, 15173–15184 (2020)
13. Shin, H., Lee, J.K., Kim, J., Kim, J.: Continual learning with deep generative replay. Advances in Neural Information Processing Syst. **30** (2017)
14. Rebuffi, S.A., Kolesnikov, A., Sperl, G., Lampert, C.H.: icarl: incremental classifier and representation learning. In: 2017 IEEE Conference on Computer Vision and Pattern Recognition (CVPR), pp. 5533–5542 (2017)
15. Rolnick, D., Ahuja, A., Schwarz, J., Lillicrap, T., Wayne, G.: Experience replay for continual learning. Adv. Neural Inform. Process. Syst. **32** (2019)
16. Yan, S., Xie, J., He, X.: Der: dynamically expandable representation for class incremental learning. In: Proceedings of the IEEE/CVF Conference on Computer Vision and Pattern Recognition, pp. 3014–3023 (2021)

17. Li, Z., Hoiem, D.: Learning without forgetting. IEEE Trans. Pattern Anal. Mach. Intell. **40**, 2935–2947 (2018)
18. Kirkpatrick, J., et al.: Overcoming catastrophic forgetting in neural networks. Proc. Nat. Acad. Sci. **114**(13), 3521–3526 (2017)
19. Aljundi, R., Babiloni, F., Elhoseiny, M., Rohrbach, M., Tuytelaars, T.: Memory aware synapses: learning what (not) to forget. In: Ferrari, V., Hebert, M., Sminchisescu, C., Weiss, Y. (eds.) ECCV 2018. LNCS, vol. 11207, pp. 144–161. Springer, Cham (2018). https://doi.org/10.1007/978-3-030-01219-9_9
20. Titsias, M.K., Schwarz, J., de G. Matthews, A.G., Pascanu, R., Teh, Y.W.: Functional regularisation for continual learning with gaussian processes. In: International Conference on Learning Representations (2020)
21. Jaderberg, M., Vedaldi, A., Zisserman, A.: Speeding up convolutional neural networks with low rank expansions. In: BMVC 2014 - Proceedings of the British Machine Vision Conference 2014. British Machine Vision Association, BMVA (2014)
22. Denton, E., Zaremba, W., Bruna, J., LeCun, Y., Fergus, R.: Exploiting linear structure within convolutional networks for efficient evaluation. Adv. Neural Inform. Process. Syst. (2014)
23. Zhang, X., Zou, J., He, K., Sun, J.: Accelerating very deep convolutional networks for classification and detection. IEEE Trans. Pattern Analy. Mach. Intell. (2016)
24. Qiu, Q., Cheng, X., Calderbank, R., Sapiro, G.: Dcfnet: deep neural network with decomposed convolutional filters. In: 35th International Conference on Machine Learning, ICML 2018 (2018)
25. Zhang, J., et al.: Class-incremental learning via deep model consolidation. In: Proceedings of the IEEE/CVF Winter Conference on Applications of Computer Vision, pp. 1131–1140 (2020)
26. Chaudhry, A., Dokania, P.K., Ajanthan, T., Torr, P.H.S.: Riemannian walk for incremental learning: understanding forgetting and intransigence. In: Ferrari, V., Hebert, M., Sminchisescu, C., Weiss, Y. (eds.) ECCV 2018. LNCS, vol. 11215, pp. 556–572. Springer, Cham (2018). https://doi.org/10.1007/978-3-030-01252-6_33
27. Zenke, F., Poole, B., Ganguli, S.: Continual learning through synaptic intelligence. In: International Conference on Machine Learning. PMLR, pp. 3987–3995 (2017)
28. Yu, L., et alSemantic drift compensation for class-incremental learning. In: 2020 IEEE/CVF Conference on Computer Vision and Pattern Recognition (CVPR), pp. 6980–6989 (2020)
29. Lee, S.-W., Kim, J.-H., Jun, J., Ha, J.-W., Zhang, B.-T.: Overcoming catastrophic forgetting by incremental moment matching. Adv. Neural Inform. Process. Syst. **30** (2017)
30. Jung, H., Ju, J., Jung, M., Kim, J.: Less-forgetting learning in deep neural networks, ArXiv, vol. abs/ arXiv: 1607.00122 (2016)
31. Serra, J., Suris, D., Miron, M., Karatzoglou, A.: Overcoming catastrophic forgetting with hard attention to the task. In: International Conference on Machine Learning. PMLR, pp. 4548–4557 (2018)
32. Masana, M., Tuytelaars, T., van de Weijer, J.: Ternary feature masks: continual learning without any forgetting, vol. 4(5), p. 6, arXiv preprint arXiv:2001.08714 (2020)
33. Wu, Y., et al.: Large scale incremental learning. In: Proceedings of the IEEE Conference on Computer Vision and Pattern Recognition, pp. 374–382 (2019)
34. Hou, S., Pan, X., Loy, C.C., Wang, Z., Lin, D.: Learning a unified classifier incrementally via rebalancing. In: Proceedings of the IEEE/CVF Conference on Computer Vision and Pattern Recognition, pp. 831–839 (2019)

35. Chaudhry, A., Ranzato, M., Rohrbach, M., Elhoseiny, M.: Efficient lifelong learning with a-gem. In: International Conference on Learning Representations (2019)
36. Chaudhry, A., et al.: On tiny episodic memories in continual learning, arXiv preprint arXiv:1902.10486 (2019)
37. Chaudhry, A., Khan, N., Dokania, P., Torr, P.: Continual learning in low-rank orthogonal subspaces. Adv. Neural. Inf. Process. Syst. **33**, 9900–9911 (2020)
38. Wang, S., Li, X., Sun, J., Xu, Z.: Training networks in null space of feature covariance for continual learning. In: Proceedings of the IEEE/CVF Conference on Computer Vision and Pattern Recognition, pp. 184–193 (2021)
39. Mehta, N., Liang, K., Verma, V.K., Carin, L.: Continual learning using a bayesian nonparametric dictionary of weight factors. In: International Conference on Artificial Intelligence and Statistics. PMLR, pp. 100–108 (2021)
40. Hyder, R., Shao, K., Hou, B., Markopoulos, P., Prater-Bennette, A., Asif, M.S.: Incremental task learning with incremental rank updates. In: Avidan, S., Brostow, G., Cissé, M., Farinella, G.M., Hassner, T. (eds. Computer Vision – ECCV 2022. ECCV 2022. LNCS, vol. 13683. Springer, Cham (2022). https://doi.org/10.1007/978-3-031-20050-2_33
41. Lopez-Paz, D., Ranzato, M.: Gradient episodic memory for continual learning. Adv. Neural Inform. Process. syst. **30** (2017)

Learning When to Observe: A Frugal Reinforcement Learning Framework for a High-Cost World

Colin Bellinger[1]( ), Isaac Tamblyn[2,3], and Mark Crowley[4]

[1] National Research Council of Canada, Ottawa, Canada
`colin.bellinger@nrc-cnrc.gc.ca`
[2] Department of Physics, University of Ottawa, Ottawa, Canada
`isaac.tamblyn@uottawa.ca`
[3] Vector Institute for Artificial Intelligence, Toronto, ON, Canada
[4] Department of Electrical and Computer Engineering, University of Waterloo, Waterloo, Canada
`mark.crowley@uwaterloo.ca`

Abstract. Reinforcement learning (RL) has been shown to learn sophisticated control policies for complex tasks including games, robotics, heating and cooling systems and text generation. The action-perception cycle in RL, however, generally assumes that a measurement of the state of the environment is available at each time step without a cost. In applications such as materials design, deep-sea and planetary robot exploration and medicine, however, there can be a high cost associated with measuring, or even approximating, the state of the environment. In this paper, we survey the recently growing literature that adopts the perspective that an RL agent might not need, or even want, a costly measurement at each time step. Within this context, we propose the Deep Dynamic Multi-Step Observationless Agent (DMSOA), contrast it with the literature and empirically evaluate it on OpenAI gym and Atari Pong environments. Our results, show that DMSOA learns a better policy with fewer decision steps and measurements than the considered alternative from the literature. The corresponding code is available at: https://github.com/cbellinger27/Learning-when-to-observe-in-RL.

Keywords: Reinforcement Learning · DQN · Sensing and Observation Costs · Noiselessly Observable Markov Decision Processes

1 Introduction

In many applications of reinforcement learning (RL), such as materials design, computational chemistry, deep-sea and planetary robot exploration and medicine [2,13,15], there is a high cost associated with measuring, or even approximating, the state of the environment. Thus, the RL system as a whole faces observation costs in the environment, along with processing and decision making costs in the agent. On both sides, the costs result from a cacophony of factors including the use of energy, systems and human resources. In this work, we propose the Deep Dynamic Multi-Step Observationless Agent (DMSOA), the first RL agent in its class to reduce both measurement and decision making costs.

Since standard RL agents require a large number of *state-action-reward-next state* interactions with the environment during policy learning and application, the measurement and decision making costs can be very high. Traditionally, these underlying costs are hidden from the agent. Indeed, little consideration has been given to the idea that the agent might not need, or even want, a potentially costly observation at each time step. In the real-world, however, agents (animal or artificial) are limited by their resources. To save time and energy, decision making associated with common or predictable tasks is believed to be conducted re-actively or based on fast, low-resource systems. Only with deliberate cognitive intervention are the slower, resource-intensive planning systems used [8,22].

Recently, there have been a number of interesting conference papers, workshop discussions and theses discussing how to address this problem in RL [4–6,9,11,15,20]. The general approach is to augment RL by *a)* assign an intrinsic cost to measure the state of the environment, and *b)* provide the agent with the flexibility to decide if the next state should be measured. Together, these provide a mechanism and a learning signal to encourage the agent to reduce its intrinsic measurement costs relative the to the explicit control rewards it receives.

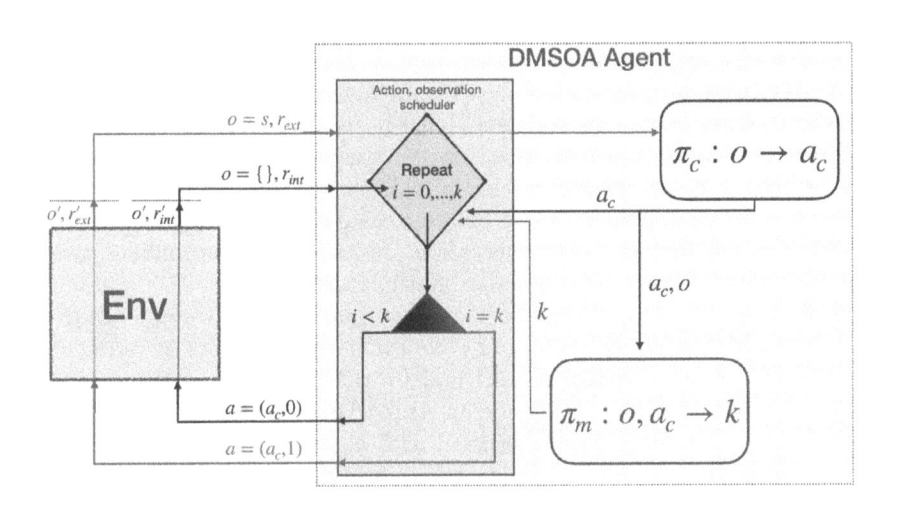

Fig. 1. Illustration of the DMSOA Framework.

When the agent opts not to measure the state of the environment, it must make its next control decision based on stale information or an estimate. Thus, at the highest level, this constitutes a partially observable Markov decision process (POMDP). Learning a POMDP, however, is much more difficult than learning a Markov decision process (MDP) with RL [17]. When designed as shown in

Fig. 1, the agent's experience is composed of fully observable measurements and partially observable estimates of the state of the environment. Thus, the problem is related to mixed observable Markov decision processes (MOMDPs), which are an easier sub-class of POMDPs [16]. The authors in [15] denoted this class of RL problem as action-contingent, noiselessly observable Markov decision processes (AC-NOMDPs). Distinct from an MOMDP, action-contingent in AC-NOMDP relates the fact that the agent explicitly chooses between measuring and not measuring the environment. "Noiselessly observable" relates to the fact that when the agent decides to measure at a cost, the state is fully observable. Although previous works have used different terms to refer to this class of problem, we believe that AC-NOMDP is the most descriptive of the underlying dynamics and use it throughout this paper.

Recently, [15] provided a theoretical analysis of the advantages of AC-NOMDP of over a general POMDP formulation and found a significant improvement in efficiency for RL with explicit observation costs and actions. All other previous works have carried out limited empirical evaluations in which the proposed algorithm is compared to a baseline MDP [5,9,11,20]. Moreover, the previous analyses primarily relied on just a few, or even single, experiments on OpenAI gym classic control environments and grid-worlds [5,11,20].

In this work, we compare DMSOA to the one-step memory-based observationless agent (OSMBOA) recently proposed in [5]. Our contribution serves to expand the state-of-the-art in AC-NOMDP algorithms and the understanding of how different classes of algorithms impact the observation behaviour. OSMBOA was selected for its demonstrated effectiveness and easy of use. At each time step, OSMBOA selects a control action and makes a decision about measuring the next state of the environment. If no measurement is made, the agent's next control action is selected based on its fixed-size internal memory of the last measured state(s). In contrast, DMSOA selects a control action and the number of times to apply the action before measuring the next state. Therefore, DMSOA learns to reduce both observation costs and decision making costs by dynamically applying its control action multiple times.

To facilitate fair comparison, we implement both agents as double DQN [25] with prioritized experience replay [19]. We evaluate the agents in terms of the accumulated extrinsic control reward and by the reduction in the number of observations and decision steps made on Atari Pong and OpenAI gym [7]. The results show that the proposed method learns a better control policy, requires fewer measurements of the environment and decision steps. Moreover, DMSOA has less variance across independent training runs.

The remainder of the paper is organized as follows. In the next section, Sect. 2, we outline the related work. Section 3 formalizes the AC-NOMDP problem and Sect. 4 presents the proposed algorithms. Section 5 provides the experimental setup. The results are shown in Sect. 6 and discussed in Sect. 7. The environmental impact of this work is described in Sect. 8 and our concluding remarks are in Sect. 9.

2 Related Work

This work fits into a small but growing sub-area of RL in which observations are optional at each time step and have an explicit cost to the agent when they are made. In the subsection immediately below, we provide an overview of methods recently applied to AC-NOMDP. Following that, we discuss the literature directly related to the proposed DMSOA algorithm.

2.1 AC-NOMDP Methods

In the existing work, the authors in [4,15,20] proposed tabular Q-learning-based algorithms for AC-NOMDPs and [5,9,11,15] proposed deep RL based methods. In [11], the authors modify TRPO, and in [9,15], actor-critic frameworks with a recurrent neural networks are used. In [5], the authors provide a wrapper class that modifies the underlying environment by expanding the observation and action spaces to facilitate any off-the-shelf deep RL algorithm to work in the AC-NOMDP setting.

Through our analysis of the literature, we have identified 4 key questions addressed when developing for AC-NOMDPs. These are: *1)* the mechanism by which the agent expresses its desire not to measure, *2)* how the observation is supplemented when no measurement is made, *3)* how the agent is encouraged to reduce its reliance of costly measurements, and *4)* how the agent is constructed.

The most common way to handle question *1)* is by expanding the action space. In the case of discrete actions, [4,5,9,15,20] expanded the action space to action tuples: ⟨control actions⟩ × ⟨measure, don't measure⟩. Alternatively, in [11], the agent specifies the control action plus a sample purity value $q \in \mathbb{R}^1$, where a larger q triggers a less accurate measurement with lower associated costs.

With respect to question *2)*, when the agent does not request a fresh measurement in [4,9,11,15], the environment sends a Null state observation or an observation composed of zeros. In [4], the agent uses an internal statistical model to estimate the next state and in [9,15] the agents utilize a deep recurrent networks for estimating belief states and encoded states, respectively. In [5], the agent utilizes a fix-size memory of recent measurements when no measurement is made. To reduce partial observability, each observation is augmented with a flag indicating whether or not it is the result of a fresh measurement of the environment. Since the agent in [11] adjusts the noise level rather than turning on and off measurements, it makes its next action selection purely based on the noisy measurement returned.

Question *3)* relates to the rewards structure. This is generally divided into intrinsic rewards, which are used to encourage the agent to reduce its reliance on costly measurements and extrinsic rewards that push the agent to achieve the control objective. At each time step in [4,9,11,15], an intrinsic cost is subtracted from the extrinsic reward if the agent measures the state. Alternatively, in [21] a positive intrinsic reward is added when the agent foregoes a measurement. A critical point that remains unclear in the literature is how to acquire the extrinsic reward when no measurement is made. In most cases, this is simply assumed to be available. We argue that if no measurement is made, the extrinsic reward cannot be known. As a result, in this work only the intrinsic portion of the reward is provided when no measurement is made.

The final question relates to the architecture of the agent. In [4,5,15], as single agent policy select both the control action and the measurement behaviour. Alternatively, in [9,11,20], separate policy are learned to determine the control actions and measurement actions. In addition, [4,9,15] also learn models for estimating the next state.

2.2 Works Related to DMSOA

The proposal of [20] is most algorithmically related to the DMSOA. In it, the author demonstrated the potential of dynamic action repetition for RL with observation costs using tabular q-learning. The agent learns to forego a sequence of one or more measurements in predictable regions of the state space by repeatedly applying the same action. Their proposed method is found to requires fewer measurement step to reach the goal than the MDP baseline. However, it is only suitable for discrete state and actions spaces, and was only evaluated on gridworld problems. In this work, we show how action repetition and measurement skipping can be implemented in deep RL for continuous and image-based observation spaces.

DMSOA is a method that aims to improve the efficiency of RL. To this end, it is weakly related to other techniques to improve the sampling efficiency [10,18,19]. The classic sample efficiency work, however, aims to reduce the overall number of training steps needed to learn a suitable policy, rather than reducing the measurement or decision steps made by the agent.

DMSOA utilizes concepts from the RL literature on dynamic frame skipping to repeatedly apply the selected control action [12]. In DMSOA, however, the agent's measurement skipping policy is shaped by the intrinsic reward. Moreover, unlike frame skipping applications, which are concerned with processing speed not measurement costs, DMSOA does not have access to privileged extrinsic control rewards from intermediate steps. This making the problem more challenging.

In addition, DMSOA has a connection to the options framework [24], and particularly dynamic options [1]. Similar to the options framework, at each decision point the DMSOA agent chooses to apply a sequence of actions that will transition the agent through multiple states. In DMSOA, the agent's policy selects a single control action and the number of times to apply the action in order to reduce its measurement costs while still achieving the control objective. Through the incorporation of measurement costs, the agent is able to learn how many times the action should be applied in order to arrive at the next meaningful state. For DMSOA, a meaningful state is one for which the information provided by it is greater than the cost to measure it.

3 Problem Setup

An AC-NOMDP is defined by $\langle \mathcal{S}, \mathcal{A}, \mathcal{O}, \mathcal{P}, \mathcal{R}_{ext}, \mathcal{R}_{int}, \mathcal{P}_{s_0}, \gamma \rangle$ where $\mathcal{S}$ is the state space, $\mathcal{A} = \langle A_c \times A_m \rangle$ is the set of action tuples composed of control actions a_c and binary measurement actions $a_m \in \{0, 1\}$ that specify if an observation of the next state is requested. The observation space $\mathcal{O}$ is related to $\mathcal{S}$ by the observation emission function $p(o|s', a)$ (more on this below). $\mathcal{P} : S \times A \times S \to \mathbb{R}$ denotes the transition probabilities, $\mathcal{R}_{ext} : S \times A_c \to \mathbb{R}$ denotes the extrinsic reward function, $\mathcal{R}_{int} : S \times A_m \to \mathbb{R}$ denotes the intrinsic reward function that encourages the agent to reduce the number of measurements it makes. The r_{int} value is typically set to slightly outweigh the r_{ext} value to achieve the balance between the need for information to solve to control problem and the cost of information. If r_{int} is very large or very small relative to r_{ext}, the agent may never measure at the cost of solving the control objective or always measure and fail to reduce the observation costs.

The function $\mathcal{P}_{s_0} : S \to \mathbb{R}$ denotes the probability distribution over the initial state and $\gamma \in (0, 1]$ is the discount factor. The observation emission function $p(o|s', a)$ specifies the probability of observing $o \in \mathcal{O}$ given the action a in state s. Unlike the more general POMDP, the observation space in a AC-NOMDP is limited to $\mathcal{O} = \mathcal{S} \cup \{empty\}$, where $empty$ is the missing measurement of the environment. In this setup, the potential probabilities of $p(o|s', a_m = 1) \in \{0, 1\}$, with $p(o|s', a_m = 1) = 1$ if and only if $o = s'$ and $p(o|s', a_m = 1) = 0$ for all $o \neq s'$. In contrast, $p(o|s', a_m = 0) = 1$ if and only if $o = stale$.

The agent learns a policy $\pi(o) : O \to A$ that maps observations to action tuples. The initial observation $o_0 = s_0$ contains a fresh measurement of the environment. The control action selected by the agent is applied in the environment and the underlying state transitions according to $\mathcal{P}$. At each time step, the reward, r_t is the intrinsic reward, $r_t = r_{(int,t)}$, if $a_m = 0$, otherwise the extrinsic reward, $r_t = r_{(ext,t)}$, is given in response to the state s_t and control action a_c selected by the agent. When the measurement action, $a_m = 1$, is selected, the agent receives a fresh measurement of the underlying state $o_{t+1} = s_{t+1}$ of the environment. Alternatively, when $a_m = 0$, the agent does not obtain a fresh measurement and the next action must be selected based the agent's internal mechanism, such as an internal memory or model.

The OSMBOA agent selects one control and one measurement action, $\langle a_{c,t}, a_{m,t} \rangle$ per time step, whereas the DMSOA agent moves from decision point to decision point with a frequency less than or equal to the environment's clock. At each decision point, the DMSOA agent selects a control action and the number of times to apply it, k. The state is only measured on the kth application (e.g. $\langle a_c, a_m = 0 \rangle_t, ..., \langle a_c, a_m = 0 \rangle_{t+(k-1)}, \langle a_c, a_m = 1 \rangle_{t+k}$).

The agent's objective is to learn a policy π that maximizes the discounted expected costed return which incorporates both the intrinsic and extrinsic rewards:

$$J(\pi) = \mathbb{E}_{a_t \sim \pi, s_t \sim P} \left[\sum_t \gamma^t r(s_t, a_t) \right], \tag{1}$$

where $\gamma < 1$ is the discount factor. In this work, we focus on deep Q-learning based solutions [14] combined with standard improvements such as *n-step* DQN for better convergence [23], double DQN to improve stability [25] and prioritized replay to improve sample efficiency [19]. Although this work examines problems with discrete action spaces, the proposed algorithms can be modified for continuous action spaces.

4 Deep Dynamic Multi-step Observationless Agent

The Deep Dynamic Multi-Step Observationless Q-learning Agent (DMSOA) for noiselessly observable RL environments with explicit observation costs is presented in Fig. 1. The framework has three key components: the control policy $\pi_c : o \to a_a$ that maps the observation to a control action, the measurement skipping policy $\pi_m : o, a_c \to k$ that maps the observation and selected control action to $k \in \{1, ..., K\}$ the number of steps to apply a_c to the environment, and the action-observation scheduler. The action-observation scheduler applies the action pair $(a_c, 0)$ $k-1$ times and collects the intrinsic rewards r_{int} from the environment. On the kth iteration, it applies the action pair $(a_c, 1)$, records the extrinsic reward r_{ext}, and passes the new observation to π_c and π_m. The extrinsic reward is equal to the control policy reward for applying a_c and arriving in the measured state after step $i = k$. The intrinsic reward is $r_{int} \in \{0, c\}$, where c is a bonus (i.e. "cost saving") given to the agent when it chooses not to measure. To ensure the agent is motivated to omit measurements whenever possible, we set $c \geq r_{ext}^{max}$. The optimal setting of c will depend on the application and the requirements of the domain.

In this work, the policies are implemented as deep Q networks (DQN), however, other forms of policy learning could be utilized. The agent's objective is to maximize the costed rewards $\sum_{t=0}^{\infty} \gamma^t r_t$. To achieve this we learn parameterized value functions $Q_c(o; \theta)$ and $Q_m(o, a; \zeta)$ as feed-forward deep neural networks. As described above, for an m-dimensional observation space and an n-dimensional action space, Q_c is a mapping from an m-dimensional observation to an n-dimensional vector of action values. The function Q_m is a mapping from an $m+1$-dimensional observation-action to a K-dimensional vector of measurement values. In the case of image data, each channel is augmented with the action details. The argmax of each output indicates the action to apply and the number of times to apply it.

During training, the experience tuples $(o_t, a_{(c,t)}, a_{(m,t)}, r_t, o_{t+1})$ are stored in a prioritized experience replay buffer. To improve stability, target networks θ^- and ζ^- for Q_c and Q_m are copied from θ and ζ every τ steps. In addition, we use the double DQN [25] to improve value estimates. The target for the control network is:

$$Y_i^{Q_c} \equiv r_t + \gamma \, Q_c\big(o_{t+1}, \text{argmax}_a Q_c(o_{t+1}, a; \theta_t); \theta_t^-\big). \tag{2}$$

For the same update step, the target for the measurement network is:

$$Y_i^{Q_m} \equiv r_t + \gamma \, Q_m\big((o_{t+1}, a_{(c,t+1)}), \text{argmax}_a Q_m((o_{t+1}, a_{(c,t+1)}), a; \zeta_t); \zeta_t^-\big). \tag{3}$$

The corresponding losses are:

$$\mathcal{L}_i^{Q_c}(\theta_i) = \mathbb{E}_{(o_t, a_{(c,t)}) \sim \mathcal{D}}\left[(Y_i^{Q_c} - Q_c(o_t, a_{(c,t)}; \theta_i))^2\right], \tag{4}$$

and

$$\mathcal{L}_i^{Q_m}(\zeta_i) = \mathbb{E}_{(o_t, a_{(c,t)}, a_{(m,t)}) \sim \mathcal{D}}\left[(Y_i^{Q_m} - Q_m((o_t, a_{(c,t)}), a_{(m,t)}; \zeta_i))^2\right] \tag{5}$$

5 Experimental Setup

In this section, we compare the performance of DMSOA to OSMBOA. In order to highlight the differences in the measurement behaviour of each method, we implement both with double DQN and a prioritized replay buffer. The hyperparameters were selected via grid search with 3 random trials. For the evaluation, we report the mean and standard deviation of the reward during training and the observation behaviour of the best policy. Each agent is reinitialized with 20 difference seeds and trained on the OpenAI gym environments Cartpole, Acrobot, Lunar Lander and Atari Pong. The experiments were run on CentOS with Intel Xeon Gold 6130 CPU and 192 GB memory. In addition, a NVIDIA V100 GPU was used in the training of the Atari agent. Clips of the DMSOA agents can be viewed here[1].

6 Results

Figure 2 shows the mean and standard deviation for each agent on the Cartpole and Acrobot environments. The aim in the Cartpole environment is for the agent to operate a cart such that a vertical pole remains balanced for as long as possible. The extrinsic reward is set to 1 and the intrinsic reward is set to 1.1. We truncate each episode at a maximum of 200 time steps. In the Acrobot environment, the objective is to apply torque to flip an arm consisting of two actuated links connected linearly above a target height in as few steps as possible. The agent receives an extrinsic reward of -1 or an intrinsic reward of -0.85 at each time step. The episode ends after 200 steps or when the arm is successfully flipped over the line.

DMSOA learns a policy for both environments that produces a higher costed reward than OSMBOA. This indicates that DMSOA requires fewer measurements whilst carrying out the control policy. In addition, the standard deviation is lower indicating more stability across independent training runs. The episode length plots on the right show that DMSOA learned policies to keep the Cartpole upright longer and flip the Acrobot over the goal faster.

The results for the Lunar Lander environment are presented in Fig. 3. The Lunar Lander environment is a rocket trajectory optimization problem [7]. The

---

[1] https://www.youtube.com/playlist?list=PLr6sWY5moZhFtTuCBbIjb4cZQOZkbjkOV.

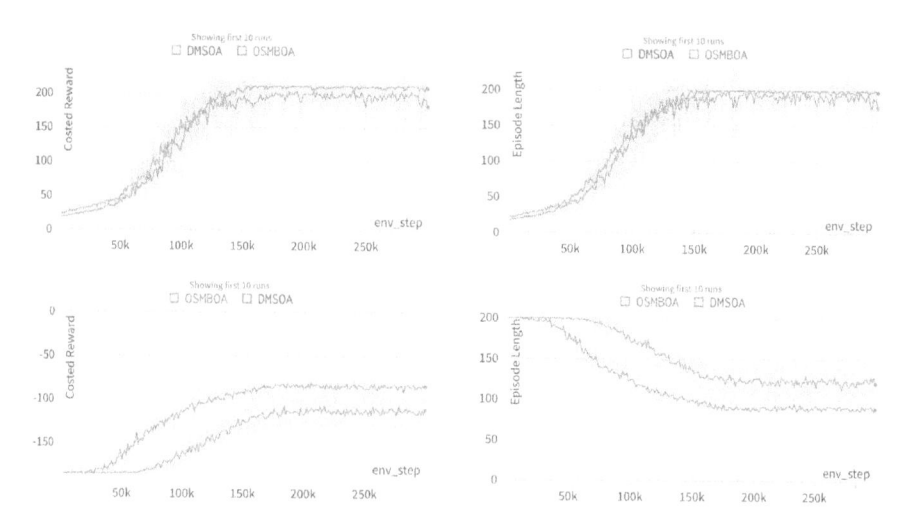

Fig. 2. Mean and standard deviation of performance on Cartpole (upper) and Acrobot (lower). Left: costed reward and right: episode length. In both cases, DMSOA has a higher mean costed reward, and is superior in terms of the control objective (longer episodes on Cartpole and shorter episodes on Acrobot.)

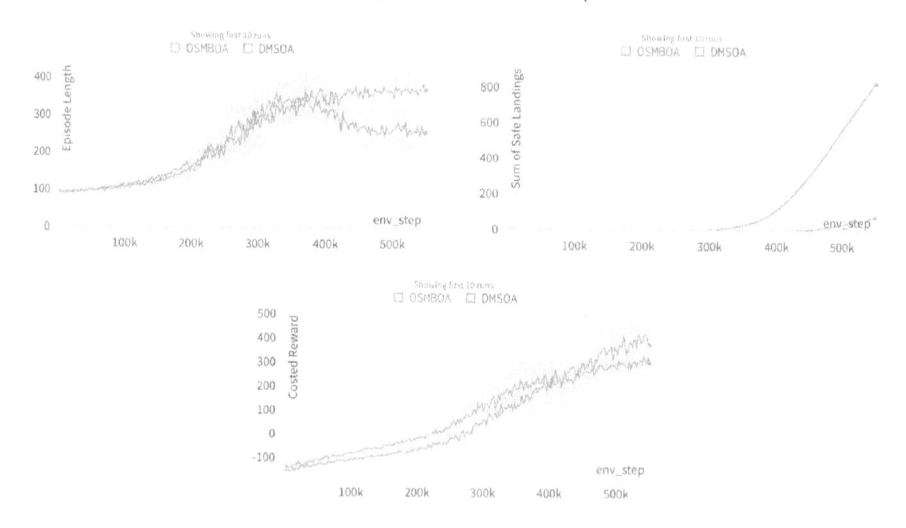

Fig. 3. Mean and standard deviation of the performance on the Lunar Lander environment. Top left: episode length, top right: sum of the number of successful landings, lower: costed reward. DMSOA and OSMBOA achieve similar mean costed rewards. DMSOA, however, learns to successfully land the ship more frequently and in fewer steps.

objective is to fire the lander's rockets such that it lands squarely in the target area. The fuel supply is infinite, but the best policy uses it sparingly. The environment has four discrete actions available: do nothing, fire left orientation engine, fire main engine, fire right orientation engine. The intrinsic reward is 0.1. The extrinsic reward is -0.3 for firing the main engine and -0.03 for side engines, the reward is also scaled by the lander's distance from the landing pad. Ten points are added to the extrinsic reward for each leg that is in contact with the ground, and an additional 100 points are added for landing, while 100 points are subtracted for crashing. The episode ends when the agent lands or crashes, or is truncated after a maximum of 400 time steps.

The plot on the top left in Fig. 3 shows that mean episode length is longer for OSMBOA than DMSOA, and the top right plot shows that DMSOA has significantly more successful landings. This indicates that DMSOA learns a policy that quickly navigates the ship to a safe landing. The lower plot shows that OSMBOA has a slightly higher costed reward. As suggested by the first two plots, this is due to the fact that it takes longer to land and not because the policies is superior.

Table 1. Ratio of steps with measurements to steps without measurements of the converged policy during training.

Env.	DMSOA	OSMBOA
Cartpole	1:1.27	1:0.37
Acrobot	1:0.45	1:1.03
Lunar Lander	1:1.56	1:0.33

Table 1 shows the ratio of the number of steps made without measuring for each measurement made. On Cartpole and Lunar Lander, DMSOA makes more than one step without measuring for each measurement step, whereas on Acrobot it makes an average of 0.5 non-measuring steps for each measuring step. This suggests that the dynamics of Acrobot are less predictable, causing DMSOA to measure more frequently. Interestingly, Acrobot is the only environment where OSMBOA does better than a 1:1 ratio.

6.1 Examination of Measurement Policies

Figure 4 shows the measurement behaviour of the best OSMBOA (left) and DMSOA (right) policies for Cartpole (top), Acrobot (middle) and Lunar Lander (lower) environments. Each row specifies a 1-episode roll-out of the best policy. Each column in the OSMBOA plots is the environment time step during the episode. For OSMBOA, the number of decision steps is equivalent to the number of steps in the environment. In contrast, each column in the DMSOA plots corresponds to a decision by the agent, with one or more environment time steps associated with it. In addition to highlighting the measurement efficiency, this also shows the decision efficiency. On Cartpole, DMSOA makes approximately 70 action selections (decisions) per episode of 200 environment steps (the mean steps per episode are shown in Fig. 2).

For OSMBOA, an orange cell indicates that a fresh measurement of the environment and blue specifies that no measurement was requested at corresponding time step. In the case of DMSOA, the colour indicates the number of consecutive steps that were taken without a fresh measurement. Blue indicates that a measurement is made after the control action is applied once, yellow indicates that a measurement is made after the control action is applied twice and red indicates that a measurement is made after the control action is applied three times.

The distinct pattern in each plot suggests the different capabilities of each class of AC-NOMDP agent, along with the fact that each environment is unique in terms of its dynamics and complexity. The consistent measurement patterns for OSMBOA and DMSOA on Cartpole suggest that the environment has very regular dynamics. OSMBOA switches between selecting the next action from a freshly measured observation and selecting it from a stale observation. Alternatively, DMSOA learns to apply an action 3 times before measuring. This clearly demonstrates the potential of DMSOA to take more environment steps without measuring than OSMBOA.

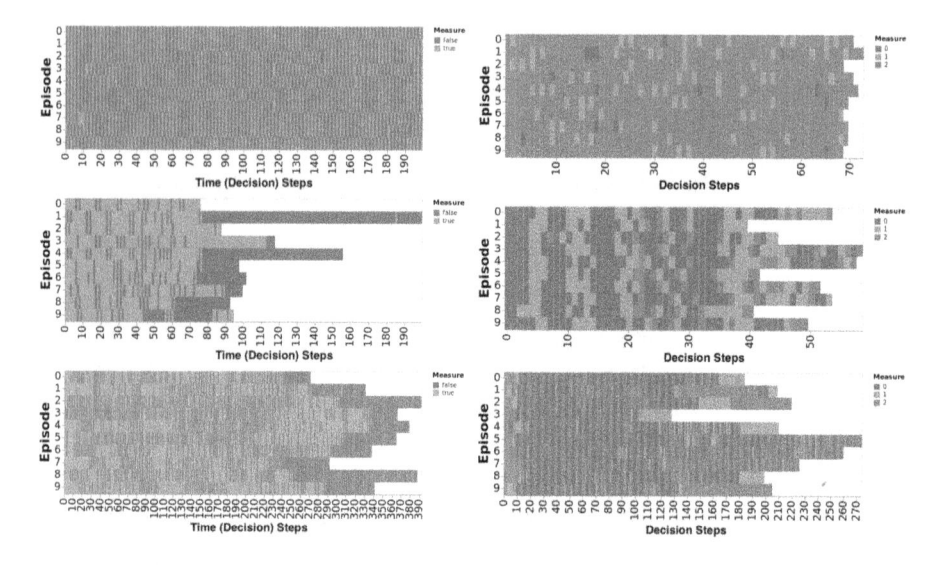

Fig. 4. Measurement behaviour of the best OSMBOA (left) and DMSOA (right) policies. Top: Cartpole, centre: Acrobot, lower: Lunar Lander. For OSMBOA, blue indicates that no measurement was made and orange indicates that a measurement was made. In the case of DMSOA, blue indicates that a measurement is made after one step, orange indicates that a measurement is made after two steps, and red indicates that a measurement is made after three steps. This figure reveals the very distinct measurement behaviour between the two classes of AC-NOMDP agents. (Color figure online)

Acrobot and Lunar Lander show much more complex measurement behaviour. For both OSMBOA and DMSOA on Acrobot during approximately the first 3/4s of the each episode they display a pattern of frequently measuring followed by briefly not measuring. Our analysis finds that both OSMBOA and DMSOA skip measurements while the arcobot is in the lower left region of the observation space. This is roughly where the momentum of the Acrobot shifts from heading way from the goal, back towards to the goal. In this area, it is deemed safe to apply torque back towards the goal without observing. In the last quarter of each episode, both agents take more steps without measuring. It is noteworthy that in most episodes OSMBOA takes significantly more steps without observing than DMSOA. However, this has a negative impact on the total number of action decisions made by OSMBOA on route to achieving to goal. This particularly visible in episodes 1 and 4. DMSOA does not to suffer from similar behaviour.

On the Lunar Lander environment both methods take few or no measurements near the end of the episode when the agent is close to landing. In addition, DMSOA repeatedly takes 2-3 steps before measuring at the beginning of each episode, whereas OSMBOA repeatedly measures early in each episode. Each method measures frequently during the middle of the episode as agent attempts to direct the lander safely towards the landing area. OSMBOA generally alternates between measuring and not measuring at each time step, whereas DMSOA typically takes many measurement steps followed by 1 to 2 steps without measuring before returning to measuring again. Similar to Acrobot, once OSMBOA estimates that it is on target to reach the goal it commits to never measuring again. When this estimate is erroneous, the leads to much longer episodes than necessary and the risk of crashing the ship.

6.2 Image-Based RL Results

The objective in the pong Atari game is to bounce the ball off of your paddle and past the opponents paddle into its goal [3]. The action space is 6-dimensional including do nothing, fire, move right, move left, fire right and fire left. The observation space is a (210, 160, 3) image. In the case of OSMBOA, a 210 by 1 vector of ones or zeros is added to each channel to indicate if the observation is fresh or stale. The agent gets an extrinsic reward of 1 for winning a match and 0 for each intermediate step. Each episode is composed of 21 matches and the intrinsic reward is 0.001.

The results in Fig. 5 show that DMSOA wins significantly more matches than OSMBOA (top left), achieves a higher costed reward (top right) and more intrinsic reward (lower). Thus, DMSOA learns to be a better Pong player and requires fewer measurements. Due the longer episodes and training times, a measurement behaviour plot similar to Fig. 4 is not feasible within the confines of this paper. However, recordings of each agent and its measurement behaviour are available in the paper Github repository.

From our analysis for the measurement policies of each agent, we found that both learn to measure less frequently when the ball is travelling away from their paddle. Alternatively, if the ball is near their paddle or the opponents paddle, each agent measures more frequently. Inline with the observations on Acrobot and Lunar Lander, when OSMBOA reaches a state from which it expects to win the match, it switch to not measuring for the remainder of the match. If the prediction is correct, it can achieve a greater reduction in measurements than DMSOA. If it is wrong, however, OSMBOA general loses the match. An erroneous prediction of this nature is particularly risky in a complex and dynamic environment.

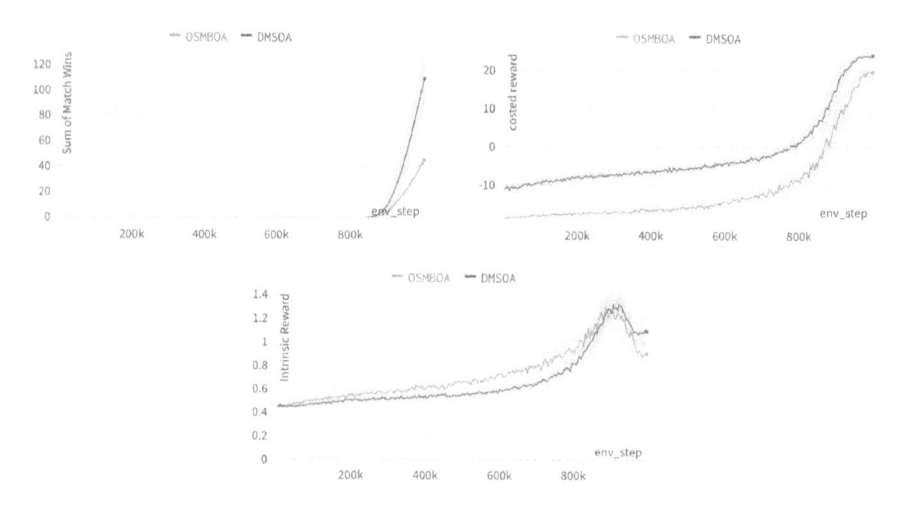

Fig. 5. Mean and standard deviation of the performance on the Atari Pong environment. Top left: sum of the number of wins, top right: costed reward, lower: intrinsic reward. DMSOA learns a policy that wins more games with a better costed reward and fewer measurements.

7 Discussion

The results indicate that DMSOA has a clear advantage over OSMBOA in terms of its convergence rate and the reduction in measurements and decision steps. We believe that the control action repetition capabilities of DMSOA improve its exploration of the environment and its understanding of the implications (positive and negative) of taking multiple steps without measuring. This helps it to quickly converge to good control and measurement policies. In addition, the fact that DMSOA's multi-step action sequences always ends with a measurement of the final state provides it with a good grounding from with to select the next control action. On the other hand, because the extrinsic reward for intermediate steps is not available, there is the potential for more noise in the reward signal for longer DMSOA action repetition trajectories. Due to the fact that OSMBOA is limited to one-step action, noise in the reward is less of a concern. Although, DMSOA appears to handle the noisy reward signal, future work should examine this in more detail.

For unshaped (or uniform) reward environments, such as Cartpole, Acrobot and Pong, setting the intrinsic reward is simple and the agent is insensitive to the value so long as it is slightly larger than the extrinsic reward. Alternative, the intrinsic reward requires fine tuning on environments with complex reward shaping such as Lunar Lander. As heuristic, we suggest starting the fine tuning from the mean of the extrinsic reward collected over multiple random walks in the environment.

In multiple environments, we found that OSMBOA commits to not measuring towards the end of each episode. This is surprising since if OSMBOA takes more than one step without measuring, it enters a partially observable state. This is akin to playing the game with its eyes closed. The agent is, thus, unaware if any unexpected event occurs. On Acrobot and pong, this resulted in it not achieving the goal, or it taking much longer than otherwise necessary. An example of this is seen in episodes 1 and 4 of the Acrobot plot in Fig. 4.

8 Environmental Impact

This work aims to strike a balance between scientific understanding and energy consumption. To do this we have selected a number of OpenAI gym classic control environments from which RL policies can be efficiently learned, along with one large image-based RL environment. Although the set is relatively small the dynamics are diverse enough to illustrate the differences between the two classes of AC-NOMDP algorithms considered in this work. We also note that the work was conducted in a jurisdiction in which the majority of the electric comes from sources such as hydro-electric and nuclear.

In addition to reducing the measurement costs, this work can lead to a reduction in the associated carbon footprint for RL in this area. Unlike OSMBOA, the multi-step capabilities of DMSOA may robustly lower the number of forward passes through the network for decision making, offer savings in terms of communication with the environment and lower latency. Moreover, it can help with exploration, thereby reduce the time to policy convergence.

9 Conclusion

In this work, we consider the problem of RL for environments where agent's decision making and measuring of the state of the environment have explicit costs, namely AC-NOMDPs. We provide the first survey of methods recently proposed for AC-NOMDPs. Building on the existing work, we propose DMSOA, an RL algorithm learns a control and a measurement policy to reduce measurement and decision steps. Our empirical results confirm the previously published results for OSMBOA on Cartpole, Acrobot and Lunar Lander, and show that OSMBOA is also capable on the more complex, image-based Atari Pong environment. However, we find that our proposed method DMSOA learns a *better control policy* than OSMBOA, and *requires fewer costly measurement and decision steps.*

This demonstrates the great potential to reduce measurement and decision costs associated with RL by allowing the agent to take control of its action and observation behaviour. We expect this to be a necessary capability of RL agents applied in many real-world applications. The next steps that we envision are developing more sophisticated loss functions for DMSOA, incorporating recurrency into the network to deal with time, expanding the analysis to additional methods and more realistic setting such as self-driving chemistry where observation can be costly and potentially destructive [2].

Acknowledgments. This work was supported with funding from the National Research Council of Canada's AI for Design Program.

References

1. Barto, A.G., Mahadevan, S.: Recent advances in hierarchical reinforcement learning. Discr. Event Dyn. Syst. **13**(1–2), 41–77 (2003)
2. Beeler, C., et al.: Chemgymrl: An interactive framework for reinforcement learning for digital chemistry. arXiv preprint arXiv:2305.14177 (2023)
3. Bellemare, M.G., Naddaf, Y., Veness, J., Bowling, M.: The arcade learning environment: an evaluation platform for general agents. J. Artif. Intell. Res. **47**, 253–279 (2013)
4. Bellinger, C., Coles, R., Crowley, M., Tamblyn, I.: Active measure reinforcement learning for observation cost minimization. In: Proceedings of the Canadian Conference on Artificial Intelligence. Canadian Artificial Intelligence Association (CAIAC) (Jun 8 2021). https://caiac.pubpub.org/pub/3hn8s5v9
5. Bellinger, C., Drozdyuk, A., Crowley, M., Tamblyn, I.: Balancing information with observation costs in deep reinforcement learning. In: Proceedings of the Canadian Conference on Artificial Intelligence. Canadian Artificial Intelligence Association (CAIAC) (may 27 2022). https://caiac.pubpub.org/pub/0jmy7gpd
6. Bellinger, C., Drozdyuk, A., Crowley, M., Tamblyn, I.: Scientific discovery and the cost of measurement – balancing information and cost in reinforcement learning. In: ICML 2nd Annual AAAI Workshop on AI to Accelerate Science and Engineering (AI2ASE) (Feb 13 2023)
7. Brockman, G., et al.: Openai gym. arXiv preprint arXiv:1606.01540 (2016)
8. Daniel, K.: Thinking fast and slow. United States of America (2011)
9. Fu, Y.: The Cost of OPS in Reinforcement Learning. Master's thesis, University of California, Berkeley (2021)
10. Gal, Y., McAllister, R., Rasmussen, C.E.: Improving pilco with bayesian neural network dynamics models. In: Data-Efficient Machine Learning workshop, ICML. vol. 4, p. 34 (2016)
11. Koseoglu, M., Özcelikkale, A.: How to miss data?: Reinforcement learning for environments with high observation cost. In: 2020 International Conference on Machine Learning (ICML) Workshop, Wien, Österrike, 12-18 juli (2020)
12. Lakshminarayanan, A., Sharma, S., Ravindran, B.: Dynamic action repetition for deep reinforcement learning. In: Proceedings of the AAAI Conference on Artificial Intelligence, vol. 31 (2017)
13. Mills, K., Ronagh, P., Tamblyn, I.: Finding the ground state of spin Hamiltonians with reinforcement learning. Nature Mach. Intell. **2**(9), 509–517 (2020). https://doi.org/10.1038/s42256-020-0226-x
14. Mnih, V., et al.: Human-level control through deep reinforcement learning. Nature **518**(7540), 529–533 (2015)
15. Nam, H.A., Fleming, S., Brunskill, E.: Reinforcement learning with state observation costs in action-contingent noiselessly observable markov decision processes. Adv. Neural. Inf. Process. Syst. **34**, 15650–15666 (2021)
16. Ong, S.C., Png, S.W., Hsu, D., Lee, W.S.: Planning under uncertainty for robotic tasks with mixed observability. Int. J. Robot. Res. **29**(8), 1053–1068 (2010)
17. Papadimitriou, C.H., Tsitsiklis, J.N.: The complexity of Markov decision processes. Math. Oper. Res. **12**(3), 441–450 (1987)
18. Pathak, D., Agrawal, P., Efros, A.A., Darrell, T.: Curiosity-driven exploration by self-supervised prediction. In: International Conference on Machine Learning, pp. 2778–2787. PMLR (2017)

19. Schaul, T., Quan, J., Antonoglou, I., Silver, D.: Prioritized experience replay. arXiv preprint arXiv:1511.05952 (2015)
20. Shann, T.Y.A.: Reinforcement learning in the presence of sensing costs. Master's thesis, University of British Columbia (2022). https://doi.org/10.14288/1.0413129, https://open.library.ubc.ca/collections/ubctheses/24/items/1.0413129
21. Sharma, S., Srinivas, A., Ravindran, B.: Learning to repeat: Fine grained action repetition for deep reinforcement learning. arXiv preprint arXiv:1702.06054 (2017)
22. Simon, H.A.: Bounded rationality. Utility and probability, pp. 15–18 (1990)
23. Sutton, R.S., Barto, A.G.: Reinforcement learning: An introduction. MIT press (2018)
24. Sutton, R.S., Precup, D., Singh, S.: Between mdps and semi-mdps: a framework for temporal abstraction in reinforcement learning. Artif. Intell. **112**(1–2), 181–211 (1999)
25. Van Hasselt, H., Guez, A., Silver, D.: Deep reinforcement learning with double q-learning. In: Proceedings of the AAAI Conference on Artificial Intelligence, vol. 30 (2016)

Workshop on Uplift Modeling and Causal Machine Learning for Operational Decision Making

Exploiting Causal Knowledge During CATE Estimation Using Tree Based Metalearners

Roger Pros[1,2](✉) and Jordi Vitrià[1]

[1] Departament de Matemàtica i Informàtica, Universitat de Barcelona,
08007 Barcelona, Spain
{roger.pros,jordi.vitria}@ub.edu
[2] Zenital, Barcelona, Spain
http://www.ub.edu

Abstract. In recent years, causal insights have been used to improve machine learning methods by introducing assumptions. Following this trend, we propose a new method to improve the estimation of Conditional Average Treatment Effect (CATE) based on ML methods. In CATE estimation, a common approach is to use metalearners, which are able to estimate CATE using conventional machine learning models if certain identification properties (the backdoor criterion) are satisfied. In this approach, the causal knowledge of the problem (e.g., the causal graph) is used only for the identification of the estimand, not for the estimation itself. We describe a new approach that exploits causal knowledge during the estimation phase by adding constraints during model training. These constraints are based on the conditional independence structure encoded in the causal graph. We apply the constraints to tree based algorithms and show that models trained with these constraints achieve higher performance and lower variability when used to estimate CATE. Our experiments also show that this approach can improve performance even in cases where the causal knowledge of the data is unknown and must be obtained by causal discovery algorithms.

Keywords: CATE estimation · Metalearners · Markov Blanket · Causal Knowledge

1 Introduction

Machine learning techniques excel at finding associations in independent and identically distributed data, but these models can struggle when used in real-world settings. It has been argued that these problems are due in part to the model's lack of causal knowledge about the data [1,6,20–22]. To address this problem, there has been interest in the research community in Causal Machine Learning [8], machine learning methods that achieve certain properties by exploiting causal knowledge. In these methods, the information that the models learn from the data is augmented with external expert causal knowledge. This knowledge typically includes assumptions about the data generation process that are not exploited by pure ML methods.

Some of the most successful use cases of Causal Machine Learning are causal feature selection and invariant mechanism learning [27,31]. Causal feature selection differs from classical feature selection in the relationship of the resulting features to the target variable. Classical feature selection aims to find a relevant subset of features based on the correlations between predictive and target features. In contrast, causal feature selection aims to find all or part of the direct causes and effects of a target variable [29]. Invariant mechanism learning aims to identify the data-generating mechanism that represents the data.

On the other hand, classical machine learning techniques have played a key role in causal inference. Under certain identifiability conditions, the causal inference problem can be expressed as a predictive problem [19]. This predictive problem is then solved in a variety of ways, including the use of classical machine learning or deep learning. One of the most extended causal inference approaches is the use of metalearners [11]. Metalearners are algorithms that use arbitrary supervised learning methods to estimate the Conditional Average Treatment Effect (CATE) function.

Other CATE estimators are designed with a specific causal problem in mind, such as [23,24,28], where the model structure exploits the binary nature of the treatment variable.

1.1 Causal Machine Learning for Causal Inference

In this paper, we will propose a method that aims to build better machine learning models when these models are used to perform causal inference. As we have seen, causal knowledge is used by several approaches to improve certain properties of classical machine learning models. In most of these cases, the task of the models is still prediction. On the other hand, metalearners use predictive models for CATE estimation, but use causal knowledge only during the identification phase. In this setting, we find our first motivation: the use of predictive models constrained by causal knowledge in CATE estimation. The task of CATE estimation assumes a causal generation of the data and tries to measure it. In this setting, the causal assumptions that classical machine learning models cannot learn from the data may prove valuable. Furthermore, the specific ways in which causal knowledge is applied to prediction models in the literature do not take advantage of all the information that is encoded in a causal graph. This information is valuable to the task of CATE estimation, and thus the ability to successfully exploit it could lead to better estimation performance.

The proposed approach can be better understood if we present the different alternatives we have when considering which features to include in a predictive model:

1. We can include the direct causes of the target variable. In this perspective, all the information required to predict the target variable is present, but there can be useful correlations in the data that are not captured by this approach.

2. We can include the minimal Markov Blanket [17] of the target variable. In this case, it can be shown that we cannot drop any variable without losing information about the target variable. This property doesn't guarantee that this is the best way to model it.
3. We can include all available variables. This approach makes use of all the data, but it can be a problem if the data is noisy or uninformative.
4. Any perspective in between, such as adding only some variables with an expert criterion.

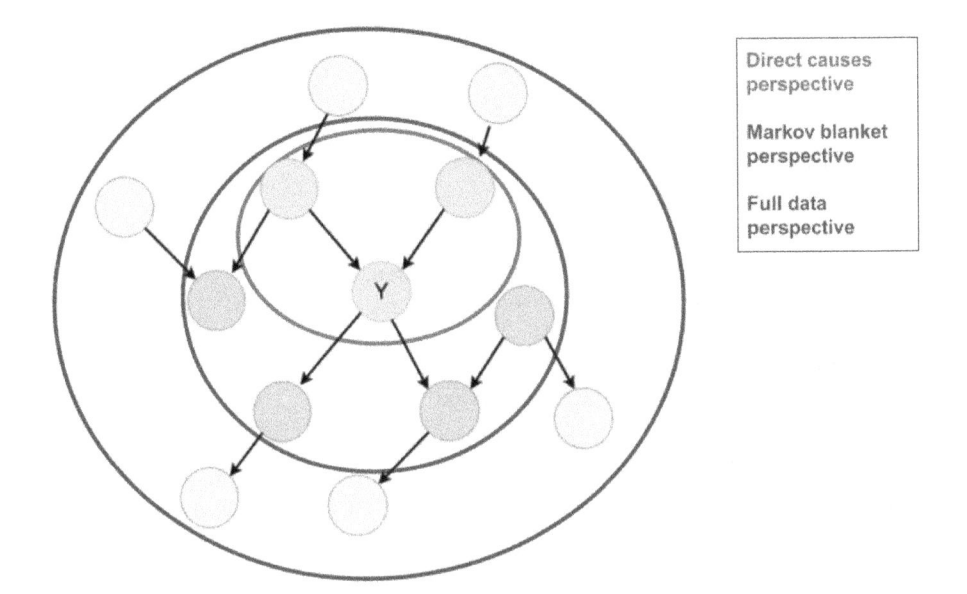

Fig. 1. Visual representation of various predictive problem alternatives.

Our approach is related to the last alternative. Specifically, we introduce a new method to exploit the knowledge encoded in the causal graph to train causal-based constrained models. From the causal graph, we obtain the Markov blanket of the target variable and thus its different sources of information. This information is encoded as interaction constraints and used to constrain a special kind of models: XGBoost estimators. We then apply these constrained models to the task of CATE estimation and compare them with unconstrained models. We show that they outperform the unconstrained models by having lower prediction error and performance variability.

In Sect. 4, we describe our approach. In particular, we describe how the causal graph is encoded as interaction constraints and how these can be used in the XGBoost package [4] to train constrained gradient boosting models. We also provide an illustrative example of the application of the method and discuss its advantages and limitations. In Sect. 5, we apply the method to benchmark datasets and compare it to the unconstrained alternative.

2 Preliminaries

Our approach builds on top of CATE estimation using metalearners. In addition, we also exploit the information encoded in the causal graph of the data. In this section we introduce the preliminary concepts that will be used throughout the paper. In Sect. 2.1 we describe the graph-based approach to causality that we use and in 2.2 we describe the particular graph topology for CATE estimation using backdoor methods.

2.1 Causal Graph and Markov Blanket

A **causal graph** [10] is a directed acyclic graph (DAG) that represents the causal relationships between variables in a system. We refer to a "causal graph" as a DAG that satisfies the causal edges assumptions, i.e. that all parents are causes of their children. We use the following notation:

- G denotes the causal graph
- $Pa(i)$ denotes the parents of node i in the causal graph
- $Ch(i)$ denotes the children of node i in the causal graph
- $MB(i)$ denotes the Markov Blanket of node i
- T denotes the treatment variable
- Y denotes the outcome variable
- $X = (x_1, \ldots, x_n)$ denotes the vector of covariates

A **Markov Blanket** [17] is a set of variables that completely shields a target variable from the rest of the variables in a probabilistic graphical model. The Markov Blanket of a node is the set of its parents, its children, and its children's other parents.

$$MB(Y) = Pa(Y) \cup Ch(Y) \cup_{x \in Ch(Y)} Pa(x) \qquad (1)$$

If a Markov Blanket is minimal, meaning that it cannot drop any variable without losing information, it is called a Markov boundary.

2.2 Metalearners

Metalearners are discrete treatment CATE estimators [11] that can take advantage of any supervised learning or regression method in machine learning and statistics. Metalearners build on base algorithms such as Random Forests or Gradient Boosted Trees to estimate CATE, a function that these algorithms are not designed to estimate directly.

Metalearners rely on the unconfoundedness assumption [13], assuming that $X_{1,\ldots,n}$ is a sufficient adjustment set. In other words, assuming that it satisfies the **backdoor criterion** [18]: A set of variables X satisfies the backdoor criterion relative to T and Y if: 1) X blocks all backdoor paths from T to Y, and 2) X does not contain any descendants of T.

This unconfoundedness assumption gives identifiability and allows for CATE estimation.

3 Related Work

Neural Network Architectures Adapted to the Causal Problem. In some approaches, such as [23,24,28], the causal problem is built directly into the architecture of the network. These architectures are designed for binary treatment effect estimation and divide the final layers of the network into two subnetworks, one for the presence of the treatment and one for the absence of the treatment. These methods are currently state of the art for several tasks, and introduce the idea of designing a specific model according to the causal problem, instead of using a generic machine learning model. We adopt this idea in our approach.

Using the Markov Blanket to Train Classical ML Models. Several approaches use the information present in the Markov Blanket to generate a causal bias in classical machine learning models. These approaches usually take the form of causal feature selection and are related to causal discovery. In [12], the Markov Blanket is used to solve the problem that arises when the number of possible features is large and the percentage of actually informative features is small, particularly in financial data sets using a random forest classifier. In [30] the feature selection problem is approached from the point of view of faithfulness in the causal graph. If a dataset violates the faithful condition, Markov blankets of a class attribute may not be unique. In this work the multiple sources of information encoded in a Markov blanket are defined as sets of features instead of a single feature.

Biasing Models Using Constraints. In [7], interaction constraints between features are applied to tree-based algorithms. They show that these constraints can improve the performance of gradient boosting models and define a method for identifying them.

Predictive Models for Causal Inference. In [14], the relationship between predictive and causal performance is investigated. They show that, within a model class, predictive performance is indicative of causal performance when choosing hyperparameters. They also propose a benchmark for causal inference.

Causal Query Estimation Using the Causal Graph. In [16], the causal graph is incorporated directly into the estimation process. They fit a general model using neural networks and normalizing flows that can be used to estimate causal queries. This general model takes into account the conditional independencies encoded in the causal graph during both the training and prediction phases.

4 Methodology

In this section, we describe the process of obtaining the constraints used in the model from a causal graph and applying them to tree-based algorithms. First, in Sect. 4.1, we detail the assumption that makes the implementation possible. In Sects. 4.2 and 4.3, we show how it can be implemented using the XGBoost package for an illustrative example. Finally, in Sect. 4.4, we discuss the advantages and limitations of the method.

4.1 General Implementation

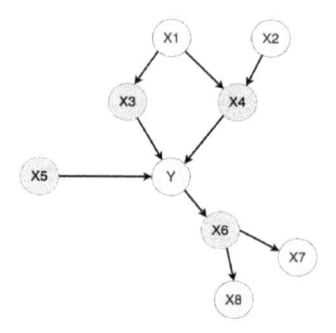

Fig. 2. In blue, the nodes included in the Markov Blanket (Color figure online)

In Fig. 2 we can see the Markov Blanket for the target variable in a Causal Graph. If the Markov Blanket is Markov boundary (i.e. it cannot drop any variable without losing information),then each of the elements contained in the Markov Blanket has the following properties: 1) contains predictive information with respect to the target node and 2) cannot be dropped without losing information.

$$P(Y|X) = P(Y|MB(Y)) \tag{2}$$

Definition 1. We define $MB_{x_i}(Y)$ as the information that reaches Y through one of the elements of the Markov Blanket of Y.

$$MB_{x_i}(Y) = P(Y|x_i) \quad \forall x_i \in MB(Y) \tag{3}$$

We will then use this information to define the assumption that will be used to constrain the models.

Distribution Modelling Simplification. Most classical ML learners model the distribution of the target variable as $P(Y|X)$. In particular, tree based models use a combination of weak learners, each of which models the target variable conditional to a random subset of the predictive features:

$$P(Y|X) \sim f(P(Y|G_1), .., P(Y|G_m)), \quad G \in rand(x_1, .., x_n) \qquad (4)$$

Our assumption is to prioritize the causal structure in the learning possibilities of the model by removing some of the cases that do not satisfy the conditional independence structure defined by the causal graph. In particular, we restrict the learning of the model to a function of the distributions $MB_{x_i}(Y)$.

$$P(Y|X) \sim f(MB_{x_1}(Y), .., MB_{x_l}(Y)), \quad x \in MB(Y) \qquad (5)$$

Since we are considering the case of CATE estimation using backdoor adjustment, not all variables are to be included in the metalearners. The nodes from the Markov blanket to be included are in the parents of the target variable $Pa(Y)$, so we'll use the following sets: $MB_{x_i}(Y), \forall x_i \in Pa(Y)$.

Since this approach does not involve feature selection, but simply modifies the distributions to be learned, we do not discard any available information. This means that to model each independent $MB_{x_i}(Y)$, we use all the features that generated it, i.e., the union of all causal paths to Y that pass through x_i.

$$MB_{x_i}^E(Y) = P(Y|x_i \cup An(x_i)) \quad \forall x_i \in MB(Y) \qquad (6)$$

Note that this set, as we saw in Sect. 2.2, still satisfies the backdoor criterion because only includes parents and ancestors.

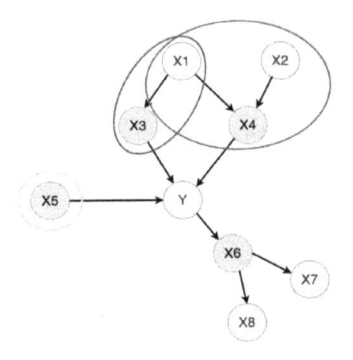

Fig. 3. Constraint groups as defined by our method.

Then, each set is transformed into interaction constraints by allowing only features belonging to the same set to interact with each other, not with any features from another set. In the case of tree-based algorithms this is implemented as follows: For each tree, the first split is unconstrained and follows the random tree algorithm. Then, from the second onwards, the candidate features for the split are constrained to those present in the constrain group of the first split.

The application of the defined assumption has two properties: 1) it limits the total number of ways a machine learning model can learn the relationship between predictive and target features. 2) It doesn't discard the real causal explanation in which the data has been generated according to the causal graph. This reduction of learning ways without discarding the causal generation is the causal-based constrain we introduce in the models.

4.2 Implementation Using XGB Interface

We implement the method using the gradient boosting algorithm from the XGBoost python package [4]. The XGBoost library implements machine learning algorithms under the gradient boosting framework. Among its hyperparameters there is the possibility to pass feature interaction constraints as a list of sets of variables. For each set, each variable is only allowed to interact with variables in the same set. We handle variable names to prevent one set from jumping into another if they have one or more variables in common. An example of implementation of the method can be found here.

4.3 Illustrative Example

In order to demonstrate the properties of the method, we generate synthetic data with a graph topology that is well suited to exploit the advantages of the method.

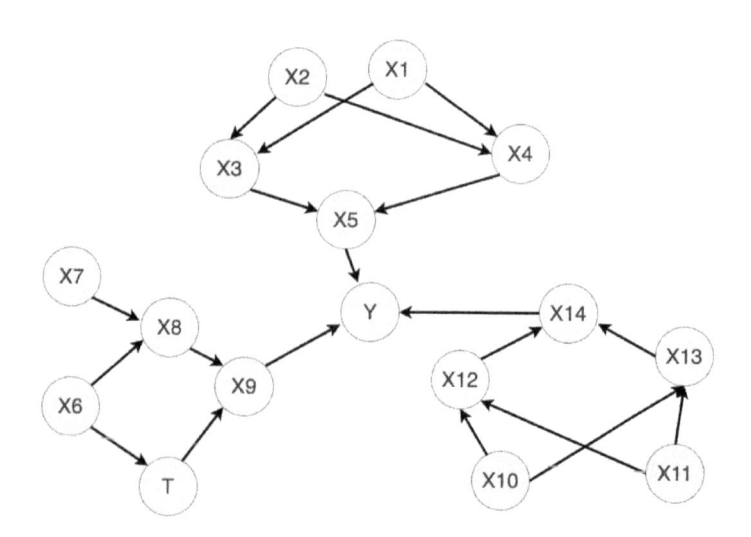

Fig. 4. Causal graph associated to the illustrative example. This setting has a complex structure and clearly separated sources of predictive information.

Data generation process:

$$x_1 = N(0,1)$$
$$x_2 = N(0,1)$$
$$x_3 = x_1 \times x_2 + \epsilon_3$$
$$x_4 = x_1 + x_2 + \epsilon_4$$
$$x_5 = x_3 \times x_4 + \epsilon_5$$
$$x_7 = N(0,1)$$
$$x_6 = N(0,1)$$
$$x_8 = x_7 + x_6 + \epsilon_8$$
$$T = \mathbb{1}(x_6 > 0.2) \times Bin(1, 0.8)$$

$$x_9 = T \times x_8 + \epsilon_9$$
$$x_{10} = N(0,1)$$
$$x_{11} = N(0,1)$$
$$x_{12} = x_{10} \times x_{11} + \epsilon_{12}$$
$$x_{13} = x_{10} + x_{11} + \epsilon_{13}$$
$$x_{14} = x_{12} \times x_{13} + \epsilon_{14}$$
$$Y = x_5 + x_9 + x_{14} + \epsilon_{15}$$
$$\epsilon_i \sim N(0, 0.1), \forall i$$

In this setting the constraint groups are (note that x_9 is a descendant of T, so it will not be used for CATE estimation):

$$[(x_1, x_2, x_3, x_4, x_5), (x_6, x_7, x_8, T), (x_{10}, x_{11}, x_{12}, x_{13}, x_{14})]$$

This setting is well suited to take advantage of the method because the casual graph has clearly independent sources of information and a complex structure. By adding the constraints, in addition to constraining the model toward the causal explanation of $P(Y|X)$, we prevent the model from using any spurious correlation that might arise between an interaction of features belonging to different $MB_{x_i}(Y)$ and the target variable.

Visual Intuition for Causal-Based Constraints. In Fig. 5 we can see a visual representation of the effect generated by this method. By plotting the correlations between the predictions of each tree in the gradient boosting algorithm, we can see how these constraints change the model toward an explanation of $P(Y|X)$ as $f(MB^E_{x_1}(Y), .., MB^E_{x_l}(Y))$, $x \in MB(Y)$.

4.4 Discussing the Advantages and Limitations of the Approach

Advantages. As defined in 4.1, this approach is able to reduce the number of ways a model can learn the distribution $P(Y|X)$ without discarding the causal explanation. This introduces a change in the model that can bring it closer to the causal explanation, and can improve the accuracy of the CATE estimation, as observed in the simulation results section of [11].

In addition, when estimating $MB_{x_i}(Y)$, variable interactions are limited to those variables with a direct or indirect causal relationship. This makes it difficult for the model to rely on any interaction between variables in different sources of information as a predictor of the target. Thanks to the causal graph, we know that any predictive power of such interactions would be a spurious correlation. Note that spurious correlations can still occur when combining the multiple $MB^E_{x_i}(Y)$.

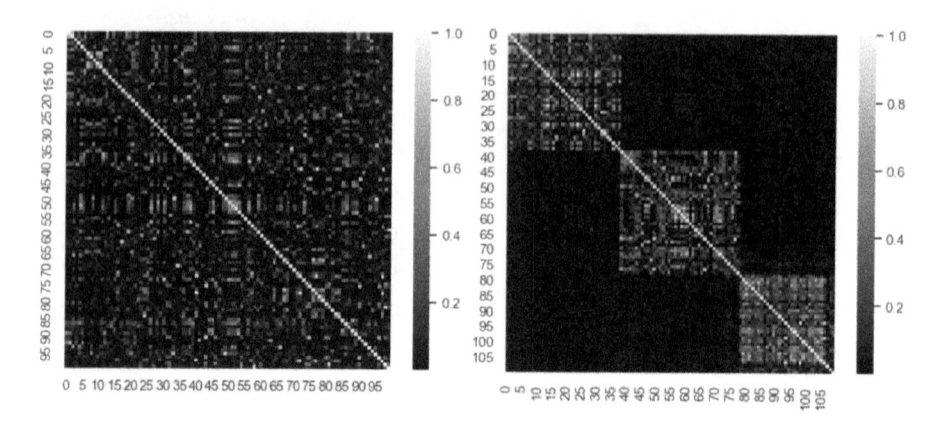

Fig. 5. Heatmaps of the correlations of the individual prediction trees for each gradient boosting algorithm. On the left, unconstrained, On the right, constrained with our method and rearranged according to the constraint group. Experiments on these models in Sect. 5.2

Main Limitation. The main limitation of this approach is that it relies on a correct causal graph. In real world data, the causal graph is not always known or easy to define. Since the advantage of this approach is that it uses more of the information encoded in the causal graph than the unconstrained alternative, any misspecification in the causal graph may have a greater impact on model performance.

5 Experiments

In this section, we test the performance of the constrained models against the unconstrained models. In addition to the illustrative dataset, we run two different settings. The first setting is the synthetic datasets used in [15] to test model performance under different scenarios and variable relationships. In this setting, the causal graph is known and 100% correct. The second setting is the causal benchmark suggested in [14]. The data sets in this setting are semi-synthetic, and the causal graph is unknown.

5.1 Experiment Settings

Both the constrained and unconstrained prediction models use the same process. First, we use Bayesian optimization, implemented by the Hyperopt [3] Python package, with 50 starting points and 50 iterations. Each iteration consists of a 5-fold cross-validation that minimizes the mean square error of the prediction of the target variable. We use the search space defined in [26] for the XGboost hyperparameters. The result of the optimization is then used for both S and T learners. Each experiment is repeated 100 times.

Tables. Each element of the tables represents the mean MSE and (in parethesis) the standard deviation MSE over the 100 runs. The comparison column is a ratio between the best performing constrained model and the best performing unconstrained model (Table 1).

5.2 Illustrative Dataset

First, we evaluate on the illustrative dataset designed to take advantage of the method.

Table 1. Illustrative dataset

Noise	0.5	1	2	4
SLearn	0.263 (0.067)	0.287 (0.063)	0.374 (0.108)	0.834 (0.569)
TLearn	0.693 (0.157)	0.891 (0.197)	1.872 (0.327)	3.773 (0.808)
SLearn_constr	**0.134 (0.063)**	**0.151 (0.057)**	**0.221 (0.077)**	**0.6 (0.473)**
TLearn_constr	0.673 (0.151)	0.852 (0.191)	1.743 (0.287)	3.482 (0.687)
Comparison	0.51 (0.938)	0.527 (0.905)	0.593 (0.718)	0.719 (0.832)

5.3 Application to Synthetic Data Sets

In [15], several synthetic scenarios are used to evaluate model performance. These scenarios correspond to cases of different complexity and behavior. We summarize here the main characteristics of each scenario and the associated constraints according to our definition:

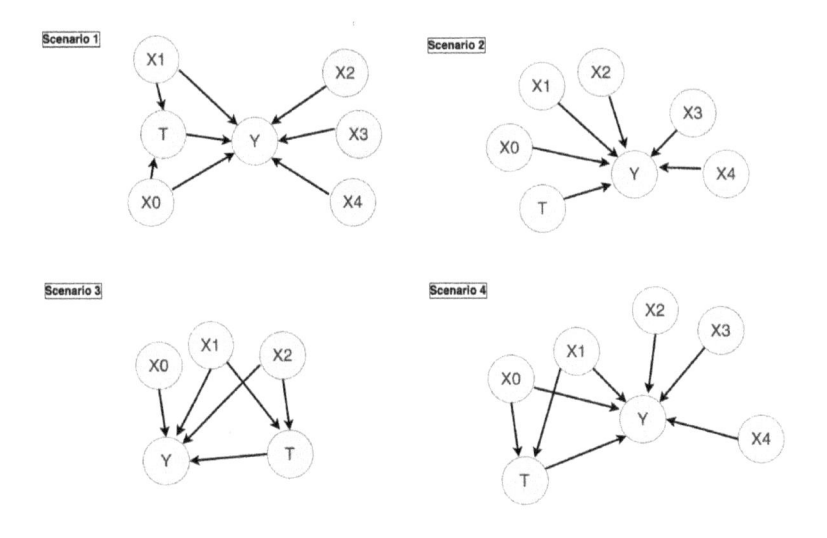

Fig. 6. DAGs associated with each of the mechanisms, see [15] for details

- Scenario 1: Complex outcome regression model with easy treatment effect.
  The constraint groups are: $[(x_0), (x_1), (x_2), (x_3), (x_4), (T, x_0, x_1)]$
- Scenario 2: A randomized trial.
  The constraint groups are: $[(x_0), (x_1), (x_2), (x_3), (x_4), (T)]$
- Scenario 3: Easy propensity score with a difficult control outcome.
  The constraint groups are: $[(x_0), (x_1), (x_2), (T, x_0, x_1)]$
- Scenario 4: Unrelated treatment arm and control arm,.
  The constraint groups are: $[(x_0), (x_1), (x_2), (x_3), (x_4), (T, x_0, x_1)]$

In Fig. 6 we can see the causal graphs associated with each scenario (Tables 2, 3, 4, 5). Each scenario is tested under different values of number of observations, number of variables and noise, as described in [15]

Table 2. Scenario 1

Noise	NSamples	SLearn	TLearn	SLearn_constr	TLearn_constr	Comparison
0.5	1000	0.051 (0.019)	0.102 (0.025)	**0.029 (0.012)**	0.095 (0.023)	0.572 (0.676)
	500	0.075 (0.032)	0.135 (0.039)	**0.042 (0.020)**	0.121 (0.038)	0.569 (0.625)
1	1000	0.063 (0.023)	0.177 (0.057)	**0.041 (0.019)**	0.161 (0.048)	0.650 (0.799)
	500	0.084 (0.040)	0.229 (0.087)	**0.060 (0.028)**	0.213 (0.088)	0.710 (0.699)
2	1000	0.078 (0.050)	0.529 (0.220)	**0.068 (0.038)**	0.530 (0.197)	0.881 (0.76)
	500	0.104 (0.078)	0.710 (0.333)	**0.090 (0.057)**	0.729 (0.364)	0.869 (0.754)
4	1000	0.155 (0.169)	1.523 (0.681)	**0.131 (0.125)**	1.576 (0.795)	0.874 (0.821)
	500	0.198 (0.221)	2.178 (1.194)	**0.177 (0.166)**	2.101 (1.012)	0.902 (0.752)

Table 3. Scenario 2

Noise	NSamples	SLearn	TLearn	SLearn_constr	TLearn_constr	Comparison
0.5	1000	**0.061 (0.017)**	0.083 (0.024)	0.128 (0.011)	0.074 (0.02)	1.22 (0.658)
	500	**0.085 (0.028)**	0.115 (0.034)	0.139 (0.019)	0.108 (0.035)	1.268 (0.683)
1	1000	**0.099 (0.037)**	0.173 (0.058)	0.142 (0.024)	0.162 (0.053)	1.435 (0.663)
	500	**0.139 (0.058)**	0.24 (0.082)	0.159 (0.041)	0.222 (0.086)	1.144 (0.701)
2	1000	**0.142 (0.055)**	0.639 (0.236)	0.144 (0.045)	0.607 (0.227)	1.018 (0.849)
	500	0.191 (0.114)	0.838 (0.349)	**0.19 (0.09)**	0.84 (0.311)	0.992 (0.795)
4	1000	0.226 (0.142)	1.981 (0.71)	**0.208 (0.123)**	1.921 (0.626)	0.92 (0.863)
	500	0.333 (0.301)	2.752 (1.068)	**0.316 (0.266)**	2.808 (1.081)	0.948 (0.878)

Table 4. Scenario 3

Noise	NSamples	SLearn	TLearn	SLearn_constr	TLearn_constr	Comparison
0.5	1000	0.056 (0.028)	0.151 (0.044)	**0.039 (0.022)**	0.133 (0.035)	0.692 (0.787)
	500	0.082 (0.049)	0.22 (0.064)	**0.059 (0.033)**	0.194 (0.051)	0.714 (0.704)
1	1000	0.067 (0.046)	0.272 (0.078)	**0.052 (0.035)**	0.257 (0.077)	0.774 (0.762)
	500	0.092 (0.076)	0.39 (0.128)	**0.08 (0.065)**	0.357 (0.108)	0.878 (0.858)
2	1000	0.045 (0.075)	0.788 (0.267)	**0.036 (0.045)**	0.735 (0.271)	0.796 (0.612)
	500	0.102 (0.112)	1.076 (0.365)	**0.098 (0.105)**	1.056 (0.395)	0.961 (0.942)
4	1000	0.121 (0.141)	2.073 (0.742)	**0.111 (0.134)**	2.004 (0.783)	0.914 (0.942)
	500	0.244 (0.279)	3.069 (1.151)	**0.216 (0.262)**	3.042 (1.097)	0.882 (0.94)

Table 5. Scenario 4

Noise	NSamples	SLearn	TLearn	SLearn_constr	TLearn_constr	Comparison
0.5	1000	0.095 (0.021)	0.07 (0.015)	0.293 (0.017)	**0.064 (0.014)**	0.909 (0.982)
	500	0.148 (0.037)	0.1 (0.023)	0.317 (0.03)	**0.095 (0.024)**	0.951 (1.067)
1	1000	0.174 (0.042)	0.151 (0.045)	0.329 (0.03)	**0.135 (0.035)**	0.896 (0.718)
	500	0.257 (0.062)	0.211 (0.058)	0.364 (0.043)	**0.198 (0.057)**	0.94 (0.788)
2	1000	**0.385 (0.092)**	0.508 (0.181)	0.418 (0.048)	0.499 (0.186)	1.087 (0.539)
	500	**0.435 (0.094)**	0.647 (0.255)	0.459 (0.074)	0.606 (0.234)	1.055 (0.793)
4	1000	**0.485 (0.101)**	1.211 (0.503)	0.501 (0.091)	1.222 (0.494)	1.033 (0.925)
	500	**0.529 (0.128)**	1.756 (0.86)	0.533 (0.124)	1.695 (0.86)	1.008 (0.978)

5.4 Application to RealCause Datasets (with Causal Discovery)

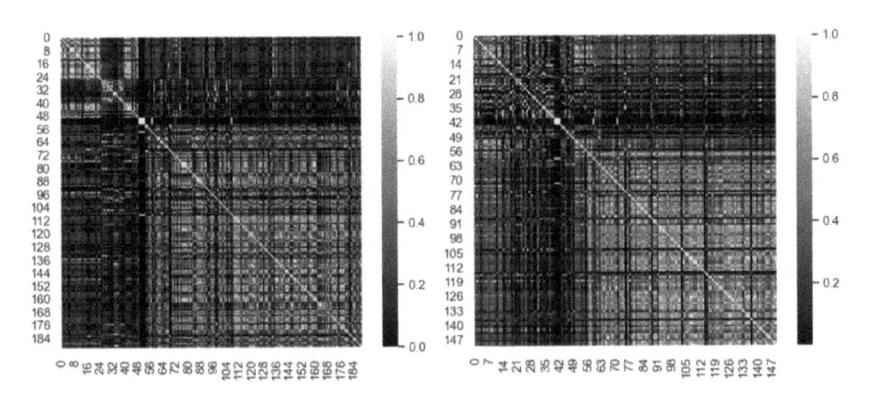

Fig. 7. Heatmaps of the correlations of the individual prediction trees for the constrained gradient boosting algorithms. On the left, the Lalonde psid dataset, on the right, the Lalonde cps dataset. The constraints used in the particular models in these plots are discovered using the notears algorithm

We use the data generated in [14] to test the method in a realistic benchmark. The generated data corresponds a semi-synthetic version of the datasets *lalonde cps* and *lalonde psid*.

There is no causal graph for these datasets, so we use causal discovery to obtain one. It's important to note that our approach relies on the correctness of the causal graph, so errors in causal discovery can directly affect the performance of the constrained models. We use the NOTEARS [33], PC [9], GES [5] and ICALiNGAM [25] algorithms, which are implemented using the CausalNex [2] and gCastle [32] python packages (Tables 6 and 7).

Table 6. RealCause datasets - Lalonde PSID

Algorithm	Ges	icalingam	notears	pc
SLearn	4.64e8 (1.62e8)	4.71e8 (1.72e8)	4.61e8 (8.15e7)	4.72e8 (1.20e8)
TLearn	2.23e8 (7.33e7)	2.19e8 (5.46e7)	**2.18e8 (4.81e7)**	2.13e8 (5.72e7)
SLearn_constr	4.52e8 (7.72e7)	4.67e8 (1.04e8)	4.61e8 (7.92e7)	4.59e8 (8.02e7)
TLearn_constr	**2.12e8 (3.77e7)**	**2.18e8 (5.25e7)**	2.20e8 (6.70e7)	**2.10e8 (4.21e7)**
Comparison	0.954 (0.515)	0.998 (0.96)	1.011 (1.392)	0.984 (0.736)

Table 7. RealCause datasets - Lalonde CPS

Algorithm	ges	icalingam	notears	pc
SLearn	1.60e8 (2.96e7)	1.60e8 (2.85e7)	1.57e8 (2.89e7)	1.64e8 (2.71e7)
TLearn	**9.06e7 (9.59e6)**	9.05e7 (8.97e6)	9.09e7 (9.41e6)	8.95e7 (7.98e6)
SLearn_constr	1.68e8 (2.78e7)	1.40e8 (2.10e7)	1.52e8 (2.53e7)	1.57e8 (2.10e7)
TLearn_constr	9.09e7 (9.07e6)	**8.90e7 (7.96e6)**	**9.05e7 (8.12e6)**	**8.92e7 (7.15e6)**
Comparison	1.003 (0.946)	0.983 (0.887)	0.996 (0.863)	0.997 (0.896)

5.5 Experiments Discussion

We applied our method to the illustrative dataset and the synthetic and semisynthetic datasets. The results show that the method performs as expected in different settings. In the illustrative dataset, the models that incorporate the causal constraints have a clear advantage over the models that do not. In the synthetic datasets, we observe that the unconstrained models perform better in scenario 2, which simulates a randomized controlled trial where the treatment is independent of the other covariates. However, in the other scenarios where the treatment is correlated with some covariates, the constrained models have a higher performance than the unconstrained models. In the semisynthetic datasets, despite the possible errors in the causal graph discovery, the constrained models still slightly outperform the unconstrained models.

6 Conclusion

In this paper, we presented a novel approach to introduce constraints into tree-based predictive models by exploiting information from the causal graph associated with the dataset. We then used these constrained models for CATE estimation in different settings and compared them with their unconstrained counterparts. In several experiments under different conditions, we showed that the constrained models outperform the unconstrained ones with higher accuracy and lower performance variability, and that it is possible to use the method even when the causal graph is unknown by using causal discovery algorithms.

The results in this paper open new research opportunities related to exploiting the information encoded in the causal graph:

- Extend the method to work on other, non tree-based, algorithms.
- Explore applications of the constrained models other than CATE estimation.
- Explore other ways to incorporate Causal Graph information into models.
- Explore the use of Causal Discovery and its impact on the performance of the method.

Acknowledgements. This research was funded by an Industrial Doctorate grant 2021 DI 41 of AGAUR (Generalitat de Catalunya) between Universitat de Barcelona and Zenital and PID2022-136436-NB-100, 2021SGR01104 grants.

Ethical Statement. There are no direct ethical implications associated with this research.

References

1. Ahmed, O., et al.: Causalworld: A robotic manipulation benchmark for causal structure and transfer learning. arXiv preprint arXiv:2010.04296 (2020)
2. Beaumont, P., et al.: CausalNex (10 2021). https://github.com/quantumblacklabs/causalnex
3. Bergstra, J., Komer, B., Eliasmith, C., Yamins, D., Cox, D.D.: Hyperopt: a python library for model selection and hyperparameter optimization. Comput. Sci. Discov. **8**(1), 014008 (2015)
4. Chen, T., Guestrin, C.: XGBoost: A scalable tree boosting system. In: Proceedings of the 22nd ACM SIGKDD International Conference on Knowledge Discovery and Data Mining, pp. 785–794. KDD '16, ACM, New York, NY, USA (2016). https://doi.org/10.1145/2939672.2939785, http://doi.acm.org/10.1145/2939672.2939785
5. Chickering, D.M.: Optimal structure identification with greedy search. J. Mach. Learn. Res. **3**(Nov), 507–554 (2002)
6. Goyal, A., Bengio, Y.: Inductive biases for deep learning of higher-level cognition. Proc. Royal Society A **478**(2266), 20210068 (2022)
7. Goyal, K., Dumancic, S., Blockeel, H.: Feature interactions in xgboost. arXiv preprint arXiv:2007.05758 (2020)
8. Kaddour, J., Lynch, A., Liu, Q., Kusner, M.J., Silva, R.: Causal machine learning: A survey and open problems. arXiv preprint arXiv:2206.15475 (2022)
9. Kalisch, M., Bühlman, P.: Estimating high-dimensional directed acyclic graphs with the pc-algorithm. J. Mach. Learn. Res. **8**(3) (2007)
10. Koller, D., Friedman, N.: Probabilistic graphical models: principles and techniques. MIT press (2009)
11. Künzel, S.R., Sekhon, J.S., Bickel, P.J., Yu, B.: Metalearners for estimating heterogeneous treatment effects using machine learning. Proc. Natl. Acad. Sci. **116**(10), 4156–4165 (2019)
12. Maragoudakis, M., Serpanos, D.: Towards stock market data mining using enriched random forests from textual resources and technical indicators. In: Artificial Intelligence Applications and Innovations: 6th IFIP WG 12.5 International Conference, AIAI 2010, Larnaca, Cyprus, October 6-7, 2010. Proceedings 6, pp. 278–286. Springer (2010)
13. Neal, B.: Introduction to causal inference (2015)

14. Neal, B., Huang, C.W., Raghupathi, S.: Realcause: Realistic causal inference benchmarking. arXiv preprint arXiv:2011.15007 (2020)
15. Nie, X., Wager, S.: Quasi-oracle estimation of heterogeneous treatment effects. Biometrika **108**(2), 299–319 (2021)
16. Parafita, Á., Vitrià, J.: Estimand-agnostic causal query estimation with deep causal graphs. IEEE Access **10**, 71370–71386 (2022)
17. Pearl, J.: Probabilistic reasoning in intelligent systems: networks of plausible inference. Morgan kaufmann (1988)
18. Pearl, J.: Bayesian analysis in expert systems: comment: graphical models, causality and intervention. Stat. Sci. **8**(3), 266–269 (1993)
19. Pearl, J.: Causality. Cambridge university press (2009)
20. Pearl, J.: The seven tools of causal inference, with reflections on machine learning. Commun. ACM **62**(3), 54–60 (2019)
21. Peters, J., Janzing, D., Schölkopf, B.: Elements of causal inference: foundations and learning algorithms. The MIT Press (2017)
22. Schölkopf, B., Locatello, F., Bauer, S., Ke, N.R., Kalchbrenner, N., Goyal, A., Bengio, Y.: Toward causal representation learning. Proc. IEEE **109**(5), 612–634 (2021)
23. Shalit, U., Johansson, F.D., Sontag, D.: Estimating individual treatment effect: generalization bounds and algorithms. In: International Conference on Machine Learning, pp. 3076–3085. PMLR (2017)
24. Shi, C., Blei, D., Veitch, V.: Adapting neural networks for the estimation of treatment effects. In: Advances in Neural Information Processing Systems, vol. 32 (2019)
25. Shimizu, S., Hoyer, P.O., Hyvärinen, A., Kerminen, A., Jordan, M.: A linear non-gaussian acyclic model for causal discovery. J. Mach. Learn. Res. **7**(10) (2006)
26. Shwartz-Ziv, R., Armon, A.: Tabular data: deep learning is not all you need. Inform. Fusion **81**, 84–90 (2022)
27. Subbaswamy, A., Chen, B., Saria, S.: A unifying causal framework for analyzing dataset shift-stable learning algorithms. J. Causal Inference **10**(1), 64–89 (2022)
28. Tesei, G., Giampanis, S., Shi, J., Norgeot, B.: Learning end-to-end patient representations through self-supervised covariate balancing for causal treatment effect estimation. J. Biomed. Inform. **140**, 104339 (2023)
29. Yu, K., et al.: Causality-based feature selection: methods and evaluations. ACM Comput. Surv. (CSUR) **53**(5), 1–36 (2020)
30. Yu, K., Wu, X., Ding, W., Mu, Y., Wang, H.: Markov blanket feature selection using representative sets. IEEE Trans. Neural Netw. Learn. Syst. **28**(11), 2775–2788 (2016)
31. Zeng, S., Bayir, M.A., Pfeiffer III, J.J., Charles, D., Kiciman, E.: Causal transfer random forest: Combining logged data and randomized experiments for robust prediction. In: Proceedings of the 14th ACM International Conference on Web Search and Data Mining, pp. 211–219 (2021)
32. Zhang, K., et al.: gcastle: A python toolbox for causal discovery. arXiv preprint arXiv:2111.15155 (2021)
33. Zheng, X., Aragam, B., Ravikumar, P.K., Xing, E.P.: Dags with no tears: Continuous optimization for structure learning. In: Advances in Neural Information Processing Systems, vol. 31 (2018)

A Parameter-Free Bayesian Framework for Uplift Modeling Application on Telecom Data

Mina Rafla[1,2]($\boxtimes$), Nicolas Voisine[1], and Bruno Crémilleux[2]

[1] Orange Labs, 22300 Lannion, France
{mina.rafla,nicolas.voisine}@orange.com
[2] UNICAEN, ENSICAEN, CNRS - UMR GREYC, Normandie Univ,
14000 Caen, France
bruno.cremilleux@unicaen.fr

Abstract. Uplift modeling is a predictive technique designed to identify individuals whose behaviour may be influenced by a particular treatment. This approach is very useful in several applications such as telecommunication data or personalized medicine, as it allows targeting the specific proportion of a population on which the treatment will have the greatest impact. This differs from supervised learning algorithms, which focus primarily on predicting outcomes, as uplift models are designed to predict the causal effect of a treatment on the outcome. Several uplift modeling algorithms have been developed in the literature [21]. A common limitation of these methods is their reliance on the user to set parameters. Meta-learners, a family of uplift methods, are even more complex since they require the user to select a machine learning algorithm to be used. In this paper, we present a unified view of a user-parameter-free Bayesian framework for uplift modeling, which is applied to data discretization, feature selection, decision trees and random forests. The various components of our framework are implemented in a new Python package called Kuplift, evaluated on real telecom data, and their performance compared to state-of-the-art uplift modeling algorithms.

1 Introduction

Uplift Modeling measures the impact of an treatment (marketing, medical) on a person's behavior. This is useful for decision-makers because it helps them to identify the groups that will be most positively affected by these treatments. As a result, they can increase their profits while minimising their marketing budget. A major difficulty is that data are only partially known: it is impossible to know for an individual whether the chosen treatment is optimal because its responses to alternative treatments cannot be observed. However, uplift can be empirically estimated by considering two groups: a treatment group (the ones with a treatment) and a control group (without treatment). The goal of uplift modeling is to estimate the conditional average treatment effect, which is the difference between the outcome estimation in the treatment and control groups.

There is a wide range of uplift methods [21] such as meta-learners and direct approaches. Meta-learners are a set of algorithms that use traditional supervised learning algorithms for uplift estimation. These include the Two-Model Approach [7], the X-learner [10], the R-learner [12] and the DR-learner [9]. On the other hand, direct approaches are a set of algorithms specifically designed for uplift modeling like uplift decision trees [17], causal forests [20], and deep learning based approaches [11,22].

The main drawback of all these approaches is that they require parameters to be set. Meta learners also present an additional requirement, which is the choice of the machine learning algorithm to be used. All of this is a clear limitation for non-machine learning experts to use these tools. Even for machine learning experts, they need to test different parameter values and different learning algorithms with meta learners to find the optimal combination that fits the data at hand. That is why parameter-free uplift modeling algorithms are needed. In a previous work [15], we introduced a Bayesian parameter-free approach to uplift discretisation and feature selection (respectively UMODL discretization and UMODL-FS). More recently [14] we proposed a novel parameter-free uplift decision tree algorithm, the Uplift Bayesian Decision Tree (UB-DT). We also presented its extension to random forests, introducing the Uplift Bayesian Random Forest (UB-RF) algorithm.

In this paper, we present a unified view of our Bayesian approach and its application to discretisation, feature selection and decision trees. We evaluate our approaches on real telecom data and compare them with state-of-the-art approaches. We implemented the presented approaches in a new Python package called Kuplift[1].

The rest of the paper is organised as follows. Section 2 provides an introduction to telecom data and how uplift modeling can be performed to deal with it. Section 3 introduces MDL approach and Sect. 4 presents our Uplift Bayesian framework and its components: UMODL discretisation, UMODL FS, UB-DT and UB-RF. We also show how these approaches can be applied to categorical data. Finally, we present our evaluation experiments in Sect. 5. Section 6 concludes.

2 Uplift Methodology

Telecom data refers to the vast amount of information generated and collected by telecommunication companies through their network infrastructure, customer interactions, and billing systems. This data includes various dimensions, customer demographics, usage patterns, call records, service subscriptions, customer interactions and billing information. Leveraging this wealth of telecom data can provide valuable insights into customer behavior and churn prediction, thereby enabling telecom companies to proactively manage customer retention strategies.

Uplift modeling is a technique used to identify and target customers who are most likely to respond positively to a specific marketing intervention. It helps

---
[1] https://github.com/UData-Orange/kuplift.

determine which customers are likely to be influenced by a marketing campaign and would not have made a purchase or taken any action otherwise. To apply uplift modeling using telecom data, the following steps can be followed:

- Outcome Definition. The outcome variable needs to be defined based on the marketing goal. For example, it could be whether a customer made a purchase or renewed their subscription within a specific time period after receiving the treatment. This outcome will be used to measure the uplift.
- Treatment Assignment. A group of customers needs to be exposed to a marketing treatment, while another group serves as a control group that does not receive the treatment. The treatment can be a specific marketing campaign, promotional offer, or any other intervention. Uplift is then modeled from the data of 2 groups.
- Data Preparation. The telecom data needs to be preprocessed and prepared for uplift modeling. This includes cleaning the data, handling missing values, and transforming variables into a suitable format. Data bias should also be addressed either at this step using propensity score matching or in the next step of model learning.
- Uplift model learning. The model predicts the uplift score, which represents the difference in the probability of a positive outcome between the treatment and control groups.
- Model Evaluation. The uplift model needs to be evaluated using appropriate metrics. These metrics help assess the model's performance in identifying customers who are most likely to respond positively to the marketing treatment.
- Targeting and Decision Making. Once the uplift model is built and evaluated, it can be used to target customers for the marketing intervention. The model can identify customers who have a high likelihood of being positively influenced by the treatment. These customers can then be prioritized for the marketing campaign, maximizing the impact and return on investment.
- Iterative Refinement. Uplift modeling is an iterative process. The model's performance should be continuously monitored and refined based on the observed outcomes. This helps improve the targeting strategy and optimize the uplift achieved from the marketing interventions.

3 Preliminaries: Bayesian Framework

The MDL (Minimum Description Length Principle) Principle [16] is derived from Shannon's information theory [18] and allows finding the simplest model that best describes the data. The MDL principle is used to select the best model, among a family of models, by taking into account the complexity of the models and the complexity of the data according to the model. According to the MDL principle, the best model M that describes the data D is the model with the minimum description length $L(M, D)$, s.t. $L(M, D) = L(M) + L(D|M)$, where $L(M)$ is the model's description length and $L(D|M)$ is the description length of the data encoded by the model.

The MODL (Minimum Optimized Description Length) [1] approach is a non-parametric *Bayesian approach* for discretization and conditional probability estimation, based on *the Minimum Description Length (MDL)* principle. Let us first introduce the link between a Bayesian and a MDL model selection problem.

A Bayesian Approach for Model Selection. From a Bayesian perspective, the best model M, among a family of models, is found by maximizing the posterior probability $P(M|D)$, i.e., to find the one that is most likely given the data. Using Bayes rule, maximizing $P(M|D)$, while taking into account that $P(D)$ is constant for all the candidate models, is equivalent to maximizing the product of the prior and the posterior probabilities: $P(M)P(D|M)$.

A MDL Approach for Model Selection. The previous approach can also be seen from an information theory perspective by using the MDL approach [16]. As previously mentioned, the goal of the MDL approach is to select the model with the minimal description length $L(M|D)$. Replacing the previously introduced probabilities by their negative log, allows interpreting them as Shannon's code length [18], s.t.: $-\log P(M|D)$ corresponds to $L(M|D)$.

The MODL approach comes to apply the concept of model selection to different types of models, like discretization [1], decision trees [19] and pattern mining [5].

4 The UMODL Approach

The MODL approach is not suitable for uplift modeling since the uplift problem deals with two treatment groups and the estimation of the conditional probabilities of the outcome variable Y given an attribute X also depends on the treatment variable T. That is why we introduce UMODL (Uplift Minimum Optimised Description Length). UMODL defines a space of models and a prior distribution. From this model space, a Bayesian optimal evaluation criterion is defined. A search algorithm is then used to find the model with the optimal criterion. In the following sections, we show how to apply the UMODL approach for uplift discretization, feature selection and decision trees.

4.1 The UMODL Discretization Approach

From a Bayesian perspective, we can find the optimal uplift discretization model, represented by M, given a set of data, denoted by D. This is achieved by maximizing the posterior probability of the model conditioned on the data, expressed as $P(M|D)$. Maximizing $P(M|D)$ implies maximizing the product of the prior and the likelihood $P(M)P(D|M)$. The evaluation criterion $C(M)$ which is the cost of an uplift discretization model M is defined by taking the negative log of the posterior probability. This turns the maximization problem to a minimization one.

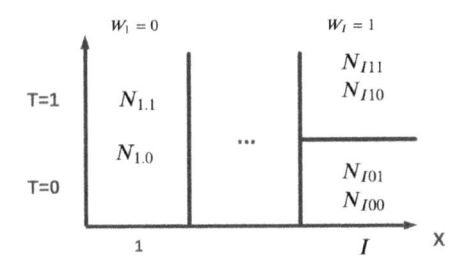

Fig. 1. Parameters of an uplift discretization model. The presence of a treatment effect ($W_i = 1$) in interval i requires describing the distribution of the outcome variable Y separately for each treatment (part right). In contrast, the absence of a treatment effect ($W_i = 0$) indicates to consider the distribution of the outcome variable Y for the interval i independently of the treatment variable (part left).

To define the prior distribution of model parameters $P(M)$, we first exploit the hierarchy of parameters of a model. The parameter hierarchy implies that the parameters are chosen in a certain order. Each type of model has its own set of parameters and its own hierarchy, e.g. the parameters of an uplift discretization model (presented hereafter) are different from the parameters of a decision tree model (see Sect. 4.3).

How to Define. M? We define M by:

- the number of intervals I,
- the bounds of the intervals (the number of individuals in each interval i) denoted $\{N_i\}$,
- the presence or absence of a treatment effect, denoted by the boolean parameter $\{W_i\}$,
- class frequencies per interval $\{N_{i.j}\}_{W_i=0}$ or for each treatment per interval $\{N_{itj}\}_{W_i=1}$, where N_{itj} corresponds to the number of examples in each interval i with treatment t and class value j.

In other words, a model M is defined by the following parameters (cf. Fig. 1):

$$\{I, \{N_i\}, \{W_i\}, \{N_{i.j}\}_{W_i=0}, \{N_{itj}\}_{W_i=1}\}$$

These parameters are exploited according to a particular hierarchy when defining the prior distribution of M denoted $P(M)$. Next we will discuss the details of this parameter hierarchy and the basis for defining the prior distribution.

How to Define the Prior Distribution? To define the prior distribution of the model parameters $P(M)$:

- We first exploit the *hierarchy of the parameters* of a discretization model. This hierarchy requires the parameters to be selected in a particular order.

First, we determine the number of intervals I, followed by the location of these I intervals or boundaries. Next, we determine whether each interval contains a treatment effect or not (expressed by the boolean parameter W_i). Finally, based on W_i, the outcome distribution is decided to be either the outcome variable's distribution for the interval or the distribution of the outcome variable for each treatment within the interval.

- Next, we assume the ***independence of the distributions across intervals***. This assumption is based on the *IID hypothesis* [3]. This assumption enables the evaluation of the model's prior and the likelihood as a product of multiple terms (Eq. 1 and Eq. 2)[2]. By taking the negative logarithm, the prior can be assessed as the sum of these terms, as illustrated in the UMODL criterion in Eq. 3.

Using the two components above, the prior distribution and the likelihood can be defined as follows (resp. Eq. 1 and Eq. 2):

$$P(M) = P(I) \times P(\{N_i\}|I) \times$$
$$\prod_i P(W_i|I) \left[(1-W_i) \times P(\{N_{i.j}\}|I, \{N_i\}) + W_i \times \prod_t P(\{N_{itj}\}|I, \{N_{it.}\}) \right] \quad (1)$$

$$P(D|M) = \prod_i P(D_i|M)$$
$$= \prod_i \left[(1-W_i) \times \frac{1}{(N_i!/N_{i.1}!..N_{i.J}!)} + W_i \times \prod_t \frac{1}{(N_{it.}!/N_{it1}!..N_{itJ}!)} \right] \quad (2)$$

- Finally, we assume a ***uniform distribution at each stage of this hierarchy***. In other words, we assume that
    1. The number of intervals I is equally likely to be any value between 1 and N.
    2. Given the number of intervals I, each possible way of dividing the data into I intervals has an equal probability.
    3. There is an equal probability that an interval i contains a treatment effect or not. Therefore, the value of the term W_i has an equal chance of being either 1 or 0.
    4. Given an interval i and the value of W_i, every distribution of the class values in the interval is equiprobable, or alternatively, every distribution of the class values for each treatment in the interval is equiprobable.

Using the uniform distribution assumption and by taking the negative log of product of the prior and the likelihood, we express $C(M)$ in terms of the parameters of an uplift discretization model and obtain Eq. 3:

---

[2] For the details of the prior and the likelihood please refer to [15].

$$C(M) = \log N + \log \binom{N+I-1}{I-1} + I \times \log 2$$

$$+ \sum_{i=1}^{I}(1-W_i)\log\binom{N_i+J-1}{J-1} + \underbrace{\sum_{i=1}^{I}(1-W_i)\log\frac{N_i!}{N_{i.1}!..N_{i.J}!}}_{Likelihood} \quad (3)$$

$$+ \sum_{i=1}^{I} W_i \sum_t \log\binom{N_{it.}+J-1}{J-1} + \underbrace{\sum_{i=1}^{I} W_i \sum_t \log\frac{N_{it.}!}{N_{it1}!..N_{itJ}!}}_{Likelihood}$$

A greedy search algorithm is then used to find the optimal uplift discretization from a Bayesian perspective, with the minimal value of $C(M)$.

4.2 UMODL Feature Selection (UMODL-FS)

As previously discussed in Sect. 2, the telecommunications sector collects significant amounts of data (containing hundreds to thousands of features) derived from services such as mobile internet, home internet, SMS and phone calls. This data contains a significant amount of noise and irrelevant features, which can cause significant challenges for supervised machine learning models. That is why a feature selection approach is necessary to increase model efficiency.

The UMODL discretization method can be used to derive a feature selection technique, named UMODL-FS. The UMODL-FS is a filter feature selection technique [23]. It calculates the importance of a feature X by first discretizing it using the UMODL discretization approach. The discretization technique results in a number of intervals that separate the different treatment effects in a variable space. The method then computes an importance score for X, denoted $imp.s(X)$. This is achieved by calculating the summed Euclidean distances between the outcome distributions within the treatment and control groups over the intervals found. Formally,

$$imp.s(X) = \begin{cases} \sum_{i=1}^{I} \frac{N_i}{N} D(p_i : q_i), & \text{if } I > 1 \\ 0, & \text{otherwise .} \end{cases} \quad (4)$$

where the distribution divergence measure D is the squared euclidean distance.

4.3 UB-DT and UB-RF

Our Bayesian approach can also be applied to create uplift decision trees [14]. Again, the goal of our Bayesian approach is to find the most probable uplift decision tree $\mathbb{T}$ given the data i.e. the one that maximizes $P(\mathbb{T}|D)$. A global evaluation criterion $C(\mathbb{T})$ is then derived by taking the negative log of $P(\mathbb{T}|D)$. Similar to the UMODL discretization, UB-DT (Uplift Bayesian Decision Tree) is made up of two ingredients: the global criterion $C(\mathbb{T})$ and a tree search algorithm to search for the most optimal tree according to $C(\mathbb{T})$.

Hereafter, we start by presenting the structure and the parameters of $\mathbb{T}$. Then we describe the new global criterion for an uplift decision tree and the search algorithm. Finally we show how the approach is straightforwardly extended to random forests.

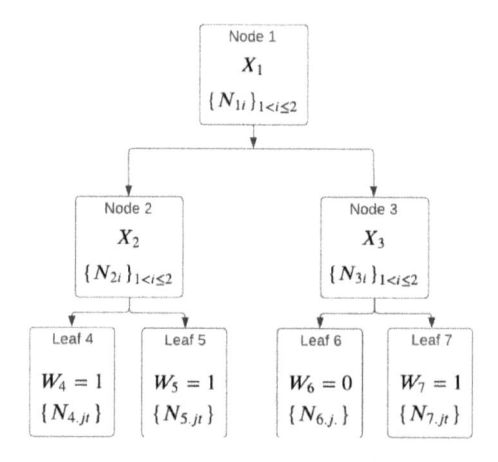

Fig. 2. Example of an uplift tree model. Internal nodes are described by the segmentation variable X_s and the distribution of instances in each of the two children $\{N_{si}\}$. Leaf nodes containing a treatment effect (i.e. $W_l = 1$) are described by the class distribution for each treatment. This applies to leaves 4, 5 and 7. Leaf nodes containing no treatment effect (i.e. $W_l = 0$) are only described by the class distribution (this is the case of leaf 6).

Parameters of an Uplift Tree Model. We define a binary uplift decision tree model $\mathbb{T}$ by its structure and the distribution of instances and class values in this structure. The structure of $\mathbb{T}$ consists of the set of internal nodes $\mathbb{S}_{\mathbb{T}}$ and the set of leaf nodes $\mathbb{L}_{\mathbb{T}}$. The distribution of the instances in this structure is described by the partition of the segmentation variable X_s for each internal node s, the class frequency in each leaf node where there is no treatment effect, and the class frequency on each treatment in the leaf nodes with a treatment effect. More precisely, $\mathbb{T}$ is defined by:

- the subset of variables $\mathbb{K}_{\mathbb{T}}$ used by model $\mathbb{T}$. This includes the number of the selected variables $K_{\mathbb{T}}$ and their choice among a set of $\mathbb{K}$ variables provided in a dataset, we note $K = |\mathbb{K}|$.
- a binary variable I_n indicating the choice of whether each node n is an internal node ($I_n = 1$) or a leaf node ($I_n = 0$).
- the distribution of instances in each internal node s, which is described by the segmentation variable X_s of the node s and how the instances of s are distributed on its two child nodes.

- a binary variable W_l indicating for each leaf node l if there is a treatment effect ($W_l = 1$) or not ($W_l = 0$). If $W_l = 0$, l is described by the distribution of the output values $\{N_{l.j.}\}_{1 \leq j \leq J}$, where $N_{l.j.}$ is the number of instances of output value j in leaf l. If $W_l = 1$, l is described by the distribution of the class values per treatment $\{N_{l.jt}\}_{1 \leq j \leq J, 1 \leq t \leq 2}$, where $N_{l.jt}$ is the number of instances of output value j and treatment t in leaf l.

How to Define the Prior Distribution. $P(\mathbb{T})$? To define the prior distribution of a tree model $\mathbb{T}$, we first exploit the hierarchy of the presented uplift tree parameters. This hierarchy describes the dependence relationships between parameters. The hierarchy of the tree model is described from the root node to its children and recursively to the leaves. We also assume the independence of the distribution of the outcome values between children nodes. This assumption allows the prior of the model to be evaluated as a product of several terms. Taking the negative log, the prior can be evaluated as the sum of these terms (cf. Eq. 5). Furthermore, we assume a uniform distribution of parameters at every stage of the hierarchy.

A Bayesian Evaluation Criterion for Uplift Decision Trees. Using the components of the prior term described above (the parameter hierarchy, the uniform distribution assumption and the independence assumption), we show next the global evaluation criterion for an uplift decision tree. Combining the prior term $P(\mathbb{T})$ and using the likelihood terms on the tree leaves, we express the negative log of the posterior probability, our criterion $C(\mathbb{T})$, as follows (cf. Eq. 5):

$$C(\mathbb{T}) = \underbrace{\log(K+1) + \log\binom{K+K_{\mathbb{T}}-1}{K_{\mathbb{T}}}}_{\text{Variable selection}}$$

$$+ \underbrace{\sum_{s \in \mathbb{S}_{\mathbb{T}_n}} \log 2 + \log K_{\mathbb{T}} + \log(N_{s.} + 1)}_{\text{Prior of internal nodes}} + \underbrace{\sum_{l \in \mathbb{L}_{\mathbb{T}}} \log 2}_{\text{Treatment effect W}}$$

$$+ \underbrace{\sum_{l \in \mathbb{L}_{\mathbb{T}}} \log 2 + \sum_{l \in \mathbb{L}_{\mathbb{T}}} (1-W_l) \log \binom{N_{l.} + J - 1}{J - 1} + \sum_{l \in \mathbb{L}_{\mathbb{T}}} W_l \sum_{t} \log \binom{N_{l..t} + J - 1}{J - 1}}_{\text{Prior of leaf nodes}}$$

$$+ \underbrace{\sum_{l \in \mathbb{L}_{\mathbb{T}}} (1-W_l) \log \frac{N_{l.}!}{N_{l.1.}! N_{l.2.}! \ldots N_{l.J.}!} + \sum_{l \in \mathbb{L}_{\mathbb{T}}} W_l \sum_{t} \log \frac{N_{l..t}!}{N_{l.1t}! \ldots N_{l.Jt}!}}_{\text{Tree Likelihood}}$$

(5)

where N_s, N_{si}, N_l and $N_{l..t}$ designate the number of instances in node s, in the ith child of node s, in the leaf l and treatment t in leaf l.

Search Algorithm. A tree search algorithm selects the best tree according to the global criterion. The algorithm, detailed in [14], chooses a split among all possible splits in all terminal nodes only if it minimises the global criterion of the tree. The algorithm continues as long as the global criterion is improved. To extend the search algorithm for random forests, a split is chosen at random from all possible splits that improve the global criterion.

4.4 How to Deal with Categorical Variables?

So far we had described the discretization, feature selection and decision trees algorithms in the context of continuous attributes as this type of data requires discretization when performing density estimation.

However, categorical variables often exists in the data, which can be considered as grouped information covering categories such as job type, phone type, and subscription type, among others. When dealing with categorical variables, the objective shifts from discretizing them to performing value grouping. In other words, given a categorical variable, the goal is to group the values of the variable that have similar behaviour: either the same outcome distribution or the same treatment effect.

Our idea is to transform categorical variables to numerical ones then to perform a discretization using UMODL. However an unsupervised encoding assigns a random ranking to categorical values, which is often not optimal. Therefore our solution is to encode categorical variable in ascending order of uplift values (since it conveys similar behaviour) before using UMODL.

5 Experiments

In this section, we conduct different experiments to evaluate our Bayesian approaches on real data, specifically derived from Orange marketing campaigns conducted in 2013 (data specifications are shown in Table 1). The original Orange dataset contains 2700 variables. However, for the purpose of efficient computation, we have selected a subset of this dataset using Khiops software[3], keeping only 101 variables. We also added 50 noise variables to this dataset to better evaluate the feature selection approaches.

First, we compare our uplift Bayesian decision trees and random forests versus the state-of-art uplift modeling algorithms. We then evaluate the impact of UMODL discretization and feature selection as preprocessing steps on these state-of-the-art uplift modeling algorithms.

5.1 UB-DT and UB-RF

In this part, we conduct a study to evaluate the performance of the UB-DT and UB-RF algorithms on our dataset. We also compare their performance with the

---

[3] https://www.khiops.com/.

Table 1. Data specifications

Size	P(Y = 1 T = 0)	P(Y = 1 T = 1)	P(T = 1)	No. columns	No. continuous variables
20000	0.13	0.35	0.89	151	44

state-of-art uplift modeling algorithms. More particularly, we evaluate the following algorithms: 1. X-learner 2. R-learner 3. DR-learner 4. Two model approach 5. Random forest algorithm based on the ED criterion 6. UB-RF 7. UB-DT. Each of the X-learner, R-learner, DR-learner and the Two model approach was used with a random forest algorithm and a logistic regression as base models. All random forests are learnt using 100 trees. Each model is learnt using a 10-fold cross validation. We use the qini metric [4, 13] to evaluate the uplift models. The higher the qini value, the larger the impact of the predicted optimal treatment.

Results. Figure 3 shows the qini curves [4] for each model, aggregating data from all test folds. The corresponding qini values are given in Table 2. Looking at the results, we see that UB-RF (shown in pale pink color) outperforms all other uplift modeling algorithms. Even a single decision tree with the UB-DT approach shows remarkable efficiency and competes well with other methods.

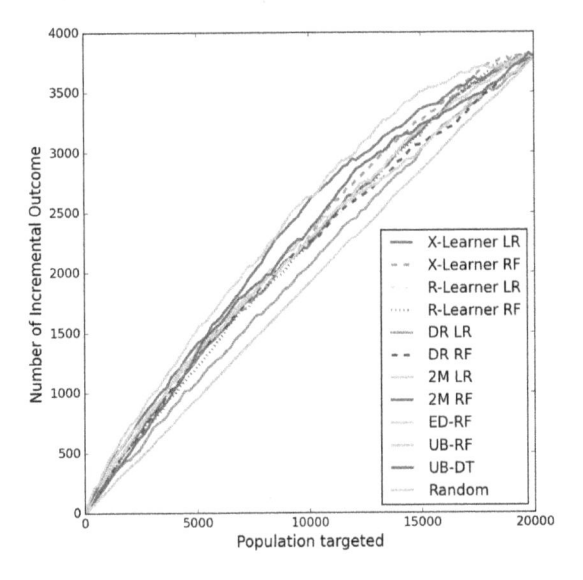

Fig. 3. Qini curves: The x-axis denotes the number of individuals targeted, while the y-axis shows the number of incremental positive outcomes.

Table 2. Qini values multiplied by 100 and variance for each uplift model. In bold the biggest qini value.

X-learner		R-learner		DR-learner		2M				
LR	RF	LR	RF	LR	RF	LR	RF	ED-RF	UB-RF	UB-DT
8.6(2.6)	10.1(3.4)	8.8(2.5)	8.2(2.0)	4.0(4.6)	7.4(4.0)	7.9(2.5)	13.3(5.6)	9.6(3.0)	**15.9(5.2)**	10.2(3.6)

5.2 Variable Transformation

This section demonstrates the impact of employing a variable transformation with the UMODL discretization as an initial preprocessing step. When the UMODL discretization is applied to a non-informative variable, the result is a single interval, i.e. the transformed variable follows a uniform distribution for all examples. In such cases, UMODL discretization discards this variable. Consequently, the process of transforming variables can be seen as inherently involving a feature selection step.

We carry out our experiments in three stages: the first with the original variables, the second with only a feature selection step, and the third with the variable transformation incorporated as a preprocessing step. As just mentioned, it should be noted that this third stage is considered to combine both feature selection and transformation. Again the model is built using a 10-fold cross-validation approach.

Results. Table 3 presents the performance of uplift modeling algorithms under three distinct scenarios: 1. without any preprocessing step (i.e. original variables) 2. with UMODL-FS as a preprocessing step 3. with variable transformation as a preprocessing step. The results indicate that feature selection significantly improves the performance of all uplift modeling algorithms compared to the original dataset (without any preprocessing). Applying variable transformation yields similar improvements for all uplift modeling algorithms, with the exception of ED-RF. When comparing the impact of feature selection and variable transformation, the benefits appear to depend on the uplift approach used. For example, when logistic regression is used as the base learner, variable transformation appears to offer better improvements. In the contrary, when random forests are used as the base learner, feature selection shows to perform better.

By performing feature selection and variable transformation, the state-of-the-art uplift models achieved the best results, close to those obtained with UB-RF (see Table 2). The two-model approach with random forests even showed the best performance when accompanied by UMODL-FS for feature selection.

5.3 Feature Selection

We evaluate the following feature selection methods: ED, LR filter, F filter and UMODL-FS. Each feature selection method gives a score to each variable in the data. The principle of the experiment is to feed the top-k features selected by

Table 3. Qini values and variance (multiplied by 100) for each uplift model. In bold the biggest qini value among all the values.

	XLearner		RLearner		DR		2M		
	LR	RF	LR	RF	LR	RF	LR	RF	ED-RF
w/o preprocessing	8.6(2.6)	10.1(3.4)	8.8(2.5)	8.2(2.0)	4.0(4.6)	7.4(4.0)	7.9(2.5)	**13.3(5.6)**	9.6(3.0)
w/ feature selection	14.2(3.3)	16.85(3.7)	14.1(3.1)	14.0(3.4)	12.3(5.2)	1.7(5.8)	12.8(1.7)	**20.1(4.5)**	14.5(3.9)
w/ transformation	14.3(4.6)	13.0(2.6)	14.0(5.1)	13.9(4.2)	14.3(4.8)	-1.7(5.4)	**14.8(5.5)**	11.9(4.3)	0.8(5.1)

each of the feature selection method into an uplift modeling algorithm and then observe the performance of the model. We use an incremental approach, first introducing only the top-1 feature. We then incrementally add an additional set of fifteen features at each step, continuing this iterative process until all features are integrated into the model. UMODL-FS allows us to continue selecting top features, as long as it gives them an importance score greater than zero. Once a score of zero is reached, no additional features are selected, thus establishing a threshold for feature selection.

Results. Fig. 4 shows the performance obtained with the two model approach and X-learner respectively. Each of these two models are used with a random forest of 100 trees. UMODL-FS shows a good performance selecting the top features leading to performant uplift models. In addition, UMODL-FS automatically determines the features to eliminate without user intervention. In contrast, the other feature selection methods cannot automatically determine an appropriate cut-off score for a feature to be discarded or considered.

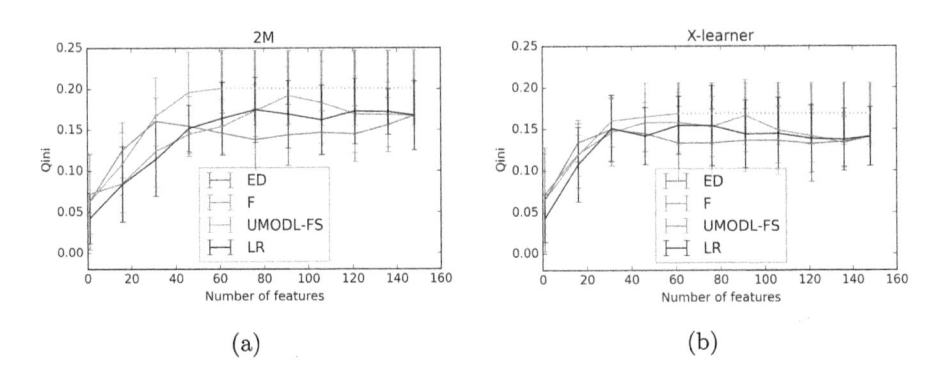

Fig. 4. Uplift models with the top features

6 Conclusion

In this paper, we provide a unified view of UMODL, a user-friendly, parameter-free Bayesian method that is applicable to a variety of uplift modeling tasks.

These tasks include preprocessing steps such as data discretization and feature selection, as well as uplift modeling algorithms including decision trees and random forests. To evaluate the effectiveness of our Bayesian approaches, we conducted a study on real telecom data, comparing our methods with state-of-the-art algorithms. The results demonstrate the competitive performance of our preprocessing techniques and our Bayesian decision trees and random forests.

In addition to presenting the UMODL methodology, we have developed Kuplift, a Python package that implements the above approaches. It provides user-friendly interfaces consistent with established libraries such as Scikit-Learn and CausalML, thus providing accessible tools for uplift modeling to the broader data science community.

There are several perspectives for this work. A special criterion for categorical data can be developed. In addition, the Bayesian approach can be extended to create new uplift modelling algorithms such as K-nearest neighbours [6] and Selective Naive Bayes [2]. In addition, the continuous treatment problem is very interesting and very needed in various domains such as medical and marketing domains. Modeling continuous variables using the MODL approach was studied in [8] and can be used as a basis of a new uplift criterion for continous treatments and outcomes. Another type of an uplift modeling problem is the estimation of individual uplift based on sequence data [5]. Essentially, this involves determining the uplift for each individual, taking into account a sequence of their behaviors. An example of sequence data: a customer initially accepted an Internet offer, then upgraded to a premium package, and then subscribed to a movie platform.

References

1. Boullé, M.: MODL: A bayes optimal discretization method for continuous attributes. Mach. Learn. **65**(1), 131–165 (2006)
2. Boullé, M.: Compression-based averaging of selective naive Bayes classifiers. J. Mach. Learn. Res. **8**, 1659–1685 (2007)
3. Boullé, M.: Recherche d'une représentation des données efficace pour la fouille des grandes bases de données. Ph.D. thesis, Ecole Nationale Supérieure des Télécommunications (2007)
4. Devriendt, F., Van Belle, J., Guns, T., Verbeke, W.: Learning to rank for uplift modeling. IEEE Transactions on Knowledge and Data Engineering, pp. 1–1 (2020)
5. Egho, E., Gay, D., Boullé, M., Voisine, N., Clérot, F.: A user parameter-free approach for mining robust sequential classification rules. Knowl. Inf. Syst. **52**, 53–81 (2017)
6. Ferrandiz, S., Boullé, M.: Bayesian instance selection for the nearest neighbor rule. Mach. Learn. **81**, 229–256 (2010)
7. Hansotia, B., Rukstales, B.: Incremental value modeling. J. Interact. Mark. **16**, 35–46 (2002)
8. Hue, C., Boullé, M.: A new probabilistic approach in rank regression with optimal bayesian partitioning. J. Mach. Learn. Res. **8** 2727–2754 (2007)
9. Kennedy, E.H.: Towards optimal doubly robust estimation of heterogeneous causal effects (2020). https://arxiv.org/abs/2004.14497

10. Künzel, S.R., Sekhon, J.S., Bickel, P.J., Yu, B.: Metalearners for estimating heterogeneous treatment effects using machine learning. Proc. Natl. Acad. Sci. **116**(10), 4156–4165 (2019)
11. Louizos, C., Shalit, U., Mooij, J.M., Sontag, D., Zemel, R., Welling, M.: Causal effect inference with deep latent-variable models. In: Advances in Neural Information Processing Systems **30** (2017)
12. Nie, X., Wager, S.: Quasi-oracle estimation of heterogeneous treatment effects. Biometrika **108**(2), 299–319 (09 2020). https://doi.org/10.1093/biomet/asaa076
13. Radcliffe, N.: Using control groups to target on predicted lift: Building and assessing uplift model. Direct Market. Anal. J. 14–21 (2007)
14. Rafla, M., Voisine, N., Crémilleux, B.: Parameter-free bayesian decision trees for uplift modeling. In: Kashima, H., Ide, T., Peng, W.-C. (eds.) Advances in Knowledge Discovery and Data Mining: 27th Pacific-Asia Conference on Knowledge Discovery and Data Mining, PAKDD 2023, Osaka, Japan, May 25–28, 2023, Proceedings, Part II, pp. 309–321. Springer Nature Switzerland, Cham (2023). https://doi.org/10.1007/978-3-031-33377-4_24
15. Rafla, M., Voisine, N., Crémilleux, B., Boullé, M.: A non-parametric bayesian approach for uplift discretization and feature selection. In: European Conference on Machine Learning and Principles and Practice of Knowledge Discovery in Databases (2022)
16. Rissanen, J.: Modeling by shortest data description. Automatica **14**(5), 465–471 (1978)
17. Rzepakowski, P., Jaroszewicz, S.: Decision trees for uplift modeling with single and multiple treatments. Knowl. Inf. Syst. **32**(2), 303–327 (2012)
18. Shannon, C.E.: A mathematical theory of communication. ACM SIGMOBILE Mob. Comput. Commun. Review **5**(1), 3–55 (2001)
19. Voisine, N., Boullé, M., Hue, C.: A Bayes evaluation criterion for decision trees. In: Guillet, F., Ritschard, G., Zighed, D.A., Briand, H. (eds.) Advances in Knowledge Discovery and Management, pp. 21–38. Springer Berlin Heidelberg, Berlin, Heidelberg (2010). https://doi.org/10.1007/978-3-642-00580-0_2
20. Wager, S., Athey, S.: Estimation and inference of heterogeneous treatment effects using random forests. J. Am. Stat. Assoc. **113**(523), 1228–1242 (2018). https://doi.org/10.1080/01621459.2017.1319839
21. Zhang, W., Li, J., Liu, L.: A unified survey of treatment effect heterogeneity modelling and uplift modelling. ACM Comput. Surv. **54**(8) (oct 2021)
22. Zhang, W., Liu, L., Li, J.: Treatment effect estimation with disentangled latent factors. In: Proceedings of the AAAI Conference on Artificial Intelligence. vol. 35, pp. 10923–10930 (2021)
23. Zhao, Z., Zhang, Y., Harinen, T., Yung, M.: Feature selection methods for uplift modeling and heterogeneous treatment effect. In: Maglogiannis, I., Iliadis, L., Macintyre, J., Cortez, P. (eds.) Artificial Intelligence Applications and Innovations: 18th IFIP WG 12.5 International Conference, AIAI 2022, Hersonissos, Crete, Greece, June 17–20, 2022, Proceedings, Part II, pp. 217–230. Springer International Publishing, Cham (2022). https://doi.org/10.1007/978-3-031-08337-2_19

A Churn Prediction Dataset from the Telecom Sector: A New Benchmark for Uplift Modeling

Théo Verhelst[1](✉), Denis Mercier[2], Jeevan Shestha[2], and Gianluca Bontempi[1]

[1] Machine Learning Group, Université Libre de Bruxelles, Brussels, Belgium
theo.verhelst@ulb.be
[2] Data Science Team, Orange Belgium, Brussels, Belgium

Abstract. Uplift modeling, also known as individual treatment effect (ITE) estimation, is an important approach for data-driven decision making that aims to identify the causal impact of an intervention on individuals. This paper introduces a new benchmark dataset for uplift modeling focused on churn prediction, coming from a telecom company in Belgium. Churn, in this context, refers to customers terminating their subscription to the telecom service. This is the first publicly available dataset offering the possibility to evaluate the efficiency of uplift modeling on the churn prediction problem. Moreover, its unique characteristics make it more challenging than the few other public uplift datasets.

1 Introduction

Uplift modeling, often called the conditional average treatment effect, has become a crucial tool for data-driven decision making. This modeling technique estimates the effect that a particular intervention or treatment has on individuals, enabling the selection of only those individuals who are likely to have a positive reaction to the action. Although the methodology of uplift modeling has witnessed substantial development and diversification [9], a notable constraint remains: the low number of publicly available datasets designed specifically for uplift modeling. A recent uplift benchmark conducted by [14] listed only 4 public uplift datasets: Criteo [4], Hillstrom [10], Starbucks[1] and Lenta[2]. Furthermore, despite the fact that customer churn is often cited as a common application for uplift modeling, none of these public datasets are concerned with churn. To

---

Funded by the Brussels-Capital Region - Innoviris (Brussels Public Organisation for Research and Innovation) under grant number 2019-PHD-16.

[1] https://github.com/joshxinjie/Data_Scientist_Nanodegree/tree/master/starbucks_portfolio_exercise.
[2] https://www.uplift-modeling.com/en/latest/api/datasets/fetch_lenta.html.

address this issue, this paper introduces a new churn dataset for uplift modeling, coming from a telecom company in Belgium. This dataset offers researchers and practitioners a new resource to evaluate strategies aimed at reducing churn and increasing customer retention within the telecommunications industry. In Sect. 2 we present the marketing campaigns that form the basis of this dataset (Sect. 2), and we compare the characteristics of our dataset to two other public datasets in Sect. 3. Then, in Sections 3 and 6 we evaluate the performance of three models on these datasets, and finally we conclude by highlighting its potential to foster innovation and progress within the uplift modeling domain in Sect. 7. The dataset is available on the OpenML platform under the name churn-uplift-mlg and the benchmark code is available on GitHub[3].

2 Churn Campaigns

The dataset comes from a series of three marketing campaigns conducted between September and December 2020. The campaign pipeline is represented in Fig. 1. During each campaign, the probability of churn for each customer was estimated using a predictive model and the riskiest customers were selected. A subset of these high-risk customers was randomly assigned to the control group, while the remaining customers formed the target group. The list of customers in the target group was shared with a call center tasked with contacting each customer and presenting them with a marketing offer or recommending a new tariff plan based on their individual history. The churn outcome is determined in a two-month window following the campaign, and any subsequent churn is not attributed to this specific campaign. The data of this campaign and the churn outcome are then recorded in the historical database, and the same campaign process is repeated the next month.

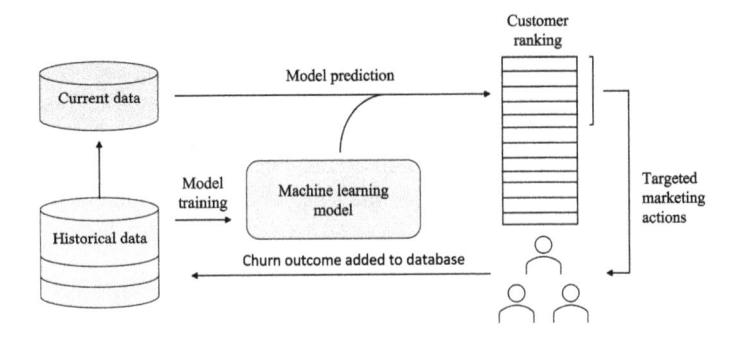

Fig. 1. Schematic representation of the churn retention campaign pipeline.

Table 1. Description of the churn dataset and two other uplift datasets.

Name	Features	Samples	Control response rate (%)	Target response rate (%)	Treatment rate (%)
Churn	178	11,896	3.6	3.4	75.74
Hillstrom	15	42,693	10.62	15.14	66.71
Criteo	12	25,309,483	4.2	4.9	84.6

3 Description

The characteristics of the dataset are summarized in Table 1, as well as the same characteristics of two popular uplift datasets, the Criteo dataset [4], and the Hillstrom dataset [10]. We report the number of features, the number of samples, the response rate in the control and target groups, and the treatment rate.

The churn dataset consists of 11,896 samples, a relatively small number compared to other publicly available uplift datasets. However, it has a larger number of features, totaling 178. These features encompass a diverse range of customer attributes, including demographics (e.g., region of residence, age), usage patterns (e.g., data consumption, number of calls), and subscription details (e.g., price of the tariff plan). The dataset comprises features of various types, including discrete numerical, continuous, and categorical variables, each exhibiting diverse distributions. To ensure privacy and data confidentiality, the dataset is anonymized by using a Principal Component Analysis (PCA) projection of the numerical features, allowing for effective analysis and modeling while protecting sensitive information. Adopting this strategy has proven effective in preserving predictive accuracy while safeguarding privacy in the domain of fraud detection [3]. All categorical features and their levels are anonymized by giving them generic names.

One distinctive aspect of the dataset is the inherent difficulty in accurately predicting the churn outcome. The complex dynamics of churn in the telecom sector make it a challenging task, requiring advanced modeling techniques to capture the underlying patterns and factors influencing customer behavior. Uplift modeling is even more difficult than predicting the outcome probability alone due to the relatively small effect of the treatment. To quantify this aspect, we estimate the mutual information $I(\boldsymbol{x}; \boldsymbol{y}_t)$ (for $t = 0, 1$), which represents the difficulty in predicting the binary outcome $\boldsymbol{y}_t$ from the set of features $\boldsymbol{x}$ [2]. It is estimated using the formula

$$I(\boldsymbol{x}; \boldsymbol{y}_t) = H(\boldsymbol{y}_t) - \mathbb{E}_{\boldsymbol{x}}[H(\boldsymbol{y}_t \mid \boldsymbol{x})] \approx H(\boldsymbol{y}_t) - \frac{1}{N} \sum_{i=1}^{N} H(\boldsymbol{y}_t \mid \boldsymbol{x} = x^{(i)})$$

where the term $H(\boldsymbol{y}_t)$ is estimated from the prior distribution of $\boldsymbol{y}_t$, and a T-learner uplift model (details of the experimental setup are presented in Sect. 5)

---

[3] https://github.com/TheoVerhelst/Churn-Uplift-Dataset-Paper.

provides the necessary probability estimates to compute

$$H(y_t \mid x) = P(y_t = 0 \mid x) \log P(y_t = 0 \mid x) + P(y_t = 1 \mid x) \log P(y_t = 1 \mid x).$$

Table 2. Estimates of the mutual information between the features and the outcomes.

	$H(y_0)$	$H(y_1)$	$\hat{I}(x; y_0)$	$\hat{I}(x; y_1)$	$\frac{\hat{I}(x;y_0)}{H(y_0)}$	$\frac{\hat{I}(x;y_1)}{H(y_1)}$
Churn	0.16	0.15	0.0008	0.0025	0.54%	1.71%
Hillstrom	0.34	0.43	0.0112	0.0123	3.32%	2.90%
Criteo	0.16	0.20	0.0429	0.0573	24.63%	29.32%

The estimates of the mutual information are given in Table 2. In the last two columns, the mutual information estimate is divided by the entropy of the prior distribution, indicating the proportion of uncertainty of the outcome explained by the features. Our dataset has a low outcome probability similar to that of the Criteo dataset, while also having a very low mutual information, like the Hillstrom dataset. This represents a unique contribution to the uplift ecosystem, where there are no other datasets that come from a small-scale marketing campaign with these particular characteristics.

To better characterize the differences in the outcome distribution among the three datasets, we use the counterfactual point estimator proposed in [15]. It estimates the probabilities of the joint distribution of the potential outcomes y_0, y_1, even though this distribution cannot be observed directly. We use the following formula, also based on the probability estimates given by the T-learner:

$$P(y_0 = y_0, y_1 = y_1) \approx \frac{1}{N} \sum_{i=1}^{N} P(y_0 = y_0 \mid x^{(i)}) P(y_1 = y_1 \mid x^{(i)}). \tag{1}$$

for $y_0, y_1 \in \{0, 1\}$. Estimated probabilities are reported in Table 3, along with the business name associated with the four counterfactuals. Note that, in the churn setting, the outcome $y = 1$ should be avoided, while in retail, its probability should be maximized. This implies that the two contexts associate different names to the same probabilities. We see that the churn dataset is characterized by a low probability that both potential outcomes are 1 (*lost cause* customers, fourth row). This suggests that a negligible number of customers are likely to churn regardless of the targeted marketing action. This differs from the two other datasets, for which this probability is higher. We also observe that the churn dataset is more balanced between positive and negative causal effects (second and third rows), whereas, in both the Hillstrom and Criteo datasets, there is a larger proportion of individuals with a positive causal effect (*persuadable* customers, third row).

Table 3. Estimated distribution of counterfactuals.

Formula	Name (in churn)	Name (in retail)	Churn	Hillstrom	Criteo
$P(y_0 = 0, y_1 = 0)$	Sure thing	Lost cause	93.1%	76.0%	90.8%
$P(y_0 = 1, y_1 = 0)$	Persuadable	Do-not-disturb	3.5%	8.9%	2.8%
$P(y_0 = 0, y_1 = 1)$	Do-not-disturb	Persuadable	3.2%	13.4%	4.8%
$P(y_0 = 1, y_1 = 1)$	Lost cause	Sure thing	0.1%	1.8%	1.7%

4 Randomization

Since the dataset comes from a randomized campaign, the treatment should be independent of the outcomes. To validate this independence, we performed the Classifier 2 Sample Test used in [4]. We trained a classifier to predict the treatment indicator and compared its Hamming loss with the loss distribution obtained under the null hypothesis, sampled by training models to predict random splits. The treatment predictor has a loss of 23.82% (close to the proportion of control samples, 24.26%), which corresponds to a p-value of 0.26 under the null hypothesis. This result is shown in Fig. 2. This indicates that the treatment cannot be predicted based on available features, hence the randomization of treatment assignment can be considered appropriate and unbiased.

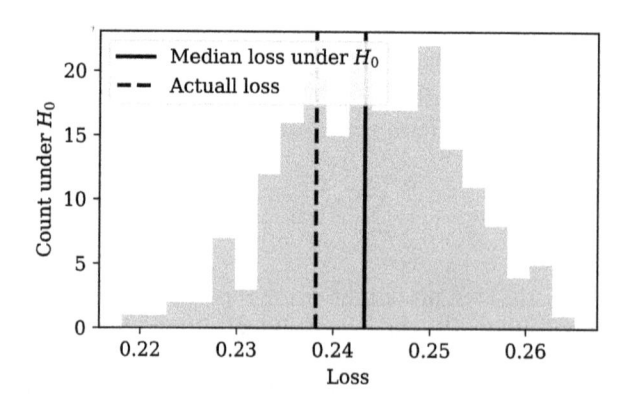

Fig. 2. Distribution of the loss under the hypothesis that the treatment is randomized.

5 Benchmark Experimental Setup

We conducted an experimental benchmark on the churn, Hillstrom and Criteo datasets. We used the classical random forest (RF) model [1], the T-learner uplift model [11], and the uplift random forest [8]. The classical RF model, which we call outcome RF, was trained to predict churn with control samples, therefore, without explicitly considering the individual treatment effect. This serves as a baseline for evaluating the performance of uplift models. This is especially relevant in sectors such as telecoms, where such predictive models are often used instead of uplift models because of their simplicity and sufficient performance. The T-learner used a random forest as base learner. All three models used 100 trees, a maximum depth of 20, and a minimum of 10 samples per leaf. To tackle class imbalance, the EasyEnsemble strategy [13] was applied with 8 folds. For each fold, a new model was trained using all positive samples and an equally sized set of randomly selected negative samples. This approach helps mitigate the adverse impact of class imbalance. The predictions of the eight models were then averaged, effectively reducing the potential biases caused by undersampling the negative samples in individual folds. K-fold cross-validation with $k = 3$ was used to obtain training and test splits of each dataset. Finally, the whole experiment was repeated 10 times to obtain a more robust estimation of the performance, as well as an estimation of its variability. The performance of each model was estimated in terms of the area under the uplift curve (AUUC) [7].

6 Results

The AUUC is reported in Table 4. To evaluate the impact of the PCA projection, we performed the same experiment on the original, non-anonymized churn dataset. It appears that the performance is only slightly lower on the anonymized dataset than on the original, and, given the high uncertainty in the AUUC, we cannot exclude that this difference is due to random variations in the benchmark sampling. We also observe that the performance of all models is highest on the Hillstrom dataset and lowest on the churn dataset. We attribute this difference to the fact that the outcome is balanced in the Hillstrom dataset, whereas it is unbalanced and more difficult to predict in the churn dataset. Interestingly, the performance of the outcome RF model is consistently the highest, showing that the uplift approach is not always preferable, as discussed in [5,6].

The estimator variance likely plays an important role in determining when classical predictive modeling outperforms uplift modeling [5,6]. To evaluate this possibility, we computed the variance of the predicted probability estimates of each model on each data sample. This was achieved by considering the 10 different predictions generated for each sample during the repeated 3-fold cross-validation procedure. The values reported in Table 5 represent the variance averaged across all samples in the dataset. We observe that the two uplift models in this benchmark suffer from a higher variance than the outcome RF, especially on the Criteo dataset.

Table 4. Mean and standard deviation of the area under the uplift curve (AUUC) in the benchmark.

	Churn (%)	Churn (not anonymized) (%)	Hillstrom (%)	Criteo (%)
Outcome RF	0.26 ± (0.47)	0.33 ± (0.37)	2.20 ± (0.32)	1.01 ± (0.25)
Uplift RF	0.19 ± (0.37)	0.22 ± (0.29)	2.19 ± (0.27)	0.89 ± (0.23)
T-learner RF	0.25 ± (0.38)	0.33 ± (0.39)	2.72 ± (0.28)	0.86 ± (0.18)

Table 5. Variance of the predictions averaged over the dataset.

	Churn	Hillstrom	Criteo
Outcome RF	2.07×10^{-3}	3.49×10^{-3}	1.22×10^{-3}
Uplift RF	3.06×10^{-3}	4.33×10^{-4}	2.05×10^{-3}
T-learner RF	3.78×10^{-3}	7.59×10^{-3}	1.94×10^{-3}

7 Conclusion

The primary objective of this new dataset is to facilitate the evaluation and comparison of uplift modeling techniques, with a focus on customer churn prediction in the telecom sector. More generally, researchers and practitioners can leverage this dataset to develop and benchmark new algorithms, feature engineering approaches, and model evaluation metrics tailored to uplift modeling in difficult settings characterized by a low information rate, a low outcome probability, and a small number of samples. This is especially interesting for smaller companies aiming to initiate personalized marketing campaigns, but which have limited historical data to train uplift models. While large-scale benchmarks such as the Criteo dataset are crucial for evaluating the performance of uplift models on a large sample, small-scale datasets are more representative of some practical applications. This dataset also provides an opportunity to assess other causal inference methods such as counterfactual estimation [12,15]. Finally, we observed in a benchmark experiment that classical predictive modeling is more effective than uplift modeling [5,6]. This has also been observed in practice by our industrial partner. In future work, we intend to investigate this question from a theoretical perspective with the hope of gaining a deeper understanding of the critical factors that impact the performance of both predictive and uplift approaches.

References

1. Breiman, L.: Random forests. Mach. Learn. **45**(1), 5–32 (2001)
2. Cover, T.M., Thomas, J.A.: Elements of Information Theory. Wiley (1991)
3. Dal Pozzolo, A., Caelen, O., Johnson, R.A., Bontempi, G.: Calibrating probability with undersampling for unbalanced classification. In: 2015 IEEE Symposium Series on Computational Intelligence, pp. 159–166. IEEE (2015)
4. Diemert Eustache, B.A., Renaudin, C., Massih-Reza, A.: A large scale benchmark for uplift modeling. In: Proceedings of the AdKDD and TargetAd Workshop, KDD, London, United Kingdom, 20 August 2018. ACM (2018)
5. Fernández-Loria, C., Provost, F.: Causal classification: treatment effect estimation vs. outcome prediction. J. Mach. Learn. Res. **23**(59), 1–35 (2022)
6. Fernández-Loria, C., Provost, F.: Causal decision making and causal effect estimation are not the same. . . and why it matters. INFORMS J. Data Sci. (2022)
7. Gubela, R.M., Lessmann, S.: Uplift modeling with value-driven evaluation metrics. Decision Support Syst. (2021)

8. Guelman, L., Guillén, M., Pérez-Marín, A.M.: Uplift random forests. Cybern. Syst. **46**(3–4), 230–248 (2015). https://doi.org/10.1080/01969722.2015.1012892
9. Gutierrez, P., Gérardy, J.-Y.: Causal inference and uplift modelling: a review of the literature. In: Hardgrove, C., Dorard, L., Thompson, K., Douetteau, F. (eds.) Proceedings of The 3rd International Conference on Predictive Applications and APIs, pp. 1–13. PMLR, Microsoft NERD, Boston, USA (2016)
10. Hillstrom, K.: The MineThatData E-mail analytics and data mining challenge (2008). https://blog.minethatdata.com/2008/03/minethatdata-e-mail-analytics-and-data.html
11. Künzel, S.R., Sekhon, J.S., Bickel, P.J., Yu, B.: Metalearners for estimating heterogeneous treatment effects using machine learning. Proc. Natl. Acad. Sci. U.S.A. **116**(10), 4156–4165 (2019). https://doi.org/10.1073/pnas.1804597116
12. Li, A., Pearl, J.: Unit selection based on counterfactual logic. In: IJCAI, International Joint Conferences on Artificial Intelligence Organization, pp. 1793–1799 (2019). https://doi.org/10.24963/ijcai.2019/248
13. Liu, X.-Y., Wu, J., Zhou, Z.-H.: Exploratory undersampling for class-imbalance learning. IEEE Trans. Syst. Man Cybern. Part B (Cybern.) **39**(2), 539–550 (2009). https://doi.org/10.1109/tsmcb.2008.2007853
14. Rößler, J., Schoder, D.: Bridging the gap: a systematic benchmarking of uplift modeling and heterogeneous treatment effects methods. J. Interact. Mark. **57**(4), 629–650 (2022)
15. Verhelst, T., Mercier, D., Shrestha, J., Bontempi, G.: Partial counterfactual identification and uplift modeling: theoretical results and real-world assessment. Mach. Learn. (2023). https://doi.org/10.1007/s10994-023-06317-w

6th Workshop on AI in Aging, Rehabilitation and Intelligent Assisted Living (ARIAL)

Semi-supervised Co-teaching for Monitoring Motor States of Parkinson's Disease Patients

Kamer Ali Yuksel[✉], Golara Javadi, and Ahmet Gunduz

aiXplain Inc., Los Gatos, CA, USA
{kamer,golara,ahmet}@aixplain.com

Abstract. Parkinson's disease is a common neurodegenerative disorder that affects about 1% of people aged 60 and above in developed countries. The number of Parkinson's patients is expected to surpass 8 million in Europe alone within the next decade due to an aging population. More than 80% of patients experience motor symptoms, which can be alleviated with personalized medication plans. However, precise and continuous measurement of motor symptoms during daily activities is crucial for developing these plans. A wrist-worn smartwatch with 3D motion sensors has been proposed to estimate motor fluctuation severity in real-life settings. Using a semi-supervised deep learning approach, this method provides accurate motor symptom estimation with a nine-level granularity, benefiting medical professionals. The approach utilizes Co-Teaching, allowing self-learning through pseudo-labels generated from a large volume of unlabeled data. In summary, this approach offers a practical solution for measuring motor symptoms accurately and creating personalized medication schedules to enhance patients' quality of life.

Keywords: Parkinson's disease · Motor fluctuation · Wearable devices · Personalized medication · Semi-supervised learning · Deep learning

1 Introduction

Individualizing medication dosage and schedule can significantly improve the life quality for Parkinson's disease (PD) patients. However, this can be challenging for doctors who rely on periodic brief visits and may encounter biases from either the patient or themselves during the evaluation process. PD patients require medication to supplement the neurotransmitter their brain can no longer preserve as the disease progresses. However, giving too much of this neurotransmitter can cause hyperkinetic symptoms like dyskinesia, characterized by involuntary and jerky movements, while too little can result in bradykinesia, a slowing of movement similar to partial paralysis. These motor symptoms arise from imbalances in dopamine levels supplied by the medication. Although the medication's plasma half-life lasts only 80 min, doctors generally prescribe fixed dosages that can cause patients' motor abilities to fluctuate considerably over a day or even within hours. The objective of providing personalized medication schedules and dosages to each patient is to minimize time spent in abnormal motor fluctuation states. Continuous and non-invasive methods for measuring dopamine levels can help tailor medication schedules to individual needs and minimize the occurrence of undesirable symptoms. If doctors continuously monitor a PD patient's motor fluctuation state, they could optimize medication schedules and dosages to increase the likelihood of spending the entire day in a normal state. However, the optimal strategy varies for each person since their dopamine production and storage capabilities are unique and change as the disease progresses. Therefore, motor state assessment is crucial for clinical decision-making in PD, as all therapies aim a stable (ON) condition while preventing bradykinetic (OFF) or dyskinetic (DYS) motor states.

The advancement of wearable devices and statistical modeling tools allowed several researchers to analyze the movements of PD patients and map the sensory input to motor states. Previous studies often introduced impractical settings for PD treatment, such as using multiple sensors over the body or instructing patients to perform specific actions. These settings did not reflect the real-world conditions that patients experience daily. Therefore, using a wrist-worn sensor enhanced the adoption of the proposed method in practice, compared to locating sensors at body parts that are more unorthodox and impractical in everyday life. The literature on data analysis in this field primarily focuses on extracting features manually, such as variance, mean, and skewness of multivariate time series. Classical machine learning models like Support Vector Machines (SVM), Multi-layer Perceptron (MLP), and Gaussian Processes (GP) have been extensively used in this domain. Instance-based and feature-based time-series classification (TSC) methods have been thoroughly reviewed by Fulcher et al. and Bagnal et al. [1,3]. Deep Learning techniques have performed better than traditional feature-based methods [2,10,14]. While previous literature on motor fluctuation modeling primarily focused on binary (ON-OFF) or three-class classification with a discrete response, Keijers et al. [11] were the first to propose modeling approaches with a continuous response. Goschenhofer et al. [6] compared the performance of classification, ordinal classification, and regression on motor fluctuation estimation using state-of-the-art TSC architectures and several baseline models from traditional machine learning and deep learning. They found that the FCN architecture in a regression setting performed best among several baseline methods. Yuksel et al. [16] have proposed using Res2Net blocks [4] in the FCN architecture for motor fluctuation estimation to represent multi-scale features at a granular level with hierarchical residual connections and increasing the receptive field ranges of the FCN layers.

This study proposes using a wearable smartwatch on the dominant hand of PD patients to accurately estimate their motor fluctuation states during daily activities. The proposed approach outperforms previous work in the same domain by utilizing a stochastic mini-batch co-teaching scheme for post-training with pseudo-labels. In contrast with most previous work, The study uses leave-one-subject-out cross-validation (LOSO-CV) and eliminates any practical limitations such as personalized models, multiple sensors, or specific activity instructions during clinical data collection. The proposed approach offers state-of-the-art performance in estimating motor fluctuation states with nine-level granularity expected by doctors and is highly applicable in real-world clinical use-cases.

2 Materials and Methods

2.1 Data

This work utilized a dataset of motor fluctuation severity that comprised recordings from 39 PD patients, with an average duration of six hours. The dataset includes 3D accelerometer and gyroscope values collected from a single Microsoft Band 2 fitness-tracking smartwatch mounted on the patient's dominant hand. All patients were diagnosed with PD based on UK Brain Bank Criteria and had an established history of motor fluctuations. The patients in this study were hospitalized for treatment of their PD symptoms, during which they performed regular activities such as sleeping, walking, eating, and therapy. To ensure real-world applicability, the researchers carefully selected the quantity and placement of the motion sensor, specifically mounting it on the patient's wrist. This method is easily adaptable in clinical practice, as wearing a smartwatch requires no more effort than wearing a regular watch. The data was collected continuously, with only short breaks due to technical issues or bathroom activities. Due to the nature of PD, the labels for motor symptom fluctuation severities were highly imbalanced. Therefore, the training and evaluation metrics utilized were adjusted to account for this imbalance, as suggested by previous studies [9]. Additionally, a second unsupervised dataset of 136 subjects was utilized, which only contained meta-information on whether the recording was from a PD patient or healthy control. This dataset was used for transfer learning [12,15] through binary classification of PD, followed by self-learning (pseudo-labeling) to improve performance on the supervised regression task of motor fluctuation estimation.

Preprocessing: To increase the training set, a sliding window technique was applied to divide the time series into one-minute bins, with 80% overlap between neighboring windows. The input features were extracted for each one-minute bin by computing the Euclidean norms of the 3D raw signals obtained from both sensors, following down-sampling from 62.5 Hz to 20 Hz. These norms are rotation-invariant features not affected by how patients wear the device during data collection. A motor fluctuation severity label was assigned to each one-minute bin to classify the severity of the motor fluctuations. The clinical severity of PD symptoms was evaluated using a combination of the MDS-UPDRS [5] and mAIMS [13] rating scales. Medical doctors use these questionnaires to assess the severity of bradykinesia and dyskinesia on a scale of 0–4, with 0 being the ON state. The ratings from both questionnaires were combined to label each minute of motion data with a score between −4 and 4, indicating the patient's motor state, monitored by a doctor in a free-living setting over one day.

2.2 Method

The proposed method for estimating the severity of motor fluctuations in PD patients consists of: i) a pre-training technique to improve the model's generalization to unseen patients despite having a limited clinically labeled dataset for training; ii) a relaxed loss function to handle the discreteness noise of clinical rater's labels; iii) a stochastic mini-batch Co-Teaching scheme for self-learning.

Loss Function: In practice, errors in motor fluctuation state classification tend to be asymmetric and accompanied by inherent noise. Due to the discrete nature of the ratings used to label the motor severities of PD symptoms, labels corresponding to similar motor states may exhibit significant variations. Goschenhofer et al. [6] proposed an asymmetric hinged loss to diagnose PD symptoms concerning clinical requirements such as the non-linearity of labels, where misclassifying a sample with a label two levels away is much worse than misclassifying it with a label only one level away. The asymmetry of labels suggests that an exaggerated diagnosis in the proper pathological direction should be better than an opposing diagnosis in the wrong pathological direction, even if the label difference between them is the same. In this work, their custom loss function is extended to compensate for the discreteness noise of labels by assuming a fixed uncertainty β in the quadratic error between the actual label y and the predicted label $\hat{y}$. Any predictions that fall within this uncertainty bound are accepted.

$$L = (\alpha + \text{sign}(\hat{y} - y))^2 \cdot \max\left(0, (\hat{y} - y)^2 - \beta\right) \quad (1)$$

where y is the true label, $\hat{y}$ is the model prediction, and $\alpha = 0.25$ and $\beta = 0.25$ are parameters that control costs defined for the asymmetry and the allowance of the label relaxation in the custom loss, respectively. Finally, a weighted average of losses for each sample in the mini-batch are taken according to the inverse frequency of each class $[-4, 4]$ in the dataset due to its high-class imbalance.

Label Noise Handling: Collecting labels from clinical settings posed a challenge due to the subjective and discretized nature of the labels provided by clinicians. As a result, inconsistencies existed between the labels and patients' continuous and natural symptoms. This led to label noise that impacted the accuracy of modeling the ground truth. The uncertainty-weighted method was employed to learn predicted continuous labels to address this issue. However, deep learning methods were susceptible to noisy clinical labels due to their large capacity, resulting in memorizing noisy samples during training. To mitigate the impact of label noise, Han et al. [7] proposed Co-Teaching, a robust training method that involved training two networks simultaneously and exchanging samples that each network considered clean. This method discarded samples with

Algorithm 1. Stochastic Mini-batch Co-teaching

Inputs:
    training set $\mathcal{D}$, models $\{f, g\}$, sampling fraction $\alpha = 0.75$,
    number of epochs K, number of mini-batches N
Initialize:
    losses $\mathcal{L}_f = (l_{f1}, \ldots, l_{fN}) = \mathbf{1}_N$, $\mathcal{L}_g = (l_{g1}, \ldots, l_{gN}) = \mathbf{1}_N$
for $k = 1, 2, \ldots, K$ **do**
    mini-batches $\mathcal{B} = (b_1, \ldots, b_N)$
    Sample $X_f \sim$ Multinomial(trials $= \alpha N, p = \frac{l_{fi}}{\sum_{i=1}^{N} l_{fi}}$)
    Sample $X_g \sim$ Multinomial(trials $= \alpha N, p = \frac{l_{gi}}{\sum_{i=1}^{N} l_{gi}}$)
    Train f on $\mathcal{B}_f = \{b_i \in \mathcal{B} : X_{gi} = 0\}$
    Train g on $\mathcal{B}_g = \{b_i \in \mathcal{B} : X_{fi} = 0\}$
    Update losses $\mathcal{L}_f, \mathcal{L}_g$
end for

---

the highest loss according to each network before optimization, preventing biased selection of training instances and accumulation of errors on clean samples. A stochastic, mini-batch version of Co-Teaching was implemented, which outperformed the original per-sample method. In the proposed version, each network selected mini-batches to optimize itself pseudo-randomly at each epoch using multinomial sampling weighted by the inverse losses computed by the other network during forward passes of the previous epoch. This approach allowed for more efficient training and better handling of noisy labels in clinical settings. Algorithm 1 shows the proposed stochastic mini-batch Co-Teaching details.

Regularization: Data augmentation and regularization were key to enhancing our method's generalization, particularly in a LOSO-CV scheme. Two techniques, additive noise and block shuffling, were applied as per Um et al. [14] findings in the PD domain. These techniques improved model robustness to input noise from motion sensors and promoted feature diversity. DropBlock, used after the last convolutional layer, dropped spatially correlated units in a feature map, encouraging the remaining units to learn robust features and improving regularization by preventing correlated activations.

Lastly, Han et al. [8] introduced a post-training strategy that starts with a fully trained dense model and then regularizes it by sparsifying to achieve better generalization performance. This is done by sorting the network weights, pruning low-weight connections, and post-training this sparse network. This work applies their strategy by continuing sparse training on the 75% pruned connections in each convolutional layer after the initial convergence. This post-training allowed for the significant improvement of the first convergence with the dense network due to the large kernel sizes of FCN and redundancy of Res2Net blocks in others.

3 Experiments and Results

Experiments were conducted using an Nvidia Tesla V100 GPU and the AdamW optimizer with a decoupled weight decay of 5e−6 and a partially adaptive momentum of 0.4. A batch size of 128, a learning rate of 1e−4, and an epsilon parameter of 5e−3 were used. Where applicable, a 20% DropBlock rate was applied to the final convolutional layer, and Gaussian input noise was set to 0.05. The LOSO-CV was used to assess generalization, with the optimal evaluation epoch determined by each fold's minimum average loss. Model predictions were smoothed with Gaussian filtering before post-processing, and regression outputs were rounded for classification metrics. Due to high-class imbalance, evaluation metrics were class distribution-weighted.

To evaluate the proposed training loss and label noise algorithm, data was tested with three different model architectures FCN [6], FCN+, and FCN++ [16]. The results are presented in Tables 1–3 where the relaxed version of the custom loss is denoted by (r). Furthermore, due to the poor performance of highly under-represented −4 and 4 boundary classes, the experiments' results are reported for 7-class classification as well. Utilizing the proposed loss relaxation (Eq. 1) consistently improved the classification metrics for most models, significantly impacting both 7 and 9 class classification. However, the original non-relaxed version of the custom loss (with $\beta = 0$) exhibited better performance on regression metrics, including the relaxed accuracy metric, which shares similar characteristics with regression metrics (MAE and MSE) due to its ±1 class prediction tolerance.

The proposed pre- and post-training methods significantly improved most models, particularly when used in combination. Except for the last scheme, the enhanced FCN+ and FCN++ models consistently outperformed the standard FCN. FCN++ excelled over FCN+ in all pre-training cases due to its larger parameter count (54.3k vs 37.4k). However, the standard FCN surpassed others in all regression and relaxed accuracy metrics when both training methods were applied, likely due to its four times larger parameter count (265k).

The proposed Co-Teaching approach, when applied to the FCN architecture, achieved the best overall performance due to its high parameter count. This model's predictions on the unlabelled dataset were used as pseudo-labels for self-learning. During post-training, these pseudo-labels and actual labels were evenly mixed to generate mini-batches per epoch, significantly improving all regression metrics and relaxed accuracy. However, a slight decline in classification metrics was observed, presumably due to the pseudo-labels not being discretized.

The primary objective of this work was to achieve superior regression performance in PD motor fluctuation severity estimation, especially regarding the custom loss designed with input from medical experts to meet the clinical requirements of PD treatment. Comparing the results with all previous work was challenging because older studies lacked LOSO-CV and class-weighted evaluation metrics. As shown in Table 3, theproposed method outperformed the previous

Table 1. Experimental results with pre-training. FCN model without the relaxed loss (r) is identical to [6]. FCN+ & FCN++ are architectures improved by [16].

Model	MAE	MSE	Acc-7	Acc-9	Acc ± 1
FCN	1.031	1.658	0.373	0.272	0.693
FCN (r)	1.055	1.692	0.330	0.264	0.657
FCN+	0.951	1.409	0.375	0.301	0.718
FCN+ (r)	1.000	1.617	0.368	0.282	0.727
FCN++	0.913	1.304	0.380	0.287	0.760
FCN++ (r)	0.945	1.426	0.382	0.302	0.732

Table 2. Experimental results with pre- and post-training (PP) where a sparse training is done after pruning convolutional weights by 75% as proposed in [16].

Model	MAE	MSE	Acc-7	Acc-9	Acc ± 1
FCN	0.894	1.227	0.378	0.282	0.800
FCN (r)	0.897	1.293	0.394	0.313	0.751
FCN+	1.020	1.630	0.352	0.282	0.677
FCN+ (r)	1.001	1.554	0.373	0.292	0.721
FCN++	0.934	1.298	0.357	0.277	0.731
FCN++ (r)	0.911	1.350	0.405	0.317	0.742

Table 3. Results with PP and co-teaching, without and with self-training (ST).

Model	MAE	MSE	Acc-7	Acc-9	Acc ± 1
FCN w/o ST	**0.863**	**1.202**	0.395	**0.338**	**0.827**
FCN with ST	**0.771**	**0.941**	**0.422**	0.320	**0.857**

state-of-the-art [6,16] (Tables 1 and 2) using a single-sensor in a free-living environment, and set new benchmarks in classification and regression metrics. The method achieved a relaxed accuracy of 86% under LOSO-CV in the nine-class motor-state classification desired by doctors (Table 3).

4 Conclusion

This study used a wrist-worn smart-watch with 3D motion sensors to estimate motor fluctuations in PD patients. The proposed method surpassed previous work by employing Deep Learning techniques and achieved state-of-the-art performance. The study made several significant contributions. Firstly, a pre-training technique improved the model's generalization to unseen patients despite limited clinical data. Secondly, a relaxed loss function handled the discreteness noise of clinical raters' labels. Lastly, a stochastic mini-batch Co-

Teaching scheme was adopted for post-training and self-learning. Experimental results demonstrated the accurate estimation of motor fluctuation severity in PD patients' home environment, which is crucial for clinical decision-making as personalized medication tailored to patients can significantly enhance their life quality.

References

1. Bagnall, A., Lines, J., Bostrom, A., Large, J., Keogh, E.: The great time series classification bake off: a review and experimental evaluation of recent algorithmic advances. Data Min. Knowl. Disc. **31**(3), 606–660 (2017)
2. Eskofier, B.M., et al.: Recent machine learning advancements in sensor-based mobility analysis: deep learning for Parkinson's disease assessment. Eng. Med. Biol. Soc., 655–658 (2016)
3. Fulcher, B.D., Jones, N.S.: Highly comparative feature-based time-series classification. IEEE Trans. Knowl. Data Eng. **26**(12) (2014)
4. Gao, S.H., Cheng, M.M., Zhao, K., Zhang, X.Y., Yang, M.H., Torr, P.: Res2Net: a new multi-scale backbone architecture. IEEE Trans. Pattern Anal. Mach. Intell. **43**(2), 652–662 (2019)
5. Goetz, C.G., et al.: Movement disorder society-sponsored revision of the unified Parkinson's disease rating scale (MDS-UPDRS): scale presentation and clinimetric testing results. Mov. Disord. Official J. Mov. Disord. Soc. **23**(15), 2129–2170 (2008)
6. Goschenhofer, J., Pfister, F.M., Yuksel, K.A., Bischl, B., Fietzek, U., Thomas, J.: Wearable-based Parkinson's disease severity monitoring using deep learning. In: Brefeld, U., Fromont, E., Hotho, A., Knobbe, A., Maathuis, M., Robardet, C. (eds.) ECML PKDD 2019. LNCS, vol. 11908, pp. 400–415. Springer, Cham (2020). https://doi.org/10.1007/978-3-030-46133-1_24
7. Han, B., et al.: Co-teaching: robust training of deep neural networks with extremely noisy labels. In: Advances in Neural Information Processing Systems, vol. 31 (2018)
8. Han, S., et al.: DSD: dense-sparse-dense training for deep neural networks. arXiv preprint arXiv:1607.04381 (2016)
9. He, H., Garcia, E.A.: Learning from imbalanced data. IEEE Trans. Knowl. Data Eng. **21**(9), 1263–1284 (2009)
10. Hssayeni, M.D., Burack, M.A., Ghoraani, B.: Automatic assessment of medication states of patients with Parkinson's disease using wearable sensors. In: 38th Annual International Conference of the IEEE Engineering in Medicine and Biology Society (EMBC), pp. 6082–6085 (2016)
11. Keijsers, N.L., Horstink, M.W., Gielen, S.C.: Automatic assessment of levodopa-induced dyskinesias in daily life by neural networks. Mov. Disord. Soc. **18**, 70–80 (2003)
12. Laengkvist, M., Karlsson, L., Loutfi, A.: A review of unsupervised feature learning and deep learning for time-series modeling. Pattern Recogn. Lett. **42** (2014)
13. Lane, R.D., Glazer, W.M., Hansen, T.E., Berman, W.H., Kramer, S.I.: Assessment of tardive dyskinesia using the abnormal involuntary movement scale. J. Nerv. Ment. Dis. (1985)
14. Um, T.T., et al.: Parkinson's disease assessment from a wrist-worn wearable sensor in free-living conditions: deep ensemble learning and visualization. arXiv preprint arXiv:1808.02870 (2018)

15. Yosinski, J., Clune, J., Bengio, Y., Lipson, H.: How transferable are features in deep neural networks? In: Advances in Neural Information Processing Systems, pp. 3320–3328 (2014)
16. Yuksel, K.A., Goschenhofer, J., Varma, H.V., Fietzek, U., Pfister, F.M.: Granular motor state monitoring of free living Parkinson's disease patients via deep learning. In: Proceedings of the Machine Learning for Health (ML4H) Workshop at the 33rd Annual Conference on Neural Information Processing Systems (NeurIPS) (2019)

Explainable Artificial Intelligence in Medical Diagnostics: Insights into Alzheimer's Disease

Ali Nawaz and Amir Ahmad[✉]

Department of Information Systems and Security, College of Information Technology,
United Arab Emirates University, Al Ain, UAE
amirahmad@uaeu.ac.ae

Abstract. Alzheimer's Disease (AD) is the most prevalent form of dementia globally, which presents a pressing health issue, especially in aging populations. Its early detection is critical to initiating appropriate care and therapeutic strategies. However, AD's complex and multifaceted nature poses considerable challenges to accurate and early diagnosis. Machine learning (ML) models have emerged as promising disease detection and diagnosis tools, including AD. However, despite their superior predictive performance, these models are often viewed as "black boxes" due to their complex internal workings, which are not readily interpretable. This study aims to explore the application of Explainable Artificial Intelligence (XAI) techniques to enhance the interpretability of the best-performing ML classifier for AD detection. The robust analysis offers significant insights into the ML model's decision-making processes, thereby enhancing their interpretability and bolstering confidence in their use for early AD detection.

Keywords: Aging Problem · Alzheimer Disease · Explainable Artificial Intelligence · Machine learning

1 Introduction

AD the most common cause of dementia, is a neurodegenerative disorder characterized by progressive memory loss and cognitive decline [1]. It is a significant public health concern, given its increasing prevalence and the burden it imposes on patients, healthcare specialist, and healthcare systems [2]. Despite extensive research, AD remains incurable, with treatments primarily focused on symptom management. Early detection of AD can enable timely interventions, potentially delaying disease progression and improving quality of life [3]. However, diagnosis is challenging, often requiring complex and invasive tests [4].

ML provides systems the ability to learn and improve from experience automatically. ML has shown promise in various healthcare applications, including disease detection and prognosis [5]. In the context of AD, ML models can potentially identify subtle patterns in clinical and demographic data that might indicate early disease stages, thus aiding in early detection [6].

XAI is a subfield of AI that emphasizes the creation of AI models whose actions can be understood and interpreted by human experts. It promotes trust and understanding by providing insights into the decision-making process of complex machine learning algorithms [7]. It is crucial in health care, particularly in predicting diseases like Alzheimer's. Two popular XAI techniques are Local Interpretable Model-Agnostic Explanations (LIME) and SHapley Additive exPlanations (SHAP) [8]. LIME, proposed by Ribeiro et al. [9], is a technique that explains the predictions of any ML classifier in an interpretable and faithful manner. It does so by approximating the prediction of the complex model with a simpler model (e.g., linear model) locally around the prediction. Similarly, SHAP, proposed by Lundberg and Lee [10], is a unified measure of feature importance that assigns each feature an importance value for a particular prediction. The SHAP value can be interpreted as the average marginal contribution of a feature value across all possible coalitions.

Several studies have applied these techniques in various domains, including healthcare. For instance, Lu et al. [11], created a stacking classifier by aggregating the predictions from five models: Random Forest (RF), AdaBoost, XGBoost, and CatBoost, which served as base learners, while Logistic Regression (LR) was utilized as the meta learner. Then applied LIME and SHAP to interpret the readmission of diabetic patients. Similarly, Gao et al. [8] used data from the Alzheimer Disease Genetics Consortium to construct polygenic risk scores (PRSs) for AD and age-at-onset (AAO) of AD. They then apply the eXtreme Gradient Boosting (XGBoost) algorithm to predict AD development. By employing XAI techniques, they found that PRSs and EHR data can be used to improve the accuracy of AD risk prediction.

This research paper explores the application of LIME and SHAP in interpreting the predictions of ML classifiers for AD detection. We trained multiple ML classifiers using a demographic, genetic, and clinical features dataset. Then we selected the best model to interpret its predictions with LIME and SHAP. This study aims to contribute to the field by demonstrating the potential of XAI in healthcare, specifically in improving the interpretability of ML models for AD detection.

2 Methodology

2.1 Dataset and Pre-processing

The dataset used in this study was sourced from a publicly available Oasis dementia database [12], which has been extensively used in Alzheimer's disease research. This dataset comprises 150 instances and fifteen different demographic, genetic, and clinical features of individuals diagnosed with Alzheimer's disease and healthy controls. The demographic features include age, sex, and education level. The genetic features consist of the APOE genotype test which is a type of genetic test that determines the type of APOE alleles an individual carries. The clinical features encompass measures such as Mini-Mental State Examination

(MMSE), Estimated Total Intracranial Volume (eTIV), Atlas Scaling Factor (ASF), and Normalized Whole Brain Volume (nWBV).

The dataset was pre-processed to ensure its suitability for machine learning analysis. The pre-processing steps were as follows:

- The dataset was first cleaned to handle any missing or inconsistent data. Eight instances with missing data in the SES column were detected. To maintain the size of the dataset, we adopted the imputation method [12], replacing the missing entries with corresponding values.
- The categorical variables in the dataset, such as sex and APOE genotype, were encoded using one-hot encoding [13] to convert them into a format suitable for the ML algorithms.
- The numerical features in the dataset were scaled using MinMaxScaler [14]. This technique, which normalizes or rescales numerical features to fall within a specific range (usually 0 to 1), is crucial for the performance of many ML algorithms. These algorithms, including the ones used in the study, are sensitive to the scale of the input features. By transforming each feature value by subtracting the minimum value and then dividing it by the range of the feature, MinMaxScaler ensures that all features have a similar scale.
- The dataset was split into five folds, k = 5, and for every five iterations, it trains the model on four folds and tests it on the remaining fold.

2.2 Machine Learning Classifiers

For the purpose of this study, we employed different types of ML models, as detailed in Table 1. This diverse range encompassed linear models, ensemble models, tree-based models, and probabilistic classifiers. The models were implemented using the Scikit-learn library [22], a popular open-source Python tool that provides efficient data analysis and modeling tools. This experimentation across multiple model types enhances the robustness of the study, ensuring that the findings are not overly dependent on any specific model type or assumption. With the best model at hand, we then utilize XAI techniques to understand the model's decision-making process.

2.3 Explainable AI Techniques

XAI techniques are crucial in enhancing machine learning models' transparency, trust, and interpretability, especially in sensitive applications such as healthcare [7]. This interpretability helps clinicians understand the reasoning behind the AI model's predictions. It gives them valuable insights into how different patient characteristics affect the model's output, thereby complementing their domain expertise. It also provides a safety check, as it allows humans to identify when a model might be making predictions based on spurious correlations. This study utilized two popular XAI techniques, namely LIME [9] and SHAP [8], to interpret the predictions of the machine learning classifier.

Table 1. ML models

S. NO.	Models	Category	[ref.]
1.	Logistic Regression, Linear Support Vector Classifier (LinearSVC), Ridge Classifier, Perceptron	Linear Models	[15]
2.	Decision Tree Classifier, Extra Tree Classifier, Random Forest Classifier, AdaBoost Classifier, Gradient Boosting Classifier	Tree-Based Models	[16]
3.	Bagging Classifier, Extra Trees Classifier	Ensemble Models	[17]
4.	Gaussian Naive Bayes, Bernoulli Naive Bayes	Probabilistic Classifiers	[18]
5.	K-Nearest Neighbors (KNN), Support Vector Classifier (SVC), Calibrated Classifier CV, Quadratic Discriminant Analysis	Miscellaneous Models	[19]
6.	XGBoost, LightGBM	Gradient Boosting Model	[20]
7.	Perceptron	Neural Networks	[21]

3 Results

3.1 Performance of ML Classifiers

The comparative analysis trained and evaluated 20 machine learning classifiers on the dataset. The performance metrics included Accuracy, Balanced Accuracy ((sensitivity+specificity)/2), and F1 Score [23].

The classifier with the highest overall performance was the QDA [22], which achieved an Accuracy of 0.82, Balanced Accuracy of 0.79, and an F1-score of 0.81. This performance is significant as it demonstrates the potential for machine learning classifiers to effectively predict Alzheimer's disease based on neuroimaging and demographic data.

The second-best performing classifier was the Perceptron with an Accuracy of 0.82, Balanced Accuracy of 0.77, and an F1 Score of 0.8. This was closely followed by the LGBMClassifier model, which achieved an accuracy, Balanced accuracy, and an F1-score of 0.75, 0.75, and F1-score of 0.74, respectively. The least performing models were the ExtraTreeClassifier, and DummyClassifier, with an Accuracy of 0.50, and 0.38, respectively.

While the performance of these classifiers was lower than the other models, it's important to note that each classifier has its strengths and weaknesses. Some models may perform better on certain types of data or tasks. The key takeaway from these results is that complex models like QDA can perform extremely well on this task, but simpler models can still provide reasonable results.

These results indicate that when appropriately trained and evaluated, machine learning classifiers can effectively predict Alzheimer's disease. However, performance alone is not enough, especially in healthcare applications where interpretability is crucial [24]. Therefore, this study also focused on explaining the predictions of the best classifier, i.e., QDA using XAI techniques.

3.2 LIME Interpretation

We applied LIME to understand the predictions made by our best-performing model, the QDA, on a sample instance.

The instance had the following features:

- Mini-Mental State Examination (MMSE) score: 26
- Atlas Scaling Factor (ASF): 1.26
- Estimated Total Intracranial Volume (eTIV): 1391
- Sex (M/F): Male (0)
- Education (EDUC): 16 years

According to the LIME analysis shown in Fig. 1, the most influential features for the prediction were the MMSE score and eTIV, with weights of 0.56 and 0.11, respectively. An MMSE score lower than 26.75 is indicative of cognitive impairment, often serving as a precursor to Alzheimer's disease. The model gave this feature more weight in cases where eTIV was between 1345.75 and 1400, which might reflect a correlation between these specific values and Alzheimer's disease. The ASF was another influential feature with a weight of 0.10. In this context, a score between 1.21 and 1.30 was found to be more influential. Gender (M/F), has no effect on interpretation, indicating female gender, had a weight of 0.09. This might suggest a higher prevalence of Alzheimer's disease in females, which aligns with some epidemiological studies. Finally, age was also an influential feature with a weight of 0.01, specifically for individuals aged between 70 and 76.

3.3 SHAP Interpretation

For the same instance, we interpreted using LIME, we applied SHAP [10] to obtain another perspective on the important features. The base value, which represents the model's output without considering any features, was 0.5121. Here is the SHAP value interpretation for the features as shown in Fig. 2:

Fig. 1. LIME interpretation

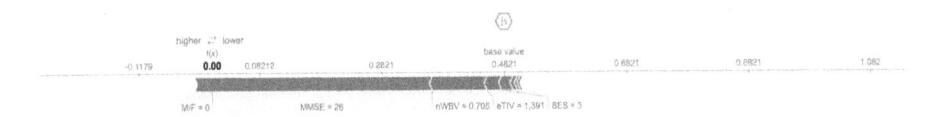

Fig. 2. SHAP interpretation

- MMSE: The SHAP value was −0.12, indicating that a MMSE score of 26 (slightly below average) decreased the model's output, suggesting an increased likelihood of Alzheimer's disease.
- M/F: The SHAP value was −0.03 for a male patient. This indicates that being male had a small negative effect on the model's output, implying a slightly higher likelihood of Alzheimer's disease compared to a female patient.
- eTIV: The SHAP value for an eTIV of 1391 was −0.01, indicating that this value slightly decreased the model's output, suggesting a slightly higher likelihood of Alzheimer's disease.
- nWBV: The SHAP value for an nWBV of 0.705 was −0.01, indicating that this value slightly decreased the model's output, suggesting a slightly higher likelihood of Alzheimer's disease.

4 Conclusion

To conclude, this study demonstrates the potential of machine learning for the early detection of Alzheimer's disease. It highlights the importance of explainability in building trust and understanding in ML models. By providing interpretable predictions, we can better align machine learning with clinical decision-making and pave the way for the integration of AI in healthcare. Despite the promising results, this study has several limitations. The dataset used was relatively small, and future research should validate these findings in larger, more diverse datasets such as MRI [25]. Furthermore, while our study focused on interpreting individual predictions of the QDA model, future work could also explore global interpretation techniques to provide an overall picture of how the classifiers work.

Acknowledgment. The UAEU supported this research under grant number 12R000.

References

1. Yang, P., Sun, F.: Aducanumab: the first targeted Alzheimer's therapy. Drug Discoveries Ther. **15**(3), 166–168 (2021)
2. Meng, W., et al.: Female perspective: the burden of Alzheimer's disease and other dementias in china from: to 2019 and prediction of their prevalence up to 2044. Front. Public Health **11**, 2023 (1990)
3. Angelopoulou, E., et al.: How telemedicine can improve the quality of care for patients with Alzheimer's disease and related dementias? A narrative review. Medicina **58**(12), 1705 (2022)
4. Manemann, S.M., et al.: Alzheimer's disease and related dementias and heart failure: a community study. J. Am. Geriatr. Soc. **70**(6), 1664–1672 (2022)
5. Ahmad, Z., Rahim, S., Zubair, M., Abdul-Ghafar, J.: Artificial intelligence (AI) in medicine, current applications and future role with special emphasis on its potential and promise in pathology: present and future impact, obstacles including costs and acceptance among pathologists, practical and philosophical considerations. a comprehensive review. Diagn. Pathol. **16**, 1–16 (2021)
6. Dashwood, M., Churchhouse, G., Young, M., Kuruvilla, T.: Artificial intelligence as an aid to diagnosing dementia: an overview. Prog. Neurol. Psychiatry **25**(3), 42–47 (2021)
7. Ali, S., et al.: Explainable artificial intelligence (XAI): what we know and what is left to attain trustworthy artificial intelligence. Inf. Fusion, 101805 (2023)
8. Gao, X.R., et al.: Explainable machine learning aggregates polygenic risk scores and electronic health records for Alzheimer's disease prediction. Sci. Rep. **13**(1), 450 (2023)
9. Ribeiro, M.T., Singh, S., Guestrin, C.: "Why should i trust you?" Explaining the predictions of any classifier. In: Proceedings of the 22nd ACM SIGKDD International Conference on Knowledge Discovery and Data Mining, pp. 1135–1144 (2016)
10. Lundberg, S.M., Lee, S.-I.: A unified approach to interpreting model predictions. In: Advances in Neural Information Processing Systems, vol. 30 (2017)
11. Haohui, L., Uddin, S.: Explainable stacking-based model for predicting hospital readmission for diabetic patients. Information **13**(9), 436 (2022)
12. Basheer, S., Bhatia, S., Sakri, S.B.: Computational modeling of dementia prediction using deep neural network: analysis on oasis dataset. IEEE Access **9**, 42449–42462 (2021)
13. Venugopalan, J., Tong, L., Hassanzadeh, H.R., Wang, M.D.: Multimodal deep learning models for early detection of Alzheimer's disease stage. Sci. Rep. **11**(1), 3254 (2021)
14. Raju, V.N.G., Prasanna Lakshmi, K., Jain, V.M., Kalidindi, A., Padma, V.: Study the influence of normalization/transformation process on the accuracy of supervised classification. In: 2020 Third International Conference on Smart Systems and Inventive Technology (ICSSIT), pp. 729–735. IEEE (2020)
15. Matloff, N.: Statistical Regression and Classification: From Linear Models to Machine Learning. CRC Press (2017)
16. Clark, L.A., Pregibon, D.: Tree-based models. In: Statistical Models in S, pp. 377–419. Routledge (2017)
17. Ali, H.A., Mohamed, C., Abdelhamid, B., Ourdani, N., El Alami, T.: A comparative evaluation use bagging and boosting ensemble classifiers. In: 2022 International Conference on Intelligent Systems and Computer Vision (ISCV), pp. 1–6. IEEE (2022)

18. Murphy, K.P.: Machine Learning: A Probabilistic Perspective. MIT Press (2012)
19. Kumar, M.: Using machine learning to predict heart-related diseases. IUP J. Comput. Sci. **16**(3), 22–34 (2022)
20. Bentéjac, C., Csörgő, A., Martínez-Muñoz, G.: A comparative analysis of gradient boosting algorithms. Artif. Intell. Rev. **54**, 1937–1967 (2021)
21. Goodfellow, I., Bengio, Y., Courville, A.: Deep Learning. MIT Press (2016)
22. Tharwat, A.: Linear vs. quadratic discriminant analysis classifier: a tutorial. Int. J. Appl. Pattern Recogn. **3**(2), 145–180 (2016)
23. Sokolova, M., Japkowicz, N., Szpakowicz, S.: Beyond accuracy, F-score and ROC: a family of discriminant measures for performance evaluation. In: Sattar, A., Kang, B. (eds.) AI 2006. LNCS (LNAI), vol. 4304, pp. 1015–1021. Springer, Heidelberg (2006). https://doi.org/10.1007/11941439_114
24. Miotto, R., Wang, F., Wang, S., Jiang, X., Dudley, J.T.: Deep learning for healthcare: review, opportunities and challenges. Briefings Bioinf. **19**(6), 1236–1246 (2018)
25. Islam, J., Zhang, Y.: A novel deep learning based multi-class classification method for Alzheimer's disease detection using brain MRI data. In: Zeng, Y., et al. (eds.) BI 2017. LNCS (LNAI), vol. 10654, pp. 213–222. Springer, Cham (2017). https://doi.org/10.1007/978-3-319-70772-3_20

Cross-Modal Video to Body-Joints Augmentation for Rehabilitation Exercise Quality Assessment

Ali Abedi[1(✉)], Mobin Malmirian[2], and Shehroz S. Khan[1,3]

[1] KITE Research Institute, University Health Network, Toronto, Canada
{ali.abedi,shehroz.khan}@uhn.ca
[2] Faculty of Applied Science and Engineering, University of Toronto, Toronto, Canada
mobin.malmirian@mail.utoronto.ca
[3] Institute of Biomedical Engineering, University of Toronto, Toronto, Canada

Abstract. Exercise-based rehabilitation programs have been shown to enhance quality of life and reduce mortality and rehospitalizations. AI-driven virtual rehabilitation programs enable patients to complete exercises independently at home while AI algorithms can analyze exercise data to provide feedback to patients and report their progress to clinicians. This paper introduces a novel approach to assessing the quality of rehabilitation exercises using RGB video. Sequences of skeletal body joints are extracted from consecutive RGB video frames and analyzed by many-to-one sequential neural networks to evaluate exercise quality. Existing datasets for exercise rehabilitation lack adequate samples for training deep sequential neural networks to generalize effectively. A cross-modal data augmentation approach is proposed to resolve this problem. Visual augmentation techniques are applied to video data, and body joints extracted from the resulting augmented videos are used for training sequential neural networks. Extensive experiments conducted on the KInematic assessment of MOvement and clinical scores for remote monitoring of physical REhabilitation (KIMORE) dataset, demonstrate the superiority of the proposed method over previous baseline approaches. The ablation study highlights a significant enhancement in exercise quality assessment following cross-modal augmentation.

Keywords: Rehabilitation Exercise · Exercise Quality Assessment · Video Augmentation · Cross-Modal Data Augmentation

1 Introduction

The referral of patients who have experienced a stroke, cardiac event, or injury to rehabilitation programs is a widely adopted strategy with the objective of enhancing patients' quality of life and reducing re-hospitalization and mortality rates [1]. A significant part of these programs focuses on prescribed regular exercises that are designed to facilitate the restoration of mobility and strength among patients [1]. In recent years, there has been a notable emergence of Artificial Intelligence (AI)-driven virtual rehabilitation as a promising approach for remotely delivering rehabilitation programs to patients within the confines of their own homes [2]. Studies have shown that virtual rehabilitation can offer health benefits comparable to in-person rehabilitation and that it can overcome several barriers, such as transportation, the cost of therapy, and financial concerns [3]. Virtual rehabilitation can involve the utilization of diverse sensors to capture patients' movements, which are subsequently subjected to analysis using AI algorithms during exercise sessions [2,4]. The analysis outcomes derived from these algorithms can be used to provide patients with feedback regarding the quality or completion of their exercises [4,5]. Additionally, clinicians can utilize the analysis results to closely monitor patients' progress and implement appropriate personalized interventions.

Rehabilitation programs typically involve prescribing patients with specific exercises, as well as other components such as education [1,6–9]. The assessment of exercise performance relies on objective criteria, including adhering to the prescribed exercise sets and repetitions [19], maintaining consistency in the execution of exercises, demonstrating proper technique and movement quality, and ensuring the correct posture of various body parts [6,7]. Previous research on generic human activity analysis has highlighted the importance of incorporating joint modelling within the parts of the human body [6,10]. In the context of rehabilitation exercise quality assessment, the incorporation of joint modelling within patients' body parts aligns with the approach taken by clinicians when assessing the quality and technique of exercises [7]. Body joints exhibit resilience towards variations in illumination and background, making them a reliable data modality for analysis. Body joint information can be acquired through specialized hardware, including depth cameras and wearable sensors [6,7]. Alternatively, computer vision techniques can be employed to extract body joint information from RGB videos [11,12]. This work specifically concentrates on the latter approach, which eliminates the requirement for costly hardware/equipment and enables the integration of body joint analysis into platforms that solely rely on commonly available RGB cameras. The body joint sequences are extracted from consecutive frames of the videos of exercises. These sequences are then input into a deep sequential neural network for analysis, enabling the inference of exercise quality in the form of a real number.

Obtaining sufficiently large-scale annotated data is often a challenge in many practical scenarios due to the expensive and time-consuming nature of data collection and annotation [21]. This issue is particularly pronounced in healthcare-related contexts and patient data, where acquiring data from patients, such as rehabilitation exercise videos from post-stroke patients at home, poses greater difficulties compared to other applications [7]. Additionally, annotating patient data incurs higher costs since it requires expert annotators such as physiotherapists and stroke rehabilitation clinicians to score the quality of stroke rehabilitation exercises. To annotate rehabilitation exercises, clinicians rely on video data modality since simply having skeletal body joint data is insufficient for assessing the quality and technique of exercises [7]. Consequently, while most deep learning models are trained on body joint data modality [6], in real-world scenarios, there is typically a higher availability of annotated video data. As a result, the majority of existing exercise rehabilitation datasets lack sufficient samples to be used for training generalizable deep learning models [6,7,15]. The purpose of this work is to overcome this difficulty by applying visual augmentation techniques to annotated videos in order to increase the number of training samples. The main contribution of this work is cross-model data augmentation from videos to body joints; augmenting video data modality, and using the augmented data in the form of body joints data modality to train generalizable deep learning models. Extensive experiments on the only publicly available rehabilitation exercise video dataset, KInematic assessment of MOvement and clinical scores for remote monitoring of physical REhabilitation (KIMORE) [7], demonstrated the effectiveness of the cross-modal augmentation and superiority of the proposed method compared to previous methods.

This paper is structured as follows. Section 2 introduces related works on rehabilitation exercise quality assessment. In Sect. 3, the proposed method for rehabilitation exercise quality assessment is presented. Section 4 describes experimental settings and results on the proposed methodology. In the end, Sect. 5 presents our conclusions and directions for future works.

2 Related Work

In this section, a brief review is conducted on the current state of research pertaining to two key areas: rehabilitation exercise quality assessment and cross-modal data augmentation.

2.1 Rehabilitation Exercise Quality Assessment

Liao et al. [6] classified the methodologies employed for assessing the quality of rehabilitation exercises into three categories: discrete movement scores, rule-based, and template-based approaches. Discrete movement score approaches utilize traditional machine learning classifiers to categorize rehabilitation exercises into discrete groups, such as correct or incorrect [6,8,14]. These methods, however, are limited in their ability to detect subtle variations in patient performance and provide nuanced assessments of movement quality, such as scores between 0 and 1 [6]. Rule-based approaches, on the other hand, require clinicians to determine in advance a set of rules for each particular rehabilitation exercise. These rules serve as a benchmark for evaluating an exercise's level of correctness [6,7,15]. The drawback of rule-based approaches lies in the fact that they are exercise-specific and cannot be applied to other exercises [6,15]. A template-based approach evaluates exercises against a reference exercise that is correct. Template-based approaches can be categorized as either model-free (direct matching) or model-based [15,16]. Model-free approaches apply a distance function, such as dynamic time warping, between the sequence of movements performed by the patient and the reference sequence of movements of the correct exercise [6,15]. Machine-learning and deep-learning approaches are in the category of model-based approaches [6,15–18]. Some of the model-based approaches extract a single feature vector from the entire video sample/body joint sequence and develop a machine-learning model to analyze the feature vector in a non-sequential manner [18], but most of them address exercise quality assessment as a spatial-temporal data analysis problem using models such as variants of recurrent neural networks [6,16] and spatial-temporal graph neural networks [6,15,17].

2.2 Cross-Modal Data Augmentation

Data augmentation across modalities has been employed in a variety of applications, including for emotion recognition using image and audio data [22]. Wang et al. [22] presented an approach for transferring knowledge between annotated facial images and audio domains by learning a joint distribution of samples in different modalities and mapping an image sample to an audio spectrum. Other examples of cross-modal data augmentation include across image and text [23], and video and Lidar data [24].

In this paper, we propose the application of cross-modal data augmentation across video and body joint data modalities to increase the number of body joint sequences that can be utilized for training generalizable deep sequential models.

3 Method

The proposed method takes as input an RGB video sample containing a rehabilitation exercise performed by a patient. The output is a real number that reflects the quality of the rehabilitation exercise. A sequence of body joints is extracted from consecutive frames of the video, through the use of a pre-trained pose estimation model. A sequence of feature vectors is extracted from the sequence of body joints, by extracting hand-crafted features from the body joints in each frame. The features are exercise-specific. For instance, the upper body is given more consideration in the arm-lifting exercise [7], where features such as elbow angle and distance between the hands are calculated [18]. To analyze the sequence of feature vectors, a many-to-one Recurrent Neural Network (RNN) is employed. Each feature vector extracted from one frame of the input data is fed to a corresponding timestamp of the RNN. Following the RNN, fully-connected layers are utilized, culminating in a single neuron in the final layer, which generates an output representing exercise quality.

To enhance the number of annotated training samples and improve the generalizability of RNNs, visual augmentation techniques are implemented on the video samples within the training dataset. Care is taken to select video transformation techniques that do not alter the inherent nature of the data or its annotation, specifically the exercise quality depicted in the video. The chosen video transformations encompass horizontal flipping and slight rotations applied uniformly to all video frames. However, temporal data augmentation is not employed on videos to avoid altering the structure of rehabilitation exercises and the way they have been annotated by clinicians [7]. By utilizing the augmented video data, the corresponding body joints are extracted and employed to train RNNs effectively. The details of the parameters of RNNs are explained in Sect. 4.1.

4 Experiments

This section evaluates the performance of the proposed method on the KIMORE dataset [7] in comparison to previous methods. The KIMORE dataset [7] contains RGB and depth videos along with body joint position and orientation data captured by the Kinect camera. The data were collected from 78 participants, including 44 healthy participants and 34 patients with motor dysfunction (stroke, Parkinson's disease, and low back pain). Each data sample in this dataset is composed of one participant performing multiple repetitions of one of the five exercises: (1) lifting of the arms, (2) lateral tilt of the trunk with the arms in extension, (3) trunk rotation, (4) pelvis rotations on the transverse plane, and (5) squatting. The data samples were annotated by clinical experts in terms of exercise quality as a number in the range of 0 to 50 [7]. In this dataset, there are 353 samples with an average of 70 samples per exercise, which is quite a few samples for training deep learning models.

4.1 Experimental Settings

The experiments were conducted using RGB videos available in KIMORE [7]. MediaPipe [12], a pre-trained deep neural network for pose estimation, was used to extract body-joints sequences from consecutive video frames. Exercise-specific features, designed for five different exercises in KIMORE, were extracted from body joint sequences to construct feature vectors for each video sample. More information about exercise-specific features can be found at [7,18]. Long Short-Term Memory (LSTM) is used to analyze the sequences of exercise-specific features. The number of neurons in the input layers of the LSTM depends on the dimensionality of features extracted from each exercise [18]. In the LSTM, there are 4 unidirectional layers that contain 16 neurons in hidden layers. Each LSTM layer except the last is followed by a dropout layer with a probability of 0.17. The LSTM is trailed by a 16×1 linear layer to output the exercise quality score. Since the model solves a regression problem, no activation function was used. The Adam optimization algorithm was used with 300 epochs, batches of size 8, and a learning rate of 0.01 to minimize a mean absolute error loss function [25].

Using samples of the five exercises in KIMORE, five different models were trained and evaluated. The models were trained and evaluated using a five-fold cross-validation procedure. During each iteration of five-fold cross-validation, video augmentation is applied only to the training samples. A total of seven new videos were generated from each video sample by adding horizontal flipping, -1, -2, -3, 1, 2, and $3°$ rotations to the existing video.

Table 1. The Spearman's rank correlation between predictions and ground-truth exercise quality scores in five different exercises in the KIMORE dataset [7] for different settings of the proposed method compared to previous methods.

	Ex. 1	Ex. 2	Ex. 3	Ex. 4	Ex. 5
Capecci et al. [6]	0.44	0.41	0.46	**0.62**	0.30
Guo and Khan [17]	0.55	**0.64**	0.63	0.37	0.42
Proposed method - no augmentation	0.41	0.48	0.52	0.37	0.41
Proposed method – flipping, -1, and 1 degrees rotation augmentation	**0.76**	0.61	**0.73**	0.54	**0.67**
Proposed method – flipping, -2, -1, 1, and 2 degrees rotation augmentation	0.74	0.59	0.72	0.53	0.65
Proposed method – flipping, -3, -2, -1, 1, 2, and 3 degrees rotation augmentation	0.72	0.54	0.70	0.50	0.62

4.2 Experimental Results

Following the literature [6, 16–18], the Spearman's rank correlation was used as the evaluation metric. The performance of the proposed method in different settings compared to the previous works is shown in Table 1. It is noteworthy that the samples in the five folds of cross validation in our experiments are not exactly the same samples as those in the previous methods. Compared to no augmentation and with the small number of samples in the individual exercises in KIMORE, cross-modal video-to-body-joint data augmentation significantly improved the performance. For instance, for the first exercise, Ex. 1 in Table 1, the augmentation resulted in an 86% improvement in the correlation from 0.41 to 0.76. For the proposed method, the best results were obtained using the first type of data augmentation in which three samples were generated from each video sample by flipping and rotating -1 and $1°$. The proposed method significantly outperformed the previous methods on the first, third, and fifth exercises, with

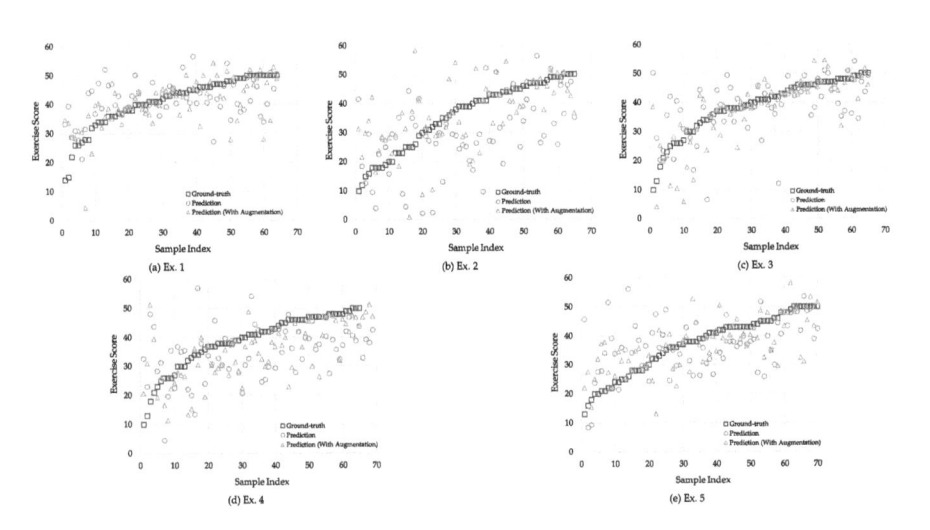

Fig. 1. The scatter plots of the predictions of the proposed method without and with cross-modal augmentation compared to ground-truth exercise quality scores in (a)–(e) five exercises in the KIMORE dataset [7].

72%, 59%, and 123% improvements in correlation, respectively. While for the second exercise, the performance of the proposed method is superior to [7] and close to [18], the performance of the proposed method on the fourth exercise is inferior to [7]. This is due to the fact that the fourth exercise involved pelvis rotations, i.e., movements along the z axis, which is relatively difficult to capture by the MediaPipe [12].

Corresponding to the third and fourth rows of Table 1, Fig. 1 illustrates the scatter plots of the proposed method without and with cross-modal augmentation for five exercises in KIMORE. According to Fig. 1, cross-modal augmentation results in predictions that are more closely correlated with ground-truth exercise quality scores.

5 Conclusion and Future Works

The purpose of this study was to investigate the effectiveness of cross-modal data augmentation from RGB videos to body joints for developing sequential neural networks for rehabilitation exercise quality assessment. With data augmentation, more generalizable neural networks were trained. This resulted in significant improvement in performance compared to no augmentation and outperformance compared to previous methods. This study represents the first work on video-to-body-joint cross-modal data augmentation [13,22–24]. Future research may involve the inclusion of cross-modal data augmentation within a generative adversarial network setting and using spatial-temporal graph convolutional networks for rehabilitation exercise quality assessment.

References

1. Dibben, G.O., et al.: Exercise-based cardiac rehabilitation for coronary heart disease: a meta-analysis. Eur. Heart J. **44**(6), 452–469 (2023)
2. Ferreira, R., Santos, R., Sousa, A.: Usage of auxiliary systems and artificial intelligence in home-based rehabilitation: a review. In: Exploring the Convergence of Computer and Medical Science Through Cloud Healthcare, pp. 163–196 (2023)
3. Seron, P., et al.: Effectiveness of telerehabilitation in physical therapy: a rapid overview. Phys. Therapy **101**(6), pzab053 (2021)
4. Sangani, S., et al.: Real-time avatar-based feedback to enhance the symmetry of spatiotemporal parameters after stroke: instantaneous effects of different avatar views. IEEE Trans. Neural Syst. Rehabil. Eng. **28**(4), 878–887 (2020)
5. Fernandez-Cervantes, V., et al.: VirtualGym: a Kinect-based system for seniors exercising at home. Entertainment Comput. **27**, 60–72 (2018)
6. Liao, Y., et al.: A review of computational approaches for evaluation of rehabilitation exercises. Comput. Biol. Med. **119**, 103687 (2020)
7. Capecci, M., et al.: The KIMORE dataset: KInematic assessment of MOvement and clinical scores for remote monitoring of physical REhabilitation. IEEE Trans. Neural Syst. Rehabil. Eng. **27**(7), 1436–1448 (2019)
8. Vakanski, A., et al.: A data set of human body movements for physical rehabilitation exercises. Data **3**(1), 2 (2018)

9. Miron, A., et al.: IntelliRehabDS (IRDS)-a dataset of physical rehabilitation movements. Data **6**(5), 46 (2021)
10. Yan, S., Xiong, Y., Lin, D.: Spatial temporal graph convolutional networks for skeleton-based action recognition. In: Proceedings of the AAAI Conference on Artificial Intelligence, vol. 32, no. 1 (2018)
11. Pavllo, D., et al.: 3D human pose estimation in video with temporal convolutions and semi-supervised training. In: Proceedings of the IEEE/CVF Conference on Computer Vision and Pattern Recognition (2019)
12. Lugaresi, C., et al.: MediaPipe: a framework for building perception pipelines. arXiv preprint arXiv:1906.08172 (2019)
13. Chen, D., et al.: Cross-modal data augmentation for tasks of different modalities. IEEE Trans. Multimedia (2022)
14. Um, T.T., et al.: Parkinson's disease assessment from a wrist-worn wearable sensor in free-living conditions: deep ensemble learning and visualization. arXiv preprint arXiv:1808.02870 (2018)
15. Sardari, S., et al.: Artificial intelligence for skeleton-based physical rehabilitation action evaluation: a systematic review. Comput. Biol. Med., 106835 (2023)
16. Liao, Y., Vakanski, A., Xian, M.: A deep learning framework for assessing physical rehabilitation exercises. IEEE Trans. Neural Syst. Rehabil. Eng. **28**(2), 468–477 (2020)
17. Deb, S., et al.: Graph convolutional networks for assessment of physical rehabilitation exercises. IEEE Trans. Neural Syst. Rehabil. Eng. **30**, 410–419 (2022)
18. Guo, Q., Khan, S.: Exercise-specific feature extraction approach for assessing physical rehabilitation. In: 4th IJCAI Workshop on AI for Aging, Rehabilitation and Intelligent Assisted Living, IJCAI (2021)
19. Abedi, A., et al.: Rehabilitation exercise repetition segmentation and counting using skeletal body joints. arXiv preprint arXiv:2304.09735 (2023)
20. Réby, K., et al.: Graph transformer for physical rehabilitation evaluation. In: 2023 IEEE 17th International Conference on Automatic Face and Gesture Recognition (FG). IEEE (2023)
21. Athanasiadis, C., Hortal, E., Asteriadis, S.: Audio-visual domain adaptation using conditional semi-supervised generative adversarial networks. Neurocomputing **397**, 331–344 (2020)
22. Wang, S., et al.: Semi-supervised classification-aware cross-modal deep adversarial data augmentation. Future Gener. Comput. Syst. **125**, 194–205 (2021)
23. Wang, H., et al.: Paired cross-modal data augmentation for fine-grained image-to-text retrieval. In: Proceedings of the 30th ACM International Conference on Multimedia (2022)
24. Wang, C., et al.: PointAugmenting: cross-modal augmentation for 3D object detection. In: Proceedings of the IEEE/CVF Conference on Computer Vision and Pattern Recognition (2021)
25. Paszke, A., et al.: Pytorch: an imperative style, high-performance deep learning library. In: Advances in Neural Information Processing Systems, vol. 32 (2019)

Multimodal Sensor Fusion for Daily Living Activity Recognition in Active Assisted Living for Older Adults

Kang Wang[1], Himalaya Sharma[1], Jasleen Kaur[1], Shi Cao[2], and Plinio Morita[1,2,3,4](✉)

[1] School of Public Health Sciences, University of Waterloo, Waterloo, ON, Canada
plinio.morita@uwaterloo.ca
[2] Department of Systems Design Engineering, University of Waterloo, Waterloo, ON, Canada
[3] Centre for Digital Therapeutics, Techna Institute, University Health Network, Toronto, ON, Canada
[4] Management, and Evaluation, Institute of Health Policy, University of Toronto, Toronto, ON, Canada

Abstract. Given the global population's significant growth in the aging demographic, there is an urgent need for advanced technologies capable of monitoring the daily activities of older adults. Active Assisted Living, which integrates multimodal sensors, has emerged as a promising solution to promote independent living among older adults. However, the lack of an efficient fusion method has hindered the full potential of Active Assisted Living technology. This study aims to develop a novel multimodal sensor fusion framework utilizing diverse smart home devices to achieve accurate recognition of daily living activities for older adults. To validate the effectiveness of the framework, a case study was conducted involving 5 individuals in a carefully constructed smart home environment. Five machine learning models were employed to evaluate the recognition performance across 23 indoor activity scenarios. The evaluation results demonstrate the effectiveness of the sensor fusion framework, with an average recognition accuracy exceeding 0.850, and the highest accuracy achieving 0.958.

Keywords: Active Assisted Living · Multimodal Sensor Date Fusion · Healthy Aging · Remote Healthcare Monitoring · Activity Recognition

1 Introduction

In recent years, the global population has experienced a significant demographic shift, with a substantial increase in the proportion of older adults [1]. As individuals age, they often face difficulties in maintaining their independence and performing Activities of Daily Living (ADLs) without assistance. To address these challenges, the concept of Active Assisted Living (AAL) has emerged, aiming to provide older adults with a smart home environment that promotes independent living while ensuring their safety and well-being [2]. Smart home technologies leverage a range of sensors, including environmental sensors, wearable devices, and active sensors like cameras and motion sensors to monitor and capture information about older adults' activities [2]. The recognition and monitoring of daily living activities represent a crucial aspect of AAL, as they offer valuable insights to caregivers and healthcare providers regarding an individual's well-being, facilitate the detection of potential health issues, and enable timely interventions [3]. Traditional approaches to activity recognition have predominantly relied on single-modality sensors, such as accelerometers or video cameras [4]. However, the current state of sensor technologies in AAL environments faces a critical challenge related to the fusion of data from multiple sensors [5]. While individual sensors provide valuable insights into specific aspects of daily activities, the lack of a robust multimodal sensor fusion method hampers accurate recognition and interpretation of these activities. Without effective fusion techniques, the full potential of AAL systems cannot be realized, thereby limiting their impact on the lives of older adults.

To address this limitation, a novel multimodal sensor fusion framework was proposed in this study for recognizing the daily living activities of older adults. Employing a range of AAL sensors, including environmental sensors, occupancy sensors, and wearable devices, within a smart home environment, the objective of this study is to develop and validate the proposed framework for activity recognition. By integrating data from multiple sensors, the aim is to enhance the accuracy and reliability of activity recognition in AAL environments, enabling personalized and proactive care for older adults, improving their safety and well-being, and promoting independent living.

2 Related Studies

Several research papers have been published in the field of human activity recognition (HAR) and sensor fusion for assisted living and healthcare monitoring. San et al. [6] investigated HAR using smartphones and sensor fusion, specifically analyzing the performance of individual and combined use of accelerometer, gyroscope, and magnetometer sensors. The results demonstrate that sensor fusion improves recognition accuracy, and feature selection is vital for improving classification accuracy and reducing computational complexity. Nahiduzzaman et al. [7] proposed an Recurrent Neural Network (RNN) framework for fall detection and daily activity monitoring in elderly individuals with neurological disorders using data from wearable devices and cameras. The system incorporates Internet of Things (IoT) devices, cloud analysis, and anomaly detection. The RNN model outperforms Support Vector Machines and Random Forest models, highlighting the significance of machine learning and IoT in managing neurodegenerative diseases. Wang et al. [8] developed a hybrid sensor data fusion system for recognizing older adults' activities. This system integrates data from both wearable and ambient sensors, incorporating information of daily routines and room location. The findings demonstrate that fusing wearable device data with a new feature set and ambient information improves recognition performance. Although the existing work has made significant contributions to activity recognition and sensor fusion in assisted living and healthcare monitoring, several gaps (such as lack of robust multimodal sensor fusion methods; limited consideration of resource constraints and specific requirements; insufficient evaluation of real-world effectiveness) still need to be addressed. The proposed paper aims to fill these gaps by developing and validating a novel multimodal sensor fusion framework in a real-world environment.

3 Methods

3.1 Materials

AAL Sensors. The AAL sensors used in this study were sourced from Swidget, a renowned smart home solution company known for their modular and interchangeable systems integrated into various electrical devices. Swidget's sensors offer a versatile range of capabilities, capturing both environmental and occupancy data. Environmental sensors measure and monitor parameters such as power usage, temperature, humidity, and air quality, providing valuable insights for environment control. Occupancy sensors, including motion sensors, door contact sensors, and electrical usage log sensors, detect the presence or absence of individuals and provide binary data with timestamps. Real-time data with 30-s granularity was seamlessly retrieved from these sensors using the Application Programming Interfaces (APIs) and integrated into the research database for comprehensive analysis and evaluation.

Wearable Sensors. Empatica E4 is a wristband equipped with multiple sensors to capture various physiological signals. It measures heart rate, blood volume pulse, and inter beat interval using a photoplethysmogram sensor. The heart rate is detected every second, while the blood volume pulse is sampled at 64Hz. It also has an electrode sensor to monitor changes in skin's electrical properties at 4Hz, an infrared thermopile sensor to measure skin temperature at 4Hz, and a 3-axis accelerometer to capture motion activity at 32Hz. The device can be connected to the Empatica Manager app to download raw data in CSV format for further analysis. Fitbit sense, a trusted consumer activity monitor, is widely used by healthcare professionals to measure patient activity levels. Its accurate estimation of intensity and energy consumption in real-life settings, along with its API gateway for accessing historical data, makes it an ideal research tool. In this study, Fitbit sense recorded individuals' steps at a 1-min frequency during experiment sessions.

3.2 AAL Environment

A smart home environment was established in Research Institute for Aging at Waterloo (Fig. 1 shows the layout). The apartment comprises a kitchen, living room, bedroom, and bathroom, equipped with furniture necessary to satisfy an occupants' daily living requirements. The smart home environment was designed as a sensor-rich space to capture various ADLs. Original switches and outlets were replaced with intelligent smart devices, which were coupled with three types of environmental sensors and motion sensors based on the locations of electrical devices in each room. Specifically, motion sensors were placed in the environment following principles of wider coverage, higher placement, and less false alarm, with consideration of 5-m detection range of the motion sensor. Door contact sensors were attached on each door, closet, and drawer to capture open/close events. For more accurate and comprehensive environmental data, multiple temperature and humidity sensors, as well as air quality sensors were placed in different rooms, with additional sensors installed in areas where these parameters are more likely to change, such as the kitchen and bathroom. During the design phase, five volunteers were invited to perform potential activities in the room. Their involvement assisted in testing and adjusting the sensor location and quantity, following a user-centered design method.

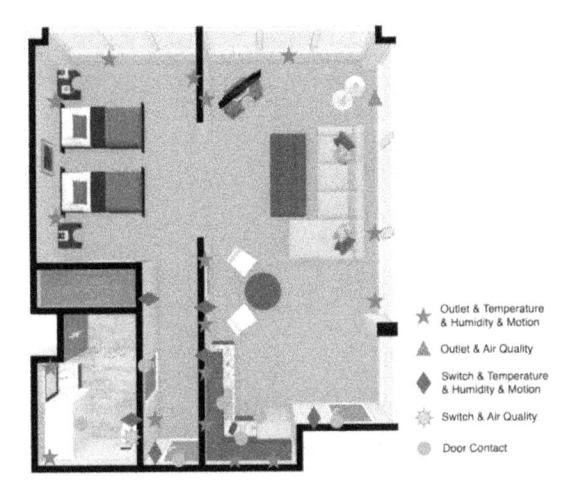

Fig. 1. Smart home environment and sensor locations.

3.3 Temporal Windowing and Statistical Feature Extraction

In this study, we proposed a method called Temporal Windowing and Statistical Feature Extraction (TWSFE) to extract features from time series data (Fig. 2). The window concept is employed in this transformation to facilitate the extraction of statistical features from each window, encompassing both time-domain and frequency-domain characteristics of the data. By utilizing Fourier transform, the time-domain signal is converted into the frequency-domain, enabling the examination of frequency-based properties. This conversion provides valuable insights into the periodicity and oscillatory behavior of the data. Within each window, 16 statistical features is extracted from each dataset, encompassing measures including mean, standard deviation, average absolute difference, minimum and maximum values, maximum and minimum difference, median, median absolute deviation, inter-quartile range, positive and negative counts, values above mean, number of peaks, skewness, energy, and signal magnitude area. These statistical features effectively capture various aspects of the data distribution and dynamics, revealing critical characteristics relevant to the monitored activities. By considering this comprehensive set of features, a rich representation of the data is achieved, facilitating subsequent analysis and modeling tasks.

Furthermore, for activity recognition, a supervised classification task, determining the activity label for each window assumes utmost importance. By identifying the most frequently occurring activity within a given window, the assigned label represents the dominant activity during that specific timeframe. This approach leverages the majority class present within the window, thereby providing a reasonable approximation of the overall activity occurring, considering the limited duration of the window.

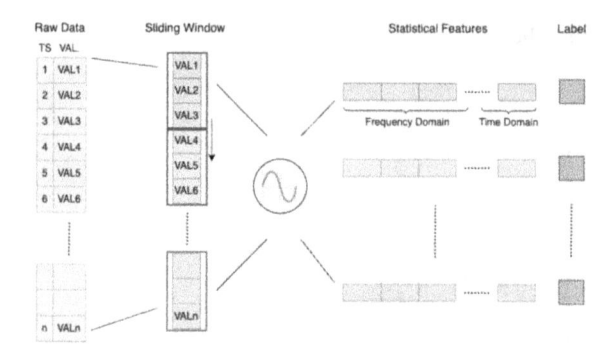

Fig. 2. Temporal windowing and statistical feature extraction method

3.4 Sensor Fusion Framework

Figure 3 illustrates our sensor fusion framework, designed to leverage the complementary information from multiple sensors and enhance the accuracy and reliability of our system. The framework integrates data from diverse sensors into a unified representation.

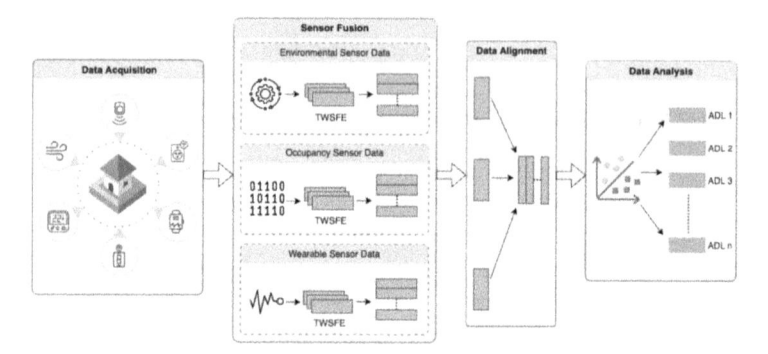

Fig. 3. Sensor fusion framework

Initially, data collection from various sensors occurs through APIs or corresponding channels, enabling the acquisition of environmental, occupancy, and wearable data. This forms the foundation for the subsequent stages of our fusion framework. The sensor fusion process begins with data pre-processing and feature extraction, performed separately for each data type. In the pre-processing step, acquired sensor data undergoes noise removal, correction of sensor biases or calibration errors, and necessary transformations or conversions. The TWSFE methods is then applied to the data. The window size (e.g. 30, 60 s) in TWSFE can be customized according to specific frequency information of each data type to make sure the alignment of each data for final dataset. Following pre-processing, the data alignment stage aims to synchronize the data from different sources to correspond to the same point in time. Additionally, the starting reference timestamp is synchronized for each dataset. Once the data from different devices has been synchronized to have a common granularity, the fused representation is created by combining the transformed features from each source. By performing these systematic steps, the multimodal sensor fusion approach enables the integration of data from different device sources, allowing for more comprehensive and accurate recognition of daily living activities using machine learning models in the context of AAL for Older Adults.

4 Case Study

4.1 ADLs Scenarios

The scripts for activities of daily living in this study were developed based on the principles outlined in Edemekong et al. [9]. The scripts encompass 23 different basic and instrumental ADLs, as well as posture and movement-oriented activities, which occur in all areas of the home and are representative of an individual's daily activities. To ensure comprehensive coverage, different levels of activities were developed, as each requires different levels of effort from individuals and can cause the variation of activity intensity, which also can improve the robustness and accuracy of the models. The detailed ADL scenarios are as follow: 1) Phase 1 - Single activities: 1. Arriving home, 2. Eating dinner, 3. Going to sleep, 4. Cooking, 5. Going out; 2) Phase 2 - Posture-oriented: 1. Reading on sofa, 2. Completing a puzzle, 3. Reading on bed, 4. Meal time, 5. Bathroom job; 3) Phase 3 - Movement-oriented: 1. Morning exercise, 2. Tidying a room, 3. Taking shower, 4. Wondering in rooms; 4) Phase 4 - Basic ADLs: 1. Cleaning rooms, 2. Changing footwear, 3. Prepare meal, 4. Make up; 5) Phase 5 - Instrumental ADLs: 1. Arriving home from groceries, 2. Cleaning kitchen, 3. Emptying garbage, 4. Morning routine, 5. Wrap up things.

4.2 Data Collection

Due to the challenges of Covid-19 pandemic, we were having difficulty on recruiting older adults during this study, considering they are vulnerable population. Instead, we recruited students from University of Waterloo as participants. Five participant (3 females, 2 males) was involved in the study whose mean age is 24 years old ranging between 20 to 34 years. To minimize the bias on performing daily living activities between different age groups, we instructed participants to perform slower than their usual speed. To safeguard participants' privacy and confidentiality, their information were de-identified. Before the experiment, participants completed a consent form and demographic questionnaire. The researchers then escorted them to the smart home environment and oriented them to the locations of labeled sensors, appliances, and furniture. Participants were instructed to wear Empatica E4 and Fitbit sense on their preferred hand to increase data accuracy. During the experiment, facilitators delivered activity instructions to participants via phone and observed their activity performance through cameras in an adjacent room. Instructions were given in a fixed sequence of scenarios, with no further instructions provided unless requested. A one-minute transition time was allowed between each scenario to reset all activated sensors. An experimenter recorded activity information, including start and end timestamps, on an annotation sheet. Sensor readings were collected, formatted, and stored in the cloud database via the API channel. Each experiment participant has approximately three hours' data size. The study's ethical aspects were reviewed and approved by the Human Research Ethics Board of the University of Waterloo under ORE #43843.

5 Results

5.1 Evaluation Models, Metrics, and Hyperparameters

A set of commonly used machine learning classification algorithms was employed, encompassing Random Forest (RF), Support Vector Classifier (SVC), K-Nearest Neighbors (KNN), Decision Tree (DT), and Gaussian Naive Bayes (GNB). To assess the performance of the models, we use several metrics widely recognized in the field: Accuracy, Precision, Recall, and F1-score. Our dataset was divided into training and testing sets with a ratio of 7:3. The programming scripts was built upon Scikit-learn library. Additionally, in order to search the hyperparameters that yielded the best performance for each model, we employed the Hyperopt package [10] to tune different hyperparameter combinations. The primary hyperparameters are set as follows: RF (n_estimators = 200); SVC (kernel = linear, C = 1); KNN (n_neighbors = 3); DT (max_depth = 5); GNB (var_smoothing = 1e-08). The window size for TWSFE is 30 s.

5.2 Performance of Daily Living Activity Recognition on ML Models

The results of the evaluation on five machine learning models for the recognition of daily living activities are presented in Table 1.

Table 1. Evaluation results on five machine learning models

	Accuracy	Precision	Recall	F1-score
RF	0.922	0.927	0.922	0.919
SVC	0.934	0.937	0.934	0.933
KNN	**0.958**	**0.962**	**0.958**	**0.957**
DT	0.841	0.843	0.841	0.838
GNB	0.601	0.699	0.602	0.599

The evaluation results demonstrate the effectiveness of our sensor fusion framework in accurately recognizing daily living activities using machine learning models for individuals. Among the models, RF achieved an accuracy of 0.922, with precision, recall, and F1-score values of 0.927, 0.922, and 0.919, respectively. SVC exhibited slightly higher accuracy at 0.934, with precision, recall, and F1-score values of 0.937, 0.934, and 0.933, respectively. The KNN model outperformed the other models with the highest accuracy of 0.958, along with excellent precision (0.962), recall (0.958), and F1-score (0.957). This demonstrates the effectiveness of KNN in capturing patterns in the collected sensor data. While the DT model achieved an accuracy of 0.841, with precision, recall, and F1-score values of 0.843, 0.841, and 0.838, respectively, the GNB model exhibited relatively lower accuracy and precision at 0.602 and 0.699, respectively, with recall and F1-score values of 0.602 and 0.599.

6 Conclusion

In conclusion, this study presented a AAL sensor fusion framework for the recognition of daily living activities using machine learning models. The evaluation results demonstrate that all the machine learning models exhibited good performance in accurately classifying daily living activities, demonstrating the effectiveness of proposed framework for remote monitoring on older individuals. However, one limitation of this study is the age of the samples, and we acknowledge that the physiological response and behavior of young people may differ from older individuals. Despite this limitation, our study represents an important step in developing intelligent AAL systems that can enhance live independence for older adults. Further research will focus on validating current finds on older participants.

References

1. United Nations. World Population Ageing 2019. www.un.org, 2019. https://www.un.org/en/development/desa/population/publications/pdf/ageing/WorldPopulationAgeing2019-Highlights.pdf. Accessed 1 Jun 2023
2. Marcelino, I., Laza, R., Domingues, P., Gómez-Meire, S., Fdez-Riverola, F., Pereira, A.: Active and assisted living ecosystem for the elderly. Sensors **18**(4), 1246 (2018)
3. Patel, A., Shah, J.: Sensor-based activity recognition in the context of ambient assisted living systems: a review. J. Ambient Intell. Smart Environ. **11**(4), 301–322 (2019)
4. Hassan, M.M., Uddin, M., Mohamed, A., Almogren, A.: A robust human activity recognition system using smartphone sensors and deep learning. Futur. Gener. Comput. Syst. **81**, 307–313 (2018)
5. Koshmak, G., Loutfi, A., Linden, M.: Challenges and issues in multisensor fusion approach for fall detection: review paper. J. Sensors **2016**, 1–12 (2016)
6. San, C.V., Michael, N.: Basic human activity recognition based on sensor fusion in smartphones. In: 2017 IFIP/IEEE Symposium on Integrated Network and Service Management (IM) (2017)
7. Nahiduzzaman, M., Tasnim, M., Newaz, N.T., Kaiser, M.L., Mahmud, M.: Machine learning based early fall detection for elderly people with neurological disorder using multimodal data fusion. Lecture Notes in Computer Science, pp. 204–214 (2020). https://doi.org/10.1007/978-3-030-59277-6_19
8. Wang, Y., Cang, S., Yu, H.: A data fusion-based hybrid sensory system for older people's daily activity and daily routine recognition. IEEE Sens. J. **18**(16), 6874–6888 (2018)
9. Edemekong, P.F., Bomgaars, D.L., Sukumaran, S., Schoo, C.: Activities of Daily Living. In: StatPearls, StatPearls Publishing (2022)
10. Bergstra, J., Komer, B., Eliasmith, C., Yamins, D., Cox, D.D.: Hyperopt: a python library for model selection and hyperparameter optimization. Comput. Sci. Discov. **8**(1), 014008 (2015)

Modeling and Detecting Urinary Anomalies in Seniors from Data Obtained by Unintrusive Sensors

Yueyi Ge, Ingrid Zukerman(✉), Mahsa Salehi, and Mor Vered

Department of Data Science and Artificial Intelligence, Monash University, Clayton, VIC 3800, Australia
{yueyi.ge,ingrid.zukerman,mahsa.salehi,mor.vered}@monash.edu

Abstract. In this project, we use unintrusive sensors to collect data about toilet attendance of seniors as a proxy for micturition, in order to detect anomalous behaviour. Firstly, we identify and address challenges associated with building a robust dataset of normal toilet-attendance behaviour from sensor logs. Next, since our users are healthy, we leverage medical information to build personalized simulated models of abnormal toilet attendance on the basis of users' normal behaviour. We then compare the performance of two anomaly-detection models in detecting abnormal increases in toilet visits.

Keywords: Anomaly detection · Modeling patients toilet attendance · Urinary anomalies · Unintrusive sensors

1 Introduction

A widely accepted solution to the challenge of caring for older adults living alone in their homes consists of developing in-home monitoring systems that help seniors stay safely at home [14]. Since elderly people often object to intrusive sensors, such as wearable devices and cameras [7], we focus on monitoring systems that rely on *unintrusive sensors*, such as motion sensors. These systems have been employed to detect inactivity in the home as a proxy for falls [10], and to link behavioural changes to underlying medical conditions, e.g., decreased walking speed with cognitive impairment [6], and abnormal behaviour patterns with urinary tract infections (UTIs) [4,11]. In this paper, we focus on detecting urinary disturbances on the basis of users' behaviour changes. However, we could not find such behavioural information in the medical literature; rather, physicians know it from experience. To understand the link between UTIs and behaviour changes, we conducted structured interviews with eight physicians.

Our approach consists of using unintrusive sensors to track toilet visits of healthy users; then employing anomaly detection algorithms to determine whether there is an abnormal increase in toilet visits; and if so, raising an alert. To implement this approach, we need to infer toilet visits from sensor data

(Sect. 3.1), and simulate disease onset in healthy people (Sect. 4.2). Inferring toilet visits is necessary because medical advice about micturition patterns is in terms of toilet visits, rather than sensor activations. It is a challenge, because according to our data, the relationship between sensor activations and toilet visits is unclear (Sect. 3.1). Simulating disease onset is necessary because (1) we could not find datasets with behaviour changes due to urinary disturbances; (2) all our users are healthy, and it is not realistic to wait for them to get sick; and (3) what constitutes a urinary disturbance depends on a person's normal behaviour, therefore we cannot apply a model developed for one user or a population of users to a different person.

2 Related Work

Using Unintrusive Sensors to Collect Data for Modeling Users' Behaviour. We focus on unintrusive sensors because as mentioned above, cameras and wearable devices are not acceptable to our stakeholders [7]. These sensors have been studied in the literature, e.g., passive infrared (PIR) motion sensors have been employed to model user inactivity [10] and walking activity [6], and environmental sensors to identify behaviour patterns [1].

Behavioural Markers of Medical Conditions, Focusing on UTIs. The most common symptoms of UTIs are urination frequency and urgency. The system developed by Rantz *et al.* [11] raised an alert when the number of sensor activations in the bathroom exceeded a threshold. This alert was followed up by physicians in order to determine whether users have UTIs, which revealed that Rantz *et al.*'s procedure yielded too many false alerts. Enshaeifar *et al.* [4] also used bathroom-sensor activations to detect UTIs. They employed non-negative matrix decomposition to extract potential factors from a data matrix, and used these factors to cluster the data into normal clusters and clusters with UTI cases. However, unlike Rantz *et al.* [11], not all alerts were verified through urinalysis tests. Finally, Taramasco *et al.* [15] analyzed presence records and nocturnal movement trajectories in various rooms in a home, and linked them to the output of dedicated sensors that record urination events.

Anomaly Detection Models. These models have been widely used in in-home monitoring systems to detect abnormal behaviour [10,16]. We compare two methods: *One-class Support Vector Machine (OCSVM)* [12], which performs well for anomaly detection, and a modified version of the method developed in [11].

3 Data Pre-processing

We obtained PIR motion-sensor data for ten users, sourced from our industry collaborator SOFIHUB (sofihub.com) (3 users) and the CASAS Smart Home project (7 users) [3]. When movement is detected by a motion sensor, it sends an 'active' signal, and once the sensor fails to detect any movement, it sends an 'inactive' signal. The signals include a time and a room, e.g., {30/06/2018 10:37:59, Bathroom, active} followed by {30/06/2018 10:39:34, Bathroom, inactive}.

To support the construction of a dataset of normal toilet-related behaviour patterns, we (1) infer whether a user has left the home, (2) infer the number of toilet visits in an hour, (3) distinguish between daytime and nighttime, and (4) handle missing data due to home absences. The first step is required in any in-home monitoring application. To perform this step, we followed the method proposed in [10]. However, the other steps depend on the user activity of interest.

3.1 Inferring the Number of Toilet Visits in Each Hour

Following the research in [11], we initially relied on sensor activations as a direct proxy for toilet visits, but this proved to be inappropriate, as the data obtained from sensor activations do not directly map to toilet visits, e.g., a single toilet visit may be associated with 4 sensor activations or 20. In addition, we cannot use sensor activations in other rooms to conclude that a user has left the toilet, because there may be visitors who activated these sensors. In fact, when we tried to use such sensor activations to infer toilet visits, we found that the calculated number of visits exceeded significantly what is considered normal, which is between 3 and 11 toilet visits a day [2,5,8].

To infer the number of toilet visits in each hour, we empirically set an *Inactivity Threshold* (T_I), and apply the following rule:

   If no sensor has been activated in another room,

      then all sensor activations in the toilet belong to the same visit.

   Elseif

{the time between an inactive signal and the next active signal in the toilet} $\leq T_I$,

      then these signals belong to the same toilet visit.

   Else the next active signal is the start of a new toilet visit.

To set T_I, we calculated the number of toilet visits obtained for thresholds between 10–60 min. Three of the thresholds (20, 30 and 40 min) yielded numbers of toilet visits within the normal range. The results reported here were obtained with $T_I = 30$ min, which means that we can posit two toilet visits per hour at most.

3.2 Distinguishing Between Daytime and Nighttime

We employed K-means clustering (with k values ranging from 2 to 9) on the normalized average hourly number of toilet visits and sensor firings (over the hours that have observations, smoothed with adjacent values) in order to determine whether there are times when users exhibit different behaviours. The best clusters for all the users were obtained for $k = 2$, and distinguished between daytime and nighttime hours (the actual hours differed for each user). This result is intuitively appealing, as there is usually a significant difference between the number of toilet visits during day and night.

3.3 Handling Missing Data

Absences from the home result in missing values. Replacing missing values for room visits prevents forming a wrong impression of what constitutes a reasonable number of daily room visits for a particular user. Importantly, the activity of interest affects the method used to replace missing values. For example, going to the toilet at a particular time indicates that this activity is unlikely to be performed for a while before or after this time. Thus, interpolation of values from adjacent times would not be suitable. Further, toilet attendance at the same time on previous or subsequent days is unlikely to be informative for most toilet visits. We therefore selected k *Nearest Neighbour* (*kNN*) to impute data to replace missing values [9]. kNN uses the context of a missing value at time h to find similar neighbours in a dataset (i.e., instances with similar numbers of toilet visits around an hour t, which may be different from h), and imputes a value to the missing observation on the basis of the values obtained from these neighbours.

Defining the Context of a Missing Value. The context of a missing value comprises the hours before and after this value, e.g., a context for a missing observation O_h? may be $\{O_{h-2}, O_{h-1}, \underline{O_h?}, O_{h+1}, O_{h+2}\}$. The question is how much context to incorporate in a data point, i.e., how many hours before or after h? A larger context is more informative than a smaller one, but it may be more difficult to find close neighbours for it than for a smaller context. To answer this question, we considered six variants on the basis of the number of observations before and after an hour h with a missing value. These variants are denoted Var4B, Var2B, Var1B1A, Var2B2A, Var2A, Var4A. For instance, Var2B2A has two observations before the missing value and two observations after it, and Var4B has four observations before the missing value. The idea is to use the "best" variant among the applicable ones to impute values to hours with missing observations, e.g., if a user has been at home all day before 2 pm and after 3 pm, then all the variants are applicable, but if the user did not return home right after 3 pm, then only Var4B and Var2B are applicable. To obtain a ranking of the six variants, we used them to impute toilet visits for all the users for hours that had observations, and ranked the variants in descending order of accuracy.

Imputing Values to Hours with Missing Observations. Users may be absent from their homes for several consecutive hours. Thus, to impute values to hours without observations, we start with hours that are at "the edge" of a group of hours without observations, e.g., we use Var2B if the user has been home for the preceding two hours. We then proceed to hours that have become eligible for imputation due to the recently imputed values, and so on, until all the missing values have been replaced. For each imputation, we (1) select the highest-ranking applicable variant, (2) apply this variant to find k nearest neighbours, and (3) use probabilistic assignment on the basis of these neighbours' predictions to ascribe a value to the missing observation.

4 Creating Test Data with Normal/Abnormal Behaviour Patterns

To validate the performance of models that detect abnormal voiding behaviour, we need test datasets comprising both normal and abnormal behaviours. We deemed a week (seven days) to be a suitable length of time to detect a urinary abnormality or lack thereof. This means that we need test data comprising several weeks of normal and abnormal data. However, we have two problems: (1) we have between 16 and 59 days of normal test data for our users (after using 60 days for training our models, Sect. 5), and (2) we do not have any observational data representing abnormal behaviour. In this section, we describe our approach for addressing both problems. We decided to use ten weeks of data for each different situation in order to test our anomaly-detection models.

4.1 Normal Behaviour

As mentioned above, medical advice distinguishes between daytime and nighttime urination patterns. To generate ten weeks of normal data for day and night for each user, we applied a sliding window to split the remaining daytime and nighttime data (after day 60) into seven-day samples. Clearly, this procedure results in significant data replication, but conceptually, it is similar to drawing probabilistically from a distribution of the real data. Also, the sliding window ensures that we include patterns comprising real consecutive days of data.

4.2 Abnormal Behaviour

There are no datasets about changes of people's micturition patterns when they get UTIs. Fortunately, the medical literature and our team of physicians yielded the following information. According to [8,13], the following were deemed pathological: diurnal voiding frequencies higher than once every two hours, and two or more voiding incidents at night. Also, the literature and/or our team of physicians agree that disease progression differs for different patients; UTI progression may involve fluctuations in the number of toilet visits, with an overall significant increase over a relatively short time; significant changes in toilet visits continuing for two or more days are cause for concern; there can be slow or fast UTI onsets; and UTIs can start with increased micturition only during the day, followed by increased micturition at night. We harnessed this information to create abnormal data for our users by simulating an altered version of our users' voiding behaviours that would be associated with increases in urinary frequency; we also distinguished between daytime and nighttime behaviours, and incorporated slow and fast disease onset.

Modeling Disease Progression. We employ a function that increases the number of toilet visits over a period of time in accordance with the above-provided information. Specifically, we formulate a pattern of increased urinary frequency as a continuous piece-wise linear function $f(x)$ over the period $(0 : n]$, where n is the number of days we have to detect such an increase (at present, $n = 7$), and $x \in \mathbb{N}$ is a day's index. $f(x)$ is composed of p linear segments, where $p \in \{1, .., n-1\}$, and segment $i = \{1, \ldots, p\}$ comprises a linear function $f_i(x)$ that represents the number of toilet visits of a user with increased urinary frequency on day x:

$$f_i(x) = b_i x + \epsilon_i \tag{1}$$

The piece-wise linear function $f(x)$ enables us to control the speed of disease progression through the slope b_i of different segments of this function, and to introduce fluctuations in each segment through the perturbation factor ϵ_i.

To specify $f(x)$, we randomly draw a number $2 \leq p \leq n$ for the number of segments between day 1 of increased urinary frequency and day n, and then select p unique values from the set $\{2, .., n\}$ as x coordinates of the end points of p segments. These coordinates are sorted in ascending order to form a set $\{a_1, \ldots, a_p\}$. Next, we populate the parameters of Eq. 1 for each linear function $f_i(x)$ by randomly drawing a positive slope b_i from $(0, 1]$, and a perturbation factor ϵ_i from a normal distribution $N(0, 0.2)$. Our continuous piece-wise linear function $f(x)$ can now be specified as follows, where Φ is an initialization value (different for day/night):

$$f(x) = \begin{cases} \Phi + f_1(x) & 1 \leq x \leq a_1 \\ \Phi + f_1(a_1) + f_2(x - a_1) & a_1 < x \leq a_2 \\ \ldots \\ \Phi + f_1(a_1) + f_2(a_2 - a_1) + \ldots + f_{p-1}(a_{p-1} - a_{p-2}) + f_p(x - a_{p-1}) & a_{p-1} < x \leq a_p = n \end{cases} \tag{2}$$

The number of toilet visits for each increased-frequency day is obtained by drawing a number from f_1 for day(s) 1 to a_1, from f_2 for day(s) $a_1 + 1$ to a_2, and so on, until we reach day $a_p = n$; each drawn number is added to Φ.

As mentioned above, following medical advice, we model *slow* and *fast* disease onset, and generate separate patterns of increased micturition for *day* and *night*, yielding abnormal data for the combinations {*slow*, *fast*} onset × {*day*, *night*} for each user. For slow disease onset, we draw a slope between $0 < b_i \leq 0.5$; and for fast onset, we draw a slope between $0.5 < b_i \leq 1$. The initialization value Φ is set to the 95th percentile of each user's number of toilet visits for day/night.

5 Evaluation

5.1 Anomaly-Detection Models

Here, we compare the performance of two models: *One Class Support Vector Machine (OCSVM)* and *modified baseline (MBL)*. OCSVM [12] was chosen as it is a popular method for unsupervised anomaly detection that can learn the boundary of normal data points (in this case, number of users' toilet visits) during training without any labels, and identify data outside the learned boundary as anomalies during testing. In addition, initially we selected Rantz et al.'s algorithm [11] as a baseline for detecting changes in urination frequency, because this is the only approach that uses only sensors (Sect. 2). The algorithm generates an alarm if the total number of sensor activations in the toilet on a particular day exceeds four standard deviations from the average of the previous 14 days. Notice, however, that if frequency of urination gradually increases due to illness, so does the mean of the last 14 days, which in turn reduces the likelihood of raising an alert. Further, as mentioned above, the mapping between sensor firings and toilet visits is unclear, and medical advice is in terms of toilet visits. We therefore implemented a modified baseline (MBL) whereby Rantz *et al.*'s method [11] is applied to inferred toilet visits, and we calculated the mean and standard deviation of toilet visits from the 60 days of training data, instead of using the last 14 days.

5.2 Performance Metrics

We employ three metrics in our evaluation: (1) *False Alerts* is the number of times when the behaviour is normal, but the model deems it to be abnormal; (2) *Detection Delay* is the time elapsed between the occurrence of an abnormal event and its detection, which for our application, is measured in days, e.g., if a user has an abnormally large number of toilet visits for a few days, but the abnormality is detected only on day 3, then there will be a 2 day delay; and (3) *No coverage* [10] is the number of times when an abnormal event has occurred, but no alert has been raised within a specified period of time.

5.3 Anomaly Detection Performance

In this section, we compare the anomaly detection performance of MBL with the performance of OCSVM. Note that the *False alert* metric applies only to the normal datasets (day and night), while the *Detection delay* and *No coverage* metrics apply only to the abnormal datasets (day/night and slow/fast onset). To distinguish between daytime and nighttime performance, we use the clusters identified during pre-processing.

Table 1 displays the overall performance (mean and standard deviation for False alerts, Detection delays and No coverage) of MBL and OCSVM for our ten users, after detecting departures from the house and imputing values, averaged over ten runs. The main insights obtained from these results are as follows:

Overall Performance. MBL has no false alerts, but this comes at the expense of detection delays and no coverage. In contrast, OCSVM has a few false alerts, but it has full coverage of abnormal conditions and no detection delays. It is worth noting that no coverage is associated with long detection delays, as a small change in an instance with a long detection delay could turn into a no coverage situation.

Day/Night. The number of nighttime toilet visits is relatively low (normally 0–1 visits), and has a low variability, while the number of daytime toilet visits is higher and more variable. These differences do not affect the detection delays

Table 1. Performance Evaluation for MBL and OCSVM for all users.

	Nighttime							
	Modified baseline (MBL)				OCSVM			
Metric	False Alerts	Delay		No Coverage		False Alerts	Delay		No Coverage	
Statistics/Progression		Fast	Slow	Fast	Slow		Fast	Slow	Fast	Slow
μ	0	1.57	4.05	0	0.30	0.46	0	0	0	0
σ	0	0.97	1.42	0	0.33	0.88	0	0	0	0
	Daytime							
	Modified baseline (MBL)				OCSVM			
	False Alerts	Delay		No Coverage		False Alerts	Delay		No Coverage	
Statistics/Progression		Fast	Slow	Fast	Slow		Fast	Slow	Fast	Slow
μ	0	3.69	-	0.02	0.96	0.71	0	0	0	0
σ	0	0.85	-	0.06	0.10	0.28	0	0	0	0

of OCSVM, but due to MBL's reliance on variance, it has more delays and no-coverage instances for daytime than for nighttime. MBL has no false alerts for day or night, while OCSVM raised more false alerts during the day than at night.

Fast/Slow Disease Progression. Again, the delays and coverage of OCSVM were not affected by disease progression, but MBL has substantially more delays and instances with no coverage for the slow disease onset than for the fast one.

6 Discussion

The overarching aim of our research is to link changes in user behaviour to potential medical conditions. In this paper, we have focused on urinary frequency—a behaviour that is often associated with UTIs. We have made three key contributions: (1) methods for pre-processing real-world data obtained from unintrusive sensors, viz inferring toilet visits from sensor activations and handling missing data; (2) simulated datasets of abnormal micturition behaviour based on medical domain knowledge, which distinguish between nighttime and daytime behaviour and between slow and fast disease progression; and (3) results of anomaly-detection models applied to these datasets. In the near future, we propose to develop algorithms that detect visitors in the home. Finally, to test our approach with real users who eventually get sick, we must deploy our system over a long time in a geriatric facility.

References

1. Barger, T.S., Brown, D.E., Alwan, M.: Health-status monitoring through analysis of behavioral patterns. IEEE Trans. Syst. Man Cybern.-Part A Syst. Hum. **35**(1), 22–27 (2004)
2. Bladder Bowel Community: Urinary frequency — how often should you pee? (2023). https://www.bladderandbowel.org/bladder/bladder-conditions-and-symptoms/frequency/

3. Cook, D.J.: Learning setting-generalized activity models for smart spaces. IEEE Intell. Syst. **27**(1), 32–38 (2012)
4. Enshaeifar, S., et al.: Machine learning methods for detecting urinary tract infection and analysing daily living activities in people with dementia. PLoS ONE **14**(1), e0209909 (2019)
5. Fitzgerald, M., Stablein, U., Brubaker, L.: Urinary habits among asymptomatic women. Am. J. Obstet. Gynecol. **187**(5), 1384–1388 (2002)
6. Kaye, J., et al.: One walk a year to 1000 within a year: continuous in-home unobtrusive gait assessment of older adults. Gait Posture **35**(2), 197–202 (2012)
7. Larizza, M., et al.: In-home monitoring of older adults with vision impairment: exploring patients', caregivers' and professionals' views. J. Am. Med. Inform. Assoc. **21**(1), 56–63 (2014)
8. Lukacz, E.S., Whitcomb, E.L., Lawrence, J.M., Nager, C.W., Luber, K.M.: Urinary frequency in community-dwelling women: what is normal? Am. J. Obstet. Gynecol. **200**(5), 552-e1 (2009)
9. Maltamo, M., Kangas, A.: Methods based on k-nearest neighbor regression in the prediction of basal area diameter distribution. Can. J. For. Res. **28**(8), 1107–1115 (1998)
10. Moshtaghi, M., Zukerman, I., Russell, R.A.: Statistical models for unobtrusively detecting abnormal periods of inactivity in older adults. User Model. User-Adap. Inter. **25**(3), 231–265 (2015). https://doi.org/10.1007/s11257-015-9162-6
11. Rantz, M.J., et al.: Using sensor networks to detect urinary tract infections in older adults. In: IEEE International Conference on e-Health Networking, Applications and Services, pp. 142–149 (2011)
12. Schölkopf, B., Smola, A.J., Bach, F.: Learning with Kernels: Support Vector Machines, Regularization, Optimization, and Beyond. MIT Press (2018)
13. Sommer, P., et al.: Voiding patterns and prevalence of incontinence in women. A questionnaire survey. Br. J. Urol. **66**(1), 12–15 (1990)
14. Suryadevara, N.K., Mukhopadhyay, S.C.: Wireless sensor network based home monitoring system for wellness determination of elderly. IEEE Sens. J. **12**(6), 1965–1972 (2012)
15. Taramasco, C., Rimassa, C., Martinez, F.: Improvement in quality of life with use of ambient-assisted living: clinical trial with older persons in the Chilean population. Sensors **23**(1), 268 (2022)
16. Yamauchi, M., Ohsita, Y., Murata, M., Ueda, K., Kato, Y.: Anomaly detection in smart home operation from user behaviors and home conditions. IEEE Trans. Consum. Electron. **66**(2), 183–192 (2020)

Assessing Frailty Using Behavioral and Physical Health Data in Everyday Living Settings

Chao Bian[1,2](✉) ⓘ, Shehroz S. Khan[1,2] ⓘ, and Alex Mihailidis[1,2] ⓘ

[1] KITE, University Health Network, Toronto, ON M5G 2A2, Canada
chao.bian@mail.utoronto.ca
[2] Institute of Biomedical Engineering, University of Toronto, Toronto, ON M5S 3G9, Canada

Abstract. Early identification of frailty is challenging in clinical settings due to its insidious onset and progression. Assessing real-life changes in behavioral and physical health may facilitate early frailty identification from home settings. The goal of this paper is to determine the performance of machine learning models for identifying frailty using behavioral and physical health features. This study re-used the dataset from the Survey of Health, Ageing and Retirement in Europe, and implemented machine learning classifiers to classify frailty. We selected twenty-two features from the dataset. The classification performance was evaluated using the area under the receiver operating characteristic curve (AUC ROC) and precision-recall curve. As a result, the Gradient Boosting classifier achieved the highest cross-validated AUC ROC (0.9453) and precision-recall curve (0.7029). Mobility limitations and physical inactivity were the top two most important features among the 22 features. In summary, machine learning methods can accurately identify frailty using the selected behavioral and physical health features. The findings have significant implications for identifying frailty much earlier using data in individuals' real-life before clinical frailty assessment.

Keywords: Frailty · Machine Learning · Home Settings

1 Introduction

Frailty is the most problematic expression of population aging [1]. It is characterized as increased vulnerability and comprised ability to cope with everyday or acute stressors [2]. According to a 10-year prospective cohort study of community-dwelling elderly people, the most common disorder leading to death was frailty [1]. Frailty affects as much as 59.1% older population [1]. Early identification of frailty is crucial as it provides opportunities for early prevention to regain function and to prevent adverse outcomes associated with frailty. Studies have found that frailty is reversible only when identified early [3]. However, early recognition of frailty in clinical settings has been facing challenges due to frailty's insidious onset and progression [4]. Studies have found late detection of frailty is common since healthcare professionals came in contact with frail people only when adverse events had occurred [5].

Observations of early behavioral changes in older adults in whom frailty is developing, but as yet undetected, could provide insight into how frailty was developed, and suggest means for early intervention [2]. This is because assessing real-life changes may reflect the net impact of the declining reserve, considering the balance between internal physiologic capacity and external challenges older adults experience in daily life [2]. However, none of the existing clinical frailty assessment instruments were designed for early identifying frailty by evaluating real-life changes. Questions remain as to what real-life health indicators can be used to early detect frailty, and how accurately one can use real-life health indicators to assess frailty. Answering these questions can help us identify a novel approach outside of clinical settings to early assess frailty.

Previous studies have used machine learning (ML) with existing datasets to find new features for identifying frailty or predicting outcomes of frailty [6–8]. An XGBoost model achieved the highest sensitivity (78.14%) and specificity (74.41%) using electronic medical record data for frailty classification [7]. An overall accuracy above 75% in identifying frailty was achieved using support vector machine with data in a residential aged care database [6]. The dataset from Survey of Health, Ageing and Retirement in Europe (SHARE), the largest pan-European social panel study by the number of interviews and participants, covers a more comprehensive health domain than the above datasets in the literature, and includes behavioral and physical health risk factors of frailty [9, 10]. ML techniques have been used with the SHARE datasets and successfully identified people with dementia [11, 12] and at high risk of developing T2DM diabetes mellitus [13]. However, no studies were found using ML techniques on the SHARE dataset to identify frailty. This paper describes for the first time in literature how ML is used with the SHARE dataset to identify frailty. The objective was to determine the performance of machine learning classification models for identifying frailty. This work focused on frailty assessment using data collected from everyday living settings rather than clinical settings where clinical frailty scales were already used.

2 Method

2.1 Study Design, Participants and Setting

We formulated the frailty assessment problem as a classification task in which the model aimed to make a binary classification (i.e., frail vs non-frail) using selected features in the SHARE dataset. SHARE contains eight waves of data collection since 2004. We used Wave 1 of the SHARE dataset in this paper. SHARE Wave 1 contains data from a comprehensive health domain on a sample of 30,424 individuals (16,906 females and 13,518 males, aged 50 years and over) in 11 European countries and Israel. The survey modules in SHARE include demographics, physical health, behavioral risks, cognitive function, mental health, social support, financial transfers, activities, and many more. Questionnaires and physical tests such as walking and grip strength tests were administered.

Full SHARE dataset access was obtained in June 2021. We used SPSS software (IBM, v28.0.0.0) to clean and label the data. To label the frailty classes, we used the five frailty criteria defined in SHARE-Frailty Instrument (SHARE-FI), a validated clinical frailty scale derived from the SHARE dataset [14]. The five frailty criteria for labelling include fatigue, appetite, grip strength, slowness, and activities requiring a low to moderate level of energy. The samples that have missing values in any of the five variables were removed.

A sample was labelled frail if three or more criteria in SHARE-FI were fulfilled, and non-frail if less than three criteria were present. The final sample dataset was exported as a CSV file from the SPSS software. We used the Scikit-learn library (v1.0) in Python (v3.9.1) to build and compare ML classifiers.

2.2 Classifier Training and Evaluation

The classifier training and evaluation process took a four-step approach. The process started with the original SHARE Wave 1 dataset as Step 1 (baseline). Based on the same Wave 1 dataset, we then created three more sub-datasets, representing Steps 2 – 4 (Tables 2 and 3).

Step 1 includes the walking speed feature that has missing values in around 90% of samples in the original dataset. As walking speed was an effective indicator of frailty [15], we decided to keep this feature in Step 1. In Step 2, we imputed the walking speed feature with the mean of the available walking speed data in the training dataset. In Step 3, we removed the walking speed feature as it contains too many missing values despite its clinical importance. In Step 4, we removed several more features and retrained the classifiers as certain features might have close correlations with the feature used for class labelling.

Stratified three-fold cross-validation was performed on the datasets after removing samples containing missing values. The folds were made by preserving the percentage of samples for each class. The datasets were divided into two-thirds for training and one-third for testing for each fold.

Tree-based classifiers were chosen as they can inherently handle the features with mixed types, which is the case for the SHARE dataset. We chose seven classifiers that are random forest (RF), gradient boosting classifier (GBC), decision tree (DT), AdaBoost, histogram-based gradient boosting classifier (HGBC), XGBoost, and logistic regression (LR). Only HGBC and XGBoost were used in Step 1 with missing values in the walking speed feature as other classifiers in scikit-learn could not handle missing values. All seven classifiers were used in Steps 2, 3 and 4. For performance evaluation, we chose the area under the curves (AUC) of receiver operation characteristics (ROC) and Precision-Recall (PR) as they were better metrics than accuracy for the imbalanced SHARE dataset [16, 17]. Feature ranking based on feature permutation [18] was also performed on the best classifier to understand feature importance.

3 Results

Of the 30,424 samples in the original SHARE dataset Wave 1, 9% were removed due to missing values in the maximum grip strength criterion. The final sample size used to train and test ML algorithms was 27,832. Among all the samples, 91.4% were non-frail, and 8.6% were frail. The dataset is highly imbalanced. Twenty-two (22) features extracted from the SHARE dataset (Table 1) were selected for model training. The choice of the 22 features was based on a combination of Fried's frailty phenotypes [19], behavioral signs, and physical health indicators associated with frailty. The data was mixed because it contains categorical, binary, ordinal and continuous features.

Table 1. Features Selected from Survey Modules in SHARE Wave 1.

Survey Module	Features
Demographics	Gender, Year of birth
Walking speed	Walking speed
Behavioral risk	Sports or activities that are vigorous, Physical inactivity
Physical health	Weight, Height, Body Mass Index (BMI)
	Mobility, arm function and fine motor limitations Number of limitations with activities of daily living (ADL), instrumental ADL (iADL)
	Limitations with activities
	Difficulties with bathing or showering, Getting in or out of bed, Walking across a room, Eating (e.g., cutting up your food), Getting up from a chair after sitting for long periods, Preparing a hot meal, Using the toilet (including getting up or down), Pulling or pushing large objects like a living room chair, Climbing several flights of stairs without resting, Lifting or carrying weights over 10 lb/5 kilos

The GBC classifier in Step 2 produced slightly higher performances in both metrics than all other classifiers across four steps (Tables 2 and 3). The highest mean AUC ROC and overall AUC PR achieved by GBC in Step 2 on the dataset with imputed walking speed was 0.9453 and 0.7029, respectively, as shown in Fig. 1. The worst performance was achieved by the decision tree classifier. Compared to a no-skill classifier (a dashed flat line in PR curves in Fig. 1), all the ML models across the four steps showed significant improvement in identifying frailty considering the highly imbalanced dataset. We also ranked the feature importance for GBC in Step 2 and found that mobility and physical inactivity were the two most important features. They were significantly more important than other features across the three folds of the cross-validation.

In Step 4, we removed four features that include mobility, physical inactivity, sports or activities that are vigorous, and climbing several flights of stairs without resting. Firstly, we removed the two most important features found in Step 2 (i.e. mobility and physical inactivity) to eliminate potential correlations between the two most important features and the frailty criteria for class labelling. We found only a small drop in both AUC ROC and AUC PR without the two features. The highest AUC ROC of 0.9182 and AUC PR of 0.5850 (Table 3) were achieved by GBC. Other classifiers except the decision tree achieved very similar performances. The feature importance rankings showed that the sports or activities that are vigorous, iADL, BMI, and climbing several flights of stairs without resting were among the most important features. Furthermore, we removed two more features, which are sports or activities that are vigorous and climbing several flights of stairs without resting. We found that the AUC ROC and AUC PR also only dropped slightly to AUC ROC = 0.9008 and AUC PR = 0.5513 for the GBC classifier. The results are shown in Table 3.

Table 2. Performance of frailty classification in Steps 1 - 3.

	Classifiers	Mean AUC ROC (std. Dev.)	Overall AUC PR (std. Dev.)
Step 1 (baseline) – The dataset without imputation	HGBC	0.9432 (±0.0012)	0.6966 (±0.0110)
	XGBoost	0.9350 (±0.0016)	0.6654 (±0.0075)
Step 2 - The dataset with imputed walking speeds	RF	0.9345 (±0.0020)	0.6838 (±0.0154)
	GBC	0.9453 (±0.0004)	0.7029 (±0.0086)
	DT	0.7326 (±0.0029)	0.5250 (±0.0072)
	AdaBoost	0.9416 (±0.0029)	0.6952 (±0.0101)
	HGBC	0.9391 (±0.0040)	0.6882 (±0.0114)
	XGBoost	0.9344 (±0.0024)	0.6709 (±0.0092)
	LR	0.9291 (±0.0014)	0.6496 (±0.0144)
Step 3 - The dataset with walking speed removed	RF	0.9340 (±0.0019)	0.6798 (±0.0119)
	GBC	0.9445 (±0.0011)	0.7017 (±0.0061)
	DT	0.7325 (±0.0042)	0.5207 (±0.0067)
	AdaBoost	0.9411 (±0.0028)	0.6908 (±0.0092)
	HGBC	0.9423 (±0.0008)	0.6929 (±0.0079)
	XGBoost	0.9327 (±0.0031)	0.6642 (±0.0075)
	LR	0.9305 (±0.0041)	0.6525 (±0.0163)

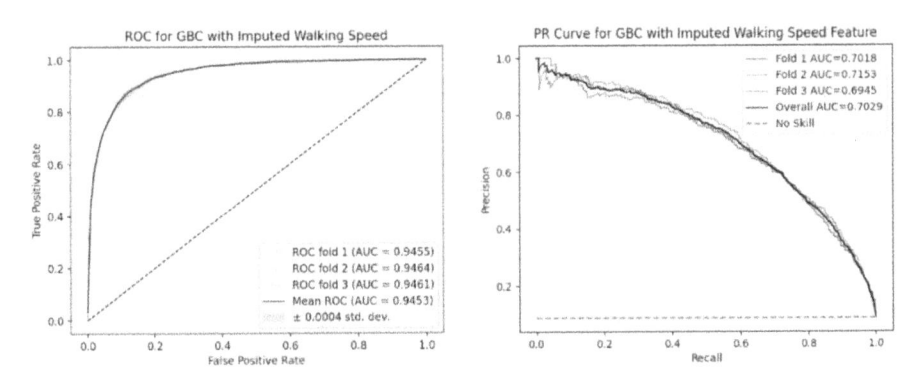

Fig. 1. The best AUCs ROC and PR curves achieved in Step 2.

Table 3. Performance of frailty classification in Step 4.

Step 4 - The dataset with reduced features	W/o 2 features[a]	W/o 4 features[b]	W/o 2 features[a]	W/o 4 features[b]
RF	0.9004 (±0.0039)	0.8767 (±0.0018)	0.5570 (±0.0102)	0.5069 (±0.0065)
GBC	**0.9182 (±0.0027)**	**0.9008 (±0.0030)**	**0.5850 (±0.0049)**	**0.5513 (±0.0054)**
DT	0.6815 (±0.0045)	0.6618 (±0.0082)	0.4402 (±0.0093)	0.4025 (±0.0132)
AdaBoost	0.9115 (±0.0044)	0.8970 (±0.0051)	0.5787 (±0.0140)	0.5492 (±0.0127)
HGBC	0.9132 (±0.0043)	0.8976 (±0.0031)	0.5699 (±0.0203)	0.5378 (±0.0126)
XGBoost	0.9038 (±0.0043)	0.8819 (±0.0039)	0.5449 (±0.0138)	0.5013 (±0.0078)
LR	0.9100 (±0.0008)	0.8913 (±0.0014)	0.5724 (±0.0085)	0.5298 (±0.0075)

a. w/o 2 features: without mobility and phactiv features; b. w/o 4 features: without mobility, phactiv, br015_ and ph048_4 features.

4 Conclusions

This study investigated the use of behavioral and physical health data in the SHARE dataset and ML classifiers to assess frailty. This is the first-time ML is used on the SHARE dataset for frailty classification. The high AUC ROC and AUC PR of the best ML model showed that frailty can be identified by monitoring changes in behavioral and physical health indicators in real life. Mobility limitations, physical inactivity, and iADLs are the most effective features in identifying frailty. This study is significant as the results indicated that it is possible to detect the early onset of frailty by monitoring changes in these health indicators from people's everyday living settings before clinical visits. The ML-enabled preclinical frailty onset detection and risk stratification are positioned to supplement clinical assessments rather than to replace existing clinical frailty instruments. Future work can include implementing more diverse and advanced techniques for data processing and model training, investigating predictability for frailty using longitudinal data across multiple waves/years in the SHARE dataset, and connecting ML models with home sensors to build an intelligent home-based frailty monitoring system.

Acknowledgements. This paper uses data from SHARE Waves 1 (DOIs: https://doi.org/10.6103/SHARE.w1.710), see Börsch-Supan et al. (2013) for methodological details. The SHARE data collection has been funded by the European Commission, DG RTD through FP5 (QLK6-CT-2001–00360), FP6 (SHARE-I3: RII-CT-2006–062193, COMPARE: CIT5-CT-2005–028857, SHARELIFE: CIT4-CT-2006–028812), FP7 (SHARE-PREP: GA N°211909,

SHARE-LEAP: GA N°227822, SHARE M4: GA N°261982, DASISH: GA N°283646) and Horizon 2020 (SHARE-DEV3: GA N°676536, SHARE-COHESION: GA N°870628, SERISS: GA N°654221, SSHOC: GA N°823782) and by DG Employment, Social Affairs & Inclusion through VS 2015/0195, VS 2016/0135, VS 2018/0285, VS 2019/0332, and VS 2020/0313. Additional funding from the German Ministry of Education and Research, the Max Planck Society for the Advancement of Science, the U.S. National Institute on Aging (U01_AG09740-13S2, P01_AG005842, P01_AG08291, P30_AG12815, R21_AG025169, Y1-AG-4553–01, IAG_BSR06–11, OGHA_04–064, HHSN271201300071C, RAG052527A) and from various national funding sources is gratefully acknowledged (see www.share-project.org).

AGE-WELL NCE (Aging Gracefully across Environments using Technology to Support Wellness, Engagement, and Long Life NCE Inc.) - Networks of Centres of Excellence of Canada funds the project.

References

1. Clegg, A., Young, J., Iliffe, S., Rikkert, M.O., Rockwood, K.: Frailty in elderly people. The Lancet **381**, 752–762 (2013). https://doi.org/10.1016/S0140-6736(12)62167-9
2. Xue, Q.L.: The frailty syndrome: definition and natural history. Clin. Geriatr. Med. **27**, 1–15 (2011). https://doi.org/10.1016/j.cger.2010.08.009
3. Gill, T.M., Gahbauer, E.A., Allore, H.G., Han, L.: Transitions between frailty states among community-living older persons. Arch. Intern. Med. **166**, 418 (2006). https://doi.org/10.1001/archinte.166.4.418
4. Muscedere, J., et al.: Screening for frailty in Canada's health care system: a time for action. Can. J. Aging **35**, 281–297 (2016). https://doi.org/10.1017/S0714980816000301
5. Obbia, P., Graham, C., Duffy, F.J.R., Gobbens, R.J.J.: Preventing frailty in older people: an exploration of primary care professionals' experiences. Int. J. Older People Nurs. **15**(2), e12297 (2020). https://doi.org/10.1111/opn.12297
6. Ambagtsheer, R.C., Shafiabady, N., Dent, E., Seiboth, C., Beilby, J.: The application of artificial intelligence (AI) techniques to identify frailty within a residential aged care administrative data set. Int. J. Med. Inform. **136**, 104094 (2020). https://doi.org/10.1016/j.ijmedinf.2020.104094
7. Aponte-Hao, S., et al.: Machine learning for identification of frailty in Canadian primary care practices. Int. J. Popul. Data Sci. **6**(1), 1650 (2021). https://doi.org/10.23889/ijpds.v6i1.1650
8. Tarekegn, A., Ricceri, F., Costa, G., Ferracin, E., Giacobini, M.: Predictive modeling for frailty conditions in elderly people: machine learning approaches. JMIR Med. Inform. **8**, e16678 (2020). https://doi.org/10.2196/16678
9. Börsch-Supan, A.: Survey of Health, Ageing and Retirement in Europe (SHARE) Wave 1. Release version: 7.1.0. SHARE-ERIC. Data set. (2019). https://doi.org/10.6103/SHARE.w1.710
10. Börsch-Supan, A., et al.: Data resource profile: the survey of health, ageing and retirement in Europe (SHARE). Int. J. Epidemiol. **42**, 992–1001 (2013). https://doi.org/10.1093/ije/dyt088
11. Cleret de Langavant, L., Bayen, E., Yaffe, K.: Unsupervised machine learning to identify high likelihood of dementia in population-based surveys: development and validation study. J. Med. Internet Res. **20**(7), e10493 (2018). https://doi.org/10.2196/10493
12. Danso, S.O., Zeng, Z., Muniz-Terrera, G., Ritchie, C.W.: Developing an explainable machine learning-based personalised dementia risk prediction model: a transfer learning approach with ensemble learning algorithms. Front Big Data **4**, 613047 (2021). https://doi.org/10.3389/fdata.2021.613047

13. Stiglic, G., Wang, F., Sheikh, A., Cilar, L.: Development and validation of the type 2 diabetes mellitus 10-year risk score prediction models from survey data. Prim. Care Diabetes **15**, 699–705 (2021). https://doi.org/10.1016/j.pcd.2021.04.008
14. Romero-Ortuno, R., Walsh, C.D., Lawlor, B.A., Kenny, R.A.: A frailty instrument for primary care: findings from the survey of health, ageing and retirement in Europe (SHARE). BMC Geriatr. **10**, 57 (2010). https://doi.org/10.1186/1471-2318-10-57
15. Schwenk, M., et al.: Frailty and technology: a systematic review of gait analysis in those with frailty. Gerontology **60**, 79–89 (2014). https://doi.org/10.1159/000354211
16. Juba, B., Le, H.S.: Precision-recall versus accuracy and the role of large data sets. Proc. AAAI Conf. Artif. Intell. **33**, 4039–4048 (2019). https://doi.org/10.1609/aaai.v33i01.33014039
17. Khan, S.S., et al.: Unsupervised deep learning to detect agitation from videos in people with dementia. IEEE Access **10**, 10349–10358 (2022). https://doi.org/10.1109/ACCESS.2022.3143990
18. Altmann, A., Toloşi, L., Sander, O., Lengauer, T.: Permutation importance: a corrected feature importance measure. Bioinformatics **26**, 1340–1347 (2010). https://doi.org/10.1093/bioinformatics/btq134
19. Fried, L.P., et al.: Frailty in older adults: evidence for a phenotype. J. Gerontol. A Biol. Sci. Med. Sci. **56**, M146–M157 (2001). https://doi.org/10.1093/gerona/56.3.M146

Synthesizing Diabetic Foot Ulcer Images with Diffusion Model

Reza Basiri[1,2(✉)], Karim Manji[3,4], Harton Francois[3,4], Alisha Poonja[3,4], Milos R. Popovic[1,2], and Shehroz S. Khan[1,2]

[1] Institute of Biomedical Engineering, University of Toronto, Toronto, Canada
Reza.basiri@mail.utoronto.ca
[2] KITE, University Health Network, Toronto, Canada
[3] Zivot Limb Preservation Centre, Peter Lougheed Centre, Calgary, Canada
[4] Department of Surgery, Cumming School of Medicine, University of Calgary, Calgary, Canada

Abstract. Diabetic Foot Ulcer (DFU) is a serious skin wound requiring specialized care. However, real DFU datasets are limited, hindering clinical training and research activities. In recent years, generative adversarial networks and diffusion models have emerged as powerful tools for generating synthetic images with remarkable realism and diversity in many applications. This paper explores the potential of diffusion models for synthesizing DFU images and evaluates their authenticity through expert clinician assessments (WoundVista: http://bit.ly/WoundVista). Additionally, evaluation metrics such as Fréchet Inception Distance (FID) and Kernel Inception Distance (KID) are examined to assess the quality of the synthetic DFU images. A dataset of 2,000 DFU images is used for training the diffusion model, and the synthetic images are generated by applying diffusion processes. The results indicate that the diffusion model successfully synthesizes visually indistinguishable DFU images. 70% of the time, clinicians marked synthetic DFU images as real DFUs. However, clinicians demonstrate higher unanimous confidence in rating real images than synthetic ones. The study also reveals that FID and KID metrics do not significantly align with clinicians' assessments, suggesting alternative evaluation approaches are needed. The findings highlight the potential of diffusion models for generating synthetic DFU images and their impact on medical training programs and research in wound detection and classification.

Keywords: Diabetic Foot Ulcer (DFU) · Synthetic Images · Diffusion Model

1 Introduction

Diabetic Foot Ulcer (DFU), a type of skin wound commonly found on the plantar foot, requires specialized care. Failure to heal DFUs can lead to prolonged treatments with high recurrence rates, resulting in the loss of mobility, independence, quality of life, amputation, and even mortality [1–3]. The global prevalence of DFUs is reported to be 6.3%, while in North America, it is estimated to affect 13% of the diabetic patient population [4]. In evaluating DFUs, clinicians follow a series of steps that involve recording and examining the location and size of the wounds, either in person or by analyzing captured images [5]. The interpretation of DFU images is a crucial skill for expert clinicians, enabling them to track and diagnose wound conditions and conduct research. However, the availability of real DFU datasets is limited, restricting clinical training and hampering research activities in the DFU area [6].

In recent years, there has been a notable emergence of Generative Adversarial Networks (GANs) [7] and diffusion models [8], which have proven to be powerful tools for generating synthetic images that exhibit remarkable realism and diversity in many image-processing applications [9, 10]. These techniques hold great promise, especially in medical images, as they can significantly enhance medical training programs and expedite research efforts.

The traditional approach to collecting medical images involves a laborious and time-consuming gathering of real-life samples. Due to medical record privacy and ownership concerns, this often entails redundant data collection from multiple centers. This conventional approach is burdened with limitations, including limited dataset size, imbalanced representation, data sharing constraints, and high costs associated with data acquisition. However, GANs and diffusion methods offer an alternative that overcomes these limitations, facilitating medical analysis and management advancements.

Although synthetic medical images have been extensively explored in areas like X-rays [11] and MRIs [12], the potential for generating synthetic wound images still needs to be explored, particularly in DFU. The availability of a large and diverse DFU dataset holds significant value for medical training programs and the development of standardized wound detection and classification methods. By encompassing various types of wounds, different severities, and distinct anatomical locations, an extensive collection of synthetic wound images enhances the representativeness of the dataset. This, in turn, facilitates the training of deep learning algorithms, allowing them to generalize better and recognize the diverse patterns of wounds encountered in clinical practice. While GNAs pioneered the area of synthetic image generation, diffusion models have risen in popularity due to their ability to generate higher-resolution images, a capability that is crucial in medical imaging.

In this study, we explore the potential of diffusion models for generating synthetic DFU images. To evaluate the authenticity of the synthetic DFUs, three expert clinicians assess and distinguish them as either real or fake. Additionally, we investigate the suitability of commonly used evaluation metrics such as Fréchet Inception Distance (FID) and Kernel Inception Distance (KID) for evaluating the quality of synthetic DFU image generation.

2 Related Works

Diffusion models involve introducing noise to data and then removing the noise iteratively to recover the original data. These models excel at capturing intricate relationships between signals and noise, leading to improved accuracy in reconstructing images. Moreover, diffusion models fall under probabilistic distributions. They can be conditioned to generate synthetic data of exceptional diversity and quality, making them particularly well-suited for image generation tasks. Although diffusion models hold promise for various applications, customizing them for specific domains, such as DFU image generation, may necessitate additional modifications. Having said this, diffusion models are relatively uncommon in medical imaging, as GANs remain the dominant architecture for generating images from noise or transforming images [13].

Rombach et al. [10] introduced a novel approach called latent diffusion models, where the forward and reverse processes occur in the latent space learned by an autoencoder. They enhanced the architecture by incorporating cross-attention, improving conditional image synthesis, super-resolution, and inpainting. Building upon Rombach's work, Packhäuser et al. [11] utilized the latent diffusion model to generate high-quality chest X-ray images conditioned on specific classes. They also proposed a sampling strategy to preserve the privacy of sensitive biometric information during the image generation process. The generated dataset was evaluated in a thoracic abnormality classification task, and the results demonstrated superior performance compared to GAN-based methods. Our approach to using an unconditional diffusion model takes inspiration from Rombach et al. [10] and Packhäuser et al. [11]'s works.

3 Method

3.1 Dataset

We used 2,000 640×480 DFU colored images from Yap et al. [14, 15] for training the diffusion model. Wound quantities per image ranged from zero to five in this dataset. The proportion of the wound area ranged from 0.06% to 57.38% of the entire image area. Some real DFU images are shown in Fig. 1.

3.2 Synthetic Generator

GAN models have limitations when it comes to generating high-resolution images. To generate synthetic DFU imaging that matches the resolution of our DFU dataset, we chose to utilize an unconditional diffusion model. Our diffusion model was inspired by the work of Rombach et al. [10], with modifications made to accommodate our specific data size and computational resources.

During the training process, the diffusion model was trained on 256×256 input images of the entire foot, ensuring that at least one DFU was present in the image, along with minor background details. A batch size of 32 and an initial decaying learning rate of 1e-4 were used for approximately 500 epochs. Gaussian noise was added to the original image in the forward pass of diffusion. A denoising diffusion probabilistic model scheduler was employed to define the variance schedule across 1,000 successive steps. For the denoising step, a U-Net architecture with attention layers was utilized to predict the noise distribution and project it back to the original DFU images. Mean squared error loss was employed for this process.

In the inference stage, 1,000 denoising steps were applied in a reverse pass to generate 50 synthetic DFU images. These generated images comprised the foot, minor background elements, and DFUs on the foot. The 256 by 256 generated images were manually cropped to 100 by 100 boxes, ensuring the DFUs were centered in each box.

3.3 Analysis

We replicated the process of cropping 100 by 100 boxes from real DFU images to match the dimensions of the synthetic images. We employed FID, KID, and the ratings of three expert DFU clinicians to evaluate the similarity between the synthetic and real normalized images. FID and KID are metrics that compute the pixel-based similarity between the distributions of synthetic and real images. FID was calculated using 2048 Inceptionv3 feature layers, while KID utilized a subset sampling of 50 images.

For the clinicians' evaluation, we presented 100 cropped DFU images at 72 DPI, evenly split between real and synthetic, to three DFU clinicians (co-authors #2,3,4). Each clinician marked each image as either real or fake. We then compared and assessed the clinicians' markings and the correlation between FID, KID, and the clinicians' ratings using the student t-test and Pearson correlation coefficient, respectively.

All values, including FID, KID, ratings of real images, and ratings of synthetic images, were normalized to a distribution ranging from 0 to 3. A rating of 0 indicated no correct marking. In contrast, a rating of 3 indicated that all three clinicians correctly identified whether the image was a real or synthetic DFU, as shown in Fig. 1.

4 Results

4.1 Generated Images

Synthetic images were generated from randomized Gaussian noises. The results were curated, and those with obvious color offsets of a real wound or foot were discarded. Figure 1 contains some sample synthetics images that were discarded and selected as well as some real DFU images for comparison. For illustration, we also show images before the 100 by 100 cropping application in Fig. 1.

4.2 Evaluations

Of the 100 presented images, 77% were marked as real by the clinicians. Out of 300 ratings for the three clinicians, 84% of times marked real images correctly. This value falls to 30% for synthetic image correct marking. This means that 70% of the times synthetic DFU images were marked as real. The two marking distributions are significantly different, with a p-value of 0.01. On average, as shown in Fig. 1, 2.52 ± 0.70 clinicians marked real DFU images as real, and 2.10 ± 0.88 clinicians marked synthetic DFU images as real.

Our mean values for the normalized FID and KID were 0.73 and 0.14. Pearson's correlation between FID and KID and clinicians' markings showed a positive coefficient of 0.20 but was not significant. The clinicians' ratings are shown in Fig. 2.

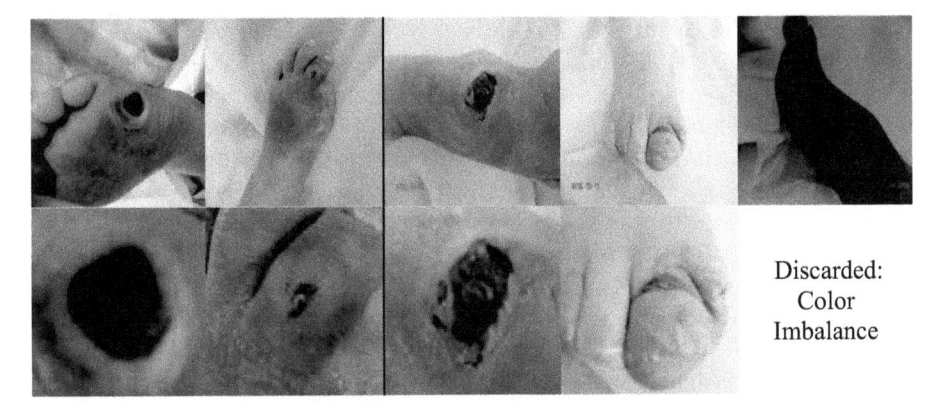

Fig. 1. Sample real and synthetic DFU images. The original real and generated DFU images are depicted on the top row and 100 by 100 cropped 72 DPI versions are on the bottom. Generated images with color imbalances as shown in the last column were discarded.

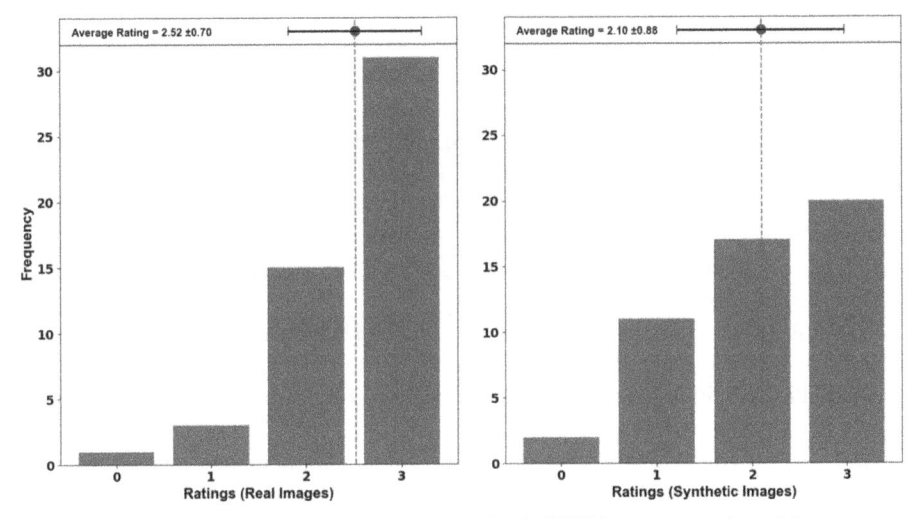

Fig. 2. Three clinicians' ratings of real and synthetic DFU images. A rating of 0 means zero real rating for real or synthetic images from the three clinicians. While a noticeable number of synthetic images were marked as real, the confidence level in real DFU markings was higher, meaning clinicians were more frequently in agreement with the real DFUs.

5 Discussion

5.1 Application in the DFU Area

In medical imaging, high-resolution images that accurately depict local information is crucial for effective disease detection. Diffusion models have demonstrated superior performance compared to GANs in achieving this objective, leading to their increasing popularity. In our study focusing on DFUs, the diffusion model showed satisfactory performance despite having a limited dataset. With minor adjustments to the generated images, our current network successfully augmented the existing DFU datasets, enhancing their size and diversity. As evident from clinicians' ratings, the diffusion model synthesized wound images visually indistinguishable from real wounds. However, the confidence level in identifying real images was significantly higher, resulting in noticeably different rating distributions with a p-value of 0.01 for the student t-test. This disparity can be attributed to the small training dataset and the limited resolution of our model. This issue is resolvable by more training samples and expanding the computational power to train larger diffusion models for higher-resolution outputs.

Interestingly, we observed that commonly used evaluation metrics such as FID and KID did not significantly align with the assessments provided by clinicians. We discovered a statistically insignificant positive correlation of 0.20 for the Pearson r coefficient between these metrics and the ratings assigned by the clinicians. This suggests that alternative quantitative approaches for evaluating synthetic wound images may be required to better align with the clinicians' assessments.

5.2 Limitations and Future Directions

The medical community places significant importance on safeguarding the privacy of medical data. Some research findings indicate that diffusion models tend to memorize individual images from the training data and reproduce them during the generation process [16]. Consequently, adversaries could exploit this behavior to extract sensitive training data. Moreover, these studies reveal that diffusion models exhibit lower privacy than generative models like GANs. Therefore, there is a need for new advancements in privacy-preserving training methods to address these vulnerabilities, especially in sensitive health domains, such as medicine.

Utilizing diffusion models as a generative prior can help mitigate data heterogeneity, reduce the risk of privacy breaches, and enhance the quality and trustworthiness of the learned models in terms of fairness and generalization. Additionally, due to similar privacy concerns, diffusion models can streamline the process of generating synthetic medical data for educational purposes or augmentation while maintaining privacy and data integrity.

Even at the current stage, the diffusion model can generate images to enhance the existing dataset augmentations. Overfitting is a well-known problem with classification models, especially in DFU, where datasets are limited [6]. The standard solution to reduce overfitting is data augmentation that artificially enlarges the dataset. Classic augmentation techniques mostly include affine transformations such as translation, rotation, scaling, flipping and shearing [17]. Synthetic DFUs can complement classic augmentation by adding newly diffused DFU examples created by the diffusion model. As a next step, we will explore the effect of diffused DFU augmentation on classification model performances. Our team also made a web application called "WoundVista", publicly available for researchers to rate DFU images as real or fake at [http://bit.ly/WoundVista]; a screenshot is shown in Fig. 3. We will use global and clinical performance in rating synthetic and real images to compare and analyze generative quantitative metrics such as FID or KID in DFU image evaluations.

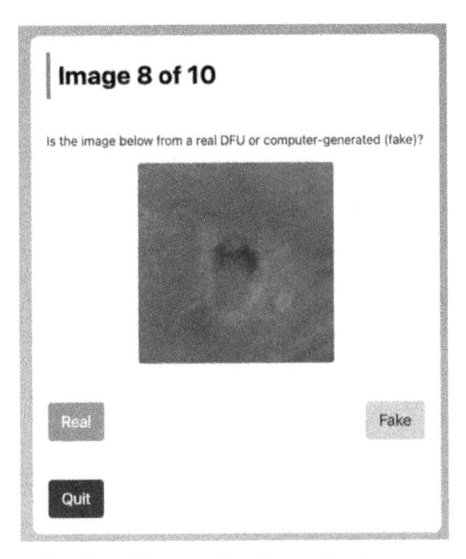

Fig. 3. Wound Rater Application. We are collecting evaluations on our generated DFU images from clinicians and the public by using our web application. Global and clinical performance of real and synthetic DFU images are used to evaluate quantitative generative evaluation metrics such as FID.

6 Conclusion

We investigated the applications of diffusion models for generating synthetic DFU images. By generating diverse and realistic synthetic DFU images, these models can address the limitations of traditional data collection methods, such as limited dataset size, imbalanced representation, and high costs associated with data acquisition.

Our findings demonstrated that the diffusion model successfully synthesized DFU images that were visually indistinguishable from real wounds. Additionally, we demonstrated that FID and KID evaluation metrics did not align with the clinicians' assessments. This suggests the requirement for alternative quantitative approaches that better align with the expert clinicians' evaluations.

The utilization of diffusion models in generating synthetic DFU images shows promise for augmenting existing datasets and facilitating advancements in DFU analysis.

References

1. López-Valverde, M.E., Aragón-Sánchez, J., López-de-Andrés, A., et al.: Perioperative and long-term all-cause mortality in patients with diabetes who underwent a lower extremity amputation. Diabetes Res. Clin. Pract. **141**, 175–180 (2018). https://doi.org/10.1016/j.diabres.2018.05.004
2. Lin, C.-W.C.-H., Hsu, B.R.-S., Tsai, J.-S., et al.: Effect of limb preservation status and body mass index on the survival of patients with limb-threatening diabetic foot ulcers. J. Diabetes Complications **31**, 180–185 (2017). https://doi.org/10.1016/j.jdiacomp.2016.09.011

3. Basiri, R., Haverstock, B.D., Petrasek, P.F., Manji, K.: Reduction in diabetes-related major amputation rates after implementation of a multidisciplinary model: an evaluation in Alberta, Canada. J. Am. Podiatr. Med. Assoc. **111**(4), Article_1 (2019) https://doi.org/10.7547/19-137
4. Zhang, P., Lu, J., Jing, Y., et al.: Global epidemiology of diabetic foot ulceration: a systematic review and meta-analysis. Ann. Med. **49**, 106–116 (2017). https://doi.org/10.1080/07853890.2016.1231932
5. Armstrong, D.G., Lavery, L.A.: Diabetic foot ulcers: prevention, diagnosis and classification. Am. Fam. Physician **57**, 1325–1332 (1998)
6. Basiri, R., Popovic, M.R., Khan, S.S.: Domain-specific deep learning feature extractor for diabetic foot ulcer detection. In: IEEE International Conference on Data Mining Workshops, ICDMW 2022-November:243–247 (2022). https://doi.org/10.1109/ICDMW58026.2022.00041
7. Chen, Y., Yang, X.H., Wei, Z., et al.: Generative adversarial networks in medical image augmentation: a review. Comput. Biol. Med. **144**, 105382 (2022). https://doi.org/10.1016/J.COMPBIOMED.2022.105382
8. Croitoru, F.-A., Hondru, V., Ionescu, R.T., Shah, M.: Diffusion Models in Vision: A Survey (2022).https://doi.org/10.1109/TPAMI.2023.3261988
9. Karras, T., Laine, S., Aila, T.: A Style-Based Generator Architecture for Generative Adversarial Networks, pp. 4401–4410 (2019)
10. Rombach, R., Blattmann, A., Lorenz, D., et al.: High-Resolution Image Synthesis With Latent Diffusion Models, pp. 10684–10695 (2022)
11. Packhäuser, K., Folle, L., Thamm, F., Maier, A.: Generation of Anonymous Chest Radiographs Using Latent Diffusion Models for Training Thoracic Abnormality Classification Systems (2022)
12. Pinaya, W.H.L., Tudosiu, P.D., Dafflon, J., et al.: Brain Imaging Generation with Latent Diffusion Models. Lecture Notes in Computer Science (including subseries Lecture Notes in Artificial Intelligence and Lecture Notes in Bioinformatics) 13609 LNCS:117–126 (2022). https://doi.org/10.1007/978-3-031-18576-2_12/COVER
13. Yi, X., Walia, E., Babyn, P.: Generative adversarial network in medical imaging: a review. Med. Image Anal. **58**, 101552 (2019). https://doi.org/10.1016/J.MEDIA.2019.101552
14. Cassidy, B., Reeves, N.D., Joseph, P., et al.: DFUC2020: Analysis Towards Diabetic Foot Ulcer Detection
15. Goyal, M., Reeves, N.D., Rajbhandari, S., Yap, M.H.: Robust methods for real-time diabetic foot ulcer detection and localization on mobile devices. IEEE J. Biomed. Health Inform. **23**, 1730–1741 (2019). https://doi.org/10.1109/JBHI.2018.2868656
16. Carlini, N., Hayes, J., Nasr, M., et al.: Extracting Training Data from Diffusion Models (2023)
17. Shorten, C., Khoshgoftaar, T.M.: A survey on image data augmentation for deep learning. J Big Data **6**, 1–48 (2019). https://doi.org/10.1186/S40537-019-0197-0/FIGURES/33

Engaging Older Adults at Meal-Time Through AI-Empowered Socially Assistive Robots

Berardina De Carolis, Corrado Loglisci[✉], Nicola Macchiarulo, and Giuseppe Palestra

University of Bari 'Aldo Moro', Via E. Orabona 4, Bari 70125, Italy
{berardina.decarolis,corrado.loglisci,nicola.macchiarulo, giuseppe.palestra}@uniba.it

Abstract. Proper nutrition is important for the well-being of older adults. Inadequate or wrong food consumption during meals can lead to health issues. In this paper, we present an application that uses a humanoid Socially Assistive Robot, Alpha Mini in this case, in order to monitor the behavior and engage adults during meal-time, enhancing their experience. The robot works in a tight coupling with Artificial intelligence technologies based on Deep learning for the tasks of activity recognition and food detection and recognition.

Keywords: Social Assistive Robots · Computer Vision · Food AI

1 Introduction

Older adults face unique challenges when it comes to nutrition due to the complex interaction of various factors, resulting in a condition known as "nutritional frailty" [15]. Financial constraints, often associated with poverty, may make it difficult for individuals to meet their nutritional needs. Additionally, feelings of loneliness and social isolation reduce the motivation to prepare meals and subsequently lead to decreased food intake. These factors can contribute to depression, further worsening the state of nutritional frailty. Moreover, physiological changes in sensory thresholds, such as reduced sensitivity to smell and taste, can diminish appetite in older individuals. The inadequate food consumption can lead to serious health issues such as malnutrition, which significantly contributes to morbidity, decreased quality of life, and mortality among the elderly especially in long-term care facilities [3]. It is crucial to explore new technological aids that can promote independent eating habits among seniors living alone or in nursing homes to address their needs during mealtimes. One of the most promising approaches appears to be the technology of the Socially Assistive Robotics (SAR), which has been proposed for various purposes, such as providing social companionship [19], supporting independent living [12], and engaging older adults in physically and cognitively stimulating activities [7,10].

In this paper, we present a prototype system, integrated into the Alpha Mini social robot, that aims at providing cognitive assistance, stimulation and social interaction during meal-time. In particular, we designed two modules to empower the robot's capabilities, *i)* recognition of the specific activities of eating and drinking, and *ii)* detection and recognition of the food during eating. Both modules offer recognition capabilities learned through deep learning models, which are trained on the data collected directly from the seniors through informal conversation about the eating behavior and food intake of the seniors.

The first module implements facilities of human activity recognition in a living environment and works on the video-camera frames [2] by transforming low-level data into interpretable activities [6], which the robot sees as actions that the adult is doing [8,11]. To improve the accuracy of the recognition (in distinguishing eating and drinking), the module also performs object recognition to distinguish handheld meal-related utensils from others. For this purpose, we rely on the technologies MMAction [18] and YOLOv5 [17] respectively.

The second module provides computer vision and dialog capabilities to enable the robot to detect and recognize food, thereby establishing engaging and motivating one-on-one interactions. The computer vision technology is in charge of recognizing food and, for this reason, we rely on the YOLOv8 technology [13] with a classification model trained on images of food, organized by categories, typical of the Apulian region (South of Italy). This would open the possibility to track the intake of nutrients and problems related to allergies, intolerances.

We used the Ubtech Alpha Mini robot, a small-size humanoid social robot, which will be situated on the table facing the adult and monitoring the food on the table. The robot is able to communicate with the older adult through natural dialogs in order to allow the robot to collect data on the categories of food consumed by the adult throughout the day, monitor his meal habits and engage him in eating and drinking through a workflow-based dialog. The dialog uses three levels of information. First, speeches based on cues, encouragement, positive statements, personal communication (e.g., calling by name) aiming to stimulate the consumption of food. Second, as social factors, the robot considers gestures, the shape of the eyes and images displayed on its eyes. Third, the meal-related actions detected by means of human activity recognition module and food recognition and detection.

In the following sections, technical details for the modules, here introduced, are provided.

2 Meal-Related Activity Recognition

To recognize meal-related actions (eating and drinking) during the times of the interaction adult-robot, we resort to the approach proposed in [5] which originally worked in real-time. Additionally, it has been extended to identify handheld objects involved in the action (Table 1). The approach relies on supervised solutions of Graph-convolutional networks which straightforwardly model the structure of the human skeleton by representing the joints as the nodes of a graph and the bones as the edges. To train the model, we use the dataset NTU RGB+D [16] which includes the data of 60 daily activities. It has been originally arranged to conduct training and validation sessions, indeed it has 37,920 activity videos for training and 18,960 for validation.

Table 1. Action and objects.

Action code	Action	Object
A1	Drink water	Glass
A2	Eat meal	Fork, Knife, Spoon, Dish, Food

However, after preliminary experiments resulting in low performances, we have performed a step of feature augmentation on these videos, by extracting the characteristics of the human skeleton joints. To obtain this kind of information, we implement a two-step procedure, that is, identification of the human figures and extraction of the joints. The first step uses the technology YOLOv5, while for the second one, we apply the toolbox MMDetection [4] to the dataset AVA[1] and considered 17 types of skeleton joints. So, by following the steps described in [5], we trained four different models on four different feature sets so grouped: i) *Joint*, the 3D coordinates of the extracted joints; ii) *Joint motion*, the difference between the coordinates of the joint at time $t+1$ and time t; iii) *Bone*, the difference between the coordinates of linked joints on the basis of the structure of the human skeleton extracted; iv) *Bone motion*: the difference between the bone at time $t+1$ and time t. Moreover, we used an ensemble learning scheme with four models with resulting predictions based to the weighted average. The results on the validation set are the followings: Joint - 90.72%, Joint motion - 88.98%, Bone - 89.52%, Bone motion - 87.64%, Ensemble - 92.42%. Even if the ensemble model has the highest accuracy, we decided to use the model trained on the Joint features (HAR base model) since it allows a faster computation in real-time with slightly lower performance.

However, when analyzing the performance of the model in recognizing the eating and drinking activities on the validation set of the considered NTU RGB+D dataset, we noticed that there were some ambiguities depending on the similarity of the body pose and movements of some activities that could be easily misinterpreted by considering the object involved in the action [14]. So, to facilitate the robot to better understand the meal-related actions, we extended the module with object detection techniques. We considered the YOLO v5x6 model and, as detected object, we picked the one associated to the highest confidence.

Regarding the issue of filtering objects which are uninvolved in the analyzed actions, namely those irrelevant and those placed at the background, we grouped objects by categories (Table 1) and let the model to work also on those categories.

---

[1] https://github.com/MVIG-SJTU/AlphAction/blob/master/DATA.md.

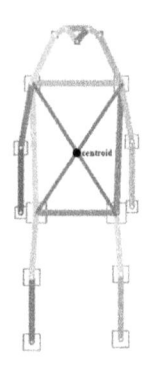

Fig. 1. Graphical representation of the centroid of a skeleton.

To complete the data preparation, a representative point (centroid) corresponding to the geometric center of the body was determined by triangulating the coordinates of the shoulder and hip joints. This also allows to simulate the z-axis, absent from the selected parameters (Fig. 1). Finally, to provide a uniform format of the data to the tensors of the YOLO v5x6 model, a subtraction operation between the centroid and each joint was performed. To demonstrate our hypothesis, two models have been trained and tested. The base model uses two channels, corresponding to the x and y skeleton joint coordinates. The extended model uses four channels, corresponding to the x and y skeleton joint coordinates, the distances from the object center and each skeleton joint, and the used object class. The dataset containing 856 instances for each class (that is, codes of the action, A1 and A2) was split as for training and testing. The results of the test show that there was an improvement of accuracy of 3% on average, showing that adding hand-held object detection and identification to activity recognition allows a better understanding of what the adult is doing and in particular to correctly recognize eating and drinking. In particular, the eating activity accuracy went from 0.92 to 0.94 and the drinking one from 0.93 to 0.97.

3 Food Recognition

The second module is in charge of recognition of food, which, with the recognition of eating and drinking activities, completes the third level of the information based on which the dialog carries on. Also food recognition is handled as a problem of object detection and recognition through deep learning techniques. In the current work, since we are going to test the application with adults resident in Apulia, we created and trained the food recognition model on Apulian food usually consumed by adults. To collect the relative image data and create the dataset, we rely on standard Web Scraping. Then, we manually selected images of variegate categories of food that however require the use of none, one or two utensils. An overall number of 31 categories was identified representative list of the selected categories of food is here reported: *tortellini in broth, pasta* and lentils, arancino, focaccia, octopus salad, mixed fried seafood, baked fish, meatballs in white, mozzarella cheese, green salad, french fries, mussels.

The scraped images were 2300 images and, by using the technology Roboflow [9], were associated to a label each, so as a supervised set to train a classification model. However, the presence of different categories of food in the same images has led to detect a number of categories of food equal to 3856, which is greater than the set of selected images. So, to work on a well-structured dataset without the presence of possible misinterpretations, the collection of the images was extended accordingly by generating new images whether the original images showed more categories of food. This is the basic idea of the *data augmentation* task. To make the new images distinguishable each other and different from those of origin, we applied image (pre-)processing techniques, in the order, auto-adjust contrast, random shear, random rotation of the image and vertical flip. Finally, the set of labelled images amounts to 14757 image data ready to be processed.

To build the classification model, we used the Deep learning algorithms available in Ultralytics YOLOv8 [13]. YOLOv8 has been preferred to YOLOv5 in this task since it has been proven as superior in detecting small objects. For the experimental session, the dataset is so partitioned: 70% for training, 20% for validation, 10% for testing.

As performance measure, we used the mAP (mean Average Precision) which is commonly used as evaluation metric in object detection tasks. In this work, it is used to assess the performance of an object detection model in terms of both accuracy and precision. In particular, we considered the mAP@50 value that refers to the mean Average Precision at a specific IoU (Intersection over Union) threshold of 0.5. The performance we reached was mAP@50 to 66.5%.

4 The Food Diary Application

The idea of using a friendly social robot for recognizing users' activities in a smart home using the robot's camera is not new [8]. The main aim of our research in this phase is to evaluate how this approach can be used to collect a diary of entries containing annotated data about meal-related activities and eaten food for learning, in the future, the daily intake and nutrition habits of the user. To this aim, we developed the Food Diary application for the Alpha Mini robot that uses a combination of natural language dialogues and computer vision modules created for this purpose. Figure 2 (left) provides an overview of the application that is made up of the following modules, some of them, due to computational complexity, run on a local computational unit, which works in the Edge computing paradigm:

- *Dialog Management*: the dialog with the adult is handled using a JSON specification of the workflow representing the dialog. The workflow includes conditions that trigger the robot's behaviors. The dialog combines natural language and non-verbal communicative signals, such as the eyes and body movements (Fig. 2 - right)

Fig. 2. Left: an overview of the Food Diary Application with Mini - Right: a positive feedback expressed through the eyes.

- *Face Detection and Person Recognition*: this functionality is already present in the Alpha Mini SDK and is used for detecting and recognizing a person by face. This information is kept on a local database on-board the robot and it is stored according to EU GDPR rules.
- *User Profile*: Recognition allows to access the user profile. The User Profile keeps the information about each user. It stores personal (user's picture, user's age, gender, name, family, friends and physician contacts) and medical features (chronic diseases, allergies, therapies, etc.) and preferences (food, music, TV programs, etc.).
- *Food Diary Manager*: this module allows inserting eaten food, nutrition facts, time of eating activity in a database present on the local Edge.
- *Food Diary Local Edge*: allowing access to services for:
  - *Activity Recognition*: the module for activity recognition described in Sect. 2 is used in real-time in the food diary the application.
  - *Food Detection and Recognition*: the module for food detection and recognition described in Sect. 4 is used during the meal activity. At the present stage of the project, this module uses the Edamam API [1] to extract nutrition information and health-related labels.
  - *Food Diary Database*: the daily food diary is stored in a database developed for the application purpose.

The Mini Local Edge allows the robot to communicate with Computer Vision services. To analyze the video streaming captured from Alpha Mini, the Socket technology was used: frames captured from the robot's camera are sent continuously to the Edge and stored in a buffer. When the edge has collected a sufficient amount of frames, computer vision modules are applied and the results are returned on the same communication channel. As far as the robot behaviors during meal eating are concerned, they aim at monitoring and motivating a user to eat the meal and drink while also promoting the social dimensions of eating. Some examples are shown in Table 2.

Table 2. Examples of robot dialog sentences.

communicative goal	behavior
Greet	Hi! my name is Mini <waiving with happy eyes> and I'm here to stay with you while you eat
Confirm food	"The food looks good! Are you eating <name of the recognized food>?
Motivate to eat	"Yummy! There is still some food in your dish! It looks good ... It's a shame I can only eat energy
Positive statements	"It's so nice to spend some time with you." (while in a happy emotional state)
Joke	"Where is Brindisi?" "In a bar!" (robot laughs and puts one hand in front of its mouth)
Congratulate	"I see that you have finished your meal. That's great! " (while waving goodbye in a happy emotional state)

5 Conclusions and Future Work

In this paper, we presented the prototype of an application that shows how a Social Robot, Alpha Mini, integrated with AI functionalities for activity recognition and food detection and recognition, can be used for assisting seniors during meal-time to enhance their meal-time experience and, in the meanwhile, monitor their eating behavior. At present, we designed task-oriented dialogs that are handled locally on the robot, however, in addition to these predefined sentences, GPT 3.5 is being integrated to perform what we call "chit-chat" dialogs about food, nutrition and other topics that could enhance the user experience. The approach needs to be tested in a real-world scenario robot-adults from the technology acceptance point of view. We plan also to evaluate it in terms of accuracy when the Computer vision tasks are made in the wild. In particular, we plan improvements aiming at increasing the accuracy of the food recognition.

Acknowledgements. This publication was produced with the co-funding European Union - Next Generation EU, in the context of The National Recovery and Resilience Plan, Investment Partenariato Esteso PE8 "Conseguenze e sfide dell'invecchiamento", Project Age-It (Ageing Well in an Ageing Society), CUP: B83C22004800006.

References

1. Edamam[api]. https://developer.edamam.com/edamam-docs-recipe-api
2. A review and categorization of techniques on device-free human activity recognition. J. Netw. Comput. Appli. **167**, 102738 (2020). https://doi.org/10.1016/j.jnca.2020.102738
3. Chen, C.C.H., Schilling, L.S., Lyder, C.: A concept analysis of malnutrition in the elderly. J. Adv. Nurs. **36**(1), 131–142 (2001). https://doi.org/10.1046/j.1365-2648.2001.01950.x

4. Chen, K., et al.: Mmdetection: Open mmlab detection toolbox and benchmark. ArXiv abs/ arXiv: 1906.07155 (2019)
5. Chen, Y., Zhang, Z., Yuan, C., Li, B., Deng, Y., Hu, W.: Channel-wise topology refinement graph convolution for skeleton-based action recognition. In: Proceedings of the IEEE/CVF International Conference on Computer Vision, pp. 13359–13368 (2021)
6. Dang, L.M., Min, K., Wang, H., Piran, M.J., Lee, C.H., Moon, H.: Sensor-based and vision-based human activity recognition: A comprehensive survey. Pattern Recogn. **108**, 107561 (2020)
7. DeCarolis, B., Carofiglio, V., Grimandli, I., Macchiarulo, N., Palestra, G., Pino, O.: Using the pepper robot in cognitive stimulation therapy for people with mild cognitive impairment and mild dementia (2020)
8. Di Napoli, C., Ercolano, G., Rossi, S.: Personalized home-care support for the elderly: a field experience with a social robot at home. User Model. User-Adap. Inter. **33**(2), 405–440 (2023)
9. Dwyer, B., Nelson, J., Solawetz, J., et al.: Roboflow (version 1.0)[software] (2022)
10. Fasola, J., Matarić, M.J.: A socially assistive robot exercise coach for the elderly **2**(2), 3–32 (2013). https://doi.org/10.5898/JHRI.2.2.Fasola
11. Ghayvat, H., et al.: Smart aging system: Uncovering the hidden wellness parameter for well-being monitoring and anomaly detection. Sensors **19**(4) (2019). https://doi.org/10.3390/s19040766
12. Gross, H., et al.: Progress in developing a socially assistive mobile home robot companion for the elderly with mild cognitive impairment. In: 2011 IEEE/RSJ International Conference on Intelligent Robots and Systems, IROS 2011, San Francisco, CA, USA, 25-30 September 2011, pp. 2430–2437 (2011)
13. Jocher, G., Chaurasia, A., Qiu, J.: Yolov8. YOLO by Ultralytics. https://github.com/ultralytics/ultralytics (2023). Accessed 30 February 2023 (2020)
14. Liu, C., Li, X., Li, Q., Xue, Y., Liu, H., Gao, Y.: Robot recognizing humans intention and interacting with humans based on a multi-task model combining st-gcn-lstm model and yolo model. Neurocomputing **430**, 174–184 (2021). https://doi.org/10.1016/j.neucom.2020.10.016
15. Lorenzo-López, L., Maseda, A., de Labra, C., Regueiro-Folgueira, L., Rodríguez-Villamil, J.L., Millán-Calenti, J.C.: Nutritional determinants of frailty in older adults: a systematic review. BMC Geriatrics **17**(1), 108 (2017). https://doi.org/10.1186/s12877-017-0496-2
16. Shahroudy, A., Liu, J., Ng, T.T., Wang, G.: Ntu rgb+d: a large scale dataset for 3d human activity analysis. In: Proceedings of the IEEE Conference on Computer Vision and Pattern Recognition, pp. 1010–1019 (2016)
17. Ultralytics: YOLOv5: You only look once v5 (2020). https://github.com/ultralytics/yolov5
18. Yan, S., Xiong, Y., Wang, J., Lin, D.: Mmskeleton (2019). https://github.com/open-mmlab/mmskeleton
19. Yu, R., et al.: Use of a therapeutic, socially assistive pet robot (paro) in improving mood and stimulating social interaction and communication for people with dementia: Study protocol for a randomized controlled trial. JMIR Res. Protoc. **4**(2), e45 (2015). https://doi.org/10.2196/resprot.4189

Investigating the Dynamics of Cardio-Metabolic Comorbidities and Their Interactions in Ageing Adults Through Dynamic Bayesian Networks

Erica Tavazzi[1], Chiara Roversi[1], Martina Vettoretti[1], and Barbara Di Camillo[1,2(✉)]

[1] Department of Information Engineering, University of Padova, Padova, Italy
{erica.tavazzi,chiara.roversi,
martina.vettoretti,barbara.dicamillo}@unipd.it
[2] Department of Comparative Biomedicine and Food Science, University of Padova, Padova, Italy

Abstract. With increased longevity, the likelihood of developing multiple chronic diseases also increases. Among these, cardio-metabolic comorbidities represent a burden both in terms of individual quality of life and public health. Understanding the impact of risk factors and unravelling possible cross-effects between comorbidities themselves can facilitate care management and prevention strategies. In this work, we present a model of ageing progression and the onset of three cardio-metabolic diseases, namely type 2 diabetes, hypertension, and heart problems, together with survival, based on socio-demographic, clinical, and biomarkers data of more than 11,000 subjects available in the English Longitudinal Study of Ageing. Leveraging dynamic Bayesian networks, our model effectively captures the probabilistic relationships between risk factors and morbidities over time, with many biological interactions known from the literature correctly encoded, such as the effect of body mass index and physical activity on the onset of cardio-metabolic diseases. Noticeably, some cross-relationships between outcomes' occurrence also emerge, with an increased risk of heart problems in the presence of hypertension. In addition to the graphical description of the ageing process, we propose a simulation strategy that allows us to predict *in silico* the progression of the clinical state of a new patient population (iAUC between 0.62–0.83 for all outcomes), as well as a stratification analysis that allows investigating the effect of selected variables on the risk of developing morbidity. This approach provides valuable support for the acquisition of knowledge aimed at designing prevention strategies and targeted interventions to improve the health status of the ageing population.

Keywords: Ageing · Cardio-metabolic Comorbidities · Dynamic Bayesian Network

1 Introduction

With the rapid growth of the ageing population [16], we are witnessing an increase in the number of cases in which two or more coexisting diseases (i.e., comorbidities) occur in the same individual. Affecting mainly people aged 50 or older, this condition impacts in terms of worse quality of life, increased risk of death, and burden for the public health. Therefore, there is a growing interest in public health research to study the progression of chronic diseases and the development/interaction of comorbidities [12].

In this context, approaches based on statistical methods and artificial intelligence (AI) can enable the analysis of relationships between risk factors and health outcomes, the investigation of cross-influences between concomitant diseases, as well as the identification of the subjects more at risk, facilitating the implementation of treatment and prevention strategies. Several predictive models have been explored in the literature, aiming to anticipate the onset of age-related diseases based on the analysis of clinical and lifestyle variables. However, there is a lack of computational approaches that focus on the combined analysis of multiple diseases, with most of the works considering only one single disease at a time (e.g., [10,13,17]) or making limited use (in terms of dynamics or variables) of longitudinal information collected during patient follow-ups (e.g., [6,9]). These limitations affect the possibility of simultaneously investigating the relationships between risk factors and multiple, concomitant health outcomes.

In this work, we present a dynamic probabilistic model of the onset and interaction of three cardio-metabolic diseases, namely type 2 diabetes (T2D), hypertension, and heart disease, in an ageing population. Starting from the clinical and socio-demographic information collected in the English Longitudinal Study of Ageing (ELSA) dataset, we employ dynamic Bayesian networks (DBNs) to investigate both the direct and indirect effects of the considered variables on the outcomes, highlighting how they interact as the population ages, along with the cross-influence of each disease on the onset of the others. The resulting network shows interesting relationships between risk factors (some of which are adjustable with practical lifestyle modifications) and comorbidities as well as between the outcomes themselves, providing them in a way that can be easily accessed and interpreted, thus representing a novelty compared to what can be achieved with traditional statistical methods. Based on the DBN, we propose a simulation approach that permits the forecasting of the ageing process on a new, unseen population, and to evaluate the model's performance. Finally, we perform a simulation-based stratification analysis to better study the effect of selected variables on the occurrence of cardio-metabolic comorbidities, focusing in particular on studying the effect of having or not having hypertension at baseline on the risk of developing heart problems.

2 Material

ELSA is an ongoing study funded by the U.S. National Institute on Aging and a consortium of UK government departments that collects multidisciplinary data from a representative sample of the English population, mostly aged 50 years and older [11,14]. The data include up to 9 interviews (waves) and clinical examinations conducted about every 2 and 4 years, respectively. For this work, we focused on 6 consecutive, homogenised waves covering an observation period of around 11 years, for a total of 11,160 subjects. The first wave available for each subject was taken as a *baseline* observation and, for subsequent visits, we tracked the passage of time by introducing the variable *time since baseline* (TSB). From the available information, we selected a number of socio-demographic variables, clinical, health indicators, and blood tests (see Table 1) to be analysed in terms of potential risk factors for the development of three of the most frequent age-related cardio-metabolic comorbidities, namely type 2 diabetes (T2D), hypertension, and heart problems, along with survival. Of the entire group of subjects, 1,476 reported having diabetes in at least one of the follow-up visits, 5,358 hypertension, and 2,836 cardiovascular problems.

Table 1. Variables included in the model.

Category	Variables
Socio-demographics	Sex, age at baseline interview, education level
Lifestyle	Marital status, retirement, frequency of physical activity, smoking history, drinking habits (alcohol consumption in the last year and N days of drinking in the last week)
Health indicators	Difficulty in Activity of Daily Living (ADL) and in Instrumental Activity of Daily Living (IADL)
Physical measurements	Body mass index (BMI), systolic and diastolic blood pressure (BP)
Biomarkers	Fasting glucose, glycated hemoglobin (HbA1c), cholesterol, high-/low-density lipoprotein (HDL/LDL), triglycerides, fibrinogen, C-reactive protein level (CRP), ferritin
Time	Time since baseline (TSB)
Outcomes	Type 2 diabetes (T2D), hypertension, heart problems, survival

3 Methods

As a modelling technique, we employed DBNs [1], a probabilistic graphical model that represents dynamic stochastic processes as a Directed Acyclic Graph (DAG) consisting of nodes representing a set of random variables, and edges corresponding to the dependencies among variables over consecutive time steps (parent(s)-child relationships). The DAG is supplemented by conditional probability tables (CPTs) that encode the influence on a variable at time t by its parents at time t-1. Noticeably, constraints can be imposed on the structure of the network to encode state-of-the-art relations, thus enabling the transfer of domain knowledge to the trained model. In the literature, DBNs have been successfully used to model evolving diseases, such as type 1 diabetes complications [7], T2D onset [13], or amyotrophic lateral sclerosis stages [5,15]. Here, we apply DBNs to simultaneously model the relationships over time among T2D, hypertension, and heart problems, and study how their onset is probabilistically determined by the considered risk factors.

To perform our analysis, we first split the data in a 3:1 proportion into a training set to learn the DBN (8,328 subjects, 37,085 visits), and a test set to estimate performance (2,832 subjects, 12,620 visits), stratifying for the age of subjects at baseline. Then, in order to overcome the problem of missing values in the dynamic risk factors (the static ones had no NA), we imputed them through an interpolation strategy supplemented by a forward/backward observation for tail or single values. Although possibly constituting a source of bias, this step was necessary as biomarkers were only available for even waves, according to ELSA collection protocols [14]. Survival information was coded at each subject's visit as a binary variable indicating whether the subject dies within 4 years of that visit, in order to balance the number of occurrences in which the death event is observed or not by the model. Finally, since we used the DBN implementation provided by the bnstruct [3] R package, which encodes probabilistic relationships among discrete variables over a discrete number of time steps, we further preprocessed the continuous variables by quantising them according to common clinical thresholds (for blood tests) or on the tertiles of their distribution computed on the training set. A quantisation interval of 4 years was chosen for the TSB, to cut its distribution into three parts with equal time length.

To learn the DBN, we imposed some constraints on its structure, by grouping the variables into layers (namely demographic, schooling, variables at time t-1, variables at time t, survival, and time), and we defined some rules on which layer can/can not influence the others based on common sense or literature knowledge (e.g., survival cannot influence sex, but vice versa is allowed). The DBN structure was then learned using a hill climbing algorithm, while the Bayesian Information Criterion [8] and the maximum a posteriori estimation were used to score the different network structures during the search and to compute the CPTs, respectively.

3.1 Simulation Algorithm

Once trained, a DBN can be used to simulate the progression of new subjects from an initial condition. Relying on the learned structure of the network and its CPTs, we implemented an algorithm that, given a complete vector of features corresponding to the values at the baseline of a new subject, probabilistically simulates the evolution of their ageing process for 6 consecutive waves at 2 years each, according to the follow-up and temporal resolution of the training data. The simulation procedure may stop before reaching 6 simulated waves if the death event is simulated in the process.

3.2 Model Validation

The learned model can be validated in the first instance by checking the correspondence of the relationships represented graphically with those expected from the literature or clinical context. Moreover, by comparing the simulated ageing process of the subjects in the test set (not used in the learning phase) with the real one, we can assess the prediction performance of the model in terms of frequency and time of occurrence of the outcomes.

Since the simulation algorithm is probabilistic, we run the simulation 100 times for each subject to obtain a probabilistic estimate of the expected follow-up. Then, for each outcome, we compared the distributions of its occurrence (defined as the detection of the event in a subject without a previous diagnosis of that disease) in the observed and simulated test populations using the Kaplan-Meier estimator. We used the log-rank test on the Kaplan-Meier curves (with a significance threshold equal to 0.05) to assess the similarity of the trends of outcome occurrence. For p-values above the significance threshold, we can assume that the model is well calibrated, that is, the observed and predicted risks are consistent, with the model neither underestimating nor overestimating the risk. We further used the integrated Area Under the Receiver Operating Characteristic (iAUC) curve for evaluating the discrimination ability of the model, i.e., its capability to predict a longer time to event for those subjects who actually experience the outcome later in reality. The more the value of the iAUC tends to 1, the better the model is at discriminating. For each clinical outcome (and considering only the subjects without that outcome at baseline), we first computed the time-dependent AUC every 2 years (i.e., the wave sampling time) to assess the performance of the DBN over time, employing as the predicted risk for each subject the area under the Kaplan-Meier curve computed over their 100 repetitions. Then, we calculated the iAUC by averaging the time-dependent AUC to obtain an overall performance [4].

3.3 Stratification Analysis

A DBN can also be used to study the specific effect of one or more selected risk factors on an outcome, by using the DBN to evolve two selected populations that differentiate at baseline in the value of the risk factor(s) of interest. By comparing their predicted progression – for instance, through stratified Kaplan-Meier curves – it is possible to investigate the impact of the different baseline values on the risk of outcome occurrence in a more extensive way than simply observing the real population.

4 Results and Discussion

Figure 1 reports the DBN learned on the training set. The joint effect of the parent nodes on the child node at subsequent time points, quantified by CPTs, is represented by the directed edges entering a node. For the dynamic variables, we graphically reported the self-influence at successive instants through loops.

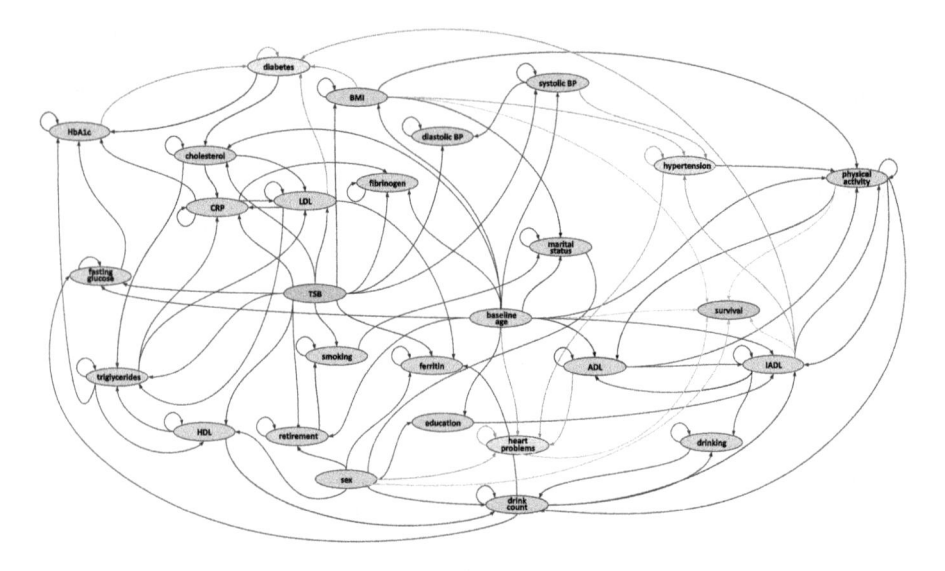

Fig. 1. DBN obtained on the training dataset. Static variables are reported in orange, dynamic variables in blue, the time variable in magenta, survival in green, and cardio-metabolic comorbidity onsets in yellow. Edges representing a direct influence of a variable on an outcome are marked in green for survival, red for cardio-metabolic comorbidities. The loops on the dynamic variables indicate the influence of the variable at time *t-1* on itself at the subsequent time *t*. (Color figure online)

The quantitative performance of the model on the test set population with a complete baseline visit (n = 2,340, slightly reduced due to missing information in the non-imputed survival outcome) is reported in Fig. 2 in terms of Kaplan-Meier estimator. For each outcome, the curves of the actual versus simulated occurrence are represented, together with the p-value of the log-rank test. In addition to the visual inspection, the log-rank test quantitatively confirms that the learned DBN is generally well calibrated (all p-values > 0.05 except for the survival outcome, which suffers from a limited observation interval). Table 2 reports the iAUC for each clinical outcome, computed over the entire observation interval. Discrimination performance appears to be generally good, except for the heart problems outcome which proved to be more difficult to simulate.

By analysing the relationships represented in Fig. 1, we can observe a joint probabilistic direct effect of IADL, BMI, HbA1c, and LDL cholesterol on the T2D onset; of IADL, BMI, and systolic BP on the hypertension onset; and of age at baseline, sex, ADL, and hypertension on the heart problems onset. Moreover, we observe the combined probabilistic direct effect of age at baseline, sex, frequency of physical activity, IADL, BMI, and heart problems on survival. Interestingly, in addition to some of the biomarkers classically used to define/predict the (early or confirmed) onset of cardio-metabolic morbidities, such as the systolic BP on hypertension and HbA1c on T2D, some adjustable risk factors (such as BMI or physical activity) show a direct effect on the risk of developing disease early.

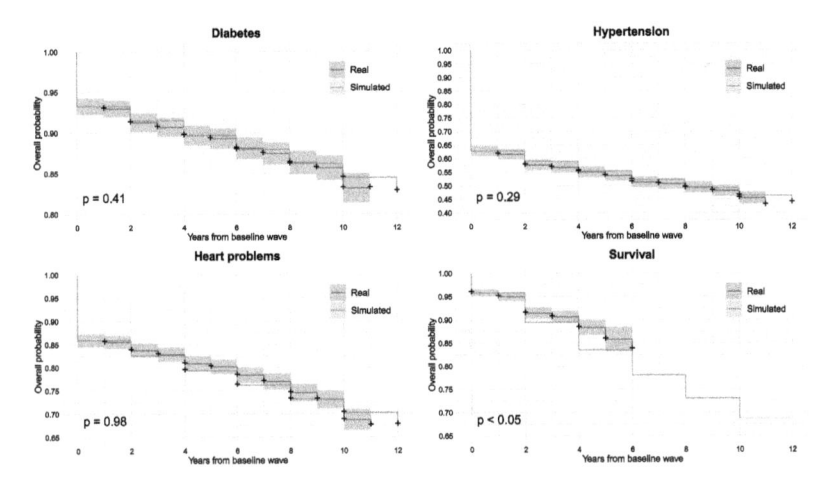

Fig. 2. Kaplan-Meier curves for each considered outcome computed on the test set. Shaded areas denote confidence intervals ($\alpha = 0.05$), + indicates censored subjects. For each outcome, the log-rank test's p-value is reported.

Table 2. iAUC computed for the cardio-metabolic comorbidities and survival on the subjects of the test set.

Outcome	T2D	Hypertension	Heart problems	Survival
iAUC	0.824	0.741	0.618	0.830

This evidence supports the prevention strategies suggested for active ageing, as the ones proposed by the European Commission in the European Innovation Partnership on Active and Healthy Ageing [2].

By examining the cross-relationships between the outcomes, a direct link can be observed between heart problems and survival, and between hypertension and heart problems. To better investigate this latter relationship, we performed a stratification analysis to assess how the risk of heart problems changes in the presence of a baseline condition with or without hypertension. We selected the test subjects without heart problems at baseline (N = 2,010). Of these, 1,314 were free of hypertension at baseline, while 696 had already had a diagnosis of hypertension. We simulated their progression 100 times per patient and compared the risk of experiencing the onset of heart problems over time among the two populations, represented in terms of Kaplan-Meier curves in Fig. 3 (left plot). As expected, we can observe that subjects with hypertension at baseline have a higher risk of developing heart problems over time, with a difference that is statistically significant, according to the log-rank test. Noticeably, similar trends are also observed in the real test data (right plot of Fig. 3), further confirming the ability of the DBN to model real trends; however, thanks to the high number of repetitions of the simulation, the confidence intervals in the DBN-simulated scenario are tighter than in the real case.

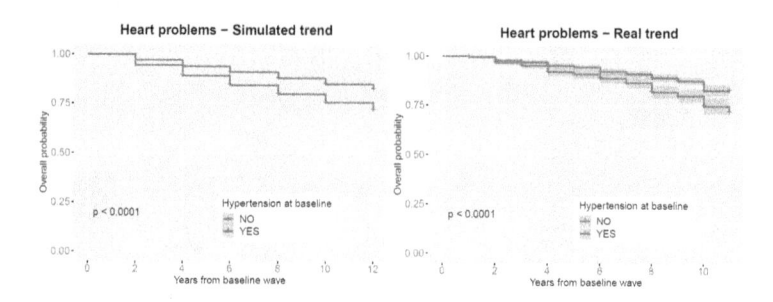

Fig. 3. Kaplan-Meier survival curves of heart problems onset on the simulations of the test set (on the left) and on the real test set (on the right) stratified according to the presence or not of hypertension at baseline, and log-rank test's p-value. Shaded areas denote confidence intervals ($\alpha = 0.05$), + censored subjects.

5 Conclusions

The network developed in this work on 6 consecutive waves of the ELSA dataset shows interesting temporal relationships between risk factors and the onset of the three considered cardio-metabolic comorbidities, namely T2D, hypertension, and heart problems, together with survival. Moreover, it highlights the enhanced risk of consecutively developing some of these diseases; specifically, we observed an augmented risk of developing heart problems over time if hypertension is already present at baseline. With its graphical output quantitatively supported by CPTs, DBNs are a highly explicable modelling technique that lends itself well to communicating results in a multidisciplinary context. Furthermore, the proposed simulation algorithm makes it possible to effectively predict the progression of the ageing process, constituting a complementary tool to more classical predictive approaches. Furthermore, the combined simulation-stratification strategy allows the effect of selected risk factors on outcomes to be observed more clearly, possibly suggesting prevention strategies for healthy ageing. As future developments, we aim at comparing the predictive performance of our model vs. other state-of-the-art machine learning approaches, also investigating the importance given to static predictors vs. their dynamic contribution as encoded by the DBN.

References

1. Dagum, P., Galper, A., Horvitz, E.: Dynamic network models for forecasting. In: Uncertainty in Artificial Intelligence, pp. 41–48. Elsevier (1992)
2. EU Commission: Strategic implementation plan for the european innovation partnership on active and healthy ageing: Steering group working document (2011)
3. Franzin, A., Sambo, F., et al.: bnstruct: an r package for bayesian network structure learning in the presence of missing data. Bioinformatics **33**(8), 1250–1252 (2017)
4. Kamarudin, A., et al.: Time-dependent roc curve analysis in medical research: current methods and applications. BMC Med. Res. Methodol, **17**(1) (2017)

5. Longato, E., Tavazzi, E., Chió, A., et al.: Dealing with data scarcity in rare diseases: dynamic bayesian networks and transfer learning to develop prognostic models of amyotrophic lateral sclerosis. In: International Conference on Artificial Intelligence in Medicine, pp. 140–150. Springer (2023). https://doi.org/10.1007/978-3-031-34344-5_18
6. Maag, B., et al.: Modeling longitudinal dynamics of comorbidities. In: Proceedings of the Conference on Health, Inference, and Learning, pp. 222–235 (2021)
7. Marini, S., Trifoglio, E., et al.: A dynamic bayesian network model for long-term simulation of clinical complications in type 1 diabetes. J. Biomed. Inform. **57**, 369–376 (2015)
8. Neath, A.A., Cavanaugh, J.E.: The bayesian information criterion: background, derivation, and applications. Wiley Interdisciplinary Rev. Comput. Statist. **4**(2), 199–203 (2012)
9. Ng, R., Sutradhar, R., Wodchis, W.P., et al.: Chronic disease population risk tool (cdport): a study protocol for a prediction model that assesses population-based chronic disease incidence. Diagnostic Prognostic Res. **2**(1), 1–11 (2018)
10. Noble, D., Mathur, R., Dent, T., Meads, C., et al.: Risk models and scores for type 2 diabetes: systematic review. BMJ **343** (2011)
11. Oldfield, Z., Rogers, N., Taylor Nelson, P., et al.: English longitudinal study of ageing: Waves 0-9, 1998–2019. UK Data Service (2020)
12. Partridge, L.: Intervening in ageing to prevent the diseases of ageing. Trends Endocrinol. Metabolism **25**(11), 555–557 (2014)
13. Roversi, C., Tavazzi, E., Vettoretti, M., Di Camillo, B.: A dynamic bayesian network model for simulating the progression to diabetes onset in the ageing population. In: 2021 IEEE EMBS International Conference on Biomedical and Health Informatics (BHI), pp. 1–4. IEEE (2021)
14. Steptoe, A., Breeze, E., Banks, J., et al.: Cohort profile: the English longitudinal study of ageing. Int. J. Epidemiol. **42**(6), 1640–1648 (2013)
15. Tavazzi, E., Daberdaku, S., Zandonà, A., et al.: Predicting functional impairment trajectories in amyotrophic lateral sclerosis: a probabilistic, multifactorial model of disease progression. J. Neurol. (2022)
16. United Nations, et al.: World population ageing 2017-highlights. Department of Economic and Social Affairs (2017)
17. Vettoretti, M., Di Camillo, B.: A variable ranking method for machine learning models with correlated features: In-silico validation and application for diabetes prediction. Appli. Sci. (11), 7740 (2021)

Adapting to Change: Reliable Multimodal Learning Across Domains

Harnessing Error Patterns to Estimate Out-of-Distribution Performance

Thomas Bonnier[✉] and Benjamin Bosch

Société Générale, Paris, France
{thomas.bonnier,benjamin.bosch}@socgen.com

Abstract. Once a classification model has been implemented, adverse distribution shifts can surface. As true labels are costly to obtain or may only be known after a certain lag, cautious monitoring should be applied to prevent unnoticed and harmful deterioration of the model's performance. In this paper, we consider distribution shift settings where the presence of shifts is uncertain and the target dataset contains only unlabeled examples. We suggest two methods for practitioners to assess the model's performance in that context. Those techniques aim to exploit patterns which result in incorrect predictions by the model or unreliable uncertainty assessment. The *Calibration Error Grid (CE Grid)* exploits regional disparities in model calibration quality to adjust the model's confidence on unlabeled data. The *Error Classifier (EC)* is a supervised learning approach which leverages representations from the data coupled with the model's confidence in order to predict the probability of error. To prove their efficacy, these techniques are empirically tested over different scenarios of shifts on various use cases. These two techniques display promising results when compared against four crucial baselines.

Keywords: Distribution shifts · Performance prediction

1 Introduction

Once a Machine Learning (ML) classification model has been deployed, dataset shifts can occur in non-stationary environments. In other words, the joint distributions of training data (the Source dataset S) and real-world data (the Target dataset T) can be different. However, given the true label is sometimes obtained with a certain cost or lag, the deterioration of the model's performance may remain unnoticed. For instance, when the outputs from an upstream model (e.g. news classification) serve as inputs to another algorithm (e.g. fake news detection), the labels related to the first model may be checked on a low-frequency basis, especially if human feedback is required to confirm the ground truth. In the financial domain, with a 24-month default horizon, the accuracy of a credit granting model cannot be assessed before two years. In the context of unlabeled Target data, an absence of monitoring could wreak havoc if the classifier made predictions for several months under detrimental distribution shifts.

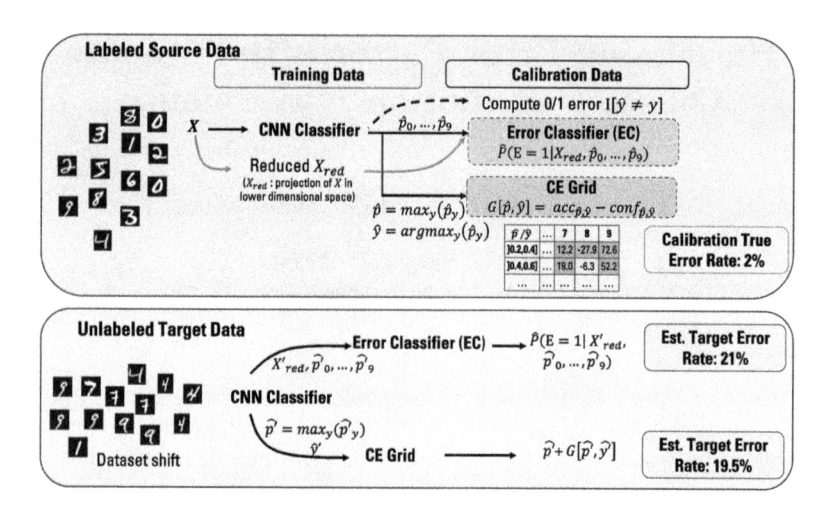

Fig. 1. Illustration of our techniques: (1) CE Grid and EC learn failure patterns of a classification model on labeled Source data. These OOD performance estimators exploit model miscalibration and error patterns. (2) CE Grid leverages the model's confidence and predicted class to adjust the confidence on unlabeled data. EC is a supervised learning technique which predicts the probability of error given the feature space specificities and the classification model's class probability estimates.

In this paper, we aim to estimate the error rate of a classifier on unlabeled data, rather than obtaining predictions for individual data points. We propose two methods which exploit error patterns resulting in unreliable uncertainty estimates or incorrect model's predictions. We assume that the classifier produces class probability estimates: e.g. neural network. As shown in Fig. 1, the *Calibration Error Grid (CE Grid)* exploits regional disparities in the quality of probability calibration in order to adjust the model's confidence when it predicts on unlabeled data. The *Error Classifier (EC)* leverages the feature space singularities coupled with the classification model's predicted probabilities, in order to learn patterns that would cause the classifier to fail. Based on those representations, EC estimates the error probability for predictions on unlabeled data.

2 Prior Work

Covariate shifts are defined as $p_S(y|x) = p_T(y|x)$ and $p_S(x) \neq p_T(x)$, while prior probability shifts are defined as $p_S(x|y) = p_T(x|y)$ and $p_S(y) \neq p_T(y)$. These changes can exacerbate the model's uncertainty and deteriorate its performance [16]. To assess the uncertainty on unlabeled data, the maximum confidence (i.e. maximum value of class probability estimates) can be leveraged [8]. As models such as neural networks can be miscalibrated, techniques such as Platt scaling [14] or temperature scaling [6] are suggested to better calibrate the class probability estimates. With such methods, the objective is to reduce miscalibration defined as the expected absolute difference between accuracy and confidence. The Expected Calibration Error (ECE) estimates miscalibration by partitioning predictions into bins based on p equally-spaced intervals of maximum confidence [13]: $ECE = \sum_{i=1}^{p} w_i |acc_i - conf_i|$ where w_i, acc_i, and $conf_i$ denote the share, accuracy, and average confidence of bin i, respectively. With regard to accuracy estimation, the Average Thresholded Confidence (ATC) technique learns a cut-off value on the Source validation data so that the proportion of samples with score (e.g. maximum confidence) above that threshold matches the accuracy [4]. The predicted accuracy is estimated as the fraction of Target examples for which the score exceeds that threshold. With the Difference of Confidences (DoC) approach, the accuracy change between the Source and unlabeled Target data is assessed by the difference between the average confidences on these two datasets [5]. Importance weighting can be used to estimate the Target error rate [2]. To achieve that, the Mandoline framework relies on importance re-weighting of the 0–1 error with the use of axes of distribution shifts. Lastly, regional uncertainty can be assessed on unlabeled data by leveraging tree representations [1].

3 Methods

Notations. We consider a Source dataset $S = \{(x_i, y_i)\}_{i=1}^{n}$ with features $x_i \in \mathcal{X} \subseteq \mathbb{R}^d$ and discrete label $y_i \in \mathcal{Y} = \{1, 2, ..., C\}$ for C-class classification. The samples are drawn i.i.d from true unknown distribution $p_S(x, y)$. The classification model $\hat{p}_y(x) = \hat{p}(y|x)$ estimates the true unknown class probabilities $p_y(x) = \mathbb{P}(Y = y | X = x), \forall x \in \mathbb{R}^d$, for any $y \in \mathcal{Y}$. A predicted label $\hat{y}$ is based on the argmax of the vector of predicted probabilities. The model maximum confidence is $\hat{p} = \max_{y \in \mathcal{Y}}(\hat{p}_y(x))$. At the time of monitoring, we assume that the Target set T is unlabeled. We define the error rate on dataset S (indexed by set $\mathcal{I}_S$) as $\varepsilon_S = \frac{1}{|\mathcal{I}_S|} \sum_{k \in \mathcal{I}_S} \mathbb{1}(y_k \neq \hat{y}_k)$, where $\mathbb{1}(.)$ is the indicator function. S is randomly and equally partitioned, for training and calibration: (S_{Train}, S_{Calib}). $\mathcal{C}$ denotes any classification algorithm that takes in training data indexed by $\mathcal{I}$ in order to output a classifier $\hat{p}_y$ fitted on that data: $\hat{p}_y = \mathcal{C}(\{(x_i, y_i) : i \in \mathcal{I}\})$.

3.1 The Calibration Error Grid (CE Grid)

We propose CE Grid to predict the performance of a classification model on the Target data. We construct a (model maximum confidence × predicted class) grid G with values equal to the difference in expectation between the accuracy and the model maximum confidence. For a prediction, a given model confidence ($\hat{p} = \max_y \hat{p}_y(x)$) could lead to a specific calibration error based on the predicted class (e.g., minority versus majority class). For instance, $G[\hat{p}, \hat{y}] < 0$ means that the model tends to be over-confident in that area, and $\hat{p}$ will thus be negatively adjusted during inference. To build the grid based on finite samples, the classifier is first fitted on S_{Train}. Using S_{Calib} data, we define N bins: indices of samples falling into bin B_{ij} have $\hat{p} \in i$ (i, interval for maximum confidence), and predicted label $\hat{y} = j$. We thus have $N = p \times c$, where p denotes the number of intervals i and c is the number of predicted classes. The grid value $G(B_{ij})$ is $acc(B_{ij}) - conf(B_{ij})$. $acc(B_{ij})$ is the accuracy in bin B_{ij}: $\frac{1}{|B_{ij}|} \sum_{k \in B_{ij}} \mathbb{1}(y_k = \hat{y}_k)$ where y_k and $\hat{y}_k$ are the true and predicted labels for sample k, respectively. $conf(B_{ij})$ is the average confidence within bin B_{ij}: $\frac{1}{|B_{ij}|} \sum_{k \in B_{ij}} \hat{p}_k$ where $\hat{p}_k$ is the maximum confidence for sample k. When there are no S_{Calib} samples in B_{ij}, then $G(B_{ij}) = 0$. Intervals i are equally spaced with arbitrary value $p = 5$: for instance, in the experiments, we used $[0.5, 0.6], ...,]0.9, 1]$ for the binary classification use case; and $[0, 0.2], ...,]0.8, 1]$ for the multi-class tasks ($C \geq 7$). For each prediction $(\hat{p}, \hat{y})$ on the Target data, we adjust the classification model's confidence with the corresponding grid value accordingly, based on the model's confidence and predicted class:

$$\hat{p}_{adj} = \min(1, \max(0, \hat{p} + G(B_{ij})_{\hat{p} \in i, \hat{y}=j})) \tag{1}$$

The adjusted uncertainty is then: $1 - \hat{p}_{adj}$, and the estimated error rate on T (indexed by set $\mathcal{I}_T$) is thus $\hat{\epsilon}_{CEGrid} = 1 - \frac{1}{|\mathcal{I}_T|} \sum_{k \in \mathcal{I}_T} \hat{p}_{adj k}$. Unlike other classwise calibration measures based on the true label [10], CE grid can thus be applied to unlabeled Target samples.

3.2 The Error Classifier (EC)

EC aims to estimate the classifier's error probability when predicting with the Target data. EC training is performed using $\boldsymbol{x}$ coupled with the classification model's class probability estimates as inputs, and the generalization error as label. To this end, we randomly partition the Source data into a training set S_{Train} to train the classification model $\hat{p}_y(\boldsymbol{x})$ and a calibration set S_{Calib} to compute the $0 - -1$ loss E for each instance, i.e., $E = \mathbb{1}(y \neq \hat{y})$. The EC model $\hat{p}_e$ defined on $\mathbb{R}^d \times \mathbb{R}^C$ is thus fitted on S_{Calib} indexed by $\mathcal{I}_{S_{Calib}}$:

$$\hat{p}_e = \mathcal{C}(\{((\boldsymbol{x}_i, \hat{p}_y(\boldsymbol{x}_i)), \mathbb{1}(y_i \neq \hat{y}_i)) : i \in \mathcal{I}_{S_{Calib}}\}) \tag{2}$$

with $\hat{y}_i = \arg\max_y \hat{p}_y(\boldsymbol{x}_i)$. As displayed in Fig. 1, $\boldsymbol{x}$ sparsity can lead to employing more relevant representations such as word embeddings for text data in neural network architectures or projections in reduced dimensions for image datasets. EC is then used to infer the model's error probability for each new instance of the Target data T, given the classification model's predicted probabilities and feature values: $\hat{p}(E = 1 | \boldsymbol{x}, \hat{p}_1, ..., \hat{p}_C)$. For instance, EC should be able to identify situations where the model is over-confident in unfamiliar feature space or in a minority class, and tends to generalize poorly. The error rate on the Target data is estimated as $\mathbb{E}_T[\hat{p}(E = 1 | \boldsymbol{x}, \hat{p}_y(\boldsymbol{x}))]$, or for $|\mathcal{I}_T|$ samples:

$$\hat{\varepsilon}_{EC} = \frac{1}{|\mathcal{I}_T|} \sum_{i \in \mathcal{I}_T} \hat{p}(E_i = 1 | \boldsymbol{x}_i, \hat{p}_{1,i}, ..., \hat{p}_{C,i}) \tag{3}$$

4 Experiments

4.1 Settings

Datasets and Models. We empirically test the relevance of our methods on five datasets with a variety of classification tasks (binary and multi-class) and modalities (tabular, text, image): the default of credit card clients data (*credit*) [18], the wine quality data (*wine*) [3], the 20 Newsgroups dataset (*newsgroups*) [11], the MNIST database (*mnist*) [12], and the Fashion-MNIST dataset (*fashion*) [17]. We consider diverse classifiers: CatBoost [15] and various neural network architectures (LSTM, CNN, pre-trained *ResNet50* [7]). For EC, we employ non-optimized random forest or LightGBM classifier algorithms [9] with 100 estimators. For *newsgroups*, EC leverages the word embeddings learned by an LSTM model as features, aggregated with mean pooling. For *mnist* and *fashion*, EC exploits sparse random projections of the flattened pixel data.

Shift Scenarios. We consider two categories of shifts. Natural shifts are generated by using a specific sampling process based on clusters, without modifying the original instances. Synthetic shifts are created by altering the original dataset. With regard to natural shifts, the Target dataset including the true labels is sampled according to three different scenarios: (i) Standard scenario: No distribution shift; (ii) Benign: Moderate shifts affect both covariates and label proportions; (iii) Adverse: Severe shifts impact covariates and label proportions, and model's performance. For the image datasets, in addition to natural shifts, we examine the impacts of synthetic covariate shifts, with three fractions of affected Target data $\delta \in \{0, 0.2, 0.8\}$ coupled with three levels of increasing shift intensity in order to characterize the standard, benign, and adverse scenarios, respectively: (i) Gaussian noise (*mnist-N*, *fashion-N*): We randomly alter the pixels of a fraction δ of Target samples by adding Gaussian noise with various levels of standard deviations depending on the scenario and use case; (ii) Image shift (*mnist-T*, *fashion-T*): We randomly alter a fraction δ of Target samples by introducing rotation angles $\{0, 15, 40\}$, (x, y) translation percentages $\{0, 0.03, 0.07\}$, and scaling levels $\{1, 1.5, 2\}$ with equal share for each transformation.

Baselines. For each use case, the Source dataset is equally divided into training (for the classifier) and calibration data (to calibrate the different methods). We optimize the parameters of Platt or temperature scaling on S_{Calib}. The Target dataset contains 1,000 samples. To compare the different techniques, we use the absolute difference (AD) between the true (ε) and predicted ($\hat{\varepsilon}$) error rates on the Target data. This metric, when averaged over K experiments as in Table 1, is thus the Mean Absolute Error (MAE): $(1/K) \sum_{i=1}^{i=K} |\varepsilon_i - \hat{\varepsilon}_i|$. We compare our estimates of the Target error rate with four different baselines: (i) *Average Confidence (AC)*: the error rate is computed as one minus the expected confidence, i.e. $1 - AC = 1 - \mathbb{E}_T[\max_{y \in \mathcal{Y}}(\hat{p}_y(\boldsymbol{x}))]$; (ii) *Difference of Confidences (DoC)*: We adjust S_{Calib} error rate with the difference of average confidences,

Table 1. Results (MAE%) with **natural shifts**, by use case averaged over 10 dataset splits, for a Target dataset size of 1,000 samples. EC demonstrates robustness across all the experimented scenarios, especially in the adverse case. Values in parenthesis are standard deviations of absolute errors. Adv=Adverse. Ben=Benign. Std=Standard.

Use case	Scenario	EC	CE Grid	AC	DoC	Mandoline	ATC
credit	Adv	3.7 (2.9)	**2.5** (2.1)	7.5 (1.8)	7.1 (1.8)	6.4 (2.1)	30.9 (7.0)
	Ben	**1.6** (1.2)	1.8 (1.3)	2.6 (1.8)	2.2 (1.6)	1.9 (1.4)	7.1 (2.5)
	Std	1.8 (1.6)	1.3 (1.2)	1.4 (1.1)	1.3 (1.3)	1.3 (1.3)	**1.1** (1.3)
wine	Adv	**4.5** (5.5)	9.1 (3.9)	13.3 (7.4)	14.3 (7.6)	10.3 (2.8)	24.3 (17.4)
	Ben	**1.0** (0.7)	1.2 (1.2)	1.6 (1.3)	1.1 (1.2)	1.7 (1.2)	4.9 (3.3)
	Std	**1.6** (1.8)	1.9 (1.6)	2.1 (1.2)	2.0 (1.5)	1.9 (1.6)	2.7 (1.4)
newsgroups	Adv	**6.0** (3.2)	13.0 (4.8)	12.2 (4.3)	15.0 (4.6)	11.1 (4.7)	6.3 (4.4)
	Ben	**1.1** (0.9)	2.2 (1.5)	3.1 (1.8)	2.2 (1.8)	1.4 (1.2)	5.4 (2.6)
	Std	1.4 (1.5)	**1.4** (1.3)	2.1 (2.1)	1.5 (1.5)	**1.4** (1.5)	1.5 (1.6)
mnist	Adv	**3.0** (3.1)	4.8 (4.5)	6.6 (4.8)	6.4 (4.8)	5.5 (3.6)	16.2 (8.4)
	Ben	5.3 (2.5)	**1.8** (1.1)	4.1 (2.3)	3.8 (2.1)	3.2 (1.6)	2.1 (1.1)
	Std	0.5 (0.3)	0.6 (0.3)	**0.4** (0.4)	0.5 (0.5)	0.5 (0.5)	0.7 (0.6)
fashion	Adv	5.0 (3.2)	8.4 (3.3)	10.3 (2.6)	10.6 (2.2)	11.3 (2.0)	**3.5** (2.2)
	Ben	1.5 (0.9)	1.9 (1.4)	**1.4** (1.1)	1.8 (1.5)	2.0 (1.9)	2.0 (1.4)
	Std	1.3 (0.9)	1.4 (0.8)	**1.2** (0.7)	1.5(0.7)	1.5 (0.8)	1.6 (1.0)

i.e. $\mathbb{E}_{S_{Calib}}[\mathbb{1}(y \neq \hat{y})] + \mathbb{E}_{S_{Calib}}[\max_{y \in \mathcal{Y}}(\hat{p}_y(x))] - \mathbb{E}_T[\max_{y \in \mathcal{Y}}(\hat{p}_y(x))]$; (iii) *Mandoline*: The estimation of the error rate is based on the 0–1 loss error importance re-weighting with one slice determined by the classifier's maximum confidence; (iv) *Average Thresholded Confidence (ATC)*: The error rate is estimated with $\mathbb{E}_T[\mathbb{1}(s(\hat{p}_y(x)) < t)]$, where s is the maximum confidence score function. t denotes the threshold selected by the ATC method by minimizing the difference between S_{Calib} error rate and the fraction of S_{Calib} samples with score below t.

4.2 Results

Results by Use Case. With regard to natural shifts, Table 1 shows that EC can be relatively robust over different tasks (binary and multi-class), data types (structured and unstructured), and shift scenarios. With this nature of shifts, it outperforms the other baselines in many experiments, especially in case of adverse shift. CE Grid remains reliable in many scenarios, but the simplicity of the method shows some limitations in certain adverse scenarios. Indeed, when moving to shifted data, the same calibration map is applied, which is a limitation.

Table 2 shows that MAE can be relatively large in the adverse scenario. However, EC and ATC outperform the other techniques in case of adverse synthetic shifts. EC seems to be more prone to overreacting in the benign scenarios with Gaussian noise. As it is the only method employing a reduced representation of the input (random projections), it may be more sensitive to benign covariate shifts.

Table 2. Results (MAE%) with **synthetic shifts**, by use case averaged over 10 seeds, for a Target dataset size of 1,000 samples. Lower MAE is better. EC and ATC outperform the other methods in the adverse scenario.

Use case	Scenario	EC	CE Grid	AC	DoC	Mandoline	ATC
mnist-N	Adv	**4.4** (3.6)	17.7 (5.0)	15.0 (5.2)	15.4 (5.1)	18.5 (5.5)	4.8 (3.1)
	Ben	6.1 (1.5)	1.1 (0.6)	**1.0** (0.7)	**1.0** (0.6)	1.1 (0.7)	2.3 (1.2)
	Std	0.6 (0.5)	0.5 (0.4)	**0.4** (0.4)	0.7 (0.4)	0.7 (0.4)	0.7 (0.5)
mnist-T	Adv	15.4 (1.2)	20.3 (1.8)	20.0 (1.8)	20.3 (1.7)	21.7 (1.7)	**14.9** (2.1)
	Ben	**1.0** (0.9)	1.3 (0.6)	1.3 (0.5)	1.6 (0.7)	1.7 (0.7)	1.4 (0.8)
	Std	0.6 (0.5)	0.5 (0.4)	**0.4** (0.4)	0.7 (0.4)	0.7(0.4)	0.7 (0.5)
fashion-N	Adv	22.5 (4.5)	24.1 (7.3)	26.0 (6.6)	25.9 (6.8)	26.1 (7.0)	**17.3** (10.2)
	Ben	**1.3** (0.8)	2.0 (1.5)	2.1 (1.2)	2.2 (1.2)	2.2 (1.3)	1.8 (1.2)
	Std	1.4 (1.1)	1.3 (0.8)	**0.9** (0.6)	1.3 (0.9)	1.3 (0.9)	1.4 (1.2)
fashion-T	Adv	**17.3** (2.9)	24.1 (3.7)	23.1 (2.8)	23.0 (3.4)	23.1 (3.7)	17.8 (5.3)
	Ben	**1.7** (1.1)	4.1 (1.7)	4.2 (1.3)	4.1 (1.6)	4.1 (1.7)	3.4 (2.2)
	Std	1.4 (1.1)	1.3 (0.8)	**0.9** (0.6)	1.3 (0.9)	1.3 (0.9)	1.4 (1.2)

5 Conclusion, Limitations, and Future Work

We have shown the relevance of two practical monitoring techniques to assess the severity of the impact of dataset shifts on a classification model's performance. The results are specific to these datasets and the nature of the shifts. There are a few caveats to be aware of. First, EC can sometimes overreact in benign scenarios with image datasets due to the fact that EC might be more sensitive to benign covariate shifts as it leverages projections of the pixel data. As an alternative, other relevant representations could be tested, such as the output of a given layer in the neural network architecture. The main weakness of CE Grid is that it uses a static calibration map, which may not be adequate for every shift scenario. The values in the grid may not be valid anymore in case of severe shift. With regard to natural distribution shifts, we could experiment with situations where the test set is from another real-world distribution instead of re-sampling from an in-distribution. Further, additional multi-class probability calibration methods could be tested, such as Dirichlet calibration [10].

References

1. Bonnier, T., Bosch, B.: Engineering uncertainty representations to monitor distribution shifts. In: NeurIPS 2022 Workshop on Distribution Shifts: Connecting Methods and Applications (2022)
2. Chen, M.F., Goel, K., Sohoni, N.S., Poms, F., Fatahalian, K., Ré, C.: MANDOLINE: model evaluation under distribution shift. In: Proceedings of the 38th International Conference on Machine Learning, ICML 2021, 18-24 July 2021, Virtual Event. Proceedings of Machine Learning Research, vol. 139, pp. 1617–1629. PMLR (2021)
3. Cortez, P., Cerdeira, A., Almeida, F., Matos, T., Reis, J.: Modeling wine preferences by data mining from physicochemical properties. Decis. Support Syst. **47**(4), 547–553 (2009)
4. Garg, S., Balakrishnan, S., Lipton, Z.C., Neyshabur, B., Sedghi, H.: Leveraging unlabeled data to predict out-of-distribution performance. In: The Tenth International Conference on Learning Representations, ICLR 2022, Virtual Event, April 25-29, 2022 (2022)
5. Guillory, D., Shankar, V., Ebrahimi, S., Darrell, T., Schmidt, L.: Predicting with confidence on unseen distributions. In: 2021 IEEE/CVF International Conference on Computer Vision, ICCV 2021, Montreal, QC, Canada, October 10-17, 2021, pp. 1114–1124. IEEE (2021)
6. Guo, C., Pleiss, G., Sun, Y., Weinberger, K.Q.: On calibration of modern neural networks. In: International conference on machine learning, pp. 1321–1330. PMLR (2017)
7. He, K., Zhang, X., Ren, S., Sun, J.: Deep residual learning for image recognition. In: 2016 IEEE Conference on Computer Vision and Pattern Recognition, CVPR 2016, Las Vegas, NV, USA, June 27-30, 2016, pp. 770–778. IEEE Computer Society (2016)
8. Hendrycks, D., Gimpel, K.: A baseline for detecting misclassified and out-of-distribution examples in neural networks. In: 5th International Conference on Learning Representations, ICLR 2017, Toulon, France, April 24-26, 2017, Conference Track Proceedings (2017)
9. Ke, G., et al.: LightGBM: a highly efficient gradient boosting decision tree. In: Advances in Neural Information Processing Systems, vol. 30. Curran Associates, Inc. (2017)
10. Kull, M., Perello Nieto, M., Kängsepp, M., Silva Filho, T., Song, H., Flach, P.: Beyond temperature scaling: obtaining well-calibrated multi-class probabilities with dirichlet calibration. In: Advances in Neural Information Processing Systems, vol. 32 (2019)
11. Lang, K.: The 20 newsgroups text dataset. https://scikit-learn.org/0.19/datasets/twenty_newsgroups.html (1995). Accessed 1 Jun 2022
12. LeCun, Y., Cortes, C., Burges, C.: MNIST handwritten digit database. ATT Labs [Online]. Available: http://yann.lecun.com/exdb/mnist**2** (2010)
13. Naeini, M.P., Cooper, G., Hauskrecht, M.: Obtaining well calibrated probabilities using Bayesian binning. In: Twenty-Ninth AAAI Conference on Artificial Intelligence (2015)
14. Platt, J., et al.: Probabilistic outputs for support vector machines and comparisons to regularized likelihood methods. Adv. large margin classifiers **10**(3), 61–74 (1999)
15. Prokhorenkova, L., Gusev, G., Vorobev, A., Dorogush, A.V., Gulin, A.: CatBoost: unbiased boosting with categorical features. In: Advances in Neural Information Processing Systems, vol. 31 (2018)

16. Rabanser, S., Günnemann, S., Lipton, Z.: Failing loudly: an empirical study of methods for detecting dataset shift. In: Advances in Neural Information Processing Systems, vol. 32. Curran Associates, Inc. (2019)
17. Xiao, H., Rasul, K., Vollgraf, R.: Fashion-MNIST: a novel image dataset for benchmarking machine learning algorithms. arXiv preprint arXiv:1708.07747 (2017)
18. Yeh, I.C., Lien, C.H.: The comparisons of data mining techniques for the predictive accuracy of probability of default of credit card clients. Expert Syst. Appl. **36**(2), 2473–2480 (2009)

HAVE-Net: Hallucinated Audio-Visual Embeddings for Few-Shot Classification with Unimodal Cues

Ankit Jha[✉], Debabrata Pal, Mainak Singha, Naman Agarwal, and Biplab Banerjee

Indian Institue of Technology Bombay, Mumbai, India
ankitjha16@gmail.com

Abstract. Recognition of remote sensing (RS) or aerial images is currently of great interest, and advancements in deep learning algorithms added flavor to it in recent years. Occlusion, intra-class variance, lighting, etc., might arise while training neural networks using unimodal RS visual input. Even though joint training of audio-visual modalities improves classification performance in a low-data regime, it has yet to be thoroughly investigated in the RS domain. Here, we aim to solve a novel problem where both the audio and visual modalities are present during the meta-training of a few-shot learning (FSL) classifier; however, one of the modalities might be missing during the meta-testing stage. This problem formulation is pertinent in the RS domain, given the difficulties in data acquisition or sensor malfunctioning. To mitigate, we propose a novel few-shot generative framework, *Hallucinated Audio-Visual Embeddings-Network (HAVE-Net)*, to meta-train cross-modal features from limited unimodal data. Precisely, these hallucinated features are meta-learned from *base* classes and used for few-shot classification on *novel* classes during the inference phase. The experimental results on the benchmark ADVANCE and AudioSetZSL datasets show that our hallucinated modality augmentation strategy for few-shot classification outperforms the classifier performance trained with the real multimodal information at least by 0.8–2%.

Keywords: Multimodal learning · Audio-Visual remote sensing data · Few-shot learning · Meta-learning · CNN

1 Introduction

Accurate remote sensing (RS) image classification with fewer training samples is crucial for land-cover classification, voice-to-satellite image retrieval, efficient route planning, etc. While existing researches primarily rely on optical images or unimodal data, incorporating audio cues can tackle several real-world challenges. For example, audio can assist in locating visually obscured objects or identifying tiny features in low-resolution satellite images. However, the lack of paired audio-visual training data hinders the development of reliable multimodal systems.

Although there exists limited usage of audio data in RS scene classification, integrating land-cover class-specific audio information with geo-tagged [5] aerial images can significantly boost the RS classification performance.

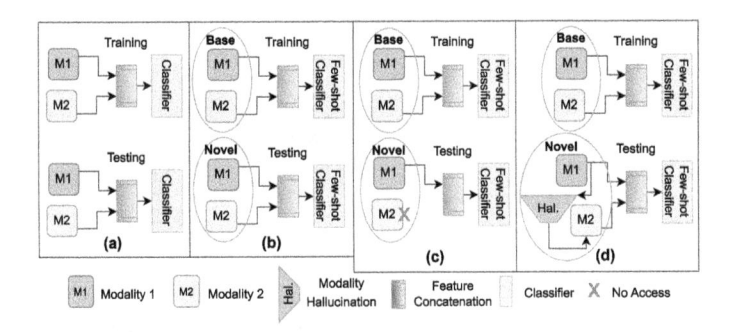

Fig. 1. Illustration of (a) Fully supervised classifier considering same classes during the training and testing phases, (b) Multimodal few-shot classification, and (c) Issues with non-availability of a single modality for the novel classes during testing. To mitigate (d) we propose modality hallucination for multimodal audio-visual few-shot classification. The hallucinated modality generator is trained on *base* (seen) classes and used only at the testing time on the novel (unseen) classes.

Metric learning [7,15] and optimization-based meta-learning [2] are common approaches in the few-shot learning (FSL) [2,7,15,17] community. Siamese networks [7] extract the image pair features using shared parameters and seeks to build an efficient distance metric based on feature similarity. In Prototypical Networks [15], the distance from the nearest class prototype is used to determine the label of a test query. On the other hand, MAML [2] focuses on learning initial parameters for rapid adaptation to unobserved tasks. Besides, SPN [11] employs Bayesian approximation to stabilize model uncertainty in FSL.

Due to the poor perception of the classification environment by uni-modal learning, researchers [10] further investigated multimodal learning in a few-shot context. For example, Multimodal Prototypical Networks [10] additionally considers hallucinated text modality. In literature [6,12], Multimodal learning has demonstrated significant performance gain. However, accessing all the modalities during testing is difficult and can impact classification performance. We address this problem by hallucinating all the unavailable modalities during test time.

In this paper, we propose to use a Conditional Generative Adversarial Network (CGAN) [9] to hallucinate missing modality data. Unlike traditional CGAN, we train a modality and class-conditioned Conditional Multimodal GAN (CMM-GAN) by episodic meta-learning with *base* class samples, allowing it to generate cross-modal features for novel classes. During meta-training, we utilize both audio and visual modality data to extract discriminative features with strong cross-modal correlation (Fig. 1). The hallucinated features are augmented with available real modality features to enrich the distribution density. Then, during meta-testing, our approach involves hallucinating missing modality data based on the available real modality data of *base* (seen) classes. These hallucinated features are utilized to perform few-shot multimodal classification on novel (unseen) classes. Our main contributions are as follows:

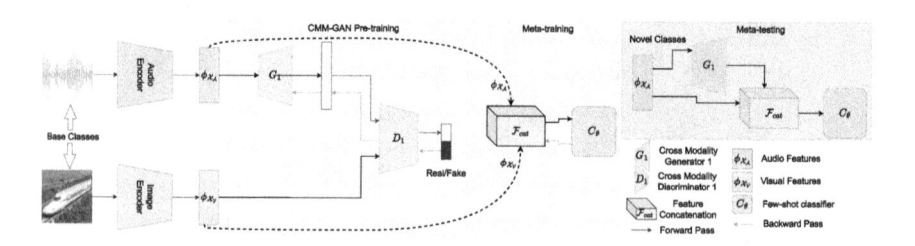

Fig. 2. The overview of our proposed HAVE-Net framework. We first pre-train CMM-GAN, composed of a Generator G_1 and a Discriminator D_1 for audio to visual cross-modal feature generation using a large number of *base* class samples. Then, we meta-train a few-shot learning classifier C_θ using the multimodal dataset (original fused modality on *base* class limited samples). During Meta-testing, the classification is performed for the novel class samples based on the available modality features augmented with the hallucinated cross-modal features from the pre-trained CMM-GAN.

- We introduce a novel modality-agnostic multimodal framework in a few-shot regime, namely, HAVE-Net, to battle against the missing modality problem in the meta-testing phase.

- We propose a novel Conditional Multimodal Adversarial loss objective to pre-train our CMM-GAN classifier from the available unimodal data (either audio to visual or vice-versa)

- We conduct extensive experiments on the benchmark AudioSetZSL [12] and ADVANCE [6] datasets, showcasing our method's superior few-shot multimodal classification performance from available unimodal data.

2 Related Works

A. Multimodal Learning: RS audiovisual deep learning has received limited attention in existing research. However, some works have been proposed in this area like, [8] focuses on learning the correspondence between the audio and visual modalities for cross-modal retrieval of RS images. Similarly, [14] proposes a clustering-based *aural atlas* approach that fuses audiovisual information. Recently, a self-supervised learning-based approach was proposed in [5] to understand the key mapping between RS audiovisual samples, which was extended to other transfer learning tasks such as scene classification [6], semantic segmentation, and cross-modal retrieval. In [6], sound-image pairs were enforced to transfer sound event information for RS scene classification. It is worth noting that the existing models are designed for specific pairs of modalities.

B. Few-shot Learning: To overcome the challenge of limited labeled data in remote sensing (RS) classification, researchers have proposed various methods, such as semi-supervised CNN, self-taught learning, and few-shot learning (FSL) [16,17]. FSL uses the "learning to learn" approach, where the model is trained on fully-supervised *base* classes to transfer learning to novel, label-deficient categories [2,13]. The use of meta-learning algorithms, like MAML [2], enables the model to learn invariant features by creating few-shot tasks (episodes) for training. Additionally, metric-learning methods [17] aim to learn an optimal feature space with minimal intra-class and maximum inter-class distances.

3 Methodology

3.1 Preliminaries

Let $\mathcal{D} = \{\mathcal{X}_A, \mathcal{X}_V; \mathcal{Y}\}$ be the multimodal dataset, where $\mathcal{X}_A$ is an audio spectrogram, $\mathcal{X}_V$ represents visual space, and $\mathcal{Y}$ is their corresponding label space. Further, let $x^i{}_A \in \mathcal{X}_A$ and $x^i{}_V \in \mathcal{X}_V$ be the ith input sample point and y^i is its associated label. In FSL, two disjoint sets of classes namely, base classes $\mathcal{Y}_{Base}$ for training and novel classes $\mathcal{Y}_{Novel}$ for testing are sampled from each dataset where, $\mathcal{Y} = \mathcal{Y}_{Base} \cup \mathcal{Y}_{Novel}$ and $\mathcal{Y}_{Base} \cap \mathcal{Y}_{Novel} = \phi$. $\mathcal{Y}_{Base}$ has ample amount of training sample points such that we assert $|\mathcal{Y}_{Base}| > |\mathcal{Y}_{Novel}|$. As the few-shot classifier trained using original modalities, $\mathcal{X}_A$ and $\mathcal{X}_V$, the presence of all the modalities certainly boosts the FSL classifier performance. However, we assume only one modality during testing, causing the classifier to underperform for the novel classes. So to make the missing modality available at the inference, we pre-train CMM-GAN over all samples of the base classes to generate the cross-modal features, i.e., either $\mathcal{X}_A$ to $\mathcal{X}_V$ or vice-versa. During meta-training, random episodes are sampled consisting of support $\mathcal{S}$ and query set $\mathcal{Q}$. The support set is defines as $\mathcal{S} = \{(x^i{}_A, x^i{}_V; y^i)\}_{i=1}^{m\mathcal{K}}$ where m training samples per $\mathcal{K} \in \mathcal{Y}_{Base}$ classes are sampled in each episode and also known as $\mathcal{K}$-way m-shot classification. The query set $\mathcal{Q} = \{(x^j{}_A, x^j{}_V; y^j)\}_{j=1}^{n\mathcal{K}}$ is formed with other disjoint random n samples per $\mathcal{K}$ class. By training from a wide range of $\mathcal{Y}_{Base}$ samples, classifier C_θ gets transferrable knowledge to classify single modality data. Also, CMM-GAN learns to generate pseudo samples of cross-modal data. In this paper, during meta-training, we use both $\mathcal{X}_A, \mathcal{X}_V$ whereas, during meta-testing, we assume one of the modalities is absent. Hence, we generate pseudo samples from other available modalities using CMM-GAN and classify samples belong to the $\mathcal{Y}_{Novel}$.

3.2 Proposed Methodology

In Fig. 2, we show the architectural diagram of our proposed HAVE-Net. Here, we explain the two phases adopted in training the HAVE-Net, i.e., i) base training for cross-modal hallucination, which is the main essence of our proposed setup, and ii) incrementally training the multimodal few-shot classifier. To begin with, we first use the VGGish model pre-trained on Audio Set [3] dataset as audio encoder to extract the audio features $\phi_{\mathcal{X}_A} \in \mathbb{R}^{1 \times 1024}$ for each of the audio spectrograms $x^i{}_A$. Similarly, for each $x^i{}_V$ we extract visual features $\phi_{\mathcal{X}_V} \in \mathbb{R}^{1 \times 1024}$ using pre-trained ResNet model on remote sensing RESISC45 [1] dataset. Note that we haven't used pre-trained ImageNet features due to wide domain differences with RS scenes.

Base Training: We split this phase into two parts; firstly, CMM-GAN is trained for cross-modal feature hallucination, where generator G_1 of CMM-GAN generates base class visual features $\phi_{\mathcal{X}_V}$ from audio features $\phi_{\mathcal{X}_A}$. Similarly, using G_2, we generate audio features from visual features. Inspired by [10], we train CMM-GAN by imposing the constraints over one modality to generate other modality pseudo features. Mathematically, CMM-GAN is pre-trained on the large number of base class audio spectrogram features $G_1(\phi_{\mathcal{X}_A})_{Base} \approx \phi_{\mathcal{X}_V}{}_{Base}$ and thereafter it is used to generate the pseudo-visual features from limited novel audio class samples $\phi_{\mathcal{X}_V}{}_{Novel} = G_1(\phi_{\mathcal{X}_A}{}_{Base \ Novel})$ in testing or vice-versa. Secondly, we perform training of FSL classifier using multimodal real audio-visual features. We fuse the audio and visual features ($\mathcal{X}_A$ and $\mathcal{X}_V$) as: $\mathcal{F}_{cat} = [\phi_{\mathcal{X}_A}; \phi_{\mathcal{X}_V}]$, where ';' indicates the concatenation operator. We train $\mathcal{F}_{cat}$ in a similar fashion as in SPN [11] to stabilize the model predictions. The classifier C_θ aims to learn from a small set of audio and visual features from limited base class samples $C_\theta(\phi_{\mathcal{F}_{cat}})$, where C_θ denotes the FSL classifier with its learnable parameters θ.

Novel Testing: We concatenate pre-trained CMM-GAN hallucinated visual features conditioned on only available novel unimodal real audio features to mitigate the need for missing visual data. Then multimodal few-shot classification is performed by the meta-trained classifier, $C_\theta(\phi_{[\mathcal{X}_A; G_1(\mathcal{X}_A)]})$. Similarly, from novel visual samples and corresponding hallucinated audio samples, we perform multimodal classification $C_\theta(\phi_{[\mathcal{X}_V; G_2(\mathcal{X}_V)]})$. This helps in shifting the initial uncertain class prototype to the true distribution centroid position in the metric space.

3.3 Objective Functions

Here, we define the three loss components in optimizing the proposed HAVE-Net, which are as follows:

CMM-GAN Loss: We optimize CMM-GAN using conditional multimodal adversarial loss $\mathcal{L}_{CMA}$ comprising Eqs. 1 and 2 to hallucinate visual features from the available audio features.

$$\mathcal{L}_{CGAN}(G_1, D_1) = \min_{G_1} \max_{D} \mathbb{E}_{y \sim \phi_{\mathcal{X}_V}}[log D_1(y)] \\ + \mathbb{E}_{z \sim P_z, \mathcal{X}_A}[log(1 - D_1)(G_1(\phi_{\mathcal{X}_A} | \phi_{\mathcal{X}_V}, z))] \quad (1)$$

Additionally, we introduce reconstruction loss $\mathcal{L}_{Rec}$ in (Eq. 2) in defining $\mathcal{L}_{CMA}$, which helps in minimizing the distance between the generated visual features and corresponding ground truth. The overall CMM-GAN objective function is defined in (Eq. 3) where λ_1 is a weight factor.

$$\mathcal{L}_{Rec}(G_1) = ||\phi_{\mathcal{X}_V} - G_1(\phi_{\mathcal{X}_A})|| \qquad (2)$$

$$\mathcal{L}_{CMA}(D_1) = \mathcal{L}_{CGAN}(G_1, D_1) + \lambda_1 \cdot \mathcal{L}_{Rec}(G_1) \qquad (3)$$

Similarly, we hallucinate visual features from the available audio features using generator G_2 and discriminator D_2.

Prototypical Loss: In each episode, $(\mathcal{S}, \mathcal{Q}) \subset \mathcal{D}$ is randomly sampled under FSL setting. We calculate the training samples' multimodal (audio-visual) prototypes c_k for k true classes, which is the mean of the support audio-visual features $(x : [\phi_{\mathcal{X}_A}, \phi_{\mathcal{X}_V}])$ and later used to find the nearest prototype for the test samples based on the euclidean distance function.

$$\mathcal{L}_{Proto} = \frac{\exp(-d(C_\phi(x), c_k))}{\sum_{k'=1}^{\mathcal{K}} \exp(-d(C_\phi(x), c_{k'}))} \qquad (4)$$

FSL uncertainty minimization loss: For i^{th} query image, standard deviation and mean across all prediction probabilities $p_{i,multiple} = \{p_i^1, p_i^2, p_i^3, \cdots, p_i^{n_{times}}\}$ are $\sigma_{Loss,i}$, and, $\mu_p = \frac{\sum_{y=1}^{n_{times}} p_{ik}^y}{n_{times}}$. The prediction variance loss for all queries,

$$\mathcal{L}_{std} = \sum_{i=1}^{n\mathcal{K}} \sigma_{Loss,i} = \sum_{i=1}^{n\mathcal{K}} \sqrt{\frac{\sum_{y=1}^{n_{times}} (p_{ik}^y - \mu_p)^2}{n_{times}}} \qquad (5)$$

Total Loss: In Eq. 6, to train the HAVE-Net, we jointly optimize the CMM-GAN (Eq. 3) and the prototypical loss (Eq. 4) with the uncertainty minimization loss $\mathcal{L}_{std}$ (Eq. 5), where λ_2 represents the hyperparameter.

$$\mathcal{L}_{Total} = \mathcal{L}_{CMA} + \mathcal{L}_{Proto} + \lambda_2 \times \mathcal{L}_{std} \qquad (6)$$

4 Experiments and Analysis

4.1 Datasets

We evaluated the proposed method on two benchmark multimodal (audio-visual) datasets namely, AudioSetZSL [12] & ADVANCE [6] datasets. The AudioSetZSL is a subset of Audio Set [3] contains weakly annotated visuals related to different audio events. We set $|\mathcal{Y}_{Base}| = 23$ and $|\mathcal{Y}_{Novel}| = 10$ as per train-test split in [12], where $|\mathcal{Y}|$ denotes the cardinality of $\mathcal{Y}$. We used the features provided in [12] for our few-shot methodologies. On a similar note, the ADVANCE dataset, which has pairs of RS audio and visual modalities and are randomly split into $|\mathcal{Y}_{Base}| = 8$ and $|\mathcal{Y}_{Novel}| = 5$.

Table 1. Comparison of different meta-learning methods for m ways $\in \{3, 5\}$ with k-shot $\in \{1, 5\}$ on ADVANCE dataset. A + (Hal. V)* is the fusion of audio modality with the hallucinated visual modality. V + (Hal. A)** represents the fusion of visual modality with hallucinated audio modality during the meta-testing.

Model	m-way	Audio (A)		Visual (V)		Fusion	
		1-shot	5-shot	1-shot	5-shot	1-shot	5-shot
Prototypical [15]	3-way	56.12 ± 0.38	73.35 ± 0.44	58.65 ± 0.24	77.13 ± 0.37	65.44 ± 0.32	81.96 ± 0.34
Relation Net [16]	3-way	39.00 ± 0.43	40.45 ± 0.44	43.91 ± 0.22	47.96 ± 0.18	49.08 ± 0.55	56.33 ± 0.37
MAML [2]	3-way	57.20 ± 0.30	74.61 ± 0.31	64.31 ± 0.25	79.27 ± 0.24	76.60 ± 0.42	83.01 ± 0.31
Matching-Net [17]	3-way	56.50 ± 0.48	69.53 ± 0.36	60.09 ± 0.32	76.35 ± 0.29	70.11 ± 0.39	81.60 ± 0.41
HAVE-Net(A + Hal. V)*	3-way	59.41 ± 0.55	75.03 ± 0.12	67.42 ± 0.35	81.50 ± 0.31	**79.61 ± 0.34**	**84.75 ± 0.19**
HAVE-Net(V + Hal. A)**	3-way	59.41 ± 0.55	75.03 ± 0.12	67.42 ± 0.35	81.50 ± 0.31	**77.43 ± 0.27**	**84.30 ± 0.45**
Prototypical [15]	5-way	43.63 ± 0.32	68.20 ± 0.26	46.32 ± 0.57	70.47 ± 0.33	55.71 ± 0.29	73.69 ± 0.48
Relation Net [16]	5-way	28.72 ± 0.38	31.93 ± 0.46	33.66 ± 0.22	36.80 ± 0.63	39.61 ± 0.32	44.36 ± 0.41
MAML [2]	5-way	47.31 ± 0.19	71.52 ± 0.33	48.97 ± 0.42	72.65 ± 0.19	59.00 ± 0.56	75.82 ± 0.34
Matching-Net [17]	5-way	43.87 ± 0.40	69.32 ± 0.24	47.15 ± 0.30	66.90 ± 0.39	56.41 ± 0.50	71.20 ± 0.30
HAVE-Net(A + Hal. V)*	5-way	53.70 ± 0.31	74.29 ± 0.24	56.22 ± 0.35	76.13 ± 0.46	**61.39 ± 0.48**	**76.80 ± 0.26**
HAVE-Net(V + Hal. A)**	5-way	53.70 ± 0.31	74.29 ± 0.24	56.22 ± 0.35	76.13 ± 0.46	**60.54 ± 0.18**	**76.32 ± 0.40**

We highlight the best results in **blue**, where it represents HAVE-Net's performance during inference time.

4.2 Training Protocol

As described in Sect. 2.2 , we extract the audio and visual features ($\mathbb{R}^{1 \times 1024}$) from the pre-defined encoders and train the CMM-GAN model for cross-modal feature hallucination and FSL classifiers for the classification task.

CMM-GAN Pre-training: For AudioSetZSL, the audio features are readily available in [12] whereas for ADVANCE dataset, we extract the audio features from ResNet18 [4] trained on RESICS45 [1] dataset. We pre-train CMM-GAN with a batch size of 128 and set Adam optimizer with a learning rate of 10^{-4} with λ_1 to 1 in (Eq. 3).

Few-shot Multimodal Training: We randomly sample base class data at $m \in \{5, 10\}$ and $m \in \{3, 5\}$ ways respectively for AudioSetZSL [12] and ADVANCE [6] datasets with $\mathcal{K} \in \{1, 5\}$. We choose λ_2 (Eq. 5) to be 10 and optimize few-shot classifier of HAVE-Net using Adam optimizer with learning rate 10^{-3}. We train the model for 60 epochs with 100 episodes per epoch.

4.3 Discussion

Competitors: To validate the performance of our proposed framework, we compare the results for the ADVANCE and AudioSetZSL datasets using different state-of-the-art (SOTA) meta-learning methods in Tables 1 and 2, respectively[1]

---

[1] To the best of our knowledge, we compare our proposed method with most relevant method. [10] concentrates on image-text pairs as multiple modalities, which is not fair to use in comparison with our problem of joint audio-visual learning.

The dominating modalities in both datasets are distinct, i.e., audio in AudioSet-ZSL and visual in ADVANCE; the FSL classifiers can indeed classify their joint representation better than separate ones.

Table 2. Comparison of different meta-learning methods for m ways $\in \{5, 10\}$ with k-shot $\in \{1, 5\}$ on AudioSetZSL dataset. A + (Hal. V)* is the fusion of audio modality with the hallucinated visual modality. V + (Hal. A)** represents the fusion of visual modality with hallucinated audio modality during the meta-testing.

Model	m-way	Audio (A)		Visual (V)		Fusion	
		1-shot	5-shot	1-shot	5-shot	1-shot	5-shot
Prototypical [15]	5-way	50.56 ± 0.31	67.18 ± 0.24	43.39 ± 0.35	62.26 ± 0.31	61.30 ± 0.53	76.11 ± 0.43
Relation Net [16]	5-way	50.47 ± 0.34	55.69 ± 0.41	42.83 ± 0.27	50.45 ± 0.32	60.75 ± 0.35	66.75 ± 0.33
MAML [2]	5-way	51.89 ± 0.21	66.93 ± 0.23	44.57 ± 0.22	63.30 ± 0.21	60.80 ± 0.21	77.65 ± 0.31
Matching-Net [17]	5-way	50.60 ± 0.36	62.76 ± 0.40	42.91 ± 0.30	63.08 ± 0.43	59.40 ± 0.51	70.22 ± 0.48
HAVE-Net(A + Hal. V)*	5-way	53.70 ± 0.44	69.95 ± 0.32	46.14 ± 0.16	65.97 ± 0.31	**62.38 ± 0.30**	**78.86 ± 0.29**
HAVE-Net(V + Hal. A)**	5-way	53.70 ± 0.44	69.95 ± 0.32	46.14 ± 0.16	65.97 ± 0.31	61.89 ± 0.22	78.31 ± 0.54
Prototypical [15]	10-way	34.09 ± 0.27	51.66 ± 0.45	28.39 ± 0.47	45.23 ± 0.36	43.13 ± 0.31	60.29 ± 0.41
Relation Net [16]	10-way	31.39 ± 0.27	37.86 ± 0.34	26.30 ± 0.32	30.67 ± 0.28	39.39 ± 0.54	42.17 ± 0.41
MAML [2]	10-way	34.35 ± 0.63	48.91 ± 0.43	32.99 ± 0.36	47.68 ± 0.32	44.19 ± 0.24	63.87 ± 0.18
Matching-Net [17]	10-way	32.15 ± 0.43	46.40 ± 0.31	29.73 ± 0.25	42.60 ± 0.24	42.57 ± 0.42	61.22 ± 0.31
HAVE-Net(A + Hal. V)*	10-way	36.69 ± 0.35	53.02 ± 0.15	32.11 ± 0.31	48.91 ± 0.22	**49.07 ± 0.39**	**66.00 ± 0.27**
HAVE-Net(V + Hal. A)**	10-way	36.69 ± 0.35	53.02 ± 0.15	32.11 ± 0.31	48.91 ± 0.22	48.75 ± 0.14	65.18 ± 0.33

We highlight the best results in **blue**, where it represents HAVE-Net's performance during inference time.

On the ADVANCE dataset, HAVE-Net with audio and hallucinated visual features (Audio + Hal. Visual) and (Visual + Hal. Audio) significantly outperforms the other SOTA approaches for the fusion of original modalities at least by 1.1% on 3-way and 0.7% on 5-way classification settings. While on the AudioSetZSL dataset, our HAVE-Net outperforms the referred methods on 5-way and 10-way classification settings by at least 0.8% and 2%, respectively. We show the ablation results in supplementary paper.

5 Takeaways

We address the challenge of remote sensing audio-visual FSL in the absence of unimodal data during testing. To overcome this limitation, we utilized CMM-GAN to generate cross-modality features from the available unimodal data of base classes, which were then used to hallucinate the missing modality for novel classes during inference. Our proposed modal-agnostic unified framework, HAVE-Net, is designed to overcome the limitations of existing few-shot learning methods and is particularly useful in scenarios where robotic sensors may malfunction or data acquisition may be limited. We evaluated the performance of HAVE-Net against several state-of-the-art meta-learning algorithms on benchmark datasets, i.e., ADVANCE and AudioSetZSL, and our results demonstrate its favorable performance compared to using actual modalities during testing.

References

1. Cheng, G., Han, J., Lu, X.: Remote sensing image scene classification: benchmark and state of the art. CoRR arxiv preprint arxiv:abs/1703.00121 (2017). http://arxiv.org/abs/1703.00121
2. Finn, C., Xu, K., Levine, S.: Probabilistic model-agnostic meta-learning. In: Neural Information Processing Systems NeurIPS (2018)
3. Gemmeke, J.F., et al.: Audio set: an ontology and human-labeled dataset for audio events. In: Proc. IEEE ICASSP 2017. New Orleans, LA (2017)
4. He, K., Zhang, X., Ren, S., Sun, J.: Deep residual learning for image recognition. CoRR arxiv preprint arxiv: abs/1512.03385 (2015)
5. Heidler, K., et al.: Self-supervised audiovisual representation learning for remote sensing data. CoRR arxiv preprint arxiv: abs/2108.00688 (2021)
6. Hu, D., et al.: Cross-task transfer for geotagged audiovisual aerial scene recognition (2020)
7. Koch, G., Zemel, R., Salakhutdinov, R., et al.: Siamese neural networks for one-shot image recognition. In: ICML Deep Learning Workshop, vol. 2. Lille (2015)
8. Mao, G., Yuan, Y., Xiaoqiang, L.: Deep cross-modal retrieval for remote sensing image and audio. In: 2018 10th IAPR Workshop on Pattern Recognition in Remote Sensing (PRRS), pp. 1–7 (2018). https://doi.org/10.1109/PRRS.2018.8486338
9. Mirza, M., Osindero, S.: Conditional generative adversarial nets. arXiv preprint arXiv:1411.1784 (2014)
10. Pahde, F., Puscas, M., Klein, T., Nabi, M.: Multimodal prototypical networks for few-shot learning. In: Proceedings of the IEEE/CVF Winter Conference on Applications of Computer Vision, pp. 2644–2653 (2021)
11. Pal, D., Bundele, V., Banerjee, B., Jeppu, Y.: SPN: stable prototypical network for few-shot learning-based hyperspectral image classification. IEEE Geosci. Remote Sens. Lett. **19**, 1–5 (2022). https://doi.org/10.1109/LGRS.2021.3085522
12. Parida, K.K., Matiyali, N., Guha, T., Sharma, G.: Coordinated joint multimodal embeddings for generalized audio-visual zero-shot classification and retrieval of videos. In: IEEE Winter Conference on Applications of Computer Vision (WACV) (2020)
13. Ren, M., et al.: Meta-learning for semi-supervised few-shot classification. arXiv preprint arXiv:1803.00676 (2018)
14. Salem, T., Zhai, M., Workman, S., Jacobs, N.: A multimodal approach to mapping soundscapes. In: IGARSS 2018 - 2018 IEEE International Geoscience and Remote Sensing Symposium, pp. 3477–3480 (2018). https://doi.org/10.1109/IGARSS.2018.8517977
15. Snell, J., Swersky, K., Zemel, R.: Prototypical networks for few-shot learning. In: Advances in Neural Information Processing Systems (2017)
16. Sung, F., Yang, Y., Zhang, L., Xiang, T., Torr, P.H., Hospedales, T.M.: Learning to compare: Relation network for few-shot learning. In: Proceedings of the IEEE Conference on Computer Vision and Pattern Recognition (2018)
17. Vinyals, O., Blundell, C., Lillicrap, T., Wierstra, D., et al.: Matching networks for one shot learning. Adv. Neural Inf. Process. Syst. **29** (2016)

CAD Models to Real-World Images: A Practical Approach to Unsupervised Domain Adaptation in Industrial Object Classification

Dennis Ritter[1](✉), Mike Hemberger[2], Marc Hönig[3], Volker Stopp[3], Erik Rodner[4], and Kristian Hildebrand[1]

[1] Berliner Hochschule für Technik, Berlin, Germany
dennis.r.ritter@gmail.com
[2] nyris GmbH, Berlin, Germany
[3] topex GmbH, Erkenbrechtsweiler, Germany
[4] KI-Werkstatt/FB2, University of Applied Sciences Berlin, Berlin, Germany

Abstract. In this paper, we systematically analyze unsupervised domain adaptation pipelines for object classification in a challenging industrial setting. In contrast to standard natural object benchmarks existing in the field, our results highlight the most important design choices when only category-labeled CAD models are available but classification needs to be done with real-world images. Our domain adaptation pipeline achieves SoTA performance on the VisDA benchmark, but more importantly, drastically improves recognition performance on our new open industrial dataset comprised of 102 mechanical parts. We conclude with a set of guidelines that are relevant for practitioners needing to apply state-of-the-art unsupervised domain adaptation in practice. Our code is available at https://github.com/dritter-bht/synthnet-transfer-learning.

1 Introduction

Recognizing machine parts requires in-depth industrial domain knowledge. However, particularly in engineering, machine-specific specialists are often needed to identify components without prolonged research, making it challenging for customers of machine manufacturers to independently identify the parts of their machines. Automatic visual recognition seems therefore a straightforward solution to apply. However, complex machines typically comprise hundreds or even thousands of individual parts. Generating and labeling sufficient images of each component for training is often too costly. In contrast, companies own the computer-aided design (CAD) data of the parts, which can be rendered with any parameters and in any quantity. Consequently, our goal (Fig. 1) is to use CAD data and train a classifier with adaptation techniques from rendered 3D objects (source domain) that can be applied to real-world images (target domain).

Our proposed contribution is twofold: First, we present a comprehensive guide designed to facilitate future research in surpassing SoTA performance

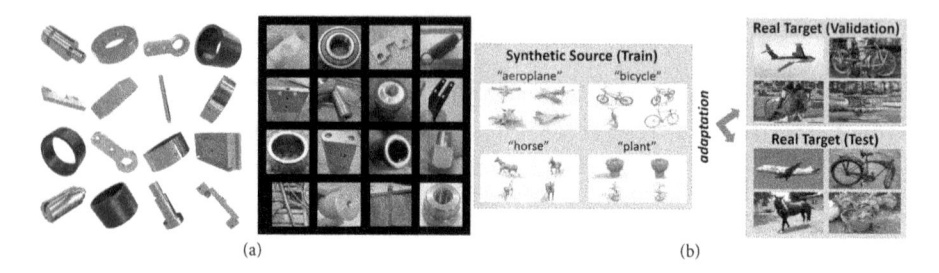

Fig. 1. (a): Our Topex-Printer dataset contains rendered and real images from 102 machine parts (Sect. 3). (b): The VisDa-2017 challenge tests UDA model performance under simulation-to-real domain shifts [22].

(MIC [8]) on the VisDA classification challenge benchmark. We analyze the performance enhancements and their impact at the different stages of our domain adaptation (DA) pipeline, providing a blueprint from a wide range of methods already present in the vast existing literature (Sect. 5). Second, we introduce a new open dataset characterized by minimal inter-class distances, offering a novel challenge for unsupervised domain adaptation (UDA) research (Sect. 3).

Specifically, we use publicly available models pretrained on the ImageNet22K (IN22K) dataset [1] and continue with linear probing using only source domain data to tune the classification head as initialization for further training (similar to [14]). We continue training in an unsupervised domain adaption (UDA) setting, i.e. no labels for target domain data available, applying CDAN [19] and MCC [11]. We test our approach with the VisDA-2017 image classification challenge dataset [22] and our self-made *Topex-Printer* dataset (Sect. 3) shown in Fig. 1.

2 Related Work

Adversarial training, which encourages domain-invariant image features, is a key approach in image-based DA techniques. Originally introduced in [3], it adapts the GAN concepts of [5] for DA tasks. ADDA [26] consolidates several approaches into a framework based on adversarial learning. CyCADA [7] applies CycleGAN's [30] cycle consistency for DA on image classification and semantic segmentation. CDAN [19] adds a conditional domain discriminator utilizing classifier predictions to assist the DA process. Lastly, SDAT [23] uses a *smooth task loss* to stabilize adversarial training, leading to improved generalization on the target domain.

Beyond adversarial training, discrepancy minimization methods aim to align feature representations, reducing distribution discrepancy between source and target domains. Deep Adaptation Network (DAN) [18] and JAN [20] use maximum mean discrepancy (MMD) and joint MMD for feature transfer. Contrastive Adaptation Network (CAN) [12] introduces the *Contrastive Domain Discrepancy* (CDD) metric for class-aware alignment. Sliced Wasserstein Discrepancy metric (SWD) [15] is based on the Wasserstein Distance. The *Minimum Class Confusion* (MCC) loss [11] reduces target domain cross-class confusion. Recently, Masked Image Consistency (MIC) [8] enforces prediction consistency between masked target images and complete-image pseudo-labels. Kumar et al. [14] suggest an optimized transfer learning scheme that initially updates the classification head, then fine-tunes all parameters—proves to be particularly effective for large distribution shifts in out-of-distribution datasets by preserving pretrained features. Our work adopts this approach, combining CDAN [19] and MCC [11] for UDA. While many methods rely on CNNs, recent studies [13,29] show that Vision Transformer (ViT) [2] models surpass these. In addition, the benchmark ranking for CNNs does not extend to Transformer models, although pretraining significantly improves domain transfer [13]. For a comprehensive survey of transfer learning, encompassing pretraining and adaptation techniques, refer to [10].

We utilize the VisDA-2017 image classification dataset, comprising three subsets: a training set of 150k rendered 2D images from 1,907 3D models, a validation set of 174k real photos from MS COCO [16], and a test set of 72k real images from Youtube-boundingboxes [24]. Each image is categorized into one of twelve classes. However, as shown later, performance on this dataset already saturates and therefore a novel benchmark is required.

3 A New Domain Adaptation Benchmark: Topex-Printer

We introduce a challenging dataset for identifying machine parts from real photos, featuring images of 102 parts from a labeling machine. This dataset was developed with the complexity of real-world scenarios in mind and highlights the complexity of distinguishing between closely related classes, providing an opportunity to improve domain adaption methods. The dataset includes 3,264 CAD-rendered images (32 per part) and 6,146 real images (6 to 137 per part) for UDA and testing. Rendered images were produced using a Blender-based pipeline with environment maps, lights, and virtual cameras arranged to ensure varied mesh orientations. We also use material metadata and apply one of 21 texture materials to the objects. We render all images at 512^2 pixels. Some examples of our rendered images can be seen on the left side of Fig. 1 (a). The real photo set consists of raw images captured under varying conditions using different cameras, including varied lighting, backgrounds, and environmental factors. More examples are available in the supplementary material. The dataset is publicly available at https://huggingface.co/datasets/ritterdennis/topex-printer/resolve/main/topex-printer.zip.

4 Our Adaptation Pipeline

We reviewed existing research, analyzing two prevalent stages of DA training. This led to our empirically-backed approach that yielded robust results on the Topex-Printer and VisDA datasets, achieving 93.47% accuracy on the target domain for the latter, which exceeds the accuracy reported in [8]. The steps comprise the following:

1. **Adapting pretrained models to rendered images:**
   (a) We start from pretrained models and train a new classification head with source domain data (see [13,14]). For this, we freeze layers, exchange the class head to the necessary number of classes and tune the class head with source data only (CH).
   (b) We executed a fine-tuning across all layers and a hyperparameter search (optimizer, scheduler, learning rate, augmentations) for our DA experiments on source domain data only (FT).
2. **Adapting to real-world images with UDA:**
   (a) We use the best parameters from experiments training only with source domain data for our UDA experiments and start training from the checkpoint with the tuned classification head.
   (b) We conduct studies on our two datasets with the methods CDAN, MCC, and CDAN-MCC combined and analyze the effect of all our parameters in Sect. 5.

While these are standard procedures in DA, we lay out the most important aspects for the single steps in the next sections.

4.1 Adapting Pretrained Models to Rendered Images

We conduct transfer learning on various models (ViT [2], Swinv2 [17] and DeiT [25], please refer to the supplementary material for version details), pretrained on IN22k, using only source domain data for training and identical training procedures and configurations. This approach allows us to establish a suitable baseline and determine appropriate training parameters. First, we load the pretrained model and replace the linear classification head with one that matches the number of classes in our dataset (12 outputs for VisDa-2017 [22], 102 outputs for Topex-Printer). We perform three different training schemes: training the classification head only (CH), fine-tuning the full model (FT), and a combination of CH and FT, tuning the classification head first and continuing with full fine-tuning (CH-FT) inspired by [14].

1. For CH, we freeze all layers but the classification head and train for 20 epochs using SGD with learning rates [10.0, 1e–01, 1e–03], momentum 0.9, no weight decay, no learning rate scheduler, and no warmup.
2. For FT, we do not freeze any layers and train for 20 epochs using AdamW optimizer with learning rates [1e–01, 1e–03, 1e–05], weight decay 0.01, cosine annealing learning rate scheduler [21] without restarts, and two warmup epochs (10% of total epochs).
3. For CH-FT, we use the best-performing CH training run based on the test set's top-1 accuracy and continue fine-tuning the whole model from the best validation checkpoint using parameters of the best-performing FT run for another 20 epochs (so 40 epochs total training after pretraining).

For both datasets, VisDa-2017 and Topex-Printer, we use a batch size of 32 and two different data augmentation setups. For all runs, we use random resized

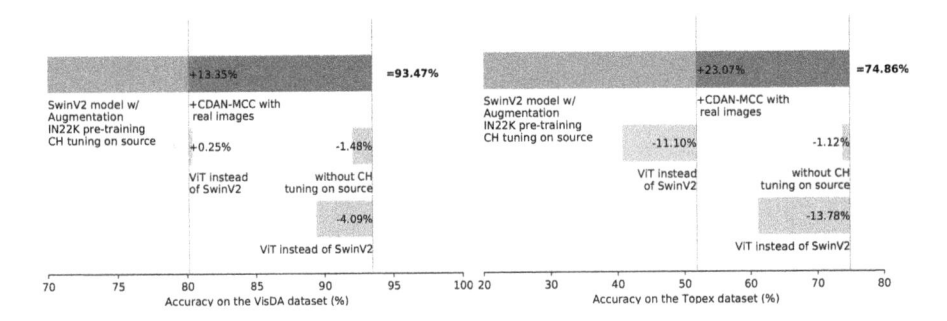

Fig. 2. Results of our DA pipeline for the (Left): VisDA and our (Right) Topex dataset. Blue bars highlight results obtained using UDA with additional target images. (Color figure online)

crops with relative scale range (0.7, 1.0), random horizontal flip, random color jitter with parameters (brightness = 0.3, contrast = 0.3, saturation = 0.3, hue = 0.3), random grayscale, and normalize the final tensor using standard deviation [0.5, 0.5, 0.5] and mean [0.5, 0.5, 0.5]. We further replace random color jitter and random grayscale by AugMix [6] with default parameters.

4.2 Adapting to Real-World Images with Unsupervised Adaptation

Upon completion of the first stage, we proceed with further experiments in an UDA setting. For these, we solely employ the SwinV2 [17] and ViT [2] model architectures, as these demonstrated superior performance (see supplementary material Table 4 for details). We start with the optimal classification head (CH) checkpoint from our experiments described in Sect. 4.1 and keep the training parameters consistent with the best-performing fine-tuning (FT) run for each model. We execute six UDA runs each for the ViT [2] and SwinV2 [17] models: 20 training epochs, 32 batch size, AdamW optimizer with a 1e–05 learning rate, 1e–02 weight decay, and a cosine annealing learning rate scheduler without restarts and a two-epoch warmup (details in supplementary material). Image augmentations - random resized crop, horizontal flip, and AugMix [6] - are utilized as described in Sect. 4.1. Essentially, we replicate the process executed for source-domain-only CH-FT training runs, while concurrently incorporating UDA techniques—namely, CDAN [19] and MCC [11]. Following the findings of [13] that CDAN [19] outperforms even newer DA techniques using modern architectures (Vit-L, ConvNext-XL), we decide to use the Transfer Learning Library (tllib) [9,10] implementations of CDAN (hidden size 1024) and MCC [11] (temperature 1.0) DA methods and also combine both.

5 Evaluation

Our experiments are always based on measuring the mean class-wise accuracy in the target domain, *i.e.* the real-world images.

Table 1. Image classification top-1 accuracy in % on VisDA-2017 target domain (real images) across all classes compared to literature. We report our best source-domain-only and UDA runs for the ViT and SwinV2 architecture.

Method		Pl	Bcl	Bus	Car	Hrs	Knf	Mcy	Per	Plt	Skb	Trn	Tck	Mean
CDAN [19]	ResNet	85.2	66.9	83.0	50.8	84.2	74.9	88.1	74.5	83.4	76.0	81.9	38.0	73.9
MCC [11]		88.1	80.3	80.5	71.5	90.1	93.2	85.0	71.6	89.4	73.8	85.0	36.9	78.8
SDAT [23]		95.8	85.5	76.9	69.0	93.5	97.4	88.5	78.2	93.1	91.6	86.3	55.3	84.3
MIC [8]		96.7	88.5	84.2	74.3	96.0	96.3	90.2	81.2	94.3	95.4	88.9	56.6	86.9
TVT [29]	ViT	92.9	85.6	77.5	60.5	93.6	98.2	89.3	76.4	93.6	92.0	91.7	55.7	83.9
CDTRANS [28]		97.1	90.5	82.4	77.5	96.6	96.1	93.6	88.6	97.9	86.9	90.3	62.8	88.4
SDAT [23]		98.4	90.9	85.4	82.1	98.5	97.6	96.3	86.1	96.2	96.7	92.9	56.8	89.8
MIC [8]		**99.0**	93.3	86.5	87.6	**98.9**	**99.0**	**97.2**	**89.8**	98.9	**98.9**	96.5	68.0	92.8
Ours w/o UDA		96.48	71.82	90.14	**99.20**	94.66	77.71	87.28	44.45	95.12	83.64	94.05	40.76	80.54
Ours		94.82	93.49	92.80	95.89	90.95	88.51	77.46	75.42	96.27	97.32	94.74	88.03	89.38
Ours w/o UDA	Swin	97.09	80.48	85.35	98.12	92.39	83.54	94.85	19.89	89.13	78.89	**97.03**	55.18	80.12
Ours		97.96	**95.15**	**95.81**	98.64	98.34	95.68	80.12	83.87	**99.39**	94.68	96.61	**93.85**	**93.47**

Results on VisDA-2017 Dataset

Our first evaluation is done on the standard domain adaptation benchmark VisDA-2017 [22], where we are able to achieve SoTA performance as highlighted in Table 1. One can see, that our ViT training outperforms TVT [29] and achieves competitive results compared to CDTRANS [28] and SDAT [23] but does not reach the performance of MIC [8] when the same ViT architecture is used. However, our pipeline with the SwinV2 architecture slightly outperforms the current state of the art by 0.68% accuracy.

Most importantly for us and the paper, we analyzed the contribution of each part of our pipeline in Fig. 2 (left). In this figure, the results of several ablations have been visualized with blueish bars referring to results achieved with additional target images through UDA techniques. The results reveal several aspects:

1. Unsupervised domain adaptation is important to adapt to real-world images: Our best models with source data only, achieve around 80% accuracy, but with CDAN [19] and MCC [11] as combined UDA techniques, we are able to outperform all other approaches on this dataset.
2. It is beneficial and fast and easy to use class head (CH) tuning on the source data before applying UDA techniques to prevent feature distortion [14]: This can be seen in the −1.48% drop in performance without CH tuning.
3. Using the right model architecture is crucial for UDA: Our ViT models after UDA achieve less than 90% accuracy (drop of 4.09%). This difference in performance is insignificant before UDA.
4. Our SoTA performance was achieved after only 3 training epochs of fine-tuning from the pretrained checkpoint on a single Nvidia Tesla V100 PCIE 32GB GPU (CH-checkpoint after 1 epoch + 2 Epochs UDA with CDAN+MCC). However, the number of training epochs

and training stability varies between our runs but almost all experiments achieve the best validation accuracy after just a few epochs of training.

Further experimental results are given in the supplementary material of the paper and reveal the following additional aspects:

1. CDAN+MCC in combination outperforms CDAN and MCC individually in most cases (see supp. Table 6 and Table 7).
2. Given the ConvNextV2 [27]-based runs' modest performance—12.42% and 19.82% for source-data-only experiments, we suspend further experiments with this architecture. (see supp. Table 2)

Results on the Topex-Printer Dataset
The high accuracies on VisDA-2017 [22] in general and the marginal improvements achieved on this dataset in the last years, suggest the use of a more challenging dataset to benchmark domain adaptation pipelines. Therefore, we developed and assembled the Topex-Printer dataset (Sect. 3). The results on the dataset are given in Fig. 2 (Right) and similar conclusions compared to the previous section can be drawn:

1. Unsupervised domain adaptation is even more important on this dataset: with a 23.07% gain in performance, the domain gap between the rendered images and the real-world images is likely larger compared to VisDA-2017.
2. It is again reasonable to do CH tuning before UDA. Surprisingly, SwinV2 setups using CDAN [19] or MCC [11] alone do not benefit from using a tuned classification head but instead perform worse than just using the pretrained checkpoint from Huggingface (see supplementary material Table 7 for these results). However, when using CDAN and MCC combined starting from the tuned classification head, the final model performs 1.12% better. For the ViT runs on the other hand, the CH initialized runs outperform runs without classification head tuning significantly.
3. The Swin-V2 model shows a remarkable performance compared to the ViT model with a performance gain of +11.10% before UDA and +13.78% after UDA.

6 Conclusion

We propose a practical approach for an image classifier in a DA setting using rendered images from 3D objects as the source domain and real images as the target domain. We conducted several experiments performing transfer learning with source data only to set a strong baseline for follow-up UDA training using the VisDA-2017 image classification challenge dataset and our newly proposed Topex-Printer dataset with more than 100 categories. In our DA experiments, we outperformed the current state-of-the-art [8] by achieving a mean accuracy of 93.47% on the VisDA-2017 dataset and 74.86% on the Topex-Printer dataset. One goal in future work is to adapt our framework to object detection scenarios [4].

Acknowledgements. This work was funded by the German Federal Ministry of Education and Research (BMBF) through their support of the project SynthNet, a part of the KMU-Innovativ initiative (project code: 01IS21002C), the KI-Werkstatt project at the University of Applied Sciences Berlin (part of the Forschung an Fachhochschulen program (project code: 13FH028KI1) as well as project TAHAI (funded by IFAF Berlin).

A Implementation Details

A.1 Adapting Pretrained Models to Rendered Images Implementation Details

We use pretrained models *"google/vit-base-patch16-224-in21k"* (ViT) [2], *"microsoft/swinv2-base-patch4-window12-192-22k"* (SwinV2) [17], *"facebook/convnextv2-base-22k-224"* (ConvNextV2) [27], and *"facebook/deit-base-distilled-patch16-224"* (DeiT) [25] from Huggingface[1] for experiments using the VisDA-2017 dataset but only ViT and SwinV2 for our Topex-Printer dataset. ViT, SwinV2, and ConvNextV2 were pretrained on ImageNet22K, while DeiT has been pretrained on ImagNet1K. We perform three different training schemes, training the classification head only (CH), fine-tuning the full model (FT), and a combination of CH and FT, tuning the classification head first and continuing with full fine-tuning (CH-FT) inspired by [14].

1. For CH we use the Pytorch[2] SGD optimizer with learning rates [10.0, 0.1, 0.001], momentum 0.9, no weight decay, no learning rate scheduler, and no warmup.
2. For FT we use the Pytorch implementation of AdamW optimizer with learning rates [0.1, 0.001, 0.00001], weight decay 0.01, cosine annealing learning rate scheduler[3] [21] without restarts, and two warmup epochs (10% of total epochs).

For both datasets for data augmentation Pytorch 2.0.0 implementation[4] is used.

---

[1] https://huggingface.co/models.
[2] https://pytorch.org/.
[3] https://huggingface.co/docs/transformers/main_classes/optimizer_schedules.
[4] https://pytorch.org/vision/main/generated/torchvision.transforms.AugMix.html.

A.2 Adapting to Real-World Images with Unsupervised Domain Adaptation Implementation Details

For UDA experiments we start from the best source-domain-only trained CH checkpoint with respect to the model architecture and continue training using the same parameters as the best FT run for each model as described in the paper. We use Pytorch 2.0.0 implementations of image augmentations random resized crop, horizontal flip, and AugMix [6] with the same parameters described in the last paragraph of Sect. A.1. We use the Transfer Learning Library (tllib) [9,10] implementations of CDAN (hidden size 1024) and MCC [11] (temperature 1.0) domain adaptation methods and also combine both using two different initial checkpoints for each model architecture. One initial checkpoint from Huggingface, pretrained on ImageNet22K [1] (*"google/vit-base-patch16-224-in21k"* (ViT) and *"microsoft/swinv2-base-patch4-window12-192-22k"* (SwinV2)) and the best-performing checkpoint after training only the classification head from our source-domain-only experiments. Again, we use global random seed 42 for all experiments and training is performed on a single Nvidia Tesla V100 PCIE 32GB GPU.

Different from other methods, we perform considerably better correctly identifying the *truck* class but underperform on the *motorcycle* and *person* class instead. The confusion matrix shown in Fig. 6 shows, that our trained model often mixes up motorcycle samples with bicycles (7%) and skateboards (10%) while the person class is mixed up rather uniformly (3%–4%) with skateboards, plants, motorcycles, and horses.

B Dataset Samples

(See Figs. 3, 4 and 5).

Fig. 3. 80 random samples of rendered images from the Topex-Printer dataset. Each image 512^2, featuring machine parts marked with bounding boxes, is trimmed according to these boxes, extended to form a rectangle, and padded with black if needed. Finally, all images are resized to a resolution of 256×256 pixels.

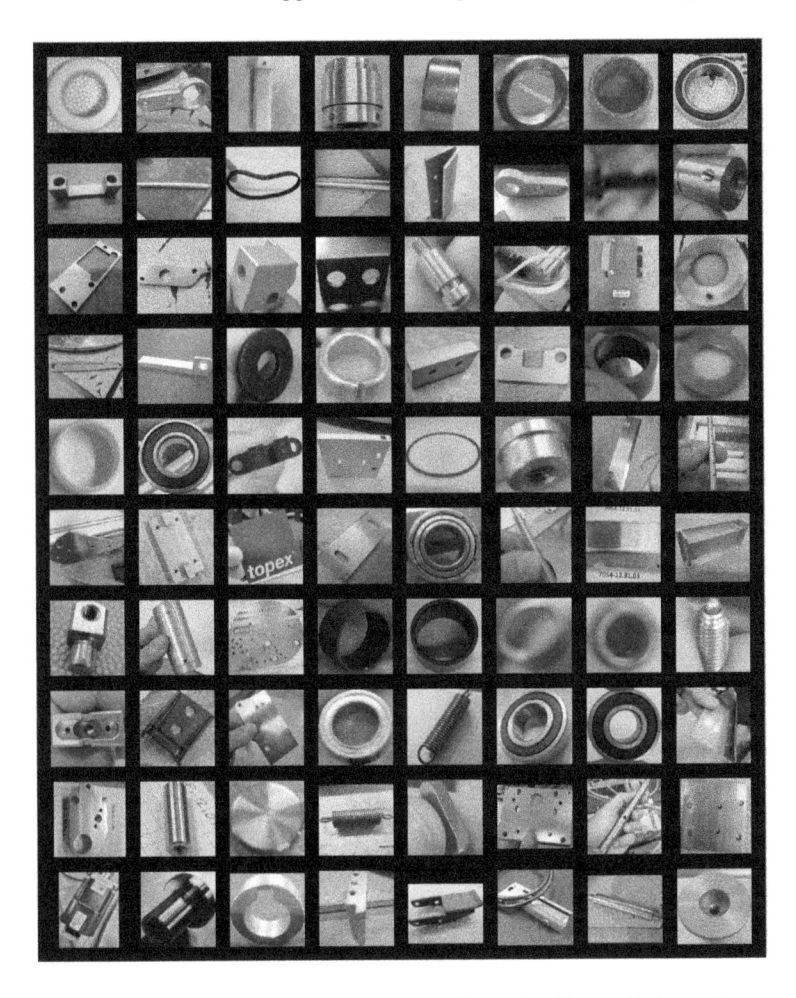

Fig. 4. 80 random samples of real images from the Topex-Printer dataset.

(a)   (b)

Fig. 5. (Best viewed in color) Left (a): HDRI of the warehouse environment map used in our rendering scene. Image by Sergej Majboroda [CC0], via Polyhaven. Right (b): Our handcrafted Blender material collection we used for the Topex-Printer dataset.

C Evaluation Results

(See Tables 3, 5 and 8).

Table 2. Acc@1 in % on target domain (real images) for all source-domain-only training experiments on VisDA-2017 classification dataset. Note that *base* transform means that random color jitter and random grayscale transforms are applied. Faded out rows are representing numerically instable runs that have been canceled due to NaN loss for example.

Model	Pre-training	train scheme	transform	lr	Acc@1
ViT-b	IN22K	CH	base	1e+1	63.31
ViT-b	IN22K	CH	base	1e−1	71.03
ViT-b	IN22K	CH	base	1e−3	80.37
ViT-b	IN22K	CH	AugMix	1e−3	80.18
ViT-b	IN22K	FT	base	1e−1	07.64
ViT-b	IN22K	FT	base	1e−3	17.69
ViT-b	IN22K	FT	base	1e−5	66.88
ViT-b	IN22K	FT	AugMix	1e−5	73.76
ViT-b	**IN22K**	**CH-FT**	**AugMix**	**1e−5**	**80.53**
SwinV2	IN22K	CH	base	1e+1	69.49
SwinV2	IN22K	CH	base	1e−1	72.02
SwinV2	IN22K	CH	base	1e−3	80.12
SwinV2	IN22K	CH	AugMix	1e−3	79.54
SwinV2	IN22K	FT	base	1e−3	18.84
SwinV2	IN22K	FT	base	1e−5	72.41
SwinV2	IN22K	FT	AugMix	1e−5	73.49
SwinV2	IN22K	CH-FT	AugMix	1e−5	76.96
ConvNextV2	IN22K	CH	base	1e+1	12.81
ConvNextV2	IN22K	CH	base	1e−1	12.42
ConvNextV2	IN22K	CH	base	1e−3	11.30
ConvNextV2	IN22K	CH	AugMix	1e−3	11.98
ConvNextV2	IN22K	FT	base	1e−1	10.04
ConvNextV2	IN22K	FT	base	1e−3	17.22
ConvNextV2	IN22K	FT	base	1e−5	19.82
ConvNextV2	IN22K	FT	AugMix	1e−5	11.98
ConvNextV2 CH-base-1e-3-e20	IN22K	CH-FT	AugMix	1e−5	25.43
DeiT	IN1K	CH	base	1e+1	59.21
DeiT	IN1K	CH	base	1e−1	59.50
DeiT	IN1K	CH	base	1e−3	75.13
DeiT	IN1K	FT	base	1e−1	12.32
DeiT	IN1K	FT	base	1e−3	21.00
DeiT	IN1K	FT	base	1e−5	69.34
DeiT	IN1K	FT	AugMix	1e−5	70.52
DeiT CH-base-1e-3-e20	IN1K	CH-FT	AugMix	1e−5	69.41
DeiT CH-base-1e-3-e1	IN1K	CH-FT	AugMix	1e−5	74.12

Table 3. Acc@1 in % on target domain (real images) for all source-domain-only training experiments on the Topex-Printer dataset. Note that *base* transform means that random color jitter and random grayscale transforms are applied. Faded out rows are representing numerically instable runs that have been canceled due to NaN loss for example.

Model	Pre-training	train scheme	transform	lr	Acc@1
ViT-b	IN22K	CH	base	1e+1	34.85
ViT-b	IN22K	CH	base	1e−1	40.69
ViT-b	IN22K	CH	base	1e−3	31.78
ViT-b	IN22K	FT	AugMix	1e−1	01.74
ViT-b	IN22K	FT	AugMix	1e−3	21.75
ViT-b	IN22K	FT	AugMix	1e−5	32.54
ViT-b	IN22K	CH-FT	AugMix	1e−5	45.90
SwinV2	IN22K	CH	base	1e+1	42.34
SwinV2	IN22K	CH	base	1e−1	45.15
SwinV2	IN22K	CH	base	1e−3	51.79
SwinV2	IN22K	FT	AugMix	1e−1	01.70
SwinV2	IN22K	FT	AugMix	1e−3	26.23
SwinV2	IN22K	FT	AugMix	1e−5	25.69
SwinV2	IN22K	CH-FT	AugMix	1e−3	51.79
SwinV2	**IN22K**	**CH-FT**	**AugMix**	**1e−5**	**59.21**

Table 4. Acc@1 in % on target domain (real images) for best results per model and training scheme in our source domain training experiments on VisDA-2017 classification dataset. Note that *base* transform means that random color jitter and random grayscale transforms are applied instead of AugMix (other augmentations stay the same as explained in Sect. A.1).

Model	Pre-training	train scheme	transform	lr	Acc@1
ViT-b	IN22K	CH	base	1e−3	80.37
ViT-b	IN22K	FT	AugMix	1e−5	73.76
ViT-b	**IN22K**	**CH-FT**	**AugMix**	**1e−5**	**80.53**
SwinV2	IN22K	CH	base	1e−3	80.12
SwinV2	IN22K	FT	AugMix	1e−5	73.49
SwinV2	IN22K	CH-FT	AugMix	1e−5	76.96
DeiT	IN1K	CH	base	1e−3	75.13
DeiT	IN1K	FT	AugMix	1e−5	70.52
DeiT	IN1K	CH-FT	AugMix	1e−5	74.12

Table 5. Acc@1 in % on target domain (real images) for best results per model and training scheme in our source-domain-only training experiments on Topex-Printer dataset. Note that *base* transform means that random color jitter and random grayscale transforms are applied instead of AugMix (other augmentations stay the same as explained in Sect. A.1).

Model	Pre-training	train scheme	transform	lr	Acc@1
ViT-b	IN22K	CH	base	1e−1	40.69
ViT-b	IN22K	FT	AugMix	1e−5	32.54
ViT-b	IN22K	CH-FT	AugMix	1e−5	45.90
SwinV2	IN22K	CH	base	1e−3	51.79
SwinV2	IN22K	FT	AugMix	1e−5	25.69
SwinV2	**IN22K**	**CH-FT**	**AugMix**	**1e−5**	**59.21**

Table 6. Acc@1 in % on target domain (real images) for all UDA experiments on VisDA-2017 classification dataset. Note that *init checkpoint* describes the model checkpoint used for the UDA experiments. CH refers to the best-performing CH training scheme from our DG experiments respecting the used model architecture and IN22K refers to the respective Huggingface model checkpoints described in Sect. A.2.

Model	DA method	init checkpoint	Acc@1
ViT-b	CDAN	IN22K	61.96
ViT-b	CDAN	CH	88.78
ViT-b	MCC	IN22K	79.63
ViT-b	MCC	CH	88.88
ViT-b	CDAN-MCC	IN22K	75.26
ViT-b	CDAN-MCC	CH	89.38
SwinV2	CDAN	IN22K	71.21
SwinV2	CDAN	CH	80.12
SwinV2	MCC	IN22K	90.65
SwinV2	MCC	CH	91.88
SwinV2	CDAN-MCC	IN22K	91.99
SwinV2	**CDAN-MCC**	**CH**	**93.47**

Table 7. Acc@1 in % on target domain (real images) for all UDA experiments on the Topex-Printer dataset. Note that *init checkpoint* describes the model checkpoint used for the UDA experiments. *CH* refers to the best-performing CH training scheme from our source-domain-only training experiments respecting the used model architecture and IN22K refers to the respective Huggingface model checkpoints described in Sect. A.2.

Model	DA method	init checkpoint	Acc@1
ViT-b	CDAN	IN22K	43.31
ViT-b	CDAN	CH	47.51
ViT-b	MCC	IN22K	32.95
ViT-b	MCC	CH	61.36
ViT-b	CDAN-MCC	IN22K	43.33
ViT-b	CDAN-MCC	CH	61.08
SwinV2	CDAN	IN22K	65.51
SwinV2	CDAN	CH	61.94
SwinV2	MCC	IN22K	72.86
SwinV2	MCC	CH	71.14
SwinV2	CDAN-MCC	IN22K	73.74
SwinV2	**CDAN-MCC**	**CH**	**74.86**

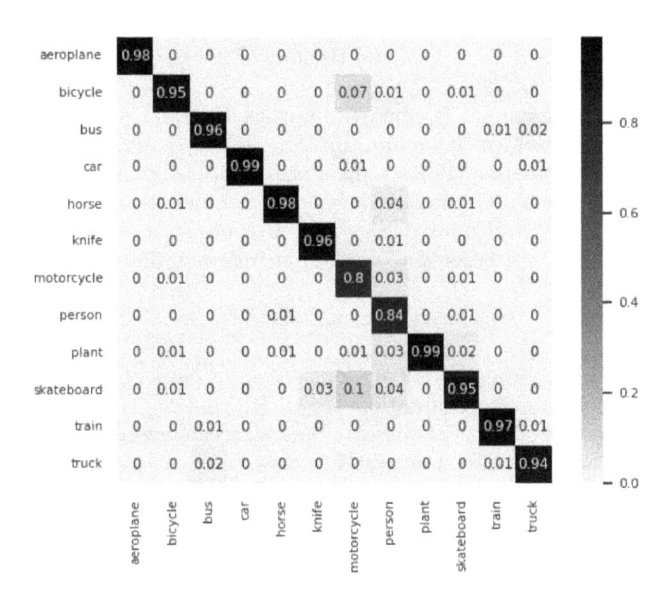

Fig. 6. Confusion matrix for our best-performing model on VisDA-2017: SwinV2-CH-CDAN-MCC

Table 8. Image classification top-1 accuracy in % on VisDA-2017 target domain (real images) across all classes compared to literature. We report our best source-domain-only and UDA runs for the ViT and SwinV2 architecture.

Method		Pl	Bcl	Bus	Car	Hrs	Knf	Mcy	Per	Plt	Skb	Trn	Tck	Mean
CDAN [19]	ResNet	85.2	66.9	83.0	50.8	84.2	74.9	88.1	74.5	83.4	76.0	81.9	38.0	73.9
MCC [11]		88.1	80.3	80.5	71.5	90.1	93.2	85.0	71.6	89.4	73.8	85.0	36.9	78.8
SDAT [23]		95.8	85.5	76.9	69.0	93.5	97.4	88.5	78.2	93.1	91.6	86.3	55.3	84.3
MIC [8]		96.7	88.5	84.2	74.3	96.0	96.3	90.2	81.2	94.3	95.4	88.9	56.6	86.9
TVT [29]	ViT	92.9	85.6	77.5	60.5	93.6	98.2	89.3	76.4	93.6	92.0	91.7	55.7	83.9
CDTRANS [28]		97.1	90.5	82.4	77.5	96.6	96.1	93.6	88.6	97.9	86.9	90.3	62.8	88.4
SDAT [23]		98.4	90.9	85.4	82.1	98.5	97.6	96.3	86.1	96.2	96.7	92.9	56.8	89.8
MIC [8]		**99.0**	93.3	86.5	87.6	**98.9**	**99.0**	**97.2**	**89.8**	98.9	**98.9**	96.5	68.0	92.8
Source Only		96.48	71.82	90.14	**99.20**	94.66	77.71	87.28	44.45	95.12	83.64	94.05	40.76	80.54
Ours		94.82	93.49	92.80	95.89	90.95	88.51	77.46	75.42	96.27	97.32	94.74	88.03	89.38
Source Only	Swin	97.09	80.48	85.35	98.12	92.39	83.54	94.85	19.89	89.13	78.89	**97.03**	55.18	80.12
Ours		97.96	**95.15**	**95.81**	98.64	98.34	95.68	80.12	83.87	**99.39**	94.68	96.61	**93.85**	**93.47**

References

1. Deng, J., Dong, W., Socher, R., Li, L.J., Li, K., Fei-Fei, L.: Imagenet: a large-scale hierarchical image database. In: CVPR, pp. 248–255 (2009)
2. Dosovitskiy, A., et al.: An image is worth 16×16 words: transformers for image recognition at scale. In: ICLR (2021)
3. Ganin, Y., et al.: Domain-adversarial training of neural networks. J. Mach. Learn. Res. **17**(1), 2096–2030 (2016)
4. Goehring, D., Hoffman, J., Rodner, E., Saenko, K., Darrell, T.: Interactive adaptation of real-time object detectors. In: 2014 IEEE International Conference on Robotics and Automation (ICRA), pp. 1282–1289. IEEE (2014)
5. Goodfellow, I.J., et al.: Generative adversarial nets. In: NeurIPS (2014)
6. Hendrycks, D., Mu, N., Cubuk, E.D., Zoph, B., Gilmer, J., Lakshminarayanan, B.: Augmix: a simple data processing method to improve robustness and uncertainty. In: ICLR (2019)
7. Hoffman, J., et al.: Cycada: cycle-consistent adversarial domain adaptation. In: ICML (2017)
8. Hoyer, L., Dai, D., Wang, H., Van Gool, L.: Mic: masked image consistency for context-enhanced domain adaptation. In: CVPR, pp. 11721–11732 (2023)
9. Jiang, J., Chen, B., Fu, B., Long, M.: Transfer-learning-library (2020). https://github.com/thuml/Transfer-Learning-Library
10. Jiang, J., Shu, Y., Wang, J., Long, M.: Transferability in deep learning: a survey. ArXiv arxiv:2201.05867 (2022)
11. Jin, Y., Wang, X., Long, M., Wang, J.: Minimum class confusion for versatile domain adaptation. In: ECCV (2019)
12. Kang, G., Jiang, L., Yang, Y., Hauptmann, A.: Contrastive adaptation network for unsupervised domain adaptation. In: CVPR, pp. 4888–4897 (2019)
13. Kim, D., Wang, K., Sclaroff, S., Saenko, K.: A broad study of pre-training for domain generalization and adaptation. In: ECCV (2022)

14. Kumar, A., Raghunathan, A., Jones, R.M., Ma, T., Liang, P.: Fine-tuning can distort pretrained features and underperform out-of-distribution. In: ICLR (2022)
15. Lee, C.Y., Batra, T., Baig, M.H., Ulbricht, D.: Sliced wasserstein discrepancy for unsupervised domain adaptation. In: CVPR, pp. 10277–10287 (2019)
16. Lin, T.-Y., et al.: Microsoft COCO: common objects in context. In: Fleet, D., Pajdla, T., Schiele, B., Tuytelaars, T. (eds.) ECCV 2014. LNCS, vol. 8693, pp. 740–755. Springer, Cham (2014). https://doi.org/10.1007/978-3-319-10602-1_48
17. Liu, Z., et al.: Swin transformer v2: scaling up capacity and resolution. In: CVPR, pp. 11999–12009 (2021)
18. Long, M., Cao, Y., Wang, J., Jordan, M.: Learning transferable features with deep adaptation networks. In: ICML, pp. 97–105. PMLR (2015)
19. Long, M., Cao, Z., Wang, J., Jordan, M.I.: Conditional adversarial domain adaptation. In: NeurIPS (2017)
20. Long, M., Zhu, H., Wang, J., Jordan, M.I.: Deep transfer learning with joint adaptation networks. In: ICML (2016)
21. Loshchilov, I., Hutter, F.: SGDR: stochastic gradient descent with warm restarts. arXiv: Learning (2016)
22. Peng, X., Usman, B., Kaushik, N., Wang, D., Hoffman, J., Saenko, K.: Visda: a synthetic-to-real benchmark for visual domain adaptation. In: CVPR-W, pp. 2021–2026 (2018)
23. Rangwani, H., Aithal, S.K., Mishra, M., Jain, A., Babu, R.V.: A closer look at smoothness in domain adversarial training. In: ICML (2022)
24. Real, E., Shlens, J., Mazzocchi, S., Pan, X., Vanhoucke, V.: Youtube-boundingboxes: a large high-precision human-annotated data set for object detection in video. In: CVPR, pp. 7464–7473 (2017)
25. Touvron, H., Cord, M., Douze, M., Massa, F., Sablayrolles, A., Jegou, H.: Training data-efficient image transformers and distillation through attention. In: Meila, M., Zhang, T. (eds.) Proceedings of the 38th International Conference on Machine Learning, vol. 139, pp. 10347–10357. PMLR (2021)
26. Tzeng, E., Hoffman, J., Saenko, K., Darrell, T.: Adversarial discriminative domain adaptation. In: CVPR, pp. 2962–2971 (2017)
27. Woo, S., et al.: Convnext v2: co-designing and scaling convnets with masked autoencoders. ArXiv arxiv:2301.00808 (2023)
28. Xu, T., Chen, W., Pichao, W., Wang, F., Li, H., Jin, R.: Cdtrans: cross-domain transformer for unsupervised domain adaptation. In: ICLR (2021)
29. Yang, J., Liu, J., Xu, N., Huang, J.: Tvt: transferable vision transformer for unsupervised domain adaptation. In: WACV, pp. 520–530 (2021)
30. Zhu, J.Y., Park, T., Isola, P., Efros, A.A.: Unpaired image-to-image translation using cycle-consistent adversarial networks. In: ICCV (2017)

EMG Subspace Alignment and Visualization for Cross-Subject Hand Gesture Classification

Martin Colot[1]([✉]), Cédric Simar[1,2], Mathieu Petieau[2], Ana Maria Cebolla Alvarez[2], Guy Cheron[2], and Gianluca Bontempi[1]

[1] Machine Learning Group, ULB, Brussels, Belgium
martin.colot@ulb.be

[2] Laboratory of Neurophysiology and Movement Biomechanics (LNMB) and ULB-Neuroscience Institute (UNI), ULB, Brussels, Belgium

Abstract. Electromyograms (EMG)-based hand gesture recognition systems are a promising technology for human/machine interfaces. However, one of their main limitations is the long calibration time that is typically required to handle new users. The paper discusses and analyses the challenge of cross-subject generalization thanks to an original dataset containing the EMG signals of 14 human subjects during hand gestures. The experimental results show that, though an accurate generalization based on pooling multiple subjects is hardly achievable, it is possible to improve the cross-subject estimation by identifying a robust low-dimensional subspace for multiple subjects and aligning it to a target subject. A visualization of the subspace enables us to provide insights for the improvement of cross-subject generalization with EMG signals.

Keywords: EMG classification · Cross-subject adaptation · Subspace alignment

1 Introduction

The recognition of hand gestures from electromyographic (EMG) signals is important for many brain-computer interfaces (BCI) applications, such as robotic hand prostheses, video game control, or sign language recognition. The muscle activity is recorded through surface electrodes, placed on the skin, and processed by a machine learning model to classify instantaneous hand postures. These models have become very accurate when considering a single subject and session [8]. However, they often lack generalization across subjects. A major difficulty when working with EMG signals is that they are highly person-specific [6,7] due to intrinsic differences in anatomical and physiological characteristics. Also, small shifts in the location of the electrodes can significantly affect the recorded signal. In order to deal with real-world settings, EMG-based systems must tackle the *cross-subject* issue, i.e., be able to generalize to other users (targets) than the ones used for training (sources). This is necessary since long phases of labeled data collection are not acceptable in real settings, and may even be impossible for impaired users. We tackle this issue as an unsupervised domain adaptation (UDA) problem where labeled samples from multiple source subjects are available, and a model has to classify unlabelled samples from a target subject. In a real-world implementation, the model would have an initial low efficiency with a new user. Then, as new unlabelled samples are collected, the model parameters would regularly be updated through UDA to improve the estimation.

In this paper, we focus on bridging the gap between intra-subject (training and testing on the same person) and cross-subject classification by analyzing an original EMG dataset where 14 participants perform 4 simple hand postures. We start by considering several dimensionality reduction strategies to better understand the dissimilarities that occur in the dataset and find a simpler representation of the samples. We then show that a common low-dimensional subspace can help to perform unsupervised domain adaptation, improving the classification accuracy on a target subject. The paper presents the following results: i) an assessment of hand gesture classification from EMG in intra-subject and cross-subject configurations in the original signal space, ii) the definition and visualization of a common low-dimensional subspace, and iii) the assessment of subspace alignment domain adaptation with a leave-one-subject-out strategy.

2 Related Work

Classification of hand gestures from EMG signals has attracted large attention in machine learning [8]. However, since the number of classes, hand gestures, and data acquisition are very heterogeneous over different studies, it is hard to define a state-of-the-art baseline accuracy. Nevertheless, it appears that, when few classes are considered, the intra-subject classification accuracy is typically above 90% [8]. EMG signals are usually classified using either a shallow machine-learning model with handcrafted features or a deep CNN with the raw signal [4,7]. Recently, CNN has become the primary choice for EMG classification. However, with few signs to recognize, it is often possible to obtain similar results with a shallow neural network or handcrafted features [4].

Cross-subject classification usually involves training a single classifier on pooled samples from many source subjects, with the aim of obtaining enough generalization to handle new subjects. However, [7] stresses that, without fine-tuning for the target subject, the accuracy stays low even with many sources subjects. We refer to unsupervised domain adaptation as transfer learning methods that use unlabeled samples from a target domain that is different but related to the source domain. Cross-subject EMG classification is typically a multi-sources domain adaptation problem as we can access labeled samples from a set of source subjects and adapt the model to a target subject using only unlabeled samples. This problem has recently attracted attention for classifying high-density EMG (HD-EMG) with the implementations of deep neural network-based methods. In [3], the AdaBN method is used to adapt a deep convolutional neural network. In the cross-subject configuration, their method improves the accuracy from 39% to 55.3% with 10 subjects and 8 hand gestures. In [14], a sampling strategy that aligns the marginal distributions of the sources and target domains is introduced. They show that it adapts the model better than AdaBN, up to closing the gap between intra-subject and cross-subject with HD-EMG.

3 The Experimental Setting

Our experiments are conducted with an original dataset of 14 participants. It contains 400ms non-overlapping windows of EMG during the hold of 4 different finger postures. The data acquisition protocol is detailed in appendix A[1] [1]. To classify those samples, we use engineered features that have led to good EMG classification in related studies [4]. Those are the mean absolute value, root mean square, waveform length, zero crossing, Wilson amplitude, maximum absolute amplitude, and integral. We compute them on each of the 8 EMG channels, which gives us a feature vector of size 56.

4 Baseline Classifiers

For the intra-subject baseline, we train one classifier for each subject; we take 90% of the samples for training and 10% for testing in a 10-fold cross-validation. We then compute the average classification accuracy. For cross-subject configurations, leave-one-subject-out cross-validation is used. We pool the samples from 13 subjects to create the training set and use those from the remaining subject for testing. All our experiments are conducted using similar classification models. We use a multi-layer perceptron neural network with one hidden layer and a logistic activation function. We keep 90% of the training set for fitting the model and 10% as the validation set. The model is trained until convergence of the classification accuracy on the validation set, with a maximum of 1000 epochs. The hidden layer is set to contain 100 nodes in the intra-subject configurations and only 10 in the cross-subject configurations. This is set to reduce the effect of overfitting in cross-subject configurations.

The baseline classification reaches 93.1% accuracy for intra-subject and 69.8% for cross-subject. While this result highlights the *cross-subject* issue, it also assesses the quality of our model as its performance is similar to the state-of-the-art (typically above 90% for intra-subject models). For the following tests, we consider that the model has access to all the unlabelled target samples at training time and that those samples contain only EMG samples from the 4 recognized classes. In a real-world setting, the model should be able to discriminate between samples that correspond to a specific gesture class or no intended gesture. We simplify the problem to concentrate on highlighting the cross-subject issue.

---

[1] This dataset is expected to be published shortly in another paper.

5 Dimensionality Reduction for Cross-Subject Learning

This section explores the role of dimensionality reduction in improving cross-subject generalization. The rationale of the analysis is that the poor accuracy of the cross-subject classification observed in the previous section might be improved by finding a subspace where the intra-subject conditional distributions are more similar. We consider the following dimensionality reduction strategies: Principal Component Analysis (PCA), Kernel PCA (KPCA) with cosine and polynomial kernel, independent component analysis (ICA), and singular value decomposition (SVD). The plot in Fig. 1.a reports the classification accuracy in intra-subject configurations, where these algorithms are fitted on each subject separately. It appears that KPCA with a cosine kernel offers the best data

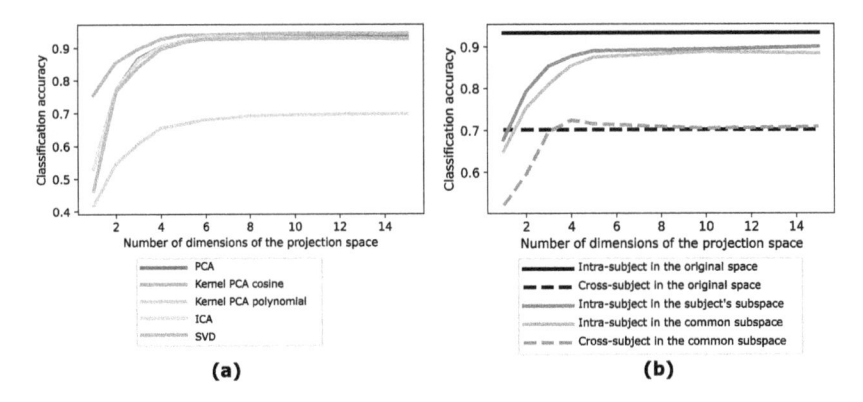

Fig. 1. (a) Intra-subject classification accuracy for different dimensionality reduction algorithms and an increasing number of dimensions of the projection space. (b) Classification accuracy for an increasing number of dimensions of the KPCA subspace.

representation with few dimensions. We evaluate the quality of this subspace for cross-subject estimation. Considering a leave-one-subject-out strategy, we fit the projection on the pooled samples from all sources subjects to find a common subspace. We project all the samples in this subspace and compute the cross-subject accuracy. The results are shown in Fig. 1.b. The main conclusions deriving from the conducted experiments are i) for a single subject, the EMG signals may be effectively embedded in a low-dimensional space so that a classification model keeps high accuracy, ii) selecting a common subspace for all subjects does not help with the cross-subject issue. It remains however an open question: do the subjects differ in terms of subspace or in terms of distributions, yet over the same subspace? In order to settle the question, we implement and assess a cross-subject dimensionality reduction step. The idea is to use all the subjects with one set aside (leave-one-subject-out) to derive a common low-dimension subspace and then test such subspace (source) on the remaining subject (target). Note that in this case, though the subspace has been obtained from the other subjects, the training set contains only the EMG signals of the target.

From the orange line in Fig. 1.b, it appears that the intra-subject accuracy in the common subspace falls just below the accuracy obtained in the target subject's specific subspace. This suggests that the subspaces of different subjects are similar but not the same. The mapping between the features and labels must be different with each subject to explain the poor cross-subject accuracy.

6 Visualization of the Low-Dimensional Subspace

We have shown in Sect. 5 that there is a low-dimensional KPCA subspace that is convenient for training a classifier for all the subjects. This section uses the first 2 components of such projection (computed from the entire dataset) to gain a visual insight into the distribution of both the pooled dataset (left side of Fig. 2.a) and the individual subjects (the right side of Fig. 2.a shows the first 6 subjects). As we can see, when looking at one subject at a time, the class clusters are often separable, even with only 2 dimensions. However, the shape and positions of those clusters are very subject-dependent. The leftmost subfigure shows that once pooled all the subjects together, the class clusters are hardly separable. This explains the poor accuracy obtained with cross-subject training of the classification model. To show that this effect stays in higher dimensions, we provide a t-SNE projection of the samples in Fig. 2.b. This projection is computed from the 10-dimensional common subspace as it provides good intra-subject classification. This enables us to show that even when considering the complete low-dimensional subspace, the class clusters are easier to separate when looking at one subject at a time than when pooling the subjects together.

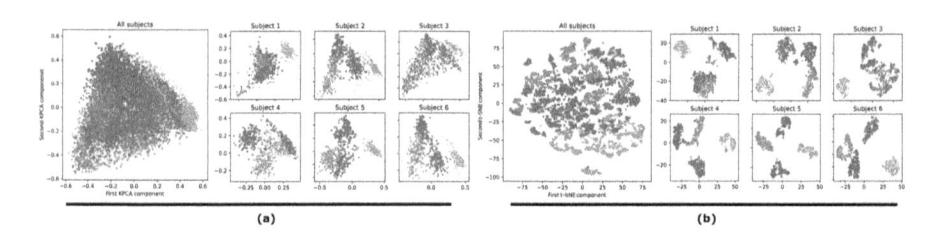

Fig. 2. (a) KPCA projections of the samples from all subjects in a common subspace. (b) t-SNE visualization of the samples from all subjects in the common KPCA subspace

7 Subspace Alignment for Domain Adaptation

Subspace alignment (SA) [5] is a UDA method that projects the samples from two different but related domains into a single subspace using PCA projections of the two domains. We suggest that applying this method to our engineered features will yield a common subspace, with a better correspondence between the source and target domains. As in Sect. 5, cosine KPCA gave better results than PCA; we adapted the simple SA to work with cosine kernel. As explained in [10], the cosine similarity function is equivalent to the linear kernel (used by PCA) if the data is L2-normalized. Hence, applying L2-normalization on each subject enables us to use standard SA to align the same subspaces as the one obtained with cosine KPCA. We implement an estimator, using all the source subjects as a single pooled domain, and apply SA to align the common KPCA subspace of those source subjects with the target subject's KPCA subspace. We validate the alignment efficiency in leave-one-subject-out cross-validation. The results in Fig. 3 show that this domain adaptation method obtains a better accuracy than the cross-subject's baseline. The model converges to 79.5% accuracy, obtained with only 10 dimensions of the KPCA subspace. The posthoc analysis of these results using a Nemenyi test [2] (given in Fig. 4) shows that this result is significantly better than the cross-subject baseline. However, it doesn't close the gap between cross-subject and intra-subject.

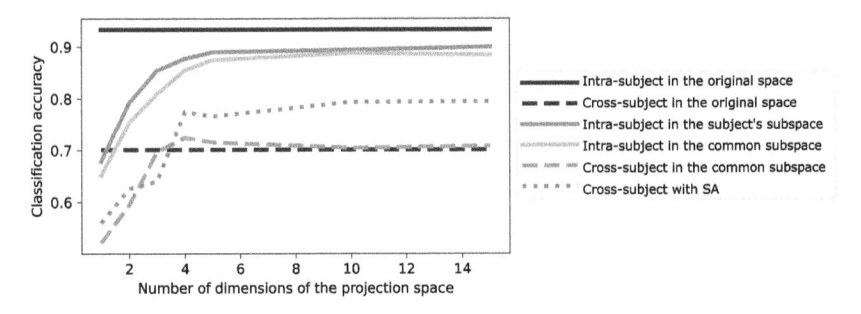

Fig. 3. Comparison of the classification accuracy obtained with KPCA SA and with the other strategies for an increasing number of dimensions of the KPCA subspace.

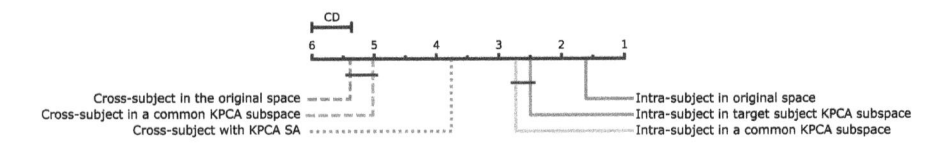

Fig. 4. Average rank of the different classifiers (the lower, the better). Classifiers that are not significantly different are connected (at $p = 0.05$ found by a Nemenyi test [2]).

We finish by comparing the KPCA SA with other UDA methods. First, we test the standard PCA SA by not applying L2-normalization to see if it has any impact on the model. After that, we test the Correlation Alignment (CORAL) algorithm [12]. This method aligns the second-order statistics of the sources and target domains. Finally, we introduce an instance-based domain adaptation algorithm. The Kullback-Leibler Importance Estimation Procedure

(KLIEP) [11] finds a weighing of the sources samples that minimizes the differences with the target domain distribution. This strategy does not affect the feature space, contrary to SA and CORAL. CORAL and KLIEP are tested both in the original feature space (with L2-normalization) and in the common KPCA subspace found on source subjects. We used 10 dimensions for the KPCA subspace as it gave the best results in Fig. 3. The results in Fig. 5 show that all of these models are less efficient than KPCA SA.

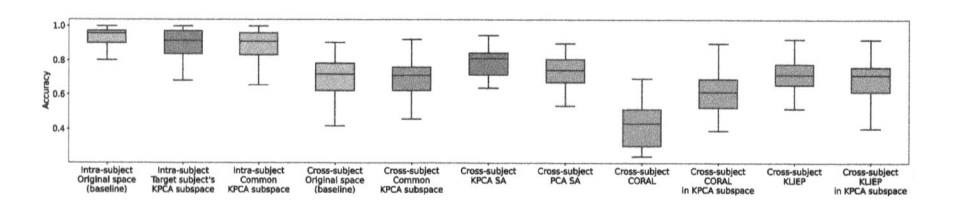

Fig. 5. Comparison of the results from the different models

8 Conclusion

The literature on EMG-based hand gesture classification is full of highly accurate results as far as a single subject is concerned. The story changes when several subjects are pooled together. This paper confirms the limitations of naive cross-subject approaches, which simply rely on pooling together the data of several subjects. At the same time, our results show that it is possible to find a common robust subspace in which classifiers can rapidly be tuned to different subjects. Though such a common subspace is low-dimensional, the associated classifiers are competitive with the ones fitted to specific individuals. Moreover, we showed that this subspace helps improve the accuracy of cross-subject classifiers. Using SA to align the target's specific subspace to the common subspace found on sources, we improved the accuracy from 69.8% to 79.5%.

Such a result is encouraging, but it should be considered as a first step in the definition of a robust methodology to solve the cross-subject problem of learning from electrophysiological signals. A limitation of this study is the small complexity of the problem as we only considered able-bodied participants performing simple gestures. We showed that it is sufficient to highlight the cross-subject issue but future research will have to extend this analysis to more complex settings by involving hand gestures with multiple degrees of freedom and an assessment with amputee users. Finally, to further close the gap between intra-subject and cross-subject estimation, future work will focus on four aspects: i) enlarging the dataset by including additional subjects to enhance the assessment of the approach, ii) extending the search of a common subspace to supervised strategies (e.g., feature selection based on a leave-one-subject-out criterion), iii) making use of more recent and more efficient alignment methods such as those described in [9,13], and iv) finding a strategy to incorporate the variability of all the source subjects better than naive pooling, which assumes a single source domain.

Acknowledgements. We gratefully thank all the members of the Laboratory of Neurophysiology and Movement Biomechanics (ULB) for the expertise and equipment they provided us during our data acquisition for this work.

References

1. Colot, M., Bontempi, G., Chéron, G., Simar, C.: Hand gestures estimation from EMG and VR a machine learning approach, Master thesis, ULB (2022). https://mlg.ulb.ac.be/wordpress/members-2/martincolot/
2. Demšar, J.: Statistical comparisons of classifiers over multiple data sets. J. Mach. Learn. Res. **7**, 1–30 (2006)
3. Du, Y., Jin, W., Wei, W., Hu, Y., Geng, W.: Surface EMG-based inter-session gesture recognition enhanced by deep domain adaptation. Sensors **17**(3), 458 (2017)
4. Fajardo, J.M., Gomez, O., Prieto, F.: EMG hand gesture classification using handcrafted and deep features. Biomed. Signal Process. Control **63**, 102210 (2021)
5. Fernando, B., Habrard, A., Sebban, M., Tuytelaars, T.: Subspace alignment for domain adaptation. arXiv preprint arXiv:1409.5241 (2014)
6. Gu, X., Guo, Y., Deligianni, F., Lo, B., Yang, G.Z.: Cross-subject and cross-modal transfer for generalized abnormal gait pattern recognition. IEEE Trans. Neural Netw. Learn. Syst. **32**(2), 546–560 (2020)
7. Hoshino, T., Kanoga, S., Tsubaki, M., Aoyama, A.: Comparing subject-to-subject transfer learning methods in surface electromyogram-based motion recognition with shallow and deep classifiers. Neurocomputing **489**, 599–612 (2022)
8. Jaramillo-Yánez, A., Benalcázar, M.E., Mena-Maldonado, E.: Real-time hand gesture recognition using surface electromyography and machine learning: a systematic literature review. Sensors **20**(9), 2467 (2020)
9. Saito, K., Watanabe, K., Ushiku, Y., Harada, T.: Maximum classifier discrepancy for unsupervised domain adaptation. In: Proceedings of the IEEE Conference on Computer Vision and Pattern Recognition, pp. 3723–3732 (2018)
10. Schutze, H., Manning, C.D., Raghavan, P.: Introduction to Information Retrieval. Cambridge University Press, Cambridge (2008)
11. Sugiyama, M., Nakajima, S., Kashima, H., Buenau, P., Kawanabe, M.: Direct importance estimation with model selection and its application to covariate shift adaptation. Adv. Neural Inf. Process. Syst. **20** (2007)
12. Sun, B., Feng, J., Saenko, K.: Return of frustratingly easy domain adaptation. In: Proceedings of the AAAI Conference on Artificial Intelligence, vol. 30 (2016)
13. Xu, R., Li, G., Yang, J., Lin, L.: Larger norm more transferable: an adaptive feature norm approach for unsupervised domain adaptation. In: Proceedings of the IEEE/CVF International Conference on Computer Vision, pp. 1426–1435 (2019)
14. Zhang, X., Zhang, X., Wu, L., Li, C., Chen, X., Chen, X.: Domain adaptation with self-guided adaptive sampling strategy: feature alignment for cross-user myoelectric pattern recognition. IEEE Trans. Neural Syst. Rehabil. Eng. **30**, 1374–1383 (2022)

Adapting Classifiers to Changing Class Priors During Deployment

Natnael Daba[2]([✉]) [iD], Bruce McIntosh[1], and Abhijit Mahalanobis[2] [iD]

[1] Department of Computer Science, University of Central Florida, Orlando, FL 32816, USA
[2] Department of Electrical and Computer Engineering, University of Arizona, Tucson, AZ 85721, USA
ndaba@arizona.edu

Abstract. Conventional classifiers are trained and evaluated using "balanced" data sets in which all classes are equally present. Classifiers are now trained on large data sets such as ImageNet, and are now able to classify hundreds (if not thousands) of different classes. On one hand, it is desirable to train such general-purpose classifier on a very large number of classes so that it performs well regardless of the settings in which it is deployed. On the other hand, it is unlikely that all classes known to the classifier will occur in every deployment scenario, or that they will occur with the same prior probability. In reality, only a relatively small subset of the known classes may be present in a particular setting or environment. For example, a classifier will encounter mostly animals if its deployed in a zoo or for monitoring wildlife, aircraft and service vehicles at an airport, or various types of automobiles and commercial vehicles if is used for monitoring traffic. Furthermore, the exact class priors are generally unknown and can vary over time. In this paper, we explore different methods for estimating the class priors based on the output of the classifier itself. We then show that incorporating the estimated class priors in the overall decision scheme enables the classifier to increase its run-time accuracy in the context of its deployment scenario.

Keywords: unknown priors · context · classifier · test time performance accuracy

1 Introduction

Conventional classifiers are trained and evaluated using "balanced" data sets in which all classes are equally present. For instance, well known data sets such as CIFAR-100 and ImageNet (to name a few) have the same number of training and test images for all classes. However, it is unlikely that the prior probability of occurrence will be the same for the classes that are encountered in a given deployment scenario. In fact, many well-known off-the-shelf networks are trained on ImageNet and then deployed in various applications where they will encounter only a relatively small subset of classes. For example, a network trained on ImageNet (with a thousand classes) deployed for traffic surveillance and monitoring is likely to encounter various types of vehicles, pedestrians, cyclists, and some animals such as birds and dogs. However, it is unlikely that most other classes known to the classifier (such as aircraft, large wild animals, marine creatures, and so forth) will be present in such deployment scenarios. Knowledge of the class priors allows the decisions to be weighted in favor of the likely classes, and thereby improves the classifier's accuracy in a given deployment scenario.

Unfortunately, the exact class priors are generally unknown and can vary over time. In this paper, we explore different methods for estimating the class priors based on the response of the classifier itself, as a means for adapting to unknown or time-varying class mixtures at different sites of operation. We then show that incorporating the estimated class priors in the overall decision scheme (as shown in Fig. 1) improves the classifier's accuracy in the context of the deployment site. It should be noted that no retraining is required, and the method can be applied to any classifier trained on a large number of classes. Results of experiments show that performance can be improved by as much as 10% for individual classes in many cases.

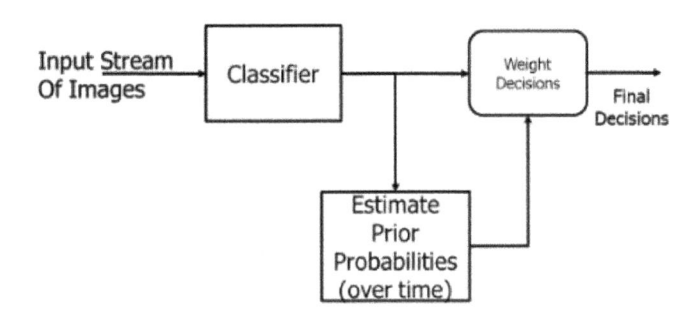

Fig. 1. The prior probabilities are estimated using the classifier's decision frequency, and re-weights the decision confidence to improve overall accuracy.

The importance of estimating class priors has been investigated by other researchers. Katti [1] states that detecting objects in real world scenes is difficult, and despite huge successes in CNN based detection, humans still generally do better. One proposed reason for this is people understand the context or the environment within which an object is found, and whether a strong correlation exists between the class of the object and context in which it is encountered. Hasan [2] says that in nature, objects and their surroundings tend to coexist in a particular configuration known as a 'context' and that visual recognition systems have taken advantage of this to improve results. Aude [3] informs us that objects co-vary with one another, and particular environments create associations that can be exploited by visual system. Sulc [4] points out that a common assumption is that training and test data are independently sampled from an identical distribution; however this is frequently not the case in practice. This discrepancy between training and test time data is posed as a domain adaptation problem, and they propose a method of maximum a posteriori estimation to improve classifier accuracy by learning and using the prior likelihoods of the test set.

Prior works such as [9,10] have explored different test-time prior adaptation methods using a Bayesian framework. For example, [9] proposed an iterative algorithm that is an instance of the expectation-maximization (EM) algorithm for estimating unknown priors at test time. [10] treats the problem of prior estimation as a maximum likelihood estimation based on a confusion matrix by defining and maximizing a likelihood function of class priors. While we also use a Bayesian framework to formulate the problem, we then show that a naive estimation technique based on the classifier's decision frequency can give good results under certain condition. We also introduce a simpler quadratic programming method for estimating priors that has not been explored in previous works.

2 Estimation of Class Priors Based on Decision Frequency

We now discuss several different approaches for estimating the prior probabilities for the different classes using the observed run-time response of the classifier. Assume that x is an image (or data vector) that we seek to classify as one of K possible classes. The true identities of these classes are denoted by w_i for $i = 1, \ldots, K$. Let $P(w_i|x)$ denote the posterior probability for class i conditioned on the observation x, and $P(w_i)$ be the prior probability of occurrence for class i. By design, the classifier's output (confidence score) in response to the input data is a proxy for $P(w_i|x)$, and will be denoted by $\hat{P}(w_i|x)$. The softmax function used at the output of the classifier ensures that $\sum_{i=1}^{K} \hat{P}(w_i|x)$, and the classifier decides in favor of class i if $\hat{P}(w_i|x) > \hat{P}(w_j|x)$ for all $j \neq i$. In doing so, it assumes that the prior likelihood of all classes is the same. Although this is true in a balanced test set, it is unlikely to be valid in a real world setting.

During training with balanced data, the priors for all classes is the assumed to be the same, say $P = 1/K$, where K is the total number of classes in the dataset. Using Bayes rule, the classifier's default decision confidence can be interpreted to be $\hat{P}(w_i|x) \cong \frac{P(x|w_i) \cdot P}{P(x)}$. To take the estimated class prior into account when the network is deployed, we multiply the output of the classifier by the scalar ratio $\alpha_i = \frac{\hat{P}(w_i)}{P}$, where $\hat{P}(w_i)$ is the estimated class prior. This yields

$$\alpha_i \hat{P}(w_i|x) \cong \left(\frac{\hat{P}(w_i)}{P}\right)\left(\frac{p(x|w_i) \cdot P}{p(x)}\right) = \frac{p(x|w_i) \cdot \hat{P}(w_i)}{p(x)} \quad (1)$$

which is the corrected estimate for the posterior probability for class i using $\hat{P}(w_i)$ instead of P. Our goal is to then modify the decision strategy to choose class i if $\alpha_i \hat{P}(w_i|x) > \alpha_j \hat{P}(w_j|x)$ for all $j \neq i$. However, since P is the same for all classes, this is the same as choosing class i if $\hat{P}(w_i|x)\hat{P}(w_i) > \hat{P}(w_j|x)\hat{P}(w_j)$ for all $j \neq i$.

A relatively simple approach for estimating $\hat{P}(w_i|x)$ while the classifier is in operation is as follows. Let the decision made by the classifier in response to x be denoted by C_j, for $j = 1, \ldots, K$. Further, let $P(C_i|w_i)$ represent the probability that the classifier will decide C_i when the true class of x is w_i. Similarly, the probability that the true class of x is w_i when the classifier decides C_i is denoted by $P(w_i|C_i)$. Using Bayes rule, we obtain $P(w_i|C_i) = \frac{P(C_i|w_i)P(w_i)}{P(C_i)}$ where $P(w_i)$ is the yet unknown prior probability of class i. Since $P(C_i|w_i)$ is the same as **recall**, and $P(w_i|C_i)$ is the same as **precision**, we can re-write this as

$$P(w_i) = \frac{P(w_i|C_i)P(C_i)}{P(C_i|w_i)} = \frac{Precision_i \times P(C_i)}{Recall_i} \quad (2)$$

It should be noted that $P(C_i)$ is the overall probability that the classifier decides class i regardless of what class the input x belongs to. To estimate this term, assume that the classifier is observed to process a total of N test images during operation, and N_i are the number of them classified as belonging to class i. A rough estimate for $P(C_i)$ is then given by $\hat{P}(C_i) = N_i/N$ so that the prior probability for class i is estimated as

$$\hat{P}(w_i) = \frac{Precision_i \times N_i}{Recall_i \times N} \quad (3)$$

Of course, the classifier's precision and recall for the different classes can be readily obtained from the "off-line" evaluations on balanced test sets. If precision and recall are approximately equal, we get $\hat{P}(w_i) = \frac{N_i}{N}$. We will use this as a "naïve estimate" to modify the decision strategy for the classifier such that it decides class i if $\hat{P}(w_i|x)\hat{P}(w_i) > \hat{P}(w_j|x)\hat{P}(w_j)$ for all $j \neq i$. This re-weights the classifier's default decision confidences (when deployed) using the naïve estimate of the class priors, and thereby adapts its performance to the chances of encountering the various classes in the environment in which it is operating.

Quadratic Programming Approach: The previous naïve estimate does not take joint error probabilities into account, and may not provide optimum results if the incorrect decisions are highly correlated, or when the precision and recall differ significantly. To address this problem, consider a deployed classifier which produces a sequence of decisions in response to an input stream of images. Assume that these images belong to a subset of the classes known to the classifier, but the prior probability of occurrence of each class is not known. We also assume that the performance of the classifier on a balanced test set is available in the form of a confusion matrix, where each row has been normalized to add to 1.0. We can then treat the entry in the j-th row and i-th column as an estimate of $P(C_i|w_j)$, i.e. the probability that the classifier's decision is C_i when the true class is w_j. By definition, we know that $P(C_i) = \sum_{j=1}^{K} P(C_i|w_j)P(w_j)$, where K is the total number of classes known to the classifier. However, $P(C_i)$ is nothing but the frequency of the decisions made by the classifier, and is essentially the normalized histogram of the classifier's decisions over time, which can be observed and measured in the deployed environment. What is not known are the prior probabilities $P(w_j)$.

To solve for $P(w_j)$, consider the j-th row of the normalized confusion matrix represented as a column vector $\mathbf{h}_j = [\, P(C_1|w_j)\ P(C_2|w_j)\ \ldots\ P(C_k|w_j)]^T$ These can be arranged as the columns of the matrix $\mathbf{H} = [\mathbf{h}_1\ \mathbf{h}_2\ \ldots\ \mathbf{h}_k]$. We also express the histogram of the observed decisions $P(C_i)$, for $i = 1, ..., k$ as the vector $\mathbf{c} = [\, P(C_1)\ P(C_2)\ \ldots\ P(C_k)]^T$, and the vector of unknown class priors as $\mathbf{v} = [\, P(w_1)\ P(w_2)\ \ldots\ P(w_K)]^T$.

Using these definitions, the equation $P(C_i) = \sum_{j=1}^{K} P(C_i|w_j) p(w_j)$ can then be written simply as $\mathbf{c} = \mathbf{H}\mathbf{v}$. Note that $\mathbf{H}$ is known apriori from the training process, and is a normalized version of the confusion matrix. Similarly, $\mathbf{c}$ is the histogram of the observed decisions when the network is deployed. A simple solution for $\mathbf{v}$ is of course obtained by inverting the matrix $\mathbf{H}$ (i.e. $\mathbf{v} = \mathbf{H}^{-1}\mathbf{c}$) but this does not guarantee positive values between 0 and 1 for the elements of $\mathbf{v}$. Therefore, we use quadratic programming to find $\mathbf{v}$ by solving the problem

$$minimize\ (\mathbf{H}\mathbf{v} - \mathbf{c})^2\ subject\ to \sum_{k=1}^{K} v(k) = 1.0\ and\ 0 \leq v(k) \leq 1.0, \quad (4)$$

where $v(k)$ (or equivalently $P(w_k)$) is an element of $\mathbf{v}$. The resulting values are the estimates of the prior probabilities of the classes that are present in the input stream.

3 Method and Results

We now apply this idea to the CIFAR-100 [5] and Tiny ImageNet [6] datasets using the Resnet18 [7] and Densenet201 [8] classifiers. Both classifiers are pretrained on ImageNet, but finetuned on CIFAR-100 and Tiny ImageNet (TIN). The first experiment is conducted on the CIFAR-100 dataset. To simulate different deployment scenarios, we define twelve "super-classes" or "context scenarios" which contain from 5 to 25 classes each. These included aquatic animals, food containers, flora, electrical items, fruits and vegetables, furniture, insects, manmade things, animals, people, outdoor places, and vehicles. The premise is that although the classifier knows a hundred classes, it will only encounter a relatively small number of them when operating in any one of these settings. For example, when the classifier is deployed to recognize aquatic animals, it will not be presented with fruits and vegetables and so forth. However, the classifier does not know which contextual scenario it is operating in. The goal is to estimate the class priors using the method described in the previous section, and employ it to increase the classifier's accuracy in the deployed setting.

The CIFAR-100 data set provides 100 test images per class. Of these, 50 test images per class were used for estimating the matrix $\mathbf{H}$ (which is based on the normalized confusion matrix). We also create a transfer set consisting of 20 samples of each class drawn from the test set. The main purpose of this set is to estimate the histogram of the decisions for each context scenario, which then provides the vector **c**. We then solve for **v** using the techniques proposed in Sect. 2, and use it to weight the classifier's outputs. Finally, the remaining 30 images for each class are used to evaluate the decision strategy and assess the impact of the proposed approach on the overall accuracy of the classifier. We are careful to make sure that the three splits of the test data are exclusive of one another. As noted previously, the simple matrix inverse results in negative values for some of the class priors, so these are mapped to 0. The quadratic programming approach constrains the resulting priors on the closed interval [0,1]. The CVXPY convex optimization library was used for this task.

Table 1. CIFAR-100/ResNet-18: Comparison of classifier accuracy using different techniques for estimating class priors. Using the estimated priors always achieves higher accuracy than the baseline

Class ids	0	1	2	3	4	5	6	7	8	9	10	11
Baseline	0.643	0.683	0.725	0.736	0.799	0.773	0.729	0.822	0.687	0.573	0.763	0.806
Naive	**0.733**	**0.785**	0.778	0.855	0.859	0.827	0.788	0.9	0.725	**0.585**	0.856	0.844
Matrix inverse	0.722	0.803	**0.799**	0.854	**0.867**	0.833	**0.81**	**0.909**	0.733	0.524	**0.859**	0.854
Quadratic programming	0.731	**0.805**	**0.799**	**0.863**	**0.867**	**0.838**	0.809	0.908	**0.735**	0.57	**0.859**	**0.856**
Ground truth	0.751	0.818	0.798	0.875	0.873	0.841	0.81	0.907	0.759	0.614	0.867	0.854

Table 2. CIFAR-100/DenseNet-201

Class ids	0	1	2	3	4	5	6	7	8	9	10	11
Baseline	0.751	0.807	0.859	0.853	0.923	0.863	0.842	0.897	0.847	0.633	0.843	0.92
Naive	0.744	**0.793**	**0.861**	0.833	0.937	0.9	0.871	0.9	0.84	**0.657**	0.873	**0.927**
Matrix inverse	0.732	0.783	0.824	**0.913**	**0.94**	**0.903**	0.867	**0.923**	0.84	0.58	**0.88**	**0.927**
Quadratic programming	0.732	0.78	0.824	**0.913**	0.937	**0.903**	**0.881**	**0.923**	**0.848**	0.577	**0.88**	**0.927**
Ground truth	0.818	0.86	0.887	0.933	0.95	0.923	0.923	0.937	0.875	0.69	0.913	0.935

The results of different comparisons are shown in Table 1 for ResNet18, and in Table 2 for DenseNet201. Since the number of samples to work with for these experiments is relatively small, we make use of 10-fold cross-validation where each fold is a different mixture of samples between the context transfer and context test sets. The columns represent a particular "context" or scenario, where the test images are restricted to one of the 12 super-classes. There are five scores for every scenario, each represented by one of the rows of the table. In any given column, the first row is the baseline performance obtained using the default score of the classifier without using any estimated priors. The bottom row is the "best possible" or ideal score that could be obtained if the exact true priors were known. The three rows in-between represent the naïve estimate, the matrix inverse solution, and the priors obtained using quadratic programming, respectively. The largest among these is indicated by the bold font. It is clear from these results that in every scenario, using the estimated priors yields higher accuracy than the baseline. We see that for ResNet-18, the proposed techniques can improve accuracy by as much as 12% compared to the baseline (scenario 1), in some cases achieving the theoretical maximum improvement (i.e. comparable to the last row). The quadratic programming approach achieves the best result in eight of the twelve scenarios. For DenseNet201, the distinction between the different technique is not as much, which indicates that precision and recall are comparable for this network. The quadratic programming approach gives the best result in seven of the scenarios, and the estimated priors improve the accuracy compared to the baseline in all cases except for scenarios 0 and 1.

The second experiment is conducted on the Tiny ImageNet (TIN) dataset. This dataset contains 64 × 64 RGB images of 200 classes with 500 images per class for the training set, 50 images per class for the validation set, and 50 images per class for the test set. For this experiment, we selected 36 classes (out of the entire 200 classes) of the dataset, and created twelve contexts/superclasses each with 3 member classes. The groupings are as follows: amphibian, arthropod, bird, car, cat, clothing, cooking utensil, dog, edible fruit, furniture, geological formation, and timepiece. The transfer set is made up of 20 samples of each member class and thus contains a total of 12 × 3 × 20 = 720 images. The test, which is separate from the transfer set, is made up of 30 samples of each member class and thus contains a total of 12 × 3 × 30 = 1080 images.

Once again, we used ResNet-18 and DenseNet-201 that are pretrained on 224 × 224 sized images from the ImageNet-1k dataset. These models are then fine-tuned on the 64 × 64 sized images from the TIN dataset. The results are shown in Tables 3 and 4, which are all results are obtained using 10-fold cross validation. In all cases, using the estimated class priors improves the accuracy of the classifier compared to the baseline, sometimes by as much 15% for ResNet-18 (e.g. scenario 6), and by more than 10% for DenseNet-201 (e.g. Scenario 7). In some cases, this improvement approaches the theoretical best possible performance (last row of the table). While all methods for estimating the priors result in improvement in accuracy, the quadratic optimization yields the most improvement compared to the naïve method and the matrix inverse solution for both networks. As a result of incorporating the quadratic programming method into our algorithm, we identified a computational overhead characterized by a time complexity of $O(n^{3.5})$ (incurred because of the quadratic programming solver method) and a space complexity of $O(n^2)$ (incurred when storing the confusion matrix) where n denotes the number of classes.

Table 3. Tiny-ImageNet/ResNet-18

Class ids	0	1	2	3	4	5	6	7	8	9	10	11
Baseline	0.718	0.829	0.871	0.656	0.656	0.714	0.652	0.721	0.777	0.741	0.698	0.817
Naive	0.819	0.918	0.931	**0.793**	0.762	0.903	0.804	0.81	0.882	0.916	0.809	**0.959**
Matrix inverse	0.831	0.923	**0.932**	0.772	0.78	0.919	0.819	0.819	0.913	**0.93**	0.828	0.951
Quadratic programming	**0.833**	**0.93**	**0.932**	0.78	**0.781**	**0.922**	**0.82**	**0.82**	0.914	**0.93**	**0.832**	0.958
Ground truth	0.844	0.948	0.93	0.803	0.761	0.946	0.818	0.813	0.936	0.931	0.832	0.954

Table 4. Tiny-ImageNet/DenseNet-201

Class ids	0	1	2	3	4	5	6	7	8	9	10	11
Baseline	0.78	0.834	0.898	0.687	0.679	0.82	0.777	0.738	0.847	0.816	0.7	0.877
Naive	**0.867**	0.969	0.92	0.796	0.768	0.949	**0.848**	0.844	0.942	0.953	0.837	0.977
Matrix inverse	**0.867**	0.973	**0.924**	0.824	0.787	**0.954**	0.84	0.859	0.96	0.958	0.841	0.973
Quadratic programming	**0.867**	**0.977**	**0.924**	**0.826**	0.789	**0.954**	0.84	**0.863**	**0.96**	**0.959**	0.842	**0.98**
Ground truth	0.873	0.98	0.926	0.838	0.781	0.954	0.85	0.869	**0.96**	0.953	0.868	0.989

4 Conclusion

The proposed techniques enables the classifier to adapt to the unknown class prior probabilities in the deployment environment, which are likely to vary by location and over time. Specifically, we showed that these can be estimated in a Bayesian framework using the histogram of a classifier's decisions observed over a period of time. Experiments using the CIFAR-100 and Tiny ImageNet data set using ResNet18 and DenseNet201 show that in some instances this can lead to as much as 15% improvement in performance compared to the classifier's baseline accuracy. On the CIFAR100 dataset with ResNet-18, we observe that in almost all contexts (except for 0 and 9), the matrix inverse and quadratic programming methods yield better performance in terms of classification accuracy. Regarding the performance of DenseNet-201 on the CIFAR-100, there are 5 contexts (0,1,2,9 and 11) for which the naive approach yields a slightly better result than the matrix inverse and quadratic programming approaches. For these cases, we have observed that the precision and recall of the classifier are approximately the same, which makes the naïve estimate more accurate. Overall, across all experiments, the quadratic programming approach offers the greatest improvement in classification accuracy (in 36 of the 48 scenarios in all four tables).

References

1. Katti, H., et al.: Machine vision benefits from human contextual expectations. Sci. Rep. **9**(1), 1–12 (2019)
2. Hasan, M., Roy-Chowdhury, A.K.: Context aware active learning of activity recognition models. In: Proceedings of the IEEE International Conference on Computer Vision (2015)
3. Oliva, A., Torralba, A.: The role of context in object recognition. Trends Cogn. Sci. **11**(12), 520–527 (2007)
4. Sulc, M., Matas, J.: Improving cnn classifiers by estimating test-time priors. In: Proceedings of the IEEE/CVF International Conference on Computer Vision Workshops (2019)
5. Krizhevsky, A., Hinton, G.: Learning multiple layers of features from tiny images (2009)
6. Russakovsky, O., et al.: Imagenet large scale visual recognition challenge. Int. J. Comput. Vision **115**(3), 211–252 (2015)

7. He, K., et al.: Deep residual learning for image recognition. In: Proceedings of the IEEE Conference on Computer Vision and Pattern Recognition, pp. 770–778 (2016)
8. Iandola, F., et al.: Densenet: implementing efficient convnet descriptor pyramids. arXiv preprint arXiv:1404.1869 (2014)
9. Saerens, M., et al.: Adjusting the outputs of a classifier to new a priori probabilities: a simple procedure. Neural Comput. **14**(1), 21–41 (2002)
10. šipka, T., et al.: The hitchhiker's guide to prior-shift adaptation. In: Proceedings of the IEEE/CVF Winter Conference on Applications of Computer Vision (2022)

AI4M: AI for Manufacturing

Applying Machine Learning Models on Metrology Data for Predicting Device Electrical Performance

Bappaditya Dey[1(✉)], Anh Tuan Ngo[2], Sara Sacchi[1,3], Victor Blanco[1], Philippe Leray[1], and Sandip Halder[1]

[1] imec, Kapeldreef 75, 3001 Leuven, Belgium
bappaditya.dey@imec.be
[2] School of Engineering and Physical Sciences, Henriot-Watt University, Edinburgh, UK
[3] Department of Physics and Astronomy, University of Bologna, Bologna, Italy

Abstract. Moore's Law states that transistor density will double every two years, which is sustained until today due to continuous multidirectional innovations (such as extreme ultraviolet lithography, novel patterning techniques etc.), leading the semiconductor industry towards 3 nm node (N3) and beyond. For any patterning scheme, the most important metric to evaluate the quality of printed patterns is edge placement error, with overlay being its largest contribution. Overlay errors can lead to fatal failures of IC devices such as short circuits or broken connections in terms of pattern-to-pattern electrical contacts. Therefore, it is essential to develop effective overlay analysis and control techniques to ensure good functionality of fabricated semiconductor devices. In this work we have used an imec N-14 BEOL process flow using litho-etch-litho-etch (LELE) patterning technique to print metal layers with minimum pitch of 48 nm with 193i lithography. Fork-fork structures are decomposed into two mask layers (M1A and M1B) and then the LELE flow is carried out to make the final patterns. Since a single M1 layer is decomposed into two masks, control of overlay between the two masks is critical. The goal of this work is of two-fold as, (1) to quantify the impact of overlay on capacitance and (2) to see if we can predict the final capacitance measurements with selected machine learning models at an early stage. To do so, scatterometry spectra are collected on these electrical test structures at (a) post litho, (b) post TiN hardmask etch, and (c) post Cu plating and CMP. Critical Dimension (CD) and overlay measurements for line/space (L/S) pattern are done with SEM post litho, post etch and post Cu CMP. Various machine learning models are applied to do the capacitance prediction with multiple metrology inputs at different steps of wafer processing. Finally, we demonstrate that by using appropriate machine learning models we are able to do better prediction of electrical results.

B. Dey, A. T. Ngo and S. Sacchi—Contributed equally to the work.

© The Author(s), under exclusive license to Springer Nature Switzerland AG 2025
R. Meo and F. Silvestri (Eds.): ECML PKDD 2023, CCIS 2136, pp. 435–453, 2025.
https://doi.org/10.1007/978-3-031-74640-6_36

Keywords: on-device overlay · scatterometry · interconnect · Back-End-Of-Line (BEOL) · lithography · critical dimension (CD) · edge placement error (EPE) · machine learning · predictive metrology

1 Introduction

The long standing IC industry push for device shrink, increased drive current and lower operating voltages often results in complex 3D device architectures. The inspection of 3D architectures imposes more challenges and demands in increased importance of metrology [4]. During R&D phase, different metrology techniques are used for exploratory process development, while, during high volume manufacturing, metrology is focused on process control. Techniques like scatterometry and CD-SEM (Critical Dimension Scanning Electron Microscope) are typically used for in-line CD measurements. However, both techniques have certain limitations and advantages. For instance, inconsistency in material properties (n&k) and long model-optimization times restrict scatterometry techniques, while resist shrinkage and its charging effect impact the measurement performance of the CD-SEM tool [9]. As advanced patterning techniques involve fabricating the device in multiple steps of different layers, critical dimensions and overlay are crucial to be monitored and controlled. Overlay can be defined as the relative alignment of consecutive masked layers within the device [1]. Figure 1 shows an illustration of overlay, critical dimension, and pitch of devices on a wafer. If the overlay errors between layers exceed an allowed budget, defects such as short circuit, line break, or bad contacts will occur, which leads to fatal failure of the devices.

To ensure the quality of fabricated devices in multiple patterning schemes, a number of metrologies are conducted after each process step. This leads to higher costs and lower yield in the production line. One solution to tackle this problem is to build mathematical models that can predict the properties of the devices in the last steps (critical dimensions or electrical performance) using the metrology data from early steps. With these mathematical models, a number of intermediate metrology steps can be reduced, thus increasing the throughput. Furthermore, for high-volume manufacturing, gaining an early insight into the qualities of final structures can be a game changer, since proper actions can be made in timely manner to improve the overall process. For example, if a model using the overlay data measured after the second lithography step can predict that there will be a lot of failures on the wafer in the final steps, the wafer can

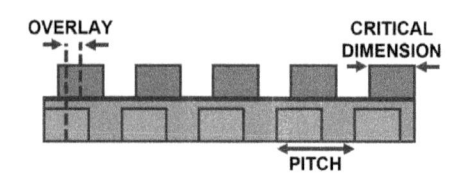

Fig. 1. Illustration of overlay, critical dimension, and pitch.

be reworked, and thus can significantly save resources and cost of production. This will not be possible if we only discover faulty wafers in later steps, where these wafers can only be scrapped.

Machine learning solutions have become an attractive tool for future process control and monitoring purposes [7]. A systematic survey was conducted on recent research works, which demonstrates different machine learning/deep learning techniques applied towards improving EPE in semiconductor manufacturing domain [3]. The methodology deployed in this study involves using the overlay metrology data from early process steps. Then, a mathematical estimator is generated using a set of machine learning algorithms. The data used to create the mathematical estimator is the training set. Once the training was completed, showing a good correlation to the reference data, the overlay metrology data from early process steps was used to predict different outcomes, such as CD and electrical performance (say, capacitance of final fabricated structures) for other wafers [2]. This technique is less dependent on structural complexity. The early estimation of electrical performance and variability provided by these machine learning techniques can significantly reduce cost for both R&D and high-volume manufacturing (HVM), by taking proper action in a timely manner either to scrap or rework the wafer, and improve or monitor the process.

2 Experimental Design and Methods

2.1 Description of the Process Flow LELE Approach

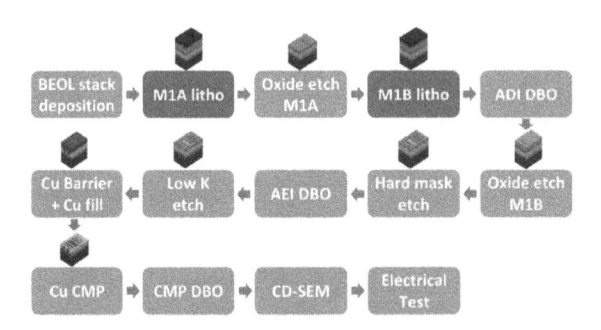

Fig. 2. Process flow showing LELE approach to achieve 48 nm pitch.

The studied layer uses a Litho-Etch-Litho-Etch (LELE) process flow to pattern a 48 nm M1 pitch by means of a double exposure of M1A and M1B layers, each of them at 96 nm pitch using a 193 nm immersion scanner. A simplified process flow describing the main fabrication steps is shown in Fig. 2. It starts with Back-End-Of-Line (BEOL) stack deposition followed by M1A lithography exposure using an ASML NXT 1950i immersion scanner. The post litho trench target CD was 40 nm. A negative tone lithography development (NTD) process was chosen to pattern the trenches. An 85 nm resist was coated on top of 30 nm (spin on glass) SOG and 100 nm (spin on carbon) SOC. This was used to pattern the M1A layer which was then transferred onto an oxide pattern storage layer by etching in a plasma chamber. The oxide etch step involved opening the SOG/SOC layer and pattern transfer into the oxide layer. A second lithography exposure was performed to pattern the M1B layer using same lithography and etch process as for M1A layer. At this stage ADI (After Develop Inspection) overlay between M1A and M1B was measured using Diffraction-Based Overlay (DBO) targets. This was followed by transferring the pattern onto the same oxide pattern storage layer. After that the patterns from M1A and M1B were transferred onto a TiN hardmask (HM) layer by plasma etching. At this stage, CD data using CD-SEM, AEI (After Etch Inspection) overlay data, as well as scatterometry spectra were collected on electrically active device structures. Finally, the TiN HM layer was used to transfer the pattern into the low k dielectric material to create the 48 nm pitch M1 trenches. Trenches were filled with Cu, followed by a CMP (chemical mechanical polishing) step. A 5 nm thin layer of SiCN layer was also deposited on top of the wafer to prevent oxidation of Cu metal lines. Scatterometry spectra collection were done on all resistance and capacitance targets before they go for electrical tests.

2.2 Description of the Electrical Test Structures

Figure 3 describes the 12 vertically placed and 12 horizontally placed (in the layout) fork-fork structures to measure capacitance. Due to overlay errors, the dielectric distance (d) between M1A and M1B changes and can be directly correlated with X overlay for vertical lines and with Y overlay values for horizontal lines. The design critical dimension here is 24 nm and the distance between the two metal lines changes in steps of 2 nm. For example, the distance between M1A and M1B is 24 nm for the AB6 and 34 nm for AB1. Similarly, it is 24 nm for BA1 and 34 nm for BA6.

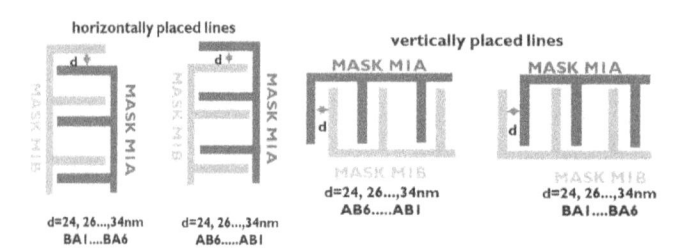

Fig. 3. Description of capacitance measurement fork-fork structures.

2.3 CD and Overlay Fingerprints Post TiN HM Etch

In order to produce a robust design of experiment we varied different parameters both at litho and etch steps. Wafers with programmed overlay were fabricated by creating a scanner sub-recipe such that wafers receive a translational offset of 0 to ±7.5 nm in X and Y direction on selected dies as shown in Fig. 4.

Non-programmed Overlay

Programmed Overlay translation(X/Y) offsets (±)7.5, 7.0,......0nm

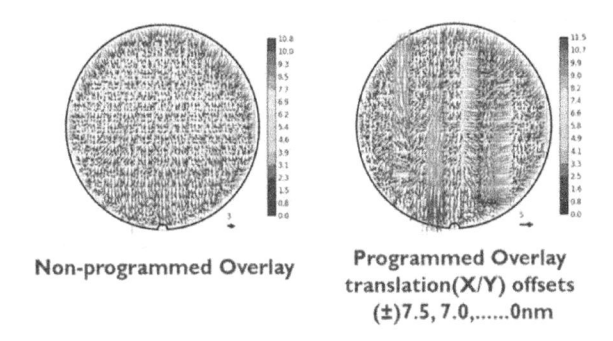

Fig. 4. Example of ADI overlay fingerprint for a POR wafer and wafer exposed with programmed overlay.

2.4 Diffraction Based Overlay DBO

The LELE double patterning technique not only entails more complex process stages, but it also needs tighter overlay control compared to the conventional single pattering [6]. Thus, it is crucial to use advanced overlay metrology methods with very high certainty to ensure the quality of fabricated devices. Recently, Diffraction-Based Overlay (DBO) emerges as a promising overlay metrology technique which offers better precision than the conventional Image-Based Overlay method [8]. DBO technique was used to monitor the overlay error of the LELE process. In DBO method, structures of stacked periodic gratings are used as the targets to measure overlay error. This method uses polarized light, with a broadband of wavelengths, perpendicularly projected to the grating targets and it measures the zero-order diffracted signal as a function of wavelength (Fig. 5a). The overlay error is measured between two layers, and spectra are obtained from target pads, each of which has gratings printed in both layers. The gratings of each target pads are similar, but intentionally shifted to each other by design as shown in Fig. 5b.

Due to symmetry, reflected spectra from pads with shifts of similar amplitude but in opposite direction are equal:

$$R(+x_0, \lambda) = R(-x_0, \lambda) \tag{1}$$

Here $R(x_0, \lambda)$ is the reflected spectrum from one target pad as a function of wavelength λ and shift x_0. In the presence of overlay error (ϵ), the symmetry is broken, and the differential spectrum of two pads is described as follows:

$$\Delta R(\lambda) = R(x_0 + \epsilon, \lambda) - R(x_0 - \epsilon, \lambda) \cong 2\epsilon \frac{\partial R}{\partial x}|_{x_0} \tag{2}$$

(a) Normal incidence reflection

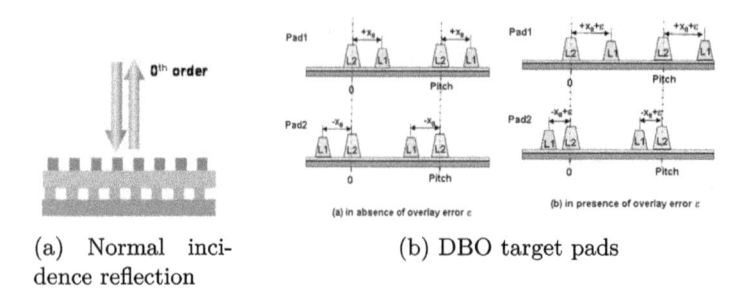

(b) DBO target pads

Fig. 5. Schematic diagrams illustrating (a) a normal incidence reflection and (b) the DBO target designed pads [6].

Using another pad with known relative offset $(x_0 + \delta)$ to get the differential spectrum $\Delta R'(\lambda)$ with respect to the x_0-shifted pad (Eq. 3), the overlay error (ϵ) can be calculated as in Eq. 4.

$$\Delta R'(\lambda) = R(x_0 + \epsilon, \lambda) - R(x_0 - \epsilon, \lambda) \cong \delta \frac{\partial R}{\partial x}|_{x_0} \quad (3)$$

$$\epsilon = \frac{\delta \Delta R(\lambda)}{2 \Delta R'(\lambda)} \quad (4)$$

3 Experimental Results and Discussions

A set of experiments and analysis using overlay data have been performed to find the optimized solutions for the process control in semiconductor manufacturing. The final goal of the experiments is to predict the electrical performance of test structures from the overlay metrology data in early process steps. Making it possible will enable/allow process engineers to make the decision of reworking or scrapping the wafers, or let them go through the next steps in the process. This will significantly help optimization of the process control, as well as save time and resources for the manufacturing operations.

3.1 Space-CD Prediction of Test Structures from Overlay Data

Predictions of the space critical dimension (CD2) of test structures from previously measured overlay metrology data are carried out through various machine learning algorithms. The best performed model was then used to predict the capacitance value of the fabricated structures.

Methodology. In this experiment, overlay metrology and CD-SEM data of four wafers are collected. Two of them are Non-Programmed Overlay wafers, while the other two are Programmed Overlay wafers, as showed in Table 1.

Machine Learning for Predicting Device Electrical Performance 441

Table 1. Description of wafers used in the experiment.

Wafers	Recipes
D02	Non-Programmed Overlay
D03	Non-Programmed Overlay
D10	Programmed Overlay
D11	Programmed Overlay

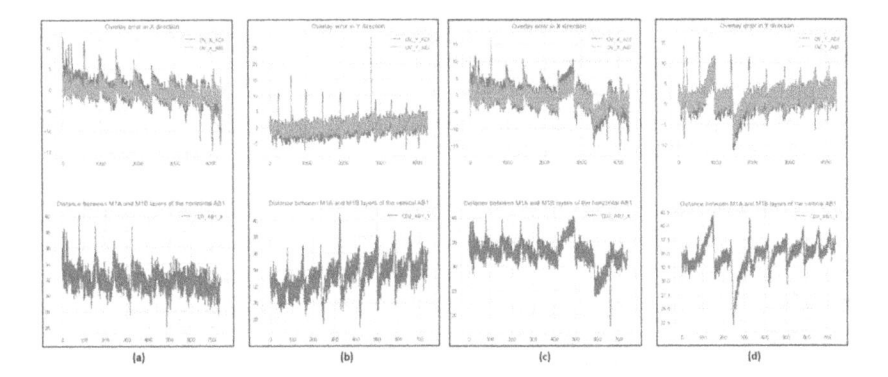

Fig. 6. Collected overlay and CD2_AB1 data. (a) and (b) show the overlay and CD-SEM data of a Non-Programmed Overlay wafer in X and Y directions. (c) and (d) show the overlay and CD-SEM data of a Programmed Overlay wafer in X and Y directions. For all graphs, the vertical axis represents the values of overlay errors (top graph) and CD2_AB1 (bottom graph) in nanometers, while the horizontal axis the sequence of data points.

In CD-SEM measurement, a number of metrics such as line width and distance of M1A and M1B layers or line width roughness are measured. The aim is to predict the distance (CD2) between M1A and M1B layers of the AB1 test structures (CD2_AB1), which has the designed value of 32 nm, using overlay data from previous steps. The line width and distance of other test structures can be predicted with the same method. The ADI-AEI overlay and CD2_AB1 data in X direction of a Non-Programmed Overlay wafer and a Programmed Overlay wafer is shown in Fig. 6. In this figure, the vertical axes represent the value of overlay errors (top graph) and CD2_AB1 distances (bottom graph) in nanometers. The horizontal axes represent the sequence of data points. Qualitatively, we can see that CD2_AB1 data aligns well with the pattern of overlay data.

Machine Learning models are built to predict the space critical dimension (CD2) of horizontal-placed and vertical-placed AB1 structure separately. The performance of those models is also compared when overlay data from different measuring steps (ADI DBO, AEI DBO, CMP DBO) are used for training and predicting. In the dataset, each of the 149 dies on the wafer was measured in 4 to 5 target points using CD-SEM, which results in more than 700 datapoints for each wafer. The CD2 of these measured points are the target labels for the Machine Learning models. Among 4 wafers that were measured in this experiment, data from three wafers (D02, D03, and D11) was used as the training set, and data from wafer D10 was used for validation.

There are in total 3 datasets, one for each DBO step (ADI, AEI, and CMP), and each one contains 30 input features:

- 26 overlay measurements of each die. Overlay error is chosen in Y direction, if the target CD2_AB1 is of the horizontal structures, and in X direction, if CD2_AB1 is of the vertical structures.
- Die positions in X and Y directions.
- Target positions of each CD-SEM measurement on each die in X and Y.

To predict the CD2_AB1, four Machine Learning regression algorithms were chosen to be compared, i.e. *Linear Regression, Support Vector Regression (SVR), Random Forest* and *Extra Tree Regressor*, as they are among the most popular and powerful. These Machine Learning models were built using a Python module called Scikit-learn [5]. For *SVR* model, Radial Basis Function kernel was used, Regularization parameter was chosen to be 3, and the epsilon parameter was 0.07. For *Random Forest* and *Extra Tree*, the forest size and minimum sample split size were chosen to be 60 and 2, respectively. Before training, the dataset is normalized and scaled to unit variance using equation (Eq. 5).

$$z = \frac{x}{s} \tag{5}$$

where z is the data after being normalized, x is the training sample, and s is the standard deviation of x. Two metrics have been used to evaluate the models: the coefficient of determination (R^2) (Eq. 6), and the mean square error (MSE) (Eq. 7).

$$R^2 = 1 - \frac{\sum_i (y_i - f_i)^2}{\sum_i (y_i - \bar{y})} \tag{6}$$

$$MSE = \frac{1}{n} \sum_{i=1}^{n} (y_i - f_i)^2 \tag{7}$$

Here, y=[$y_1,y_2,...,y_n$] is the observed data, f=[$f_1,f_2,...,f_n$] is the corresponding fitted value of y by a regression model, and $\bar{y}$ is the mean of y. The R^2 metric has the maximum value of 1, which means that the predicted values are exactly the same as the observed values. If the regression models always give the prediction value of $\bar{y}$, then R^2=0, which is called baseline. R^2 value is negative for a prediction worse than the baseline. On the other hand, MSE value is always greater than or equal to zero. The closer this metric is to zero, the better the performance of the models.

Results and Discussions. The two tables below compare the performance of four Machine Learning models using the data from the three DBO steps. Table 2 shows the results of these model with the datasets of horizontal AB1 structures, while Table 3 shows the results when the datasets are collected from the measurement of vertical AB1 structures. It can be seen that different algorithms resulted in different performance accuracies. In both horizontal and vertical dataset, it is expected that *Linear Regression* showed the worst performance compared to the other, due to its assumption that the data only follows a linear trend, which is not the case for most datasets. *SVR* model is more complex than the *Linear Regression*, and thus can better capture the underlying trend of the dataset. However, the prediction accuracy of *SVR* is still not as good as the *Random Forest* and the *Extra Tree Regressor* models for most of the cases.

Table 2. Evaluation results of the four ML models for the horizontal AB1 structures dataset.

		ADI DBO	AEI DBO	CMP DBO
Linear Regression	$R^2 training$	0.675	0.690	0.666
	$R^2 testing$	0.777	0.836	0.802
	MSE	1.591	1.168	1.414
SVR	$R^2 training$	0.952	0.949	0.952
	$R^2 testing$	0.816	0.853	0.817
	MSE	1.310	1.045	1.300
Random Forest	$R^2 training$	0.977	0.978	0.974
	$R^2 testing$	0.855	0.876	0.863
	MSE	1.031	0.881	0.974
Extra Tree Regressor	$R^2 training$	1.000	1.000	1.000
	$R^2 testing$	**0.876**	**0.891**	**0.873**
	MSE	**0.946**	**0.779**	**0.906**

This is not surprising as the last two models are based on ensemble learning, which aggregates the predictions of a group of decision trees, thus achieving better performance than the individual predictors. Between *Random Forest* and *Extra Tree Regressor*, the latter shows better accuracy with both horizontal and vertical AB1 structures datasets. When comparing the performance of the four models using overlay features from different DBO steps, it is clear that AEI overlay data gives the best accuracy for all models. This is because the overlay data in the AEI step is more stable and has much less outliers than the overlay data from ADI and CMP steps. The outliers are more frequent in ADI because the grating targets in this step still consist of photoresist of M1B layer, and the resist layer is not uniform throughout the whole wafer. Meanwhile in CMP DBO, the measurement is done after the wafer has been metalized and polished, which cause noises in the reflected spectrum.

Table 3. Evaluation results of the four ML models for the vertical AB1 structures dataset.

		ADI DBO	AEI DBO	CMP DBO
Linear Regression	$R^2 training$	0.707	0.735	0.687
	$R^2 testing$	0.667	0.759	0.668
	MSE	2.748	1.984	2.736
SVR	$R^2 training$	0.973	0.972	0.978
	$R^2 testing$	0.744	**0.906**	0.689
	MSE	2.108	**0.772**	2.564
Random Forest	$R^2 training$	0.981	0.984	0.978
	$R^2 testing$	0.834	0.882	0.834
	MSE	1.367	0.971	1.371
Extra Tree Regressor	$R^2 training$	1.000	1.000	1.000
	$R^2 testing$	**0.854**	0.894	**0.853**
	MSE	**1.203**	0.871	**1.212**

To visualize the performance of Machine Learning models in the very early step of the manufacturing process, Fig. 7 shows the results of *Extra Tree Regressor* using the ADI overlay data to predict CD2_AB1 of horizontal and vertical structures, respectively. Looking at the scatter graphs, the predicted and target values of CD2_AB1 fits closely to the 45-degree line, which proves that the *Extra Tree Regressor* model performed well on both datasets of horizontal and vertical structures. The well fitted trend is also presented in the line graphs, where the patterns of predicted values are closely mimicked by the patterns of observed data. Finally in the wafer maps, which show the average prediction error of each die, we can see that for the majority of the wafers area, the prediction errors are approximately 1 nm. This error only accounts for 3.125% of the designed distance between M1A and M1B layers. The highest average prediction error in one die for the horizontal structures is around 2.5 nm (7.813% of the designed CD2_AB1), while for the vertical structures it is close to 2.25 nm (7.031% of the designed CD_AB1).

3.2 Capacitance Prediction of Test Structures from Overlay Data

After the fabrication process, electrical tests such as capacitance and resistance measurements were conducted on the wafers to check for the quality of fabricated devices. In previous experiment, space-CD measurement data has been successfully predicted from the overlay measurements. This proves that it is also possible to predict capacitance of fabricated structures from overlay errors, as CD-SEM and capacitance are directly correlated. In this section, Machine Learning is used to predict the capacitance of different test structures using overlay measurement data.

Horizontal structures

Vertical structures

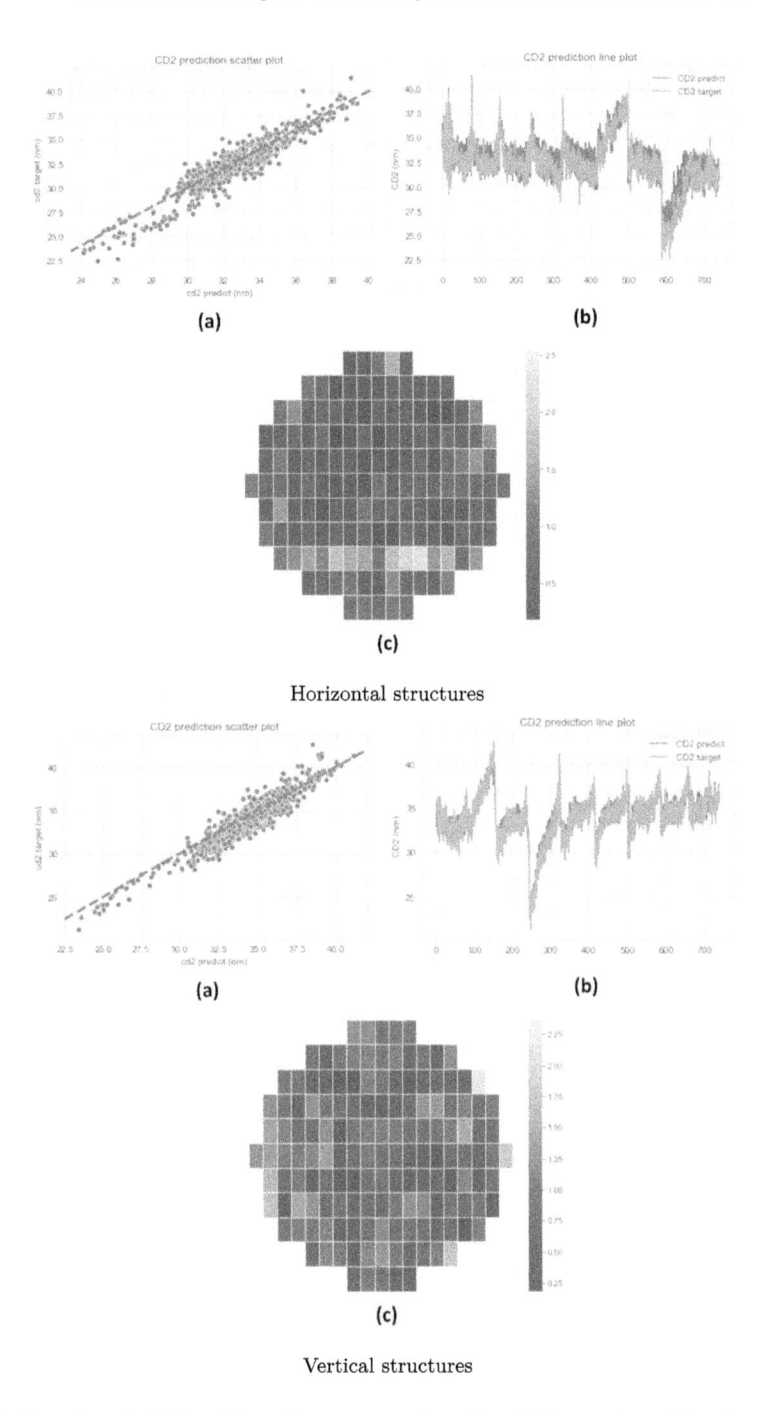

Fig. 7. Results of *Extra Tree Regressor* using the ADI overlay data to predict CD2_AB1. (a) CD2_AB1 prediction scatter plot. (b) Line plots of target and predicted CD2_AB1 values. (c) Wafer map showing each die's average prediction error.

Methodology. In this experiment, the capacitance measurement was conducted on two wafers, D02 (Non-Programmed Overlay wafer) and D10 (Programmed Overlay wafer). There are in total 127 dies, and in each five instances of one type of structures (AB1, ..., AB6, BA1, ..., BA6) were tested. This results in 635 capacitance measurements for each type of test structure in one direction on each wafer. Figure 8 displays the variation in the capacitance measurement data of the two wafers.

In these graphs, the overall capacitance of AB1, AB2, ... AB6 structures is greater than that of BA1, BA2, ... BA6, which means that the distance between M1A and M1B layers of ABx structures is smaller than BAx structures. The explanation lies in the placement error, i.e., when the M1B layer is shifted to the left by a small distance from the designed position. The small CD2 distance of ABx structures results in many failures and outliers in the capacitance data; moreover, the variance of ABx data is also much larger than the variance of BAx data. Since the target output contains outliers, if we train the regressor model directly with the data, the prediction accuracy will be low as outliers will bias the Machine Learning model during the training. Therefore, before training the model, DBSCAN algorithm was applied to clean the capacitance data. Any abnormal data points detected by the DBSCAN algorithm in one die will be replaced by the mean value of the remained clean data of that die. If there is a die which consists of only outliers, all data points on that die will be replaced by the mean value of the clean data of the whole wafer. The input features fed to the DBSCAN model are measured capacitance and die position in X and Y direction.

DBSCAN (Density-Based Spatial Clustering) is an unsupervised Machine Learning method for special clustering, which views clusters as high-density regions separated by low density areas. Therefore, the clusters discovered by DBSCAN can have any arbitrary shapes, unlike some other clustering algorithms such as k-means, which has an assumption that clusters are in convex shape. The most important hyperparameters of the model are epsilon ϵ, which determines the maximum distance between two samples to be considered neighbours, and *min_samples*, which specifies the minimum number of samples to form a dense region. The algorithm counts the number of points located within the ϵ range and if it is at least equal to the *min_samples* it considers it a core sample. All the datapoints that lie in its ϵ-neighbourhood belong to the same cluster. Datapoints not belonging to any ϵ-neighbourhood of a core sample are considered outliers. In this work, the *min_samples* parameter is chosen to be 2, the minimum value possible, in order to not replace too many data points because of constraints given by the size of the dataset. To tune the ϵ parameter, the distance to the nearest point of every data point has been found, sorted and plotted. The optimal ϵ is the point where the change of the graph is most pronounced. For the regression model to predict capacitance values based on overlay data, there are 3 datasets corresponding to each DBO step, each with 29 input features:

(a) Wafer D02

(b) Wafer D10

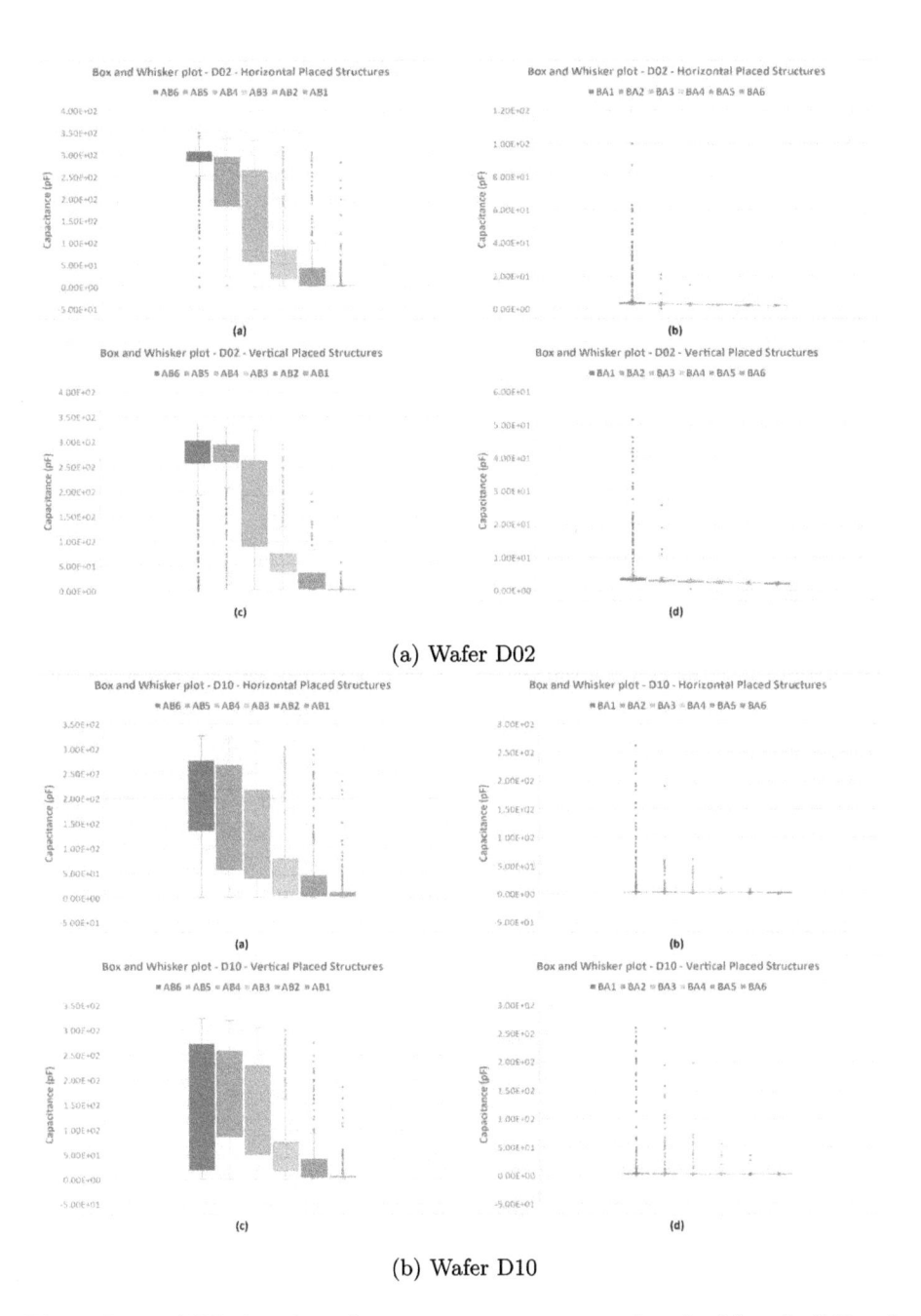

Fig. 8. Box and Whisker plots of capacitance measurement data for (a) wafer D02 and (b) wafer D10.

- 26 overlay measurements of each die. Overlay error is chosen in X direction if the capacitance values are from the horizontal structures, and in Y direction if they are from the vertical structures.
- Die positions in X and Y directions.
- Instances' indices.

Since the data is collected from only two wafers, thus, for each horizontal or vertical test structure, the dataset from two wafers were concatenated, then the training and testing set are divided with a ratio of 80-20. The *Extra Tree Regressor* model was selected for this experiment to predict the capacitance value of different test structures. The reason for this is based on the previous experiment results, *Extra Tree Regressor* performed the best compared to other Machine Learning models that were also tested. The hyperparameters of the model were chosen to be the same as the last experiment, with forest size 60 and minimum sample split size 2. To validate the performance after training, R^2 and MSE metrics were used.

Results and Discussions. Results of applying DBSCAN algorithm to clean measured capacitance data of vertical-placed BA1, BA2, and AB6 test structures from wafer D02 are shown in Fig. 9. From the graphs, we can see that DBSCAN has performed well in the task of cleaning data. For the capacitance measurements of BA2 structures, there are only a few outliers, and the algorithm can spot and replace all of them. This results in the clean dataset with smaller variance compared to the original data. For BA1 structures, there are more failures and abnormalities, yet DBSCAN can detect and clean most of them. However, for AB6 structures, there are a lot of failures, and thus, the data after cleaning is still very noisy. In general, as the gap between M1A and M1B layers of BAx structures is fairly large, capacitance data collected for those structures contains few outliers. Thus, data after applied DBSCAN is clean with most of the outliers removed. Meanwhile, for ABx structures, the distance between two metal

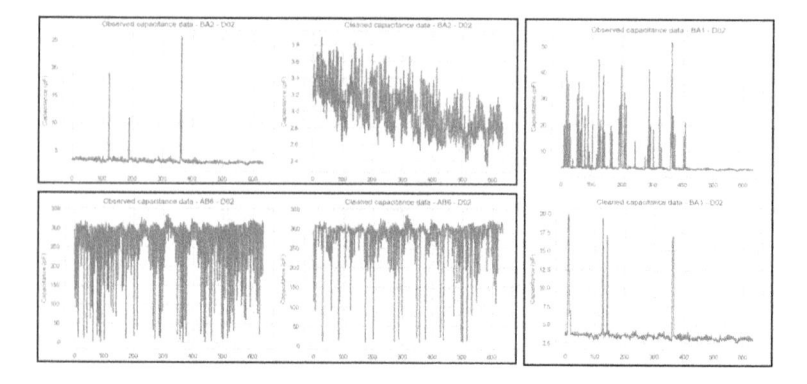

Fig. 9. Examples showing the results of data cleaning with DBSCAN applied to capacitance data of vertically placed BA1, BA2, and AB6 structures from wafer D02.

layers is small, which causes the failures happening more frequently. Therefore, the capacitance data of ABx structures is very noisy, making it hard for the DBSCAN to clean most of the outliers.

Table 4. Comparison of prediction performance of *Extra Tree Regressor* using raw overlay data and clean data after applying DBSCAN for outliers removal.

Raw data			Data after data cleaning		
Device	R^2	$MSE(nF^2)$	Device	R^2	$MSE(nF^2)$
AB6	0.612	4976.159	AB6	0.524	5802.344
AB5	0.368	4697.836	AB5	0.471	3668.759
AB4	0.472	4617.266	AB4	0.588	3513.079
AB3	0.632	1300.198	AB3	0.565	1037.417
AB2	0.582	309.921	AB2	0.613	260.188
AB1	0.113	145.959	AB1	0.220	42.433
BA6	0.802	0.006	BA6	0.828	0.004
BA5	0.365	0.026	BA5	0.823	0.006
BA4	−0.356	0.131	BA4	0.841	0.009
BA3	0.679	3.579	BA3	0.721	2.993
BA2	0.067	69.113	BA2	0.803	15.528
BA1	0.742	182.100	BA1	0.950	0.077

We have conducted an experiment to substantiate the application of DBSCAN algorithm as outlier detection method and if it may negatively affect the performance of the regression models. Table 4 shows the prediction results with raw data (without applying DBSCAN) and clean data (after applying DBSCAN). We opted for DBSCAN, as the structures from AB1 to AB6 contain many outliers, which do not really have any related trend with the overlay data. Future work can be extended towards appending other relevant input features along with overlay input to reorient outlier analysis and removal/reduction strategy. After the data cleaning step, the *Extra Tree Regressor* was trained to predict capacitance value of test structures. Table 5 and Table 6 show the prediction results after training.

It is clear that the trained Machine Learning model performed well with the BAx structures, where the R^2 scores of most of the tests are greater than 0.8, while the MSE are small. For the structures BA4, BA5, BA6, the MSE metrics from all the tests are close to 0, whereas for BA1 and BA2 structures, the MSE values are larger, but still smaller than 20 pF^2. In contrast, the prediction accuracy of the regressor model is low for the structures of AB1, AB2, ..., AB6. In most of the tests, the R^2 values are only around 0.6, while the MSE of those tests even goes up to the values of thousands pF^2. The reason for the low performance is that the capacitance dataset of ABx structures is very noisy even after cleaning

Table 5. Examples of performance results of *Extra Tree Regressor* using overlay data from different DBO step when predicting capacitance values of horizontal placed structures.

Test Structures	ADI DBO		AEI DBO		CMP DBO	
	R^2	MSE	R^2	MSE	R^2	MSE
AB6	0.652	1832.295	0.674	1718.611	0.666	1762.366
AB5	0.784	2075.884	0.778	2136.266	0.778	2141.364
AB4	0.864	1446.689	0.866	1420.37	0.865	1429.711
AB3	0.647	1972.332	0.681	1781.803	0.658	1911.048
AB2	0.593	157.465	0.615	148.941	0.614	149.283
AB1	0.658	90.119	0.659	89.752	0.623	99.097
BA6	0.964	0.003	0.966	0.003	0.968	0.003
BA5	0.865	0.004	0.82	0.004	0.867	0.004
BA4	0.851	0.006	0.826	0.006	0.863	0.006
BA3	0.803	0.014	0.865	0.012	0.815	0.013
BA2	0.828	4.458	0.876	4.655	0.805	5.036
BA1	0.853	9.586	0.849	9.853	0.806	12.664

Table 6. Examples of performance results of *Extra Tree Regressor* using overlay data from different DBO step when predicting capacitance values of vertical placed structures.

Test Structures	ADI DBO		AEI DBO		CMP DBO	
	R^2	MSE	R^2	MSE	R^2	MSE
AB6	0.524	5802.344	0.528	5748.09	0.563	5330.72
AB5	0.471	3668.759	0.417	4044.306	0.457	3768.842
AB4	0.588	3513.079	0.598	3426.801	0.562	3739.637
AB3	0.565	1037.417	0.584	991.975	0.568	1030.288
AB2	0.613	260.188	0.613	260.644	0.632	247.553
AB1	0.22	42.433	0.206	43.191	0.179	44.666
BA6	0.95	0.077	0.951	0.076	0.947	0.082
BA5	0.803	15.528	0.812	14.763	0.812	14.778
BA4	0.721	2.993	0.724	2.967	0.734	2.853
BA3	0.814	0.009	0.828	0.009	0.792	0.01
BA2	0.823	0.006	0.836	0.006	0.798	0.007
BA1	0.828	0.004	0.832	0.004	0.791	0.005

(a) Horizontal structures

(b) Vertical structures

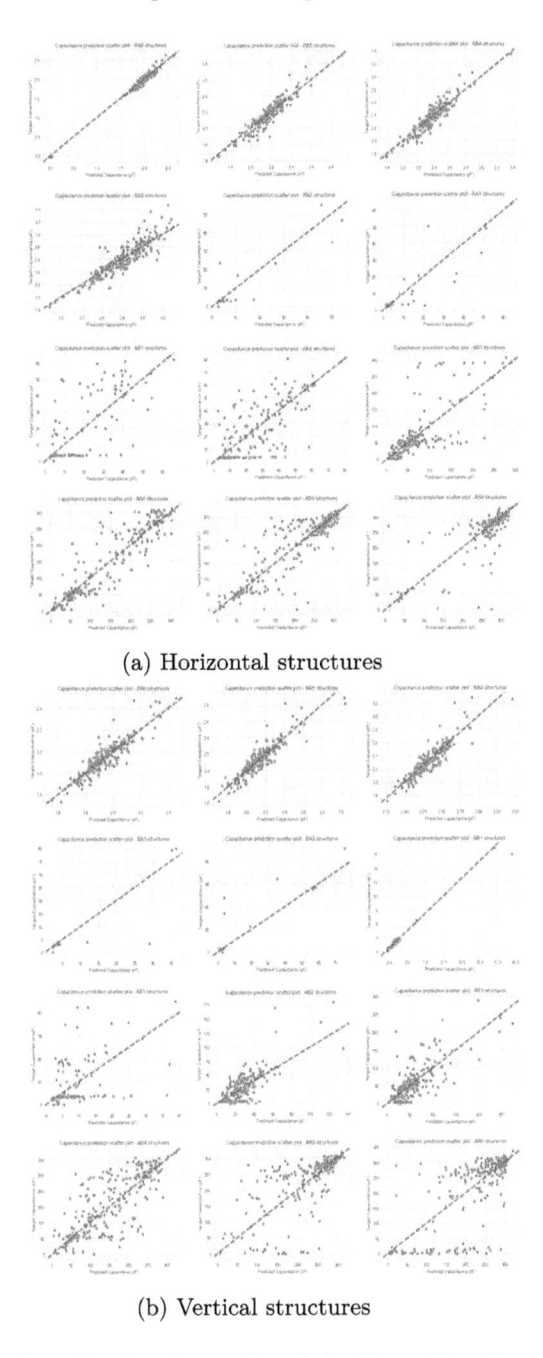

Fig. 10. Scatter plots showing the results of the Extra Tree Regressor model when predicting the capacitance value of (a) horizontal-placed structures and (b) vertical-placed structures.

by DBSCAN. Therefore, it is hard for any regression algorithms to achieve decent performance. Comparing the performance of the *Extra Tree Regressor* model when using different DBO data, we can see that the model works best when it was trained and tested by AEI overlay data. While for ADI and CMP overlay data, the performance was slightly decreased. The reason for this has been discussed earlier in the previous section, as the AEI overlay data is more stable than ADI and CMP. The visualizations of the model's performance on testing dataset are shown in Fig. 10a and Fig. 10b. The scatter plots in those figures clearly describe the trend of the tables above, since the points spread far away from the $x = y$ line for ABx structures, while they fit closely for BAx structures.

4 Conclusions

This work aims to analyse the overlay data in the semiconductor manufacturing and to make use of the overlay measurements from early steps in the process to predict electrical property of the final fabricated structures using machine learning techniques. Several data-driven techniques were developed to predict critical dimension measurements from overlay metrology data, in particular, the distance between two metal layers of the test structures. The prediction accuracy of all models is reasonable, with *Extra Tree Regressor* being the best performing algorithm, as the R^2 values in all cases were close to 0.9 and the MSE values were close to 0. We demonstrated the applicability of appropriate machine learning models to improve the throughput, as now, the critical dimensions of every wafer can be predicted from the overlay metrology data, which reduces the number of wafers needed to be measured by the physical CD-SEM tools. Future motivation is to include defective test structures (with short circuits or line breaks) as well as larger datasets (measuring more wafers from different lots from well optimized process steps) to improve the predictive performance. Furthermore, to consider including other metrology data, such as mask measurement data, resist thickness, line width roughness, etc. and further optimization using hyperparameters tuning techniques such as Grid Search, Random Search, or Bayesian Optimization are our future directives.

References

1. Bode, C., et al.: Run-to-run control and performance monitoring of overlay in semiconductor manufacturing. Control. Eng. Pract. **12**(7), 893–900 (2004). https://doi.org/10.1016/S0967-0661(03)00154-0
2. Breton, M., et al.: Electrical test prediction using hybrid metrology and machine learning. In: Metrology, Inspection, and Process Control for Microlithography XXXI, vol. 10145, pp. 16–23. SPIE (2017). https://doi.org/10.1117/12.2261091
3. Ngo, A.T., et al.: Machine learning based edge placement error analysis and optimization: a systematic review. IEEE Trans. Semicond. Manuf. (2022). https://doi.org/10.1109/TSM.2022.3217326
4. Orji, N.G., et al.: Metrology for the next generation of semiconductor devices. Nat. Electron. **1**(10), 532–547 (2018). https://doi.org/10.1038/s41928-018-0150-9

5. Pedregosa, F., et al.: Scikit-learn: machine learning in python. J. Mach. Learn. Res. **12**, 2825–2830 (2011)
6. Prasad, D.J.L., et al.: Diffraction based overlay metrology for double patterning technologies. In: Recent Advances in Nanofabrication Techniques and Applications, p. 433 (2011)
7. Rana, N., et al.: Leveraging advanced data analytics, machine learning, and metrology models to enable critical dimension metrology solutions for advanced integrated circuit nodes. J. Micro/Nanolithogr. MEMS MOEMS **13**(4), 041415–041415 (2014). https://doi.org/10.1117/1.JMM.13.4.041415
8. Saravanan, C.S., et al.: Evaluating diffraction based overlay metrology for double patterning technologies. In: Metrology, Inspection, and Process Control for Microlithography XXII, vol. 6922, pp. 125–136. SPIE (2008). https://doi.org/10.1117/12.774736
9. Vaid, A., et al.: A holistic metrology approach: hybrid metrology utilizing scatterometry, cd-afm, and cd-sem. In: Metrology, Inspection, and Process Control for Microlithography XXV, vol. 7971, pp. 21–40. SPIE (2011). https://doi.org/10.1117/12.881632

Comparing Deep Reinforcement Learning Algorithms in Two-Echelon Supply Chains

Francesco Stranieri[1,2] and Fabio Stella[1]

[1] University of Milan-Bicocca, 20125 Milan, Italy
[2] Polytechnic of Turin, 10129 Turin, Italy
francesco.stranieri@polito.it

Abstract. In this study, we analyze and compare the performance of state-of-the-art deep reinforcement learning algorithms for solving the supply chain inventory management problem. This complex sequential decision-making problem consists of determining the optimal quantity of products to be produced and shipped across different warehouses over a given time horizon. In particular, we present a mathematical formulation of a two-echelon supply chain environment with stochastic and seasonal demand, which allows managing an arbitrary number of warehouses and product types. Through a rich set of numerical experiments, we compare the performance of different deep reinforcement learning algorithms under various supply chain structures, topologies, demands, capacities, and costs. The results of the experimental plan indicate that deep reinforcement learning algorithms outperform traditional inventory management strategies, such as the static (s, Q)-policy. Furthermore, this study provides detailed insight into the design and development of an open-source software library that provides a customizable environment for solving the supply chain inventory management problem using a wide range of data-driven approaches.

Keywords: artificial intelligence · deep learning · reinforcement learning · smart manufacturing · inventory management

1 Introduction

Supply chain inventory management (SCIM) is a *sequential decision-making problem* consisting of determining the optimal quantity of products to produce at the factory and to ship to different distribution warehouses over a given time horizon. As evidenced by the helpful roadmap of [2], deep reinforcement learning (DRL) algorithms are rarely applied to the SCIM field, although they can be used to develop near-optimal policies that are difficult, or impossible at worst, to achieve using traditional methods. Indeed, the uncertain and stochastic nature of products demand, as well as lead times, represent significant obstacles for mathematical programming approaches to be effective, with specific reference to those cases where the modeling of SCIM's entities is reasonable, for example, assuming a finite capacity of warehouses [9].

Regarding the DRL algorithms that have been currently applied to tackle the SCIM problem, we found that they suffer the following *limitations*: i) given a supply chain *structure* (e.g., divergent[1] two-echelon[2]), no DRL algorithm has been deeply tested with respect to different *topologies* (i.e., by changing the number of warehouses); ii) no extensive experiments have been performed on the same supply chain structure by varying different *configurations* (e.g., demands, capacities, and costs); iii) no extension has been proposed for *comparing different DRL algorithms* and determining which one is more appropriate for a particular supply chain topology and configuration, as suggested by [1, 2].

Furthermore, relevant aspects of the SCIM problem have not yet been addressed efficiently [23], for example: i) the *sequence of events* required to reproduce and validate a simulation model is not always well-defined or given. Hence, making available a consistent and universal open-source SCIM environment can improve reusability and reproducibility, especially if implemented with standard APIs (like those of OpenAI Gym[3]. In this way, it is also possible to import DRL algorithms from reliable libraries and focus solely on their fine-tuning, instead of developing them from scratch; ii) DRL algorithms are typically compared with some standard *static reorder policies*. However, their performances are not always compared with those achieved by an oracle, i.e., a baseline who knows the optimal action to take a priori, thus making it difficult to evaluate the DRL effectiveness in real-world environments (the only paper in which an oracle is introduced is [6]); iii) none of the DRL papers available in the specialized literature considers a *multi-product approach*, whereas it has been considered relating to other solution methods [23]. Considering more than one product type increases the dimensionality and complexity of the problem, consequently requiring an efficient implementation of the SCIM environment and DRL algorithms.

This paper makes the following *contributions* to the SCIM decision-making problem:

- Design and formulation of a stochastic and divergent two-echelon SCIM environment under seasonal demand, which allows an arbitrary number of warehouses and product types to be managed.
- Comparison of a set of state-of-the-art DRL algorithms in terms of their ability to find an optimal policy, i.e., a policy which maximizes the SCIM's profit as achieved by an oracle.

---

[1] In a *linear* supply chain, each participant has one predecessor and one successor; in a *divergent* supply chain, each has one predecessor but can have multiple successors, while the opposite is true in a *convergent* supply chain. Finally, in a *general* supply chain, each participant can have several predecessors and several successors.

[2] A supply chain can include multiple stages, called formally *echelons*, through which the stocks are moved to reach the customer. When the number of echelons is greater than one, we refer to a *multi-echelon* supply chain.

[3] The OpenAI Gym library is available on https://www.gymlibrary.dev.

- Evaluation of performances achieved by state-of-the-art DRL algorithms and comparison to a static reorder policy, i.e., an (s, Q)-policy, whose optimal parameters have been set through a data-driven approach.
- Design and run of a rich experimental plan involving different SCIM topologies and configurations as well as values of hyperparameters associated with DRL algorithms'.
- Design and development of an open-source library for solving the SCIM problem[4], thus embracing the open science principles and guaranteeing reproducible results.

The rest of the paper is organized as follows: Sect. 2 is devoted to introducing and providing main reinforcement learning (RL) definitions and notation, also highlighting how RL approaches have dealt with the SCIM problem; in this section, we also describe the state-of-the-art DRL algorithms and how they have been used to address the SCIM problem. Section 3 describes the main methodological contributions of this paper. The rich experimental plan is then reported in Sect. 4, while the results of numerical experiments are presented in Sect. 5. Lastly, discussions and conclusions are given in Sect. 6.

2 Literature Review

While reinforcement learning has recently achieved remarkable results in the field of artificial intelligence, mainly when applied to video games and gaming in a more general sense [13,18,20], its deployment in industrial settings has been less extensive. Despite RL proving to be effective in solving complex sequential decision-making problems, its translation into industrial use cases is still emerging, devising a concrete opportunity for further explore its potentialities [23].

Essentially, RL adopts the Markov Decision Process (MDP) framework to represent the interactions between a learning agent and an environment [19]. As shown in Fig. 1, at each time step t, the agent observes the current state of the environment, $S_t \in \mathcal{S}$, chooses an action, $A_t \in \mathcal{A}(S_t)$, and obtains a reward, $R_{t+1} \in \mathcal{R} \subset \mathbb{R}$; then, the environment transitions into a new state, S_{t+1}. The goal of RL is thus to find an optimal policy, $\pi_* : \mathcal{S} \rightarrow \mathcal{A}$, that maximizes the *expected discounted return*, $G_t = \sum_{k=t+1}^{T} \gamma^{k-t-1} R_k$, where $0 \leq \gamma \leq 1$ is a hyperparameter called *discount rate*.

One of the most common approaches for solving the SCIM problem through RL algorithms turns out to be Q-learning. This approach is based on a tabular and temporal-difference (TD) algorithm that learns how to determine the *value* of an action A_t in a state S_t, referred to as the Q-value, in accordance with the following update rule: $Q(S_t, A_t) \leftarrow Q(S_t, A_t) + \alpha \delta_t$, where $0 \leq \alpha \leq 1$ is a hyperparameter called *learning rate*, and $\delta_t = [R_{t+1} + \gamma \max_a Q(S_{t+1}, a) - Q(S_t, A_t)]$ is the TD error. Q-values of each state-action pair are stored in a table, known as

---

[4] Our open-source library is available on https://github.com/frenkowski/SCIMAI-Gym.

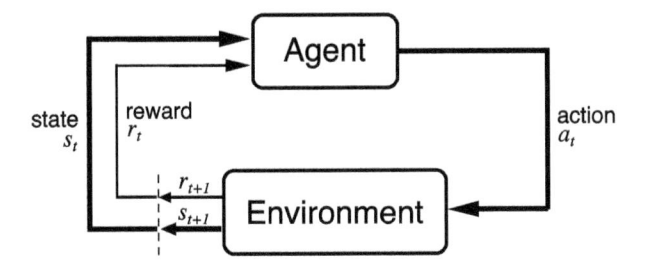

Fig. 1. Agent-environment interface in an MDP (taken from [19]).

Q-table, where each state is represented by a row and each action by a column. Through the Q-learning algorithm, Q-values associated with each state-action pair are estimated and, once convergence has been achieved (which is guaranteed under certain conditions [7]), an optimal policy can be easily obtained by identifying, for each state, the action with the highest Q-value, that is, $\pi_*(S_t) = \arg\max_a Q(S_t, a)$.

In [3], which is one of the most cited RL articles about SCIM, the authors proposed an approach based on Q-learning to address (a *centralized* variant of) the SCIM problem consisting of a linear supply chain with four participants. In particular, they defined the current system state as a vector consisting of the four inventory positions in terms of current stock levels. However, considering that inventory positions thus defined may take infinite values, applying this strategy appears unfeasible since the Q-table would be in turn infinite. Consequently, the authors *discretized* the state space into nine intervals. In this way, the possible state values amount to 9^4. Regarding actions, their approach determines the number of products to order via the $d+x$ policy; precisely, if a participant in the previous time step received a request for d product units from the succeeding stage, the $d+x$ *policy* requires ordering $d+x$ units to the preceding stage in the current time step. The learning process's objective is hence to determine the value of the unknown variable x according to the given system state. For limiting the Q-table size, x was *constrained* by the authors to belong to $[0, 3]$ so that the possible number of actions amounts to 4^4.

Obviously, by defining restricted state and action spaces, the resulting Q-table appears to be more manageable. However, analyzing various RL studies [23], it becomes evident that the Q-tables implemented are typically huge and, thus, *unscalable*. For example, the Q-table adopted by [3] has a number of cells equal to $(9^4 \cdot 4^4 =)$ 1679616, equivalent to the number of states multiplied by the number of actions. Consequently, expanding the size of the state or action spaces might not be feasible, as the Q-tables can no longer be handled.

Consequently, tabular RL methods can only be applied to discretized or constrained state and action spaces. However, discretization leads to a *loss of crucial information*, in addition to being unsuitable for real-world scenarios; thus, we need improved RL methods to address the SCIM problem effectively.

In this respect, deep reinforcement learning is a combination of RL with deep learning (DL) which promises to scale to previously intractable decision-making problems, i.e., environments with high dimensional state and action spaces. DL is rooted into artificial neural networks (ANNs) [10], which are universal approximators capable of providing an optimal approximation of *highly nonlinear functions*. In practice, function parameters θ are adjusted during the learning process in order to maximize the expected return (or, alternatively, to minimize the TD error).

The DRL algorithms we implemented belong to the policy-based methods, which can learn a *parameterized* and stochastic policy, $\pi_\theta \approx \pi_*$ with $\pi : \mathcal{A} \times \mathcal{S} \rightarrow [0,1]$, to select actions directly (as opposed to the Q-learning algorithm, which is part of value-based methods [19]). Inside them, policy gradient methods offer a considerable theoretical advantage through the *policy gradient theorem*, and the vanilla policy gradient (VPG) algorithm [21] is a natural result of this theorem; however, the *high variance* of gradient estimates usually results in policy update instabilities [22]. Also to mitigate this issue, [16] proposed an actor-critic algorithm (which means that a policy and a value function are simultaneously learned) called trust region policy optimization (TRPO), which bounds the difference between the new and the old policy in a *trust region*. Proximal policy optimization (PPO) [17] shares the same background as TRPO, but has demonstrated comparable or superior performance while being significantly *simpler* to implement and tune. Asynchronous advantage actor-critic (A3C) [12] is also one of the available state-of-the-art actor-critic algorithms. Its core idea is to have different agents interacting with different representations of the environment, each with its parameters. Periodically (and asynchronously), they update a global ANN that incorporates *shared parameters*. For interested readers, an in-depth and more rigorous discussion on the various DRL algorithms can be found in [4].

To the best of the authors' knowledge, only few papers have implemented DRL algorithms to solve the SCIM problem, despite some restrictions. More in detail, an *extension* of deep Q-network (DQN) [13] has been proposed in [14] to solve (a *decentralized* variant of) the SCIM problem. The authors revealed that a DQN agent, which basically involves an ANN instead of a Q-table to return the Q-value for a state-action pair, can learn a near-optimal policy when other supply chain participants follow a base-stock policy; under a *base-stock policy*, each participant orders in each time step t a quantity to bring its stocks equal to a fixed number s, known as the base-stock level, to determine in an optimal way. Because DQN requires a restricted action space cardinality, the authors performed numerical experiments using a $d+x$ policy, with x constrained to one of the following intervals: $[-2, +2]$, $[-5, +5]$, and $[-8, +8]$.

Alternatively, authors in [15] proposed the VPG algorithm to address a two-echelon supply chain with stochastic and seasonal demand. Due to storage capacity constraints, the authors designed a *dynamic action space*. As a result, the number of products to ship is determined also by considering the number of stocks actually present in the warehouses. To evaluate the VPG performance, three different numerical experiments are presented, and the results show that the VPG agent is able to outperform the (s, Q)-policy employed as a baseline in all three experiments. In this context, the (s, Q)-*policy* can be expressed by a rule: at each time step t, the current stock level is compared to the reorder point s. If the stock level falls below the reorder point s, then the (s, Q)-policy orders Q units of product; otherwise, it does not take any action. Also in this case, the parameters s and Q are to be determined optimally.

Using the same supply chain structure but with ten warehouses and a normal distribution, authors in [5] applied and tuned the A3C algorithm for two different numerical experiments. The authors restricted the action space by implementing a *state-dependent* base-stock policy, and the results show that A3C can achieve performance comparable to state-of-the-art heuristics and approximate dynamic programming algorithms, despite its initial tuning remaining computationally intensive.

Finally, in the experimental scenario analyzed by [1], a general four-echelon supply chain with two nodes per echelon is presented. The system state consists of product quantity currently available and in transit across the supply chain, plus *future* customer demands. To deal with the optimization problem, the authors proposed the PPO algorithm, while a deterministic linear programming agent (i.e., considering a deterministic demand) is employed as a baseline. Results of numerical experiments show that PPO still achieves satisfactory results.

3   Problem Definition

The SCIM environment we propose is primarily motivated by what was presented and discussed in [8,15]. Inspired by these works, we designed a divergent two-echelon supply chain that includes a *factory* that can produce various *product types*, a *factory warehouse*, and a certain number of *distribution warehouses*; an example of this structure is shown in Fig. 2.

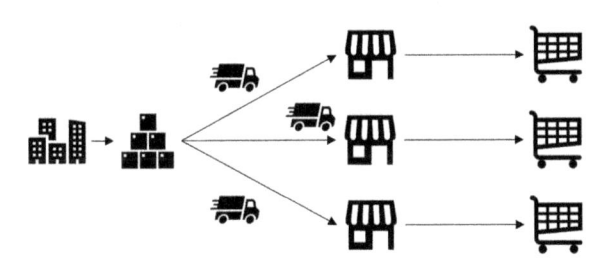

Fig. 2. A divergent two-echelon supply chain consisting of a factory and its warehouse (first echelon), plus three distribution warehouses (second echelon). Shopping carts represent customers' demands.

In our formulation, we assume that the factory produces I different product types. For each product type i, the factory decides, at every time step t, its respective production level $a_{i,0,t}$ (we assume $j = 0$ for the factory and $1 \leq j \leq J$ for the distribution warehouses), that is, how many units to produce, considering a fixed production cost of $z_{i,0}$ per unit. Moreover, the factory warehouse is associated with a maximum capacity of $c_{i,0}$ units for each product type i (this means that the overall capacity is given by $\sum_{i=0}^{I} c_{i,0} = c_0$). The cost of storing one unit of product type i at the factory warehouse is $z_{i,0}^S$ per time step, while the corresponding stock level at time t equals $q_{i,0,t}$. At every time step t, $a_{i,j,t}$ units of product type i are shipped from the factory warehouse to the distribution warehouse j, with an associated transportation cost of $z_{i,j}^T$ per unit. For each product type i, each distribution warehouse j has a maximum capacity of $c_{i,j}$ ($\sum_{i=0}^{I} c_{i,j} = c_j$), a storage cost of $z_{i,j}^S$ per unit, and a stock level at time t equal to $q_{i,j,t}$. The demand for product type i at distribution warehouse j for time step t is equivalent to $d_{i,j,t}$ units, while each unit of product type i is sold to customers at sale price p_i (which is identical across all warehouses).

Products are non-perishable and provided in discrete quantities. Additionally, we assume that each warehouse is legally obligated to fulfill all the submitted orders. Consequently, if an order for a certain time step exceeds the corresponding stock level, a penalty cost per unsatisfied unit is applied (the penalty cost for product type i is obtained by multiplying the penalty coefficient z_i^P by the sale price value p_i). Unsatisfied orders are maintained over time, and we design them as a negative stock level (which corresponds to *backordering*); this also implies that when the penalty coefficient is particularly high (e.g., $z_i^P \geq 1$), the agent may not be able to generate a positive profit if it causes backlog orders. Consequently, it should prefer a policy that leads to accumulating stocks in advance in order to pay storage costs rather than penalty costs.

3.1 Environment Formulation

In this subsection, we formalize the RL problem as an MDP. More precisely, we introduce and define the *main components* of the SCIM environment that we propose in this paper: the state vector, the action vector, and the reward function.

The *state vector* includes all current stock levels for each warehouse and product type, plus the last τ demand values, and is defined as follows:

$$s_t = (q_{0,0,t}, \ldots, q_{I,J,t}, d_{t-\tau}, \ldots, d_{t-1}),$$

where $d_{t-1} = (d_{0,1,t-1}, \ldots, d_{I,J,t-1})$. It is worth noticing that the actual demand d_t for the current time step t will not be known until the next time step $t+1$. This implementation choice ensures that the agent may benefit from learning the demand pattern so as to integrate a sort of *demand forecasting* directly into the policy. Additionally, we include the last demand values in order to enable the agent to have *limited knowledge* about the demand history and, consequently, to gain a basic comprehension of its fluctuations (similar to what was made originally by [8]). In our SCIM implementation, the agent can access the demand values of the last five time steps, even if preliminary results suggest that comparable performances are obtained by accessing the last three or four time steps.

Regarding the *action vector*, we chose to implement a *continuous action space* (i.e., the ANN generates the action value directly) consisting, for each product type, of the number of units to produce at the factory and of the number of units to ship to each distribution warehouse:

$$a_t = (a_{0,0,t}, \ldots, a_{I,J,t}). \tag{1}$$

Usually, a relatively small and *identical upper bound* is typically adopted for all the action values to reduce the computational effort. However, the drawback is that this might lead to a significant drop in terms of performance. Indeed, if the upper bound is set too small, the agent may select an inefficient action given that the optimal one is outside the admissible range. Otherwise, if the upper bound is set too high, the agent may repeatedly choose an incoherent action, i.e., one that falls within the admissible range but exceeds a specified maximum capacity, consequently slowing down the training process.

Our implementation thus provides a continuous action space with an *independent upper bound* for each action value, in order to find a trade-off between efficiency and performance. In practical terms, the lower bound for each value is simply zero. In fact, it would be illogical to produce or ship negative quantities of products. Conversely, the upper bound for each distribution warehouse corresponds to its maximum capacity with respect to each product type (by referring to Eq. (1), $0 \leq a_{i,j,t} \leq c_{i,j}$). To guarantee that the factory can adequately handle the various demands, its upper bound amounts to the sum of all warehouses' capacities with regard to each product type ($0 \leq a_{i,0,t} \leq \sum_{j=0}^{J} c_{i,j}$). We expect to improve both efficiency and performance with this intuition, as the action space is bounded (and hence restricted) but contains only coherent (and possibly optimal) actions. We specify that available stocks are not explicitly considered when the agent chooses an action. However, producing or shipping a number of stocks that it is not possible to store leads to a cost and, therefore, an *implicit penalty* for the agent. We also assume that there are no lead times both for production and transportation (or, to refer to the literature, we consider *constant lead times equal to 0*). This assumption allows us to isolate the primary dynamics of the problem without the additional effects of lead times, thus making the problem easier to address and manage.

To evaluate the performance of the DRL agents, we simulate a seasonal behavior by representing the *demand* as a co-sinusoidal function with a stochastic component, defined according to the following equation:

$$d_{i,j,t} = \left\lfloor \frac{d_{max_i}}{2} \left(1 + \cos\left(\frac{4\pi(2ij+t)}{T}\right)\right) + \mathcal{U}\left(0, d_{var_i}\right) \right\rfloor, \tag{2}$$

where $\lfloor \cdot \rfloor$ is the floor function, d_{max_i} is the maximum demand value for each product type, $\mathcal{U}$ is a random variable uniformly distributed on the support $(0, d_{var_i})$ representing the demand variations (i.e., the *uncertainty*), and T is the final time step of the episode. At each time step t, the demand may vary for each distribution warehouse j and product type i while maintaining the same behavior, as can be seen in Fig. 3.

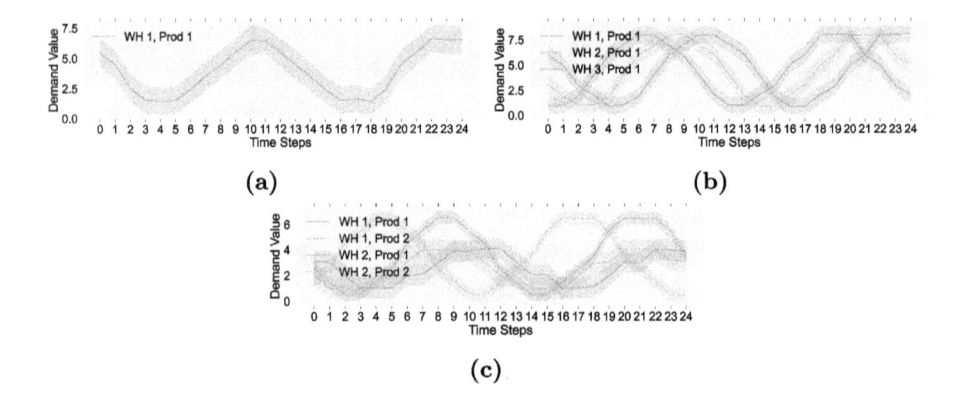

Fig. 3. Some instances of different demands behavior generated according to Eq. (2) for different topologies and configurations of the SCIM problem: (a) one product type and one distribution warehouse with $d_{max} = 5$ and $d_{var} = 3$; (b) one product type and three distribution warehouses with $d_{max} = 7$ and $d_{var} = 2$; and (c) two product types and two distribution warehouses with $d_{max} = (3, 6)$ and $d_{var} = (2, 1)$ (referring to the values in round brackets, the first denotes the first product type, whereas the second indicates the second product type).

The *reward function* for each time step t is then defined as follows:

$$r_t = \sum_{j=1}^{J}\sum_{i=0}^{I} p_i \cdot d_{i,j,t} - \sum_{i=0}^{I} z_{i,0} \cdot a_{i,0,t} - \sum_{j=1}^{J}\sum_{i=0}^{I} z_{i,j}^{T} \cdot a_{i,j,t} \\ - \sum_{j=0}^{J}\sum_{i=0}^{I} z_{i,j}^{S} \cdot \max(q_{i,j,t}, 0) + \sum_{j=0}^{J}\sum_{i=0}^{I} z_{i}^{P} \cdot p_i \cdot \min(q_{i,j,t}, 0). \tag{3}$$

The first term represents revenues, the second one production costs, while the third one transportation costs. The fourth term is the overall storage costs. The function max is implemented to avoid negative inventories (i.e., backlog orders) from being counted. The last term denotes the penalty costs, which is introduced with a plus sign because stock levels would already be negative in the eventuality of unsatisfied orders. The DRL agents' goal is thus to *maximize the supply chain profit* as defined in the reward function. By design, revenues are always calculated regardless of whether the demand is effectively satisfied; however, in the event of unsatisfied orders, the penalty costs will impact the actual return for each time step in which backlog orders are counted (in the amount of the penalty coefficient).

Finally, the *state's updating rule* is defined as follows:

$$s_{t+1} = (\min[(q_{0,0,t} + a_{0,0,t} - \sum_{j=1}^{J} a_{0,j,t}), c_{0,0}], \cdots,$$

$$\min\left[(q_{I,J,t} + a_{I,J,t} - d_{I,J,t}), c_{I,J}\right], d_{t+1-\tau}, \cdots, d_t).$$

This implies that, at the beginning of the next time step, the factory's stocks are equal to the initial stocks, plus the units produced, minus the stocks shipped. Similarly, the distribution warehouses' stocks are equal to the initial stocks, plus the units received, minus the current demand. When surplus stocks are generated, a storage cost is imposed; otherwise, a penalty cost is considered. Lastly, the demand values included in the state vector are also updated, discarding the oldest value and concatenating the most recent one.

4 Numerical Experiments

Once the environment has been specified, we implemented the agents according to three different state-of-the-art DRL algorithms: A3C, PPO, and VPG, which have been briefly introduced in Sect. 2. In this respect, we relied on the implementations made available by Ray[5], an open-source Python framework that is bundled with RLib, a scalable RL library, and Tune, a scalable hyperparameter tuning library. An advantage of Ray is that it natively supports OpenAI Gym. As a result, we exploited the OpenAI Gym APIs to develop the *simulator* representative of the environment and used for the agents' training process.

To assess and compare performances achieved by the adopted DRL algorithms, we also implemented a static reorder policy known in the specialized literature as the (s, Q)-policy. In our implementation, we opted to make reordering decisions independently; this means that the (s, Q)-policy parameters, $s_{i,j}$ and $Q_{i,j}$, can differ for each warehouse and product type (this policy is still defined *static* because these parameters do not change over time). To find the best possible parameters that maximize Eq. (3), we developed a *data-driven approach* based on Bayesian optimization (BO). In this way, the solution method does not require making any assumptions or simplifications, and hence it is no longer problem-dependent; therefore, it can be applied to any SCIM topology and configuration just as it happens for DRL algorithms (they share, in fact, the same identical simulator).

To compare DRL and BO approaches, we also implemented an *oracle*, that is, a baseline that knows the real demand value for each product type and distribution warehouse in advance and can accordingly select the optimal actions to take a priori.

---

[5] The Ray library is available on https://www.ray.io.

4.1 Scenarios Considered

A rich set of numerical experiments have been designed and performed to compare the performances of DRL algorithms and BO under *three different scenarios*. Each scenario is associated with different demand patterns with respect to each product type and distribution warehouse (i.e., seasonal and stochastic fluctuations). Furthermore, each scenario has different capacities and costs for evaluating in-depth the adaptability and robustness of DRL algorithms.

Under the *one product type one distribution warehouse* (1P1W) scenario, the supply chain is set to manage just one product type. Accordingly, it consists of one factory, a factory warehouse, and one distribution warehouse; thus the input dimension of the ANN (representing the state vector) is equal to 7, given by the number of warehouses (i.e., 2, including the factory warehouse) times the number of product types (i.e., 1), plus the last demand values for each distribution warehouse and product type (i.e., 5), while the output dimension of the ANN (expressing the action vector) is 2, equivalent to the number of warehouses (including the factory warehouse) multiplied by the number of product types. Under the 1P1W scenario, which consists of five experiments (as summarized in Table 1 of the supplementary material[6]), sale prices and costs are manipulated so as to increase or decrease revenues and, consequently, the margin of return. Moreover, in the first experiment, we bound the warehouses' capacities in such a way that they are smaller than the maximum demand value (also considering the stochastic demand variation). This decision is made to study whether DRL algorithms are able to learn an efficient strategy, i.e., a strategy capable of predicting a *growing demand* and thus saving and shipping stocks in advance. Analogously, we expect a greater quantity of stocks to be stored and shipped when storage and transportation costs are low, while we expect the opposite when these costs are high. Finally, we generate multiple penalty coefficients to determine whether a hefty punishment forces DRL algorithms to be more or less effective, with particular attention to the more challenging experiments where low revenues and high costs are considered.

The *one product type three distribution warehouses* (1P3W) scenario concerns a more complex configuration, consisting of a factory, a factory warehouse, and three distribution warehouses. Even in this case, the supply chain still manages a single product type, while the input and output dimensions of the ANN are equal to 9 and 4, respectively; hence, the difficulty of the problem is increased because there is a higher number of both ANN parameters to be optimized and actions to be determined. The design of the five experiments follows that of the previous 1P1W scenario. However, a remarkable difference is found in storage capacities and costs (as depicted in Table 2 of the supplementary material (See Footnote 6)). In fact, we set warehouses' costs to be *directly proportional* to their corresponding capacities, that is, the less storage space we have, the more expensive it is to store a product. This scenario is also designed to investigate the DRL algorithms strategy when capacities increase, given that the search

---
[6] The supplementary material is available on https://github.com/frenkowski/SCIMAI-Gym.

space of optimal actions grows accordingly. Furthermore, we are interested in studying how DRL algorithms react when demand, with the associated costs (i.e., production and transportation), becomes greater than actual capacities, considering that the supply chain now consists of three distribution warehouses and, consequently, the SCIM problem becomes more challenging to be tackled.

Finally, in the *two product types two distribution warehouses* (2P2W) scenario, the supply chain consists of two product types, a factory with its warehouse, and two distribution warehouses. With this design, the number of parameters to optimize is still higher, considering that the ANN input dimension is equal to 26, while the ANN output dimension is 6. Due to computational time, we performed just three experiments under this scenario (as reported in Table 3 of the supplementary material (See Footnote 6)). Regarding the demand, we explore demand variations which can be different or equal, according to the specific experiment. Additionally, we thought of something different concerning storage capacities and, consequently, the search space of optimal actions. Indeed, in the last experiment, warehouses' capacities for the first product type are designed in descending order, while for the second product type in ascending order; this implies that, for example, the second distribution warehouse can store the minimum amount of stocks for the first product type and the maximum amount for the second product type. We expect that this *imbalance*, especially when combined with greater uncertainty, makes the SCIM problem more unexpected and, thus, more difficult to be effectively solved.

5 Results

To compare the performances between DRL algorithms, BO, and oracle, we simulated, for each scenario and experiment, 200 different episodes. Each episode consists of 25 time steps, and we reported the *average cumulative profit* achieved, i.e., the sum of the per-step profit at the last time step T. All experiments were run on a machine equipped with an Intel® Xeon® Platinum 8272CL CPU at 2.6 GHz and 16 GB of RAM. The hyperparameters of DRL algorithms selected for tuning have been chosen following what is presented in the Ray documentation and discussed in the papers [1,5] (they are reported in Table 4 of the supplementary material (See Footnote 6), along with their corresponding values). To early stop training instances associated with *bad hyperparameters configurations*, we also implemented, through Ray, the asynchronous successive halving (ASHA) scheduling algorithm [11]. It is important to note that the simulation results presented and commented in this section have been obtained by selecting, for each algorithm and experiment, the respective *best training instance*[7].

Results of numerical experiments under the 1P1W scenario are summarized in Table 1a. BO and PPO achieve a near-optimal profit in the first experiment where the demand is greater than warehouses' capacities, whereas A3C and VPG

---

[7] All the figures regarding the three scenario and related to the convergence and the behavior of DRL algorithms and BO are available on https://github.com/frenkowski/SCIMAI-Gym.

perform slightly worse. All DRL algorithms achieve comparable results in the second and simpler experiment, with higher revenues but lower transportation and penalty costs. In the third and more complex experiment, which, on the contrary, involves lower revenues and higher transportation costs and penalties, the optimal profit is relatively small, but PPO tends to behave better than other DRL algorithms. BO, PPO, and A3C obtain satisfactory profits in the fourth and more balanced experiment, with increasing revenues and maximum demand value but reducing uncertainty, while VPG seems to perform poorly. The main difficulty here is represented by a wider search space (caused by greater storage capacities) and higher storage costs, especially for the factory. In the fifth and last experiment, the demand uncertainty increases, the penalty costs decrease, and it is more expensive to maintain stocks at the distribution warehouse rather than at the factory, but all DRL algorithms achieve comparable and near-optimal results.

Table 1b summarizes the results for the 1P3W scenario, which in design is similar to the 1P1W scenario. The first experiment is characterized by a high maximum demand value, especially if compared with the capacities of the factory and of the first distribution warehouse; with this setting, BO performs worse than DRL algorithms. However, as PPO, it obtains a nearly optimal profit in the second experiment, where a simpler configuration is investigated. In the third and more challenging experiment, none of the algorithms achieves a profit greater than zero, with PPO achieving the worst one. Still, PPO outperforms A3C and VPG in the fourth and more balanced experiment, characterized by an increased search space and higher storage costs. Finally, BO and PPO achieve the best profits in the fifth experiment, where uncertainty and search space are increased, but fewer penalties are considered.

To conclude, Table 1 summarizes performances under the 2P2W scenario. The first experiment provides a balanced configuration, with maximum demand values and variations that change according to the specific product type, storage costs at the factory greater than those at the two distribution warehouses, and revenues particularly high for the first product type. Under such a mix, PPO achieves a good profit, as it also does A3C, which overcomes BO. For the second experiment, sales prices for the second product type are increased and, accordingly, the associated revenues grow as well. Even storage and transportation costs are decreased, while penalties increase. With this configuration, PPO still obtains a nearly optimal result, and the same happens for VPG, while BO also behaves well. In the third experiment, capacities are increased, and we design alternating storage costs; this means, for example, that maintaining stocks of the first product type at the factory warehouse is the most inexpensive option while maintaining stocks of the second product type is the most expensive. The results allow us to conclude that PPO, followed by VPG, continues to perform successfully, whereas BO seems to suffer the most.

Table 1. Results related to the three scenarios considered:(a)for the 1P1W scenario, it is possible to note how BO and PPO obtain near-optimal profits in general, while A3C and VPG seem more distant in terms of performance;(b)in the 1P3W scenario, PPO performs better than BO and other DRL algorithms on average, except in the third and more challenging experiment; (c)results concerning the 2P2W scenario suggest that PPO behaves well typically, whereas BO seems slightly inferior compared to the other DRL algorithms.

(a)

	A3C	PPO	VPG	BO	Oracle
Exp 1	870 ± 67	1213 ± 68	885 ± 66	**1226 ± 71**	1474 ± 45
Exp 2	1066 ± 94	1163 ± 66	1100 ± 77	**1224 ± 60**	1289 ± 68
Exp 3	−36 ± 74	**195 ± 43**	12 ± 61	101 ± 50	345 ± 18
Exp 4	1317 ± 60	1600 ± 62	883 ± 95	**1633 ± 39**	2046 ± 37
Exp 5	736 ± 45	838 ± 58	789 ± 51	**870 ± 67**	966 ± 55

(b)

	A3C	PPO	VPG	BO	Oracle
Exp 1	1606 ± 139	**2319 ± 122**	803 ± 154	486 ± 330	3211 ± 60
Exp 2	2196 ± 104	**3461 ± 120**	2568 ± 112	3193 ± 101	3848 ± 95
Exp 3	−2142 ± 128	−4337 ± 216	−2638 ± 121	**−1682 ± 196**	772 ± 21
Exp 4	−561 ± 237	**2945 ± 135**	656 ± 140	1256 ± 170	4389 ± 64
Exp 5	1799 ± 306	**2353 ± 131**	1341 ± 79	2203 ± 152	2783 ± 91

(c)

	A3C	PPO	VPG	BO	Oracle
Exp 1	2227 ± 178	**2783 ± 139**	1585 ± 184	2086 ± 173	3787 ± 102
Exp 2	1751 ± 83	**2867 ± 90**	2329 ± 98	2246 ± 114	3488 ± 63
Exp 3	1414 ± 128	**2630 ± 138**	2434 ± 156	552 ± 268	3549 ± 103

6 Discussions and Conclusions

Results of numerical experiments demonstrated that the SCIM environment we propose is *effective* in representing states, actions, and rewards; indeed, the DRL algorithms we implemented have achieved *nearly optimal solutions* in all three investigated scenarios. In detail, PPO is the one that better adapts to different topologies and configurations of the SCIM environment achieving higher profits than other algorithms on average, although it fails to reach a positive profit in the most challenging experiment of the 1P3W scenario. VPG frequently appears to converge to a local maximum that seems slightly distant from PPO, especially when the number of warehouses increases, but it still obtains acceptable results.

It is worthwhile to mention that the BO approach also shows remarkable results, especially when the search space of optimal actions is limited, as in the 1P1W scenario. When compared to DRL algorithms, the BO approach seems to suffer more when there are two product types or when the demand exceeds the capacities. This is mainly due to the static and non-dynamic nature of the (s, Q)-policy, which does not allow developing an effective strategy, for example, for saving stocks in advance, but, conversely, culminates in a *myopic behavior*. Nevertheless, the absence of hyperparameters to be tuned offers a considerable advantage.

6.1 Future Research

This paper can be extended and improved in many directions as:

- Develop a *more comprehensive SCIM environment*, for example, by considering additional configurations mentioned in [9] (e.g., different demand distributions or different customers' reactions to backordering).
- Take into account the *non-linearity of transportation costs* (e.g., introducing a fixed cost independent of the number of stocks shipped effectively), as well as *non-zero leading times*.
- Use *real-world data* to validate DRL algorithms and check whether they improve the performances of currently used SCIM systems in practice.

Lastly, even the BO approach could be *extended* to other standard static reorder policies, such as the base-stock policy, which has exactly half of the (s, Q)-policy parameters and can therefore enable faster convergence times.

References

1. Alves, J.C., Mateus, G.R.: Deep reinforcement learning and optimization approach for multi-echelon supply chain with uncertain demands. In: Lalla-Ruiz, E., Mes, M., Voß, S. (eds.) ICCL 2020. LNCS, vol. 12433, pp. 584–599. Springer, Cham (2020). https://doi.org/10.1007/978-3-030-59747-4_38
2. Boute, R.N., Gijsbrechts, J., van Jaarsveld, W., Vanvuchelen, N.: Deep reinforcement learning for inventory control: a roadmap. Eur. J. Oper. Res. **298**(2), 401–412 (2022). https://doi.org/10.1016/j.ejor.2021.07.016
3. Chaharsooghi, S.K., Heydari, J., Zegordi, S.H.: A reinforcement learning model for supply chain ordering management: an application to the beer game. Decis. Support Syst. **45**(4), 949–959 (2008). https://doi.org/10.1016/j.dss.2008.03.007
4. François-Lavet, V., Henderson, P., Islam, R., Bellemare, M.G., Pineau, J.: An introduction to deep reinforcement learning. Found. Trends Mach. Learn. **11**(3–4), 219–354 (2018). https://doi.org/10.1561/2200000071
5. Gijsbrechts, J., Boute, R.N., Mieghem, J.A.V., Zhang, D.J.: Can deep reinforcement learning improve inventory management? performance on lost sales, dual-sourcing, and multi-echelon problems. Manuf. Serv. Oper. Manag. **24**(3), 1349–1368 (2022). https://doi.org/10.1287/msom.2021.1064
6. Hubbs, C.D., Perez, H.D., Sarwar, O., Sahinidis, N.V., Grossmann, I.E., Wassick, J.M.: Or-gym: a reinforcement learning library for operations research problems (2020). https://doi.org/10.48550/ARXIV.2008.06319
7. Jaakkola, T., Jordan, M.I., Singh, S.P.: On the convergence of stochastic iterative dynamic programming algorithms. Neural Comput. **6**(6), 1185–1201 (1994). https://doi.org/10.1162/neco.1994.6.6.1185

8. Kemmer, L., von Kleist, H., de Rochebouët, D., Tziortziotis, N., Read, J.: Reinforcement learning for supply chain optimization. In: European Workshop on Reinforcement Learning, vol. 14 (2018)
9. de Kok, T., Grob, C., Laumanns, M., Minner, S., Rambau, J., Schade, K.: A typology and literature review on stochastic multi-echelon inventory models. Eur. J. Oper. Res. **269**(3), 955–983 (2018). https://doi.org/10.1016/j.ejor.2018.02.047
10. LeCun, Y., Bengio, Y., Hinton, G.: Deep learning. Nature **521**(7553), 436–444 (2015). https://doi.org/10.1038/nature14539
11. Li, L., et al.: A system for massively parallel hyperparameter tuning. In: Dhillon, I., Papailiopoulos, D., Sze, V. (eds.) Proceedings of Machine Learning and Systems, vol. 2, pp. 230–246 (2020)
12. Mnih, V., et al.: Asynchronous methods for deep reinforcement learning. In: Balcan, M.F., Weinberger, K.Q. (eds.) Proceedings of the 33rd International Conference on Machine Learning, vol. 48, pp. 1928–1937. PMLR, New York (2016)
13. Mnih, V., et al.: Human-level control through deep reinforcement learning. Nature **518**(7540), 529–533 (2015). https://doi.org/10.1038/nature14236
14. Oroojlooyjadid, A., Nazari, M., Snyder, L.V., Takáč, M.: A deep q-network for the beer game: deep reinforcement learning for inventory optimization. Manuf. Serv. Oper. Manag. **24**(1), 285–304 (2022). https://doi.org/10.1287/msom.2020.0939
15. Peng, Z., Zhang, Y., Feng, Y., Zhang, T., Wu, Z., Su, H.: Deep reinforcement learning approach for capacitated supply chain optimization under demand uncertainty. In: 2019 Chinese Automation Congress (CAC). IEEE (2019). https://doi.org/10.1109/cac48633.2019.8997498
16. Schulman, J., Levine, S., Abbeel, P., Jordan, M., Moritz, P.: Trust region policy optimization. In: Bach, F., Blei, D. (eds.) Proceedings of the 32nd International Conference on Machine Learning, vol. 37, pp. 1889–1897. PMLR, Lille (2015)
17. Schulman, J., Wolski, F., Dhariwal, P., Radford, A., Klimov, O.: Proximal policy optimization algorithms (2017). https://doi.org/10.48550/ARXIV.1707.06347
18. Silver, D., et al.: Mastering the game of go without human knowledge. Nature **550**(7676), 354–359 (2017). https://doi.org/10.1038/nature24270
19. Sutton, R.S., Barto, A.G.: Reinforcement Learning: An Introduction. MIT press, Cambridge (2018)
20. Vinyals, O., et al.: Grandmaster level in StarCraft II using multi-agent reinforcement learning. Nature **575**(7782), 350–354 (2019). https://doi.org/10.1038/s41586-019-1724-z
21. Williams, R.J.: Simple statistical gradient-following algorithms for connectionist reinforcement learning. Mach. Learn. **8**(3–4), 229–256 (1992). https://doi.org/10.1007/bf00992696
22. Wu, C., et al.: Variance reduction for policy gradient with action-dependent factorized baselines (2018). https://doi.org/10.48550/ARXIV.1803.07246
23. Yan, Y., Chow, A.H., Ho, C.P., Kuo, Y.H., Wu, Q., Ying, C.: Reinforcement learning for logistics and supply chain management: methodologies, state of the art, and future opportunities. Transport. Res. Part E: Logist. Transport. Rev. **162**, 102712 (2022). https://doi.org/10.1016/j.tre.2022.102712

Reinforcement Learning for Segmented Manufacturing

Nathalie Paul[1,2(✉)], Alexander Kister[3], Thorben Schnellhardt[4],
Maximilian Fetz[1,5], Dirk Hecker[1,2], and Tim Wirtz[1,2]

[1] Fraunhofer Institute for Intelligent Analysis and Information Systems IAIS, 53757 Sankt Augustin, Germany
{maximilian.elias.fetz,dirk.hecker,tim.wirtz}@iais.fraunhofer.de
[2] Fraunhofer Center for Machine Learning, Munich, Germany
nathalie.paul@iais.fraunhofer.de
[3] eScience Division (S.3), Federal Institute for Materials Research and Testing, 12205 Berlin, Germany
alexander.kister@bam.de
[4] Fraunhofer Institute for Machine Tools and Forming Technology IWU, 01187 Dresden, Germany
thorben.schnellhardt@iwu.fraunhofer.de
[5] Hochschule Bonn-Rhein-Sieg, 53757 Sankt Augustin, Germany

Abstract. The manufacturing of large components is, in comparison to small components, cost intensive. This is due to the sheer size of the components and the limited scalability in number of produced items. To take advantage of the effects of small component production we segment the large components into smaller parts and schedule the production of these parts on regular-sized machine tools. We propose to apply and adapt recent developments in reinforcement learning in combination with heuristics to efficiently solve the resulting segmentation and assignment problem. In particular, we solve the assignment problem up to a factor of 8 faster and only a few percentages less accurate than a classic solver from operations research.

Keywords: Reinforcement Learning · Assignment Problem · Large component manufacturing

1 Introduction

In the past years, reinforcement learning [2,11] has shown high potential for solving real world problems in fields like robotics [3], gaming [26] and chemistry [28] or in fine tuning of ChatGPT [21]. Besides these major breakthroughs, reinforcement learning has lately been successfully used to improve or support approaches in operations research [4,18].

In manufacturing operations research and optimization play a central role mainly due to quality requirements and cost pressure [1,10,29]. So do they in manufacturing of large components. Large components are usually machined on special-purpose machine tools with appropriate workspaces. However, such machine tools suffer from various shortcomings compared to regular-sized machine tools, including high cost, low sustainability, low productivity, and several technical limitations due to their size (thermal issues, reduced stiffness) [27]. To overcome these problems, [25] provide a novel approach to manufacturing of large components: The core of the approach is the segmentation of the CAD model of a large component into smaller parts that can be machined on regular-sized machine tools. After processing these parts on machines, they are welded and finished to obtain the final geometry (product), cf. Fig. 1.

Segmented manufacturing thus omits the necessity of expensive, large machine tools by only using flexible and economic regular-sized machine tools and industrial robots. It makes parallel manufacturing possible and induces scalability, which can lead to a significant speed-up in production time and increase in productivity. In addition, segmented manufacturing leads to an improved resiliency through re-segmentation, which can be used to respond to changes such as the failure of machines.

To leverage the full potential of this approach, it is essential to segment the large component optimally under given boundary conditions to maximize productivity and quality.

In our case study, the objective is to segment the component in such a way that the total costs for segmenting, machining and welding are minimized while simultaneously satisfying the geometric constraints. The segmentation and welding costs can be deduced from the respective cuts and the physical properties of the component. However, the determination of the machining cost involves optimally distributing the components to machines which means that we have to solve another optimization problem, namely an assignment problem. Besides the demand for high-quality solutions, the duration of the optimization procedure is equally important. The calculation time of the optimization has to be fast, as a key aspect of the approach is the capability of reacting to failure or other environmental changes. Especially the assignment of parts to machines has to be able to react to those changes with minimal latency. This poses a challenge since classic approaches from operations research perform well on small scale problem setups, but lack the response rates required to solve problems of segmented manufacturing in reasonable time.

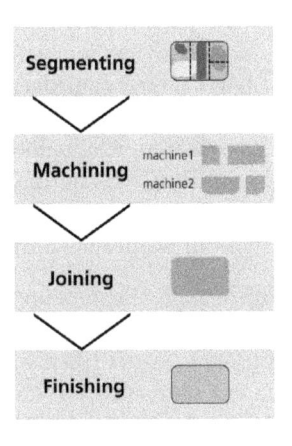

Fig. 1. A simplified depiction of the segmented manufacturing approach.

Recently, deep reinforcement learning has demonstrated high potential for solving combinatorial optimization problems with short inference times [4,18]. Currently, there exists no such approach for the assignment problem specifically. However, for other problems like routing problems deep reinforcement learning has shown to achieve a solution quality close to classic operations research methods while being significantly faster [6,13,20].

In this work, we adapt an existing reinforcement learning model in order to solve the assignment problem. This allows us to efficiently evaluate the total cost of a segmentation of a large component. Our proposed approach embeds the adapted reinforcement learning model in a two-step optimization workflow for segmented manufacturing: First, a segmentation module heuristically generates a set of candidate segmentation variants based on segmentation and welding costs. These are evaluated afterwards in terms of their machining costs through the reinforcement learning based assignment module. Segmentation, welding and machining costs are finally aggregated to determine the best variant out of the candidate pool. To summarize, our contribution consists of:

- developing a heuristic for the segmentation of large components into smaller parts which considers segmentation and welding costs,
- adapting a recent reinforcement learning approach to the assignment problem to make an efficient solution to the overall optimization problem possible, and
- empirically evaluating the reinforcement learning approach on simulated data, showing that we can achieve speed-ups up to a factor of 8 with only minor loss in accuracy compared to a mathematical solver.

The outline of the paper is as follows. We give an overview of the related work in Sect. 2. The underlying optimization problem of the segmented manufacturing approach is described and formulated in Sect. 3. Our solution workflow including our segmentation heuristic and the reinforcement learning based assignment module is discussed in Sect. 4. Empirical evaluations of the reinforcement learning model are performed on simulated data and compared to results of a naive baseline and a classic solver from operations research in Sect. 5. Section 6 summarizes the results and outlines plans for future work.

2 Related Work

The application of machine learning in general and reinforcement learning in particular has been proven to be very promising for improving computation times in the field of combinatorial optimization (CO) [4,18]. These approaches are broadly ranging, also in the sense of how they interact with exact and heuristic methods from operations research (OR). While classic machine learning is often used to support OR solvers [7,12,17], reinforcement learning is most frequently used in an end-to-end manner to generate completely new heuristics [13,18,19].

The CO problem of assigning a set of objects to a given set of resources is of general interest for a lot of applications [5]. Therefore, several approaches have been explored in the literature in the domain of assignment problems. [8] introduces the MAXQ decomposition for hierarchical reinforcement learning, which provides both procedural and declarative semantics. [9] compare reinforcement learning algorithms, such as Q-learning and Sarsa, with traditional linear programming methods for graph-based pairwise assignment problems. They demonstrate that reinforcement learning can achieve high-quality solutions for small symmetric problems but is outperformed by linear programming-based and nearest neighbor-based algorithms for large-scale asymmetric problems. [15] propose the use of deep neural networks to solve linear sum assignment problems (LSAPs) effectively. By decomposing LSAP into sub-assignment problems and treating them as classification tasks, they achieve efficient solutions with minimal accuracy loss.

Yet, to the best of our knowledge, the recent trend of using deep reinforcement learning for solving CO problems has not been explored and leveraged for assignment problems. It has been investigated for a variety of other tasks like layout planning [19], knapsack problems [24], scheduling problems [22] and especially routing problems [6,13,20,23]. E.g., in [6] the authors consider a capacitated vehicle routing problem where a single vehicle visits customers in multiple tours without exceeding its capacity. They use deep reinforcement learning to learn a local search strategy, in which solutions are iteratively locally modified by swapping nodes in the routing sequence. Yet the majority of approaches directly predict a routing solution by iteratively building it up, i.e., visiting one customer node at a time. For example, in [13] they propose an attention based encoder-decoder model for solving multiple routing problem variants. Interestingly, for the traveling salesman problem (TSP) they achieve close to optimal results for instances up to 100 nodes in short inference times. The model was further improved by integrating it into a general reinforcement learning method suggested by [14]. The Policy Optimization with Multiple Optima (POMO) framework in [14] addresses the fact that there are multiple representations of the same routing solution. E.g., for a TSP, which seeks a closed tour between a given set of nodes v_i, $i \in \{1, 2, 3\}$, the sequences $\pi^1 = (v_1, v_2, v_3)$, $\pi^2 = (v_2, v_3, v_1)$ and $\pi^3 = (v_3, v_1, v_2)$ all describe the same routing solution. As a model should find the same optimal solution independent of the starting node in the sequence, the idea of POMO is to generate multiple (parallel) rollouts with different starting nodes which contribute equally during the training process. For the TSP the authors report a superior performance in both solution quality and inference time compared to the other existing deep reinforcement learning approaches. Therefore, in Sect. 4.2, we build on the POMO model and adapt it for our assignment problem.

3 Problem Setup

To increase productivity, scalability and resiliency of large component manufacturing, we transfer it to the setup of regular-sized component manufacturing. The technology for this transfer is segmentation, as introduced in [25]. The considered workflow consists of four steps, cf. Fig. 1: At first, the CAD model of the large component is segmented to smaller parts. These parts are subsequently processed on regular-sized milling machine tools, joined together and at last finished to obtain the final product. In the following, we describe the corresponding optimization problem. To keep the description concrete we focus on a use case from the automotive industry that was also used in [25]: The segmented manufacturing of a die of a forming tool. This die is a highly stressed component, which results in high strength requirements.

The goal of the optimization task is to segment the large component in such a way that manufacturing costs (e.g. time, monetary costs) are minimized while the quality requirements are met. More specifically, it results in the following question: Given a production environment with a set of machines with certain capabilities, how does a large component have to be segmented and how do the segments have to be assigned to the machines in order to optimize the manufacturing costs while satisfying the requirements?

The requirements determine *where* the part can be segmented or how well in terms of induced segmentation costs. For our forming tool use case, the strength is particularly relevant, as this is affected significantly by the segmented manufacturing approach. Therefore, the component should only be segmented in low-stress areas. For this purpose we introduce a descriptor which assigns numerical penalty values to the part which indicate the local influence of the segmentation at the respective point (cf. colour encoding in Fig. 1). The segmentation penalty cost function is the sum of the integrals of the penalty values along the edges of the segmentation cuts. To represent the strength constraint of our example, we use the absolute equivalent stresses of a finite element simulation of the forming process of the punch.

The machine capabilities determine *whether* and at *what* cost a segment can be manufactured. In our example, the capabilities are the workspace and the machine performance. The workspace determines whether a component geometry can be manufactured on a machine due to its dimensions. The machine performance determines, together with the component geometry, the machining time cost for processing the component. Our overall objective function is derived from the described individual process steps and the requirement constraints, cf. Fig. 2: A segmentation variant x_{segm} for a given large component x is evaluated as

$$f(x_{segm}) = \lambda_1 c_{\text{segm}}(x_{segm}) + \lambda_2 c_{\text{mach}}(x_{segm}) + \lambda_3 c_{\text{weld}}(x_{segm}), \quad (1)$$

where c_{segm} denotes the corresponding total segmentation cost, c_{mach} the cost for processing all segments on the milling machines, c_{weld} for welding them together and $\lambda_i > 0$ for $i \in \{1, 2, 3\}$ the corresponding weighing factors. The costs for welding depend proportionally on the joining points and can thus be directly deduced from the segment geometry. The effort for finishing is not included as it is difficult to estimate a priori, since it depends mainly on the component distortion caused by the welding.

4 Methods

The segmented manufacturing approach leads to a complex optimization setup, since the cost function that maps a segmentation to its costs contains itself an optimization, namely the cost optimal assignment of the segments to the

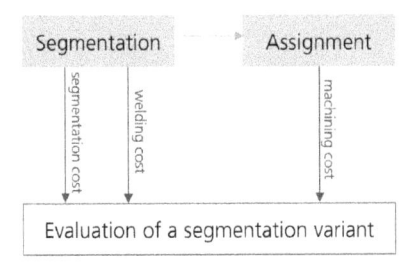

Fig. 2. A segmentation variant is evaluated based on multiple cost factors. Segmentation and welding costs can be deduced from the physical properties of the large component and the geometry of the segmented parts. To determine the machining cost for the segmented parts, an assignment problem is solved.

machines. Or in other words we have an outer optimization over the segmentation and an inner optimization over the assignments of segments to machines. To tackle the complexity of this chained optimization problem, we pursue the following approach as a first step: We heuristically generate a pool of multiple segmentation variants from which we ultimately select the one with minimal total cost according to (1). In order to find a good solution, it is essential to create a sufficiently large pool of segmentation variants. This requires to be able to compute the total cost for a segmentation variant at high speed which is challenging as computing c_{mach} in (1) involves solving an expensive assignment problem. We make this possible by applying deep reinforcement learning for solving the assignment problem.

In the following, we describe the two algorithmic components in our solution, i.e., the heuristic for segmentation and the adapted reinforcement learning approach for assignment.

4.1 Segmentation Heuristic

For a given large component, the goal is to create a candidate pool of feasible segmentation variants while considering segmentation and welding costs. We discretize the solution space by putting a grid with a user-defined mesh size over the component and generate a segmentation variant via horizontal and vertical cuts. It is feasible if all the resulting segmented components fit in at least one machine and if a user-defined segmentation cost threshold is not exceeded.

Our developed heuristic iteratively builds up a tree of segmentation variants, cf. Fig. 3. The depth of the tree is spanned by adding one more cut to the current segmentation. The breadth is controlled by considering different options for setting the cut. As the welding costs increase with an increasing amount of cuts (cf. Sect. 3), we want the tree to contain feasible variants with as few cuts as possible. This is implemented by always performing cuts within a region around the middle along the largest component size dimensions. It shrinks all component sizes as fast as possible, increasing the chance to make them fit into a machine. The segmentation costs are also taken into account and influence the different cut options for one tree level: We select those cuts within the above described region which have the smallest segmentation costs.

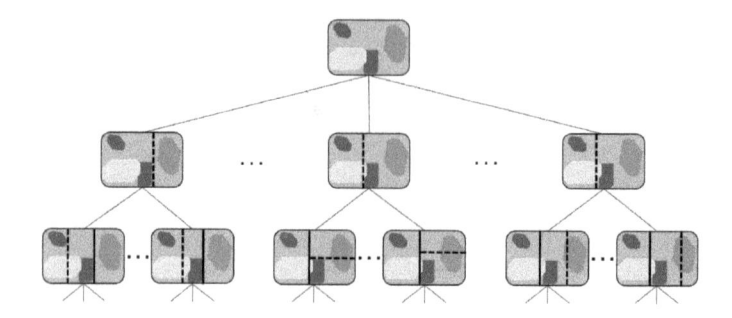

Fig. 3. An exemplary depiction of a built-up tree for generating segmentation variants of a large component. On one level different variants for setting a cut are considered based on the costs while more cuts are added when following a branch.

While building up the tree, each generated feasible segmentation variant is added to the candidate pool. The procedure terminates if the candidate pool contains a user-defined maximal amount of segmentation variants or if the large component has been decomposed into a user-defined maximal amount of segmented parts in all its branches.

4.2 Assignment

Given a set of segmented regular-sized components, the goal is to optimally assign them to machines for processing. More precisely, let n denote the number of components and m the number of (heterogeneous) machines. The task is formalized by an unbalanced assignment problem with the objective to minimize the machining time cost c_{mach}, i.e. the completion time given by:

$$\min_y \max_{i=1,\ldots,m} \sum_{j=1}^n c_{i,j}\, y_{i,j}, \tag{2}$$

where $y_{i,j} \in \{0,1\}$ denotes the binary decision variable of assigning component i to machine j and $c_{i,j} \in \mathbb{R}_{\geq 0}$ the corresponding processing cost. Assignments of components to machines are only feasible if the component fits into the respective machine's workspace. This is expressed by a binary constraint matrix.

To efficiently solve the optimization task, we want to leverage deep reinforcement learning which has not been applied to assignment problems yet. We propose to adapt an existing deep reinforcement learning approach for solving the TSP to our setup. More precisely, we make use of the in Sect. 2 introduced POMO algorithm [14]. It improves reinforcement learning models for CO problems by taking the symmetries in the sequential CO solution representations into account. In principal it can be applied to any reinforcement learning policy model. For solving the TSP, POMO employs the attention model presented by [13].

The attention model learns a stochastic policy $p(\pi|s)$ to generate a routing solution π for a routing instance s. A routing solution π is hereby represented as a permutation over the nodes of instance s. The model follows an encoder-decoder structure: The encoder uses a (multi-head) attention mechanism to learn embeddings for each node in the routing problem and deduces an embedding of the whole routing instance. The decoder is used sequentially to predict one node of the routing solution at a time. It processes the embeddings of the instance and the so far visited nodes via an attention mechanism to learn a probability distribution over the currently unvisited nodes. I.e., the learned policy, parameterized by θ, factorizes as $p_\theta(\pi|s) = \prod_{t=1}^{z} p_\theta(\pi_t|s, \pi_{1:t-1})$ where $\pi_{1:t-1}$ describes the sub-tour consisting of the first $t-1$ out of z visited nodes, cf. [13]. To learn about the symmetries in the solution representation, POMO performs multiple parallel rollouts with the policy p_θ whereby each rollout starts from a different node. The policy is trained based on the policy gradient algorithm REINFORCE. The gradient is hereby approximated by averaging over the N different rollouts of one routing instance corresponding to the different starting points. More precisely, let $R(\pi^i)$ denote the total reward of the rollout π^i, i.e., the negative tour length for the TSP. Then the expected return J is maximized with gradient ascent using

$$\nabla_\theta J(\theta) \approx \frac{1}{N} \sum_{i=1}^{N} (R(\pi^i) - b(s)) \nabla_\theta \log p_\theta(\pi|s), \qquad (3)$$

where the variance reducing baseline is given by $b(s) = \frac{1}{N} \sum_{j=1}^{N} R(\pi^j)$. The baseline is shared between all N rollouts to counteract convergence to local minima, cf. [14].

Using POMO for Assignment. To map our assignment problem to a TSP, we propose to define nodes as component-machine-tuples. Visiting a node $v = (i, j)$ induces the assignment of component i to machine j and incurs a cost of $c_{i,j}$.

I.e., one can imagine to search for a route through the assignment component-machine cost matrix $C \in \mathbb{R}_{\geq 0}^{(n \times m)}$, whereby only one node per row is allowed to be visited since the component must be assigned to exactly one machine, cf. Fig. 4. In contrast to the classic TSP, our resulting cost matrix is not symmetric. Instead, all incoming edges for a node $v = (i, j)$ have the same cost $c_{i,j}$, i.e., the cost does not depend on the predecessor node. Predecessor nodes influence the future node decisions in such a way, that they induce machine occupations and the goal of the algorithm is to optimally utilize the

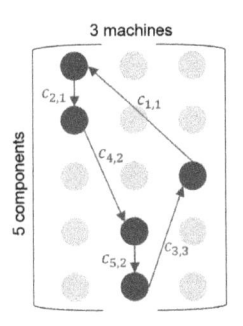

Fig. 4. Assignment as a routing task through the components-machines-matrix.

machines by minimizing the completion time in (2). To implement this setup, the following changes have been made to the original POMO algorithm respectively the underlying attention model:

- node representation: In [13], a TSP node is represented as a tuple containing its x-y-coordinates. Our nodes are represented as three-dimensional vectors of the form $(c_{i,j}, i, j)$, where $c_{i,j}$ denotes the cost of assigning component i to machine j.
- reward definition: Instead of the negative total travel distance, we use the negative completion time, i.e., the negative ending time of the of all machines longest running component processing job.
- masking procedure: The decoder of the attention model has a mechanism which masks out already visited nodes. In our setup, visiting a node (i, j) requires to not only mask out this node but all nodes associated with the same component i, i.e., (i, j) for $j = 1, ..., m$, as a component has to be assigned to exactly one machine. The procedure has been extended accordingly.
- additional constraint matrix: For our assignment setup, not all machines can necessarily process a given component as it depends on their workspace. We integrate the processing of a constraint matrix which, from the beginning masks out nodes corresponding to infeasible assignments.

5 Empirical Evaluation

In this section, we only evaluate the assignment component of our approach. As for the evaluation of the overall workflow which includes the segmentation component there is no benchmark.

In the following, we empirically evaluate the POMO model for solving the assignment problem on simulated data for various setups of 10 to 50 components and 3 to 10 machines. We describe our procedure for data generation in Sect. 5.1 and introduce the benchmarks (a naive baseline and a mathematical solver) in Sect. 5.2. The performance of POMO in comparison to the benchmarks is assessed and discussed in Sect. 5.3.

5.1 Data Generation

An assignment problem with n components and m machines is generated by simulating a real-valued cost matrix $\in \mathbb{R}^{n \times m}$ and a binary constraint matrix $\in \{0,1\}^{n \times m}$. For simulating machines with different performances, we draw the processing costs for components from machine-specific normal distributions. Each such distribution is defined by uniformly sampling a mean value from the interval [0.25, 0.75] and a variance value from [0.01,1]. To generate a constraint matrix, we at first randomly select $p\%$ out of the given components to be involved in unfeasible assignments. The value p is hereby uniformly drawn from [25, 30] for each assignment instance individually. To simulate realistic constraints, we consider a ranking in machines in terms of their workspace sizes. The constraints are therefore sampled iteratively, whereby the first considered machine corresponds to the smallest-sized machine and the subsequent one to the next respective bigger-sized one. For the smallest-sized machine, all the above drawn $p\%$ of components are declared unfeasible (by setting the value 0) and all the others as feasible (by setting the value 1). The next bigger-sized machine always keeps the 1-value-entries of its predecessor machine and flips an unfeasible 0-value to a feasible 1-value with a 50% chance. The last machine, i.e., the one with the largest workspace can always process all components, i.e., its constraint matrix values are given by ones exclusively.

5.2 Benchmarks

We compare our approach to a naive baseline and a classic linear integer programming (ILP) solver from operations research. The naive baseline assigns each component greedily to the cheapest feasible machine and serves as a lower bound on the solution quality. For an upper bound, we employ the ILP solver. This requires to reformulate the optimization task as a decision problem with integer decision variables, linear constraints and a linear objective. The complete mathematical model is omitted due to space limitations. Yet the objective in (2), e.g., can be reformulated appropriately as follows:

$$\min_{x} \max_{i=1,\ldots,m} \sum_{j=1}^{n} c_{i,j}\, x_{i,j}$$

$$\iff \min_{x,z} \sum_{i=1}^{m} z_i \sum_{j=1}^{n} c_{i,j}\, x_{i,j},$$

where

$$z_i = \begin{cases} 1, & i = \arg\max_{k=1,\ldots,m} \sum_{j=1}^{n} c_{k,j} \cdot x_{k,j}, \\ 0, & \text{o/w}, \end{cases}$$

being equivalent to

$$\min_{a} \sum_{i=1}^{m} \sum_{j=1}^{n} c_{i,j}\, a_{i,j}, \qquad (4)$$

where the product $a_{i,j} = z_i \cdot x_{i,j} \in \{0,1\}$ can be linearized by requiring

- $a_{i,j} \leq z_i$,
- $a_{i,j} \leq x_{i,j}$,
- $a_{i,j} \geq z_i + x_{i,j} - 1$.

For implementation, we use the integer solver from Google OR-Tools[1].

---

[1] https://developers.google.com/optimization/lp/mpsolver?hl=en.

5.3 Experiments

Experiments were performed on simulated data generated according to Sect. 5.1 for various setups of components and machines. Throughout the experiments we consider a maximum amount of 50 components. This is a realistic upper bound on the amount of segments for our considered forming tool since it has a floor area of about $3\,\text{m} \times 2\,\text{m}$ and the workspace dimensions of conventional machines lie between 500mm^3 and 1000mm^3. To evaluate our assignment approach empirically, we conduct multiple training procedures of increasing complexity. On the one hand, we train models for the setup of five machines and a fixed amount of various component numbers (**training procedure 1**). Since the segmentation, described in Sect. 4.1, results in different numbers of components in its segmentation variants, we need to ensure that the assignment algorithm can handle these distinct scenarios reliably. Therefore, we propose a **training procedure 2**, in which we train a model for the setup of mixed amounts of components (and five machines). Finally, to additionally address the setup of variable machines, we conduct a **training procedure 3** with both mixed component and machine numbers.

For all procedures, we used 32000 assignment training instances and the same hyperparameter values for the POMO model. They were determined via grid search with Tune [16] and correspond to the values used in [14] for solving the TSP except for a smaller chosen learning rate of 1e-05 and a smaller chosen batch size of 16.

Training Procedure 1. We consider the setup of five machines with 10, 20, 30 and 50 components respectively. We denote the POMO model trained for m machines and n components by $p_{m,n}$. Each model is evaluated on all the corresponding four test sets to assess its generalization ability, cf. first four rows in Table 1. We observe that as expected the model trained in the same setup as tested performs best (values on the diagonal, printed in bold type). Comparing these values to the corresponding ones of the benchmarks shows that the reinforcement learning model significantly outperforms the naive baseline and that it can reach a similar performance like the mathematical solver. However, we see that the generalization ability of the models to different component setups is limited.

Training Procedure 2. To obtain a model with good performance for five machines and various component setups, we provide the model with different component problem sizes during training. More precisely, for each batch we uniformly sample a component number between 10 and 50. Within the batch, 16 assignment instances of the fixed sampled problem size are generated and processed. The resulting model is denoted by $p_{5,\text{mixed}}$ and evaluated on all component test setups, cf. highlighted row in Table 1. Unlike the models trained above, the mixed model reaches a good performance across all the different component scenarios. For each test setup, it is the second best model and can compete with the results of OR-Tools.

Table 1. Experimental results for the setup of five machines and a variable amount of components. Performance is reported in terms of the completion time. The best POMO result per test setup (column) is printed in bold type.

Model	Test(5,10)	Test(5,20)	Test(5,30)	Test(5,50)
$p_{5,10}$	**0.71**	1.34	2.07	3.66
$p_{5,20}$	0.74	**1.26**	1.87	3.13
$p_{5,30}$	0.79	1.27	**1.81**	3.22
$p_{5,50}$	0.78	1.43	2.02	**2.93**
$p_{5,\text{mixed}}$	0.71	1.27	1.82	2.95
OR-Tools	0.70	1.24	1.79	2.89
naive	3.09	6.17	9.26	15.45

Training Procedure 3. We additionally consider a mixed machine setup on top of the mixed component one during training. Analogously to above, the problem sizes are sampled per batch. While component numbers are still uniformly drawn between 10 and 50, we uniformly draw machine numbers between 3 and 10. To assess the final mixed model, we also train models with different fixed machine numbers (and always mixed components) for comparison and generate corresponding test sets. Table 2 shows that analogously to above, the mixed model performs well in all scenarios in contrast to the fixed-setup-trained models. The mixed model surpasses the naive baseline significantly and gets also reasonably close to OR-Tools in all test setups.

Table 2. Experimental results for the setup of mixed components and a variable amount of machines. Performance is reported in terms of the completion time. The best POMO results per test setup (column) are printed in bold type.

Model	Test(3,mixed)	Test(5,mixed)	Test(7,mixed)	Test(10,mixed)
$p_{3,\text{mixed}}$	**3.93**	2.47	1.79	1.34
$p_{5,\text{mixed}}$	4.13	**2.02**	1.64	1.21
$p_{7,\text{mixed}}$	4.21	2.16	**1.35**	1.05
$p_{10,\text{mixed}}$	4.34	2.24	1.42	**0.88**
$p_{\text{mixed,mixed}}$	3.95	2.04	1.38	0.91
OR-Tools	3.50	1.85	1.29	0.87
naive	11.70	9.76	8.91	7.90

In Table 3, we report the inference times for the naive baseline, OR-Tools and our final mixed machine and mixed component model corresponding to the experiments shown in Table 2. As expected, the naive baseline is the most efficient approach where the number of machines has only a negligible - on the given scale - not visible effect on the run time. However, given the quality of its produced solutions, the naive baseline cannot be employed in practice. Comparing the inference times of the reinforcement learning model to OR-Tools, the reinforcement learning model performs significantly faster, up to a factor of 8. This is crucial for our workflow as it enables us to evaluate a large pool of segmentation variants. E.g., when evaluating 1000 variants for the setup of 10 machines for identifying the best segmentation, using the reinforcement learning model or OR-Tools makes a considerable difference of around 30 min in run time. It is essential when deploying the model since the segmented approach to large component manufacturing shall allow fast response times to sudden changes in the production environment.

Table 3. Average inference time in seconds per instance for our final POMO model trained in a mixed component and mixed machine setup and for the benchmark OR-Tools.

Model	Test(3,mixed)	Test(5,mixed)	Test(7,mixed)	Test(10,mixed)
$p_{mixed,mixed}$	0.22	0.27	0.34	0.42
OR-Tools	0.64	2.23	2.42	2.42
naive	0.06	0.06	0.06	0.06

6 Conclusion

Evaluating the goodness of a segmentation solution in segmented manufacturing of large components is expensive, as a variety of cost factors must be taken into account: segmentation costs representing physical properties, machining costs for processing the segments as well as welding costs for joining the segments together. We have proposed an optimization approach for time- and cost-efficient segmented manufacturing. It consists of a two-step procedure of segmentation and assignment. The developed segmentation heuristic pre-selects a set of meaningful segmentation variants based on the segmentation and welding costs. The proposed assignment component is subsequently used to compute the corresponding machining costs for each segmentation variant, allowing to identify the overall best one with minimal total cost. The key in our approach is to use deep reinforcement learning to efficiently solve the assignment problem. For this purpose we adapted the POMO routing model. We enable the model to handle different-sized assignment problems instances by training on variable numbers of segments and machines. Empirical evaluations on simulated data demonstrate that the adapted POMO model competes with a mathematical solver in terms of solution quality while significantly reducing the run time. The presented optimization workflow could support engineers already at the design stage of the

CAD model: As the CAD model influences all cost factors relevant for an optimal segmentation, it could be designed such that the future segmented manufacturing process is optimized.

In the future, we plan to replace the heuristic rule-based segmentation component by an advanced optimizer and implement benchmark scenarios for the overall workflow. Another interesting direction is to view the assignment problem as a multi-vehicle routing problem where nodes correspond to components and vehicles to machines.

Acknowledgements. The research of N. Paul, T. Schnellhardt and M. Fetz was funded by the Fraunhofer lighthouse project "SWAP - Hierarchical swarms as production architecture with optimized utilization". D. Hecker contributed as part of the Fraunhofer Center for Machine Learning within the Fraunhofer Cluster for Cognitive Internet Technologies. The work of T. Wirtz was supported by the Federal Ministry of Education and Research of Germany and the state of North-Rhine Westphalia as part of the Lamarr-Institute for Machine Learning and Artificial Intelligence. We would also like to thank the reviewers for their valuable feedback which improved the presentation of our work.

References

1. Afteni, C., Frumuşanu, G.: A review on optimization of manufacturing process performance. Int. J. Model. Optim. **7**(3), 139–144 (2017). https://doi.org/10.7763/IJMO.2017.V7.573
2. Arulkumaran, K., Deisenroth, M.P., Brundage, M., Bharath, A.A.: Deep reinforcement learning: a brief survey. IEEE Signal Process. Mag. **34**(6), 26–38 (2017). https://doi.org/10.1109/MSP.2017.2743240
3. Bambach, P., et al.: LEAP - legged exploration of the aristarchus plateau. Europlanet Sci. Congr. (2022). https://doi.org/10.5194/epsc2022-856
4. Bengio, Y., Lodi, A., Prouvost, A.: Machine learning for combinatorial optimization: a methodological tour d'horizon. Eur. J. Oper. Res. **290**(2), 405–421 (2021). https://doi.org/10.1016/j.ejor.2020.07.063
5. Cattrysse, D.G., Van Wassenhove, L.N.: A survey of algorithms for the generalized assignment problem. Eur. J. Oper. Res. **60**(3), 260–272 (1992). https://doi.org/10.1016/0377-2217(92)90077-M
6. Chen, X., Tian, Y.: Learning to perform local rewriting for combinatorial optimization. Adv. Neural. Inf. Process. Syst. **32**, 6281–6292 (2019)
7. Deza, A., Khalil, E.B.: Machine learning for cutting planes in integer programming: a survey. arXiv preprint arXiv:2302.09166 (2023). https://doi.org/10.48550/arXiv.2302.09166
8. Dietterich, T.G., et al.: The MAXQ method for hierarchical reinforcement learning. In: ICML. vol. 98, pp. 118–126 (1998)
9. Hamzehi, S., Bogenberger, K., Franeck, P., Kaltenhäuser, B.: Combinatorial reinforcement learning of linear assignment problems. In: 2019 IEEE Intelligent Transportation Systems Conference (ITSC), pp. 3314–3321. IEEE (2019). https://doi.org/10.1109/ITSC.2019.8916920
10. Jagdev, H., Browne, J., Keogh, J.: Manufacturing process optimisation—a survey of techniques. In: Proceedings of the Twenty-eighth International: Matador Conference, pp. 205–215. Springer (1990). https://doi.org/10.1007/978-1-349-10890-9_29

11. Kaelbling, L.P., Littman, M.L., Moore, A.W.: Reinforcement learning: a survey. J. Artif. Intell. Res. **4**, 237–285 (1996). https://doi.org/10.1613/jair.301
12. Khalil, E.B.: Machine learning for integer programming. In: IJCAI, pp. 4004–4005 (2016)
13. Kool, W., van Hoof, H., Welling, M.: Attention, learn to solve routing problems! In: International Conference on Learning Representations (2019). https://doi.org/10.48550/arXiv.1803.08475
14. Kwon, Y.D., Choo, J., Kim, B., Yoon, I., Gwon, Y., Min, S.: POMO: policy optimization with multiple optima for reinforcement learning. Adv. Neural. Inf. Process. Syst. **33**, 21188–21198 (2020)
15. Lee, M., Xiong, Y., Yu, G., Li, G.Y.: Deep neural networks for linear sum assignment problems. IEEE Wireless Commun. Lett. **7**(6), 962–965 (2018). https://doi.org/10.1109/LWC.2018.2843359
16. Liaw, R., Liang, E., Nishihara, R., Moritz, P., Gonzalez, J.E., Stoica, I.: Tune: A research platform for distributed model selection and training. arXiv preprint arXiv:1807.05118 (2018). https://doi.org/10.48550/arXiv.1807.05118
17. Lin, X., Hou, Z.J., Ren, H., Pan, F.: Approximate mixed-integer programming solution with machine learning technique and linear programming relaxation. In: 2019 3rd International Conference on Smart Grid and Smart Cities (ICSGSC), pp. 101–107. IEEE (2019). https://doi.org/10.1109/ICSGSC.2019.00-11
18. Mazyavkina, N., Sviridov, S., Ivanov, S., Burnaev, E.: Reinforcement learning for combinatorial optimization: a survey. Comput. Oper. Res. **134**, 105400 (2021). https://doi.org/10.1016/j.cor.2021.105400
19. Mirhoseini, A., et al.: A graph placement methodology for fast chip design. Nature **594**(7862), 207–212 (2021). https://doi.org/10.1038/s41586-022-04657-6
20. Nazari, M., Oroojlooy, A., Snyder, L., Takác, M.: Reinforcement learning for solving the vehicle routing problem. In: Advances in Neural Information Processing Systems, vol. 31 (2018)
21. Ouyang, L., et al.: Training language models to follow instructions with human feedback. Adv. Neural. Inf. Process. Syst. **35**, 27730–27744 (2022)
22. Pan, Z., Wang, L., Wang, J., Lu, J.: Deep reinforcement learning based optimization algorithm for permutation flow-shop scheduling. IEEE Trans. Emerging Top. Comput. Intell. (2021). https://doi.org/10.1109/TETCI.2021.3098354
23. Paul, N., Wirtz, T., Wrobel, S., Kister, A.: Multi-agent neural rewriter for vehicle routing with limited disclosure of costs. In: Presented at the Gamification and Multiagent Solutions Workshop within Tenth International Conference on Learning Representations, ICLR (2022). https://doi.org/10.48550/arXiv.2206.05990
24. Refaei Afshar, R., Zhang, Y., Firat, M., Kaymak, U.: A state aggregation approach for solving knapsack problem with deep reinforcement learning. In: Pan, S.J., Sugiyama, M. (eds.) Proceedings of The 12th Asian Conference on Machine Learning. Proceedings of Machine Learning Research, vol. 129, pp. 81–96 (2020)
25. Schnellhardt, T., Hemschik, R., Weiß, A., Schoesau, R., Hellmich, A., Ihlenfeldt, S.: Scalable production of large components by industrial robots and machine tools through segmentation. Front. Robot. AI **9** (2022). https://doi.org/10.3389/frobt.2022.1021755
26. Silver, D., et al.: Mastering the game of go without human knowledge. Nature **550**(7676), 354–359 (2017). https://doi.org/10.1038/nature24270
27. Uriarte, L., et al.: Machine tools for large parts. CIRP Ann. **62**(2), 731–750 (2013). https://doi.org/10.1016/j.cirp.2013.05.009

28. Volk, A.A., et al.: AlphaFlow: autonomous discovery and optimization of multi-step chemistry using a self-driven fluidic lab guided by reinforcement learning. Nat. Commun. **14**(1), 1403 (2023). https://doi.org/10.1038/s41467-023-37139-y
29. Weichert, D., Link, P., Stoll, A., Rüping, S., Ihlenfeldt, S., Wrobel, S.: A review of machine learning for the optimization of production processes. Int. J. Adv. Manuf. Technol. 1889–1902 (2019). https://doi.org/10.1007/s00170-019-03988-5

Automatic Tool Wear Inspection by Cascading Sensor and Image Data

Robbert Verbeke[1](✉), Lars De Pauw[2], Fabian Fingerhut[1], Tom Jacobs[3], Toon Goedemé[2], and Elena Tsiporkova[1]

[1] EluciDATA Lab Sirris, Brussels, Belgium
robbert.verbeke@sirris.be
[2] EAVISE KU Leuven, Sint-Katelijne Waver, Belgium
lars.depauw@kuleuven.be
[3] Precision Manufacturing Sirris, Brussels, Belgium

Abstract. This paper explores the possibility to apply data-driven methods to improve the replacement strategy of worn cutting tools used in milling industry. While the data was generated in a controlled environment, the conditions under which the data were generated varied to make them more realistic. Both indirect (sensor data) and direct (images) data was captured and individually modelled. We propose a cascading approach, combining both modalities in a sequential way, and show that this methodology leads to very accurate tool replacement strategy while keeping production efficiency high, as long as the cutting speed does not change drastically.

1 Introduction

In many manufacturing settings, the usage of cutting tools used during, e.g., milling or drilling, constitutes a non-negligible economic cost. They are typically replaced after manual inspection of an operator who makes a decision on the tool status. This monitoring is time consuming and subjective. Alternatively, the tool is replaced automatically after a fixed time of operating. Since a faulty tool can lead to lower quality of the produced part, or even severe damage when the tool breaks, this automatic replacement time is set very conservatively. This leads to an inefficient use of the tools and a waste of precious materials.

Continuous collection of diverse measurements of the tool status allows to use a data-driven approach to assess whether the tool should be replaced or not and thus can lead to an improved replacement strategy that is time and resource efficient. However, such continuous monitoring comes with a cost, not only in terms of investment related to the installation of the measurement infrastructure, but also in terms of potentially reduced production efficiency caused by obtrusive measurements.

In this paper, a two-phase approach is presented, using both sensor and image data, to accurately monitor the tool status. The two modalities work in a complementary way and we show that combining the two in a cascading fashion leads to a better performance than any of the individual models. In addition, the two-phase paradigm allows optimisation of the measurement workflow in such way that the production process is minimally affected by the executed measurements. The data was produced in a controlled real-life environment using varying machine settings.

2 Related Work

In this section, we give a non-exhaustive overview of some related works in the field of tool wear monitoring.

Kim et al. [1] and Ayman et al. [2] both give an exhaustive overview of, among others, the research done on the topic tool monitoring and tool wear prediction.

Benkdedjouh et al. [3] use Support Vector Machines (SVMs), taking cutting forces, vibration, and acoustic emission as input, to predict the tool wear and remaining useful life. ANNs using only image data as input have been used to predict the tool wear as well, achieving good results as shown in [4]. However, other authors (see e.g. [5]) found that Random Forests, using the same input features, can outperform Artificial Neural Networks (ANNs) and SVMs for tool wear prediction. More recently, deep learning was shown to be well suited for tool wear prediction as well [6].

In many application contexts, the exact value of the wear is less important than the tool condition (e.g., highly worn or not). Also for this purpose, the above methods can be applied, either on image data [7,8] or on sensor measurements [9–12] as input.

A main drawback in many of the above studies is that the data was generated under simplified controlled environments, typically using one fixed value for the machine settings like the cutting speed and feed rate. Transfer learning has been used to generalize better to different operating conditions [13], however the step to an integration of the approach in an industrial setting remains large. In real-life settings the machine settings may vary continuously, data will be noisy, and reliable labels will be very rare.

Due to the latter reason, unsupervised [14–16] and semi-supervised [17] anomaly detection methods have been applied for tool wear monitoring, instead. Despite the mentioned above challenges, promising results for unsupervised tool wear monitoring during real life manufacturing operations have been achieved [18].

In this paper, the data used is generated in a controlled setting, but the machine settings are varied, mimicking real industrial situations, to study their impact. Both sensor and image data are captured and used as input to separate models.

3 Materials and Methods

3.1 Use Case and Data

Use Case Scenario. The use case considered in this paper is on the automatic monitoring of tool wear and recommending the optimal replacement time. This

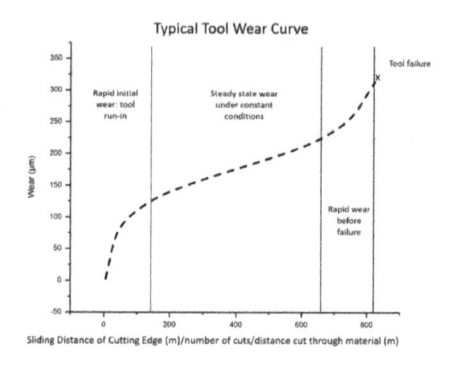

Fig. 1. The typical evolution of tool wear. Taken from Alhadeff et al. 2019 [19].

is important in manufacturing settings where tools are typically replaced in a less-than-optimal way, leading to an inefficient use of materials. Rather than trying to predict the exact tool wear through a regression model, the aim is to come up with an accurate classification task that predicts whether the tool is operating under *safe* or *unsafe* conditions. Unsafe conditions are characterized by a rapid increase in tool wear, compared to a more steady increase during safe conditions. This is illustrated in Fig. 1. In practice, this is treated as equivalent to predicting *low* or *high* tool wear based on some threshold due to convenience. However, these are not necessarily the same and the differences are discussed later on.

Data Generation. We collected 11 different data sets, using a different tool for each set and with different cutting speed V_c, feed rate f_z, spindle speed n, radial depth a_e, and axial depth of the cut a_p. Each set consists of a certain number of usages, all done with the same tool. The aim was to produce 100 usages per set. However, when the tool wear evolved too slowly (or too quickly), more (or less) usages were performed. These are all specified in Table 1. All tests were done on the same type of material, namely CK45 (steel). More information about the data generation process, as well as a download link for the full dataset used in this paper, can be found in [20].

As can be seen, sets 4 to 11 have the same V_c and n, while the other machine settings may vary. Sets 2 and 3 on the other hand, have different values for V_c and n, and the values for these parameters for set 1 are even unknown. This is the reason why in the (sensor) analysis, the first 3 sets will be analysed separately from the last 8.

Sensor Data. 5 different sensor values are captured:

1. Acoustic emission (Vallen VS30-Sic-V2: 25–80 kHz sensor),
2. Vibration (multiple PCB 333B40 accelerometers),
3. Force in x, y, and z direction (Kistler 9257B and 9255C dynamometers).

Table 1. Machine settings and number of usages for each set.

Set	V_c [m/min]	n [rev/min]	f_z [mm/rev]	V_f [mm/min]	a_e [mm]	a_p [mm]	n_{usages}
1	100	2000	0.05	100	1.0	1.0	91
2	120	2547	0.08	203	1.0	1.0	82
3	150	3184	0.05	159	1.0	1.0	92
4	174	3705	0.05	185	1.0	1.0	75
5	174	3705	0.04	148	1.0	1.0	56
6	174	3705	0.04	148	1.0	1.0	139
7	174	3705	0.045	170	1.0	1.0	98
8	174	3705	0.048	178	1.0	1.0	97
9	174	3705	0.048	178	1.0	0.5	98
10	174	3705	0.05	185	1.0	0.5	98
11	174	3705	0.043	159	1.0	1.0	97

All sensor data are gathered using a DAQ system from National Instruments in a synchronized way, with a sampling frequency of 1626 Hz. An overview of the set-up is shown in Fig. 2a.

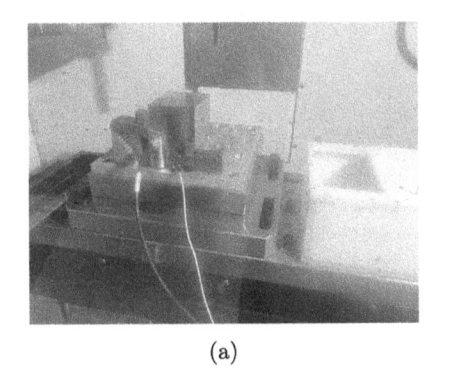

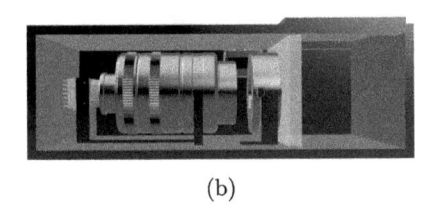

Fig. 2. (a) Sensor data capturing set-up. The acoustic sensor is connected with the black cable, the accelormeter with the white cable, and the plate with the holes is the dynamometer. (b) Cross-section of Camera box with used vision setup.

Image Data. Image data acquisition on a scale of only few micrometers is prone to errors caused by small movements of the camera w.r.t. to the tool. This is addressed by creating a fully enclosed box which is bolted to the machine table of the milling machine. This box can be seen on the right side of Fig. 2a. A firm connection to the table ensures the focal distance is respected on all images and generates stable images throughout the dataset. Figure 2b provides a visual of the used vision setup. Left to right are camera, lens, ring light and enclosed part for tool to be presented to the camera. Technical details for these parts are discussed next. Most left part is 20.5 MP Alvium 1800 U-2050 rgb camera. This is configured using the manufacturers framework Vimba to apply an exposure time of 1500 ns and a gain of 15. These settings are adjusted together with the aperture on our macro lens to provide well lit images with a large enough depth of field to capture the worn edge on the tool. The used lens is a CA-LMHE0510 produced by Keyence. This lens is manually adjusted to a field of view of 17.8 × 14.3 resulting in a pixel resolution of 3.2 micron per pixel. A LED ring light (CA-DRW13M by Keyence) is positioned in front of this lens as close to the insert as possible to provide multi-angle lighting to the point of interest. A plexi screen is added in front of the light to protect the electronical systems from metal chips and cooling fluids coming from the milling process.

The results from this setup are shown in Fig. 3. The left and right images on the top represent the first and second set of data respectively. Underneath them are displayed their cropped counterparts that are later used for training.

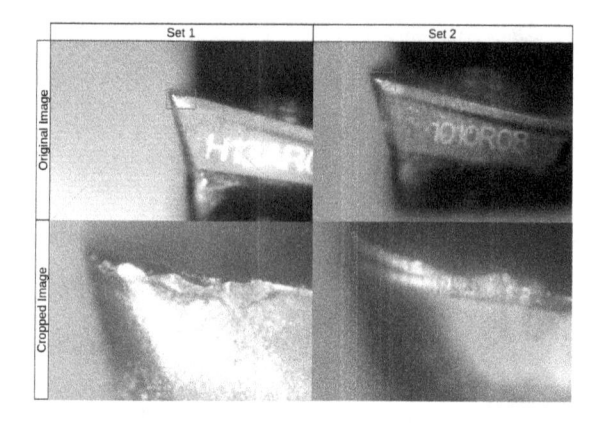

Fig. 3. Example of raw image captured with setup.

Tool Wear Data. The values for the tool wear are measured by a domain expert from the captured images. Two types of tool wear are identified: flank wear and adhesive wear. The flank wear increases monotonically while the adhesive wear can also decrease as the particles sticking to the tool get removed.

The ground truth wear values are obtained by human assessment of the tool pictures taken. The resolution of these measurements is 15 μm which results in plateaus in the tool wear evolution. To make the labels more reliable, we linearly interpolate the *flank* tool wear during the plateaus from the first usage of the plateau to the moment the measured wear increases. No interpolation is done after the last measured increase.

We assume that adhesive wear will have very little effect on the sensor measurements, since this adhesion to the tool is typically very short lived. Because

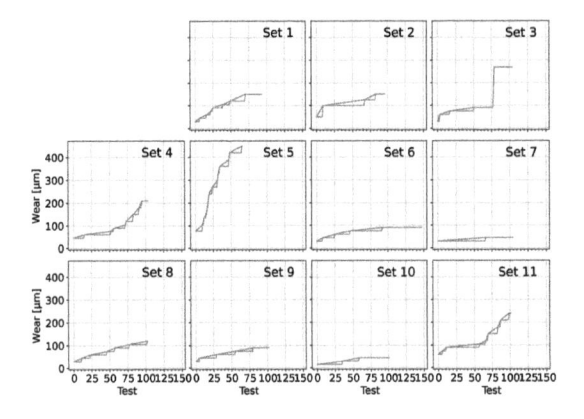

Fig. 4. Evolution of the annotated flank wear (red) and the corresponding interpolation (green) for all sets. (Color figure online)

of this, wherever adhesive wear was measured, the labels were replaced by an estimate of the flank wear by linearly interpolating using the closest measured flank wear usages.

Looking at Fig. 4, it seems that the rapid increase in wear occurs around 120 μm for sets 4 and 11. Set 5 seemingly was always in the unsafe zone, apart from the first few usages, reaching very quickly much higher wear values than the other sets. The tool wear in sets 1 and 2 seems to still increase at a safe, gradual rate, even after reaching 120 μm. Set 3 has a sudden increase in wear from 90 to 270 μm, but the wear rate gets stable after that. The other sets show a stable evolution and do not exceed 120 μm.

Given all this, it seems that the safe zone depends on many different factors, such as the cutting speed and the current amount of wear. Furthermore, given that the sudden increase in wear in set 3 did not lead to any big increase in wear afterwards, it seems that the wear geometry plays a big role as well.

Despite this, for the sake of uniformity, we chose to use a threshold of 120 μm to label the usages as in the safe or unsafe zone. This seems valid at least for sets 4 to 11, but the above considerations will have to be taken into account while analyzing the results.

3.2 Tool Wear Inspection via a Cascade of Sensor and Image Models

This study presents a multi-modal data analysis framework for tool-wear monitoring. Namely, two different models for tool wear monitoring are used, originating from different modalities, which are deployed in a complementary way. It aims to shed light on the potential and limitations of the different data modalities, e.g. different types of sensor data, that are usually employed to monitor the wear rate of the cutting tools. The outcome of such analyses can help choosing the suitable data modality or set of data modalities for a given machine setting and cutting tool.

Cascade Model. To combine the two methodologies, a 2-phase cascade approach is proposed:

1. The sensor-based model decides whether the tool is in the safe or unsafe regime,
2. If the model output is unsafe, the image modality is switched on,
3. The image-based model reevaluates the safe or unsafe condition.

There are multiple advantages to this approach:

- It becomes a multi-modal approach, making use of all the available data
- The image capturing modality, which is time-consuming, is only switched on when it is deemed necessary.

Sensor Data Preprocessing. Before any data exploration or modelling is done on the sensor data, some preprocessing steps are performed.

As a first step, the *active* part of the signal, corresponding to the times where the tool is in contact with the work piece, is identified. For this, we propose a very simple change point detection method. First, the standard deviation σ is computed over a rolling window of 200 timestamps. Next, all the timestamps where σ is above 1.5 times the median of σ are identified. The first and last of these timesteps are set to respectively be the start and end of the active part. This value of 1.5 was chosen based on a visual inspections that verified the accuracte identification of start and end. The active part is typically about 30 s long.

Sometimes, drift can be present in the sensor measurements. This is purely an artifact and not a physical property. To account for this, the mean of the signals is calculated over a rolling window of 1000 timestamps and subsequently subtracted from the signal.

As a final step, the active part, which has variable length, is split into overlapping segments of fixed length N. This has the advantage that the input samples to the model have a much shorter and fixed length. This also assumes that the signatures related to wear are present over this shorter time span. Another advantage is that the number of input samples available gets greatly increased. After experimenting with varying window sizes, $N = 2000$ was chosen empirically since basic characteristics, like the maximum amplitude, are more stable when looking at consecutive segments compared to using shorter segments. Given the sampling frequency, this corresponds to segments of 1.2 s. The stride was chosen to be 500 timestamps, resulting in overlapping segments, which further increases the number of input samples.

The tool wear labels of the segments are set to the value of the corresponding usage.

The above preprocessing results in 7400 to 15600 segments, depending on the set. The variation can mostly be explained by the different number of usages per set, but small differences in the length of the active parts also have an impact.

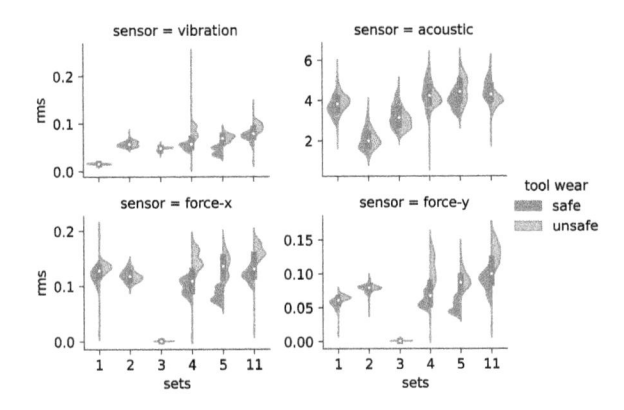

Fig. 5. Exploratory analysis of sensor data segments with respect to tool wear. Most statistical parameters are indicative of safe or unsafe tool wear.

Sensor Data Exploration and Profiling. After an initial examination of the data, it was found that the force in the z-dimension often was a constant value. This feature was thus removed from any further analysis.

Subsequently, it was checked whether the extracted segments can be indicative of tool wear. Figure 5 illustrates the root mean square (rms) value that was extracted from the identified segments, where the rms value for a given measurement vector $\mathbf{x}$ is calculated as $rms = \sqrt{1/n \times \sum_{i=1}^{n} x_i}$ with $\mathbf{x} = [x_1, ..., x_n]^T$. A binary value for safe and unsafe tool wear was chosen based on the previously defined tool wear threshold of 120 μm which was shown to be the point at which tool wear rapidly increases. We excluded two outlying instances, where the rms value for the vibration exceeded 2.

It can be observed that (1) within each setting, the low and high tool-wear segments differ in their rms distribution and that (2) the setting itself has an influence on the distribution. For instance, the rms value of the y-force differs substantially between safe and unsafe tool wear segments in set 11. The rms value for unsafe tool wear examples of set 1 is however typically lower than the rms values for safe tool-wear examples of set 11. Similar observations can be made with other statistical parameters (e.g. standard deviation, absolute maximum). We conclude, that with respect to the rms value (but also with respect to other statistical parameters that were not shown in Fig. 4) the segments are separable per set, but not separable over all sets. This hold with the exception of the acoustic emission which displays little differences between safe and unsafe tool-wear with regards to the rms value.

The effect of different tool settings cannot only be observed in the statistical metrics, but in data-driven models that take the given segments as input as well. In order to prove this point, an auto-encoder is trained, based on the *Deep clustering with Convolutional Autoencoders* (DCEC) network [21]. Figure 6 displays the U-MAP [22] representation of the 10 dimensional embedding space of the auto-encoder trained on sets 4, 5, 6 and 10 and taking set 7 as validation

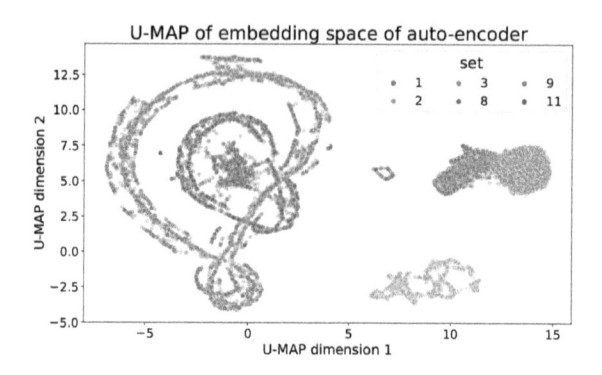

Fig. 6. The machine settings have a clear effect embedding of the auto-encoder. Set 1, 2 and 3 differ from the other sets with respect to V_c and n and are therefore embedded differently compared to sets 8, 9 and 11.

set. It becomes apparent that the segments of sets 1, 2 and 3 are embedded differently from the other sets, following their different machine settings that they were run under (see Table 1).

Sensor Data Classification. Using the sensor data, a model is trained to identify whether the tool is in the unsafe zone, i.e., where the wear is increasing much more rapidly.

Our classification model is a deep neural network architecture, built using 1D convolutional neural networks (CNNs) and taking the time series segments as multi-channel input. The 1D CNNs were used to learn temporal patterns of the time-series sensor data which are essential for efficient tool-wear monitoring.

Given the meaningless values of the z-force measurements and the low separability based on tool wear values of the acoustic emission, only the vibration, x-force, and y-force were used as an input to the model. Each input sample will thus have the shape 2000 × 3.

There are 5 convolutional blocks (consisting of a 1D CNN layer, a max-pooling layer, and a batch-normalization layer) using 8, 16, 32, 64, and 128 number of filters. All CNN layers have a kernel size of 5. After the last convolutional block, the output is flattened and followed by 5 fully connected (FC) layers (of size 64, 32, 16, 8, and 2). All CNN and FC layers use a ReLU activation function, except for the last one, which uses SoftMax. The model was trained over 200 epochs, with an initial learning rate of 10^{-5}. This was reduced when a plateau was reached for the validation accuracy, with a minimum learning rate of 10^{-11}.

Image Data Analysis. Image data analysis is performed using a 2D CNN classifier trained to predict the safety of the tool. This safety is defined the same way as for the sensor classifier with a threshold at 120 μm. Resulting in a label 0 for safe, 1 for unsafe for the binary classification.

We selected the Resnet [23] architecture out of many different possible classification networks due to proven performance on classification tasks. On this backbone, the classifier has been modified from a 1000 class classifier to a 1 class binary classifier. To interpret the binary classification output value, a threshold needs be set between 0 and 1 for safe or unsafe classification, this threshold is chosen to be 0.5 by default. Pretrained weights trained on Imagenet have been loaded into the model before training.

Training was done on the same training sets used for training sensor classifier to prevent data leakage between the two approaches. Parameters for training are left to default except for the learning rate which was set to 3×10^{-3} and batch size set to 32. The Resnet family consists of multiple layer depths for the network. Resnet101 was empirically selected as best performing for this task.

Training runs were stopped by an early stopping algorithm to prevent overfitting by ending the training when validation loss stopped decreasing. To further optimize training, the learning rate was reduced by 1/2 after a plateau of 10 epochs was reached.

The imbalancedness of the dataset poses difficulties where the network would predict the same class for all samples presented. The dataset was balanced by random sampling from both classes (safe/unsafe) which results in a 50/50 distribution between the two classes. The test dataset was left imbalanced to evaluate on realistic data.

Training Strategy. To train the model using sensor data, great care has to be taken to prevent data leakage. The sensor data coming from each set can be seen as one continuous time series, interrupted when a picture is taken between each usage. As such, different usages in the same set should not be randomly divided between training and test set. It is indeed to be expected that subsequent usages with the same tool will result in very similar time series. In other words, these samples will be highly correlated. Similarly, as the wear increases gradually, the images can not be considered as independent samples either.

To avoid any data leakage, the split is done on the set level. All usages from sets 4, 5, 6, and 10 were used for training the models. These sets were chosen because they encompass the whole wear range of all sets. The decision of including four sets in the training is based on the fact that this is half of the number of sets with similar machine setting.

The remaining sets are used to evaluate the generalizability of the model. The first 3 sets were not included on purpose in the training set, to inspect how the results differ as the machine settings vary.

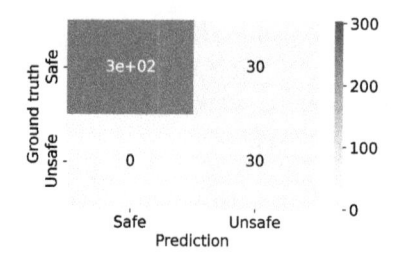

Fig. 7. Confusion matrix for the sensor-based model.

4 Results and Discussion

4.1 Sensor-Based Model

This section reports the results of the sensor data classification model, as described in Sect. 3.2. The classification score is computed for all the segments of the sets, which are not included in the training set. However, we are interested mostly in the prediction on the usage level, not for individual segments. Therefore, the prediction scores are averaged for the segments of the same usage. The results are depicted in Fig. 7. As can be observed, the majority (90 %) of the safe usages are labeled correctly, while *all* all unsafe usages are identified as such correctly. In other words, there are no false negatives, which are much more catastrophic than false positives. The performance metrics are reported in the first column of Table 2.

4.2 Image-Based Model

The vision-based classifier was trained on the same data as the sensor-based was trained on. The results are discussed here, shown in Fig. 8 and summarized in Table 2. When using the default threshold of 0.5 to decide which class the model outputs, the model reaches a higher precision than the sensor-based model (90% vs. 50%) but much lower recall (60% vs. 100%). By lowering this decision threshold, the recall can be increased, but with a lower precision as trade-off. When using a decision threshold of 0.1, the precision slightly decreases, but all other metrics increase. Several thresholds were explored and the value was chosen based on the best F1-score.

4.3 Cascade Approach

When combining two modalities, using the best threshold for the vision-based model, in a cascade approach where the sensor network provides a first selection between safe and unsafe, the total accuracy is boosted further to 99%, with high recall, precision, and F1-score as well, as seen in the final column of Table 2 (Fig. 9).

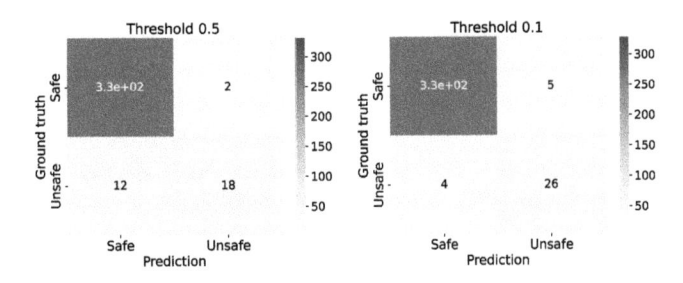

Fig. 8. Confusion matrix for the computer vision model with a decision threshold for the output of the model of 0.5 (left) and 0.1 (right).

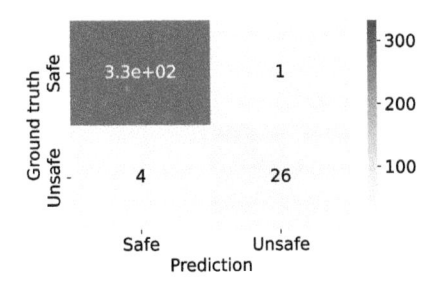

Fig. 9. Confusion matrix for the 2-step classification model

An important question is where the misclassified usages are occuring. This is shown in Fig. 10. As it can be seen, set 11 is the only set that gets into the unstable regime. For all other sets, the usages are correctly labeled as safe. For set 11, the incorrectly labeled usages are close to where the tool transitions from safe to unsafe, which is naturally the most noisy region for classification. In other words, none of the misclassifications are catastrophic with respect to wear.

Table 2. Performance metrics of the sensor-based model, the image-based model, using both a decision threshold of 0.5 and 0.1, and the cascading model.

	Sensor model	Image model (0.5)	Image model (0.1)	Cascading model
Accuracy	92%	96%	98%	99%
Precision	50%	90%	84%	86%
Recall	100%	60%	87%	87%
F1-score	67%	72%	85%	91%

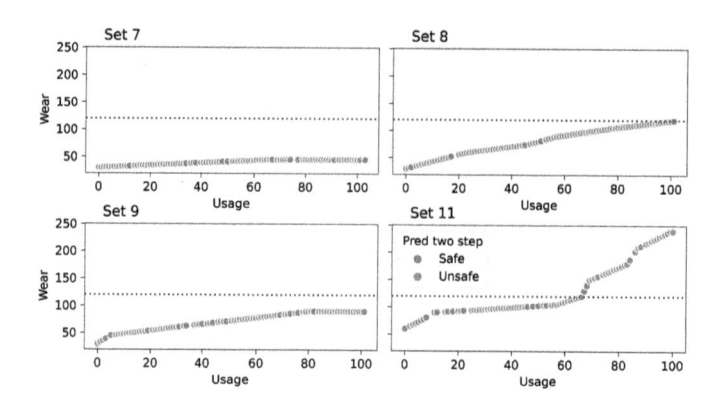

Fig. 10. Interpolated tool wear evolution of the four unseen sets with the prediction of the cascading model for each usage.

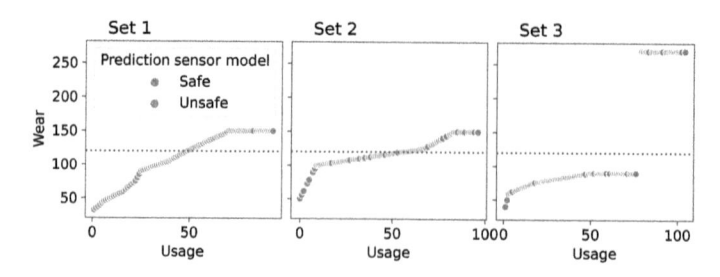

Fig. 11. Evolution of the interpolated tool wear and the prediction of the sensor model for Sets 1–3, which have different cutting speeds.

4.4 Generalization to Different Cutting Speeds

Figure 11 shows the predictions of the sensor model for sets 1, 2, and 3. These sets used a different cutting speed, so it is not clear how well the model would generalize to these sets. As can be observed, the model predicts safe conditions for all usages of sets 2 and 3, and only just starts to predict unsafe conditions for the final usages of set 1. This is despite the fact that all sets contain usages well past the threshold of 120 μm. However, as discussed in Sect. 3.1, it is not clear from the tool wear evolution that these sets have entered an unsafe regime. In this sense, the prediction of the model are accurate.

This raises the question what determines the transition from safe to unsafe conditions. From the current available sets, it seems that the threshold for this transition is dependent on the cutting speed, but too few sets where the transition happens are available to make this more concrete.

Unfortunately, with the current data it can not be evaluated whether the model would accurately pick up the transition also for sets with different cutting speeds.

The performance of the image model on Sets 1–3 is also evaluated. This is shown in Fig. 12. The accuracy is 69% and the F1-score 49%. Varying the decision threshold did not significantly improve the results for these sets.

The model clearly performs much better than the sensor-based model on the same sets, which can be explained by the fact that the resulting images are not (directly) influenced by the cutting speed, unlike the sensor measurements. On the other hand, the performance is worse on these sets than of the same model on the sets previously discussed in Sect. 4.2. This implies that the resulting wear looks differently when the cutting speed is changed, making it harder for the image model to determine whether the wear is above the threshold of 120 μm.

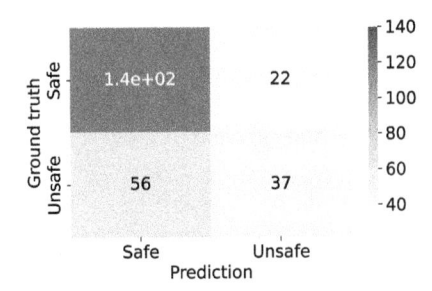

Fig. 12. Confusion matrix for the predictions of the image model on Set 1–3.

Note that, given the bad performance of the sensor model here, using the 2-phase, cascading approach would lead to bad performance as well.

4.5 Open Challenges and Next Steps

This study serves as an intermediate step to gap the bridge between academic research and industrial implementation. It was shown that for a fixed cutting speed, while varying other machine settings, the proposed approach is able to monitor the tool status effectively. However, in an industrial setting, the cutting speed will generally not be constant and possibly even vary during the cutting operation as well.

As a next step, the approach should be tested with data coming from operations that are more realistic, with more complex cutting speeds and not in a straight path.

However, in settings where the machining operations are repeated often, e.g., when a large amount of the same parts are produced, we expect that the proposed can be adopted fairly easily to work well.

5 Conclusion

In this paper, a measuring set-up and methodology was outlined to improve the replacement strategy for cutting tools. The approach involves predicting when the tool wear starts increasing more rapidly, leading to unstable behaviour. The data is generated in several sets, using different tools and machine settings. Both sensor and image data are combined to achieve a model that can very accurately identify when this rapid increase in tool wear starts, as long as the cutting speed is kept constant. For the sets where this is not the case, the results seem much worse. However, this is likely due to a mislabeling of safe or unsafe conditions, since this was purely based on a threshold on the wear. Unfortunately, only a few of the sets have different cutting speeds, so this could not be clearly validated.

Our two-step cascade approach shows to be a promising alternative to the typical regression-based approach for tool wear monitoring. It has a very good performance on the untrained data, while only employing the time-intensive image capturing module if the sensor-based model deems it necessary.

Acknowledgment. This research is funded by VLAIO (Flanders Innovation & Entrepreneurship) through the ATWI project and the Flemish Government through the AI Research Program.

References

1. Kim, D.-H., et al.: Smart machining process using machine learning: a review and perspective on machining industry. Int. J. Precis. Eng. Manuf.-Green Technol. **5**(4), 555–568 (2018)
2. Mohamed, A., Hassan, M., M'Saoubi, R., Attia, H.: Tool condition monitoring for high-performance machining systems - a review. Sensors **22**(6) (2022). https://www.mdpi.com/1424-8220/22/6/2206
3. Benkedjouh, T., Medjaher, K., Zerhouni, N., Rechak, S.: Health assessment and life prediction of cutting tools based on support vector regression. J. Intell. Manuf. **26**(2), 213–223 (2015)
4. D'Addona, D., Ura, S., Matarazzo, D.: Tool-wear prediction and pattern-recognition using artificial neural network and dna-based computing. J. Intell. Manuf. **28**, 08 (2017)
5. Wu, D., Jennings, C., Terpenny, J., Gao, R.X., Kumara, S.: A comparative study on machine learning algorithms for smart manufacturing: tool wear prediction using random forests. J. Manuf. Sci. Eng. **139**(7), 071018 (2017)
6. Ma, J., Luo, D., Liao, X., Zhang, Z., Huang, Y., Lu, J.: Tool wear mechanism and prediction in milling tc18 titanium alloy using deep learning. Measurement **173**, 108554 (2021)
7. García-Ordás, M., Alegre, E., González-Castro, V., Alaiz, R.: A computer vision approach to analyze and classify tool wear level in milling processes using shape descriptors and machine learning techniques. Int. J. Adv. Manuf. Technol. **90**, 05 (2017)
8. Mamledesai, H., Soriano, M.A., Ahmad, R.: A qualitative tool condition monitoring framework using convolution neural network and transfer learning. Appl. Sci. **10**(20), 7298 (2020)

9. Krishnakumar, P., Rameshkumar, K., Ramachandran, K.: Tool wear condition prediction using vibration signals in high speed machining (hsm) of titanium (ti-6al-4 v) alloy. Procedia Comput. Sci. **50**, 270–275 (2015)
10. Painuli, S., Elangovan, M., Sugumaran, V.: Tool condition monitoring using k-star algorithm. Expert Syst. Appl. **41**, 2638–2643 (2014)
11. Guo, K., Yang, B., Wang, H., Sun, J., Lu, L., et al.: Singularity analysis of cutting force and vibration for tool condition monitoring in milling. IEEE Access **7**, 134113–134124 (2019)
12. Shi, C., Panoutsos, G., Luo, B., Liu, H., Li, B., Lin, X.: Using multiple-feature-spaces-based deep learning for tool condition monitoring in ultraprecision manufacturing. IEEE Trans. Ind. Electron. **66**(5), 3794–3803 (2019)
13. Xie, R., Wu, D.: Optimal transport-based transfer learning for smart manufacturing: tool wear prediction using out-of-domain data. Manuf. Lett. **29**, 104–107 (2021)
14. Denkena, B., Dittrich, M.-A., Noske, H., Witt, M.: Statistical approaches for semi-supervised anomaly detection in machining. Prod. Eng. Res. Devel. **14**(3), 385–393 (2020). https://doi.org/10.1007/s11740-020-00958-9
15. Watanabe, T., Kono, I., Onozuka, H.: Anomaly detection methods in turning based on motor data analysis. Procedia Manuf. **48**, 882–893 (2020)
16. Dou, J., Xu, C., Jiao, S., Li, B., Zhang, J., Xu, X.: An unsupervised online monitoring method for tool wear using a sparse auto-encoder. Int. J. Adv. Manuf. Technol. **106**(5), 2493–2507 (2020)
17. Liang, Y., Wang, S., Li, W., Lu, X.: Data-driven anomaly diagnosis for machining processes. Engineering **5**(4), 646–652 (2019)
18. Fingerhut, F., et al.: Data-driven usage profiling and anomaly detection in support of sustainable machining processes, pp. 127–136 (2022)
19. Alhadeff, L., Marshall, M., Slatter, T.: The influence of tool coating on the length of the normal operating region (steady-state wear) for micro end mills. Precis. Eng. **60**, 07 (2019)
20. De Pauw, L., Jacobs, T., Goedemé, T.: Matwi: a multimodal automatic tool wear inspection dataset and baseline algorithms (2023)
21. Guo, X., Liu, X., Zhu, E., Yin, J.: Deep clustering with convolutional autoencoders. In: Liu, D., Xie, S., Li, Y., Zhao, D., El-Alfy, E.-S.M. (eds.) Neural Information Processing, pp. 373–382. Springer, Cham (2017). https://doi.org/10.1007/978-3-319-70096-0_39
22. McInnes, L., Healy, J., Saul, N., Großberger, L.: Umap: uniform manifold approximation and projection. J. Open Source Softw. **3**(29), 861 (2018). https://doi.org/10.21105/joss.00861
23. He, K., Zhang, X., Ren, S., Sun, J.: Deep residual learning for image recognition. In. IEEE Conference on Computer Vision and Pattern Recognition (CVPR) 2016, pp. 770–778 (2016)

Author Index

A
A. Runkler, Thomas   126
Abedi, Ali   320
Agarwal, Naman   390
Ahmad, Amir   312
Anicic, Darko   126
Antonelli, Michela   59
Azzopardi, Daniel   73

B
Bader, Sebastian   19
Bampa, Maria   87
Banerjee, Biplab   390
Barandas, Marília   3
Basiri, Reza   353
Batista, Bruna Raynara Maia   26
Bellinger, Colin   242
Benedetti, Riccardo   103
Bian, Chao   345
Biancucci, Federica   103
Blanco, Victor   435
Bogliolo, Alessandro   103
Bonneau, Antoine   217
Bonnier, Thomas   381
Bontempi, Gianluca   292, 416
Bosch, Benjamin   381

C
Caltabiano, Armando   168
Cao, Shi   328
Cebolla Alvarez, Ana Maria   416
Chaves, Samir Braga   26
Cheron, Guy   416
Coelho, Pedro   3
Colot, Martin   416
Crémilleux, Bruno   277
Cremonesi, Francesco   59
Crowley, Mark   242
Cruz, Lívia Almada   26
Curioso, Isabel   3

D
Daba, Natnael   424
De Carolis, Berardina   361
Dey, Bappaditya   435
Di Camillo, Barbara   369
Diepold, Klaus   115
Donati, Matteo   103

F
Fenske, Ole   19
Ferretti, Stefano   103
Fetz, Maximilian   470
Fingerhut, Fabian   486
Flich, Jose   138
Fragata, José   3
Francois, Harton   353

G
Gamboa, Hugo   3
Ge, Yueyi   336
Goedemé, Toon   486
Goh, Vicky   59
Granados, Alejandro   59
Gunduz, Ahmet   303

H
Habibi, Mahnaz   41
Halder, Sandip   435
Hecker, Dirk   470
Hemberger, Mike   399
Hildebrand, Kristian   399
Hönig, Marc   399

I
Innocenti, Lucia   59

J
Jacobs, Tom 486
Javadi, Golara 303
Jha, Ankit 390

K
Kaur, Jasleen 328
Khan, Shehroz S. 320, 345, 353
Kirste, Thomas 19
Kissel, Matthias 115
Kister, Alexander 470

L
Le Mouël, Frédéric 217
Leray, Philippe 435
Li, Xue 126
Loglisci, Corrado 361
Lorenzi, Marco 59

M
Macchiarulo, Nicola 361
Macedo, José Antônio Fernandes de 26
Magalhães, Régis Pires 26
Magnani, Mauro 103
Mahalanobis, Abhijit 226, 424
Malmirian, Mobin 320
Manji, Karim 353
McIntosh, Bruce 424
Medina, Laura 138
Menotta, Michele 103
Mercier, Denis 292
Mieyeville, Fabien 217
Mihailidis, Alex 345
Miliou, Ioanna 73
Milovanović, Marta 153
Mondrejevski, Lena 73
Montagna, Sara 103
Morita, Plinio 328

N
Navarro, Luis González 168
Nawaz, Ali 312
Niemann, Onno 185

O
Ourselin, Sebastien 59

P
Pal, Debabrata 390
Palestra, Giuseppe 361
Papapetrou, Panagiotis 41, 87
Patrinos, Panagiotis 201
Paul, Nathalie 470
Pauw, Lars De 486
Pavan, Massimo 168
Petieau, Mathieu 416
Poonja, Alisha 353
Popovic, Milos R. 353
Pros, Roger 261

Q
Quétu, Victor 153

R
Rafla, Mina 277
Randl, Korbinian 87
Ren, Haoyu 126
Ribeiro, Bruno 3
Ritter, Dennis 399
Rodner, Erik 399
Roveri, Manuel 168
Roversi, Chiara 369
Rugolon, Franco 87

S
Sacchi, Sara 435
Salehi, Mahsa 336
Santos, Ricardo 3
Sarhan, Kenaan 59
Schnellhardt, Thorben 470
Sharma, Himalaya 328
Shestha, Jeevan 292
Simar, Cédric 416
Singha, Mainak 390
Sirocchi, Christel 103
Sousa, Inês 3
Stella, Fabio 454
Stopp, Volker 399
Stranieri, Francesco 454
Suffian, Muhammad 103
Suykens, Johan A. K. 201
Szalai, Marcell 41

T
Taheri, Golnaz 41
Tamblyn, Isaac 242

Tavazzi, Erica 369
Tayyab, Muhammad 226
Tonin, Francesco 201
Tsiporkova, Elena 486
Tuan Ngo, Anh 435

V
V. Carreiro, André 3
Verbeke, Robbert 486
Vered, Mor 336
Verhelst, Théo 292
Vettoretti, Martina 369
Vitrià, Jordi 261

Voisine, Nicolas 277
Vox, Christopher 185

W
Wang, Kang 328
Werner, Thorben 185
Wirtz, Tim 470

Y
Yuksel, Kamer Ali 303

Z
Zukerman, Ingrid 336